International Conference on Applied Computing 2023 and WWW/Internet 2023

Porto, Portugal
15-18 July 2023

Editors:

Paula Miranda
Pedro Isaías

ISBN: 978-1-7138-8469-9

Printed from e-media with permission by:

Curran Associates, Inc.
57 Morehouse Lane
Red Hook, NY 12571

Some format issues inherent in the e-media version may also appear in this print version.

International Association for Development of the Information Society (IADIS)
Rua Sao Sebastiao Da Pedreira
No. 100, 30, 1050-209
Lisbon, Portugal

Phone: 351 21 3151373
Fax: 351 21 3151244

secretariat@iadis.org

Additional copies of this publication are available from:

Curran Associates, Inc.
57 Morehouse Lane
Red Hook, NY 12571 USA
Phone: 845-758-0400
Fax: 845-758-2633
Email: curran@proceedings.com
Web: www.proceedings.com

TABLE OF CONTENTS

FULL PAPERS

SHORT PAPERS

REFLECTION

FULL

PAPERS

MOVING TOWARDS QUALITY 5.0: AN INTERNET OF VEHICLE EXAMPLE

Tauheed Waheed and Eda Marchetti
CNR-ISTI
Via Moruzzi, 1 Pisa, Italy

ABSTRACT

To improve the quality of and better orchestrate its process, the paper introduces the Quality 5.0 paradigm, i.e. human-centric automated testing activities focused on software system and ecosystem security and privacy with the final purpose of increasing end-users satisfaction, reputation, and trustworthiness. To show the proposal's feasibility, Quality 5.0 has been exemplified in the field of the Internet of Vehicles domain. Quality 5.0 integrated with technological innovation will enhance sustainability, social responsibility and quality of life.

KEYWORDS

Industry 4.0, Quality 5.0, Cybersecurity Testing, Internet of Vehicle

1. INTRODUCTION

In the last decade, the process of developing and deploying software has undergone significant changes focusing again on the role of quality for businesses and digital transformation as well as leading the fourth industrial revolution (Zonnenshain et al. 2020). In this emphasis, the new Quality 4.0 discipline, supported by its framework, has been introduced. The purpose of Quality 4.0 has been to integrate digitization and automation effectively. Moreover, it provided a competitive advantage and ultimately enhanced profitability for organizations having business models inspired by Industry 4.0. Interestingly, Quality 4.0 was perceived as an innovative quality management strategy for effective implementation and maintaining quality for Industry 4.0, which supports the fourth industrial revolution in this essay.

However, even if innovative, Quality 4.0, strictly tied to the Industry 4.0 model, is no longer sufficient to satisfy the required quality level of the finished outputs. Factors such as customer experience (CX), employee experience (EX), user experience (UX), and cybersecurity are becoming pieces of evidence and attributes of the software and must be included in the quality process (Maganga D. P. et al., 2022.). Indeed, new emerging application domains and daily situations revealed some paramount reasons for not adopting Quality 4.0 effectively (Antony J. et al, 2023):

i) Inability to build trust among various stakeholders; requirement engineers, developers, testers, cybersecurity experts, domain experts, suppliers and business analysts.
ii) Difficulties in following the corporate and business strategy.
iii) Over-reliance on traditional quality management strategies, as these techniques were producing satisfactory results.
iv) Lack of resources and proficiency to understand the Quality 4.0 paradigm.
v) difficulties in involving end-users who are real beneficiaries of the produced outcomes.

These limitations are even more critical considering the new Industry 5.0 paradigm (Xu, X. et al., 2021), which focuses more on digitalization, AI-driven technologies, research and innovation to support the industry. In this light, this paper introduces a new concept of quality, the *Quality 5.0*, and relative framework for i) better orchestrate the quality process by integrating specific, human-centric automated testing activities, ii) focusing on the software system and ecosystem security and privacy issues and the other serious unresolved cybersecurity concerns and challenges dramatically showed up during the pandemic period; iii) better target the digital transformation and Sustainable Development Goals for 2030 from United Nations (European Union 2030, 2022), iv) achieving end-users satisfaction, reputation and trustworthiness.

In introducing its new concepts, the paper will be guided by the following research questions:

- **RQ1** Do we need Quality 5.0?
- **RQ2** Is it possible to achieve Quality 5.0?
- **RQ3** Is Quality 5.0 can be applicable in various modern-day application domains?

Thus, in Section 2 the paper motivates the introduction of the Quality 5.0 paradigm, while in Section 3, the lifecycle supporting Quality 5.0 is presented. An example of applying the proposed approach considering the Internet of Vehicles environment is presented in Section4 , and the implementation and result achieved are described in Section 5. Section 6 concludes the paper and presents the future works.

2. RQ1: DO WE NEED QUALITY 5.0?

Quality will always be one of the most crucial aspects of services and goods to be adopted in international marketplaces. Software or multinational corporations can gain a competitive edge by applying an effective quality management process and increasing their position in the market.

In this section, we introduce the concept of Quality 5.0 by replying to the first research questions presented in the introduction: **RQ1** *Do we need Quality 5.0?*

As schematized in Figure 1 (Tadi D.M., 2022), the reply to this question is yes. Indeed, although traditional quality management techniques have served their purpose for a while, they cannot be considered anymore adequate for complex, evolving and dynamic software applications and environments for many reasons: i) they are not fully adequate for managing the supply networks or IoT systems often distributed across numerous vendors and geographical locations or in continuous improvement; ii) They hardly adapt to the (real-time) technologies and the enormous amount of data that can be generated by the different devices, sensors, and other digital technologies involved into the systems; iii) they rely on knowledge of domain experts who cannot rapidly adapt to smart technology changes; iv) Most of the time they report the issues after occurring while current smart prediction and incremental adaptations can be necessary.

To solve these issues and align with the industry 4.0 evolution, Quality 4.0 has been introduced (Zonnenshain et al. 2020). This focused on the quality management procedures and data-driven methodologies able to improve the goods and services, operational effectiveness, and overall performance of businesses. Significant challenges for implementing Quality 4.0 in organizations are:

i) The possibility of continuous inspection and monitoring of the system to collect suitable and trustable data.
ii) The use of big data and AI techniques in driving quality programs;
iii) Improve customer satisfaction, by focusing on their specific needs and requirements and the resource utilization.

However, as highlighted in (Antony J. et al, 2022), the limited supplier involvement and specific issues still need to be solved, such as: i) The unclear return on investment and high implementation costs; ii) Lack of resources and implementation knowledge; iii) Poor organizational culture; iv) Lack of understanding of competitive advantage.

Additionally, as Industry 4.0 has mainly been techno-economic rather than socio-economic in Quality 4.0 cybersecurity, privacy challenges have not been appropriately considered exposing the industry output to possible cyber-attackers.

With the new Industry 5.0, one of the most effective means for preventing main criticalities and breaches is to promote the by-design adoption of the cybersecurity testing process fully integrated into the development lifecycle (from the specification to implementation and execution activities). Cybersecurity testing brings significant innovation to the economy, community and quality of life, can improve inspection and monitoring, provide opportunities to promptly identify vulnerability and cybersecurity threads and increase customer and user trustworthiness.

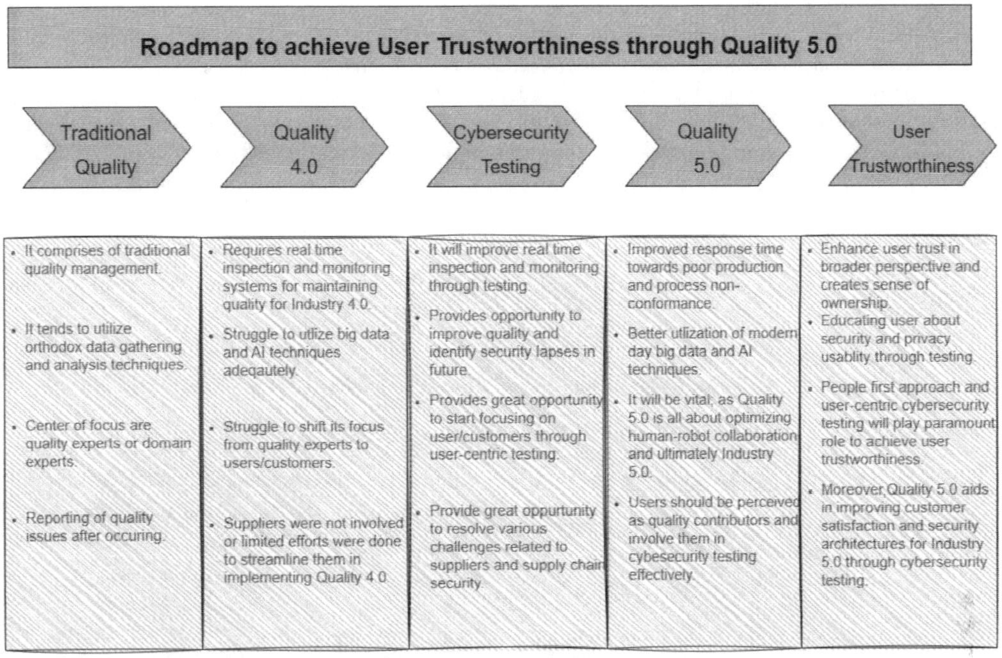

Figure 1. Roadmap

However, even if very efficient, cybersecurity testing is not sufficient to fully face the technological evolution and transformation and innovation in the Quality process is necessary. Quality 5.0 aims to provide strategies and opportunities that are more robust, human-centric and sustainable.

The concept of Industry 5.0 and Quality 5.0 is not a simple chronological continuation or substitute of the Industry 4.0 paradigm but a way to promote a user-centric approach. Thus Quality 5.0 integrated with technological innovation will enhance sustainability, social responsibility and quality of life.

Finally, teaching and sharing the knowledge of Quality 5.0 is also a mandatory activity for preparing society and industry for the future. Thus, increasing user trustworthiness is the final step of the Quality 5.0 evolution. This includes the involvement of people in the quality and testing process, educating users about security and privacy and improving customer satisfaction.

For this, schools and universities could be paramount in achieving trustworthiness, sustainability and Quality 5.0 through a human-centric approach (Carayannis E. G. et al, 2022).

3. RQ2: IS IT POSSIBLE TO ACHIEVE QUALITY 5.0?

In line with the Sustainable Development Goals (European Union 2030, 2022) for 2030, and positively replying to the RQ2 presented in the introduction, our proposal for achieving Quality 5.0 is provided in this section. As schematized in Figure 2, it brings stakeholders from various domains together to develop proactive strategies to attain digital transformation and target the transition of Quality 5.0 into Industry 5.0.

Indeed, going into Industry 5.0 involves collaboration among human robots, IoT, Artificial Intelligence (AI) and edge computing. However, this heterogeneity and complexity motivate the achievement of quality from a broader perspective and in line with customer satisfaction, reputation and trustworthiness.

As in Figure 2, the proposed Quality 5.0 lifecycle includes different activities and concepts for the final results. Considering ***Digital Development*** as a target, the life cycle's primary role is to build or develop products in collaboration with different stakeholders (like users, customers and developers) (***User Awareness***). Thus, it includes facilities and methods able to improve ***Human-Robot Collaboration*** and promote effective and efficient synergies between different stakeholders (*People Driven*).

Among them, a crucial role is the ***Testing Infrastructure***, which can be customized according to the domain-specific standards and regulations (***Domain Security***) and considering the human-centric collected requirements, quality level and global trustworthiness (***User Centric***).

Among the testing activities, a special role is dedicated to Cybersecurity. Indeed, *Cybersecurity Testing* can involve developers, users, business analysts, standards, regulations, suppliers, manufacturers and cyber-security experts. A further mandatory element for trustworthiness is the possibility of sharing knowledge, testing evidence and the achieved quality level with all stakeholders (***Knowledge Sharing***).

Finally, focusing on business aspects, the lifecycle must guarantee continuous evolution in technology and ***Business Continuity***.

Figure 2. Quality 5.0 Lifecycle

Therefore our proposal of Quality 5.0 has four main pillars:

1) a human-centric approach for collecting requirements, achieving quality and improving global trustworthiness;
2) Integration of testing and, in particular, cybersecurity testing, for increasing quality and solving vulnerabilities and criticalities in software applications and complex systems;
3) improving collaboration with suppliers and manufacturers to reach adequate quality for all stakeholders involved;
4) Include domain-specific requirements as Standards and Regulations (like General Data Protection Regulation) for better collaboration between humans/users, cyber-security experts, developers and other stakeholders.

4. INTERNET OF VEHICLE (IOV)

In replying to the last research question of the introduction, i.e., ***RQ3*** *Is Quality 5.0 can be applicable in various modern-day application domains?*, in the following sections, we showcase the positive reply by applying the proposed Quality 5.0 to the Internet of Vehicle domain. We selected this environment because it is one of the most involved in Industry 5.0 digital transformation and transformation and with high quality expectations. In this context, the proposed User-centred approach will aid in defining reliability and level of trust to keep our IoV architecture more secure during cyber-attacks.

Indeed, in recent years IoV has targeted to enhance customer satisfaction by providing users with more sophisticated services from their safety to comfort level. However, the evolution, complexity and heterogeneity of IoV pose high-level quality challenges, and the significant number of involved IoT devices increases the possibility of the cyber-attack surface of IoV ecosystem (Nizich M, 2023). Definitively, IoV ecosystem comprises various components such as Intelligent Transportation System (ITS) (Poornima E. et al 2023), IoT, humans/users, roadside units and Global Positioning System (GPS) and therefore requires: i) a more mature and proactive cybersecurity strategy, to ensure its continuity, reliability and connectivity, ii) innovative security and privacy mechanisms to achieve user trustworthiness, iii) validated security and privacy mechanisms for its effective communications and data storage.

Even if extremely useful and convenient, the IoV features expose the ecosystem and the users to quality issues and security and privacy threats (Hbaieb A. et al., 2022), that could even turn into safety problems causing loss of lives (Garg A., et al 2022), compromising completely the user trustworthiness and the future of the whole IoV industry. Therefore, a solid and effective quality and testing process should be applied before launching IoV into the market. In developing our Quality 5.0 reference lifecycle one of the first steps is to collect the quality needs and requirements useful for avoiding cyber-attacks and increasing user trustworthiness. Among them in our proposal we consider the following security aspects:

- **Authentication:** It is considered the building block for assuring that data should only be sent by authenticated vehicles. It is used to stop duplicate vehicles from sending data because senders of data will be differentiated through receiver sensors.
- **Integrity:** It secures the communication channel by ensuring that data is identical or unique, assures data privacy and ensures that only authorized users can modify the data. Message tampering and fabrication are the two common types of attacks on integrity.
- **Confidentiality:** It assures customers' privacy and personal details are protected by adopting encryption on sensitive information. It also avoids cyber-attacker access to encrypted data or information.
- **Non-repudiation:** Even though confidentiality is important in IoV security mechanism, it can be treated as conditional in some cases. For example, the intruder's privacy must be terminated, and their identities must be recognizable by all other vehicles. Therefore, it is essential to identify vehicles responsible for accidents or attacks.
- **Availability:** It assures real-time data availability during the IoV ecosystem working activity even in case of a huge number of IoT devices and users (Talib M. A et al., 2018)on the road.
- **Scalability:** As the number of vehicles and drivers increases, it also enhances the number of nodes and communication channels in vehicular networks. Moreover, the availability of a network or service is directly connected to its scalability.

4.1 Cyber-Attacks on IoV

Considering the *Human Robot Collaboration* and the *People Driven* activities presented in Figure 2 in this section, we focus on the cyber-attacks of IoV, which varies depending upon the attack surface area and skill set of attackers (Hsu C.H et al., 2023). This section describes the most frequent dangers and assaults on the IoV ecosystem. The cyber-attacker can be passive, aggressive, malevolent, local and foreign. The communication and precision of the network can be halted if an attacker gets access to the IoV network. The cyber-attacks on IoV can be categorized as follows:

- **Sybil attack:** The Sybil attack is carried out by creating various fake ids on behalf of a single node to achieve fake jamming. Moreover, the jamming signal is set up by building fake vehicles around the target vehicle, forcing the user to change his route.

- **Man-in-middle attack:** Its quite dangerous kind of attack, as it directly affects (Maurya C. et al., 2023). the user privacy and trustworthiness. As this cyber-attack involves the intruder as a middle-man and gains access to messages or communication between sender and receiver.
- **Replay attack:** The replay attack (Xi N. et al., 2022) comprises messages already present in the network where the attacker dwells to gain illegal access to network services and resources.
- **Message injection attack:** This attack comprises intruder skills to gain access to the network resources by sending legitimate messages. Further, malicious messages are sent through various components under the control of an attacker or intruder.
- **Denial-of-Service (DoS) attack:** The Denial-of-Service attack (Ortega-Fernandez I et al. 2023) is carried out by sending the bulk of messages to disrupt communication channels. Moreover, these messages are more than their capacity and lead to congestion, ultimately halting the network's efficiency ultimately halts the efficiency of the network. The attacker takes advantage of this congestion and gains access to critical system resources to cause further damage.

4.2 Cybersecurity Testing for IoV

In this section, we focus on the ***Testing Infrastructure*** activity of Figure 2 by presenting cybersecurity testing for IoV.

Vehicle manufacturers and industry must adopt proactive cybersecurity testing strategies to address vulnerabilities in-car software and various passive cyber-attacks to achieve Quality 5.0 and user trustworthiness. It is essential to understand that the above-mentioned cyber-attacks are not just related to user's personal information but also their physical safety from a broader perspective. Static Analysis (SAST) is done before the application is compiled because it doesn't need a full-fledged application or code to be executed.

It aids developers in finding vulnerabilities (NHTSA, 2023) timely and stops them from affecting the functionality of the final product or application. But the drawback of SAST is that it's only performed in the early stage of software development for IoV. The Interactive application security testing (IAST). It is performed during software development's testing (Synopsys, 2023) and Quality Assurance (QA) stage. It is carried out to manage IoV vulnerabilities and associated security risks by utilizing dynamic testing.

5. IMPLEMENTATION AND RESULTS ACHIEVED

In this section, to showcase the use of our proposal, we provide an example of a possible testing approach for avoiding cyber-attacks on the rolling code system of vehicle security keys. Usually, the replay attack is done by capturing the signal of a rolling code for a vehicle and compromising the security of IoV ecosystem. This attack needs appropriate devices that have the potential to capture and transmit signals.

Due to the unavailability of the IoV commercial system, we recreated the security key system in our lab using open source and components available in the open market. The intention is just to make an example of the testing process execution that could easily be replicated in a natural IoV environment.

It is performed by utilizing basic 433 MHz. Transmitter. Furthermore, it involves (Arduino UNO and Arduino Mega) to capture and transmit the signal of a rolling code. As depicted in Figure 3, the receiver and sender code are executed to extract test cases for improving its cybersecurity and attaining Quality 5.0. It's quite a paramount step in the right direction to extract test cases from real-time cyber-attacks in the shape of replay attack. The preliminary results extracted 20 test cases. The results show the vehicles haven't resynchronized rolling code when it receives lock/unlock commands from consecutive sources. Moreover, these test cases and real-time replay attacks will aid in improving our user-centric cybersecurity strategy and user trustworthiness, as depicted in the Quality 5.0 Life-Cycle.

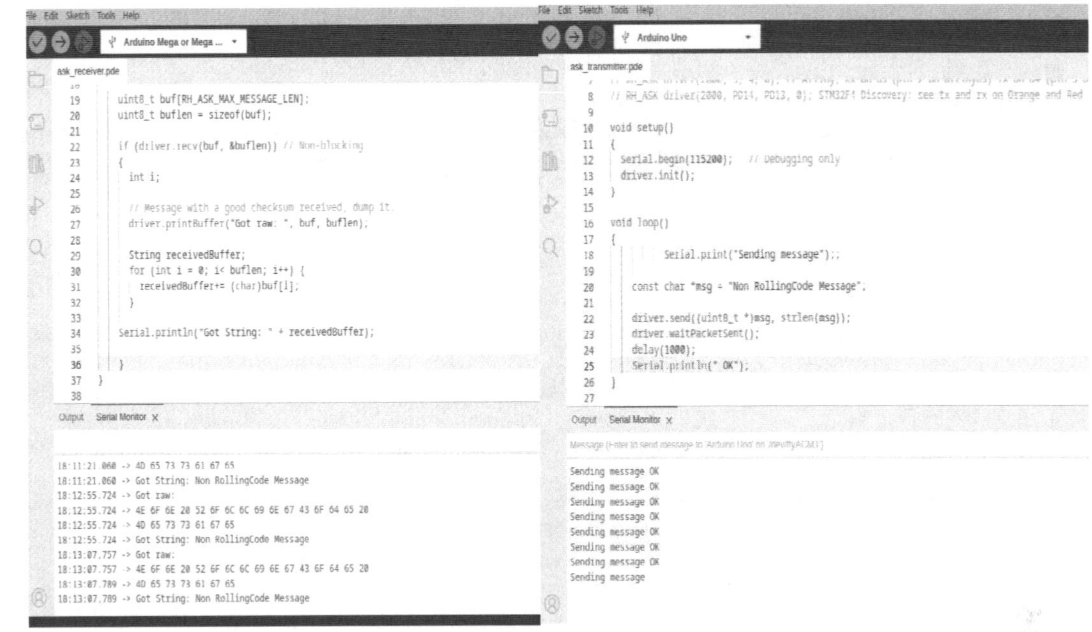

Figure 3. Quality 5.0 Lifecycle

6. CONCLUSIONS AND FUTURE WORKS

We have developed Quality 5.0 Lifecycle while considering various essential aspects that will aid researchers and developers in better adopting Industry 5.0. We have explored the domain of IoV and made efforts to improve its quality through user-centric cybersecurity. We have tried to develop more efficient and user-centric cybersecurity testing through rolling code implementation. The experiment has shown us great potential to achieve Quality 5.0. and user trustworthiness from the perspective of IoV. We have a long road ahead, and in our future work, we will focus on improving cybersecurity through our Quality 5.0 Lifecycle, as various domains have great potential to adapt to Industry 5.0, particularly co-bots.

ACKNOWLEDGEMENT

It is paramount to acknowledge this work was partially supported by the project SERICS (PE00000014) under the NRRP MUR program.

REFERENCES

Antony J. et al. (2022). Quality 4.0 and its impact on organizational performance: an integrative viewpoint. *The TQM Journal,* 34(6). pp. 2069 – 2084.

Antony J. et al. (2023). An exploration of organizational readiness factors for quality 4.0: an intercontinental study and future research directions. *Int. Journal of Quality & Reliability Management*, 40(2) pp. 582- 606.

Carayannis E. G. et al. (2022). The futures of Europe: Society 5.0 and industry 5.0 as driving forces of future universities. *Journal of the Knowledge Economy*, 13(4) pp. 3445- 3471.

European Union 2030 (2022). *Europe's digital decade: digital targets for 2030*. EU, pp. 15-21, 2022.

Garg A., et al. (2022) *Security threats & attacks in IoV environment: Open research issues and challenges*. In Third International Conference on Intelligent Computing Instrumentation and Control Technologies (ICICICT), pp. 803-810.

Hbaieb A. et al. (2022). A survey of trust management in the internet of vehicles. *Computer Networks*, 203 pp. 108558.

Hsu C.H et al. (2023). Introduction to the special section on cyber security in internet of vehicles, *ACM Transactions on Internet Technology* 22 (4) pp. 1-6.

Maganga D. P. et al. (2022). Quality 4.0 conceptualisation: an emerging quality management concept for manufacturing industries. *The TQM Journal*, 35(2). Pp. 389- 413.

Maurya C. et al. (2023). Efficient anonymous batch authentication scheme with conditional privacy in the internet of vehicles (iov) applications. *IEEE Transactions on Intelligent Transportation Systems*.

NHTSA (2023). Automative cybersecurity. US, pp. 5-10, 2023.

Nizich M. (2023). The current and future technology of cybersecurity. In *The Cybersecurity Workforce of Tomorrow*, Emerald Group Publishing Limited. Pp. 37–61.

Ortega-Fernandez I et al. (2023). A review of denial of service attack and mitigation in the smart grid using reinforcement learning. *Energies*, 16(2) pp. 635.

Poornima E. et al. (2023). Fog robotics-based intelligence transportation system using line-of-sight intelligent transportation. *Multimedia Tools and Applications*, pp. 1-29, 2023.

Synopsys (2023). Connected car cybersecurity. https://www.synopsys.com/glossary/what-is-connected-car-cyber-security, pp. 1-6, 2023.

Tadi D. M. (2022). Phases of quality development: Concluding with the concept of quality 5.0. *Tehnika*, 77(5) pp. 643-647.

Talib M. A et al. (2018). Systematic literature review on internet-of-vehicles communication security. *International Journal of Distributed Sensor Networks,* 14(12) pp 1550147718815054.

Xi N. et al. (2022). A zkp-based anonymous mutual authentication scheme for the IoV. *IEEE Internet of Things Journal*, 9(22) pp. 22903-22913.

Xu, X. et al. (2021). Industry 4.0 and industry 5.0 -inception, conception and perception. *Journal of Manufacturing Systems,* 61. Pp. 530-535.

Zonnenshain A.et al. (2020). Quality 4.0 -the challenging future of quality engineering. *Quality Engineering*, 32(4), pp. 614- 626.

REQUIREMENTS ENGINEERING WITH MDA: TOWARDS A UNIFIED FRAMEWORK

Fatima Meskine[1,2] and Safia Nait-Bahloul[1]
[1]LITIO Laboratory, University of Oran 1 Ahmed Ben Bella
PO.Box. 1524, El-M'Naouer, 31000 Oran, Algeria
[2]Computer science department, Hassiba Benbouali University of Chlef
PO.Box 78C, Ouled Fares, 02180 Chlef, Algeria

ABSTRACT

Requirements engineering (RE) is a branch of computer science which care of requirements understanding and specification in order to build software systems. By observing its progression, we see that no unified framework is proposed in the literature for the requirements engineering domain. A unified framework is necessary in order to avoid dispersion of ideas and suggestions, and keeping the advancement of the domain in the right direction. In this article, we go back to the basics of the requirements engineering domain, in order to identify a unified framework for the requirements specification technique. The requirements specification technique is the most important technique of the requirements engineering domain. Therefore, we present and we compare the basic methods of the requirements engineering domain, which are the structured analysis, i* framework and goal-oriented method, and we discuss the integration of these methods in the model driven architecture (MDA) as a software engineering approach, then we propose the MDA-RE framework for the requirements specification technique. Our proposed framework allows producing computation independent models (CIMs), which are until now not defined. The proposed framework is a result of our comparisons, and helps requirements engineers to perform their tasks comfortably.

KEYWORDS

Structured Analysis, i* Framework, Goal-Oriented, Computation Independent Model (CIM), Model Driven Architecture (MDA), DOORS Platform

1. INTRODUCTION

Requirements engineering (RE) (Nuseibeh and Easterbrook 2000; IEEE, 2009; Hull et al., 2011) is an area of computer science which interests of knowing what is really needed when building a new software system? Therefore, requirements are the first question to response when starting any IT project. And requirements engineering tasks are the first step in the software engineering process (Wang and King, 2000). Unfortunately, since its appearance as a research domain in the 1990's (Mead, 2013), requirements engineering did not establish a specific method or framework that it works with as a reference (Bambazek et al., 2023), this affects the domain itself and even the software engineering domain, which creates chaos in the software products (Stocchi et al., 2022). Currently, researches in requirements engineering are oriented to detect only privacy requirements from user stories (Casillo et al., 2022; Levy et al., 2022). Regarding methods for the domain, the recent proposed method, which is LiteStrat (Nöel, 2021; Nöel, 2023) focuses only on strategic goals in the requirements specification. A current state of arts in the requirements specification technique (Franch et al., 2023) reveals a serious problem which is the use of natural language in the documents of the requirements specification (IEEE, 2009), despite the models which are proposed for this technique in research works (Nuseibeh and Easterbrook 2000, Hull et al., 2011).

Hence, the problem we raise in this article and what we deplore in the requirements engineering domain is the absence of a unified and a standardized framework for the requirements specification technique. The requirements specification technique is among the requirements engineering domain techniques, and it is concerned by modeling and analyzing requirements (Nuseibeh and Easterbrook, 2000). So, it is a very sensible task, because it must provide a document on which the validation of the requirements engineering phase of the software engineering process depends. For this reason, we go back to the origins of the requirements engineering domain and we establish a line which connect the major achievements of the domain and give us a solid and a unified framework for the requirements specification technique.

We begin our study by presenting and comparing the three classical methods of the requirements engineering domain, which are: the structured analysis (Yourdon, 1989), i* framework (Yu, 1997) and the goal-oriented method (Van Lamsweerde, 2001). The goal of this comparison is to extract the basic concepts of the requirements specification technique. Since these methods provide models for specifying requirements, we try to unify these models by using the unified modeling language (UML) (OMG, 2011c). Therefore, we study the requirements engineering in the object-oriented paradigm (Booch, 2004), which is as the origin of the UML notations. After that we discuss the integration of these methods in the model driven architecture (MDA) (Brown 2004; Blanc 2005; OMG 2023a) as a software engineering method, because MDA uses UML as a notation language in its models. With this, we create the "MDA-RE framework" for the requirements specification technique which can be easily integrated in the software engineering process, without losing the requirements engineering foundations which are incorporated in the compared methods. As a result, our "MDA-RE framework" allows producing computation independent models (CIMs), which are MDA requirements specification models, and which are until now not defined. Hence, our framework is for the requirements specification technique of the requirements engineering domain, and in which Models are necessary.

In the presence of other software engineering methods as Agile (Reifer, 2002) and ECORE (Eclipse foundation, 2023), we orient ourselves to MDA because it is a standardized method, and because it uses a formal notation for its models. This notation is based on the object-oriented paradigm (Booch, 2004). Besides, MDA is a method of the model driven engineering paradigm (MDE) (Bézivin, 2004), i.e. it is based on models transformations. This ensures the transition from the requirements specification phase to the solution design phase in the software engineering process. Also, MDA is different from the other model driven engineering approaches (Assar, 2014; Davies et al., 2014; Hutchinson et al., 2014; Vázquez-Ingelmo, 2022), because MDA enable the meta-modeling layer for its models. And it is this layer which will incorporate the concepts of the requirements engineering domain, by integrating the compared methods in it.

Our research work is a proposition which is founded on a meta-review of: the basics requirements engineering methods, the requirements specification in the object-oriented paradigm and the research works of requirements engineering in the MDA software engineering method.

Our paper is organized as follows: In Section 2 we provide a comparison of the structured analysis, i* framework and the goal-oriented method. In Section 3, we discuss the integration of these methods in the MDA software engineering method. In Section 4, we present our result which is the MDA-RE framework for the requirements specification technique. In Section 5 we conclude our paper.

2. COMPARISON OF THE REQUIREMENTS ENGINEERING METHODS

2.1 Structured Analysis: Viewpoints

The structured analysis (SA) (Yourdon, 1989) is a method of the requirements engineering domain. It has a full systemic vision of the existing system; it is rich of concepts and models for the requirements specification technique. The main tool of the structured analysis is the data flow diagrams (DFD). DFD is a model which describes the principle elements of an information system, which are: actors, processes, data flows and data stores. The data flow diagrams are written in top-down level functional decomposition, including more details in each next level. Data dictionaries are also from the structured analysis. They allow describing all data in the data flow diagram, in flow or in store. Data dictionary can be seen as metadata of the data of the system. Processes of DFD are specified by using decision tables. The decision tables are based on the mathematical logic (Russell, 1910). The structured analysis uses also the entity-relationship (E/R) diagram (Chen, 1976) for representing relations between data. As a variant of the entity-relationship diagrams, we can cite the data models proposed by Silverston (2001). Therefore, we note that the structured analysis (SA) is a systemic view of the existing system, with the concepts of "stock and flow" and "structural/functional" aspects of the system (Bertalanffy, 1968). It is based on describing systematically and analytically the information system in order to specify requirements. The functional decomposition of DFD weakens the barrier between the requirements phase and the design phase. One can follow the steps of the method and arrives to the design of the solution beginning from the first top level DFD. This is why the structured analysis is classified as a software engineering method. In this case, we note that the structured analysis is the only one software engineering method which has its own requirements specification models. However, the requirements specification in SA does not support enough the stakeholder interests.

2.2 i* Framework: Viewpoints

Yu (1997) proposes the i* framework for modeling and analyzing stakeholder interests and how they might be addressed, or compromised, by various system-and-environment alternative. It concerns the earliest phases of the requirements specification technique. It consists of two main modeling components: the strategic dependency model (SD) and the strategic rationale model (SR). The SD model is used to describe the dependency relationships among various actors in an organizational context. It is based on two concepts: actor and dependency. Four dependencies are defined: resource, task, goal and soft-goal dependencies. The SR model provides a more detailed level of modeling by describing the internal relationships which are internal to actors, providing explicit representations of "why" and "how" and alternatives. Goals, tasks, resources, and soft-goals appear in the SR model not only as external dependencies, but also as internal elements to actors, linked by means-ends relationships and task-decompositions to be "Intentional elements". The SR and SD models are also in the form of graphs. An object-oriented implementation of the framework is proposed by using the Telos language (Mylopoulos, 1990). Therefore, since i* framework is proposed to specify requirements in the earlier stages of IT projects, it introduces the environment into the study of the information system, so that it adds the concept of the actor dependency at the level of the SD model, and it integrates goals, tasks and resources in the actor element, at the level of the SR model. We conclude that i* framework encompasses the concepts of the SA method, as the task which can be the process and the resource which can be the data and generalizes them at the level of the stakeholder which represents the environment of the system. However, the framework does not propose passage mechanisms to an advanced stage of the requirements specification.

2.3 Goal-Oriented Method: Viewpoints

The goal-oriented method (Van Lamsweerde, 2001) suggests that a clear knowledge of the system goals is necessary for the requirements specification. A goal is an objective which the system under analysis should achieve. For specifying goals many tools are used. The temporal logic (Ben-Ari et al., 1983) is an example of formulating goals as assertions. From assertions and predicates, object models are derived with attributes. The goal-oriented method includes goals refinement technique which helps to find sub goals. Graphs are also used to express relations between sub goals. The goal-oriented method supports conflict management to detect goals divergence, and agent assignments to determine responsibilities of agents for each goal. The goal-oriented method gathered many sub methods; which are integrated in some software engineering methods as ECORE (Rehman et al., 2010). Hence, knowing that the goal concept is introduced by i* framework, the goal-oriented method relies only on knowledge of goals in the requirements specification. Therefore, the goal-oriented method helps to bring the requirements from the agent level to the requirements engineer level, without wasting too much time. In this case, the transition from the requirements specification phase to the design phase is facilitated. However, we think that this method is attractive for embedded systems (Micco et al., 2020) wherein the volume of data is small and can be confined, and the intervention of users is limited, even the actor is seen as an agent in this method.

2.4 Summary of the Comparison

Therefore, these are the main requirements engineering methods which are proposed in the literature of the requirements engineering domain until now (Hull et al., 2011). Any other method which has been proposed after is based on at least one of these methods (Nöel, 2021; Nöel, 2023). The approaches which are based on user stories (Casillo et al., 2022; Levy et al., 2022) do not provide a method as a guide for the practitioners of the domain. Hence, we notice that the three compared requirements engineering methods have a theoretical background on which the models for specifying requirements are based. In addition, these methods have the same theoretical background which is the systemic approach, because "goal", "process", "flow", "stock" and "resource" are the concepts of the systemic approach (Table 1). The "actor" concept belongs to the environment of the system. And the environment concept is also from the systemic approach. We note also that i* framework is the method which gathers the structured analysis and the goal-oriented methods; even if the "flow" and "stock" concepts are absent in i* framework, because i* framework focuses on the environment of the system. However, undesirable facts which we discover when comparing the three requirements engineering methods (Table 1) are that they are not well integrated in the software engineering process, because they are not affected to a software engineering method, according to well defined criteria. Besides, we notice that for producing models, the widely used tool is the graph. Graphs (Diestel, 2017) are mathematical structure which must be enriched by more semantic to be able to produce requirements specification models. Therefore, the object-oriented paradigm offers richer notation which is the unified modeling language (UML) (OMG, 2011c), but it is not well used in these methods. Hence, we propose to integrate these methods in a suitable software engineering method, which can provide the formal notation and the power of unification, in order to have a unified framework for the requirements specification technique. Therefore, we propose the model driven architecture (MDA) as a software engineering method for this integration.

Table 1. Comparison of the requirements engineering methods

Methods	Theoretical background	Requirements concepts	Models	Notation tools	Transition to the design phase	Software engineering method
Structured analysis	Systemic approach	Process Flow Stock Data Actor	DFD E/R diagrams Data dictionaries Decision tables	Graphs Tables Mathematical logic	Top-down decomposition	Structured analysis
i* framework	Systemic approach	Dependency Task Resource Goal Actor	SD model SR model	Graphs	-	-
Goal-oriented	Systemic approach	Goal Agent	Goals models	Graphs Temporal logic	Goals refinement	ECORE

3. INTEGRATING REQUIREMENTS ENGINEERING METHODS IN MDA

3.1 Requirements Specification in the Object-Oriented Paradigm: Viewpoints

The object-oriented paradigm (Booch, 2004) has produced the unified modeling language (UML) (OMG, 2011c). UML defines several diagrams to represent systems. However, UML does not classify diagrams on which are destined to specify requirements or which are to represent solutions. Nevertheless, we note that the use-case and the activity diagrams are the preferred to specify requirements (Alkkiomäki and Smolander, 2007; Sindre, 2007). OMG (2023) proposes the business process model and notation standard (BPMN) (OMG, 2011a) for modeling business processes. BPMN is based on the object-oriented notation and standardizes DFD notation of the SA method. OMG proposes also the standard SysML (OMG, 2022, Hampson, 2015) as an adaptation of the UML language for specifying requirements. Regarding the object-oriented platforms for requirements specification, we cite the dynamic object-oriented requirements system (DOORS) (IBM, 2022). It uses the class diagrams (OMG, 2011c) to specify requirements. We cite also the DEMO tool (Ries et al. 2018) which is based on UML for producing requirements specification models from specifications which are written in the domain specific language (DSL) (Kosara, 2016). Because visual modeling is very important in computer science, the object-oriented paradigm is created in order to provide formal and standard notations for elaborating models. It is a set of abstract concepts as the famous object concept, and which has provided UML. Hence, the question here is on what basis the aforementioned notations were created, and used for the requirements specification. For answering this question we link in Table 2 between the object-oriented notations for requirements specification and the compared requirements engineering methods (Table 1).

Table 2. Object-oriented notations for requirements specification

Object-oriented notations	Requirements concepts	Corresponding model	Requirements engineering method	Software engineering method
Class diagrams	Requirements	-	-	-
Use-cases diagrams	Actors	-	-	-
Activity diagrams	Actors Data	-	-	-
BPMN	Processes Data Flows Actors	DFD	Structured analysis	-
SySML	Requirements	Goals models	Goal-oriented	-

We extract from Table 2 the most suitable object-oriented notations for the requirements specification technique, which are BPMN and SySML. We can see clearly that BPMN encompasses all the requirements concepts which are included in DFD. If we consider the requirements concept as equal to the goal concept, we can say that requirements diagrams of SySML are the object-oriented notation of the goals models. And by definition the requirements diagrams of SySML are based on class diagrams.

3.2 MDA as a Software Engineering Method

The model-driven engineering paradigm (Bézivin, 2004) for the development of software systems is based on using meta-models, models and transformations in every stage of the development of software systems. The model-driven architecture (MDA) (Brown 2004; Blanc 2005; OMG 2023a) adopts the model-driven engineering paradigm to build software systems, and uses the object-oriented paradigm concepts and definitions as a base of models notation (OMG, 2011b; OMG, 2011c). We must note that MDA and all its languages are standardized by OMG. Therefore, for each stage of the software life cycle (Blanc, 2005), MDA offers models for its specification:

- Computation independent model (CIM): is the model of specifying user needs and requirements.
- Platform independent model (PIM): is the design model of the application regardless of the platform.
- Platform specific model (PSM): is the code model, specific to the implementation platform.

As these models are proposed by MDA and as MDA uses UML as a notation language. These models must be written in UML. But, MDA does not split UML diagrams according to these models. However, as MDA is a model-driven approach, it proposes the four-layer meta-model hierarchy to define models (OMG, 2011b). This hierarchy allows unifying all models in the layer M3 which is the topmost layer; it contains the UML meta-meta-model which is the meta-object facility (MOF) (OMG, 2011b; OMG, 2019). It allows also extending the UML meta-model which is in the layer M2 of the hierarchy. As an example of the extension of the UML meta-model, we cite the common warehouse meta-model (CWM) (OMG, 2003) which is a meta-model for data. We cite also the UML profiles which take the UML meta-model as a reference and extend it for different domains (Meskine and Nait-Bahloul, 2020). CWM and UML profiles are in the same layer of the UML meta-model. UML diagrams which are notations for models are in the layer M1 of the four-layer meta-model hierarchy, and run time instances are in the layer M0. The relation between layers is "instance of", from layer M0 to layer M3. MDA proposes also the object constraints language (OCL) (OMG, 2014). OCL is a formal textual language allowing defining the necessary rules for meta-models and models. For elaborating transformations between models, MDA proposes the Query/View/Transformation language (QVT) (OMG, 2016). The atlas transformation language (ATL) (Eclipse, 2022) is also a model to model transformation language. Therefore, one can transform a CIM which is the requirements specification model to the PIM which is the conceptual model, and automates the transition from the requirements phase to the design phase. But, it is necessary to define meta-models for the CIM and the PIM to carry out this transformation. So, we discuss in the following the definition and the use of the CIM in research works.

3.3 Computation Independent Model (CIM)

3.3.1 Definition of the CIM in Research Works and Viewpoints

In MDA, the CIM (Computation independent model) is the model of requirements specification (Blanc, 2005). But MDA does not propose a specific language or a method for the CIM. It only stipulates that a requirements specification model is named a CIM. Asadi et al. (2008) separate the CIM from the requirements specification. So, the CIM and the requirements specification are two steps in the project initiation phase. The role of the CIM is to give a definition of the existing system regarding its domain. The role of the requirements specification is to determine the real requirements. Therefore, it is proposed use-case and activity diagrams in this last step. Kherraf et al. (2008) define the CIM as a model that regroups business processes and requirements, and it is proposed a transformation from a CIM to a PIM. Kardoš and Drozdová (2010) take the CIM for representing business processes, and propose DFD for the CIM and UML diagrams for the PIM. The proposed UML diagrams are: use-case, activity and sequence diagrams. The transformation from the CIM to the PIM is carried out by using the domain diagram which is proposed by the authors. The same idea is forwarded by Rhazali et al. (2016), but it is proposed the BPMN models in the CIM, and class diagrams in the PIM. The transformation from the CIM to the PIM is realized by ATL. Therefore, we conclude that there is a difficulty in the CIM definition. However, we can notice from the aforementioned research works that the CIM as a requirements specification model must gather three elements:

- The domain of the requirements specification task.
- The requirements of the users.
- The processes.

We notice also, that even if the CIM is a MDA model, UML diagrams are not the only candidates to establish it, because UML diagrams are instances of the UML meta-model, and this one is not specific to the requirements specification. Furthermore, CIM as a requirements specification model is proposed in some researches which are interested for data warehouses (DW) development (Inmon, 2002). These CIMs are instantiated from meta-models which are defined for parts of the structured analysis, i* framework and goal-oriented method. As the development of data warehouses is a real software engineering experience, we give a summary of these research works as examples of using these methods in the context of MDA.

3.3.2 CIM by the Compared Requirements Engineering Methods: Data Warehouses Case

Klimavicius and Sukovskis (2008) take the CIM as a requirements specification model for data warehouses development; it is also named the business model, and regroup the business models and the universal data models (Silverston, 2001) to have the complete CIM. Seth et al. (2013) propose the E/R diagram to express the CIM as a requirements specification model, named also the business model. Zepeda et al. (2008) propose the goal-oriented method mixed with activity diagrams for user requirements specification in data warehouses. So, it is used an extension of CWM (OMG, 2001) as a notation for the E/R diagram, this model is used as a PIM. Always in the spirit of MDA, we find the research work of Mazón et al. (2007) which defines a UML profile for i* framework. Therefore, requirements specification model according to i* framework is instantiated from this UML profile, and it is used as CIM for requirements specification in data warehouses. i* framework UML profile of Mazón et al. (2007) is enriched by Trujillo et al. (2009) with security concepts to specify security requirements in data warehouses. Therefore, CIM as defined by i* framework is instantiated from this UML profile. El Beggar et al. (2020) propose a UML profile for requirements specification in data warehouses, based on the use-case meta-model and BPMN, and it is used for producing the CIM. Some meta-models for user requirements specification are proposed (Maté and Trujillo, 2012; Solodovnikova et al., 2015). The meta-model of Maté and Trujillo (2012) is for traceability of user requirements in data warehouses. And the meta-model of Solodovnikova et al. (2015) is a requirements meta-model for data warehouses. Knowing that, these requirements meta-models (Maté and Trujillo, 2012; Solodovnikova et al., 2015) are based on UML, and are in the context of the data warehouse structure updating, more than the initial construction of the data warehouse. Therefore, these two meta-models concern requirements traceability with MDA (Assar, 2014). Hence, we conclude that these research works (Table 3) add the requirements engineering method as a background of the CIM, by defining meta-models for the concepts of these methods, in order to have the formal notation for establish it. We inform that the notation language (Table 3) which is an UML based meta-model in the most research works is independent from data warehouses domain, but it used for producing CIM for the data warehouse. Hence, it is the requirements engineering method which encompasses the elements which must be present in the CIM (Section 3.3.1).

Table 3. CIM in research works for data warehouses

Research works	MDA requirements specification model	Requirements method	Notation language	From requirements phase to design phase
Klimavicius and Sukovskis (2008)	CIM	Structured analysis	Business process diagrams Universal data model (Silverston, 2001).	No proposition
Seth et al. (2013)	CIM	Structured analysis	E/R model notation.	Transition from E/R model to relational model (Codd, 1970)
Zepeda et al. (2008)	User requirements specification	Goal-oriented	Graphs Activity diagrams	Semantic mapping (Rahm and Bernstein, 2001)
	PIM	Structured analysis	CWM extension for E/R	
Mazón et al. (2007)	CIM	i* framework	UML profile	QVT transformations
Trujillo et al. (2009)	CIM	i* framework	UML profile	Textual rules
El Beggar et al. (2020)	CIM	Structured analysis Goal-oriented	UML profile	ATL transformations
Maté et al. (2012)	Requirement traceability model	-	Class diagram as meta-model	Marking
Solodovnikova et al. (2015)	Requirement traceability model	-	Class diagram as meta-model	Flowcharts

3.4 Viewpoints

We note that even if MDA does not impose a method for the requirements engineering domain, the research works of Table 3 specify requirements in the context of MDA by using the structured analysis, goal-oriented and i* framework methods. We find that there are defined meta-models for the structured analysis, i* framework and the goal oriented methods, and a real requirements specification models are elaborated as CIM, there are also transition definitions from the requirements specification phase to the design phase (From CIM to PIM). Hence, the software engineering method which is MDA provide to these methods the formal notation for elaborating requirements specification models and the mechanisms to transit from the requirements specification phase to the design phase. And this is better than using graphs. Therefore, these research works are a big step in integrating the structured analysis, goal-oriented and i* framework methods in MDA as a software engineering method, and they are applied to develop a real software system, which is the data warehouse. Therefore, it is necessary to establish a unified framework for the CIM as a requirements specification model, by using these methods.

4. COMPARISONS RESULTS: MDA-RE FRAMEWORK

Given the comparison of the requirements engineering methods (Section 2), and the study of the requirements engineering domain in MDA (Section 3), we propose "The MDA-RE framework" (Figure 1) as a unified framework for the requirements specification technique. Our framework brings theory to practice, in order to support the back of requirements engineers. And it is unique because it is the result of an accurate comparison of requirements engineering and software engineering theories (Booch, 2004; Bézivin, 2004; Bertalanffy, 1968). Therefore, we propose in our framework to integrate entirely the structured analysis, i* framework and goal-oriented methods in MDA as a software engineering method.

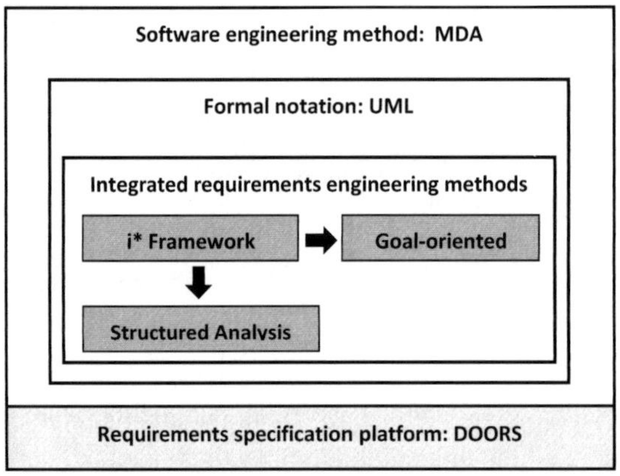

Figure 1. The MDA-RE framework

As a first step, it is necessary to work on how we can pass from i* framework to the structured analysis and to the goal-oriented method, because i* framework concerns specifying requirements in the earlier stages of the IT project, and it brings together the concepts of the structured analysis and the goal-oriented methods.

For this step, we can rely on the research work of Werneck et al. (2009). Therefore, depending on the complexity of the system, the practitioner can choose to go towards the structured analysis or towards the goal-oriented method, starting from i* framework. In our opinion, the structured analysis is more suitable for the systems where the data are important as information systems, and the goal-oriented method is suitable for small and embedded systems. So, it is necessary to establish rules for passing from i* framework to the goal oriented method, and for passing from i* framework to the structured analysis method.

By relying on our comparisons in Table 1 and Table 2, the four-layer meta-model hierarchy of MDA and OCL, we propose to define meta-models for the three requirements engineering methods as requirements specification meta-models. The research works of Table 3 and the OMG requirements notation standards BPMN and SysML (Table 2) cover a good part of this second step.

As a third step, we propose to implement these requirements specification meta-models in the DOORS platform. For this step, we can rely on the research work Fatyani et al. (2015) and the Eclipse modeling framework (EMF) (Eclipse, 2023a). We can also integrate the Telos platform which concerns i* framework.

The last step is to define QVT transformations, based on the rules of the first step, in order to allow CIM refinement. These QVT transformations must be implemented in the DOORS platform.

Once our framework is built, requirements engineers can use it to elaborate the CIM as a requirements specification model. The CIM can be a SD, SR, DFD or goals model; even it can be a data model or a process model, but by using the notation which is defined in the requirements specification meta-models. Our framework allows elaborating many CIMs for the requirements specification phase of the IT project, these CIMs can be aligned and refined until obtaining the final CIM.

Therefore, we guarantee by our proposed framework formal documents for the requirements specification phase of the software engineering process (Wang and King, 2000). The requirements specification document (IEEE, 2009) is a justification for the software product, and it is a support for the developers to ensure compliant solutions with the needs of stakeholders.

As a start, we can be tried by students in their graduation projects which are usually IT projects, since our framework uses models which are based on UML, and UML is a suitable modeling language in the educational sector (Vázquez-Ingelmo et al., 2020). Hence, we invite the researchers of the requirements engineering domain to adopt the MDA-RE framework, and orient researches to build it.

5. CONCLUSION

We propose in this research work a unified framework for the requirements specification technique of the requirements engineering domain. Our framework is a proposition which is based on:

- The comparison of the basic methods of the requirements engineering domain, which are the structured analysis (Yourdon, 1989), i* framework (Yu, 1997) and the goal-oriented method (Van Lamsweerde, 2001).
- The study of the object-oriented notations which are dedicated to the requirements specification as BPMN (OMG, 2011a) and SysML (OMG, 2022).
- The study of the research works which use MDA with the compared requirements engineering methods, for elaborating requirements specification models as CIM.

From our comparisons, we extract the concepts of the requirements specification technique and the main elements which must be included in the CIM. As a result, we obtain the MDA-RE framework (Figure 1). The MDA-RE framework allows defining meta-models for the requirements specification technique, by respecting the concepts of requirements engineering domain, and producing CIMs as requirements specification models. Because our MDA-RE framework is a result of accurate comparisons, we have found the ideal formula for combining the basic methods of the domain, allowing covering all aspects of the requirements specification technique. UML as defined by MDA via its four layer meta-model hierarchy allows offering the formal and the standard notation for these methods, by defining the meta-models of the requirements specification technique. So, formal models for the requirements specification technique can be established and help to elaborate official document for it. Our framework also solves the problem of the transition to the design phase, by using the models transformation as defined by MDA, unlike approaches which use ontologies for requirements engineering (Dermeval et al., 2014) and isolate it from the software engineering process (Wang and King, 2000). Our framework can be implemented in DOORS platform and be easily usable by requirements engineers in order to perform this important technique of the requirements engineering domain. Besides our resulting MDA-RE framework, our research work provides a useful study which clarifies the main confusions in the domain, as the confusion between UML diagrams and requirements engineering methods, which is a trap that a lot of practitioners fall into.

ACKNOWLEDGEMENT

We thank the General Directorate of Scientific Research and Technological Development (DGRSDT) of Algeria for supporting this research.

REFERENCES

Alkkiomäki V. and Smolander K., (2007). Integration Use Cases – An Applied UML Technique for Modeling Functional Requirements in Service Oriented Architecture. *Proceedings of the 13th international working conference on requirements engineering, foundation for software quality*, Trondheim, Norway, pp. 190-202.

Asadi M. et al, (2008). An MDA-based System Development Lifecycle. *Proceedings of the 2nd Asia International Conference on Modelling & Simulation*, Kuala Lumpur, Malaysia, pp. 836–842.

Assar S., (2014). Model Driven Requirements Engineering–Mapping the field and beyond. *Proceedings of the 2014 IEEE 4th International Model-Driven Requirements Engineering Workshop (MoDRE)*, Karlskrona, Sweden, pp. 1–6.

Bambazek P. et al, (2023). Requirements engineering for sustainable software systems: a systematic mapping study. *Requirements Engineering*, https://doi.org/10.1007/s00766-023-00402-1

Ben-Ari M et al, (1983). The temporal logic of branching time. *Acta Informatica*, Vol. 20, pp. 207–226.

Bertalanffy, LV., (1968). *General System Theory–Foundations–Development–Applications*. George Braziller, NY.

Bézivin J., (2004). Sur les principes de base de l'ingénierie des modèles. *Revue L'Objet*, Vol. 10, No. 4, pp. 145–157.

Blanc X., (2005). *MDA en action: Ingénierie logicielle guidée par les modèles*. Eyrolles, Paris.

Booch, G., (2004). *Object-Oriented Software Analysis and Design with Applications*. Addison Wesley Longman, CA.

Brown, A., (2004). Model driven architecture Principles and practice. *Software and Systems Modeling*, Vol. 3, No. 4, pp. 314–327.

Casillo F. et al, (2022). Detecting privacy requirements from User Stories with NLP transfer learning models. *Information and Software Technology*, Vol. 146, https://doi.org/10.1016/j.infsof.2022.106853

Chen P.P., (1976). The entity-relationship model: toward a unified view of data. *ACM Transactions on Database Systems*, Vol. 1, No. 1, pp. 9–36.

Codd, E.F., (1970). A Relational Model of Data for Large Shared Data Banks. Communicatxions of the ACM, Vol. 13, 6, pp. 377–387.

Davies J. et al, (2014). Model-driven engineering of information systems: 10 years and 1000 versions. *Science of Computer Programming*, Vol. 89, pp. 88–104.

De Micco L. et al, (2020). A Literature Review on Embedded Systems. *IEEE Latin America Transactions*, Vol. 18, No. 2, pp. 188–205.

Dermeval D. et al, (2014). A Systematic Review on the Use of Ontologies in Requirements Engineering. *Proceedings of the 2014 Brazilian Symposium on Software Engineering*, Maceio, Brazil, pp. 1-10.

Diestel R. (2017). *Graph Theory*. Springer, Berlin, Heidelberg.

Eclipse Foundation, (2022). The Atlas Transformation Language (ATL) Project: Transforming models with ATL. http://www.eclipse.org/atl/documentation/old/ATL_Flyer_Normal_Version.pdf (Last accessed 13/07/2023)

Eclipse Foundation, (2023). http://www.eclipse.org (Last accessed 13/07/2023)

Eclipse Foundation, (2023a). Eclipse Modeling Framework (EMF). https://www.eclipse.org/modeling/emf/ (Last accessed 13/07/2023)

El Beggar O. et al, (2020). DAREF: MDA framework for modelling data warehouse requirements and deducing the multidimensional schema. *Requirements Engineering*, Vol. 26, pp. 143–165.

Fatyani T. et al, (2015). Comparing DEMO with iStar–In Identifying Software Functional Requirement. *Proceedings of the 15th International Symposium on Business Modeling and Software Design*, Milan, Italy, pp. 149–155.

Franch X. et al, (2023). The state-of-practice in requirements specification: an extended interview study at 12 companies. *Requirements Engineering*, https://doi.org/10.1007/s00766-023-00399-7

Hampson K., (2015). Technical Evaluation of the Systems Modeling Language (SysML). *Procedia Computer Science,* Vol. 44, pp. 403–412.

Hull E. et al, (2011). *Requirements Engineering*. Springer, London.

Hutchinson et al, (2014). Model-driven engineering practices in industry: Social, organizational and managerial factors that lead to success or failure. *Science of Computer Programming*, Vol. 89, pp. 144–161.

Inmon W.H., (2002). Building the Data Warehouse. Wiley, NY.

Institute of Electrical and Electronics Engineers (IEEE), (2009). 830–1998–IEEE Recommended Practice for Software Requirements Specifications. https://ieeexplore.ieee.org/document/720574 (Last accessed 13/07/2023)

International Business Machines Corporation (IBM), (2022). Overview of DOORS. https://www.ibm.com/docs/en/ermd/9.7.0?topic=overview-doors (Last accessed 13/07/2023)

Kardoš M. and Drozdová M., (2010). Analytical Method of CIM to PIM Transformation in Model Driven Architecture (MDA). *Journal of Information and Organizational Sciences*, Vol. 34, No. 1, pp. 89–99.

Kherraf S. et al, (2008). Transformation from CIM to PIM Using Patterns and Archetypes. *Proceedings of the 19th Australian Conference on Software Engineering*, Perth, Australia, pp. 338–346.

Klimavicius M. and Sukovskis U., (2008). Applying MDA and Universal Data Models for Data Warehouse Modeling. *Proceedings of the WSEAS 10th International Conference on Automatic Control, Modelling & Simulation*, Istanbul, Turkey, pp. 332–337.

Kosara T. et al, (2016). Domain-Specific Languages–A Systematic Mapping Study. *Information and Software Technology*, Vol. 71, pp. 77–91.

Levy Y. et al., (2022). An impact-driven approach to predict user stories instability. *Requirements Engineering*, https://doi.org/10.1007/s00766-022-00372-w

Maté A. and Trujillo J., (2012). A trace metamodel proposal based on the model driven architecture framework for the traceability of user requirements in data warehouses. Information Systems, Vol. 3, No. 8, pp. 753–766.

Mazón J.N. et al, (2007). A model-driven goal-oriented requirement engineering approach for data warehouses. Proceedings of advances in conceptual modeling–foundations and applications, Auckland, New Zealand, pp. 255–264.

Mead N. R. (2013), A history of the international requirements engineering conference (RE)RE@21. *Proceedings of the 2013 21st IEEE International Requirements Engineering Conference (RE)*, Rio de Janeiro, Brazil, pp. 21-221.

Meskine F. and Nait-Bahloul S., (2020). A support architecture to MDA contribution for data mining. *International Journal of Data Mining–Modelling and Management*, Vol. 12, No. 2, pp. 207–236.

Mylopoulos J. et al, (1990). Telos–Representing Knowledge About Information Systems. *ACM Transactions on Information* Systems, Vol. 8, No. 4, pp. 325–362.

Nöel R. et al, (2021). The LiteStrat Method–Towards Strategic Model-Driven Development. Proceedings of the 29 International Conference on Information Systems Development, Valencia, Spain, pp. 1–13.

Nöel R. et al, (2023). Including business strategy in model-driven methods–an experiment. *Requirements Engineering*, https://doi.org/10.1007/s00766-023-00400-3

Nuseibeh B. and Easterbrook S., (2000). Requirements Engineering–A Roadmap. *Proceedings of the Conference on The Future of Software Engineering*, Limerick, Ireland, pp. 35–46.

Object Management Group (OMG), (2001). Common Warehouse Metamodel (CWM) Specification–Extensions, http://www.omg.org/cgi-bin/doc?ad/2001-02-02 (Last accessed 13/07/2023)

Object Management Group (OMG), (2003). Common Warehouse Metamodel (CWM) Specification–Version 1.1. https://www.omg.org/spec/CWM/1.1/PDF (Last accessed 13/07/2023)

Object Management Group (OMG), (2011a). Business Process Model and Notation–Version 2.0, https://www.omg.org/spec/BPMN/2.0/PDF (Last accessed 13/07/2023)

Object Management Group (OMG), (2011c). OMG Unified Modeling Language™ (OMG UML) Superstructure–Version 2.4.1. http://www.omg.org/spec/UML/2.4.1/Superstructure/PDF (Last accessed 13/07/2023)

Object Management Group (OMG), (2014). Object Constraint Language (OCL)–Version 2.4. https://www.omg.org/spec/OCL/2.4/PDF (Last accessed 13/07/2023)

Object Management Group (OMG), (2022). SysML® OMG System Modeling. https://www.omg.org/spec/SysML/1.7/Beta1/PDF (Last accessed 13/07/2023)

Object Management Group (OMG), (2023a). http://www.omg.org/ (Last accessed 13/07/2023)

Object Management Group (OMG), (2023a). MDA® - THE ARCHITECTURE OF CHOICE FOR A CHANGING WORLD, http://www.omg.org/mda/ (Last accessed 13/07/2023)

Object Management Group (OMG). (2016). Meta Object Facility (MOF) 2.0 Query/View/Transformation Specification-Version 1.3. https://www.omg.org/spec/QVT/1.3/PDF. http://www.omg.org/spec/QVT/ (Last accessed 13/07/2023)

Object Management Group, (2011b). OMG Unified Modeling Language™ (OMG UML) Infrastructure–Version 2.4.1. https://www.omg.org/spec/UML/2.4.1/Infrastructure/PDF (Last accessed 13/07/2023)

Object Management Group, (2019). OMG Meta Object Facility (MOF) Core Specification–Version 2.5.1. https://www.omg.org/spec/MOF/2.5.1/PDF (Last accessed 13/07/2023)

Rahm E. and Bernstein P.A., (2001). A survey of approaches to automatic schema matching. *The VLDB Journal*, Vol. 10, pp. 334–350.

Rehman N.U. et al, (2010). Comparative study of goal-oriented requirements engineering. *Proceedings of the 4th International Conference on New Trends in Information Science and Service Science*. Gyeongju, Korea (South), pp. 248–253.

Reifer D.J., (2002). How good are agile methods?. *IEEE Software*, Vol. 19, No. 4, pp. 16–18.

Rhazali Y. et al, (2016). Model Transformation with ATL into MDA from CIM to PIM Structured through MVC. *Procedia Computer Science*, Vol. 83, pp. 1096–1101.

Ries B. et al, (2018). A Text-First DSL-Based Approach for UML Requirements Engineering (Tool Demo). *Proceedings of the 11th International Conference on Software Language Engineering*, Boston, USA, pp. 103–107.

Russell B. et al, (1910). *Principia Mathematica*. Cambridge University Press.

Seth A. et al, (2013). MDA Based Approach Towards Implementation of MultiDimensional Database for Banking System. *International Journal of Computer Applications*, Vol. 61, No. 13, pp. 16–21.

Silverston L., (2001). *The Data Model Resource Book*. Wiley, NY.

Sindre G. (2007). Mal–Activity Diagrams for Capturing Attacks on Business Processes. *Proceedings of the 13th international working conference on requirements engineering–foundation for software*, Trondheim, Norway, pp. 355–366.

Solodovnikova D. et al, (2015). Handling Evolving Data Warehouse Requirements. *Proceedings of the East European Conference on Advances in Databases and Information Systems: New Trends in Databases and Information Systems, Poitiers, France*, pp. 334–345.

Stocchi L. et al, (2022). Marketing research on Mobile apps: past, present and future. *Journal of the Academic Marketing Science*, Vol. 50, pp. 195–225

Trujillo J. et al, (2009). A UML 2.0 profile to define security requirements for Data Warehouses. *Computer Standards & Interfaces*, Vol. 31, pp. 969–983.

Van Lamsweerde A., (2001). Goal-oriented requirements engineering: a guided tour. Proceedings of the 5th IEEE International Symposium on Requirements Engineering, Toronto, Canada, pp. 249–263.

Vázquez-Ingelmo A. et al, (2020). C4 model in a Software Engineering subject to ease the comprehension of UML and the software development process. In Proceedings of 2020 IEEE Global Engineering Education Conference, Porto, Portugal, pp. 919-924.

Vázquez-Ingelmo A. et al, (2022). MetaViz - A graphical meta-model instantiator for generating information dashboards and visualizations. *Journal of King Saud University - Computer and Information Sciences*, Vol. 34, No. 10, pp. 9977-9990.

Wang Y. and King G., (2000). *Software Engineering Processes Principles and Applications*. CRC Press, USA.

Werneck V.M.B. et al, (2009). Comparing GORE Frameworks– i-star and KAOS. *Proceedings of the 2009 Workshop em Engenharia de Requisitos*, Valparaíso, Chile, pp. 1–12.

Yourdon E., (1989). *Modern Structured Analysis*. Yourdon Press, NJ.

Yu E., (1997). Towards Modelling and Reasoning Support for Early-Phase Requirements Engineering. *Proceedings of the 3rd IEEE International Symposium on Requirements Engineering*, Annapolis, MD, USA, pp. 226-235.

Zepeda L. et al, (2008). A Mixed Approach for Data Warehouse Conceptual Design with MDA. *Proceedings of the international on conference of computational science and its applications*, Perugia, Italy, pp. 1204–1217.

A PROCESS FLOW COMPOSABLE OPENDATA MASHUP TOOL AND ITS EFFECTS EVALUATION

Satoshi Yashiro[1], Norihisa Komoda[2] and Takenao Ohkawa[1]
[1]*Graduate School of System Informatics, Kobe University*
1-1 Rokkodai-cho, Nada, Kobe 657-8501, Japan
[2]*Osaka University*
1-1, Yamadaoka, Suita, Osaka 565-0871, Japan

ABSTRACT

Open data is a data that is provided by public sectors or social infrastructure companies like transportation service providers. Recently, many people are trying to utilize open data in various applications. Even if a user is not a specialist who have enough data science skills, the user may use common data processing software such as a spread sheet software or a text editor to handle open data. Such common software requires many hours to handle the data, whereas does not require higher skills. In this paper, an open data mashup tool which can reduce hours to handle open data in utilizing the data is proposed. This tool supports a user to design data process flow easily by providing a user interface with composable processing unit components. Also, its effect in some specific cases is clarified.

KEYWORDS

Open Data, Mashup, Data Processing, Data Process Flow, Composable

1. INTRODUCTION

Since around 2010, open data has been used commonly in world-wide. Government agencies or public companies such as transportation companies or electric power companies have been trying to disclose their own data (Alexopoulos, et al., 2014). Many people are trying to utilize the data regardless of whether it is for profitable business purpose or not (Immonen, et al. 2014; Immonen, et al. 2014; Yang, et al., 2019). Particularly in Japan, after the Great East Japan Earthquake occurred in March 2011, government agencies launched their data portal sites for people to find, access, and get the data easily. For example, data on the annual municipal budget and spending results of local governments, data on facilities in nursing homes and parks are being disclosed by many local governments. Those data are utilized for the assessment of financial health of local government or life support for the elderly and child-rearing generation.

For utilizing open data, some specific skills are often required (Balarabe and Jordanov, 2022), and lack of the skills is one of barriers of open data utilization (Sébastien, at el., 2013). For example, it is said that governments should provide data gathering, analyzing and summarizing environment for better utilization (Kim, et al., 2012), and sometimes a kind of skill training to users is required (Mila, et al., 2018). Also, various data sometimes have different column names for the columns those have same meaning, then users need to give unified name to the column names. Some platforms to resolve such data name mismatch are proposed (Anneke, et al., 2016). Some geographic data have only postal address texts, but a GIS (Geographic Information Systems) software typically requires longitude and latitude values, then users need to translate the address texts to longitude and latitude values. For auditing appropriated budget execution, users need to combine planned budget data and actual spending data precisely. These data preparation works are relatively time-consuming work especially for common open data users who use common data processing software such as a spread sheet software or a text editor.

To reduce such time-consuming data preparation work, a mashup tool that equips composable data process flow editor will work well. By using this tool, open data can be easily processed and edited, and data processing flow can be defined in a shorter time than manually defined. In this paper, a process flow composable open data mashup tool is proposed. This tool supports users to design data process flow easily by providing a processing units composable user interface. Also, effectiveness of the tool is clarified through several case studies.

2. PROBLEMS OF USING COMMON DATA PROCESSING SOFTWARE IN UTILIZING OPEN DATA

In this chapter, it is explained that a typical procedure in using open data and problems in using common data processing software to handle open data.

2.1 Typical Procedure for Using Open Data

A typical procedure for using open data is as follows.

1. Search for and obtain the data you want to use on the Data Portal site or other related sites using keyword searches, etc.
2. Check the contents of the obtained data and perform arrangement processes such as converting column names and cell values to standard names or expression and converting address texts to longitude and latitude values as necessary. You can also combine multiple columns, split a column into multiple columns, extract only specific columns, and organize the data for ease of use in an application.
3. If necessary, combine multiple data that have been transformed and formatted above to create data to be used by an application for open data.
4. The data obtained above is input to an application for open data, for example, a visualization software such as GIS software or table viewer and visualized.

Among the above procedures, procedures performed using the built-in functions of common data processing software are described in step 2 and 3. When it assumes to use a spread sheet software in the step 2 and 3, keyword search function to identify certain values, filter function to identify and group certain records, replacement function to convert a value to another value are used. Such procedures typically take large costs (Johnson, et al., 2017). Even if the user is an expert data scientist, "trial and error" with the data is required (Zeng, et al., 2018) and such process takes much time.

2.2 Problems in Using Common Data Processing Software to Handle Open Data

A user who does not have enough data processing skills usually tries to use a common data processing software such as a spread sheet software or a text editor. Two example cases of problems in using such software to handle open data are explained in this section. One is aggregation processing by groups, and the other is combining plural CSV (Comma Separated Value) data.

2.2.1 Aggregation Processing by Groups

When processing open data such as traffic accident records or crime records and trying to aggregate the number of traffic accidents or incidents for each condition such as vehicle type, configuration of road surface, type of crime, or time period of the accident happening, users need to iterate filtering operation with a spreadsheet software so many times. Instead of simply aggregating the number of rows, if it is necessary to aggregate numerical values such as the number of victims per accident or the amount of damage per incident, the values in the numeric column are aggregated.

As mentioned above, aggregation processing by groups is typically iterative filtering work by certain columns as conditions and total its rows or values of certain columns. Therefore, workload of the procedure depends on the number of conditions and rows.

Figure 1 shows an example case of traffic accident aggregation by several conditions. The Japan national police agency discloses traffic accident record as open data. The record of year 2021, there are totally 305,196 accident records listed. It is to limit the records in Kanagawa prefecture only, the total number of the accident records are 21,660.

The records contain 58 columns such as severity of the accident, damage level of vehicle and human, period of the accident, day of week the accident happened, etc. 5 of 58 are the columns that represent results of the accident, 14 of 58 are the columns that represent conditions of the accident, and remaining are the columns that give complimentary information. The 14 columns that represent conditions can be divided into four categories. Those are three columns that relate to period of the day or day of week, one column that relates to road status, four columns that relate to location or surface condition of the road, and two columns that relate to driver's age and usage of the vehicle. Each column's value is allocated from pre-defined code values, and total number of combinations of the code values are 126 cases in period of the day or day of week, 5 cases of road status, 4,680 cases of location or surface condition of the road, and 32 cases of driver's age and usage of the vehicle.

Typical analysis of the traffic accident record is to identify which condition correlates with a certain result by selecting the combination of conditions. For example, if you choose the period of the day and the day of week as condition columns, then you may understand traffic accidents tend to happen easier in the evening time on holiday or the day before holiday than other period of the day or day of week. If you try to count the number of accidents in each condition, total maximum cases should become 94,348,800 (=126*5*4,680*32) cases as mentioned above. Of course, that is the worst case and less cases will appear in actual data. However, actual cases usually become thousands or more. It is not realistic for users to test all the cases by filtering operation with a spread sheet software.

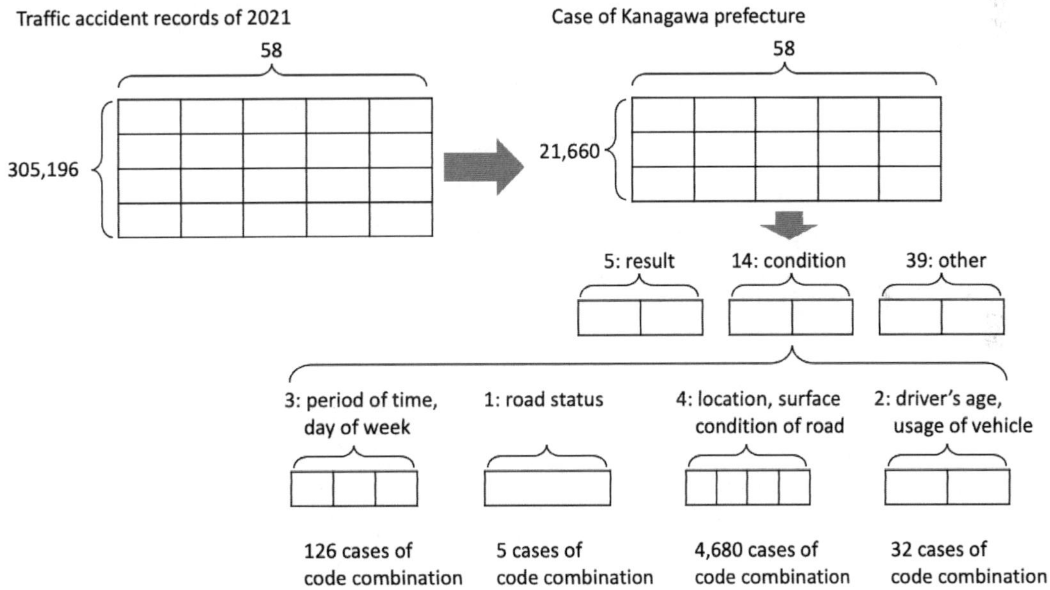

Figure 1. Configuration of traffic accident records

2.2.2 Aggregation Processing by Groups

When combining multiple CSV data that match all column names, combining process can be easily performed by using the data binding function provided by a common spreadsheet software or by selecting, copying, and pasting the data to be concatenated on the spreadsheet software. On the other hand, if you want to combine the list of public facilities and the list of AED (Automated External Defibrillator) equipped location in the column direction, and display only the public system where the AED is equipped on a GIS software, you may need to compare the key items of both list, select only records that have the same key, and perform copy and paste operations so many times. If the order of records in both list is the same, and there are no records in one list that is not in the other list, then you only need to copy the necessary columns and paste them into the other list. In such case, combining data using a spreadsheet software is less troublesome.

Figure 2 shows a concrete example that the fiscal year of 2018 planned budget revenue data and the fiscal year of 2018 actual budget revenue data published on the Tokyo Metropolitan Government's data portal site are combined in a column direction to examine the deviation of the actual budget revenue with respect to the planned budget revenue. Since the planned budget revenue data has 480 records excluding the header row, and the actual budget revenue data has 478 records excluding the header row, there are at least two rows of non-overlapping records. Both data have 14 columns, and the name of the column related to the amount is different from "Planned amount" in the planned budget revenue data and "Actual amount" in actual budget revenue data. After the combining operation, there are 528 rows excluding the header row, and 430 records come from both data, 50 records come from only revenue budget data, and 48 records come from only actual budget revenue data. Comparing all 480 and 478 records and identifying 430 rows with matching key items manual operation is a major hassle with a spreadsheet software.

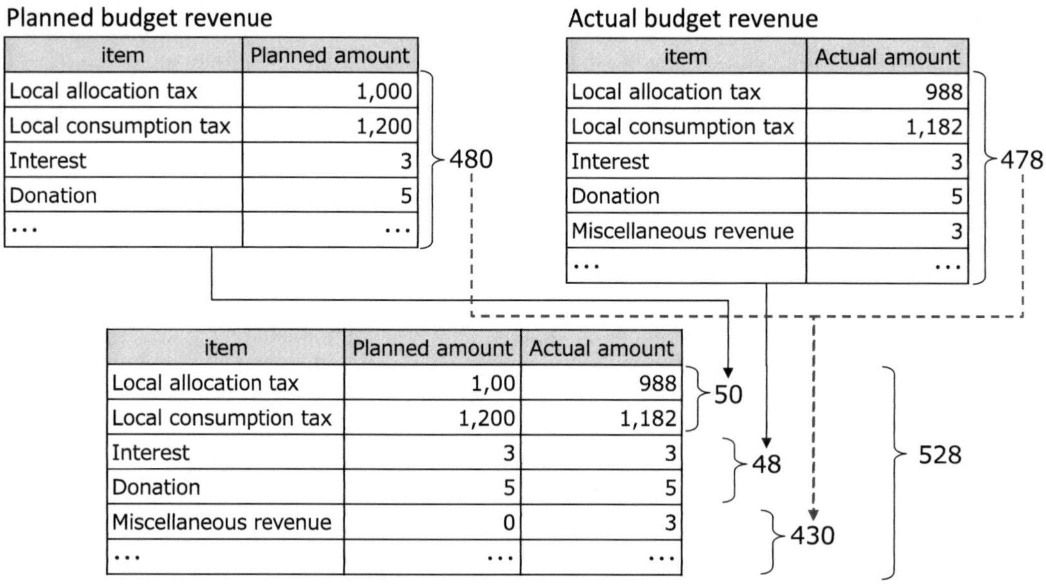

Figure 2. Combination results of planned budget revenue and actual budget revenue

Using a commercially available spreadsheet software, the procedure for combining both data in the column direction is as follows.

1. Download "Planned budget revenue" data file and "Actual budget revenue" data file.
2. Create a combined data file by copying "Planned budget revenue" data file and add "Actual amount" as the 15th column. The combined data is conveniently referred to as "Planned and actual budget revenue" data.
3. Open "Planned and actual budget revenue" data file and "Actual budget revenue" data file on the spreadsheet software and set "Auto-Filter" using the header row as sorting keys.
4. Set the same filter conditions in the 13 columns except the "Planned amount" column and "Actual amount" column to uniquely specify the records, copy the value of "Actual amount" in "Actual budget revenue" data to "Actual amount" column of "Planned and Actual budget revenue" data.
5. Iterate step 3 until all the filter conditions in the 13 columns have been tested for both "Planned and actual budget revenue" data and "Actual budget revenue" data.

3. PROCESS FLOW COMPOSABLE OPENDATA MASHUP TOOL

In this chapter, it is explained that a proposal of an open data mashup tool that supports a user to design data processing flow easily by providing composable user interface.

3.1 Key Idea to Overcome the Problems of Common Data Processing Software in Using Open Data

The problems of common data processing software in using open data are summarized into two points. First one is to force a user to perform many iterative manual operations. Second one is to ask a user to judge a certain data is what the user want or not.

An idea to overcome the problems mentioned above is to provide data processing components that are designed as performing iterative processing and typical judgement regarding data identification. In addition to this, it is needed to provide a mechanism that supports a user to select and combine those necessary components precisely. This paper proposes a mashup tool that equips the mechanism and the components.

3.2 Functionality of the Opendata Mashup Tool

The mashup tool proposed can design a data processing flow by placing icons of data processing unit components that is pre-programmed data processing as often used when using open data, such as downloading open data or converting address texts to latitude and longitude values, and connecting the icons with lines that imitate input/output relations of each processing part. Table 1 shows the outline structure of the mashup tool.

The mashup tool has four main sub-systems: 1) Data processing flow editor, 2) Data processing unit programs, 3) Data processing flow execution program, and 4) Data visualization programs. The data processing unit programs are a collection of data processing programs such as download processing of specified open data, extraction of specific columns from downloaded open data, and arithmetic processing between specified multi-column data. The tool equips several basic processing units in advance, and a developer or a user can add new processing units they develop.

A mashup tool user designs a series of data processing flows by combining multiple data processing unit programs using the data processing flow editor shown in the screen display example as Figure 3. The design work is done by placing component units to the flow design area, and connecting them with lines. The lines between the components represent data flow or input/output relation of variables in each unit program. Therefore, users can select to use only necessary variables or data columns for their purpose. This operation is done by drag and drop with mouse on the data process flow designer, then even a non-professional user can design the workflow.

After the user completes the design work and runs an execution process, the designed data processing flow is executed by the data processing flow execution program. And the execution result is displayed using a group of data visualization programs such as colored pins on a GIS software, mesh paintings on a GIS software, graphs on a Web browser, and tables on a Web browser. If the user wants to try another data or another algorithm, the user will put another data download component unit or data processing unit and change connection from previous units to newly placed units. So, users can easily conduct trial and error process.

Table 1. Components of the open data mashup tool

#	Sub system	Explanation
1	**Data process flow editor**	An editor to design data process flow by putting icons of data process unit programs and connecting those icons.
2	**Data process unit programs**	Executable unit programs for typical open data processing.
3	**Data process flow execution program**	A program execution environment to run the programs according to the flow design that is edited by the flow editor.
4	**Data visualization programs**	Application programs to visualize processed open data.

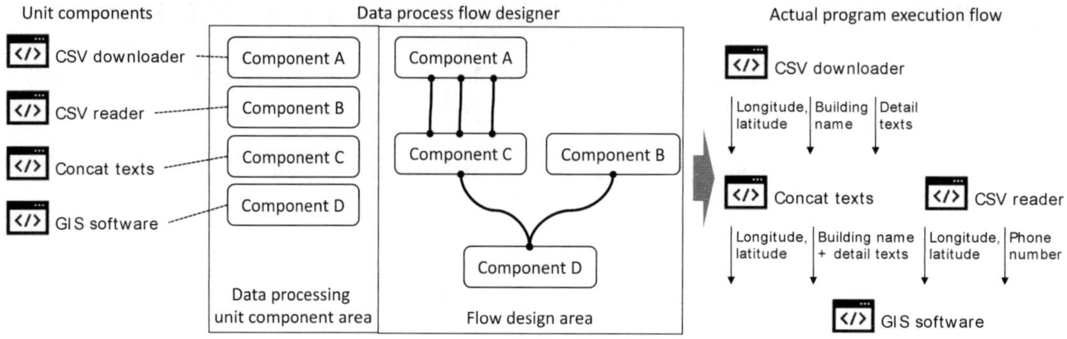

Figure 3. Example view of the data process flow editor

4. EFFECTIVENESS OF THE MASHUP TOOL

In this chapter, it is explained that the effectiveness of the mashup tool proposed in the chapter 3 based on how the tool solves the problems explained in the chapter 2.

4.1 Effects of Aggregation Processing by Groups

4.1.1 Procedure in Using the Mashup Tool

To perform the same analysis explained in 2.2.1 with the mashup tool, the procedure becomes like below and the process flow design on the flow design area becomes like figure 4.

1. Select "CSV download" component from the data processing unit component area and put the component on the flow design area to download traffic accident records, and set the URL of the traffic accident record file.
2. Select "Filter by key" component and put the component, and set the key as Kanagawa prefecture. Connect "CSV download" component to "Filter by key" component.
3. Select "Count rows by all conditions" components and put the component 14 times, and set 14 column IDs (IDentifiers) to each component. Connect "Filter by key" component to 14 "Count rows by conditions" components.
4. Select "Table view" component and put the component, and connect 14 "Count rows by conditions" components to "Table view" component.

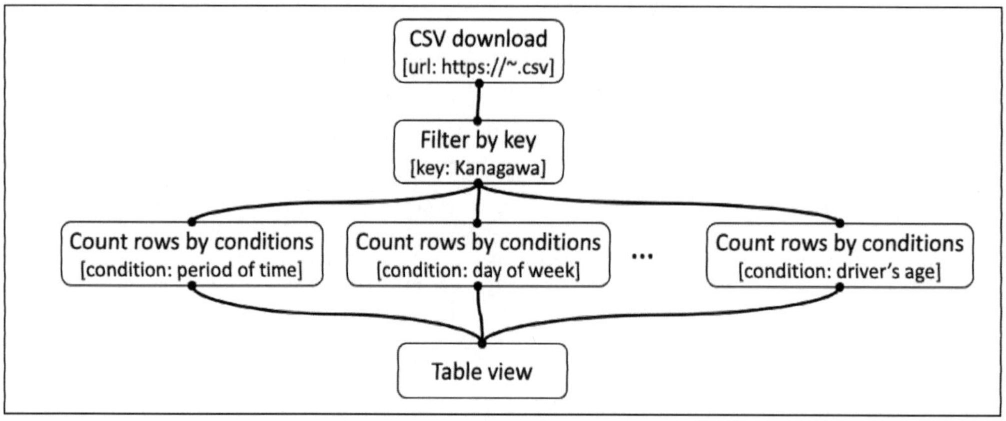

Figure 4. Data process flow design of traffic accident records analysis

4.1.2 Effects of Using the Mashup Tool

In the case of aggregation processing by groups, the mashup tool can reduce iterative manual operation of testing various conditions. If columns that relate to conditions or variation of value in a condition column are less, then total number of condition cases become less, and users may perform the process even with a common spread sheet software. But based on the example case study of the traffic accident record case, total number of conditions tends to be more.

Potential time to be reduced by using the mashup tool is the time to test totally 94,348,800 cases mentioned in section 2.2.1. Actual total records are 21,660 as mentioned in 2.2.1, so actual time reduction becomes less than the potential time. Here, let's assume how much three factors regarding period of the day and day of week will correlate with accident happening. Total number of the combination of the three factors are 126 as already mentioned in 2.2.1, so 172 (=21,660/126) accidents happen in each condition on average. If it assumes that it takes five seconds to choose one condition from three columns, it takes ten seconds to count the filtered row numbers and to record the numbers, and finally it takes 6,300 (=5*10*126) seconds after 126 times iteration of choosing condition and counting row numbers operation. The mashup tool can reduce the 6,300 seconds as almost zero.

4.2 Effects on Combining Multiple CSV Data with Multiple Identical Columns

4.2.1 Procedure in Using the Mashup Tool

To perform the same preparation process explained in 2.2.2 with the mashup tool, the procedure becomes like below and the process flow design on the flow design area becomes like figure 5.

1. Select "CSV download" component from the data processing unit component area and put the component on the flow design area two times, and set the URLs (Uniform Resource Locators) of "Planned budget revenue" data file and "Actual budget revenue" data file.
2. Select "Data merge" component and put the component, and connect the two "CSV download" components and "Data merge" component.

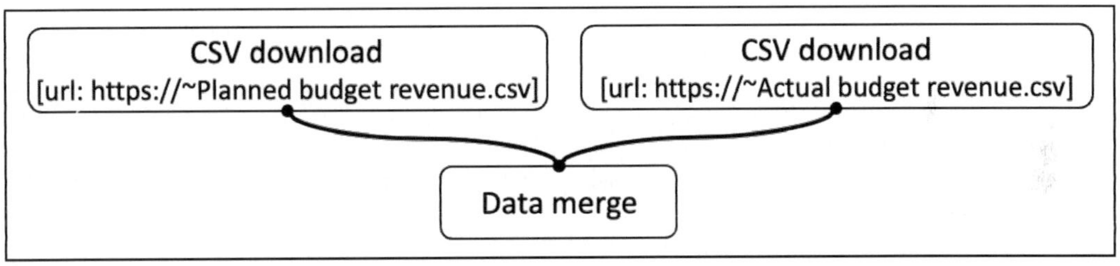

Figure 5. Data process flow design of planned and actual budget revenue analysis

4.2.2 Effects of Using the Mashup Tool

By using the mashup tool, you can reduce the number of steps from five to two. In addition, step 4 and 5 of the procedures using a spreadsheet software require multiple iterations according to the number of records, but when using a mashup tool, iterative operations by the user are not required. Also, many times of matching key items manual operation are not required. This operation is totally covered by the "Data merge" unit program.
Potential time to be reduced by using the mashup tool is the time to identify totally 528 records mentioned in section 2.2.1 and to copy values to the "Planned and actual budget revenue" data file. A record is identified by the combination of 13 columns that exclude "Planned amount" and "Actual amount" from original files. Here, let's assume that it takes ten seconds to choose 13 columns value to unique a record and it takes five three seconds to copy the value to the "Planned and actual budget revenue" data file. Then, totally 28,740 (=10*2*3*430 + 10*3*50 + 10*3*48) seconds are required by manual operation. The mashup tool can reduce the 6,300 seconds as almost zero.

5. REFLECTIONS ON THE EFFECTS OF MASHUP TOOLS

The effects of using the mashup tool instead of common data processing software for processing open data can be said to reduce iterative filtering work. One of major purposes to utilize open data is to identify major factors that affect a certain result. To meet this goal, it is necessary to test various conditions by selecting various column values. It is usually a time-consuming procedure to test various conditions with common data processing software such as spread sheet software, but the mashup tool can replace such manual operations as just putting some data processing unit components, connecting those components, and set some properties.

Other effect of using the mashup tool is to take over a user's task to judge a record is what the user wants or not. When combining two CSV files, it is needed to identify a record that has the same keys with the target record. A data processing unit component such as "Data merge" will perform this kind of task automatically and efficiently.

6. CONCLUSION

In this paper, problems of common data processing software in using open data are explained based on some concrete example cases. Also, a mashup tool that supports a user to design data processing flow easily by providing composable user interface is proposed. The effects of the mashup tool are clarified in comparing to number of steps or necessary manual operations in the example cases.

REFERENCES

Alexopoulos, C., et al. (2014). Designing a second generation of open data platforms: Integrating open data and social media. *Proceedings of International Conference on Electronic Government: EGOV 2014*, Dublin, Ireland, pp. 230-241.

Anneke Z., et al. (2016). Improving the speed and ease of open data use through metadata, interaction mechanisms, and quality indicators. *Journal of Organizational Computing and Electronic Commerce*. Vol. 26, No. 1-2, pp. 116-146.

Balarabe, A. T. and Jordanov, I. (2022). A Hybrid Dilation Approach for Remote Sensing Scene Image Classification. *IADIS International Journal on Computer Science & Information Systems*, Vol. 17, No.2, pp. 1-15.

Immonen, A., et al. (2014). Requirements of an Open Data Based Business Ecosystem. *IEEE Access*, Vol.2, pp.88-103.

Immonen, A., et al. (2014). Towards open data based business: Survey on usage of open data in digital services. *International Journal of Research in Business and Technology*, Vol. 4, No. 1, pp. 286-295.

Johnson P. A., et al. (2017). The Cost(s) of Geospatial Open Data. *Transactions in GIS*. Vol. 21, No. 3, pp. 434-445.

Kim H. J., et al. (2012). The Open Data Interface (ODI) Framework for Public Utilization of Big Data. *Proceedings of DATA ANALYTICS 2012*. Barcelona, Spain, pp. 94-96.

Mila G.H., et al. (2018). Promoting the use of open government data: Cases of training and engagement, *Government Information Quarterly*, Vol. 35, No. 2, pp. 233-242.

Sébastien M., at el. (2013). Risk analysis to overcome barriers to open data. *Electronic Journal of e-Government*, Vol. 11, No. 2, pp. 348-359.

Yang, Y., et al. (2019). Using open data to derive local amenity demand patterns for walkability simulations and amenity utilization analysis. *Proceedings of ECAADe SIGraDi 2019*. Porto, Portugal, pp. 665-674.

Zeng J. et al. (2018). Value creation from big data: Looking inside the black box. *Strategic Organization*, Vol. 16, No. 2, pp. 105-140.

AGENTS AND TRUST IN THE METAVERSE

Thomas Keller, Danny Wang and Elke Brucker-Kley
ZHAW Institute of Business Information Technology
Winterthur, Switzerland

ABSTRACT

This study discusses the relevance of agents and trust in the metaverse and explores how trust is formed between individuals and agents in a virtual world like the metaverse, specifically in the context of healthcare consultations. The research aims to identify the factors that influence the trustworthiness of an agent and how these factors can be applied in the design of digital avatars to enhance patient trust. The study draws on psychological theories such as similarity attraction theory, attractiveness theory, exchange theory, attribution theory, and expectancy theory to understand the formation of trust. Different avatars with variations in visualization, voice, and gestures, were created and a laboratory experiment with male participants aged 24-30 was conducted. The results of the experiment showed that trust in agents can be explained by psychological theories. Agents that displayed similarities to human features and conveyed competence and expertise were more trusted by the participants. However, avatars with exaggerated or non-human characteristics were met with distrust. The study concludes that psychological theories can be applied in the metaverse to build trust, and the design of avatars should consider factors that enhance trustworthiness. Overall, this research provides insights into the importance of trust in the metaverse, particularly in healthcare contexts, and offers recommendations for designing trustworthy digital avatars.

KEYWORDS

Agents, Virtual Reality, Trust

1. INTRODUCTION

The trustworthiness of one person towards another is a complex interplay of different psychological theories and concepts (Simpson, 2007). Accordingly, understanding how trust is built between people requires a high level of theoretical understanding of these areas. It is assumed that a person's trust in an agent, an embodied bot, is additionally influenced by a number of technological factors. According to Seymour et al. (2020), the degree of realism of an agent has a strong impact on human trust. To date, the lack of trust in agents is one reason why patients prefer a real visit to the doctor (Felnhofer et al., 2023). Since the term metaverse is a rather recent construct, there is currently uncertainty as to whether an agent can partially replace or at least supplement a real doctor.

This raises the question of the extent to which psychological concepts relating to interpersonal trust can also be applied in a virtual world such as the Metaverse. This is explored in this work by conducting a laboratory experiment. The results of this work may enhance the understanding of how digital avatars should be designed in healthcare to gain patient trust. Based on the results of the laboratory experiment, this can lead to recommendations for action for healthcare in the metaverse.

2. OBJECTIVE

The goal of this work is to investigate the relevance of influencing factors on the trustworthiness of an agent in the metaverse. For this purpose, a corresponding VR application is designed. Accordingly, the research question for this work is: "How should an agent be designed regarding visualization, voice, and gesture for health consultations in order to foster trust among patients?".

In a first step, the relevant psychological theories are identified and assessed. Based on this, a VR app is developed in a second step, with which the relevance of the possible influencing factors is determined with a laboratory experiment. In a final step, statements are made and critically assessed based on the collected data.

3. RELATED WORK

Avatars and agents represent one of the core elements of the metaverse, enabling a self-presence for the user in the former case (Blog, o. J.) and an embodied bot in the latter case. This serves as the basis for social interaction in the metaverse. Visualizations can be anthropomorphic, abstract, animalistic as well as fantasy creatures. Non-verbal and paraverbal features can be designed to match the visualization (Sajjadi et al., 2018). On this basis, human-computer interaction is redefined.

Trust in an agent in the metaverse is believed to be influenced by various psychological theories and constructs. These may include factors such as attractiveness, degree of realism, or similarity to the user (Aljaroodi et al., 2019). According to Seymour et al. (2018), the term "realistic visual presence" (RVP) is representative of increased trust as well as willingness to interact with an agent.

Felnhofer et al. (2023) discuss a meta-analysis that examined the social responses of users towards virtual humans in immersive VR. The study aimed to determine whether the perceived agency of a virtual human, whether controlled by a person (avatar) or a computer (agent), affects social presence, evaluation of the virtual entity, and behaviours towards it. The analysis considered factors such as task type, appearance of the virtual entity, type of interaction, and agency manipulation. The results indicated that avatars were favoured over agents in terms of social presence. However, no significant effects were found for behavioural outcomes. Further analysis revealed that the differences in social presence were larger for neutral tasks compared to negative tasks, and differences in evaluation were more pronounced for positive tasks compared to mixed and neutral tasks. In summary, the findings suggest that deliberate social responses, such as social presence and evaluation, are influenced by the perceived agency of virtual humans. However, automatic behaviours do not appear to be affected. The study emphasizes the need for consistent conceptualizations of key variables in future research.

3.1 e-Health

Telemedicine enables the interaction between doctor and patient, who are located in geographically different places (Sparwasser et al., 2022). The metaverse offers a way to improve existing telemedicine services (Skalidis et al., 2022). This includes interactions in the context of a health consultation. The visualization of the health advisor, whether human or bot, takes the form of an avatar (Rheu et al., 2020). This makes it possible to achieve a stronger persuasive effect than through conventional telemedicine tools, such as pure telephone consultation. VR goggles are also used in an attempt to provide a better patient experience in a three-dimensional environment (Bansal et al., 2022). In addition, the use of this technology can also improve access to healthcare in remote environments. People who suffer from physical limitations also typically benefit. Because the interaction is virtual via the metaverse, savings in travel costs and waiting time can also be realized. Virtual health consultation also reduces the risk of infectious disease transmission between patients and medical staff.

Another area of application in healthcare is virtual training and continuing education (Thomason, 2021). The benefits in terms of staff training are far-reaching. Through the use of VR, learners in the metaverse can gain a better overview of replicating actual procedures. This can illustrate processes in a more accessible way and enable interactive exchanges within lessons.

3.2 Psychological Theories

To model a person's trust in an agent, various social psychological concepts are used. These concepts deal with the way people interact with each other to build interpersonal relationships and trust. Based on this, it will be determined in relation to the research question how the digital avatars should be visually designed.

Similarity attraction theory fundamentally states that people are more likely to be attracted to people who are similar to themselves (Montoya & Horton, 2013). It assumes that similarities between people are attractive, while differences can be off-putting. According to (Roebken, 2010, S. 473), similar socio-demographic characteristics such as race, gender, or education level can also increase mutual attraction. However, the viewpoint that similarity of values and attitudes is a major factor in attraction between people is also contested (Montoya & Horton, 2013; Santee, 1976).

Samuel Frenning's **attractiveness theory** (Fink & Penton-Voak, 2002) is concerned with how people evaluate the attractiveness of others and how these evaluations affect interpersonal relationships. It includes various elements that positively or negatively influence the attraction between individuals. In contrast to the similarity-attraction theory, the attractiveness theory states that the evaluation of attractiveness is based on three basic factors: physical, social, as well as task-related factors. Also of note are the four guiding principles of closeness, similarity, reciprocity, and reinforcement, which are important components of Freening's attractiveness theory. A positive view of these factors can thereby lead to the reinforcement of mutual trust.

Exchange theory states that interpersonal relationships are based on an exchange process in which costs and benefits are weighed (Cook et al., 2013). Here, human interactions and relationships are viewed from the perspective of the beneficial exchange of actions in order to maximize positive outcomes. Today, exchange theory is considered one of the most significant theoretical views of social interaction and social structure. Its importance was exemplified in the 1960s to 1970s by sociologists such as George Homans, Peter Blau, and Richard Emerson. For Homans the focus is on interpersonal exchange as well as the individual behaviour of actors as they interact with each other. Here, Homans sees social exchange as an exchange of rewarding and costly activities between at least two individuals. This interpersonal relationship thereby provides for positive development when both parties maximize their own interests and minimize negative consequences.

Attribution theory (Hewett et al., 2018) is concerned with how a person uses information to explain causal relationships for events. Here, attribution refers to gathering and combining information to form a causal judgment. The focus is on subjective explanations that are perceived to be correct rather than objective correctness (Raab et al., 2010). For the context of this work, the dimension of controllability by the actor is relevant (Hatzakis, 2009). The controllability dimension is primarily about the perceived degree of influence the actor will have on the outcome. If the actor perceives that he has low control over the outcome, his perceived helplessness and vulnerability increases. Consequently, this has a negative impact on trust.

Expectancy theory (Behling & Starke, 1973) fundamentally assumes that people choose actions that are most likely to fulfill their subjective expectations. In terms of trust formation, this can be related to the fact that people trust those individuals who are most likely to fulfill their expectations. An important feature here is also the preceding subjective evaluation of the results and consequences of action (Rank, 1997, S. 3). For many people, this idea of utility maximization is a feature of rational action. In the literature, the terms value-expectancy theory or utility theory are therefore also used for this theory, depending on the context. Utility theory states that people choose a product or service from which they will get the maximum value for their money (Bühlmann et al., 1969, S. 29). In terms of trust building, it can be concluded that people trust service providers who are most likely to fulfill their personal satisfaction.

4. CONCEPTION OF THE VR APP AND THE AGENT

The creation of the agent and its variations is based on the technological and psychological criteria. When creating the avatars, it was also ensured that they were created as analogously as possible to the homogeneous characteristics of the subjects. Accordingly, only male avatars were created in the context of this work, analogous to the selection of the subjects. In this way, the result with regard to the creation of trust through voice, appearance and interaction is not distorted by other psychological influencing factors, e.g. gender. Table 1 describes the characteristics of the avatars that have to be taken into account during the creation process, while Figure 1 shows their visual representation.

Table 1. Avatar visualization and animation features

#	Style	Type	Voice	Gestures	Lip-Sync
1	Realistic	Young male	Human voice	Complex animations	complex
2	Realistic	Old male	Human voice	Complex animations	complex
3	Cartoon	Young male	Human-like voice	Simple animations	simple
4	Cartoon	Old male	Human-like voice	Simple animations	simple
5	Non-Human	Animal	Generated voice	No animations	simple
6	Non-Human	Phantasy	Generated voice	No animations	simple

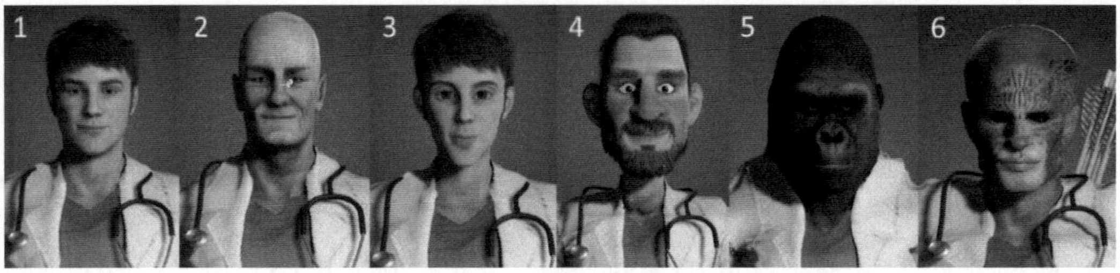

Figure 1. Avatar visualization

The interaction with the test persons in the context of a simulated consultation takes place in a practice room, which is characterized by elements such as medicine boxes or disinfection products (Figure 2).

Figure 2. Doctor's office for the simulated consultations

5. THE LABORATORY EXPERIMENT

The selection of 20 subjects is limited to males with a university degree or university students between the ages of 24 and 30. After acceptance, they were informed about the content and goal of the experiment. This will give them a rough overview of the course and design of the experiment in advance. In addition, the test persons are informed that the experiment can be carried out decentrally at the respective place of residence of the test person. On the one hand, this aims to increase motivation and willingness to participate. On the other hand, it ensures that the experiment can be conducted in a controlled environment without disturbing factors.

Immediately before the experiment is conducted, the subject is prepared for the upcoming interactions with the agents. His role as a patient in a health consultation is explained and the explanation of the evaluation form shows which factors have to be considered and evaluated during the interactions. The subject goes through the six variants of the consultation in random order and fill out the corresponding questionnaires in each case as shown in Figure 3. The three free variables concern the appearance of the agent, his voice, his gestures. The environment, the practice room, remains constantly realistic. The dependent variable is the perceived trust. The questionnaire contains five additional questions about the reasoning of trust, which are based on the psychological models.

During the laboratory experiment, covert observation of the test person takes place. Individual statements and reactions of the test person during the experiment are recorded. Subsequently, the subject is given an evaluation form to assess his experience. In this way, the subject is to record his experience as well as individual thought processes according to predefined criteria.

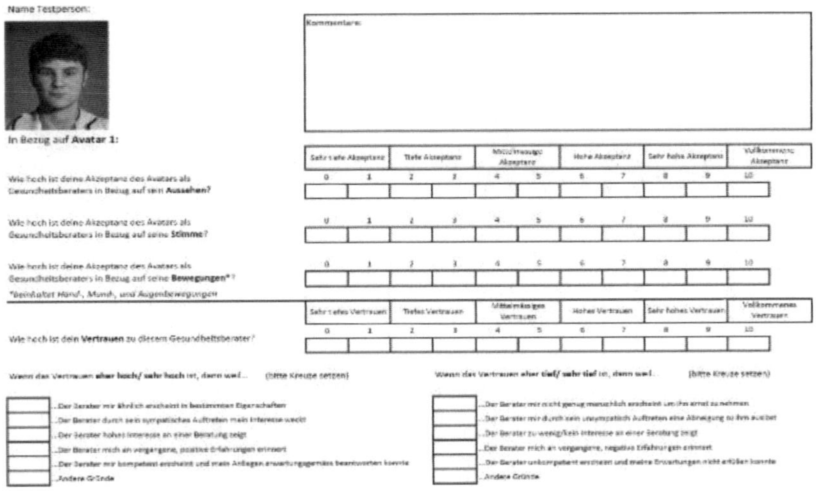
Name Testperson:

Kommentare:

In Bezug auf **Avatar 1:**

Sehr tiefe Akzeptanz	Tiefe Akzeptanz	Mittelmässige Akzeptanz	Hohe Akzeptanz	Sehr hohe Akzeptanz	Vollkommene Akzeptanz

Wie hoch ist deine Akzeptanz des Avatars als Gesundheitsberaters in Bezug auf sein **Aussehen?** 0 1 2 3 4 5 6 7 8 9 10

Wie hoch ist deine Akzeptanz des Avatars als Gesundheitsberaters in Bezug auf seine **Stimme?** 0 1 2 3 4 5 6 7 8 9 10

Wie hoch ist deine Akzeptanz des Avatars als Gesundheitsberaters in Bezug auf seine **Bewegungen*?** 0 1 2 3 4 5 6 7 8 9 10

*Beinhaltet Hand-, Mund-, und Augenbewegungen

Sehr tiefes Vertrauen	Tiefes Vertrauen	Mittelmässiges Vertrauen	Hohes Vertrauen	Sehr hohes Vertrauen	Vollkommenes Vertrauen

Wie hoch ist dein **Vertrauen** zu diesem Gesundheitsberater? 0 1 2 3 4 5 6 7 8 9 10

Wenn das Vertrauen **eher hoch/ sehr hoch** ist, dann weil… (bitte Kreuze setzen)

…Der Berater mir ähnlich erscheint in bestimmten Eigenschaften
…Der Berater durch sein sympatisches Auftreten mein Interesse weckt
…Der Berater hohes Interesse an einer Beratung zeigt
…Der Berater mich an vergangene, positive Erfahrungen erinnert
…Der Berater mir kompetent erscheint und mein Anliegen erwartungsgemäss beantworten konnte
…Andere Gründe

Wenn das Vertrauen **eher tief/ sehr tief** ist, dann weil… (bitte Kreuze setzen)

…Der Berater mir nicht genug menschlich erscheint um ihn ernst zu nehmen
…Der Berater mir durch sein unsympatisch Auftreten eine Abneigung zu ihm auslöst
…Der Berater zu wenig/kein Interesse an einer Beratung zeigt
…Der Berater mich an vergangene, negative Erfahrungen erinnert
…Der Berater unkompetent erschien und meine Erwartungen nicht erfüllen konnte
…Andere Gründe

Figure 3. Questionnaire in its original German version

6. RESULTS

Figure 4 shows that the formation of trust towards the realistic avatars can be explained by different psychological theories. The high trustworthiness of Avatar 1 is mainly characterized by the expression of three psychological theories: The Similarity Attraction Theory, the Attraction Theory, and the Exchange Theory. The strong expression of the Similarity Attraction Theory can be justified by the fact that Avatar 1 was created as a young health care worker visually similar to the homogeneous group of subjects. Out of 20 subjects, 13 sensed many similarity features in Avatar 1 during the laboratory experiment, especially with regard to his appearance and age. His realistic appearance eliminated many irritating confounding factors that occurred during interactions with the other avatars. The attractiveness theory is even more pronounced. 17 subjects found his appearance likeable and friendly. According to various statements, his human voice in particular generated a lot of sympathy among the subjects. Through his friendly appearance, he visibly showed a high level of interest in a health consultation, which significantly increased the subjects' willingness to interact. 14 subjects felt most noticed mainly because of his extroverted manner. As a result, beneficial interactions in the sense of the exchange theory were most pronounced with this avatar of all avatars. With an average score of 7.8 out of 10, Avatar 1's trustworthiness was rated as high by the subjects.

Avatar 2 has a slightly higher trustworthiness, which achieved an average score of 7.95 out of 10. The underlying psychological theories that characterize the trustworthiness of Avatar 2 are striking. The visibly higher age of Avatar 2 implied 15 subjects with a higher level of competence and more extensive expertise. For obtaining services concerning their own health, they are more likely to trust an experienced health advisor, as he or she has a more qualified impression. As a result, the expectation for expert health advice was highest for Avatar 2, which is why the expectancy theory was highest for him. 13 subjects further described their positive experiences with elderly service providers in different contexts. According to the subjects' subjective experiences, experts and specialists tend to be people of an older age, which is why they appear to be more trustworthy for obtaining a service. As a result, the attribution theory is also highest for Avatar 2. 11 subjects found his calm voice very pleasant and benevolent, which also confirms the attractiveness theory.

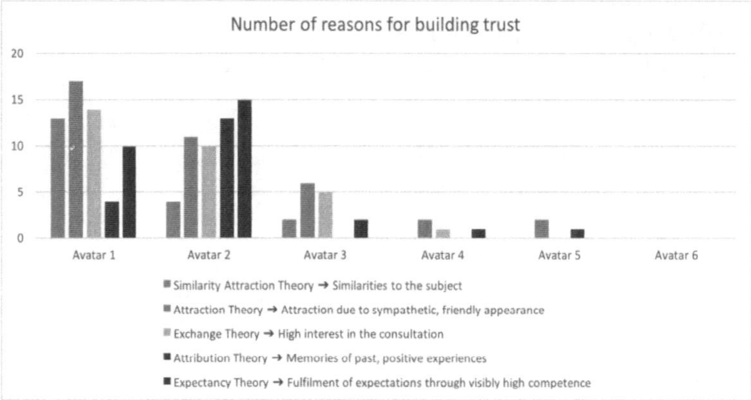

Figure 4. Reasons for building trust in the avatars

Avatar 3 elicited very mixed reactions from the subjects. Because his voice was pitched higher based on Avatar 1's voice, 6 subjects felt that interacting with him was friendly and inviting. His cartoon-like appearance caused some of the interaction with him to be described as humorous, resulting in a certain degree of attraction and trust building according to the attractiveness theory. However, the audibly artificial voice as well as the slightly exaggerated representations of facial features triggered a certain feeling of discomfort in some subjects. The reduced degree of realism caused 9 subjects to no longer perceive it as a lifelike human being. The slight discrepancy with the human appearance thus led to the formation of distrust in relation to the similarity-attraction theory. His high-pitched voice also caused 9 subjects to perceive him as an adolescent, thus questioning his competence as a health care provider. Therefore, following the expectancy theory, expectations toward him were low, which negatively affected his trustworthiness. With an average score of 5.05 out of 10, his trustworthiness was rated as mediocre.

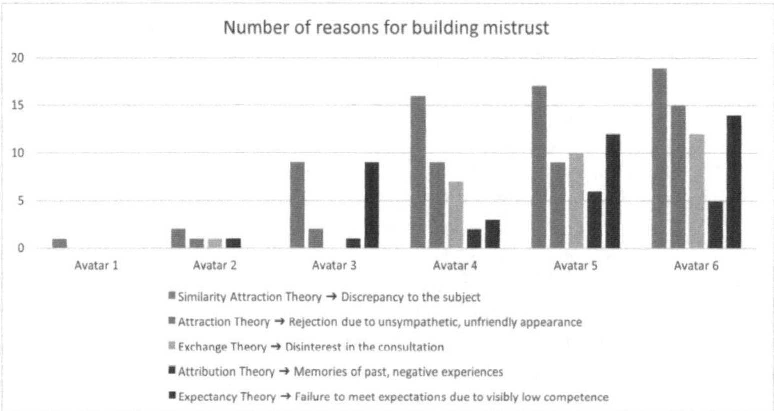

Figure 5. Reasons for mistrusting the avatars

Figure 5 shows how distrust increases with avatar 4. This is the first avatar for which trustworthiness was rated as low by the test subjects. The older cartoon avatar triggered low acceptance as a health advisor due to the exaggerated expressions of the facial features. Due to a deep voice pitch, his voice seemed inhuman and sinister to most subjects, which is why 16 subjects showed a strong rejection toward him according to the similarity-attraction theory. He thus appeared unattractive and unappealing for a trustworthy interaction in all areas, which led to the formation of distrust in 9 subjects according to attractiveness theory. The reduced level of non-verbal movements was interpreted by 7 subjects as a lack of interest in a health consultation, indicating a negative expression of the exchange theory. In general, his trustworthiness was rated low, with an average score of 3.7 out of 10. However, due to his advanced age, his professional competencies were not conspicuously questioned.

With an average value of 2.9, the trustworthiness of Avatar 5, which represents the first non-human avatar, was rated even lower. The gorilla triggered strong discomfort and rejection in 17 subjects due to its static movements and robotic voice. Thus, a strong negative expression according to the similarity-attraction theory is evident. This made it difficult for 10 subjects to perceive a serious interaction guidance in the context of a health consultation, which led to the formation of distrust according to the exchange theory. Based on diverse subjective experiences, the sight of the gorilla triggered a scary feeling in 6 subjects. Attributing to the attribution theory, this significantly reduced the trustworthiness of the gorilla towards these subjects. However, it should also be emphasized that the gorilla elicited sympathy in 2 subjects. The gorilla was received by them with humor, which is why the attractiveness theory has a small influence here. Beyond that, however, the question arose to what extent a gorilla would represent a competent and trustworthy health advisor in practice. According to the expectancy theory, 12 subjects were suspicious of whether a gorilla could trustworthily follow up on a patient's needs.

Avatar 6 has the lowest trustworthiness, which triggered distrust in all test subjects with an average value of 1.55 out of 10. The negative expression of the psychological theories took place to a high degree with this fantasy avatar. All reference to a human being is absent with this avatar. The unrealistic and inhuman representation seemed completely unsuitable for 19 test persons for a trustworthy execution of a health consultation. Due to the non-existent movements and the monotonous, robotic voice, no sympathy could be developed for him either, which is why 15 subjects found him unfriendly according to the attractiveness theory. For 14 subjects, the avatar seemed incompetent and unserious as a health advisor, which led to the formation of mistrust towards him according to the expectancy theory.

7. CONCLUSION

From the results of the laboratory experiment, it can be concluded that the psychological theories for building trust also find their applicability in the metaverse. The evaluation of the results show that the test persons trust or distrust the avatars in the context of a health consultation based on different psychological theories. It can be stated that the level of the individual theories varies depending on the avatar. In the case of a virtual health consultation, which is perceived as trustworthy and positive, a strong influence of the similarity-attraction theory and the expectancy theory can be observed. Avatars tend to be trusted more when they show basic similarities to human features. A visible deviation of avatars in this respect significantly reduces their trustworthiness. Expectation is also pronounced, especially when receiving a healthcare service. The avatars exhibit higher trustworthiness if they obviously give the impression that they have the assumed competencies and expertise. It should be emphasized, however, that the high expression of these theories is only confirmed for the group of subjects studied. It is conceivable that, for example, for a younger group of subjects, e.g., children, adolescents, high external discrepancies with a human being such as a cartoon avatar may trigger higher trust.

REFERENCES

Aljaroodi, H. M., Adam, M. T. P., Chiong, R., & Teubner, T. (2019). Avatars and Embodied Agents in Experimental Information Systems Research: A Systematic Review and Conceptual Framework. Australasian Journal of Information Systems, 23. https://doi.org/10.3127/ajis.v23i0.1841

Bansal, G., Rajgopal, K., Chamola, V., Xiong, Z., & Niyato, D. (2022). Healthcare in Metaverse: A Survey on Current Metaverse Applications in Healthcare. IEEE Access, 10, 119914–119946. https://doi.org/10.1109/ACCESS.2022.3219845

Behling, O., & Starke, F. A. (1973). The Postulates of Expectancy Theory. Academy of Management Journal, 16(3), 373–388. https://doi.org/10.5465/254999

Blog, B. R. (o. J.). Scientific report: „Avatars: Shaping Digital Identity in the Metaverse". Blockchain Research Lab. Abgerufen 13. Juli 2023, von https://www.blockchainresearchlab.org/2023/03/31/scientific-report-avatars-shaping-digital-identity-in-the-metaverse/

Bühlmann, H., Loeffel, H., & Nievergelt, E. (1969). Nutzentheorie und Ihre Anwendung. In H. Bühlmann, H. Loeffel, & E. Nievergelt (Hrsg.), Einführung in die Theorie und Praxis der Entscheidung bei Unsicherheit: Unterlagen für einen Kurs der Schweizerischen Vereinigung für Operations Research (S. 29–43). Springer. https://doi.org/10.1007/978-3-642-80553-0_3

Cook, K. S., Cheshire, C., Rice, E. R. W., & Nakagawa, S. (2013). Social Exchange Theory. In J. DeLamater & A. Ward (Hrsg.), Handbook of Social Psychology (S. 61–88). Springer Netherlands. https://doi.org/10.1007/978-94-007-6772-0_3

Felnhofer, A., Knaust, T., Weiss, L., Goinska, K., Mayer, A., & Kothgassner, O. D. (2023). A Virtual Character's Agency Affects Social Responses in Immersive Virtual Reality: A Systematic Review and Meta-Analysis. International Journal of Human–Computer Interaction, 0(0), 1–16. https://doi.org/10.1080/10447318.2023.2209979

Fink, B., & Penton-Voak, I. (2002). Evolutionary Psychology of Facial Attractiveness. Current Directions in Psychological Science, 11(5), 154–158. https://doi.org/10.1111/1467-8721.00190

Hatzakis, T. (2009). Towards a Framework of Trust Attribution Styles. British Journal of Management, 20(4), 448–460. https://doi.org/10.1111/j.1467-8551.2008.00596.x

Hewett, R., Shantz, A., Mundy, J., & Alfes, K. (2018). Attribution theories in Human Resource Management research: A review and research agenda. The International Journal of Human Resource Management, 29(1), 87–126. https://doi.org/10.1080/09585192.2017.1380062

Montoya, R. M., & Horton, R. S. (2013). A meta-analytic investigation of the processes underlying the similarity-attraction effect. Journal of Social and Personal Relationships, 30(1), 64–94.

Raab, G., Unger, A., & Unger, F. (2010). Attributionstheorien. In G. Raab, A. Unger, & F. Unger (Hrsg.), Marktpsychologie: Grundlagen und Anwendung (S. 77–96). Gabler. https://doi.org/10.1007/978-3-8349-6314-7_6

Rank, B. (1997). Erwartungs-Wert-Theorien: Ein Theoriekonzept der Wirtschaftspsychologie und seine Anwendung auf eine berufsbiographische Entscheidung. München und Mering: Rainer Hampp Verlag.

Rheu, M. (MJ), Jang, Y., & Peng, W. (2020). Enhancing Healthy Behaviors Through Virtual Self: A Systematic Review of Health Interventions Using Avatars. Games for Health Journal, 9(2), 85–94. https://doi.org/10.1089/g4h.2018.0134

Roebken, H. (2010). Similarity Attracts: An Analysis of Recruitment Decisions in Academia. Educational Management Administration & Leadership, 38(4), 472–486. https://doi.org/10.1177/1741143210368264

Sajjadi, P., Hoffmann, L., Cimiano, P., & Kopp, S. (2018). On the Effect of a Personality-Driven ECA on Perceived Social Presence and Game Experience in VR. 2018 10th International Conference on Virtual Worlds and Games for Serious Applications (VS-Games), 1–8. https://doi.org/10.1109/VS-Games.2018.8493436

Santee, R. T. (1976). The Effect on Attraction of Attitude Similarity as Information About Interpersonal Reinforcement Contingencies. Sociometry, 39(2), 153–156. https://doi.org/10.2307/2786215

Seymour, M., Riemer, K., & Kay, J. (2018). Actors, Avatars and Agents: Potentials and Implications of Natural Face Technology for the Creation of Realistic Visual Presence. Journal of the Association for Information Systems, 19(10). https://aisel.aisnet.org/jais/vol19/iss10/4

Seymour, M., Yuan, L., Dennis, A., & Riemer, K. (2020). Facing the Artificial: Understanding Affinity, Trustworthiness, and Preference for More Realistic Digital Humans. http://hdl.handle.net/10125/64316

Simpson, J. A. (2007). Psychological Foundations of Trust. Current Directions in Psychological Science, 16(5), 264–268. https://doi.org/10.1111/j.1467-8721.2007.00517.x

Skalidis, I., Muller, O., & Fournier, S. (2022). CardioVerse: The cardiovascular medicine in the era of Metaverse. Trends in Cardiovascular Medicine. https://doi.org/10.1016/j.tcm.2022.05.004

Sparwasser, P., Haack, M., Frey, L., Haferkamp, A., & Borgmann, H. (2022). Virtual und Augmented Reality in der Urologie. Der Urologe, 61(2), 133–141. https://doi.org/10.1007/s00120-021-01734-y

Thomason, J. (2021). Metahealth-how will the metaverse change health care? Journal of Metaverse, 1(1), 13–16.

EVALUATION OF GPU-CENTRIC EMBEDDED ARCHITECTURES IN THE FIELD OF NEUROMUSCULAR EMG-BASED AI

Simon Pfenning[1], Raul C. Simpetru[2], Niklas Pollak[2], Alessandro Del Vecchio[2] and Dietmar Fey[1]
[1]Chair of Computer Architecture, FAU
Erlangen, Germany
[2]Neuromuscular Physiology and Neural Interfacing Laboratory, FAU
Erlangen, Germany

ABSTRACT

The recent progress in the design of deep neural networks has led a huge step forward in inference accuracy and opened new opportunities also in the design of AI aided medical hardware. However deep neural models have a high demand in both computational as well as memory resources. To make these systems applicable in the field, it is necessary to find a suitable hardware-software ecosystem, which can meet these demands at a sufficiently low energy consumption. For this purpose, we evaluated a modern heterogeneous embedded platform with a deep convolutional network for hand position recognition, based on the collection of electromyography signals. The goal of our evaluation was to find out, how much effort must be spent for optimization, if the architecture itself would be sufficient for the usage as human wearable device and which of the available accelerators on the embedded platform are best suited for the task.

KEYWORDS

EMG, CNN, Deep Learning, GPU, Embedded Hardware

1. INTRODUCTION

Hand position recognition using surface electromyography (sEMG) signals has become an increasingly popular area of research (Liu et al., 2021; Saif et al., 2022; Rahimian et al., 2022; Sîmpetru et al., 2022; Sîmpetru et al., 2023). This non-invasive technology has many potential applications, including prosthetic devices, human-machine interfaces, and robotics. Deep learning algorithms have shown to deliver reliable results in classifying sEMG signals into different hand gestures (Liu et al., 2021), (Rahimian et al., 2022). Compared to classical pattern recognition approaches such as support vector machines (SVM) or random forests, deep neural networks (DNN) are far less time consuming in design and achieve a better mapping of the complex and non-linear relationships between sEMG signals and the hand positions. The convolutional neural network (CNN) (Goodfellow et al., 2016) which will be considered in this paper is trained on regressing not only specific gestures but estimating the position of the entire hand.

On a high-performance computing system this network is able to deliver precise results in real-time. However, for the deployment of this algorithm in the field close to the human body, there are still some major challenges remaining. Since the implementation needs to be performed on devices constrained by size, and energy consumption, the compute capabilities of the underlying hardware are drastically restricted. Moreover, the CNNs commonly used for hand position recognition, are both computationally and memory demanding if they are to deliver accurate estimations in real-time. For this reason, embedded systems designed for executing the inference of such algorithms, are often equipped with specific accelerator cores, to improve the computation of the network most efficiently (Reuther et al., 2020). However, to achieve desirable results, this specific hardware design requires a highly optimized implementation of the algorithm. Our objective was to find an alternative low-power hardware setup to the current existing one, equipped with a desktop graphics processing unit (GPU). The device should be able to fulfill the needs of the high resource demand of the CNN, while staying very efficient at the same time. Therefore, we decided to evaluate the algorithm on a current embedded GPU platform, which still delivers a decent amount of computational power and memory size. To see how the

algorithm behaves when optimizing for an embedded use case we investigated the real-time capability and energy consumption of the resulting implementation. The platform contains a small GPU as well as some specific deep learning accelerator (DLA) cores. To obtain reasonable results, the original network as described in
(Sîmpetru et al., 2023) is modified to make use of the architectural design. For this purpose, we describe multiple approaches for optimization. We give insights on the deployment to the hardware and the specific benefits obtained by the conducted steps.

We then evaluate the suitability of the implemented system in terms of direct mounting on the human body for various use cases including orthotic and prosthetic devices. Finally, a proposal is given on whether the current system is sufficient, or if more optimization work needs to be done.

2. DEEP CNN FOR EMG REGRESSION

2.1 Experimental Protocol

We previously collected sEMG data from nine subjects performing three hand gestures as well as a multitude of dynamic movements in sync with their hand kinematics (Sîmpetru et al., 2023). The sEMG was acquired from 5 electrode grids (Figure 1).

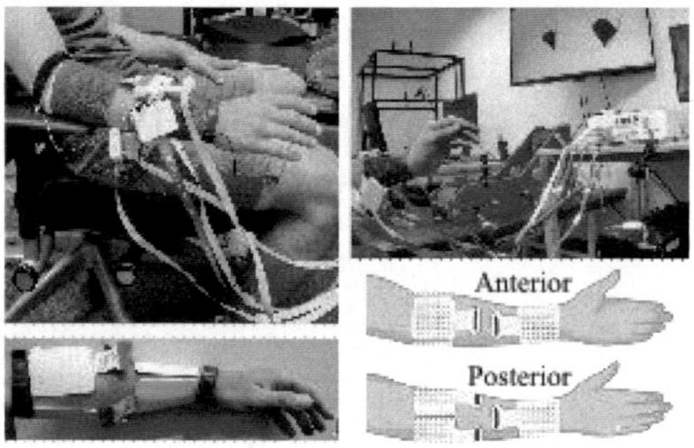

Figure 1. Experimental setup taken from *Sîmpetru et al.* (Sîmpetru et al., 2023). The subjects have 5 electrode grids attached to their forearm. Each electrode grid has 64 electrodes resulting in a total of 320 EMG signals

Three high-density EMG grids were placed around the thickest part of the forearm and two around the wrist, proximal to the ulnar head. Before placing the electrode grids, the skin was shaved and cleaned with an alcoholic solution. We recorded a total of 320 monopolar sEMG signals using a multichannel amplifier, amplified (×150) and band-pass filtered (0.7–500 Hz) at source. The signals were sampled at 2048 Hz and captured during the movement execution using a custom script written in Python. We recorded 30 seconds per movement, resulting in a total of 12 minutes of data for training a previously published network (Sîmpetru et al., 2022) from zero that we have updated for real-time capabilities (R. C. Sîmpetru et al., 2023).

2.2 EMG Preprocessing

In order to provide an embodied feeling for the subjects during real-time testing we set the EMG multichannel amplifier to provide the sEMG signals as 32 non-overlapping segments per second. This allowed our system to make a prediction every 31.25 ms resulting in smooth movement intent prediction. Ideally, prediction works only on the basis of the neurophysiological information contained in a single sEMG segment, but we have found empirically that the temporal information contained in a single segment is not sufficient. To collect enough temporal information, we create a queue containing 3 such segments, which gives 93.75 ms of information. The queue is always shifted by one segment to ensure a smooth prediction of movement. We further augment the 93.75 ms sEMG with its 20 Hz low-passed version to provide a less variable view of the information. The low-pass filter was a 4th order Butterworth filter, which we used to filter forward and backward to achieve phase-free filtering.

2.3 Model Architecture

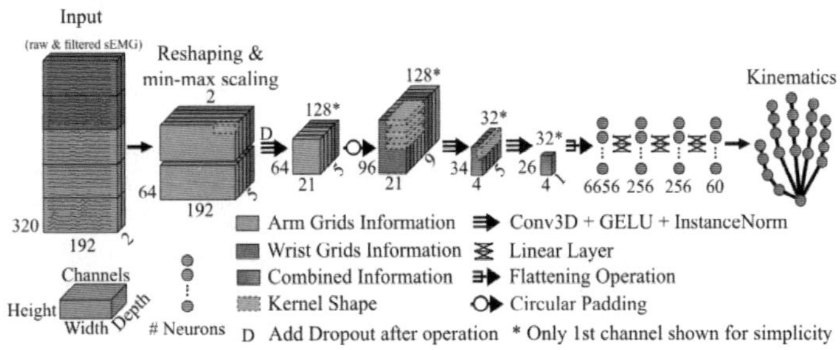

Figure 2. Experimental setup taken from Sîmpetru et al. (Sîmpetru et al., 2023). The subjects have 5 electrode grids attached to their forearm. Each electrode grid has 64 electrodes resulting in a total of 320 EMG signals

The model (Figure 2) for motion intention detection has been described in detail in *Sîmpetru et al.* (Sîmpetru et al., 2023) thus we only provide information necessary to understand the computational necessity of the individual layers.

The network consists of two parts: a CNN, which maps the sEMG signals into a high-dimensional latent space, and a subsequent multilayer perceptron (MLP), which transforms the latent space into Cartesian space.

The input of the network is a 3D tensor with a shape of 320x192x2 (electrodes, number of samples, filtered and unfiltered signal). In total one input tensor consists of 61442 floating point values.

The first step of the network is to reshape the input by dividing the 320 electrodes into the 5 grids they correspond to, creating a 4D tensor of the form 2 x 5 x 64 x 192. This reshaped tensor is then standardized grid-wise. After the reshape, the first operation performed in the network is a 3D CNN layer. It contains 128 channels and runs a time-wise kernel of size 32 with a stride of 8. Then, the output of the first layer is circularly padded by 2 in the grid dimension (from 5 to 9) and 16 in the electrode dimension (from 64 to 96). On the padded tensor we run a 5 x 32 x 18 kernel that integrates the electrode-wise only information int cross-grid patterns. To reduce computational complexity, the kernel is dilated in the electrode dimension by a factor of 2. The layer has 32 channels. The last layer also has 32 channels and is used to further extract information from the previously generated patterns by applying a 5 x 9 x 1 kernel. Each layer mentioned is followed by a Normalization layer (Ulyanov et al., 2017) and the activation function GELU (Hendrycks and Gimpel, 2020). The output is flattened and passed through a 3 layered MLP with sizes of 6656, 128 respectively. The last layer of the network outputs a 60D vector that represents the 20 hand joint coordinates in Cartesian space (x, y, and z).

3. HARDWARE OVERVIEW

For the implementation of the embedded inference system, we decided to use two platforms from Nvidia, the Xavier AGX and Xavier NX. Both being built upon the same architecture, but with a different configuration of the integrated CPU- and GPU-cores as well as the usable memory bandwidth. Xavier AGX has 33 % more GPU compute units and a memory interface twice as large. In theory it should be able to offer more compute power but at the cost of doubling the power consumption to a maximum of 30 Watts. Even though these numbers sound quite high for an embedded system, it is already a significant improvement to the previous system using an RTX 3090 with more than 350 Watt. The DLA cores are identical in design and directly attached to the main memory interface.

In the evaluation section we will investigate, if the differences between both Xavier platforms make for a better sweet spot regarding the entire efficiency of the system. In the next two subsections we will give a brief overview on the respective architectures of the accelerator cores as well as where their strengths reside.

3.1 GPU Architecture

GPUs have proven themselves to be well suited for the usage in Deep Learning (Kayid et al., 2018). Their properties as streaming processors make them an ideal choice for processing graph-based algorithms such as neural networks. Both Xavier chips contain GPUs, which are based on NVidias Volta architecture, which introduced a couple of new features specifically designed for the improved execution of training and inference of neural network algorithms.

3.1.1 Quantization

A technique that had a significant impact on the efficiency of executing deep neural networks on embedded architectures is the improved acceleration of values quantized in a lower bit width, for example FP16 or INT8, instead of FP32 (Choukroun et al., 2019). The use of lower precision data types for both activations and weights has had a twofold positive impact. First, the same compute units can perform double or quadruple the number of calculations at the same time and with the same amount of energy. Second, the memory footprint of the network can be shrunk to an excessive degree, which makes up for the smaller amount of memory available in embedded devices. Even though this leads to a certain drop in the accuracy of the inferred results, many deep learning algorithms have proven to be very robust against more aggressive quantization due to the under determined character.

3.1.2 Tensor Cores

The most prominent improvement of NVidia's Volta GPU family is probably the introduction of so-called Tensor Cores (Choquette et al., 2018). Tensor Cores are vector processing units, based on the design principles of systolic arrays (Chowdhury et al., 2020). They can conduct a 4x4 mixed-precision matrix-matrix multiplication and accumulation (MAC) per clock-cycle. For each 64 scalar compute units there are eight Tensor Cores, effectively increasing the peak number of calculations per cycle by a factor of five. This special type of compute units is very beneficial for the deployment of neural networks, especially CNNs. The most common components for these types of networks are convolutional and fully connected layers, which can be easily mapped onto MAC operations and thus being very efficiently computed by the Tensor Cores.

3.1.3 DLA Cores

Each of the chips also offers two accelerators, which are designed specifically for improving the execution of CNNs. Every of these DLA cores contains five optimized blocks for conducting certain types of convolutions, activation functions, pooling, normalization and reshape (Zhou et al., 2018). During runtime it is possible to either use each of the functional units separately, such that independent parts of the network can be executed in parallel. Or a pipelined approach can be adopted where small chunks of consecutive network-layers are mapped onto the respective functional units. The advantage of this procedure consists in the more effective data transfers between consecutive layers of the network, which can now be passed from one execution unit to the next by register transfers.

In the present case, the implementation is realized as a headless core. This implies that the configuration and control of a DLA core is handled by the CPU. The supposed reason for this kind of design is power saving since an additional control unit and an SRAM memory can be saved. On the other hand, the DLA's function units now need to directly access the slow main memory, because the cores don't offer their own L2 cache. This has the potential of a huge negative impact in cases where a pipelined execution of the network is not easily feasible, since every unit has to access the slower main memory for obtaining its data separately. In 5 we give an evaluation how well the execution of the given network was improved by these cores.

4. OPTIMIZATION METHODS

In the next sections we describe the steps conducted for optimization, to obtain an overview of the achievable results and to see which of them turns out to be the most promising.

4.1 Network Structure

The first step towards achieving a more efficient execution, are hardware agnostic methods that optimize the generic mathematical operations in the network. Traditionally the computation of neural networks is executed layer-by-layer, requiring intermediate results to be stored in memory and transferred between layers. This process incurs additional memory accesses and computational overhead, resulting in increased latency and reduced overall efficiency. As a countermeasure we use NVidia's model-compiler TensorRT, to modify the network structure. Expendable operations are eliminated from the compute graph, for example dropout layers, which are only relevant during training. Furthermore, operations of sequential or adjacent layers are fused into a single kernel and eliminates the need for intermediate memory transfers, redundant computations, and the number of kernel calls. For our network model the predominant fused layer types are convolutions and activations.

4.2 Quantization

The second measure exploits the ability of the embedded GPU to compute on smaller data types in a vectorized way (Choukroun et al., 2019), such that a regular scalar processing unit can achieve double the compute throughput.

Another very important factor to note here are the Tensor Cores, which are implemented within the GPU architecture and allow for a maximum data width of 16 bit for matrix-matrix multiplication. For this reason, we chose 16 bit as a first step for quantization reduction, because we lose a minimal amount of information while at the same time, we expect more than seven times the compute performance. This is since the scalar units on Xavier NX are delivering a peak single precision compute performance of roughly 850 GFLOPS and the 48 Tensor Cores having a total of 6.1 TFLOPS.

For quantizing there are basically two possible implementations, either during the training phase, or afterwards. The major benefit of quantization-aware training is a reduced loss in accuracy of the estimation results. For our case we decided to stick with a post training implementation, since our goal was optimizing an already trained network onto embedded hardware without the necessity of retraining. During the evaluation, we will address the impact of this decision when considering the loss of accuracy.

4.3 DLA

In the final stage of our optimization the integration of the DLA cores is conducted. We decided to opt for a pipelined programming option, mentioned in 3.1.3, to keep the number of accesses to the main memory as low as possible. Memory transfers already are a burden since the DLA cores alone are not able to solve all the network's layers. This leads to an additional continuous data traffic on main memory between DLA and GPU. Because of this, our primary intention of making use of the accelerator cores was not necessarily an improvement in execution time, but rather to achieve a significant advance in energy efficiency.

5. EVALUATION

For the overall evaluation we compare the three optimized variants on both platforms with each other and against the original unoptimized network runtime, as well as the formerly used desktop GPU. To be able to classify the results correctly, it must first be determined which threshold value the inference time must meet to be considered real-time capable. It is not easy to establish a real threshold for latency since a prosthetic hand that can be considered a complete replacement has not yet been implemented. Since the current frequency of input data from the sensors is a maximum of 32 Hz, we assume that inference within this time frame can be tentatively assumed to be real-time capable.

5.1 Inference Latency

At first, we have a look on the inference latency (Figure 3). As expected, the desktop GPU delivers the best results by far and is always able to stay below the real-time threshold at the cost of a twenty-fold increase in power consumption (360W). From the original Torch model, we can already obtain a 33 % lower latency by reducing the operations of the networks compute graph with the help of TensorRT. This is without losing any information. When applying the quantization to FP16 the GPU's Tensor Cores come into play. This can be observed in the graph as a decrease of the latency by a factor of six, which is just the amount in peak computational performance delivered by the Tensor Cores. With this boost, the inference time is easily below the real-time threshold. The DLA implementation however suffers a lot from the additional memory transfers and is not able to keep up even though it also uses weights and activations of FP16 precision. As we will see later, the problem arises from the layer structure of the network.

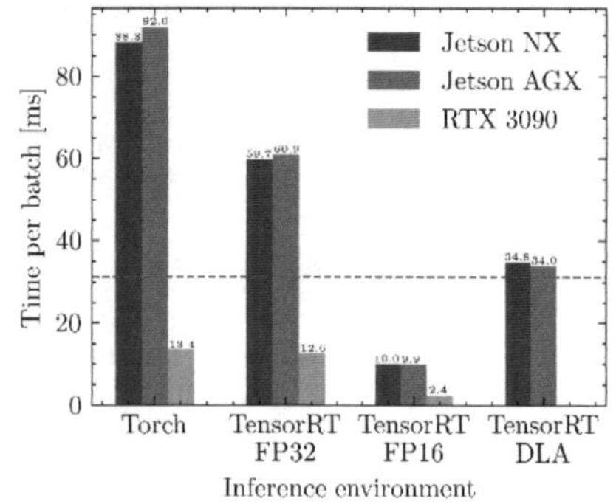

Figure 3. We obtain a 33% faster latency by the adaption of the CNN structure and x6 advance due to FP16 quantization. The DLA implementation is far slower

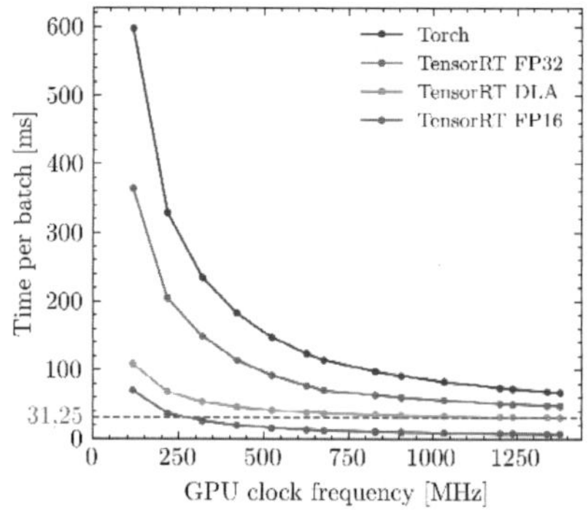

Figure 4. The sweet spot for FP16 resides at 300 MHz. The DLA implementation converges against the real-time threshold but doesn't reach it

To find the sweet spot for real-time capability, the frequency of the processing units is now varied for every iteration (Figure 4). The only optimized model available to reach well below the real-time threshold is the FP16 GPU implementation using a frequency of 300 MHz. The DLA implementation, even though also utilizing 16 bit parameters, cannot achieve the same performance. We will see later why this is the case.

5.2 Quantization Error

With the improvements in runtime due to quantization, a certain error is introduced into the estimation of finger joint positions. Before we start talking about the effects of this error, we first need to define how to measure it. For this we calculate the Euclidian distance between the estimated 3D-coordinate of the *i* joints of the quantized network to the original one. This error already has relatively high quantity going from an average of 0.001mm to 2mm in the FP16 model (Figure 5).

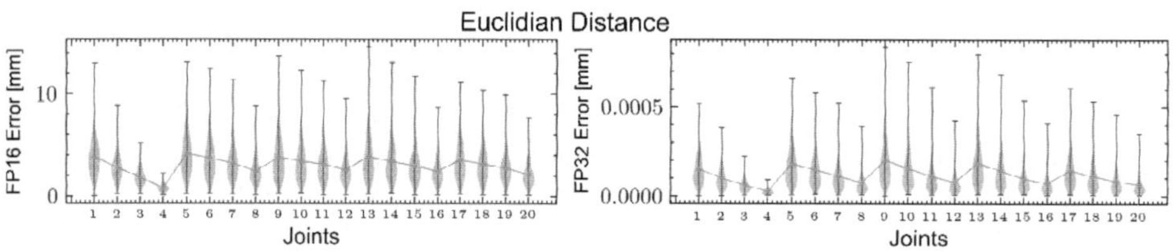

Figure 5. The quantization introduced error is significant but still acceptable 2mm on average per finger joint

Nevertheless, it is acceptable for the early stage of development. For the future a solution based on quantization-aware training should be aimed at. Especially considering another reduction in parameter size to 8 bit for further improving on the inference efficiency.

5.3 Layer-Wise Latency Analysis

In Figure 3 we detect that Xavier AGX, even though having a substantially more powerful GPU, could not achieve a speedup compared to its smaller counterpart. Thus, to identify the existence of any bottlenecks, we measured the execution time for each layer of the network. It appears that layer conv_1 of size 5 x 32 x 18 has by far the most impact, as it amounts to over 90% of an entire inference run (Table 1).

Table 1. The execution time for the networks three most impactful layers for FP32 configuration, sorted by their impact on the latency

Layername	Time [ms]	Percentage [%]	Layername	Time [ms]	Percentage [%]
cnn_encoder/conv_1	58.625	96.54	cnn_encoder/conv_1	57.306	95.94
cnn_encoder/drop-out	0.733	1.21	cnn_encoder/drop-out	0.984	1.65
reshape_and_nor-malize	0.491	0.81	reshape_and_nor-malize	0.407	0.68
Jetson Xavier AGX			Jetson Xavier NX		

We detected that the shape of the first layer leads to the same mapping of operations onto the processing units of both the GPUs. Therefore, the larger GPU cannot derive a benefit from its additional two compute clusters, because they do not get used for the layer. A different mapping of the operations onto more compute clusters is possible but will also lead to a more inefficient implementation inside a single cluster and eventually lead to an even worse result. For better occupancy, a redesign of the layer proportions or a split into two consecutive layers are the most promising alternatives to resolve the bottleneck.

For the FP16 GPU and DLA implementations we can observe a similar behavior. However, since the 3D convolutional layers are not yet supported by the DLA compute units, they are not offloaded to them but stay on the GPU instead. The following layers can be processed by the DLA cores, but at the cost of a higher number of main memory transfers due to the pipelined principle of the architecture not in use.

Layername	Time [ms]	Percentage [%]
cnn encoder/conv 1	8.276	83.98
reshape and normalize	0.341	3.46
cnn encoder/instance norm 0	0.219	2.23
cnn_encoder/conv_0	0.216	2.2
cnn encoder/gelu 0	0.104	1.05
cnn_encoder/conv 2	0.068	0.69
mlp encoder/linear 0	0.037	0.37
mlp_encoder/linear_1	0.021	0.21
cnn encoder/instance norm 1	0.018	0.18
mlp_encoder/linear 2	0.012	0.13
cnn_encoder/instance_norm_2	0.011	0.11
cnn encoder/gelu 1	0.011	0.11
cnn encoder/flatten	0.008	0.08
cnn_encoder/gelu_2	0.006	0.07
mlp_encoder/gelu_1	0.006	0.07
mlp encoder/gelu 0	0.006	0.06

FP16

Layername	Time [ms]	Percentage [%]
cnn encoder/conv 1	8.253	36.3
cnn encoder/gelu 0	7.645	33.6
reshape and normalize	2.686	7.78
cnn_encoder/gelu_1	1.534	4.44
cnn encoder/gelu 2	1.516	4.39
cnn encoder/instance norm 0	0.327	0.95
cnn encoder/conv 0	0.23	0.67
mlp_encoder/linear_0	0.151	0.44
mlp encoder/gelu 0	0.09	0.26
mlp encoder/gelu 1	0.082	0.24
mlp_encoder/linear_2	0.077	0.22
cnn encoder/conv 2	0.073	0.21
mlp encoder/linear 1	0.073	0.21
cnn_encoder/instance_norm_1	0.033	0.09
cnn_encoder/instance_norm_2	0.024	0.07
cnn encoder/flatten	0.008	0.02

DLA

Figure 6. The layers of the GPU FP16 and the DLA implementation. Layers executed by DLA are marked in red

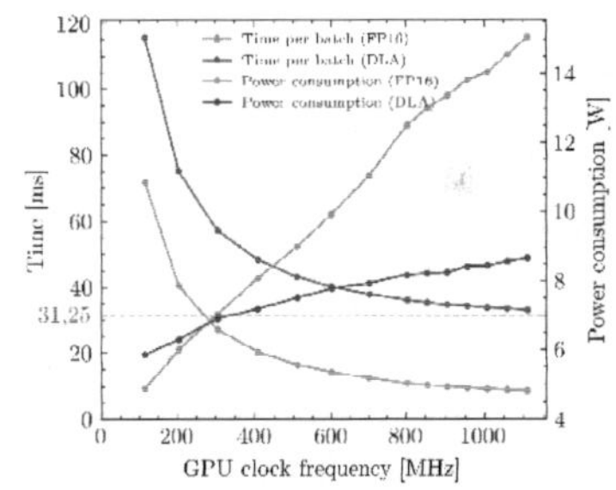

Figure 7. Comparison of the power efficiency of the DLA and the FP16 GPU implementation

5.4 Power Consumption

Power efficiency is one of the major points of interest, when it comes to designing embedded systems. For this part we neglected the differentiation between the Jetson boards, since show a very similar behavior. At the sweet spot of 300 MHz the quantized GPU implementation has a power consumption of 7 Watt (Figure 7). For lower clock speeds the GPU appears to be the more efficient choice. When it comes to higher frequencies, the additionally used DLA cores start to pay off and the system gets a lot more power efficient. We anticipate surpassing the achieved results with a few more adaptions, such as the exchange from 3D to 2D convolutions and further 8 bit quantization-aware training, in the near future.

6. CONCLUSION

With our rapid prototyped GPU/DLA optimization, we were able to already obtain decent results. A power consumption of below 10 Watt is a great achievement, compared to the desktop GPU with more than the twenty-fold energy expense. However, to be of reasonable use in a portable device, it is still far too high.

Therefore, our future efforts from now on will go in two directions. We will further tune the existing design for even higher efficiency, to quickly examine how robust the CNN behaves on more severe measures and further optimization techniques. For the development of a future portable device, we are also striving for a custom digital design based on an FPGA. We expect this to allow for a reduction of the power consumption for the entire system to less than 1 Watt. This in turn would enable us to dispense with the bulky cooling system, as well as significantly extend battery operation time. To ease our efforts on the digital circuit design, we can draw on our preliminary work. For an effective framework on implementing systolic DNN accelerators, we rely on the work achieved by (Knödtel et al., 2020). The mapping of the entire network on hardware will be based on the process described in (Pfenning et al., 2021). By this approach a high-level Python implementation of a neural network in TensorFlow can be executed on dedicated hardware according to the principles described in (Holzinger and Reichenbach, 2021). This way, we expect to be able to quickly achieve decent results on low-power FPGA SoCs, such as Xilinx Zynq Ultrascale+ family.

REFERENCES

Choquette, J., et al. (2018). Volta: Performance and programmability. IEEE Micro, vol. 38, no. 2. pp. 42–52.

Choukroun, Y., et al. (2019). Low-bit quantization of neural networks for efficient inference. pp. 3009–3018.

Chowdhury, R., et al. (2020). A computational model for tensor core units. 32nd ACM Symposium on Parallelism in Algorithms and Architectures. p. 519–521. Available: https://doi.org/10.1145/3350755.3400252

Goodfellow, I., et al. (2016). Deep Learning. MIT Press. Available: https://www.deeplearningbook.org/

Hendrycks, D., and Gimpel, K. (2020). Gaussian Error Linear Units (GELUs). arXiv:1606.08415. Available: http://arxiv.org/abs/1606.08415

Holzinger, P., and Reichenbach, M. (2021). The HERA methodology: Reconfigurable logic in general-purpose computing. IEEE Access, vol. 9. pp. 147 212–147 236.

Kayid, A., et al. (2018). Performance of cpus/gpus for deep learning workloads.

Knödtel, J., et al. (2020). A model-to-circuit compiler for evaluation of DNN accelerators based on systolic arrays and multibit emerging memories. 9th International Conference on Modern Circuits and Systems Technologies (MOCAST). pp. 1–6.

Liu, Y., et al. (2021). NeuroPose: 3D Hand Pose Tracking using EMG Wearables. Web Conference, ser. WWW '21. New York, NY, USA: Association for Computing Machinery. Available: https://doi.org/10.1145/3442381.3449890

Pfenning, S., et al. (2021). Transparent FPGA Acceleration with TensorFlow. DATE Friday Workshop on Systemlevel design Methods for Deep Learning on Heterogeneous Architectures (SLOHA 2021)

Rahimian, E., et al. (2022). Hand Gesture Recognition Using Temporal Convolutions and Attention Mechanism. IEEE International Conference on Acoustics, Speech and Signal Processing (ICASSP). pp. 1196–1200.

Reuther, A., et al. (2020). Survey of machine learning accelerators. IEEE High Performance Extreme Computing Conference (HPEC). pp. 1-12. doi: 10.1109/HPEC43674.2020.9286149.

Saif, R., et al. (2022). Multi-Channel EMG Signal analysis for Italian Sign Language Interpretation. International Conference on Emerging Trends in Smart Technologies (ICETST). pp. 1–5.

Sîmpetru, R. C., et al. (2022). Accurate Continuous Prediction of 14 Degrees of Freedom of the Hand from Myoelectrical Signals through Convolutive Deep Learning. 44th Annual International Conference of the IEEE Engineering in Medicine & Biology Society (EMBC). pp. 702–706.

Sîmpetru, R. C., et al. (2023). Proportional and Simultaneous Real-Time Control of the Full Human Hand From High-Density Electromyography. [Online]. Available: https://doi.org/10.36227/techrxiv.21904335

Ulyanov, D., Vedaldi, A., and Lempitsky, V. (2017). Instance Normalization: The Missing Ingredient for Fast Stylization. arXiv:1607.08022 [cs]. Available: http://arxiv.org/abs/1607.08022

Zhou, G., et al. (2018). Research on NVidia deep learning accelerator. 12th IEEE International Conference on Anti-counterfeiting, Security, and Identification (ASID). pp. 192–195.

ACTIVE ANCHORS: SIMILARITY BASED REFINEMENT LEARNING

Connor Clarkson, Michael Edwards and Xianghua Xie
Computer Science Department, Swansea University
Swansea, United Kingdom

ABSTRACT

Defect detection in steel manufacturing has achieved state-of-the-art results in both localisation and classification on various types of defects, however, this assumes very high-quality datasets that have been verified by domain experts. Labelling such data has become a time-consuming and interaction-heavy task with a great amount of user effort, this is due to variability in the defect characteristics and composite nature. We propose a new acquisition function based on the similarity of defects for refining labels over time by showing the user only the most required to be labelled. We also explore different ways in which to feed these new refinements back into the model to utilize the new knowledge in an effortful way. We achieve this with a graphical interface that provides additional information to the domain expert as the data gets refined, allowing for decision-making with uncertain areas of the steel.

KEYWORDS

Similarity Learning, Data Refinement, Active Learning, Defect Detection, Interactive, Acquisition Function

1. INTRODUCTION

Gathering large pools of data has become a relatively straightforward task, with many automated ways of obtaining various sources of data. The development of pattern mining and feature representation learning approaches which leverage large collections of observations has resulted in data becoming a prized resource in recent years. Labelling such data has become an exponential problem, being a time-consuming and interaction-heavy task that involves a great amount of user effort. This development has led to the rise of active learning as a semi-supervised alternative to data labelling, where a selection of samples is labelled to refine the model's behaviour. Many domains require skilled expert knowledge to label such data; including medical image analysis (Budd, Robinson & Kainz 2021), manufacturing quality control (Sun, Gu, Tang & Li 2018), and even genomics research (Zhang & Zhou 2006). In the context of the manufacturing industry, steel is a diverse and heavily used product with many different use cases. Variability in how steel is processed can result in various types of defects such as lamination, heavy scales and edge damage. Often these defects are highly variant in shape and characteristics, lighting issues in capturing the defect, and other types of artifacts not considered defects, like soot or water (Sun, Gu, Tang & Li 2018). These often result in a challenging environment within manufacturing, and therefore it is commonplace to have visual inspection systems to help ensure a level of quality in the final product. The setup and running of such systems are complex due to the many different ways we can manufacture such products, and as such the deployment of such inspection systems will often be adapted for their circumstances (Neogi, Mohanta & Dutta 2014). These systems will often have a classification component, which attempts to recognise the different kinds of defects present on the surface of the material so that suitable approaches can be taken later in the development pipeline to correct the issue, whether this is cutting out defective regions or repurposing the product. Such systems often rely on large datasets, with engineering domain experts providing ground truth labels for the training of supervised approaches, with labelling often falling into two camps; dense labelling of pixels within the images captured by the system, or sparse labelling using bounding boxes. The dense labelling provides a fine resolution label of the defect but requires significant input by the domain expert and so is often prohibitive. The bounding-box approach allows an expert to label the defect with less overhead but can introduce incorrectly labelled pixels to what should be a ground-truth target for supervised approaches to utilise (Xu, Bai & Ghanem 2019). Defects that have forms of curvature, such as lamination or scratches, can be a challenge for a region of interest (ROI) based detection system, due to noise and artifacts around the defect. Other challenges for ROI-based systems include the composite nature of some defects that can formalize from micro defects, resulting in regions that have multiple defects. This leads to predictions with less than desired bounding boxes, and uncertainty in their location and classification. The nature of a bounding box also means that labelling is often not pixel-perfect, resulting in sampled observations which are incorrectly labelled.

In this work, we propose a data refinement strategy based on querying the similarity of embedding vectors with a human-in-the-loop approach to fix mistakes in bounding-box labelled datasets for steel defect detection. We uniformly sample patches of the labelled image and learn an embedding space of patch clusters. Querying the embedding space allows us to create a deep segmentation of the steel surface, which can then assist the inspection team.

2. RELATED WORK

2.1 Image Processing for Surface Defect Detection

Convolutional Neural Networks (CNNs) have become widely popular in many domains including defect detection, due to being able to learn robust local image features during training. One of the first CNN-based approaches used for quality inspection was used to detect cracks based on image patches of concrete, followed by a sliding window approach to follow the crack during deployment (Cha, Choi & Büyüköztürk 2017). This work was added upon by Song et al, who proposed a method based on U-net which showed robustness to background noise while detecting cracks (Song, Lin, Yang, Zhu, Guo & Xi 2019). To deal with multiple types of defects and get better localisation results, a new structural visual inspection system which uses Faster Region-based CNN (faster R-CNN) (Cha, Choi, Suh, Mahmoudkhani & Büyüköztürk 2018). They showed good average precision on different types of surface defects, including those on steel. Test-time detection is another challenge in steel manufacturing due to the speed steel moves through production (Sun, Gu, Tang & Li 2018). As a result, test-time detection needs to be at least as fast as production speeds to not introduce a bottleneck. (Li, Su, Geng & Yin 2018) proposed a real-time detection approach based on You Only Look Once, which can reach speeds of up to 83 FPS on cold-rolled steel surfaces. All these different approaches have achieved very good performance but assume that the dataset has a large amount of high-quality labelled images, this is quite impracticable in an industrial manufacturing setting due to the impact of labour-intensive labelling practices on domain experts (Luo, Fang, Liu, Yang & Sun 2020).

2.2 Similarity Learning

Similarity methods are a possible alternative to conventional supervised learning techniques, in which we train a model to learn what samples are similar and dissimilar based on a given metric which describes the similarity between two observations. The most prominent approach in recent literature is FaceNet (Schroff, Kalenichenko & Philbin 2015), which uses a CNN to learn an embedding of pairs of faces. The work is based on the triplet loss, which optimizes the embedding space such that samples with the same label are closer to each other while those with different labels are pushed further away (Weinberger & Saul 2009). To encourage faster convergence and better generalisation, FaceNet proposes an online variant of mining observed triplets based on a large batch size (Schroff, Kalenichenko & Philbin 2015). The mining strategy involves finding valid triplets given a batch of embedding vectors based on selected anchors. We mine for useful positives and negatives from some metric, where the goal is to move the positives closer to the anchor while moving the negatives away. This creates clusters of similar features within the embedding space. (Hermans, Beyer & Leibe 2017) evaluated different variants of the triplet loss, finding that sampling the hardest triplets within a batch and applying a soft margin was the best for person re-identification. This gives the benefit of finding pairwise relations between unlabelled objects from the feature similarities and providing a level of robustness due to the transitive property between the anchor and positive pairs. The main challenge of similarity learning is the mining of triplets on large datasets, due to the growth in complexity as the dataset grows in size.

2.3 Active Learning

Active refinement and analysis are widely explored domains that leverage user input to handle low-confidence predictions and then feed the changed annotations made by the user back into the model (Branson, Horn, Wah, Perona & Belongie 2014, Vezhnevets, Buhmann & Ferrari 2012). The main principle of active learning involves finding the samples that will gain the best knowledge for the model, known as the acquisition function. Most approaches involve finding k samples to relabel based on an uncertainty metric, followed by a subsequent training session. This cycle of labelling and then training completes the framework of active learning. By leveraging user input, active learning assists in model development by providing insight into hard samples the model struggles with, allowing for better focus on complex regions of the domain. This process can also be a two-way interaction between user and model, with users benefiting from seeing which samples the model is having problems with, which can be a way of interpreting the current version of the model during the refinement cycle. The main driving force in active learning is through the acquisition function, identifying samples that warrant further user insight, and measuring which samples the user should label next is commonly categorized into three buckets; uncertainty (Blundell, Cornebise, Kavukcuoglu & Wierstra 2015, Gal, Islam & Ghahramani 2017), sample representation (Sener & Savarese 2017), and training effects (Settles, Craven & Ray 2008). Once a session of active refinement is complete, an update of model weights incorporates the new knowledge. This is commonly done by updating labels of the whole dataset, but can also be achieved by populating a growing database of samples that have been observed (and potentially refined) by the user. Both of these ideas are explored in this work.

3. METHOD

Our framework consists of a new acquisition function based on embedded vectors, where we use mined triplets of anchors, positives, and negatives to refine a pre-labelled dataset of images containing surface defects on sheets of steel. During the labelling phase, the user updates the labels of the top five hardest positive and negative samples via a graphical interface. We explore two different types of initial mask labels, one using domain-expert labelled bounding boxes (ROI), and the other a dense segmentation provided by an off-the-shelf pre-trained U-Net architecture. User refinements are then incorporated into the learning strategy by either updating the original label set, or by developing a new set of samples which have been observed by the user during the active learning loop.

The following sections describe the triplet loss, the mining strategies, and finally how we refine the labels within our dataset.

3.1 Triplet Loss

Images are embedded in a d-dimensional Euclidean space, which is represented by $f(x) \in R^d$ where x is an image. A triplet consists of an anchor x_i^a, a positive which has the same label as an anchor x_i^p and a negative which has a different label to the anchor x_i^n. The goal of this loss is to ensure that the distance between the anchor and the negative is greater than the distance between the anchor and the positive over all possible triplets. Therefore, the loss L minimised is as follows,

$$L = \sum_{i}^{N} d\left(f(x_i^a), f(x_i^p)\right) - d(f(x_i^a), f(x_i^n)) + \alpha$$

Here, d is a metric function, in our case, this is the Euclidean distance between the embedding vectors of the anchor and either the positive or negative. N is the number of samples in a batch and α is a margin used to enforce a distance between positive and negative pairs. Generating all possible triplets would result in some triplets that already satisfy our goal and therefore do not add much to learning, it is becoming exponentially more expensive as the size of the dataset increases. Therefore, we deploy a strategy to mine different and useful triplets. The following section discusses a few of these strategies.

3.2 Active Online Mining Strategies

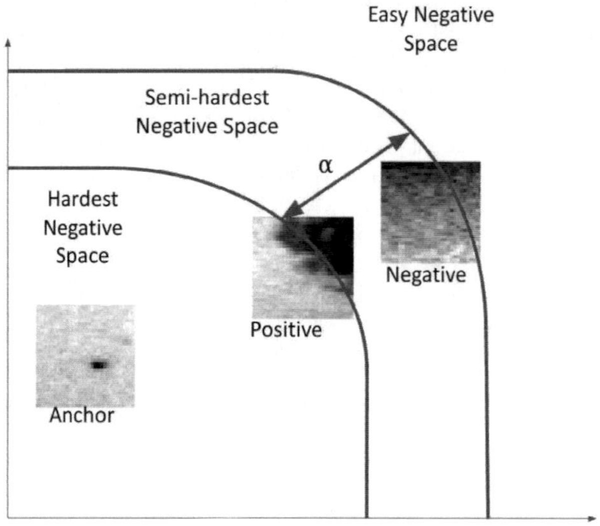

Figure 1. Negative Samples that are closer to the anchor than a positive are within the hardest negative space. Semi-hard negatives are between the positive and a α margin. Negative samples from this space are easier than hardest negatives as they are not as close to the anchor so the triplet loss will not be as great. We avoid easy negatives as they provide no new knowledge to the model and therefore return a loss of 0.

In online mining strategies, we compute meaningful triplets for each batch during the training process. The benefits of this are threefold. Firstly, mining the dataset in a batch typically leads to better generalisation and smoother learning (Schroff, Kalenichenko & Philbin 2015), Secondly, if the dataset has some mislabelled data, this would dominate the mining process. This is because if a sample was labelled negative incorrectly then the model is correct in putting it close to its anchor, yet the mining strategy would consider this a hard negative and thus the loss would try to push that sample away from the anchor. We utilise this benefit in our acquisition function. Finally, due to the change in embedding space as the model learns, the triplets would change between being hardest to semi-hardest to easy triplets (Hermans, Beyer & Leibe 2017). If x_i^p is closer to x_i^a plus some α margin than the distance between x_i^a and x_i^n, then this is considered an easy triplet as it already meets the following condition,

$$\left\|f(x_i^a) - f(x_i^p)\right\|_2^2 + \alpha < \|f(x_i^a) - f(x_i^n)\|_2^2$$

Easy triplets do not add much new knowledge to the model as they already meet the criteria and therefore should be avoided. Instead, we focus on selecting triplets that break the condition in (2). Given that we select positives such that $\text{argmax}_{x_i^p} \left\|f(x_i^a) - f(x_i^p)\right\|_2^2$, we select negatives that meet the following condition,

$$\|f(x_i^a) - f(x_i^n)\|_2^2 < \left\|f(x_i^a) - f(x_i^p)\right\|_2^2$$

These are known as the hardest triplets, as we select the closest negative to the anchor. Always selecting the hardest possible images for the model to learn from is a complex task and leads to a difficult learning environment, due to always having the largest possible loss per batch. To ease this task we can select negatives such that,

$$\left\|f(x_i^a) - f(x_i^p)\right\|_2^2 <$$

$$||f(x_i^a) - f(x_i^n)||_2^2 <$$
$$||f(x_i^a) - f(x_i^p)||_2^2 + \alpha$$

We consider these triplets semi-hard, as the negative is between a positive and the margin. They are not hard negatives as the positive is closer to the anchor, yet they are also not easy negatives as they are not beyond the margin. Throughout this mining process, for a given anchor we will always select the hardest positive such that,

$$\text{argmax}_{x_i^p} ||f(x_i^a) - f(x_i^p)||_2^2$$

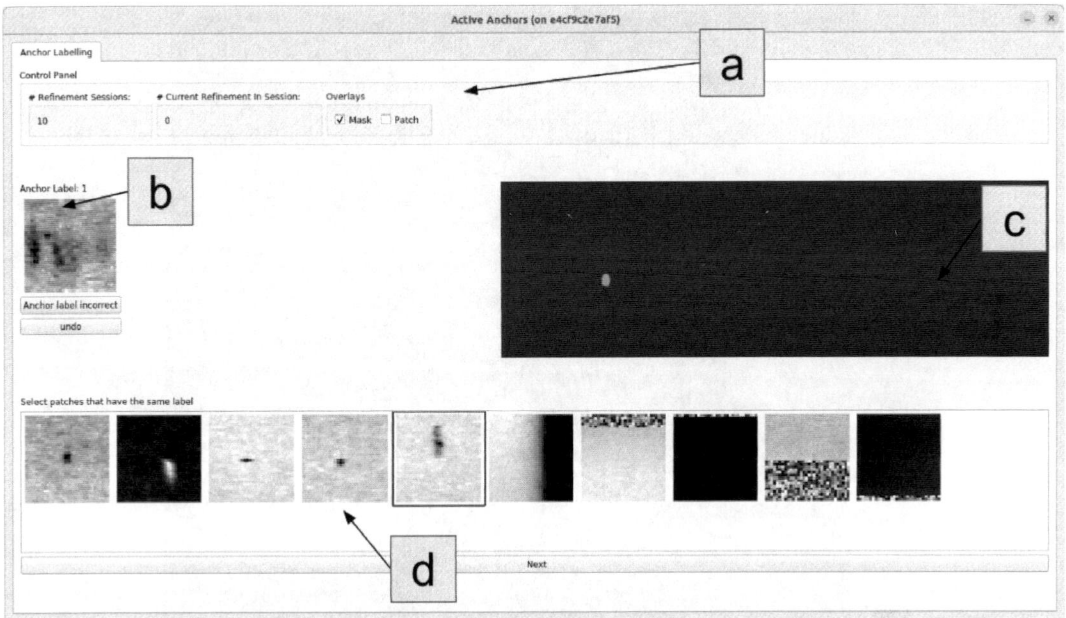

Figure 2. a: The control panel consists of the number of refinement sessions done, the number of current refinements done within a session and a mask overlay and an option to show where the selected patch is located within the image. Users can select either the anchor or any of the 10 patches in d and the user will see where that selected patch is located in c. b: The selected anchor of this batch. The user can update the anchor's label and undo the actions performed. c: Display the image of the currently selected patch. d: Users select patches that they think have the same label as the anchor.

Each of the strategies depends on how we select the negative relative to the anchor and the positive. Figure 1 demonstrates the different mining strategies.

As we need to evaluate the distance between the anchor and every other patch within the batch, we can then also order them to find the k-worst patches. These patches would be considered those the model is struggling with the most, and therefore we query these patches to the user with the graphical interface shown in Figure 2.

3.3 Dataset Label Refinement

Within our framework, we utilise an online patch-generation procedure that is based on two different types of initial masks; expert-labelled ROI and a pre-trained segmentation (Figure 3). During the labelling phase, the user is shown an anchor patch selected at random or based on model entropy. We then use a mining strategy, to find hard positives and semi-hard negatives creating our triplets. The user interacts with the model via the graphical interface shown in Figure 2. Users are shown a selected anchor patch and its corresponding 5 hardest positive and hardest negative patches per the similarity scoring in (2) and (3). The user selects the candidate patches that they think have the same label as the anchor, effectively either agreeing with the model's prediction or correcting its labelling. After a batch of refinements is carried out, and the underlying labels updated, the model goes into the subsequent training phase. This cycle of labelling and then training defines our framework.

4. APPLICATION

As an evaluation case study, we apply our refinement approach to the domain of surface inspection within steel manufacturing, due to the labelling challenges this domain has; namely non-defect artifacts, bounding-box- based labelling difficulties, and the domain expertise required. The following sections discuss the dataset used to evaluate our framework, followed by how we implemented our approach and deployed our experiments.

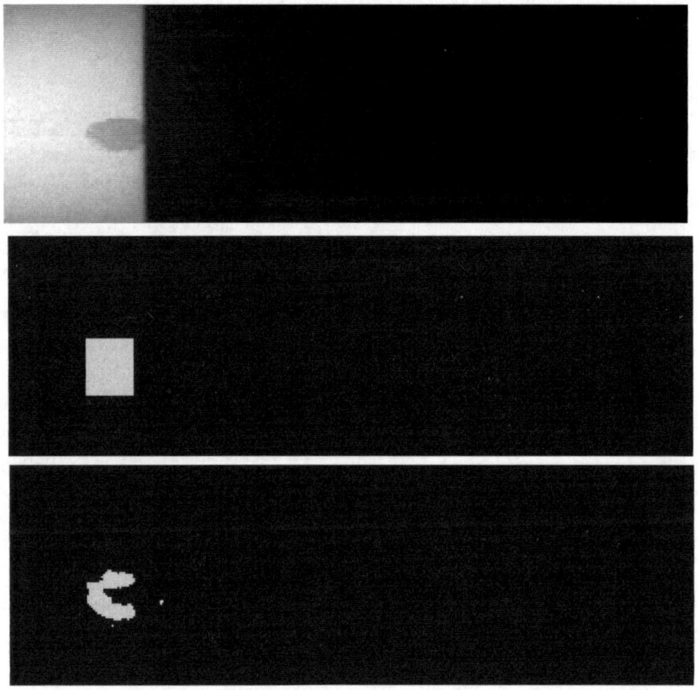

Figure 3. From top to bottom: example raw steel that contains at least one defect. An ROI label of the defects is represented as mask. A pre-trained segmentation mask of input. Masks allow us to uniformly sample pixel coordinates via the label in the mask. We then extract patches based on those coordinates.

4.1 Dataset

We evaluate our framework on grayscale images of steel, captured during the cold rolling manufacturing process. The dataset consists of 5000 images, with each containing between one and three defects. There are multiple different types of defects within this dataset, but in this instance we categorise this as a binary classification problem, identifying defect/non-defect on a per-pixel basis. Images are captured at various angles and positions along the mill, creating variance in both scene illumination and placement of the steel sheet within the camera's field of view. For the initial labelling, we utilise both bounding box labelled regions of interest and a U-Net architecture. The bounding box labels are created by domain experts from a live system. Due to the nature of the defect geometry, ROIs can often provide sub-optimal labelling, with positives labelled as negative, and vice-versa. By contrast, the pre-trained segmentation model provides dense labelling which can handle the varying shapes of the defect but is reliant on suitable generalisation and performance of the utilized model for the specific application domain.

4.2 Implementation

For our implementation, we train a modified version of ResNet with 15 layers (He et al. 2016) returning a predicted binary label and embedding vector of the input given. We uniformly sample patches based on the selected mask type and then use hard mining to find positives and semi-hard mining for negative patches to form our triplets. In refinement learning is it more important to focus on the training than the validation loss as the training set is what is being refined over time. We use a reasonably large batch of 128 triplets, allowing for more available data to mine, and approach to assist in finding the hardest possible triplets which leads to an increased inter-class embedding distance (Dong & Shen 2018).

Once training has converged, we move to the labelling phase with the graphical interface. The user is asked to select patches they think look similar to the anchor. These patches are considered the worst due to their distance away from the anchor. Patches that the user selected that have a different label to the anchor are updated via the mask. Patches that have the same label but are not selected get updated as well. Users continue this process until 50 refinements have been made, which then triggers the training phase. As part of the experiments, we explore three different ways of showing the refined labels to the model. The first is via our patch generation procedure, where we update the mask and then re-sample that mask during training. The second is that we show only patches that have been refined by the user via the selection of similar patches to the anchor, similar to online incremental learning. Our third approach is based on correcting the patches of defects by selecting a defect pixel and we shift the patch to the new centre, which will then get added as a refinement.

We deploy our experiments to explore how the model should be shown the refined labels with the two different initial masks, these are via mask updates and only refined patches. Each set of experiments also looks into anchor selection as these patches are what define a mined positive and negative sample, therefore we explore anchors that the model finds uncertain as well as randomly selected. The following section discusses what we found during our experiments.

5. RESULTS

5.1 Quantitative Analysis

Quantitatively evaluating refinements in a semi-supervised setting is challenging as we have no way of confirming if the refinement is correct and how good it is without expert domain knowledge. Our only way to measure these results is based on the initial sparse masks within our test set due to the refinement only being performed and saved on the train set. To generate our test set we use 1113 images of steel and select 128 patches uniformly per image, we then compare the mask label from the patch coordinate with the prediction from the final version of the model. This results in allowing us to compute the F1, Recall and Precision for each experiment.

In both experiments the user is shown patches to refine based on the selected anchor. In table 1 the user selects patches similar to the anchor and the update is applied to the central pixel, but in table 2 the user corrects the labelling by selecting the centre of the defect if one exists in the presented patch. Each contains two ways of feeding the model new information by updating the underlying mask that samples are drawn from, or only using refined samples to build a dataset of user-verified samples. Our results show that updating the mask (table 2) provides the highest quantitative metric scores against the pre-refinement labelling; however the pre- refinement labels can be either over- or under-approximations of the actual ground truth, reinforcing the need for qualitative analysis to inspect the impact of refinement on the labelling of the underlying data. Generally, user refinement provides low recall while having a higher precision, we theorise that this is because the model is not shown the global context of the dataset which mask update provides. As we uniformly sample defects from all over the image during training. With this global context from the mask update, we see that recall is normally higher than precision. Generally, our approaches work better with the initial segmentation from the U-Net, this is presumably due to the start being more faithful to the geometry of the defect in comparison to the bounding box approach.

Table 1. Mask update refers to refinements made to the mask over time. During training, we uniformly sample coordinates from the mask that relates to the centre pixel of our patches. User Refined refers to the labels of patches that the user changed in the graphical interface, while observed are labels of patches that the user agrees with

	Initial Mask					
	ROI			Pre-trained Segmentation		
	F1	Recall	Precision	F1	Recall	Precision
Mask Update	0.91	0.96	0.86	**0.96**	0.95	0.97
User Refined	0.96	0.93	**0.99**	0.72	**0.96**	0.58
Mask Update with Entropy Selection	**0.97**	**0.97**	0.98	0.95	0.93	**0.98**
User Refined with Entropy Selection	0.90	0.82	**0.99**	0.27	0.21	0.39

Table 2. Labels in these experiments get updated by the user shifting the centre of the patch to the defect via a graphical interface, where the user is shown the 5 hardest negatives and positives based on the anchor. We then compare patch prediction with a initial mask to compute quantitative results

	Initial Mask					
	ROI			Pre-trained Segmentation		
	F1	Recall	Precision	F1	Recall	Precision
Mask Update	**0.97**	0.95	0.98	0.68	0.90	0.55
User Refined	0.83	0.72	**0.99**	0.89	0.81	**0.99**
User Update and User Refined	0.96	**0.96**	0.97	**0.94**	0.90	**0.99**
Mask Update with Entropy Selection	0.91	**0.96**	0.87	0.91	**0.92**	0.90
User Refined with Entropy Selection	0.86	0.77	**0.99**	0.89	0.82	0.97

5.2 Qualitative Analysis

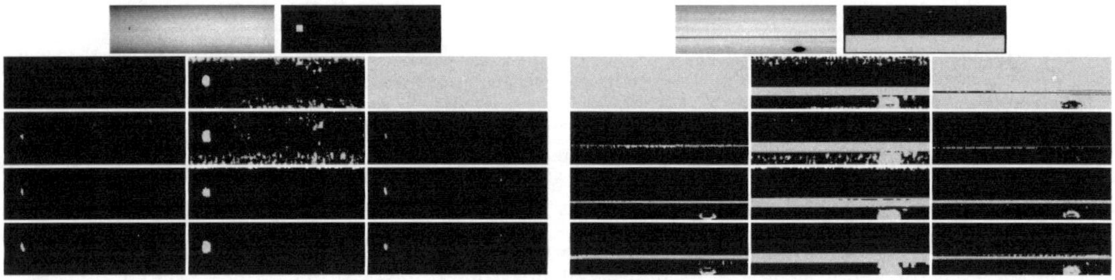

Figure 4. We show a forward pass of a single image of steel producing a dense segmentation over refinement sessions with three different experiments. This is accomplished via the graphical interface where the user is given the 5 worst negatives and positives based on an anchor, then selects new centre pixel for that patch. Row one displays the image and the initial ROI mask. Column one is based on user refinement, column two is mask updates, and column three is user refined with entropy anchor selection. Each row shows a subsequent refinement after a session.

To meaningfully show the quality of the refinement process we need some qualitative analysis as shown in Figures 4 and 5. We use a single image of steel along with its initial ROI mask, each row then contains a refinement session, until we get to the last row which is the final version of the model for that experiment. We see that the model does refine better for experiments where we just feed refined examples. Often if we uniformly sample from the mask we get a circular segmentation around and filling the ROI, which is why we often see higher precision in these experiments. Selecting the anchor based on the highest entropy often leads to worst results, we believe this is due to the task for the model to learn being harder. This is because we mine the hardest negatives and positives from the hardest anchor in a batch. Our approach is also able to find defects that have not been labelled while also ignoring non-defect artifacts like luminance. We can also see that area within the ROI also gets refined such as in figure 4 (right) where we have two defects labelled as one.

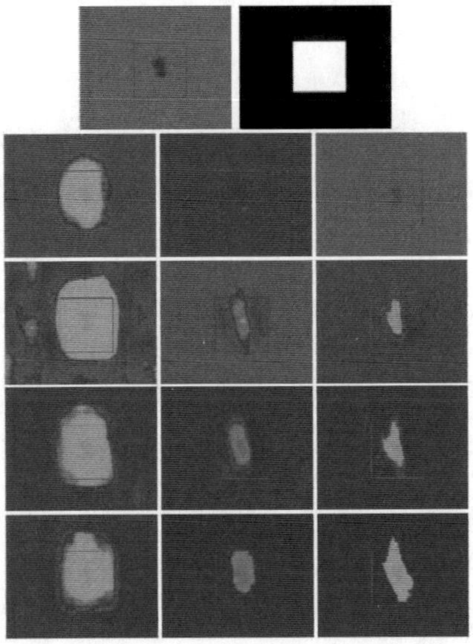

Figure 5. Zoomed in crop of the dense segmentation over refinement sessions when users select defect centers from within presented samples. Red box indicates initial ROI labelling, heatmap shows confidence of model output for positive defect detection. From top to bottom: steel image and initial ROI mask, refinement passes 1-4. From left to right: update of label mask only, user verified dataset, and user verified dataset with entropy based anchor selection.

In figure 5 we show that by adding more user interaction into the training our refinement will get better, this has the caveat that more time from domain experts is needed. Each of these patches are shown with an overlay displaying the pixel confidence of a defect, with ROI based approaches we see that there is a level of uncertainly around the box due to many of the pixels labelled as positive are actually negative. We find that the best way to deal with this uncertainly is to perform pixel labelling and shifting patches so that the defect is in the centre, this results in better ROIs and dense segmentations.

6. CONCLUSION

In this paper, we demonstrate a new active learning framework for querying patches of images based on the triplet loss. Using initial masks, we mine for the worst negatives and positives in relation to a selected anchor. Masks are used to uniformly sample centre patch coordinates creating our batch. We also explore three different ways of feeding the model refinements during training. Our first method looks into refining the mask itself to improve the ROI into a dense segmentation. Secondly, only patches that have been refined and observed by the user, create an extra challenge for the model as our initial dataset is small but grows incrementally and the patches are considered the hardest. While the mask update is considered an easier approach as it gives a global context of the image allowing for the sampling of patches not considered as hard. The final method aims to alleviate the uncertainty around ROI by centring the patch to the object.

We utilise our framework within the defect detection domain with a focus on steel during the manufacturing process due to the highly variant nature of defects, adding to the complexity of ROI approaches that lead to uncertainty around defects. Refining such datasets require highly skilled expert knowledge. Our framework helps speed this process up by only quarrying the most needed patches to be refined.

ACKNOWLEDGEMENT

Funded by EPSRC Centre for Doctoral Training in Enhancing Human Interactions and Collaborations with Data and Intelligence Driven Systems (EP/S021892/1).

REFERENCES

Blundell, C., Cornebise, J., Kavukcuoglu, K. & Wierstra, D. (2015), Weight uncertainty in neural network, in 'International Conference on Machine Learning', pp. 1613–1622.

Branson, S., Horn, G. V., Wah, C., Perona, P. & Belongie, S. (2014), 'The ignorant led by the blind: A hybrid human–machine vision system for fine-grained categorization', International Journal of Computer Vision. URL: http://vision.cornell.edu/se3/wp-content/uploads/2015/02/ijcv2014.pdf

Budd, S., Robinson, E. C. & Kainz, B. (2021), 'A survey on active learning and human-in-the-loop deep learning for medical image analysis', Medical Image Analysis 71, 102062.

Cha, Y.-J., Choi, W. & Büyüköztürk, O. (2017), 'Deep learning-based crack damage detection using convolutional neural networks', Computer-Aided Civil and Infrastructure Engineering 32(5), 361-378.

Cha, Y.-J., Choi, W., Suh, G., Mahmoudkhani, S. & Büyüköztürk, O. (2018), 'Autonomous structural visual inspection using region-based deep learning for detecting multiple damage types', Computer-Aided Civil and Infrastructure Engineering 33(9), 731–747.

Dong, X. & Shen, J. (2018), Triplet loss in siamese network for object tracking, in 'European Conference on Computer Vision', pp. 459–474.

Gal, Y., Islam, R. & Ghahramani, Z. (2017), Deep bayesian active learning with image data, in 'International Conference on Machine Learning', pp. 1183–1192.

He, K., Zhang, X., Ren, S. & Sun, J. (2016), Deep residual learning for image recognition, in 'IEEE/CVF Conference on Computer Vision and Pattern Recognition'.

Hermans, A., Beyer, L. & Leibe, B. (2017), 'In defense of the triplet loss for person re-identification', CoRR abs/1703.07737.

Li, J., Su, Z., Geng, J. & Yin, Y. (2018), 'Real-time detection of steel strip surface defects based on improved yolo detection network', IFAC Workshop on Mining, Mineral and Metal Processing 51(21), 76–81.

Luo, Q., Fang, X., Liu, L., Yang, C. & Sun, Y. (2020), 'Automated visual defect detection for flat steel surface: A survey', IEEE Transactions on Instrumentation and Measurement 69(3), 626–644.

Neogi, N., Mohanta, D. K. & Dutta, P. K. (2014), 'Review of vision-based steel surface inspection systems', EURASIP Journal on Image and Video Processing 2014(1), 1–19.

Schroff, F., Kalenichenko, D. & Philbin, J. (2015), Facenet: A unified embedding for face recognition and clustering, in 'IEEE/CVF Conference on Computer Vision and Pattern Recognition', pp. 815–823.

Sener, O. & Savarese, S. (2017), 'Active learning for convolutional neural networks: A core-set approach'.

Settles, B., Craven, M. & Ray, S. (2008), Multiple-instance active learning, in 'Advances in Neural Information Processing Systems', Vol. 20, pp. 1289–1296.

Song, L., Lin, W., Yang, Y.-G., Zhu, X., Guo, Q. & Xi, J. (2019), 'Weak micro-scratch detection based on deep convolutional neural network', IEEE Access 7, 27547–27554.

Sun, X., Gu, J., Tang, S. & Li, J. (2018), 'Research progress of visual inspection technology of steel products—a review', Applied Sciences 8, 2195.

Vezhnevets, A., Buhmann, J. M. & Ferrari, V. (2012), Active learning for semantic segmentation with expected change, in 'IEEE/CVF Conference on Computer Vision and Pattern Recognition', pp. 3162–3169.

Weinberger, K. Q. & Saul, L. K. (2009), 'Distance metric learning for large margin nearest neighbor classification.', Journal of Machine Learning Research 10(2).

Xu, M., Bai, Y. & Ghanem, B. (2019), Missing labels in object detection, in 'IEEE/CVF Conference on Computer Vision and Pattern Recognition Workshops'.

Zhang, M.-L. & Zhou, Z.-H. (2006), 'Multilabel neural networks with applications to functional genomics and text categorization', IEEE Transactions on Knowledge and Data Engineering 18(10), 1338–1351.

DEEP LEARNING BASED MODEL FOR AMNIOTIC FLUID SEGMENTATION IN 2D FETAL ULTRASOUND IMAGES

Rihem Mahmoud[1], Taha Reheh[2] and Selma Belgacem[1]
[1]MARS ResearchLaboratory, LR17ES05, University of Sousse
[2]Higherinstitute of applied science and technologie of Sousse, University of Sousse
Sousse, Tunisia

ABSTRACT

Automatic computerized segmentation of fetal anatomical structures from ultrasound images and biometric measurements is still challenging, due to the inherent characteristics of fetal ultrasound images at different semesters of pregnancy. Generally, clinicians manually measure the fetal anatomical structures by fitting either an ellipse (AF-Pocket plane or a line (for the case of femoral plane), and it can take considerable time to take these measurements. The difficulty in automated fetal anatomical structures measurement stems from various uncertain factors, including poor and non-uniform contrast across the border of the fetal structures, the high variability of the ultrasound images, and large intersect variation. It is extremely difficult to extract the edge of the fetal anatomical structures using local patterns alone. In this paper, we propose an automated method for AF-Pocket semantic segmentation using deep learning methods. The proposed method contains four steps: Pre-processing, binary classification, semantic segmentation and AF-Pocket measurement. The results of our proposed architecture were evaluated using a prepared dataset and achieves the best results compared with a variety of state-of-the-art deep learning-based approaches.

KEYWORDS

Ultrasound Images, Semantic Segmentation, AF-Pocket, Amniotic Fluid, U-Net

1. INTRODUCTION

The first 28 days of life "the neonatal period" is the most vulnerable time for a fetus's survival. Children face the highest risk of dying in their first month of life. Globally, 2.4 million children died in the first month of life in 2019, approximately 6,700 neonatal deaths every day, with about a third of all neonatal deaths occurring within the first day after birth, and close to three quarters occurring within the first week of life. This problem is mainly addressed in the obstetrics field, which is a field of study concentrated on pregnancy, childbirth and the postpartum period. Fetal biometric measurement (i.e., abdominal circumference (AC)) is useful for predicting intrauterine growth restriction and fetal maturity as well as for estimating gestational age. Generally, Ultrasound (US) imaging is an imaging modality widely used for the diagnosis, screening and treatment of a large number of diseases, due to its portability, low cost and non-invasive nature (Zaffino P, 2020). Ultrasound imaging is the most commonly used technique for observing various factors related to fetal diagnosis such as the fetus's abdominal circumference, head circumference, Amniotic Fluid, biparietal diameter, femur and humerus length, and crown-rump length. Furthermore, amniotic fluid is one of the significant factors to determine the fetus's well-being and development. It has a myriad of functions: it protects fetus and umbilical cord, prevents infections and provides the necessary growth factors to allow normal development and growth of fetal organs. (Maria Chiara Fiorentino, 2023)

In the clinical practice, to assess the sufficiency of amniotic fluid quantity, the amniotic fluid index is used. This index is the level of amniotic fluid inside the amniotic pocket.The AF-Index is calculated dividing the maternal abdomen into 4 quadrants using the midline and the umbilicus, and then the deepest pocket of amniotic fluid is evaluated in each quadrant (Maria Chiara Fiorentino, 2023). AFI is the sum of deepest depth of amniotic fluid in each quadrant of ultrasound images.

The AF-Index is normally 7 to 25 cm. Fluctuations outside of this range define oligohydramnios or polyhydramnios. Incorrectly measurement of AFI when there is higher or lower than normal amounts can contribute to an over- or under-analysis of fetal status and inappropriate treatment. Therefore, the fully automatic segmentation of the AF pocket has been in substantial demand. With a view to automatize the index computation, amniotic fluid segmentation is a crucial task. Unfortunately, this task is highly challenging, unlike other ultrasound-based automatic fetal biometric measurements(Siyu, 2021). The detection of AF (Amniotic fluid) is usually a time-consuming process, and it is patient specific task(Khan IU, 2022). The difficulty arises due to amorphous features (i.e., an unspecified variety of shapes and sizes) of the AF pocket and various factors, such as reverberation, the AF mimicking region, floating matter, and incomplete or missing boundary, which lead to limited accuracy of AF pocket segmentation(Siyu, 2021).

Therefore, the automated amniotic fluid estimation must be able to handle noisy ultrasound images affected by signal dropouts, artifacts, motion blurring, missing boundaries, attenuation, acoustic shadows, and speckling (Rueda, 2014).

Among Deep learning approaches for fetal anatomical structure analysis, a number of work focuses on Amniotic Fluid segmentation from 2D US images. Li et al.(Li, 2017) applied a deep learning architecture to segment the amniotic fluid and fetal body in 2D US images. The model encoded and decoded the input US with VGG16 as backbone into down-scaled and up-scaled feature maps using several convolution and pooling structures. Additional convolution layers with 1x1 sized kernels are adopted to enhance the feature representations. During the training phase, Cross-domain transfer learning was performed to improve the accuracy. For amniotic fluid segmentation, the model tested on 400 images obtains Accuarcy and IoU of 78% and 54% respectively.

cho et al. (Hyun Cheol Cho, 2021) proposed a 2-step framework to segment the amniotic fluid pocket and measure the amniotic fluid index from 2D US images. The segmentation step is performed with a variation of U-Net architecture, called AF-net, which combines convolution and multi-scale side-input and side-output layers. Results obtained on a test set of 125 images are a Dice similarity of 0.877 ± 0.086 for AF segmentation and a mean absolute error of 2.666 ± 2.986 and mean relative error of 0.018 ± 0.023 for AFI value. This approach is further improved in (Sun, 2021)by developing a dual path network, which consists of AF-net as the primary path and an auxiliary network as the secondary path. The primary path consists of AF-net and the secondary path is an auxiliary CNN used to is designed to focus on the local area that is likely to be contaminated with the reverberation artifacts. The proposed dual path segmentation network achieved an average dice similarity coefficient (DSC) of 0.8599 ± 0.1074 (mean ± standard deviation) for AF pocket segmentation, on a test set of 180 images. Khan et al. (Khan IU, 2022)utilize transfer learning models in order to classify the AF levels as normal or abnormal on US images using DL models. The dataset used consisted of 166 US images of pregnant women. The results showed that MobileNet achieved an overall accuracy of 94%.

In this paper, we propose a new model for AF-Pocket semantic segmentation and measurement. First we perform a pre-processing step to remove annotations and crop the image to extract the womb with the fetal body. Then a binary classification step is performed to determine visibility of AF-pocket in the US image. Finally, we propose for the semantic segmentation task, a modified version of the classic U-Net model, combined with EfficientNet B7.

2. PROPOSED APPROACH

This section provides details of the proposed methodology along with a comprehensive analysis of data preprocessing methods, binary classification technique, semantic segmentation models applied, and AF-index measurement.

2.1 Preprocessing

The preprocessing involved several steps to prepare the data to be ready for further processing. The preprocessing phase consists of three main steps: find and eliminate 3D and doppler effects from US images, remove annotations and crop the image to only leave the womb with the fetal body inside.

2.1.1 Eliminate 3D and Doppler effects

For 3D ultrasounds, multiple two-dimensional images are taken at various angles and then pieced together to form a three-dimensional rendering. Generally, ultrasounds in 3D are performed only to closely examine suspected fetal anomalies, such as cleft lip and spinal cord issues, or to monitor specific biometric structure. On the other side, in our case, there is no need to use the 3D information to detect AF-pocket.

Thus, we find and eliminate 3D and doppler effects. The openCV library in Python contains the template matching algorithm that slides the template image over the input image and compares the template and patch of input image under the template image. Figure 1 shows an example of 3D US fetal images and the template matching filter used to detect and eliminate 3D effects.

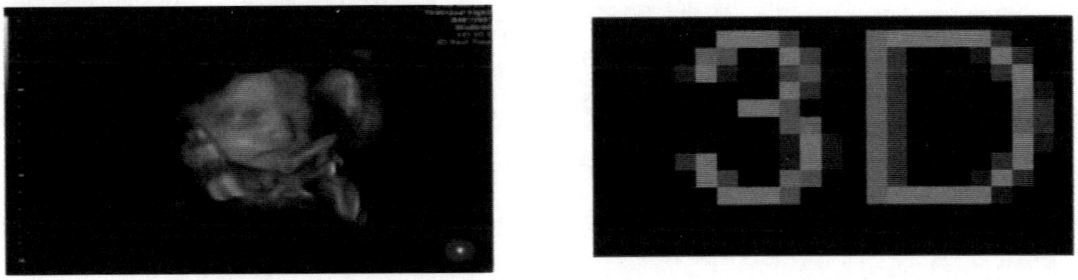

Figure 1. Example of Ultrasound 3D image and the template-matching filter used

Doppler ultrasound uses sound waves to detect the movement of blood in the vessels. It is used in pregnancy to study blood circulation in the baby, uterus and placenta. Using it in high-risk pregnancies, where there is concern about the baby's condition, shows benefits. In our case, to detect and eliminate the Doppler Effect two methods were applied: HSV thresholding to Detect fetal object based on the range of pixel values in the HSV color space and template matching with another different template.

2.1.2 Cropping and Annotations Removal

The sonographers need to take biometric measurements while executing their study on the patient. Achieving that requires placing observations on the ultrasound image, which can affect, later, the classification and segmentation of the AF-pocket and gives unexpected results. Thus, it was necessary to remove these measurements from US images. The OpenCV library provides a method *inpaint* which restores the selected region in an image using the neighboring region. This means that we give the annotations that wedetected first, using the HSV thresholding method as an input, along with the whole image, and receive and image without the annotations as output. Figure 2 shows the result of detecting and removing annotations using *HSV thresholding* and *inpaint* methods respectively.

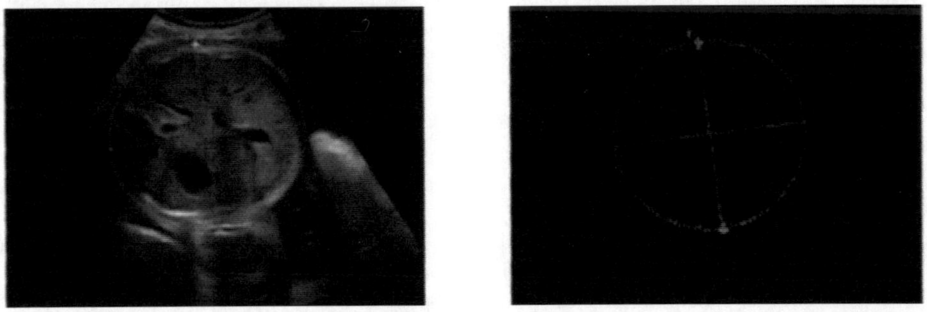

Figure 2. Result of detection annotations stepfromUltrasound 2D image using HSV thresholdingmethod

The last step in our pipeline preprocessing (see figure3) was cropping 2D US images. The cropping in our case means we only extract the womb element in the image and remove every other element. Many methods can be used, basing on the nature of the womb element; we propose a method that consists of finding the largest contour, in this case the womb. First, we applied two functions from OpenCv "threshold" and "find Contours areas" that provide all contours in the images. Then, we select the largest contour which corresponds to womb element depending on their respective areas.

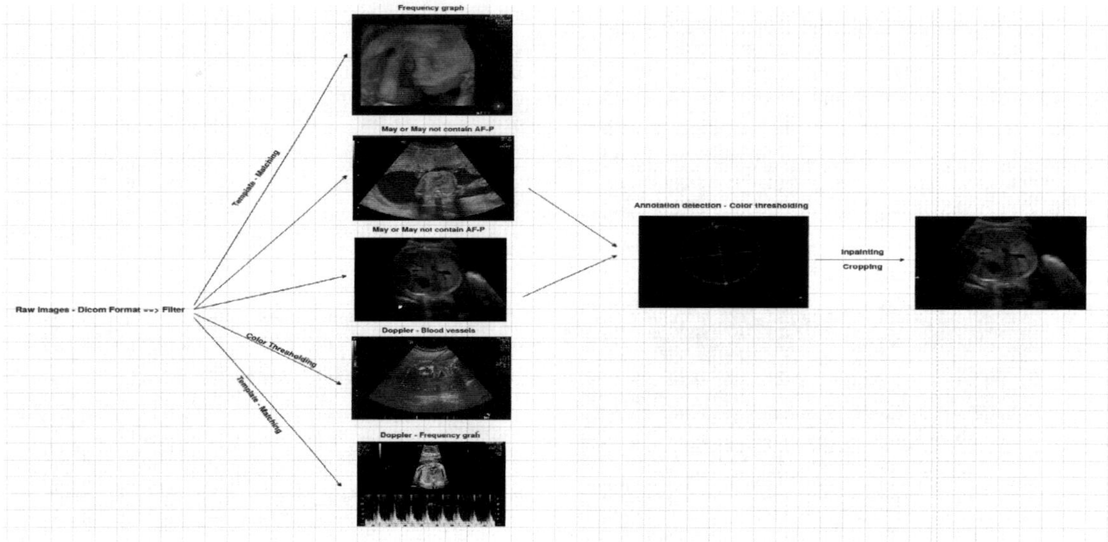

Figure 3. Overview of the preprocessing pipeline

2.2 Binary Classification

After the preprocessing phase, the dataset composed of a set of images, without 3D, doppler and annotations. Each image may or may not contain an amniotic fluid pocket. Therefore, we propose a binary classification step to determine if the AF-Pocket is visible or not in the image.

We perform the binary classification task using MobileNet model(Andrew G. Howard, 2017) with transfer learning technique. Transfer learning is a machine-deep learning technique which transfers the knowledge, in our case, the model's weights, from one task to another, and plays the role of a starting point for the new task. This may occur among different deep learning tasks, but usually works well whenthe tasks are slightly similar. For instance, a model trained to classify retinal images could serve as a starting point for another classification task for another type of image, in our case the US-images. Here, the starting point notion means, we need to furthertrain some of the last layers of the model, to work for our specific case. Keras applications provide trained deep learning networks on the imageNET dataset, these weights can be useful for different tasks on different dataset. We apply MobileNet basing on a streamlined architecture that uses depth-wise separable convolutions to build light weight deep neural networks. The results of binary classification step are presented in section 3.

2.3 Semantic Segmentation

The automatic estimation of AF index (AFI) requires automated segmentation of the AF pocket from US images, which is a challenging task due to its amorphous features and US artifacts, such as reverberation, shadowing, particle noise, and signal dropout.

As a first experiment, we proposed to implement a variety of classic semantic segmentation methods. First we perform segmentation method using texture information based on partitioning the image into regions with different textures containing similar groups of pixels (figure 4).Second, thresholding segmentation method was used, which convert the US image from color or grayscale modality to a binary image (black and white). The white pixels represent the pixels with a higher value than the threshold.

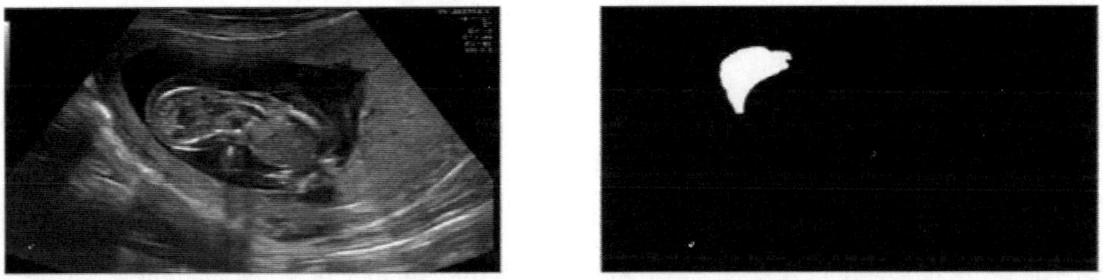

Figure 4. Example of result of semantic segmentation-based texture method

Then, we perform segmentation using canny edges to identify and locate sharp discontinuities in an image. Finally, segmentation using watershed method. It is a region-based segmentation method where an image is regarded as a topographic landscape with ridges and valleys.Even though all the methods seems to give relatively good results, except the markov based segmentation which is time-consuming for creating the masks, segmentation by thresholding and segmentation by texture methods resist to ultrasound challenges and gave the best results among classic methods. Unfortunately, the problem was that the methods presented previously don't produce satisfactory results using the same image when the same hyperparameters were used. Thus, the obligation of human intervention. We varied the hyperparameters for each method, and choose the best corresponding masks for a total of 844 images. In a second experiment, the proposed method addresses this problem by employing a DL model consists of U-net model combined with EfficientNet model as feature extractor.

2.3.1 U-net with EfficientNet-B7

In their research, the Google Brain team compared the performance of EfficientNet(Le, 2020) with other existing convolutional neural networks (CNNs) on the ImageNet dataset, a large-scale visual recognition challenge dataset with 1.2 million images belonging to 1000 categories. The results showed that EfficientNet achieved higher accuracy and better efficiency over existing CNNs models. Basing on the EfficientNet's success on different image recognition benchmarks, we choose to apply EfficientNet B7variant from the efficientNet modelfamilyas feature extractor with U-net model for classification.

U-net (Olaf Ronneberger, 2015)is a Convolutional neural network developed for biomedical image segmentation, based onthe fully convolutional network, works even with very small datasets. Our model is mainly composed of: contraction path, also known as the downsampling path, atypical convolutional network that consists of repeated application of convolutions, each followed by a rectified linear unit (ReLU) and a max pooling operation. During the contraction, the spatial information is reduced while feature information is increased. The expansion path, also known as the upsampling path that combines the feature and spatial information through a sequence of up-convolutions and concatenations with high-resolution features from the contracting path. Figure5 shows examples of results of semantic segmentation using U-net model with EfficientNet-B7. The visualization illustrates the interesting overlapping between the ground-truth of the dataset and our results.

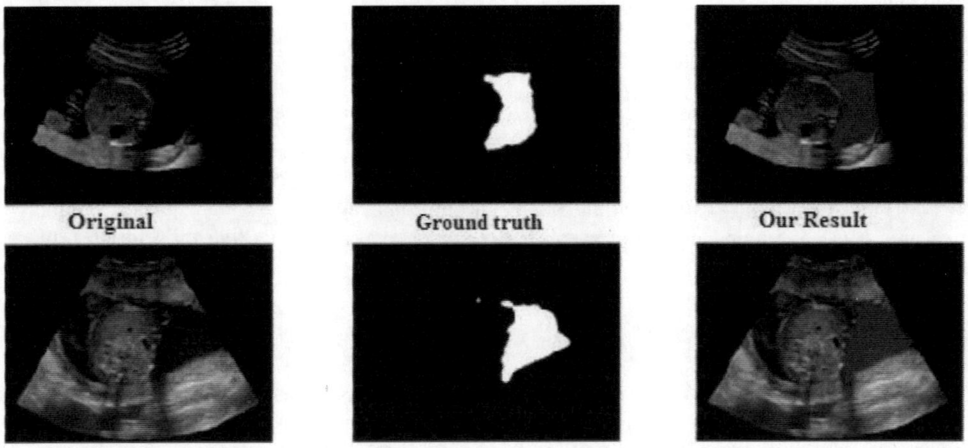

Figure 5. Example of visualization of semantic segmentation results using U-net method

2.4 AF-Index Measurement

To quantitatively demonstrate the semantic segmentation performance, we continue our approach with a final step named AF-Index measurement. This measurement aims to find the largest pocket of amniotic fluid on each ultrasound image.

AF-index is the score (expressed in mm) given to the amount of amniotic fluid seen on ultrasound images. To calculate the AF-index, Maximal Vertical Pocket (MVP) technique (Dasari, 2007) is a well-known method, highly recommended and mainly used by gynecologists.

This technique involves finding the single largest pocket of amniotic fluid on ultrasound image, free of cord and fetal parts, and then measuring the greatest vertical diameter with the ultrasound transducer perpendicular to the floor. In our case, we adopted this technique using three proposed methods. We performed a first experimentation where the AF-index is equal to the diameter of a circle with the same area as the AF-Pocket. This method shows a low precision since the AF-Pockets have different shapes and sizes. In the second experimentation, the AF-index is equal to major axis of ellipse that fitting the AF-pocket. The result of this method is better than the first method, but the detected ellipse doesn't always overlap with the shape of the AF-Pocket.

Finally, we adopted a third experimentation based on a "Modified" bounding box diameter method. This method relies on the fact that the shape of the amniotic fluid pocket is convex from one side and concave from the other, thus finding the bounding box that covers the pocket, and search for the deepest vertical diameter from the middle (see figure 6). The results of this method are presented in the following section.

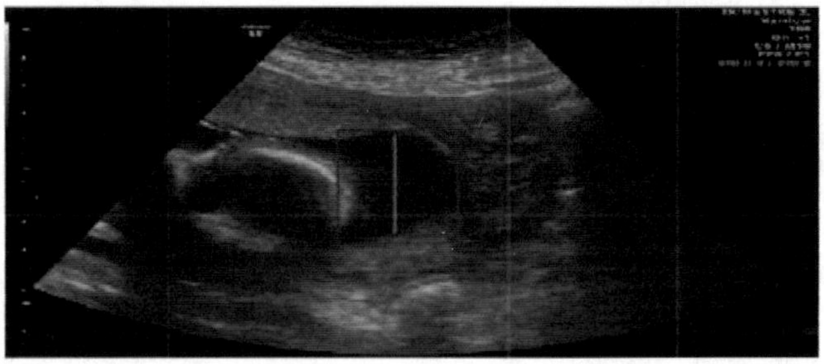

Figure 6. The predicted MVP using variable bounding box method

3. EVALUATION RESULTS

In this section, we present the evaluation and the results analysis of our semantic segmentation proposed approach.

3.1 DataSet Description

The data used in our experiments are derived from clinical examinations (The dataset is provided by deepecho organization). The dataset consists of 3265 ultrasound 2D images, in DICOM format, coming from two different distributions including 2665 US images from "Clinic A" and 300 US images from "Clinic B". Besides the ultrasound representation of the womb and fetal body the images contains biometric measurements i.e: femur length, abdomen circumference, and meta-data like the trimester, place of image and author of image, etc.

3.2 Evaluation Results

In our proposed approach, after the preprocessing step, the binary classification module determines if the AF-Pocket is visible or not in the image using the MobileNet model. In our experimentation, we choose to split our dataset as follow: 70% for training the model, 20% used for cross validation; and 10 % used for testing. The images are labeled as containing or not the AF-Pocket; in other terms, whether the AF-Pocket is visible or not. To build a robust segmentation model, data augmentation techniques were adopted, including random brightness settings, contrast,and horizontal flipping. For the binary classification task, we used a brightness range of 5% less and 5% more, random rotation up to 15°, horizontal flipping and the nearest pixel values for the filling mode. During our experimentation, we tested a variety of DL methods such as MobileNet, InceptionV3, resNet5....To measure the performance of our model, we considered the accuracy rate, precision and recall metrics. Table 1 shows the performance comparison with other best models on our Dataset using MobileNet classifier. Indeed, our model based on mobileNet, achieved 93% in term of accuracy and significantly outperforms the tested DL methods despite many challenges due to the inherent characteristics of fetal ultrasound images. For semantic segmentation, our model based on U-net model with EfficientNet-B7 outperforms others state of the art methods in term of mean Dice Coefficient (Table 2).

Table 1. Comparison of binary classification

DL Model	Accuarcy	Precision[c0,c1]	Recall[c0,c1]
MobileNet	**92.49%**	**[0.9160.934]**	**[0.939 0.909]**
VGG16	88.94%	[0.80, 0.87]	[0.87, 0.90]
ResNet50	85.46%	[0.79, 0.92]	[0.82, 0.67]
InceptionV3	82.16%	[0.92, 0.76]	[0.67, 0.87]
EfficientNetB7	91.14%	[0.90, 0.91]	[0.93, 0.88]
DenseNet201	84.36%	[0.80, 0.91]	[0.96, 0.71]

Table 2. Comparison of semantic segmentation results

Methods	Dice (mean) ± std
Our approach	**0.90 ± 0.0127**
Li et al. (2017)	0.87 ±0.00
choet al. (2021)	0.877 ± 0.086
Sun et al. (2021)	0.8599 ± 0.1074

For AF-index measurement,we adopt a technique based on the comparison between expert prediction as groundtruth and our model prediction. Thus, to quantitatively demonstrate the detection performance, we calculate the Absolute and Relative errorbetween the predictedand experts AF-Index measures (Table 3). Figure 8shows an example of the visualization of AF-index detection. The blue and green lines were manually drawn by two sonography experts, and the red lines are predicted by our «Modified» bounding box diameter method. By examining the results obtained by our model, we can clearly see the great precision with which the identification of the limits of points was obtained. In addition, we can gain a few millimeters by always predicting a perfect vertical line, which is not the case of the human experts.

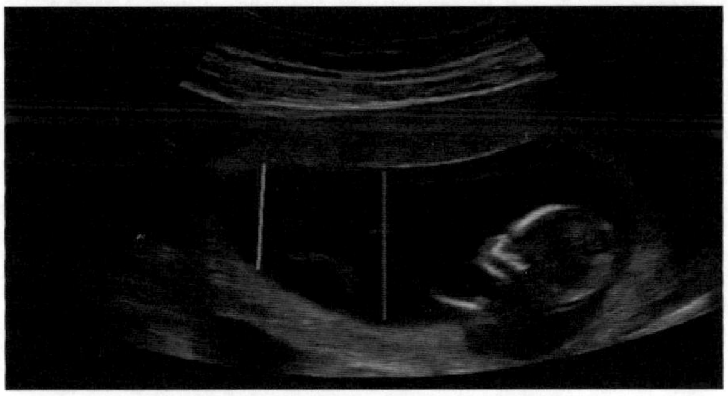

Figure 8. Visualisation of AF-index

Table 3. Absolute & Relative error between the predicted & experts AF-Index measures

	Expert 1 & Predicted	Expert 2 & Predicted
Absolute error(mm)	2.54 ± 2.39	4.07 ± 6.17
Relative error(mm)	0.013 ± 0.013	0.026 ± 0.054

4. CONCLUSION

We have proposed, in this work, a new model for AF-Pocket semantic segmentation from UltraSound images. Our strategy is based on three phases: a first phase consists of preprocesing step to Find and eliminate 3D and doppler effects, remove annotations and crop the image to extract the womb with the fetal body. The second phase, the objective of which is to determinate the visibility of AF-Pocket by a binary classification using MobileNet method. The final phase was the semantic segmentation and Af-Index measurement which aim to the extraction and the detection of AF area. The results of the experiments confirm the robustness and the good performance of our model compared to those of the main models studied in the literature. The future prospects for this work can be articulated around an intersting direction which is UltraSound videos. Using our proposed classification and semantic segmentation models, we can also process 2d ultrasound videos, frame by frame, the models get their input and output their predictions.

REFERENCES

Andrew G. Howard, M. Z. (2017). *MobileNets: Efficient Convolutional Neural Networks for Mobile Vision.*

Dasari, P. N. (2007). The maximal vertical pocket and amniotic fluid index in predicting fetal distress in prolonged pregnancy. *International journal of gynaecology and obstetrics, 96(2).*

Hyun Cheol Cho, S. S.-Y. (2021). Automated ultrasound assessment of amniotic fluid index using deep learning,. *Medical Image Analysis, 69.*

Khan IU, A. N. (2022). Computer-Aided Classification of Amniotic Fluid Using Ultrasound Images from Saudi Arabia. *Big Data and Cognitive Computing, 6(4):107.*

Le, M. T. (2020). *EfficientNet: Rethinking Model Scaling for Convolutional Neural Networks.*

Li, Y. a. (2017). Automatic fetal body and amniotic fluid segmentation from fetal ultrasound images by encoder-decoder network with inner layers. *39th Annual International Conference of the IEEE Engineering in Medicine and Biology Society*, (pp. 1485-1488).

Maria Chiara Fiorentino, F. P. (2023). A review on deep-learning algorithms for fetal ultrasound-image analysis. *Medical Image Analysis, 83.*

Olaf Ronneberger, P. F. (2015). U-Net: Convolutional Networks for Biomedical Image Segmentation. *Medical Image Computing and Computer-Assisted Intervention (MICCAI), Springer, 9351*, 234--241.

Rueda, S. a. (2014). Evaluation and Comparison of Current Fetal Ultrasound Image Segmentation Methods for Biometric Measurements: A Grand Challenge. *IEEE Transactions on Medical Imaging, 33 (4)*, 797-813.

Siyu, S. &.-Y. (2021). Complementary Network for Accurate Amniotic Fluid Segmentation From Ultrasound Images. *IEEE Access, PP-10.1109/ACCESS.2021.3098844.* .

Sun, S. a.-Y. (2021). Complementary Network for Accurate Amniotic Fluid Segmentation From Ultrasound Images. *IEEE Access* , 108223-108235.

Zaffino P, M. S. (2020). Review on Advances in Intra-operative Imaging for Surgery and Therapy : Imagining the Operating Room of the Future. *Annals of biomedical engineering, 48(8).*

SECURITY INFORMATION AND EVENT MANAGEMENT EDO4SIEM - A GENERIC MODEL FOR EVALUATION, DEPLOYMENT AND OPERATION

Maximilian Rosenberg, Bettina Schneider, Christopher Scherb and Petra Maria Asprion
University of Applied Sciences and Arts
Northwestern Switzerland

ABSTRACT

In organisations, the topic of cybersecurity is becoming increasingly important as the number of cyberattacks continues to grow; it is no longer just a matter of protecting, but rather of detecting cyberattacks at an early stage and responding accordingly. There is no generic model for the evaluation, deployment, and operation of a sufficient ´Security Information and Event Management´ (SIEM) available that can be applied generically. Applying a recognized design science approach, the goal of this research was to develop and validate a generic model ´EDO4SIEM´ for the evaluation, deployment, and operation of a SIEM system (SIEMs) in any organisation. As desire for future research, the model should be applied in various organizations to confirm its applicability and to further develop it.

KEYWORDS

Cybersecurity, EDO4SIEM, Security Information and Event Management, SIEM

1. INTRODUCTION

Cybersecurity is a major concern for organisations (Bygrave, 2022). One accepted way to track security-related activities of an organisation is with the help of a ´Security Information and Event Management´ (SIEM) system. A SIEMs collects, stores, and analyses security-related logs that provide information related to information, network, data security, and regulatory compliance (Chuvakin, 2010). Only when properly implemented, a SIEM unfolds their value. The establishment is a resource-intense and demanding procedure. If a SIEMs is not implemented correctly, it can result in an organisation having an expensive SIEMs in place which does not achieve the expected values (Mokalled, et al., 2019). This may result that the SIEMs may ultimately not be used. It is essential to choose the ´right´ system and to customize it sufficient. A literature search conducted on the platforms ´Google Scholar´, ´IEEE Xplore´, ´ResearchGate´, ´Scopus´ and ´Swisscovery` has shown that there are some models available, but all dependent on a certain SIEM product. An analysis of existing models showed: (1) no SIEM model/procedure could be found that depicted the phases ´evaluation´, ´deployment´ and ´operation´. (2) some models from SIEM product vendors provide inputs for the evaluation phase, (3) no model/procedure for the operations phase could be found. As a result, this research contributes a prototypical model - EDO4SIEM - on how to evaluate, deploy and operate a SIEMs in any organisation.

The following representations are structured as follows: in section 2, the methodology is elaborated; section 3 explains the core of the given problem and defines the requirements. In section 4, existing models and some security related frameworks are analysed. Section 5 explains how the prototypical model was systematically developed, whereas section 6 explains the validation and the final model. Finally, section 7 concludes main elements and gives a short outlook for further research.

2. METHODOLOGY

To ensure a systematic approach, Design Science Research (DSR) (Hevner, March, Park, & Ram, 2008) was applied. DSR starts with the identification of a problem, which in this research is the lack of a sufficient model for the establishment of a SIEMs in organisations. Figure 1 shows five process steps that were performed to develop the EDO4SIEM based on Kuechler and Vaishnavi´s approach based on DSR (Hevner, March, Park, & Ram, 2008).

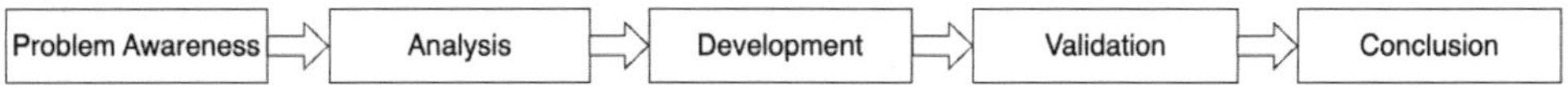

Figure 1. DSR process adopted from Kuechler and Vaishnavi *(Kuechler & Vaishnavi, 2008)*

The first step - *Problem Awareness* - derived why a new model is needed for the establishment of a SIEMs. Awareness of the problem was raised by conducting a literature review on log management, log analysis and the current state of different SIEMs. In the second step - *Analysis* - existing models for the establishment of a SIEMs were searched and analysed. In this context, security frameworks were examined to derive recommendations regarding the establishment of a SIEMs. In addition, a case study was conducted at a Swiss retail organisation; the organisation was in the process to evaluate and establish a SIEMs. Due to this case study, practical experience could also be investigated. The third step - *Development* - was used to combine the previously acquired knowledge and findings in a new model EDO4SIEM. In the fourth step - *Validation* - interviews were conducted with subject matter experts to test and improve the newly developed EDO4SIEM. Based on the interviews, further insights could be gained, which could iteratively be incorporated. The last step - *Conclusion* - EDO4SIEM was revised and finalized based on the inputs and findings of step 4 and resulted in a practitioner-oriented, and generic model for the establishment of any SIEMs in organisations.

3. PROBLEM AWARENESS

SIEMs are relatively new products and must be distinguished from traditional logs. Logs are records of events that occur in an organization's systems, networks, or applications. While originally, logs were used for troubleshooting, nowadays they serve e.g., recordings to user interactions, performance, or malicious activities. As threats to corporate networks and systems continue to grow, the need to analyse logs has emerged to improve threat detection and fast incidence response (Kent & Souppaya, 2006), (Sahoo, Chottray, Jena, & Pattnaiak, 2012). Organisations use mostly centralized Log Management Systems (LMSs) that receive or retrieve and store the logs from various hosts; the logs should be analysed, kept for a defined period, and deleted afterwards. LMSs offer in addition various basic functionalities such as ´Log Collection´, ´Log Filtering´, ´Log Archival´, or ´Event Correlation´.

A SIEMs builds on the fundamentals of LMSs. While a LMS collects and stores all types of logs, a SIEMs focuses on security-relevant logs. Consequently, the most obvious difference between a SIEMs and a LMS is the focus of a SIEMs on security events and their analysis (Chuvakin, 2010). The concept and functionality of a SIEMs is the combination of Security Information Management (SIM) and Security Event Management (SEM). SIM collects security-related logs for report generation whereas SIEM analyses these security-related logs. SIEMs are mainly used by Security Operations Centers (SOC), which aim to maintain and improve the security of an organization (Kent & Souppaya, 2006), (Miloslavskaya, 2018), (Vielberth, 2021). Most SIEMs have the previously mentioned functionalities of LMSs. In addition, a SIEMs offer further functionalities such as the integration of user and entity behaviour analysis (UEBA) or machine learning-based data analysis[1] (González-Granadillo, González-Zarzosa, & Diaz, 2021) (Chuvakin, 2010), (Yelevin & Batamig, 2021), (Salitin & Zolait, 2018). There are different solutions of SIEMs from different vendors, but their basic functionalities and mechanisms are similar. Incoming events are analysed using various rules or data models and compared with past events. Alerts can be triggered, which inform about events, or a multitude of them (Kent & Souppaya, 2006), (Salitin & Zolait, 2018), (Shahid & Shah, 2021).

[1] https://community.exabeam.com/s/article/Exabeam-Use-Case-Series-Contextualization

Establishing a SIEM can provide organisations benefits, but these are cancelled by incorrect configuration. One essential benefit is that a SIEM allows to analyse security-related logs in real time. Based on the analysis, security teams can immediately initiate countermeasures.

The evaluation of a SIEMs can be resource consuming for both - deployment and operation phase. If the alerts of a SIEM are not analysed and processed, the introduction of a SIEMs is worthless. A SIEMs is usually established for mapping use cases; for example, an organisation could use the SIEMs for reporting and regulatory compliance, insider threats and threat hunting. Consequently, the new EDO4SIEM to be developed should include as first an evaluation phase. (Kavanagh, Rochford, & Bussa, 2015) revealed that the SIEMs market grew from 3.55 billion in 2019 to 3.58 billion in 2020; the study indicates further that new that organisations are re-evaluating their current SIEM vendors because of incomplete and failed deployments. Consequently, the new EDO4SIEM should include a deployment and operation phase. A systematic analysis to derive potential models for the establishment of a SIEM that include the phases ′evaluation′, ′deployment′ and ′operations′ did not yield to any results. Therefore, a second search was conducted for models/procedures that represent at least one of these three phases.

The first search for models/procedures, which can be used for the evaluation of SIEM products, delivered few results which could partly be adopted; all the analysed contributions provided some criteria for evaluating a SIEMs. But they were mostly contributions/guides from SIEM vendors (Alien Vault, 2021) . An assessment method for SIEM products was provided by (Safarzadeh, Gharaee, & Panahi, 2019). The second search for the deployment phase resulted in one best practice manual for the deployment of Azure Sentinel6 (Yelevin & Batamig, 2021) and a contribution (Holik, Horalek, Neradova, Zitta, & Marik, 2015), which describes the deployment of a SIEM in a cloud infrastructure. The third search focused on how to operate a SIEMs or any operational application after deployment did not yield any results. Overall, the search revealed that there is currently no model/procedure for the establishment of a SIEMs available which can be applied independently of products and includes one or more of the three as relevant discovered phases. Based on these results, additional literature analysis, and results from the case study, requirements were defined for a EDO4SIEM which should include all three phases (Table 1).

Table 1. EDO4SIEM Requirements (R1 to R5)

#	Requirements Description
R1	The model is based on elements of existing (project management) methods.
R2	The model covers the three phases ′evaluation′, ′deployment′ and ′operation′.
R3	The model can be applied regardless of manufacturer/vendor or product.
R4	The model is based on agile methods and approaches.
R5	The model includes references to other methods and/or security frameworks.

4. ANALYSIS

To develop the first prototype, an analysis of relevant elements to be considered from existing material was performed: First, minimum criteria were established that the new model should fulfil. These were expanded, especially for the deployment phase, with project management methods. Furthermore, security frameworks were studied, and three accepted ones were selected, from which relevant elements derived that were considered in the new model.

4.1 Relevant Criteria for EDO4SIEM

One of the requirements for EDO4SIEM is that it should be based on elements of existing models that are usually used (R1 in Table 1) for the establishment or deployment of a software. Consequently, literature research was conducted to find models which could be adopted. The models investigated (Broy & Kuhrmann, 2021), (Heil, 2012), (Leyh, 2019), (Berg, Knott, & Sandhaus, 2014), (Schatten, et al., 2010), (Vivenzio, Vivenzio, Vivenzio, & Vivenzio, 2013), were divided into three categories: (1) sequential (waterfall model or V-Model XT), (2) iterative (spiral model, rational unified process, openUP model, prototyping), and (3) agile (scrum, incremental approach, extreme programming, kanban, DevOps). Based on the analysed models, minimum criteria for the evaluation phase were derived (Table 2) and three models were compared regarding the criteria surveyed. In the following paragraphs, the three selected models are presented and weighed against each other in terms of their suitability for the evaluation phase.

Waterfall model: Royce (Royce, 1987) first described the model by mapping software development processes. At the initialization of a project, different phases are defined, which are passed through. The phases are run through sequentially from top to bottom during the project. Feedback makes it possible to ′jump back′ to a previous phase. In terms of design, the model offers flexibility, as the phases can be freely defined. By milestones, control and decision points can be established that facilitate the decision of whether a phase is complete and the subsequent phase can start. The completion of one phase is necessary to move to the next. According to (Schatten, et al., 2010), the waterfall model should mainly be used for projects where the requirements can be clearly defined.

Table 2. Required criteria for the evaluation phase

#	Minimum criteria for the new model EDO4SIEM
C1	The model includes phases and/or activities.
C2	The model can be applied to two of the three phases (evaluation, deployment, operation).
C3	The model has agile characteristics or can be combined with agile methods.
C4	The model has return options or control mechanisms.
C5	The model is generally applicable.

V-Model XT: The previous V-Model contains various procedure modules that can be individually combined to tailor the model to the specific project. The activities, which can be seen before the ′V′, are processed and run through sequentially, as in the waterfall model. Also, after the ′V′ elements can be shown, which are run through in a sequential form after all iterations have been completed (Broy & Kuhrmann, 2021). The V-Model XT can be seen as a combination of a sequential and iterative approach (Kneuper, V-Modell XT, 2019). An advantage of V-Modell XT is the exact description of how and in which form the model can be applied in practice. In terms of tailoring, (Kleuker, 2011) mentions that care should be taken when tailoring the model to avoid creating superfluous artifacts.

Scrum: The term Scrum (Takeuchi & Nonaka, 1986) is used to point out that the sequential and phase-oriented project management should be replaced with a unified and collaborative approach of working to support rapid changes in the market. The main difference to the previous two models is that Scrum focus on the prioritisation of tasks. Likewise, the model can deal with changing requirements, which was not possible or only to a limited extent possible with the previously discussed models. Scrum defines a general framework of how the activities in the project should be carried out. The team organizes itself during the sprints; this allows the team to fully concentrate on the current tasks, which were selected at the ′Sprint Planning Meeting′. By prioritizing the requirements, which are carried out by the ′Product Owner′ in collaboration with the business, the requirements that are most important for the business can be implemented first. The use of Scrum is efficient for smaller teams, as communication during a Sprint and at the various meetings can be well coordinated. Scrum proves to be useful when results should be delivered within the shortest possible time. For example, Scrum could also be used for the development of a concept, whereby partial results are delivered again and again until finally the complete concept has been developed (Schatten, et al., 2010), (Volland, 2021), (Lucht & others, 2019).

4.2 Security Frameworks

Another requirement for the EDO4SIEM is that it includes references to security frameworks (R5 in Table 1). These references should help to apply accepted methods and, to consider well-known security frameworks. Based on literature analysis, three widely accepted cybersecurity related frameworks were selected: (1) the NIST Cybersecurity Framework (CSF)[2], (2) the ISO/IEC 27001/2[3] (Humphreys, 2016) standard, and (3) the MITRE Att&ck Framework[4]. In the following paragraphs, the three selected frameworks are briefly presented.

[2] https://www.nist.gov/cyberframework
[3] https://www.iso.org/isoiec-27001-information-security.html
[4] https://attack.mitre.org/

4.2.1 NIST CSF

The NIST CSF helps organizations manage cybersecurity. This CSF supports organisations in the process of identifying, assessing, and responding to risks. With the help of the framework, organisations can specify their risk tolerance. By knowing the risk tolerance, an organization can prioritize cybersecurity events and make decisions based on this information to faster fight critical threats (NIST, 2018). In the context of a SIEMs, it makes sense to take a closer look at the ´Detect´ function: the function contains various categories, for example ´Anomalies and Events´. This category is about detecting anomalous activities and understanding the potential impact. Within this category, there are subcategories that provide more specific aspects and address different areas, e.g., event detection and analysis (DE.AE-2), or event collection and correlation (DE.AE-3). If the NIST CSF is already in use in an organization, the introduction of a SIEM can help to cover recommended categories or various subcategories. However, the NIST CSF can also be a support for organisations that do not currently use the framework because it provides many references in the individual (sub) categories to other frameworks and standards that could be considered when establishing a SIEM.

4.2.2 ISO/IEC 27001/2

The ISO/IEC 27001/2 defines requirements for an information security management system (ISMS), e.g., for the establishment, maintenance, and improvement of an ISMS. Along with these requirements, it provides information on how information security risks could be assessed and addressed within the organization. The annex of ISO/IEC 27001:2013 describes (recommended) control objectives and controls, e.g., on information on logging and monitoring (A.12.4). Further, the following four points are described about logging and monitoring[5]: (1) Event Logging (A.12.4.1), (2) Protection of Log Information (A.12.4.2), (3) Administrator and Operator Logs (A.12.4.3), and (4) Clock Synchronization (A.12.4.4). In addition to the requirements from ISO/IEC 27001:2013, the ISO/IEC 27000 series also provides further information relating to ISMS.

4.2.3 MITRE Att&ck Framework

The MITRE Att&ck Framework is a knowledge base that contains tactics and techniques used by attackers. The framework contains 14 tactics, 191 techniques and 386 sub-techniques. Organisations can use it to learn which techniques are used by hackers when attacking organisations. As an example, the tactic ´Reconnaissance´ describes techniques that are used to gather information, which in turn could be used to plan attacks. Further techniques such as ´active scanning´ and ´phishing for information´ are described. However, the framework does not describe which solutions and tools should be used to detect an attack. The MITRE Att&ck framework can be used as a source of information for defining use cases because of the tactics, techniques, and sub-techniques described. An obvious use case could be detecting phishing emails without relying on the user. The framework provides examples of such attacks for the techniques ('Procedure Example') and how they can be mitigated ('Mitigations') and detected ('Detection'). Furthermore, data sources and related data components are mentioned, which should support the recognition of that kind of an attack. Overall, the MITRE Att&ck Framework can be used by organisations for the definition of use cases.

4.3 Derived Elements of EDO4SIEM

By analysing existing models, methods and frameworks, relevant elements could be collected that could be used in the new EDO4SIEM (Table 3, 4 and 5).

Table 3. Adoptable Criteria Project Management

Approach	Application Conditions
Sequential	Requirements can be clearly defined from the beginning.
Agile	Requirements cannot be clearly defined; they could change during the project.

[5] https://www.iso.org/cms/render/live/en/sites/isoorg/contents/data/standard/05/45/54534.html

Table 4. Adoptable Tools and Methods

Phase	Tools and Methods relevant for the new EDO4SIEM
Evaluation	Analysis of stakeholders, requirements, utilities, preference matrix, documentation
Deployment & Operation	Documentation, Review, Burn- Down-Chart, Scrum Board

Table 5. Adoptable Security Framework Elements

Phase	Section in a dedicated framework relevant for the new EDO4SIEM
Evaluation	NIST CSF: requirements (detection phase)
	ISO/IEC 27001: requirements (logging and monitoring)
	MITRE Att&ck: use cases and required log sources
Deployment	NIST CSF: procedures and processes to be followed after an incident
	ISO/IEC 27001: requirements (protection of log information, clock synchronization)
Operation	NIST CSF: continuous monitoring of the security of the organisation
	ISO/IEC 27001: regular review of the collected information
	MITRE Att&ck: use cases and sources

5. DEVELOPMENT

To structure the first prototype, six main design elements and four levels were created (Figure 2): Level 1: Phases (1), Level 2: Activities (2), Level 3: Delivery Objects (3) and Tasks (4), Level 4: Method References (5) and Security Framework Reference (6). The development of the three phases (evaluation, deployment, and operation) as defined (R2 in Table 1) are described in the following sub-sections.

5.1 Evaluation

The evaluation phase should help to evaluate the appropriate SIEM system that meets their requirements. But before these can be defined, the project team needs to know which roles are allowed to define requirements for the new SIEM system as well as which people/roles will be affected by the establishment of the SIEM. A stakeholder analysis can be applied to identify these roles/people (e.g., CISO, CTO, DPO). By analysing the system landscape, it is possible to identify the core systems that are of primary importance during the initial deployment and whose logs should be transmitted to the SIEM system on a mandatory basis. In addition, the findings of a system landscape analysis can be supportive at a later stage for the definition of the use cases when it comes to identifying the necessary logs that are required for mapping a specific use case (e.g., detection of phishing emails). Consequently, the evaluation phase should start with an analysis of the initial situation, whereby both a stakeholder analysis and a system landscape analysis should be performed.

Upon analysing the initial situation, the requirements which need to be fulfilled by a SIEM must be defined. During the stakeholder analysis, it should have become clear which persons may define requirements for the system. Therefore, these persons should subsequently be surveyed using a questionnaire or an interview. The functional and non-functional requirements are needed again in the next step for the evaluation and selection of the SIEM. Once the requirements and the most important use cases have been defined, various SIEMs should be evaluated based on these findings. For this purpose, a preference matrix should first be created that ranks and weights the requirements for the SIEM system.

Therefore, a preference matrix should be created in a meeting with all the necessary stakeholders. In this meeting, the stakeholders can exchange information with each other as well as discuss and decide together which requirements are most important for the organisation. The assessment can be performed and visualized using a utility analysis. The product with the highest score is the most suitable SIEM system for the organisation based on the criteria previously defined by the stakeholders. For the evaluation of the system requirements, the developers' websites can be visited. Likewise, the developers or partners of the systems in question can be asked directly to obtain more information. Since, in addition to the functional and non-functional requirements, the use cases also play a role in the evaluation, research should be conducted to determine which SIEMs can map which use cases.

5.2 Deployment

The establishment of the evaluated SIEMs is the overarching goal of the deployment phase. Before the SIEMs can be installed and put into operation, the contracts for obtaining the licenses must be concluded. Kavanagh and Bussa (Kavanagh, Rochford, & Bussa, 2015) report that vendors outside their region often offer their product through partners or subsidiaries; these partners assist new customers in deploying the SIEMs. In addition to the purchase, license and service contracts, local data protection laws should be taken into account, since personal data is transmitted, stored and analysed in a SIEM.

Since the new EDU4SIEM should be able to be used independently of manufacturer or product (R4 in Table 1), the focus of the deployment phase is on the connection of the log sources. Even SaaS deployments require installations in the organisation's data center, depending on which logs should be transferred to the SIEMs. In Azure Sentinel (Sahay, 2020), for example, agents are installed on the servers that send the logs to a gateway server, which forwards the logs received to the cloud-SIEMs. Exabeam[6] and Splunk (Mehta, 2021) use collectors that forward the on-premises logs to the cloud. Therefore, EDU4SIEM includes the task ′Installation′. The activities ′Contract signing′ and ′Installations and preparations′ should be carried out sequentially. The integration of the log sources should take place in iterations, whereby an iteration contains four tasks (Table 6), which must be executed until a log source can be marked as implemented. In addition to the various activities, deliverables and tasks in the deployment phase, EDU4SIEM includes references to security frameworks and methods as defined in the requirements.

Table 6. Necessary iterations

#	Tasks
1	Configuration firewall / proxy rules: Before the logs are sent to the SIEM system from on-premises applications, servers, systems or appliances, it is necessary to open/enable the communication channels required for this purpose
2	Configuration Log Forwarding: After the ports are opened on the firewall, log forwarding can be configured. Unnecessary logs should be filtered and not transferred to the SIEM. The configuration of log forwarding must be documented and available to all authorized persons
3	Parsing the logs: As soon as the logs arrive in the SIEM, the parsing of the logs can be started. If the SIEM vendor already offers the appropriate parser, e.g., known and standardized logs, there is no need to create your own. Nevertheless, it is necessary to control how the logs are parsed and whether the required information is extracted.
4	Review: When the previous three steps are complete and the logs are parsed correctly, a review should take place. The goal of the review is to verify that all relevant logs are sent from a system to the SIEM and that the logs are parsed correctly. In addition, a completeness and quality check of the documentation should be performed

5.3 Operation

In the first step of the operating phase, the handover should be prepared. User documentation should be created, responsibilities defined, and operational processes documented. User documentation supports the project team in training the defined operators of the system (Scherb, Heitz, Grimberg, Grieder, & Maurer, 2023). In addition, the users can refer to this documentation at a later point in time and train new users in the same way. By defining and recording responsibilities, it is clearly agreed which persons are responsible for what. Furthermore, the processes for handling the SIEM system should be clarified and recorded. When defining responsibilities and operational processes, the NIST CSF should consider the respond categories. Once the documentation has been prepared, responsibilities and processes defined, the SIEM system can be handed over. This should involve introducing and training the users who will be working with the system in the future before the system is effectively used by these individuals in their day-to-day work. The activity also includes the task of handing over all artifacts and documents that were developed during the project. This ensures that the people working with the SIEM have access to all required information and documents. When the first two activities of the operational phase are completed, the SIEM system can be handed over to operations. The SIEM system must be further developed by the operations team from this point on.

[6] https://docs.exabeam.com/collectors/

The reason for this is that new applications and systems are constantly being introduced and old ones replaced in an organisation. As a result, every time applications or systems change new log sources must be added. In addition, new use cases may need to be implemented due to new attack techniques, user needs, or changed and new corporate security policies. Consequently, the operational activities include the operation, maintenance, and further development of the SIEM. The operation of a SIEM should therefore take place in an agile form, as visualized in the process model (Asprion, Giovanoli, Scherb, & Bhat, 2023). With the help of an agile operational organization, incidents can be processed, new log sources can be integrated, and additional use cases can be implemented within a reasonable period.

6. VALIDATION

The DSR approach demands a validation of EDO4SIEM. The validation approach used the results from the case study experience and interviews with two subject matter experts; the aim was to determine whether the model is applicable and what can still be improved. We structured the interviews along to (1) relevant requirements, (2) the applied approach, and (3) the three phases (evaluation, deployment, operation)

6.1 Approach

Requirements: The interviews showed that the developed model fulfils all five requirements (Table 1). It includes all three defined phases, and the elements are based on existing project management methods used in practice (R1 and R2). Both experts mentioned that the model shows a high-level perspective, thus fulfilling the requirement that the model can be applied independently of the manufacturer or product (R3). Despite the high-level perspective, relevant activities which must be performed in a ´SIEMs project´ are included in EDU4SIEM. One reason for this opinion is that the activities contain various results and tasks providing users with information about which artefacts could be created. Likewise, the references to various methods and frameworks are helpful to understand how a result can be achieved or a task can be performed (R5). Since EDU4SIEM reflects the three phases of a SIEMs project from a high-level perspective, organisations may incorporate additional activities, tasks and results that are specific to the product and/or organisation. Agility is maintained in EDU4SIEM in that way that deliverables and tasks can be performed within the activities. Furthermore, the connection of the log sources and the operation must be iterative, which is why the requirements regarding agility are also met (R4).

Approach: The experts are convinced that a purely sequential or agile model is generally not suitable for the introduction of software. The activities themselves are often carried out in projects through agile methods or an iterative process. The case study also showed that a sequential approach to evaluating the SIEM system was beneficial. The agile/iterative approach to deployment and operations also proved suitable. Furthermore, it was confirmed that the operation of a SIEMs must be carried out by an agile team. Otherwise, according to the experts, the system cannot be further developed on an ongoing basis, which in turn means that the effectively possible added value of a SIEM is reduced.

Evaluation: The interviews revealed that the most important components of an evaluation of a SIEM are present in the evaluation phase depicted. Nevertheless, there were a few suggestions for improvement from the experts. When analysing the system landscape, in addition to the interviews, a document analysis would be very helpful if high-quality documentation is available. Many organisations use a configuration management database (CMDB) in which the documentation of the various components of a organisation is stored. Both experts mentioned that systems should already be prioritized during the analysis of the system landscape. They said that the systems should be prioritized during this analysis based on their relevance for the organisation. The background to this prioritization is that initial use cases can already be derived from such an analysis. In the case study, the organisation's systems were also prioritized for the subsequent definition of the use cases and log sources to be considered during the initial deployment. In addition, such prioritization can be used to determine which logs from which systems must be sent to a SIEMs. Within the analysis of the initial situation, the IT strategy of the organization would still have to be examined, according to one expert. This should already take place before the stakeholder analysis and analysis of the system landscape. The IT strategy of an organization can already be used to gather initial findings. The analysis of the IT strategy makes it possible to find out what goals the IT organization wants to achieve by introducing a

SIEM. Additionally, arguments for an investment in a SIEMs can be gathered, which have a direct impact on the achievement of the corporate strategy goals. Apart from that, one expert said that by analyzing the IT strategy, high level use cases and requirements can already be derived, which in turn could be considered as a basis for the next activity. About the security frameworks, the interviews showed that the process model contains references to the internationally known frameworks at the necessary points that are relevant in the SIEM context. In addition to the MITRE Att&ck Framework, one expert also mentioned the SPEED SIEM Use Case Framework by Jurgen Visser for defining the use cases. This framework should support an organization in structuring, categorizing, defining, and describing use cases. In summary, the framework provides a template for how an organisation can organize and manage use cases in a structured way. The case study showed that a proof of concept (POC) after a system was selected would have been beneficial to show the people who will later work with the system what the system can do and how their current workflow will be enriched by a SIEMs.

Deployment: Both experts said that the deployment phase can be carried out in the manner described and includes the elements that must be present in a SIEM project from a high-level perspective. Nevertheless, there were two suggestions for improvement. In the contract signing activity, one expert found the topic of service level agreement (SLA) missing, which is particularly essential for cloud-based SIEMs. The other expert noted that the architecture was not considered in the installation and preparation activity. According to the expert, the architecture should be a concept that includes the structure, the defined use cases and the log sources required for them and the roles and authorization management. For the creation of this concept, the artifacts created so far can be used and combined into one document. Based on this concept, the iterations for the log sources and the use cases integration could be used in the further course of the deployment phase. The log sources and use cases could then be transferred from the concept to a Scrum Board, which the project team should use in the iterative process of deployment phase. Regarding the references to methods and security frameworks, the experts said that no important framework was missing or that further references to methods should be added to the model.

Operation: According to the experts, the operation phase includes all activities, results and tasks that are required for the handover of the SIEM system. In addition, it was mentioned that the activity 'Operation, Maintenance and Further Development' shows that a SIEM is not only introduced once through an initial deployment but must always be further developed and adapted from the organisation. In this context, it was criticized that the same element for the agile way of working should be used for the deployment phase as for the modelling in the operation phase. This would show more clearly that the iterations which are carried out during the connections of the log sources should be carried out again in the operational phase. Regarding the Security Framework references, there were no comments from the experts that further requirements must be fulfilled to operate a SIEM. Instead, the creation of a RACI matrix (Responsible, Accountable, Consulted, and Informed) was suggested, which would be beneficial for defining responsibilities. The expert justified this statement by saying that such a matrix clearly and transparently defines the tasks, responsibilities, and communication flow for decisions and changes in the organisation.

6.2 The Final EDO4SIEM

Based on the validation results, the first EDO4SIEM (https://bit.ly/3C9UHaI) was iteratively revised and newly visualized (Figure 2). As outlined above (section 5) EDO4SIEM consists of three phases: The evaluation phase includes four activities (medium grey boxes) that support an organisation in evaluating SIEMs that meets their defined requirements. These activities must be completed sequentially, as in each case the results of the previous activity are assumed for the next activity. In this phase, there is the possibility to jump back from one activity to the previous one if results or task were not completed correctly or completely. For each activity there are various tasks and the corresponding results. In the subsequent deployment phase, it is assumed that the evaluated SIEMs is (now) implemented based on the two activities assigned. The final operation phase deals with the handover of the SIEMs to operations. Like in the previous phase, the first two activities support the transfer of the transition of the SIEMs to operations. The first activity ensures that user documentation is created, and responsibilities and operational processes are defined and recorded. After the users have been trained and have received all documentation and information, the SIEMs can be handed over for continuous operational use, maintenance and further development.

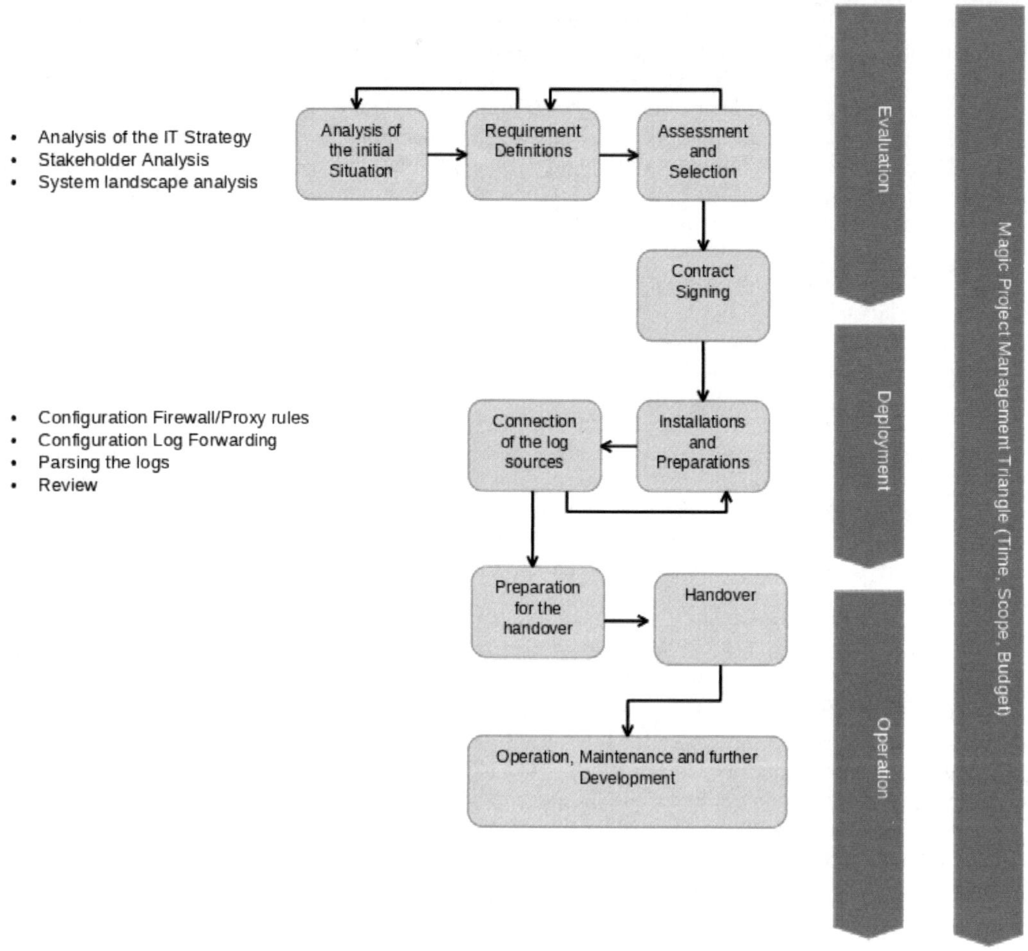

Figure 2. EDO4SIEM – Validated Prototype

7. CONCLUSION AND OUTLOOK

Within the framework of this research, we derived the research gap, that there is no model available to establish a SIEMs. By conducting a literature review, the basic differences of log management and a SIEMs were outlined. In addition, the current state of various SIEMs were considered. To develop a new prototypical model for the establishment of a SIEMS, classical models and security frameworks were investigated. It was researched whether the waterfall model, the V-Model XT and the Scrum approach can be used for SIEM establishment projects. Furthermore, the three frameworks NIST CSF, ISO/IEC 27001/2 and the MITRE Att&ck Framework were examined regarding suitable elements for EDU4SIEM. The result was a newly developed and validated model – the EDO4SIEM.

In addition, EDO4SIEM was reflected by means of a practical case study at a Swiss industrial organisation. The development of the artifact and the practical case study took place at the same time in many parts. The following further measure is desired for the future: EDO4SIEM should be applied in several organisations to test to prove its general use in practice. Through systematic supervision and evaluation, the model could be further improved and, if necessary, expanded. Currently, the model contains a manageable number of references to three security frameworks. It would be conceivable that in a next stage further frameworks, standards, or best practices could be identified, which could be used in a SIEM establishment project. To keep the model clear and simple, an additional diagram could be created in which the various references would be categorized and catalogued. EDU4SIEM provides the following benefits: 1) it is based on existing project management methods and can therefore be applied in a simple and straightforward manner, 2) it holistically covers the phases 'Evaluation', 'Deployment' and 'Operation', 3) it is neutral and can be used independently of any vendor or product, 4) it is based on agile methods and approaches, which makes it flexible and adaptable, 5) as a special feature, it contains references to further methods and/or security frameworks.

This research contributes to solving the problem that so far there is no model for the establishment of a SIEMs. Using Kuechler and Vaishnavi´s (Figure 1) approach, we created a methodologically grounded artifact that is publicly available. Our research is intended to produce a benefit for practitioners who are responsible for a SIEMs establishment in their organization. Likewise, the model is at disposal for critical appraisals, further developments and adaptations of the research and practitioner community.

REFERENCES

Alien Vault. (2021). The SIEM Evaluator's Guide. https://cdn-cybersecurity.att.com/docs/guides/The-SIEM-Evaluators-Guide.pdf: At&t.

Asprion, P., Giovanoli, C., Scherb, C., & Bhat, S. (2023). Agile Management in Cybersecurity. Proceedings of Society (pp. 21-32). Pretoria, South Africa: EasyChair.

Berg, B., Knott, P., & Sandhaus, G. (2014). Hybride Softwareentwicklung: Das Beste aus klassischen und agilen Methoden in einem Modell vereint. Springer-Verlag.

Broy, M., & Kuhrmann, M. (2021). Vorgehensmodelle in der Softwareentwicklung. In Einführung in die Softwaretechnik (pp. 83–124). Springer.

Bygrave, L. A. (2022). Cyber Resilience versus Cybersecurity as Legal Aspiration. 2022 14th International Conference on Cyber Conflict: Keep Moving!(CyCon), 700, pp. 27–43.

Chuvakin, A. (2010). The complete guide to log and event management. White Paper.

González-Granadillo, G., González-Zarzosa, S., & Diaz, R. (2021). Security information and event management (SIEM): analysis, trends, and usage in critical infrastructures. Sensors, 21, 4759.

Heil, A. (2012). Anwendungsentwicklung für Intelligente Umgebungen im Web Engineering. Springer-Verlag.

Hevner, A. R., March, S. T., Park, J., & Ram, S. (2008). Design science in information systems research. Management Information Systems Quarterly, 28, 6.

Holik, F., Horalek, J., Neradova, S., Zitta, S., & Marik, O. (2015). The deployment of security information and event management in cloud infrastructure. 2015 25th International Conference Radioelektronika (RADIOELEKTRONIKA), (pp. 399–404).

Humphreys, E. (2016). Implementing the ISO/IEC 27001: 2013 ISMS Standard. Artech house.

Kavanagh, K. M., Rochford, O., & Bussa, T. (2015). Magic quadrant for security information and event management. Gartner Group Research Note.

Kent, K. A., & Souppaya, M. (2006). Guide to Computer Security Log Management:.

Kleuker, S. (2011). Der pragmatische Weg zu erfolgreichen Softwareprojekten (2 ed.). Wiesbaden : Vieweg+Teubner Verlag Wiesbaden.

Kneuper, R. (2018). Die geschichtliche Entwicklung des V-Modells. Tech. rep., IUBH Discussion Papers-IT & Engineering.

Kneuper, R. (2019). V-Modell XT.

Kuechler, B., & Vaishnavi, V. (2008). On theory development in design science research: anatomy of a research project. European Journal of Information Systems, 17, 489–504.

Leyh, C. (2019). Passende ERP-Systeme auswählen und einführen. Controlling & Management Review, 63, 52–57.

Lucht, D., & others. (2019). Theorie und Management komplexer Projekte. Springer.

Mehta, D. (2021). Setting up a Splunk Environment with AWS. Splunk Certified Study Guide: Prepare for the User, Power User, and Enterprise Admin Certifications, 395–419.

Miloslavskaya, N. (2018). Analysis of SIEM systems and their usage in security operations and security intelligence centers. Biologically Inspired Cognitive Architectures (BICA) for Young Scientists: Proceedings of the First International Early Research Career Enhancement School on BICA and Cybersecurity (FIERCES 2017), (pp. 282–288).

Mokalled, H., Catelli, R., Casola, V., Debertol, D., Meda, E., & Zunino, R. (2019). The guidelines to adopt an applicable SIEM solution. Journal of Information Security, 11, 46–70.

NIST. (2018). Framework for improving critical infrastructure cybersecurity. URL: https://nvlpubs. nist. gov/nistpubs/CSWP/NIST. CSWP, 4162018.

Royce, W. W. (1987). Managing the development of large software systems: concepts and techniques. Proceedings of the 9th international conference on Software Engineering, (pp. 328–338).

Safarzadeh, M., Gharaee, H., & Panahi, A. H. (2019). A novel and comprehensive evaluation methodology for SIEM. Information Security Practice and Experience: 15th International Conference, ISPEC 2019, Kuala Lumpur, Malaysia, November 26–28, 2019, Proceedings 15, (pp. 476–488).

Sahay, R. (2020). Azure Monitoring. Microsoft Azure Architect Technologies Study Companion: Hands-on Preparation and Practice for Exam AZ-300 and AZ-303, 139–167.

Sahoo, P. K., Chottray, R. K., Jena, G., & Pattnaiak, S. (2012). Syslog a Promising Solution to Log Management. International Journal of Advanced Research in Computer Science, 3.

Salitin, M. A., & Zolait, A. H. (2018). The role of User Entity Behavior Analytics to detect network attacks in real time. 2018 International Conference on Innovation and Intelligence for Informatics, Computing, and Technologies (3ICT), (pp. 1–5).

Schatten, A., Biffl, S., Demolsky, M., Gostischa-Franta, E., Östreicher, T., & Winkler, D. (2010). Best practice software-engineering: Eine praxiserprobte Zusammenstellung von komponentenorientierten Konzepten, Methoden und Werkzeugen. Springer-Verlag.

Scherb, C., Heitz, L., Grimberg, F., Grieder, H., & Maurer, M. (2023). A Cyber Attack Simulation for Teaching Cybersecurity. Proceedings of Society 93 (pp. 129-140). Pretoria, South Africa: EasyChair.

Shahid, N., & Shah, M. A. (2021). ANOMALY DETECTION IN SYSTEM LOGS IN THE SPHERE OF DIGITAL ECONOMY.

Takeuchi, H., & Nonaka, I. (1986). The new new product development game. Harvard business review, 64, 137–146.

Vielberth, M. (2021). Security information and event management (SIEM).

Vivenzio, A., Vivenzio, D., Vivenzio, A., & Vivenzio, D. (2013). Vorgehensmodelle in der Softwareentwicklung. Testmanagement bei SAP-Projekten: Erfolgreich Planen• Steuern• Reporten bei der Einführung von SAP-Banking, 5–10.

Volland, M. F. (2021). Das Scrum-Framework in Großunternehmen-Entscheidung und Implementation: Eine Fallstudie Eines Multinationalen Automobilkonzerns. Springer.

Yelevin, & Batamig. (2021). Use entities to classify and analyze data in Microsoft Sentinel. Use entities to classify and analyze data in Microsoft Sentinel. Retrieved from https://docs.microsoft.com/en-us/azure/sentinel/entities

DRIFT-DRIVEN REGRESSION FOR PREDICTING THE EVOLUTION OF PANDEMICS

Khaled Jouini and Ouajdi Korbaa
University of Sousse, MARS Research Lab, LR17ES05, ISITCom
4011 H. Sousse, Tunisia

ABSTRACT

Pandemics will never cease to emerge and threaten public health and the global economy. Predicting the evolution of a pandemic is of paramount interest as it enables policymakers understand the potential spread of a virus and make informed decisions to mitigate its impact. *Concept drifts* refer to situations where the relationship between the input features (*model input*) and the learning targets (*model output*) changes or evolves over time. Concept drifts are common in pandemic curves, not only because new variants appear over time, but also due to factors such as seasonality, policy responses to the pandemic, and changes in the way the disease is treated. Without proper intervention, the accuracy of conventional (*batch*) machine learning models will deteriorate after drift occurs, since they were trained on outdated data. *Incremental learning* is an alternative to batch learning, where the training phase never ends, and the model is incrementally updated as new data becomes available. While incremental models are in general less accurate than batch models, they adapt better to concept drifts as they are continuously refined using the most recent data. Batch and incremental learning are often considered as two distinct and mutually exclusive approaches (Montiel et al., 2018a). In this work we propose CDR (*Collaborative Drift- Driven Regression*), a novel collaborative regression strategy where incremental and batch regressors work together to complement each other's strengths, ergo the overall predictive performance. Experiments conducted on COVID-19 pandemic data, show that CDR is an efficient collaborative learning strategy that yields better results than the underlying batch and incremental models used separately.

KEYWORDS

Concept Drift, Incremental Learning, Collaborative Learning, Pandemic Forecasting

1. INTRODUCTION

The risk of extreme pandemics like COVID-19 is increasing due to climate change, ease of global travel, and increasing rates of disease emergence from animal reservoirs (Marani et al., 2021). The accurate prediction of a pandemic's evolution is crucial for improved preparedness and prompt responses. It is however a particularly challenging task due to factors such as, changes in the way the virus spreads or mutates, changes in testing or reporting practices, and changes in the way the disease is treated. In machine learning and related fields, changes over time in the relationship between input data and the learning target are known as *Concept Drifts* (*a.k.a. data non-stationarity*) (Bifet & Gavaldà, 2007).

Most state-of-the-art machine learning algorithms, referred to as *batch learners* in the sequel, operate under the premise of data stationary, and assume that all training data is available prior to the learning process. Without proper intervention, the predictive performance of batch learners inevitably deteriorates as drifts occur, since they were trained on historical data and no longer accurately reflect the current relationship between input and target variables. A common intervention to handle drifts is to periodically *retrain* the batch model to take into account recent observations. Besides the computational burden, model retraining raises two significant challenges: (*i*) determining when a model is no longer valid and requires retraining (*i.e.* stability-plasticity dilemma); and (*ii*) deciding how much new data to collect, given that collecting more data enhances the chances of generating an accurate model, but also delays the replacement of the old poorly performing model.

Incremental learning (*a.k.a. online learning* or *lifelong learning*) is an alternative to batch learning, wherein the model is trained on small amounts of data at a time, rather than in a single batch. In incremental learning, the training phase is perpetual, and the model undergoes continuous and incremental refinement as new data becomes available. This continual updating enables incremental models to exhibit superior adaptability to drifts when compared to batch models. Another desirable feature of incremental learning is its *"anytime property"* which refers to the ability of a model to make predictions at any point in time during the learning process. By being responsive to changes, easy to maintain (models do not need to be retrained), and able to start making predictions after the first few training instances, incremental learning seems to be well-suited to the requirements of modeling the evolution of a pandemic. The downside of incremental learning, however, is that it builds models by making assumptions on upcoming data (an incremental model is in fact an approximation of the corresponding batch model) (Bifet & Gavaldà, 2007). In contrast to incremental algorithms, batch algorithms need time to collect enough data before building a model, but once the model is built, it is often more accurate than the corresponding incremental model.

Batch and incremental learning are commonly considered as distinct and mutually exclusive approaches (Montiel et al., 2018a). In this paper, we propose CDR (*Collaborative Drift-Driven Regression*), a novel collaborative regression strategy in which incremental and batch regressors work together to complement their strengths, with the ultimate goal of accurately predicting the evolution of pandemics. CDR continuously refines the underlying incremental model as data arrives, retrains a new batch model on recent observations whenever it detects a drift and dynamically selects the best performing model to produce predictions. Experiments conducted on COVID-19 data show that CDR yields better results compared to using the underlying incremental and batch regressors separately.

The remainder of this paper is organized as follows. Section 2 briefly reviews the main concepts related to incremental learning and provides an overview of related work. Section 3 details our CDR approach. Section 4 outlines the experimental evaluation and examines the main findings. Conclusions and future work are discussed in Section 5.

2. PRELIMINARIES AND RELATED WORK

In sensitive areas like pandemics forecasting, interpretability matters as much as accurate predictions, and white-box models are often preferred to black-box models (Salah, I. et al., 2023). Decision Trees are among the most popular white-box models. This section first introduces the key concepts related to incremental trees and then briefly reviews the main approaches utilizing them for pandemics forecasting.

2.1 Incremental Trees

A decision tree is learned top-down by recursively replacing leaves by test nodes. The recursion is completed when a node is deemed homogeneous enough, or when splitting no longer improves predictions. Batch trees scan the entire dataset to discover the attribute leading to the highest homogeneity. The aforementioned process cannot be adopted directly in contexts like pandemics forecasting where only a small fraction of data is accessible during learning. The *Hoeffding Tree* (HT) (Domingos & Hulten, 2000) is the de-facto standard in stream mining and has inspired many state-of-the-art incremental algorithms. The main idea behind HT is that a small fraction of data can often be enough to choose the best splitting attribute (*i.e.* the attribute leading to the highest homogeneity). This idea is supported by the *Hoeffding Bound* which states that, with probability $(1-\delta)$, the true mean of a random variable of range R will not differ from the estimated mean after n independent observations by more than (Domingos & Hulten, 2000):

$$\epsilon = \sqrt{\frac{R^2 \ln(1/\delta)}{2n}}$$

For the purpose of deciding which attribute to split on, the random variable being estimated is the difference in information gain between the best and second-best attributes, *resp.* referred to in the sequel as X_a and X_b. If the computed difference of information gains between X_a and X_b is higher than ϵ, the algorithm asserts with confidence $1-\delta$, that X_a will always remain a better split option than X_b. The *Fast Incremental Model Tree with Drift Detection* (FIMT-DD) (Ikonomovska et al., 2011) is among the state-of-the-art incremental regression trees. Like the *Hoeffding Adaptive Tree* (HAT) (Domingos & Hulten, 2000),

FIMT-DD is an adaptive incremental tree that encompasses local change detectors. The salient features of FIMT-DD are synthesized in the following points.

Splitting Criterion. FIMT-DD uses the *standard deviation reduction* (SDR) as splitting criterion. Similarly, to HT and HAT, FIMT-DD uses the Hoeffding Bound to control the risk that, as data arrives, the merit of splitting on X_b exceeds the merit of splitting on X_a. In practice, before splitting a node, FIMT-DD waits until the following condition is met.

$$\frac{SDR(X_b)}{SDR(X_a)} < 1 - \epsilon$$

Linear model at the leaves. FIMT-DD trains a perceptron at each leaf of the tree. The weights of the perceptrons are continuously updated as new data arrives using the incremental stochastic gradient descent and with the objective of minimizing the mean squared error. In addition to their proven effectiveness, perceptrons have the crucial advantage of naturally adapting to drifts (Ikonomovska et al., 2011).

Drift handling. FIMT-DD uses the Page-Hinkley (PH) change detection test (Mouss et al., 2004) at inner nodes to detect changes in the error rate. When a change is detected in a node *inner*, an alternate tree rooted at *inner* is grown with new incoming instances: every new instance that reaches *inner* is used for growing both subtrees. The new subtree replaces the original one when (and if) it performs better.

2.2 Related Work

The volume of literature on predicting the evolution of the COVID-19 pandemic is monumental and covers a wide range of techniques (Miralles-Pechuán et al., 2023). Despite the abundance of studies, little work has been dedicated to incremental learning (Miralles-Pechuán et al., 2023). Existing incremental approaches can be broadly classified into two families: *compartmental models* and *machine learning models*. Machine learning models rely on historical data to forecast future outcomes. Compartmental models divide the population into different groups and use differential equations to model the transition of individuals between these groups. The approach of (Camargo et al., 2022) is representative of compartmental methods and involves a two-component architecture, where the first component is a feature engineering process that selects the predictor variables used by the predictive models of the second component. Specifically, the first component analyzes the temporal dependencies between the SEIRD variables (*Susceptible, Exposed, Infected, Recovered, and Dead*) and identify, for each target variable, the best subset of predictors. The second component of the architecture employs an ensemble learning approach, where various models are trained using different batch and incremental algorithms. The final output is chosen based on the predictions of the top-performing model. When the predictions of the top-performing model are not deemed accurate enough, the approach builds new predictive models. The approach of (Camargo et al., 2022) lacks a drift detection mechanism for automatically detecting drops in performance. The authors do not specify how and when the predictions of the top-performing model are no longer considered as good enough and, hence, when the employed models need to be retrained. Furthermore, (Camargo et al., 2022) retrains its models on the entire available dataset, which implies that over time, these models are trained on a diminishing proportion of recent data and are consequently less and less sensitive to changes.

The study of (Miralles-Pechuán et al., 2023) is representative of machine learning approaches and com- pares batch and incremental algorithms using COVID-19 data from 50 countries. Results showed that incremental methods are more effective in adapting to changes and have lower computational cost compared to techniques such as LSTMs. A salient feature of (Miralles-Pechuán et al., 2023) is that it tests three different approaches. The first approach (*resp.* the second approach), involves training each model using data from a single country (*resp.* using data from the 50 countries). In the third approach, clustering is first applied to identify the most similar countries to the one being predicted and then each model is trained using data from those countries. Results showed that the third approach outperforms the two others. While the study of (Miralles-Pechuán et al., 2023) includes HT and HAT, surprisingly, it overlooks FIMT-DD. Similar to (Camargo et al., 2022), the work of (Miralles-Pechuán et al., 2023) does not include a drift detector for an automated management of the life cycle of machine learning models.

3. COLLABORATIVE DRIFT-DRIVEN REGRESSION (CDR)

The goal of a regression task is to learn a model M that predicts a real value, and not one of a discrete set of values as in classification. Formally, let S be a continuous stream of data: $S = \{(\overrightarrow{x^t}, y^t)\}$, where $\overrightarrow{x^t}$ is a feature vector, $y^t \in \mathbb{R}$ is the target variable and t the arrival timestamp. The goal is to incrementally learn $M: \vec{x} \rightarrow y$ as new data becomes available (Gomes et al., 2018). The predicted value of M is denoted as $\hat{y}$. When the actual value y gets revealed, the performance P is measured according to a loss function l: $P(M) = l(y, \hat{y})$. Performance of incremental models is typically measured using *prequential evaluation* (*a.k.a. test-then-train* evaluation), where each instance is used to test the model before it is used for training (Gomes et al., 2018). For the ith instance: $\widehat{y^i} = M^{i-1}(\overrightarrow{x^i})$.

Our drift-driven collaborative regression approach CDR draws inspiration from the work of (Montiel et al., 2018a) on fast and slow classifiers. CDR combines incremental learning and batch learning to harness the strengths of both: (*i*) the accuracy of batch regressors, and (*ii*) the anytime property and adaptability to drifts of incremental regressors. Illustrated in Figure 1, the learning process of CDR involves the utilization of incremental learning to continuously and incrementally train and refine a regressor I, as new samples become available. Concurrently, batch learning is used to train a sequence of (batch) regressors $\{B_1, B_2, \ldots, B_n\}$. As illustrated in Figure 1, whenever a drift is detected, the current batch regressor B_i is invalidated and is subsequently replaced by a new regressor B_{i+1}. While I is trained on single samples as they arrive, a batch regressor B_i is trained on a (micro-) batch M_i containing the k most recent samples. This implies that the training process of B_{i+1} is deferred until k samples are gathered.

CDR uses *ADaptive WINdowing* (ADWIN) (Bifet & Gavaldà, 2007) for drift detection. The basic idea behind ADWIN is to maintain a variable-length sliding window W which increases in size as long as no drift is detected. To detect a drift, ADWIN repeatedly partitions W into two adjacent sub-windows W_0 and W_1 and compares their average to decide whether they are likely to originate from the same distribution. If W_0 and W_1 exhibit distinct enough averages and are of sufficient size, then a drift is detected and W is shrunk by dropping W_0 items from the window. In practice, ADWIN tests if the difference between the averages of W_0 and W_1 is larger than a variable value ϵ_{cut} computed as (Bifet & Gavaldà, 2007):

$$\epsilon_{cut} = \sqrt{\frac{1}{2m} ln \frac{4|W|}{\delta}}$$

, where m is the harmonic mean of W_0 and W_1. Unlike other existing drift detectors, ADWIN is assumption-free. Its only parameter is a confidence bound $\delta \in [0, 1]$, which enables adjusting the sensitivity to drifts.

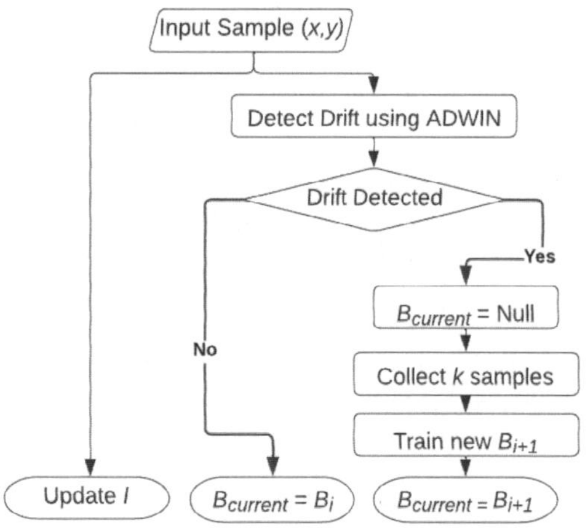

Figure 1. CDR - Learning Process

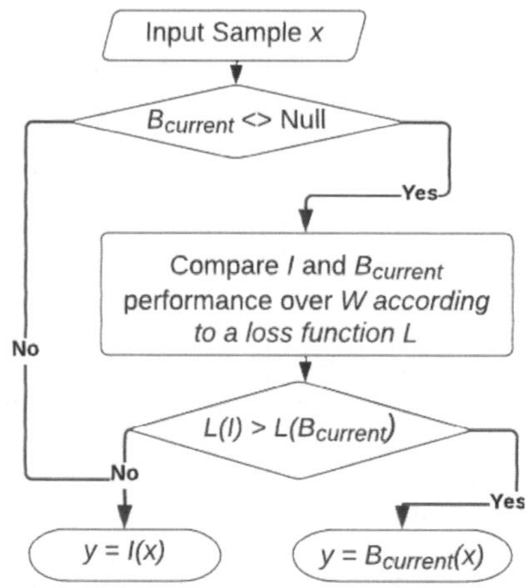

Figure 2. CDR - Inference Process

The inference process of CDR is depicted in the flowchart of Figure 2. As illustrated in Figure 2, when a batch regressor B_i is invalidated and until k samples are collected to train a new batch regressor B_{i+1}, only the incremental regressor I is used for inference. When a new batch regressor $B_{current}$ becomes available, CDR tracks the predictive performance of I and $B_{current}$ over a sliding window W containing the most recent observations. The top-performing model over W is then selected for inference. The aforementioned process is repeated for each new incoming instance. It is important to note that CDR is independent of the underlying learners and is compatible with any combination of incremental and batch methods.

4. EXPERIMENTAL EVALUATION

4.1 Tools and Datasets

We considered the dataset *Coronavirus Pandemic (COVID-19)* (Mathieu, E. et al., 2023), provided by Our World in Data (OWID). The original dataset includes daily information about the pandemic in 219 countries. Our target variables are the daily new confirmed cases and deaths per million people. We model the evolution of the daily new confirmed cases and deaths as function of the previously reported daily new confirmed cases per million people. For each country C and each record of C with a timestamp t, we consider the number of cases per million reported at 8 time points[1]: t minus 1 week, t minus 2 weeks,.., t minus 8 weeks. The obtained dataset contains nine input variables, ≈177k samples and covers the period starting from March 28, 2020 to November 30, 2022. When restricted to Tunisian data, the dataset contains ≈910 samples.

At the current state of our work, we implemented CDR using MOA (*Massive On line Analysis*) (Bifet et al., 2018), *Scikit-Multiflow* (Montiel et al., 2018b) and *Scikit-Learn* (Pedregosa et al., 2011). We configured CDR using FIMT-DD for incremental learning, DT (Pedregosa et al., 2011) for batch learning, and ADWIN for drift detection. All methods were run using their default settings. We compared the performance of batch and incremental models using a sliding window of one week and selected the best performing model to make predictions for the current input. Batch models were trained on windows of three weeks, with two weeks before and one week after a detected drift. The models' performance was evaluated using the Mean Absolute Error (MAE) and the Root Mean Squared Error (RMSE). In general, RMSE is more sensitive to large errors and outliers, while MAE is more interpretable.

4.2 Results and Discussion

A large number of experiments have been performed to demonstrate the effectiveness of CDR. Due to the lack of space, only few results are presented herein. In the first set of experiments, we compare the performance of CDR and established incremental methods using a prequential evaluation scheme. The obtained results are summarized in Table 1, and partially illustrated in Figures 3 and 4. As shown in Table 1, when compared to FIMT-DD, CDR achieves an improvement of 2.99%, 9.78%, 5.72% and 5.51% (resp. 44.59%, 63.97%, 15.75% and 16.41%) with regards to $RMSE_{Deaths}$, MAE_{Deaths}, $RMSE_{Cases}$ and MAE_{Cases} on world data (resp. single-country data). In contrast to HAT and FIMT-DD, HT lacks specialized mechanisms for handling drifts. When compared to HT, CDR achieves an improvement of 20.36%, 31.52%, 33.62% and 29.54% (resp. 57.32%, 79.41%, 26.12% and 30.7%) with regards to $RMSE_{Deaths}$, MAE_{Deaths}, $RMSE_{Cases}$ and MAE_{Cases} on world data (resp. single-country data). As we can observe in figures 3 and 4, CDR benefits from the continuous selection of predictions from both the incremental and the batch regressors. Near drift points, CDR opts in most cases for the batch model, which is only trained on recent data. However, the performance of the batch learner deteriorates quickly as we move away from drift points, primarily due to overfitting. Consequently, CDR transitions to the incremental learner. It's important to emphasize that the model selection near drift points is solely based on the performance (Mean Absolute Error) of both regressors, evaluated within a sliding window of one week.

[1] We do not consider the cases reported less than a week before t. Although including such observations could lead to more accurate models, they are not practical for timely policy responses.

Our second set of experiments compares the performance of a conventional batch regression tree against CDR. The prequential evaluation approach, commonly used in incremental learning, can be applied to batch learning by repeatedly retraining and reevaluating the model. For each training/testing round, the dataset is split into a training set and a test set in an order-preserving fashion. Instances used for testing the ith batch model are appended to the training set of the $(i+1)^{th}$ model. The evaluation of the $(i+1)^{th}$ batch model is then performed on instances that arrived after its training and before the training of a new model. The process is repeated for multiple rounds until all the data has been used for both training and testing (except the first batch of data, which is only used for training, and the last batch, which is only used for testing). In (Miralles-Pechuán et al., 2023), training/evaluation rounds are referred to as *milestones*. In this study, we followed the aforementioned process (used also in (Miralles-Pechuán et al., 2023)) and adopted a realistic scenario where a new batch model is trained from scratch every ≈3 months, resulting in a set of 9 milestones (and, hence, 9 batch models). Tables 3 and 4 report the performance of the considered batch models and of CDR over the 9 milestones. As illustrated in Tables 3 and 4 CDR by far outperforms the corresponding batch model and respectively achieves an average improvement of 111.87%, 78.14%, 59.02% and 20.64% (resp. 124.83%,

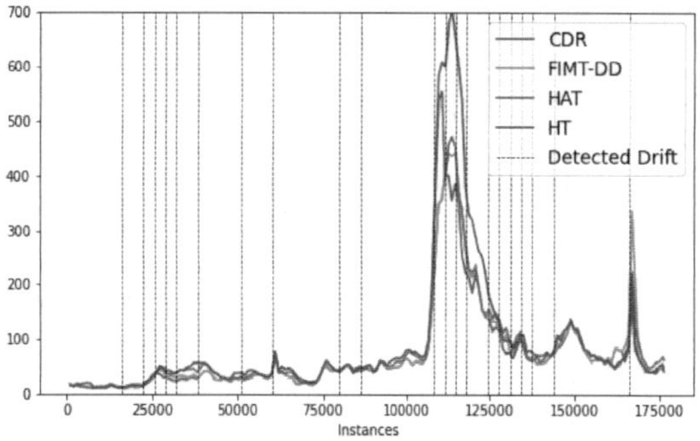

Figure 3. World - Daily New Confirmed Cases
MAE achieved by CDR and incremental learners

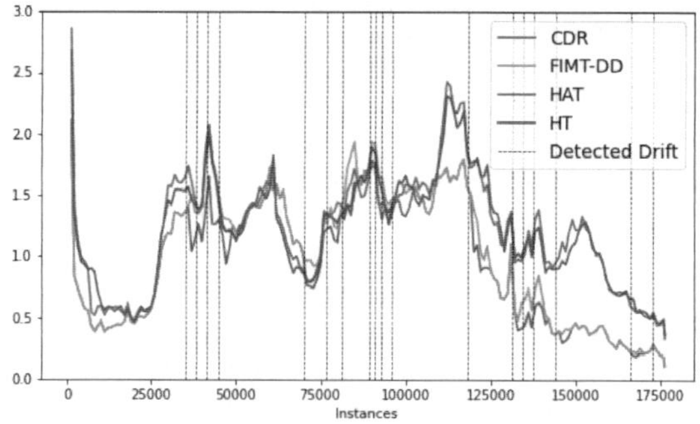

Figure 4. World - Daily New Confirmed Deaths
MAE achieved by CDR and incremental learners

90.29%, 109.17% and 65.13%) with regards to resp. $RMSE_{Deaths}$, MAE_{Deaths}, $RMSE_{Cases}$ and MAE_{Cases} on world data (resp. single-country data).

Table 1. MAE and RMSE achieved by CDR and Incremental Learners

		Daily New Confirmed Deaths		Daily New Confirmed Cases	
		$RMSE_{Deaths}$	MAE_{Deaths}	$RMSE_{Cases}$	MAE_{Cases}
World	HT	2.01	1.21	174.1	91.51
	HAT	2.03	1.23	150.12	80.67
	FIMT-DD	1.72	1.01	137.75	74.53
	CDR	**1.67**	**0.92**	**130.29**	**70.64**
Tunisia	HT	2.47	2.44	61.56	58.71
	HAT	2.46	2.43	59.35	56.68
	FIMT-DD	2.27	2.23	56.50	52.29
	CDR	**1.57**	**1.36**	**48.81**	**44.92**

Besides confirming that CDR yields better results than those attained by each of the contributing models separately, the aforementioned experiments allow to draw the following important conclusions.

Retraining on recent data vs. retraining on the entire dataset. While (re-)training a batch model on the whole available dataset is beneficial in some cases to learn stable concepts or recurrent drifts, it is not the most suitable approach when it comes to predicting a pandemic's evolution. This can be observed in Tables 2 and 3, where in most cases, CDR becomes increasingly more efficient than the batch model over time. The reason behind this is that the batch model is (re-)trained on datasets with a diminishing proportion of recent data, causing it to become less and less sensitive to changes.

Learning using data from a single country vs. Learning using data from multiple countries. As it can observed in Tables 1 and 2 and 3, CDR exhibits higher improvements over incremental and batch models when training is performed using data from a single country. This is mainly due to the occurrence of drifts at different time points across countries, and to the fact that using data from multiple countries results in models that do not accurately represent any specific country. Overall, even though using data from multiple countries provides more training data, using data from a single country yields better results, as detecting (and, hence, adapting to) drifts is easier. It should be noted that this confirms the results found in (Miralles-Pechuán et al., 2023).

Table 2. Daily New Confirmed Deaths - MAE and RMSE achieved by CDR and the batch Decision Tree

<table>
<tr><th></th><th colspan="2">Daily New Confirmed Deaths (per 1M)</th></tr>
<tr><th></th><th>$RMSE_{Deaths}$</th><th>MAE_{Deaths}</th></tr>
<tr><td>World</td><td>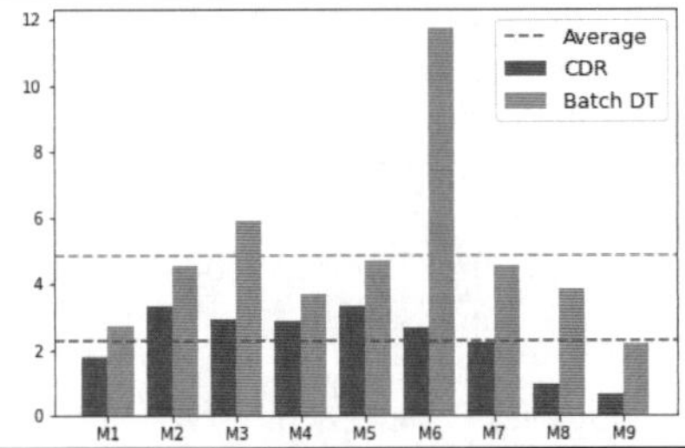
</td><td>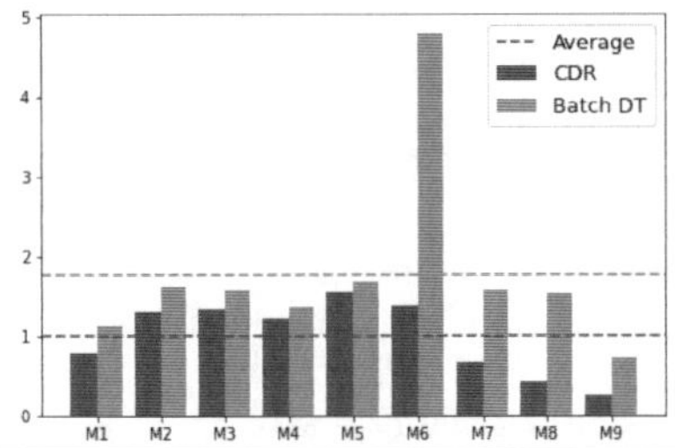
</td></tr>
<tr><td>Tunisia</td><td>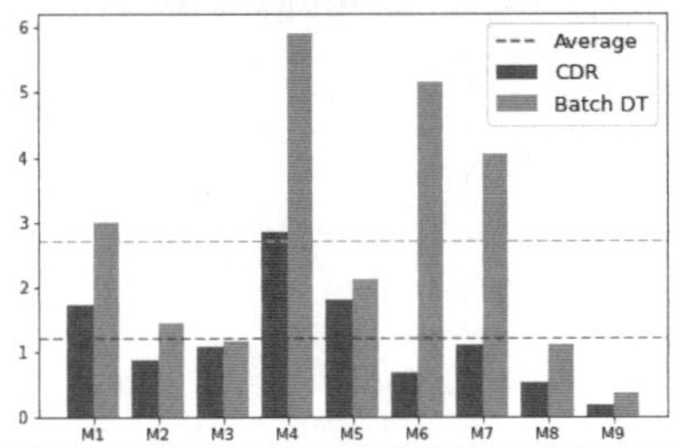
</td><td>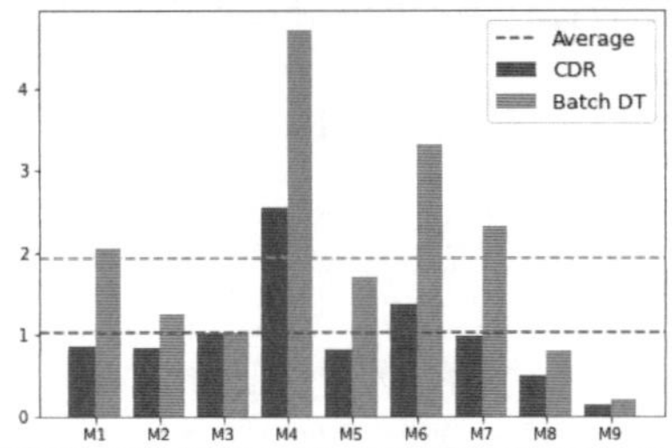
</td></tr>
</table>

Table 3. Daily New Confirmed Cases - MAE and RMSE achieved by CDR and the batch Decision Tree

<table>
<tr><th></th><th colspan="2">Daily New Confirmed Cases (per 1M)</th></tr>
<tr><th></th><th>$RMSE_{Cases}$</th><th>MAE_{Cases}</th></tr>
<tr><td>World</td><td>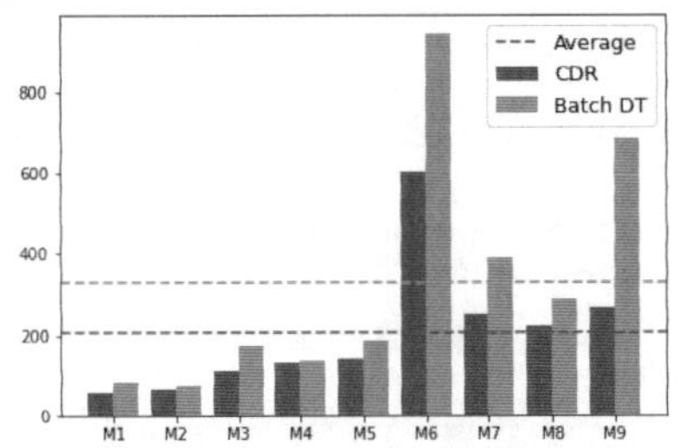
</td><td>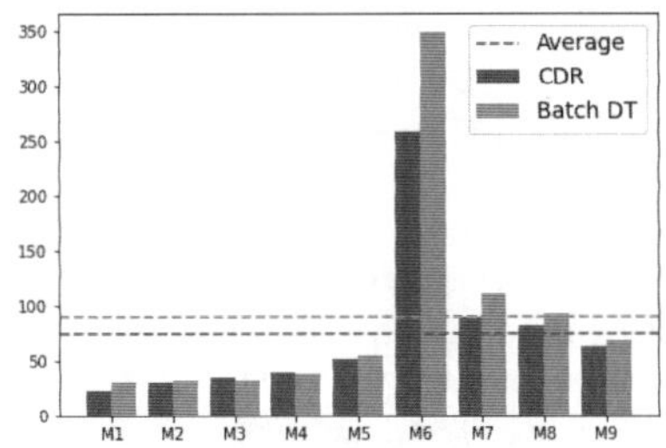
</td></tr>
<tr><td>Tunisia</td><td>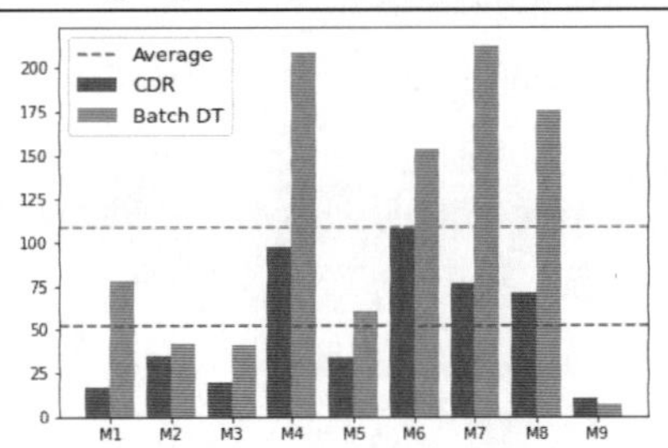
</td><td>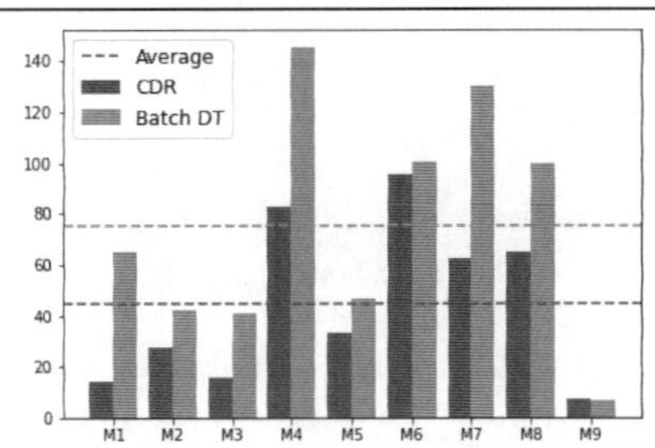
</td></tr>
</table>

5. CONCLUSION

Pandemics will never cease to emerge and threaten both public health and the global economy. Therefore, it is crucial to learn from past pandemics to develop effective tools for preventing and controlling future outbreaks. This involves not only researching treatments and therapies, but also implementing efficient epidemiological surveillance systems. In this paper we proposed CDR, an innovative collaborative regression strategy for predicting the evolution of pandemics. CDR continuously refines the underlying incremental model as data arrives, uses ADWIN as drift detector and retrains a new batch model on recent observations whenever it detects a drift. At the current state of our work, we implemented CDR using FIMT-DD as incremental regressor and the Decision Tree as batch regressor. Experiments on COVID-19 data, showed that CDR is an effective collaboration strategy that yields better results than those attained by the incremental and the batch model separately.

In this paper, we mainly focused on connecting the dots between batch regressors and incremental regressors and on the relevance of using them in conjunction to predict the evolution of a pandemic. The results obtained are highly encouraging for exploring other forms of collaboration between batch learning and incremental learning. a part of our future work, we intend to investigate the use of incremental and batch ensemble models instead of single models to further alleviate the effects of concept drifts. On the other hand, our experimental study revealed that even though using data from multiple countries provides more training data, using data from a single country yields better results. This is mainly due to the occurrence of drifts at different time points across countries. In our future work, we intend to identify subgroups of countries exhibiting similar patterns and apply CDR to each subgroup independently. We believe that doing so will allow to leverage more training data while maintaining the ability to efficiently detect and adapt to drifts.

REFERENCES

Bifet, A. et al., 2018. *Machine learning for data streams: with practical examples in MOA*. MIT Press, Massachusetts, USA.

Bifet, A. and Gavaldà, R., 2007. Learning from time-changing data with adaptive windowing. *Proceedings of the 2007 SIAM International Conference on Data Mining (SDM)*. pp. 443–448.

Camargo, E. et al., 2022. An incremental learning approach to prediction models of seird variables in the context of the covid-19 pandemic. *In Health and Technology*, Vol. 12, No. 4, pp. 2190–7196.

Domingos, P. and Hulten, G., 2000. Mining high-speed data streams. *Proceedings of the sixth ACM SIGKDD international conference on Knowledge Discovery and Data mining*. Boston, USA, pp. 71–80.

Gomes, H. M. et al., 2018. Adaptive random forests for data stream regression. *26th European Symposium on Artificial Neural Networks (ESANN 2018)*, Bruges, Belgium, pp. 267–272

Ikonomovska, E. et al., 2011. Learning model trees from evolving data streams. *Data mining and knowledge discovery*, Vol. 23, No. 1, pp. 128–168.

Marani, M. et al., 2021. Intensity and frequency of extreme novel epidemics. *Proceedings of the National Academy of Sciences*, Vol. 118, No. 35, e2105482118.

Mathieu, E. et al., 2023. OurWorldInData.org. *Coronavirus Pandemic (COVID-19)*. Retrieved from: "https://ourworldindata.org/coronavirus" [Online Resource].

Miralles-Pechuán, L. et al., 2023. Forecasting covid-19 cases using dynamic time warping and incremental machine learning methods. *Expert Systems*, Vol. 40, No. 6, e13237.

Montiel, J. et al., 2018a. Learning fast and slow: A unified batch/stream framework. *2018 IEEE International Conference on Big Data*, Seattle, WA, USA, pp. 1065–1072.

Montiel, J. et al., 2018b. Scikit-multiflow: A multi-output streaming framework. *Journal of Machine Learning Research*, Vol. 19, No. 72, pp. 1–5.

Mouss, H. et al., 2004. Test of page-hinckley, an approach for fault detection in an agro-alimentary production system. *2004 5th Asian Control Conference (IEEE Cat. No. 04EX904)*, Melbourne, VIC, Australia, pp. 815–818.

Pedregosa, F. et al., 2011. Scikit-learn: Machine learning in Python. *Journal of Machine Learning Research*, Vol. 12, pp. 2825–2830.

Salah, I. et al., 2023. On the use of data augmentation for stance and fake news detection. *Journal of Information and Telecommunication*, Vol. 7, No. 3, pp. 359–375.

A NOVEL APPROACH FOR SECURE STEGANOGRAPHY: INTER-FORMAT CONVERSION COMPENSATION FOR ENHANCED DATA SECURITY

Hasan Azooz[1], Khawla Ben Salah[2], Monji Kherallah[3] and Mohamed Saber Naceur[4]
[1]*Almuthanna University, Iraq*
[2]*University of Gafsa, Tunisia*
[3]*Faculty of Sciences of Sfax, University of Sfax, Tunisia*
[4]*National Engineering School of Tunis, Tunisia*

ABSTRACT

Steganography research and development are becoming more common in the information society, due to the widespread use of digital media formats and the challenges of managing digital resources and controlling the ownership and use of computer files. At thesame time, addressing steganography challenges is an important issue in the context of the evolving network communication infrastructure for Internet users - participants in open and uncontrolled interaction in the media space. The research concludes that it is necessaryto develop a new qualitative concealing algorithm that enables the hiding of large data. Amounts of data (MB) in still images in commongraphic formats The JPEG format was chosen as the most popular in everyday use scenarios for digital graphics, especially digital images.A qualitative analysis of classes of steganography algorithms focused on embedding data in graphic images for the purpose of covertly transmitting large amounts of data in digital images in JPEG format was carried out, resulting in the development of algorithms for working with digital image structures in JPEG and BMP graphic formats. A mechanism has been developed to compensate for the loss of data bits during inter-format conversions. Additionally, programmatic functions have been established for data insertion and extraction. Machine learning can be used to fine-tune the embedding process, making the resulting stego images harder to decipher for attackers. By usinga machine learning model that has been trained to distinguish between cover and stego images, the embedding process can be fine-tuned tomake the stego image less distinguishable from the original cover image.

KEYWORDS

Steganography, JPEG Images, Embedding Information

1. INTRODUCTION

Encryption and steganography are common and widely used techniques for processing information (messages) with the intent to encrypt it and hide its existence. These techniques have broad applications in computers and other related fields they are used to protect emails, credit card information, corporate data security (Pavan et al.,2005)), and more. Steganography is an art unto itself. It teaches one to communicate in a way that conceals the existence of a connection and ensures the transmission of information through communication channels. This method ensures that the content of the messages is sent soas not to attract attention or arouse the suspicions of unauthorized eavesdroppers. For example, it is possible to include text within an image or an audio file (Miranda & Parada ,2022). On the other hand, encryption is the study of mathematical techniques associated with the security of information to ensure the safety of confidential data. Concealing information is of paramount importance, as hiding data, whether encrypted or unencrypted, acts as a catalyst for the protection and security of that information.This method of concealment is used in many domains, notably in electronic commerce, where its applications and significance grow daily. Assuming that the client suspects the presence of some hidden text, they face the subsequent challenge of discerning the method of concealment, the password, and the encryption key (Yang & Ciou,2009); determining any one of these factors can be time-consuming. The main attention is paid to such a direction of steganography as hiding data for the purpose of transmission and optimizing the embedding process in a good steganographic algorithm. The task of hiding data in seemingly harmless containers for the purpose of covert transmission arose a long time ago, but at the same time, it is still relevant today.There is a need to protect correspondence, and network subscribers have the right, along with cryptographic means of protecting circulating information (Hsu& Wu, 1999), to use a steganographic approach to hide the very fact of correspondence.

2. RELATED WORKS

Steganography is the practice of hiding secret information within another form of data, such as an image or audio file, in order to prevent detection by unintended recipients. One common method of steganography involves embedding secret messages within cover images. Machine learning can be used to optimize the embedding process, making the resulting stego images less detectable to potential attackers. By training a machine learning model to distinguish between cover and stego images, and then using this model to predict the likelihood of an image being detected as stego, the embedding process can be adjusted to make the stego image less distinguishable from the original cover image. This can help ensure the confidentiality of sensitive information, while also preserving the appearance of the cover image. In this paper, we propose a method for image steganography based on deep learning and a decision tree. Image steganography is the art of hiding secret information within images without causing perceptible changes. There are many existing methods for image steganography, which can be roughly divided into two types: spatial domain methods and transform domain methods.

Spatial domain methods modify the pixel values directly to embed secret data. For example, the detection of information steganography in a monochrome still image leads to the replacement of less significant pixels by secret ones using artificial neural networks, (Miranda & Parada ,2022), but it introduces a method for monochrome on still images at a one type. Another example is the spatial outlier information hiding algorithm based on complex transformation (Shou et al.,2017), which uses complex numbers to represent pixels and embeds secret data in the imaginary part. This method can resist some simple attacks but may introduce noticeable artifacts. Transform domain methods transform the image into another domain such as frequency or wavelet domain and embed secret data in the coefficients. For example, Hidden Digital Watermarks in Images (Hsu& Wu, 1999) embeds secret data in discrete cosine transform (DCT) coefficients of JPEG images. This method can achieve high capacity and robustness but may degrade the image quality. Another example is analyze the false negative rates of Stegdetect (Aziz et al.,2020); extensive analysis of Stegdetect is conducted by embedding random messages in 2000 JPEG images using JPHide steganography to establish the false-negative rate of the tool. This method can reveal some existing steganographic schemes but may not be effective against new ones. Another example is Learning Multiple Layers of Features from Tiny Images (Zhu et al.,2018), which uses CNNs to learn features from small images for classification tasks. This method can extract useful information from low-resolution images but may not be suitable for high-resolution images. Another example is Hiding Data with Deep Networks (Krizhevsky et al.,2009) uses Dense Convolutional Network (DenseNet), which connects each layer to every other layer in a feed-forward fashion for image classification, this method can extract useful information from low-resolution images but may not be suitable for high-resolution images. Our proposed method differs from previous works in several aspects. First, we use a decision tree instead of a CNN to encode and decode secret data. A decision tree is a machine-learning technique that splits data into subsets based on certain criteria. By using a decision tree, we can reduce the complexity and computational cost of our method while maintaining high accuracy and security. Second, we use adversarial examples instead of natural images as cover images for embedding secret data. Adversarial examples are modified inputs that are designed to fool deep neural networks into making wrong predictions or classifications. By using adversarial examples, we can increase the imperceptibility and robustness of our method against detection by deep learning-based steganalysis techniques (Chaumont, M. 2020).

To summarize our contributions: A new deep learning and decision tree-based approach to image steganography is proposed. We used adversarial examples as cover images for embedding secret data. We tested our method on a variety of datasets and evaluated it in comparison to other methods that are considered to be state-of-the-art. The aim of the research is to develop and implement steganography methods and algorithms that allow large amounts of data to be hidden in graphic images in JPEG format for subsequent transmission of this data.

3. METHODOLOGY

In this paper, refer to the presented Algorithm 1. It uses a combination of the format method and data hiding in the spatial domain. Research has shown that the transform domain is not suitable for hiding the large amounts of data typically associated with hidden messages transmitted through graphic containers. The transform domain is better suited for embedding digital watermarks, which are short sequences of bytes. The set of restrictions applied to the use of stego in two scenarios of use is also fundamental [(Hsu& Wu, 1999; Shan et al., 2020). The embedding and extraction processes are automated and performed using the developed application. This mechanism is unmediated, and the extraction and merging methods are independent of the transmission channel. As a result, the recipient will receive an extracted message identical to the one sent, provided that the image sent with the embedded message (stego- message) does not change from the moment the sender completes the data merging process until the recipient begins extracting it (Zhu et al.,2018; Krizhevsky & Hinton,2009). If the specified safety is not observed, the program does not guarantee the fact that the recipient will be able to extract useful information (message) for him.

When developing the embedding system, difficulties were discovered regarding inter-format conversions. Since JPEG is a loss compression format (Yang & Ciou,2009; Aziz et al.,2020), they generally do not allow the recovery of an embedded message since the recovery occurs after the JPEG-RGBBMP-JPEG inter-format conversion procedures. In the developed system, these problems are solved; the process of introducing the message includes a number of preventive measures. The different steps of our developed system are presented in Figure 1. The first step is to convert a JPEG data stream into a BMP data stream. In this case, the size of the stream increases due to a change in the principle of encoding information about the color properties of image sections. Due to the fact that in the BMP format, each image point is encoded with three bytes, which are responsible for the contribution of the primary colors (R - red, G – green, and B - blue) to the target color of the point (Mouline et al.,2005; Shou et al.,2017), changing the stream size up is significant and allows you to embed required amount of information. It is known that the human eye is the least sensitive to changes in shades of blue, so B-components of RGB structures are used for embedding. To minimize the amount of change, the default algorithm uses only the smallest 1 bit of such a byte, which reduces the chance of detecting a change to a minimum, even on images with a large blue fill area (Laalaoui & Bouguila, 2014). The developed mechanism for compensating losses during inter-format conversions is designed for successful data extraction on the receiving side. The modified b-bytes are extracted from the stream and copied into a temporary buffer - buffer 1. Also, information about how the message bits were embedded is stored in another temporary buffer (buffer 2). Next, the modified BMP byte stream is subjected to JPEG compression with the highest quality factor. The resulting JPEG stream at this stage is not yet saved to the output file. Additional steps are taken to enable subsequent retrieval. An attempt is made to retrieve a message that contains:

1. Cloning a JPEG stream into a temporary stream.

2. Decoding the temporary JPEG stream into a BMP byte stream.

3. Extracting the modified b-bytes into which the message bits were embedded, taking into account information from buffer2.

4. Next comes the parsing of the retrieved message, i.e., comparing the extracted b-bytes with the b-bytes stored in buffer 1 and saving the differences to a new buffer - buffer 3. These differences are the inevitable results of JPEG- RGB-BMP- JPEG inter-format loss.

To estimate the effective "algorithm capacity", the following formula is used:

$$V = f(x, i) = \frac{(x^{jpeg \to bmp\ trans} \to x_{bmp}) - H_{BMP}}{D_{BMP}} x i$$

Where: X: jpeg file size, i: The number of low bits used, H_{BMP}: BMP file header size, bytes.

D_{BMP}: The number of bits per 1-pixel BMP image. One positive aspect of this hybrid algorithm is the ability to embed asignificant amount of data, surpassing the JHPS and JSTEG (Qiao et al.,2014) algorithms in this criterion.

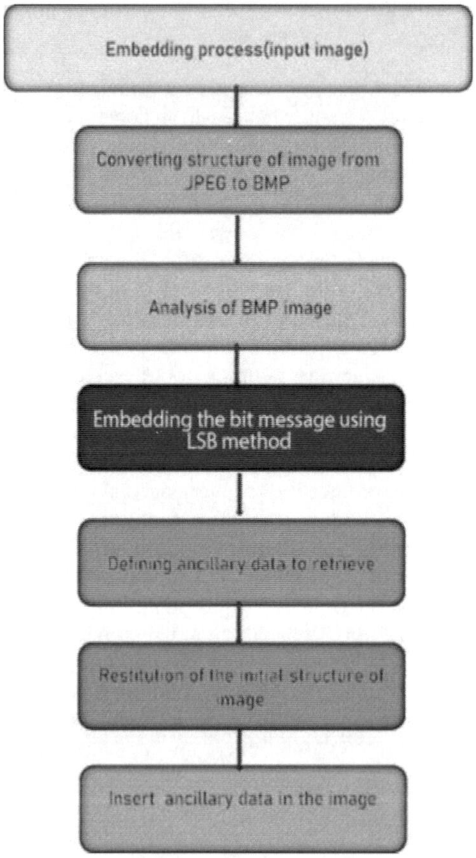

Figure 1. The Proposed embedding process using JPEG structure

Some details of the proposed approach are also presented in another form - image state transition diagrams, (as displayed in Figure 2).

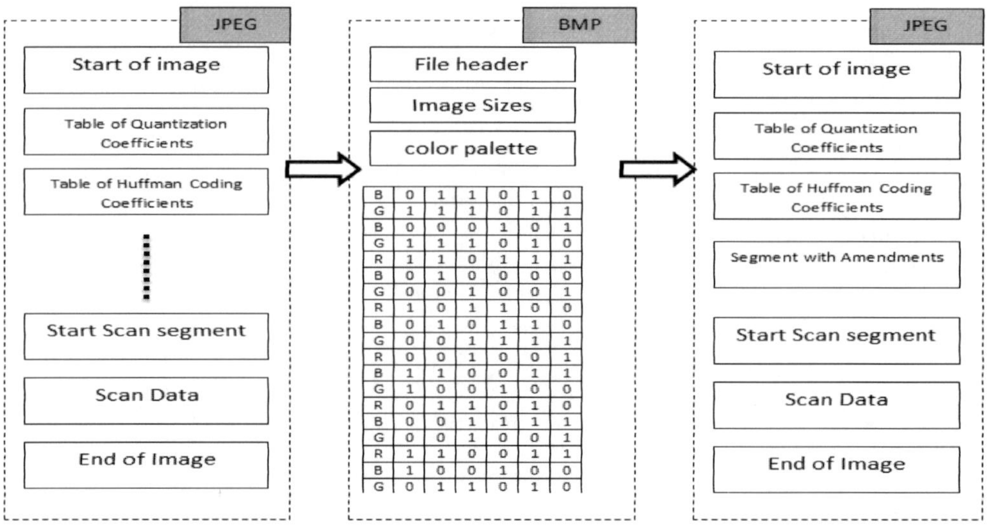

Figure 2. The general process of the conversion between JPEG and BMP format

A - Steganography embedding

The embedding procedure has six distinct phases: Dataset Creation, Feature Extraction, Model Training, Embedding Optimization, Message Extraction and Testing and Evaluation.

1. Dataset Creation: The first step would be to create a dataset consisting of cover images and corresponding stego images. For this, we had chosen a set of cover images and embedding messages into them using our steganographic algorithm. Then, the resulting stego images would be added to the dataset along with the corresponding cover images (Song et al.,2019).

2. Feature Extraction: Next, extracting features from the cover and stego images in the chosen dataset. It is a process of transforming raw data into features that can be easily understood and analyzed. And when features have been extracted from the cover and stego images in a chosen dataset, they can be used as input for a machine learning model (decision tree classifier). Then the model can be trained to distinguish between cover and stego images based on their extracted features.

3. Model Training: the extracted features from the dataset are used to train a machine learning model. The goal of the model would be to distinguish between cover and stego images. And here, we use decision trees classification algorithm to train the model (Domingos,2012).

4. Embedding Optimization: Once the model is trained, it can be used to optimize the embedding process in your steganographic algorithm. The model can predict the likelihood of a cover image being detected as a stego image, which can be used to adjust the embedding process to make the stego image less detectable.

5. Message Extraction: The machine learning model can also be used to improve the message extraction process. By analyzing the stego image, the model can predict where the message is most likely to be embedded, which can improve the accuracy of the message extraction.

6. Testing and evaluation: We compare our steganographic algorithm's performance with and without the machine learning optimization.

B - Embedding process

The embedding process in this code uses machine learning (decision tree classifier) (Breiman et al.,1984) to optimize the embedding process for a given cover image using LSB steganography. The decision tree classifier is trained on the cover image and the message bits, and it predicts the least significant bits of the cover image that can be modified to embed the message without causing a noticeable change in the cover image. The optimized message bits are then used to modify the least significant bits of the cover image to generate the stego image algorithm (3).

C - Decision tree classifier

A decision tree is used for categorization, prediction and facilitating decision making procedures (Jain et al.,2017), Decision tree comprised of three types of nodes: Decision node, Chance node and Terminal node. For classifying data, decision tree classifiers employ a supervised learning method. At each node deep within the tree, we first run a test on one of the input features to see where we should go next. In order to decide where secret information should be concealed in a cover image, the tree is expanded until all the data in a subset belong to the same class. A classifier trained on a dataset of cover and stego photos, for instance, would be able to tell the two types of images apart using only the features that were retrieved during training. Once the classifier has been trained, it may be used to determine where in the carrier image the secret message should be hidden. Make choices on where to hide secret messages within carrier images using the learned decision tree classifier. The classifier makes conclusions regarding the carrier image's covert information position using a secret information mapping paradigm. The decision tree classifier's equation looks like this in mathematics:

$$y = g(Fc)$$

where (Fc)is a matrix of size MxK, where K is the number of features extracted from each image, and M is a pair of cover and stego images, where each image has N pixels. Let c be a matrix of size MxN, where each row represents the pixel values of a cover image. This can be represented in mathematical as follows:

$$Fc=f(C)$$

The first step would be to extract features from the cover images that could be used to predict the likelihood of each pixel being a good location for embedding. This could be done by applying a function (f) to each matrix (C) row to extract features from each image. Where y is a matrix of size MxN containing the predicted likelihoods for each pixel in each cover image, and g is the function that represents the decision tree classifier.

Once the features have been extracted from the cover images, they can be used as input for a decision tree classifier that is trained to predict the likelihood of each pixel is a good location for embedding.

D - Steganography extraction

Using steganography, algorithm (4) extracts a hidden message from an image. It first loads the stego and original imagesand then calculates the differences between their pixel values. The message is concealed in the least significant bits of the resulting binary representation of the differences.

Once a pre-trained machine learning model is loaded into the method, it can decode the steganographic image. The model predicts the least significant bits of the differences, which are then used to extract the hidden message.

Finally, the algorithm compares the extracted message from the machine learning approach with the message extracted using the LSB steganography approach to check their accuracy. If the messages match, it means that the algorithm successfully extracted the hidden message from the image.

In conclusion, this algorithm can be employed to extract hidden messages from images that have been encoded using steganography techniques.

4. EXPERIMENTAL RESULTS

Twenty USC-SIPI standard grayscale images (USC-SIPI Image Database, n.d.) and ten L3i Laboratory doc copies are used to evaluate the suggested approach (photocopies of magazine pages from the PRImA dataset (Eskenaziet al.,2016). The images used in this paper were chosen from those bundled with the custom software. Each image measures 256 pixels on its longest side and is saved in JPEG format.

In comparison to other approaches, our suggested algorithm yielded superior PSNR and SSIM results. Table [1] shows that our proposed method outperforms the other state-of-the-art methods in terms of both The Peak Signal-to-Noise Ratio (PSNR)and The Structural Similarity Index Metrics (SSIM) values. These metrics are commonly used to evaluate the quality of imperceptibility of image steganography, with higher values indicating better performance. For example, our approach outperformed the LSB, PVD, and CRT methods evaluated using the PSNR and SSIM metrics in (Setiadi et al. 2021).

Our approach achieved higher embedding capacity than the steganography scheme based on the improved U-Net architecture proposed in (Liu et al.,2022). These findings prove that our proposed technique is outperformed in terms of embedding capacity, which is the amount of information that can be concealed in a single JPEG image and its ability to successfully incorporate high-quality images.

We also visually inspected the stego images created by our algorithm and other approaches and performed a quantitative evaluation. Our technique produced nearly distortion-free stego photos, while other methods produced ones with obvious artifacts. In this way, we are able to visually verify the superiority of this paper, which presented a steganography system that uses machine learning as an optimization strategy for the steganography of massive amounts of data within JPEG images.

When compared to other steganography methods, our approach is superior in terms of the amount of data that can be hidden. Our algorithm's embedding capacity is determined by the quality of the underlying JPEG file, and it employs inter-format transformations and a loss compensation technique to prevent the detection of hidden content. To further enhance the steganography algorithm further and ensure the hiddenness of embedded messages, we have incorporated machine learning optimization similar to the method proposed by (Choudhary et al., 2016) that combines RSA cryptography with decision tree-based steganography.

Table 1. PSNR, SSIM, and embedding capacity comparison of recommended approach with state-of-the-art steganography approaches

State of the art-methods	PSNR Value	SSIM Value
Our proposed method	85.73	0.99999
Our proposed method based on decision tree	87.26	0.99999
'Nashat et al.'	38.61	-
'Liu et al.'	49.60	0.9963
'Choudhary'	86.55	-
'Shang et al.'	21.78	-
'Setiadi'	51.1	0.9990

Our suggested approach was measured against state-of-the-art steganography techniques using a variety of metrics, including PSNR, SSIM, and embedding capacity, to determine its efficacy. Regarding security, the proposed approach enhances the security of steganography based on machine learning. In addition to these quantitative comparisons, we compared with related work other approaches to security and compared our approach to enhancing steganographic security with (Shang et al.,2020), which is based on deep learning to make steganographic images less detectable through steganography analysis techniques. In (Nashat & Mamdouh, 2019), the researchers assumed that using an inverted LSB from the cover image for embedding instead of the method used in our proposed approach based on replacing the LSB with secret information. The results of comparison with related research showed superiority in quality and perceptual similarity values.

Our suggested steganography technique employing machine learning outperformed the state-of-the-art steganography approaches in terms of resulting image quality (as shown in Figure 3), embedding capacity, and security. The algorithm's security was bolstered by the incorporation of machine learning optimization, and the hidden message was kept out of sight. Our analysis reveals that our technique has the ability to be used in secure data transmission in real-world settings.

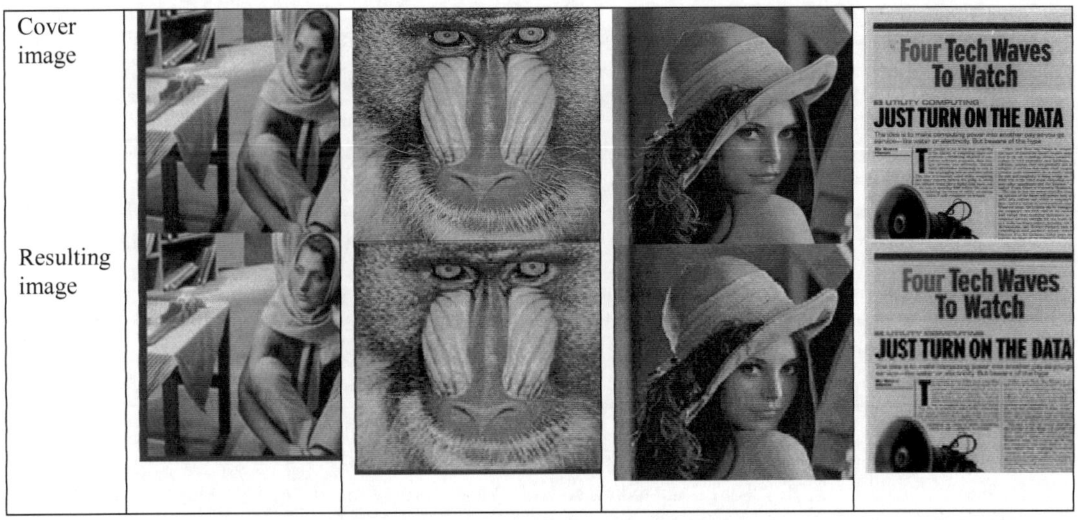

Figure 3. The results of the steganography images

5. CONCLUSION

This work presents key findings, including that the developed algorithm is based on the six distinct stages of embedding procedures. These include dataset creation, feature extraction, model training, embedding optimization, message extraction, and testing and evaluation. The algorithm employs computer vision techniques to extract salient features such as color histograms, texturefeatures, and edge information from the cover and stego images. These extracted features serve as the training data for a machine-learning model. With the help of a decision tree algorithm, the model was designed to differentiate between cover images and stego. Once this model is trained, it enhances the embedding process in the steganography algorithm, allowing large amounts of data(megabytes) to be hidden in JPEG files. A comparative analysis underscores the superiority of our developed algorithm over existing steganography techniques, particularly in terms of the maximal data embedding capacity. The number of bits suitable for embedding depends on the source JPEG file, with the specific nature of this dependency being governed by the JPEG conversion process. The adoption of inter-format transformations, coupled with a loss compensation mechanism, circumvents the introduction of discernible embedding artifacts and prevents the detection of concealed data.

REFERENCES

Aljarf, A., Zamzami, H., & Gutub, A. (2023). Integrating machine learning and features extraction for practical reliable color images steganalysis classification. Soft Computing, 1-12.

Aziz, B., Jung, J., Lee, J., & Chun, Y. T. (2020). A false negative study of the steganalysis tool Stegdetect. *Applied Sciences*, *10*(22), 8188.

Breiman, L., Friedman, J., Olshen, R., & Stone, C. (1984). Classification and regression trees–crc press. *Boca Raton, Florida*.

Charbuty, B., & Abdulazeez, A. (2021). Classification based on decision tree algorithm for machine learning. Journal of Applied Science and Technology Trends, 2(01), 20-28.

Chaumont, M. (2020). Deep learning in steganography and steganalysis. In Digital media steganography (pp. 321-349). Academic Press.

Domingos, P. (2012). A few useful things to know about machine learning. *Communications of the ACM*, *55*(10), 78-87.

Eskenazi, S., Gomez-Krämer, P., & Ogier, J.-M. (2016). Evaluation of the stability of four document segmentation algorithms. In Proc. of International Workshop on Document Analysis Systems (DAS), pages 1–6. Retrieved [9 12, 2023], from http://l3i-share.univ-lr.fr/datasets/DocCopiesWebsite/DocCopiesDataset.html

Hsu, C. T., & Wu, J. L. (1999). Hidden digital watermarks in images. *IEEE Transactions on image processing*, *8*(1), 58-68.

Jain, M., & Kumar, A. (2017). RGB channel based decision tree grey-alpha medical image steganography with RSA cryptosystem. International Journal of Machine Learning and Cybernetics, 8, 1695-1705.

Jain, M., Choudhary, R. C., & Kumar, A. (2016, December). Secure medical image steganography with RSA cryptography using decision tree. In 2016 2nd international conference on contemporary computing and informatics (IC3I) (pp. 291-295). IEEE.

Krizhevsky, A., & Hinton, G. (2009). Learning multiple layers of features from tiny images.

Laalaoui, Y., & Bouguila, N. (2014). Pre-run-time scheduling in real-time systems: Current researches and artificial intelligence perspectives. *Expert Systems with Applications*, *41*(5), 2196-2210.

Liu, L., Meng, L., Zheng, W., Peng, Y., & Wang, X. (2022). A novel high-capacity information hiding scheme based on improved U-Net. Security and Communication Networks, 2022, 1-12.

Miranda, J. D., & Parada, D. J. (2022). LSB steganography detection in monochromatic still images using artificial neural networks. Multimedia Tools and Applications, 1-21.

Mouline, P.; and Koetter, R. (2005). Data-hiding codes," *Proceedigns of the IEEE*, vol. 93,no. 12, pp. 2083– 2126, December.

Nashat, D., & Mamdouh, L. (2019). An efficient steganographic technique for hiding data. Journal of the Egyptian Mathematical Society, 27, 1-14.

Pavan, S., Sridhar, G., & Sridhar, V. (2005, March). Multivariate entropy detector based hybrid image registration. In Proceedings. (ICASSP'05). IEEE International Conference on Acoustics, Speech, and Signal Processing, 2005. (Vol. 2, pp. ii-873). IEEE.

Qiao, T., Zitzmann, C., Retraint, F., & Cogranne, R. (2014, October). Statistical detection of jsteg steganography using hypothesis testing theory. In 2014 IEEE International Conference on Image Processing (ICIP) (pp. 5517-5521). IEEE.

Setiadi, D. R. I. M. (2021). PSNR vs SSIM: imperceptibility quality assessment for image steganography. Multimedia Tools and Applications, 80(6), 8423-8444.

Shan, S., Wenger, E., Zhang, J., Li, H., Zheng, H., & Zhao, B. Y. (2020). Fawkes: Protecting privacy against unauthorized deep learning models. In *29th USENIX security symposium (USENIX Security 20)* (pp. 1589-1604).

Shang, Y., Jiang, S., Ye, D., & Huang, J. (2020). Enhancing the security of deep learning steganography via adversarial examples. Mathematics, 8(9), 1446.

Shou, Z., Liu, A., Li, S., & Cheng, X. (2017). Spatial Outlier Information Hiding Algorithm Based on Complex Transformation. In *Security, Privacy, and Anonymity in Computation, Communication, and Storage: 10th International Conference, SpaCCS 2017, Guangzhou, China, December 12-15, 2017, Proceedings 10* (pp. 241-255). Springer International Publishing.

Song, H. T., Tang, G. M., Kou, G., Sun, Y. F., & Jiang, M. M. (2019). Digital steganography model and embedding optimization strategy. *Multimedia Tools and Applications*, *78*, 8271-8288.

USC-SIPI Image Database. (n.d.). University of Southern California. Retrieved [9 12, 2023], from https://sipi.usc.edu/database/

Wayner, P. (2002). Disappearing Cryptography: Information Hiding, Steganography & Watermarking. Second Edition.

Yang, C. N., & Ciou, C. B. (2009). A comment on “Sharing secrets in stegoimages with authentication”. *Pattern Recognition*, *42*(7), 1615-1619.

Zhu, J., Kaplan, R., Johnson, J., & Fei-Fei, L. (2018). Hidden: Hiding data with deep networks. In *Proceedings of the European conference on computer vision (ECCV)* (pp. 657-672).

ENHANCING THE DIGITAL SKILLS OF TEACHERS IN AN ONLINE SETTING

Julie Madelen Madshaven, Frank Reichert and Haakon Sundbø
University of Agder – Department of ICT
Jon Lilletuns vei 9, 4879 Grimstad, Norway

ABSTRACT

The Department of ICT (Information and Communication Technologies) at the University of Agder (UiA) in Norway conducted a study to assess and improve the digital competence of teachers. An initial survey was conducted to determine the current level of teachers' digital skills. Based on the findings, an online course was developed and implemented. The primary aim of this research was to evaluate the effectiveness of the online teaching methods and determine if such approaches can support and enhance learning. The results provide insights into the potential of online interventions in teacher education, especially in digital competence.

KEYWORDS

Online Education, Teacher Professional Development, Blended Learning, Scaffolding, Digital Skills

1. INTRODUCTION

It is more important than ever in today's digital age that teachers have a good understanding of digital tools, how to use them effectively in the classroom and how to teach their students how to use digital tools in a meaningful way. the University of Agder (UiA) in Norway launched a state-funded project aimed at enhancing the digital competence of primary and secondary school teachers. The goal of the digital tools course is to raise teachers' digital competence and knowledge to be able to confidently use digital tools in their classrooms and to raise the digital skills of their students in turn. A survey was conducted before the course's initiation to determine the current digital competence levels of the participating teachers. The survey was carried out to identify meaningful topics that needed to be covered and to identify course participants who needed to develop their basic digital skills needed as a prerequisite to follow the courses in the next semester. Additionally, the survey results were vital when the course had to run fully digitally because of the COVID-19 pandemic. The survey discovered who needed basic competence development, and a post survey was conducted to discover whether the strategies implemented in the online course can support learning.

The next chapter presents the background of this project. Chapter three presents learning strategies implemented in the course. Chapter four presents the research methods and participants. Chapter five presents the results of the research, and the last chapter concludes with a discussion and reflections on the implementation of the online strategies.

2. BACKGROUND

Decentralized competence development (Dekomp) is a state funded program introduced by the Norwegian Directorate for Education and Training (Utdanningsdirektoratet, n.d.). The program is implemented locally for competence development for teachers in primary school and secondary school.

The Norwegian Directorate for Education and Training established the Decentralized competence development (Dekomp) program to support the professional development of primary and secondary school teachers. This state-funded initiative promotes collaboration between schools and higher education institutions.

The Institute of ICT at the University of Agder Norway offers courses in digital competence and have over the years collaborated with several municipalities and taught over 1000 teachers in the region on the use of digital tools in the classroom. The development of custom-made lessons is always done with involvement from principals, the school leaderships, and specific teachers with special interest in the field. The lessons are typically held face-to-face at the respective schools taking part in the program, but due to the pandemic in 2021, the lessons had to shift to fully online. During the years prior to the pandemic, we found that one of the key factors of success when teaching beginners in digital tools is the chance to experiment with and test out the tools under guidance.

3. ONLINE LEARNING STRATEGIES

Teaching a diverse group with varying expertise levels presents challenges. In the digital tools course, participants' proficiency ranged from novice to advanced. To address this disparity, it was essential to identify the novices and ensure they undertook a foundational course. This approach aimed to equip them with the necessary skills before delving into more advanced digital tool applications. Various strategies were employed in the foundational course to support the teachers during online sessions.

3.1 Constructivist Approach and Learner-Centricity

Constructivism, as defined by Phillips (1995), is a pedagogical theory that underscores the learner's proactive engagement in knowledge acquisition, building upon their pre-existing understanding. Instead of merely absorbing information passively, learners actively shape their knowledge through real-world interactions, exploration, experimentation with new tools and ideas, collaboration, and self-reflection. Digital learning platforms align well with the constructivist approach, offering learners the autonomy to dictate their learning pace and access necessary resources, catering to their unique learning requirements.

Learner-centeredness in online environments emphasizes individual learners' unique attributes and needs. Online platforms, aligned with constructivist principles, offer tailored, self-directed, and authentic experiences (Archambault et al., 2022).

3.2 Scaffolding

Scaffolding (Wood, et. al., 1976) is a teaching strategy derived from Vygotsky's Zone of Proximal Development (Vygotsky, 1978) that involves providing guidance and support from teachers or other knowledgeable persons to aid students when learning a new concept or skill. Scaffolding strategies include offering support in the initial stages of learning, modeling how to solve a task, breaking down the learning into smaller tasks, and providing the learners with hints and clues on how to solve a task. Eventually, the students' progress towards greater independence. Face-to-face teaching and online teaching are two quite different experiences. In face-to-face teaching, instructors can oversee what students are doing, how they are progressing and reacting to the teaching. This allows instructors to provide immediate feedback and offer support to students who may be struggling with a task or concept. Naturally, online teaching does not provide the same level of visibility into what the students are doing. This can make it difficult to identify students that are struggling.

3.3 Computational Thinking

In Norway, computational thinking (CT) has been integrated into the primary and secondary school curricula (Bocconi et al., 2018). CT encompasses a suite of problem-solving skills where learners decompose complex issues into smaller, more tractable tasks. This involves analyzing and structuring information to devise solutions (Tedre et al., 2016). CT emphasizes creativity and experimentation in the problem-solving process. Encountering and rectifying errors is not only anticipated but is also viewed as a valuable learning opportunity.

3.4 Multimedia Learning Content

Online learning has the possibility of offering varied content and accommodating different learning styles for the learners. Large scale research on ideal video length for educational videos from researchers at MIT (Guo, et al., 2014) concluded that videos should be shorter than six minutes for an ideal learning experience. It is considered harder to keep learners engaged when videos are long. Short videos also offer easy rewatching, skimming through the video, and stopping when needed. Providing the necessary support in online learning can also be a challenge, especially when the students have minimal knowledge of the topic and are new to online learning. With the support of synchronous video lessons, course leaders can support and scaffold student learning (van de Pol, et al., 2010). Scaffolding can also be applied in asynchronous online learning by providing learning videos, clarifications, and modeling (Hung and Nguyen., 2022).

4. RESEARCH METHODS

This study aims to assess whether transitioning a hands-on technology course from in-person to online instruction enhances the skills of teachers who classify themselves as beginners. It examines the effectiveness of online education for novices and explores potential scaffolding support measures. Two surveys were conducted: the first to pinpoint beginners within a varied skill group, and the second to evaluate the impact of the online introductory course on perceived competence. Employing an action research approach, the study seeks to determine the influence of the online course's measures on learning outcomes.

4.1 Pre and Post Survey

To determine the level of competence in digital tools among teachers, a major survey was carried out before the start of the semester. The survey was designed to identify which topics needed to be concentrated on and to identify course participants who lacked basic knowledge needed as a prerequisite to follow the courses that would run in the fall semester.

The questions in the survey were developed in collaboration with resource teachers, who are teachers with particular interest and knowledge in the field. The survey consisted of 52 questions linked to 6 thematic areas within knowledge of digital tools:

- Cloud storage and sharing files
- Co-authoring
- E-mail and calendar
- Digital meetings
- General computer skills and computer settings
- Student guidance and school routines for digital privacy

The questions contained statements of the type "I can..." with the answer options being "yes/no." A calculation of points was made at the end of the survey, and participants were informed whether they could benefit from participating in the beginning course. If the participants scored over 17 points, they were asked to participate.

Following the introductory course, teachers completed the survey once more to assess the course's impact. The subsequent survey, after the online lessons, included two additional questions about their confidence in their knowledge before and after the lessons. Out of the responses to the post-course survey, 121 were fully completed, 36 were partially filled out, and 36 respondents merely accessed the link without providing answers. It is worth noting that the survey results might be influenced by self-report bias.

4.2 Participants

Potentially 650 primary and secondary school teachers in the region participated in the course. This number is based on the number of teachers employed in the region. The survey was completed during an initial informative synchronous video conference to ensure many responses. The response rate to the pre beginning course survey is 93%, which was calculated based on how many participants clicked on the link of the survey.

434 participants completed the survey, 26 respondents completed it partially, and 5 people clicked the link without answering questions. The results showed that 128 of the 434 respondents were deemed beginners. These teachers were invited to participate in the beginning course to help them develop a basic knowledge level before joint lessons in the autumn.

4.3 Dekomp – Digital Tools Course

One of the premises of Dekomp is that the participating teachers receive competence and skill building lessons in their region, which typically means that the course leaders travel to their place of work to hold lessons after school hours. The project offers a three-semester course that is typically delivered through face-to-face lessons in the participants' schools. However, the COVID-19 pandemic forced the project to be taught online. With about 650 teachers having signed up for the course on digital tools, it became apparent that it would not be sufficient with synchronous virtual lessons to cover the topic in a satisfactory way. It was decided early on that the course would employ blended learning.

The blended learning course consisted of three components:

- **Virtual meetings**: The course leaders held a virtual meeting at the beginning of each lecture to introduce the material and answer questions. This ensured all participants understood the content and could ask questions directly to the course leaders. Additionally, computational thinking was introduced as a problem-solving method to help participants understand that learning something new can be challenging and requires stamina to keep going when faced with problems. The participants were also encouraged to sit together in a classroom with other participants in the course. That way they could discuss between them, learn from each other, and help each other.
- **Online course material**: A website was created with learning videos and tasks on the topics covered in the course. Each video dealt with a specific tool, with an accompanying task. This allowed participants to learn at their own pace, get hands-on experience with the digital tools and choose the activities that were most relevant to them. The topics covered were discovered through the survey at the beginning of the semester. Furthermore, the content from the course is readily available after lessons, giving the learners access after the course is completed.
- **Support**: The course leaders were available by phone and chat to answer questions and provide support. This allowed participants to get help when they needed it, without having to wait for the next online lesson or give up. Additionally, more knowledgeable teachers in each school were recruited to offer support physically.

Figure 1. Online learning content from Dekomp digital tools course

5. RESULTS

This research indicates that utilizing constructivist methods, scaffolding, and diverse multimedia content within a blended learning framework can enhance digital skill acquisition among novices. Establishing an online learning environment, complete with instructional videos, tasks, and immediate online support from peers and instructors, appeared to elevate overall skill proficiency. Notably, despite the constant availability of course leaders via phone and chat throughout the lessons, there were minimal inquiries from participants. This suggests that the pre-prepared resources were effective, and participants collaborated and assisted one another efficiently.

5.1 Pre Beginning Course Survey Results

The results from the survey conducted before the course started revealed that 128 participants were deemed beginners in digital skills. The survey revealed that the participants had good control of how to use e-mail services and digital calendars. The participants also felt competent enough to teach their students how to use e-mail and digital calendars.

The areas where the teachers were the least experienced were in using cloud storage, co-authoring, general computer skills and student guidance. The participants had some knowledge within each area but lacked the basic knowledge of how to use them to their benefit. Additionally, the results from the pre-survey revealed that although they felt competent in an area, they felt less competent in teaching their students in these areas. The table below highlights some of the more significant skills the teachers struggled with from the post-survey.

Table 1. Results from the cloud storage thematic area pre beginning course

Statements	"Yes"	"No"
"I can synchronize my documents so that I can gain access to them locally on my computer"	54%	46%
"I know how to search for a file in a cloud storage service"	61%	39%
"I can share a file or folder by link"	69%	31%
"I can ensure that a file does not go astray by removing access to a document I've shared with others"	36%	64%
"I can see who I have shared a file with"	55%	45%

5.2 Post Beginning Course Survey Results

The survey conducted right after the beginning of the course had 121 responses. The respondents reported that they had increased their skill in all the areas covered in the course. The areas with most significant skill development was cloud storage, co-authoring, general computer skills and student guidance. The table below shows the same questions from the pre-survey answered after the course.

Table 2. Results from the cloud storage thematic area post beginning course

Statements	"Yes"	"No"
"I can synchronize my documents so that I can gain access to them locally on my computer"	71%	29%
"I know how to search for a file in a cloud storage service"	74%	26%
"I can share a file or folder by link"	76%	24%
"I can ensure that a file does not go astray by removing access to a document I've shared with others"	51%	49%
"I can see who I have shared a file with"	70%	30%

In addition to answering the same questions found in the pre-beginning course survey, two additional questions were added to discover whether the participants themselves feel that they have increased their digital skills. The participants reported a general feeling of increased skill after participating in the beginning course.

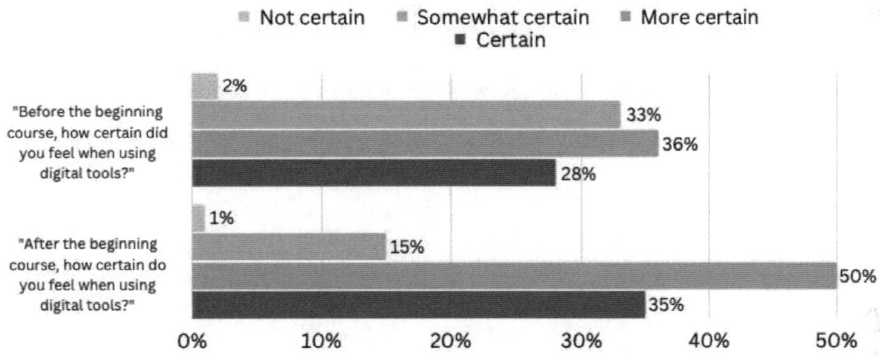

Figure 2. Post survey results on how certain participants felt in their digital skills pre and post beginning course

6. DISCUSSION AND CONCLUSION

This research explored the implementation of online pedagogical strategies in an introductory digital tools course for teachers with limited proficiency. The course incorporated elements such as concise instructional videos, modeling, organized tasks, and collaborative support from peers and instructors.

These teaching methods drew from the foundational principles of scaffolding and constructivism. The course's strategic integration proved beneficial for participants. Based on pre- and post-course surveys, participants noted improvements in various digital skill domains. While the survey data is self-reported and may have inherent biases, participants expressed enhanced skills and, in turn, heightened self-confidence.

For those new to technology, navigating digital tools in a classroom, especially in front of tech-savvy students, can be daunting. This online course aimed to bolster their foundational digital skills, fostering confidence in classroom tool usage, and encouraging exploration of other digital resources. Even though the course emphasized specific tools, the acquired knowledge is adaptable to diverse digital platforms, suggesting participants are better equipped for current and emerging tools.

While the pandemic has ended and the course has transitioned from its online format, the associated website continues to evolve, adding new instructional content, videos, and tasks. This site has become integral to Dekomp, enhancing the educational journey by catering to varied learning styles, ensuring continuous access, and offering immediate support through videos and hands-on tasks.

REFERENCES

Archambault, L., Leary, H., Rice, K. (2022). Pillars of online pedagogy: A framework for teaching in online learning environments. Educational Psychologist, 57(3), 178-191. DOI: 10.1080/00461520.2022.2051513

Bocconi, S., Chioccariello, A., Earp, J. (2018). The Nordic Approach to Introducing Computational Thinking and Programming in Compulsory Education. Report prepared for the Nordic@BETT2018 Steering Group.

Guo, P. et al. (2014). How video production affects student engagement: An empirical study of MOOC videos. Proceedings of the first ACM conference on Learning @ scale conference. Atlanta Georgia, USA, pp. 41-50.

Hung, B.P., Nguyen, L.T. (2022). Scaffolding Language Learning in the Online Classroom. New Trends and Applications in Internet of Things (IoT) and Big Data Analytics, Vol. 221, pp. 109-122.

Phillips, D.C. (1995). The Good, the Bad, and the Ugly: The Many Faces of Constructivism. Educational Researcher, 24(7), pp. 5–12.

Tedre, M., Denning, P.J. (2016). The Long Quest for Computational Thinking. Proceedings of the 16th Koli Calling Conference on Computing Education Research. Koli, Finland: pp. 120-129.

Utdanningsdirektoratet. (n.d.). Tilskuddsordning for lokal kompetanseutvikling i barnehage og grunnopplæring. Udir. Retrieved from https://www.udir.no/kvalitet-og-kompetanse/lokal-kompetanseutvikling/tilskuddsordningene-for-lokal-kompetanseutvikling-i-barnehage-og-grunnopplaring/.

Van de Pol, J. et al. (2010). Scaffolding in Teacher–Student Interaction: A Decade of Research. Educ Psychol Rev, 22, pp. 271-296.

Vygotsky, L.S. (1978). Mind in society: The development of higher psychological processes. Harvard University Press: Cambridge Massachusetts.

Wood, D., Bruner, J.S., Ross, G. (1976). The Role of Tutoring in Problem Solving. Journal of Child Psychology and Psychiatry, 17(2), pp. 89-100.

THE EFFECTIVENESS OF ADVERTISING IN ONLINE GAMES

Jorge Esparteiro Garcia[1,2], José Palha[1] and Ricardo Queirós[3]
[1]ADiT-Lab, Instituto Politécnico de Viana do Castelo,
Rua Escola Comercial e Industrial Nun'Álvares, 4900-347, Viana do Castelo, Portugal
[2]INESC TEC, Campus da FEUP, R. Dr. Roberto Frias, 4200-465 Porto, Portugal
[3]School of Media Arts and Design, Polytechnic Institute of Porto, Portugal

ABSTRACT

The world of video games has more and more users, and today it is considered as an alternative to the existing reality. Online games like Second Life have independent economies with independent businesses and there is a growing interest to create rich experiences with high levels of presence, to create an alternative to reality, where you can work, be with friends, socialize and much more. With this new era that could be true virtual reality, and with advertising agents always trying to innovate the way they convey their advertising messages, it will be necessary to keep up with the medium to also reach new consumers. This integration of advertising in video games is not recent, however, and the practice itself has become increasingly popular in sports games, car racing games and many others that already have the presence of brands and advertising messages. This study intends to work as an introductory study to the theme, proposing some questions regarding the influence of the way advertising is inserted in the game. In this sense, an initial descriptive investigation of acquired data was developed, using a game created on the Unity platform, specifically for this research. The game was developed in 3 different versions, in which each one integrates advertising messages in a distinct way. Subsequently, a questionnaire survey was conducted to assess the respondents' opinion about the game, the effectiveness of advertising and the players' opinion regarding the practice of inserting advertising in video games. The influence and effectiveness of in-game advertising was also analyzed in order and to acquire their opinion regarding the practice used. The descriptive research indicates preliminarily that the way advertising is integrated may influence the effectiveness of in-game advertising. It was also possible to perceive that although the opinion is generally neutral, the respondents that have as a habitual leisure activity the consumption of videogames have a higher retention to in-game advertising when compared with non-gamers. At the end of this study, proposals and recommendations for future research involving this theme are presented.

KEYWORDS

Videogames, Efficiency, Ad Types, In-Game Advertising, Advertising Prevalence, Marketing

1. INTRODUCTION

The digital world exists in a pattern of constant evolution, from the invention of the computer to the theorization and initiation of the development of the meta universe, science fiction ideas become reality and inspire business models (Bell et al., 2013). Several business models have gone completely online, such as the evolution of online casinos (Salmon, 2021; Garcia, 2022). Online casinos were previously restricted to their local geographic location, now they are only geographically limited depending on their legal limitations.

As well as reinventing businesses, totally digital economies have been created through blockchain technology, creating non-fungible tokens, applicable to pieces of art and other services (Chohan, 2021).

Likewise, and appreciating the large number of users in the digital world, companies have focused heavily on creating and maintaining their online presence. Companies like Meta, Google, Amazon, and many other brokers connect companies and customers on their platforms. With technological innovation, advertising campaigns follow this innovation and take advantage of new means of interaction in the digital environment to reach an audience that is increasingly involved and dependent on technology, with the mobile phone and its continued permanence and online presence being important in various social aspects (Fryman & Romine, 2021), sometimes with adverse consequences in these same social aspects, such as anxiety being one of the main negative indicators of its use (Faelens et al., 2021; Fryman & Romine, 2021; Hussain & Wegmann, 2021; Kowert & Daniel, 2021; Sunday et al., 2021). One of the means of communication and technological development with the greatest investment is the games industry, creating alternative worlds, diverse narratives from recreation, reinvention of the past and present and exploring alternatives of the future, creating alternative universes of fantasy and situations that would be inapplicable to our reality. This ability to imagine and create a new world in the creator's vision ends up sparking interest in creating a universe with its fundamental basis being the replacement of the real world, where the normal physical constraints of everyday life do not exist, this concept is called the metaverse, the meta-universe. While far from this concept, the development of games and their experiences are increasingly complex, adding to development time, where in the past games were created in 1-2 years, more complex games today are developed over 5 years. However, these games are created with new forms of interaction, experiences, and complex systems to entertain their players. As the gaming industry continues to establish itself as a legitimate form of entertainment in the eyes of the general public, companies, advertising agencies, and other stakeholders try to create campaigns and experiences dedicated to the growing community of gaming consumers, from simple Google Ads integrations in a mobile game to large advertising campaigns involving award-winning games, and its growth in investment has kept pace with the evolution of the community and the industry (In-Game Advertising Market to Grow by USD 3.54 Billion during 2021-2025 | Technavio, 2021), and therefore research into integrations could create new forms of income for game development companies.

The aim of this project is to investigate new ways of monetizing and integrating advertising into games. This form of entertainment is differentiated by the possibility of interaction and greater involvement on the part of the player. Current studies generally apply static advertising, such as billboards and billboards, and do not apply the differentiation of this entertainment model. This project also aims to assess the opinion of players when faced with different types of game advertising integration. Consumers are important to companies that develop games, so assessing their perception depending on the integration applied is fundamental. Thus, an evaluation of the effectiveness of different implementations of advertising in games, as well as a survey of opinions on this implementation, could shed light on the possibilities of monetization to increase the longevity of games if a developer wants to evaluate their options for a source of income. In a nutshell, the motivation behind this study is a proposal for different advertising integrations in future studies that delve deeper into this subject, as well as presenting alternative forms of advertising that game developers can apply to their games. Adding to the literature already produced and to future games. Adding to the positive factors that research can help with, there is a personal interest in the video games industry as a consumer and building a bridge between personal and professional interest with marketing and advertising.

This project aims to evaluate the effectiveness of the different possibilities for integrating advertising into games and the opinion of their integration, assessing whether the integration itself would be advantageous, and if so, which type of integration would be best, evaluating the memorization of the brand presented and the opinion of the players on its integration which could influence the decision to implement this type of system.

The following research questions are therefore posed:

- Do players memorize advertising better when interactivity with advertising increases?
- Do players' opinions of the game increase in games where there is more interaction with advertising?
- Does the players' opinion of the integration increase where there is more interaction?

2. METHODOLOGY

This research works as an experimental study and aims to analyze the effectiveness of advertising in games within their virtual world depending on the different possibilities for integrating advertising into games, with the main research factor being the level of interactivity, as well as the players' opinion of the interaction, with consumer opinion being a decisive factor in the implementation of an advertising integration system.

2.1 Game Design

To carry out the study, a game called "Last Try" was created using Unity, a game engine for developing games and interactive virtual experiences. Past studies (de Pelsmacker et al., 2019; Kim & Ko, 2019; M. Lee & Faber, 2007, Heckler & Childers, 1992, Moorman et al., 2007, Amaral et al., 2013) have shown the congruence of advertising in the game, both visually and thematically, and the type of game that is presented. In terms of aesthetics, the choice of game design was based on the low-poly aesthetic, popular after the Minecraft boom. This design is characterized by having few polygons in its design, thus enabling the game to be light in performance, as well as having a pleasant and simple look. As for the choice of game type, a tool called Steam Spy was used, which reports various data on the Steam platform that houses a large part of the computer games market. Steam Spy has a section reporting how many games each type of game has and the average number of players each type of game has. According to the information reported, it was decided to create a game with action, adventure and the game is a single player experience, being one of the most sought after and because a complicated game could influence the effectiveness of advertising, with some RPG elements, in its totality the game represents about 13857 games, but this number is merely representative. Just as this game fits several tags, the games included in the list also have several tags, so a sci-fi game can also be a shooter, contributing to the value of both tags. The low-poly game features a main character, a samurai whom the player controls armed with a sword. The main character finds himself in a cave where, along the way, he encounters enemies that he has to defeat. When these enemies are defeated, they leave behind resources, such as life potions that the player keeps in the inventory system and can use whenever they want. The fighting system is based on melee combat, with each enemy and the player having different life statistics, and depending on the weapon used, the damage caused and the range of the weapon. The player can also lock their camera on an enemy to make it easier to fight, can block attacks and can roll to dodge attacks, the attack can be a simple attack or a kick that stuns and knocks the enemy back for a few seconds. Players could also run during the game to escape fights. To limit the abuse of movement, a stamina system has been inserted that decreases when the player attacks, runs, jumps, or rolls. The stamina reaching "0" prevents the player from making combination attacks, which limits the speed of their attacks and if the player is running, they will have to wait a while if their stamina reaches "0" before they can run again. As for the inventory system, it could be used at any time, and had a quick inventory system where players could change weapons and use potions by pressing predefined keys. The player also had the option of fighting with or without the weapon, without the weapon the game only becomes more complicated, as fists have less range and cause less damage than the sword. The player can also pause their game at any time. The aim of the game is to defeat the main opponent at the end of the map. Once defeated, the game is paused with a window informing you that the game is over, and that the enquiry has been completed. While developing the project, it is necessary not only to use the right data analysis tools, but also the research design and data collection instruments. Based on the research problem, the methodology chosen to propose the research questions for the development of this study is the descriptive analysis of quantitative data, descriptive analysis is a direct observation of the issue addressed in a natural way with the absence of experimental manipulation that can be used as a basis for developing investigations with an experimental functional analysis (Sloman, 2011). Due to the complexity of games in a 3D world, every virtual world is a different experience, and when doing the literature review, it became clear that there are numerous variabilities that could alter the results of the research, a common formatting of the experiences during the tests is necessary. One of the most tested types of games are sports games, because they have a high number of players, because it is a demarcated market with product placement and because their format is similar in all games. With this research we intend to ask questions about the interactivity of advertising in games and the opinion on the different integrations. Descriptive statistics do not make it possible to reach a conclusion from hypotheses that we might make, but they do serve to summarize and demonstrate data in order, for example, to check for trends or patterns in the data acquired. Data collection, as mentioned above, is one of the most important processes in the research process. The use of questionnaires is predominant in quantitative studies. The types of questionnaires are divided by the way they are applied, for the case of this research, a web questionnaire was chosen, to facilitate its sharing and follow-up with the game that was also presented on the web, other advantages, in addition to being easy to share, it has a relatively low cost, obtains a faster response rate, a greater ease of processing data, and generally has a better controlled environment, with the possibility of the questions being organized in a random way, pop-ups with instructions on relevant questions, characteristics that cannot be replicated in other questionnaire formats. The game was mostly given to university students, during lectures the game was given online, and the questionnaire was also presented online. 79 responses were obtained, with the majority of respondents aged 18-19. There was a greater concentration of females in the questionnaire, corresponding to 65.8% of respondents. In terms of education, most of the respondents (77%) have completed secondary school or equivalent, and as the majority are university students, their professional status is Student (81%).

3. DEVELOPMENT

The game was then transformed into 3 different versions with different advertising integrations, with different brands, and with varying levels of interaction. To strike a balance, there was a shift in the level of incidence of advertising as the level of interaction increased, the level of incidence of advertising decreased. Regarding the visual and topical congruence of the advertising in relation to the game, there is a very low level of congruence, the advertising visually does not respect the rules of low poly. And in terms of topic, brands were chosen that are not related to the game, except for Super Mario's enemies, who are integral characters in another game, which could add to the congruence; the brands chosen were so because of their popularity and recognition in areas of similar activity. When enemies die, they drop life potions, using the product placement technique Last Try V1 (intermediate interaction level) with the higher level of interaction that this medium provides, the life potions were replaced by Monster energy drinks and Pepsi soft drinks, players could view these drinks once they defeated certain monsters, pick up these drinks, view them in the inventory and in the quick inventory system (Figure 1).

Figure 1. Screenshot of Last Try V1 with Monster energy drinks

The fight with the enemies is the centerpiece of the game and, for a large part of the game session, the player will be planning, attacking the enemies, and defending against their attack, so in Last Try V2 (high interaction level) certain enemies have been swapped for Super Mario characters, who attack without a weapon (Figure 2).

Figure 2. Screenshot of Last Try V2 with Super Mario characters

Most of the studies in this area are carried out in a context where advertising is displayed statically on a 2D platform with little interaction between the player and the advertising, not taking advantage of the interaction that could exist in this type of integration. However, to assess the possible differences between this type of integration and other types of integration, it is necessary to integrate this type of advertising. McDonald's, Tesla, Apple, Spotify and Coca Cola advertisements were included in various parts of the map, Last Try V3 (Figure 3).

The players were asked to play a game to test it, without mentioning the purpose of the study. Once they accepted, they were given a link to one of the versions of the game where they could play directly in their browser. This page included the version of the game being played, the game and the link to the form if, for technical reasons, the game didn't automatically open the questionnaire.

Once ready to play, the players were instructed to play with the mission of defeating the main enemy, the instructions on how to play and their keys were present in the game while they played, once the final opponent was defeated, the questionnaire opened and at any time they could fill in the questionnaire, when they felt they had fully experienced the game, or continue playing if they didn't feel they had fully experienced the game.

The questionnaire itself obtained data categorized into 5 groups, the first referring to demographic data, the second referring to data regarding personal habit of consuming video games, the third group analyzing players' opinions about the game, the fourth group where players would have to choose the brands they viewed during the game session, and finally, the fifth group referring to questions about the implementation of advertising in games in general.

Figure 3. Screenshot of Last Try V2 with an ad of McDonald’s

The brands were chosen for their popularity and recognition. However, it is described in previous studies (Mau et al., 2008) that familiarity with the brand ends up influencing opinion of the brand and negatively influences opinion of the game (Mau et al., 2008).

4. MAIN RESULTS

One of the main factors theorized is the influence of the type of integration that varies from version to version and how this might influence the effectiveness of the advertising communication present in the game. But the differences in opinion of integrations and opinion of the game itself are also evaluated. The percentage of brands recalled correctly out of the total number of brands presented, depending on the version, is shown in Figure 4.

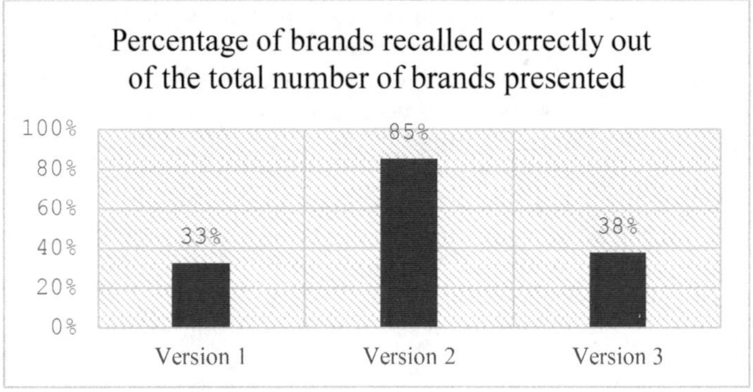

Figure 4. Average percentage of brands recalled correctly out of the total number of brands depending on the game version

The data shows that the version with the greatest interactivity (Version 2) with the advertising message has a higher result, this is due to 2 reasons: as it refers to a group of enemies to a brand - Super Mario, this advertising had less incidence in the game, but it was also the one where people interacted for the longest time, while in Version 3 the banners have no interaction and in Version 1 the interaction with it is just clicking a key to get the potion, but in Version 2 you have to fight the adversary that is the advertising.

Therefore, in this version it will also be important to check the number of incorrectly recalled brands - the brands that are not shown in the version, but, contrary to what was theorized, although very close, Version 1 is inferior to Version 3 which has less interactivity with the advertising message (Figure 5). This could be due to a number of factors, the biggest of which is the intrusive nature of the advertising in Version 3, which often takes up a large part of the player's view. However, on the other hand, brands may be incorrectly remembered, and it may be important for the advertiser to also consider this factor, as it could be a hindrance to their message.

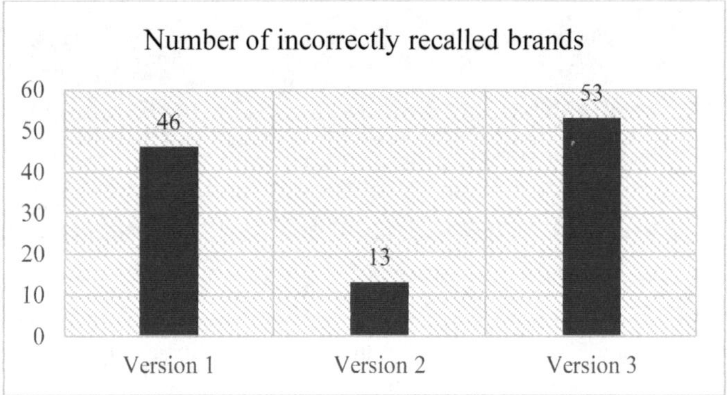

Figure 5. Number of incorrectly recalled brands depending on the game version

In the last group of the questionnaire, players had to provide their opinion on the implementation of advertising in games, in general, the opinion is mixed, deviating a little to the negative side, in general, the score is from 1 to 5 (Totally Disagree(1)-Disagree(2)-Neither Agree, Disagree(3)-Agree(4), Completely Agree(5)), the results are presented in the following tables (Table 1 and 2).

Almost all the positive questions between the 3 versions, the opinion of those who played Version 2 was higher, followed by Version 3 and lastly Version 1. Version 2 was also the only one to have a neutral opinion on average (Neither Agree nor Disagree).

Table 1. Questions related to the integration of advertising in games, with a positive content

Number	Question
Q1	I have a favorable opinion of advertising during the games
Q2	I am in favor of brands being communicated during matches
Q3	Brand communication is more effective in matches than in other media (social networks, TV, radio, press)
Q4	I choose a particular brand based on the communication made in a game
Q5	Brand communication in games is enjoyable
Q6	I consider advertising in games to be an effective way of communicating brands
Q7	Brand communication in games is fun
Q8	Brand communication in games is a well-integrated experience while playing the game
Q9	Brand communication in games is reliable
Q10	Brand communication in games is credible
Q11	In general, I like the advertising communication of brands in the various communication channels

Table 2. Average opinion of players on the implementation of advertising in positive games.

	Q1	Q2	Q3	Q4	Q5	Q6	Q7	Q8	Q9	Q10	Q11
V1	2,65	2,73	2,58	2,27	2,62	2,85	2,62	2,58	2,73	2,54	2,62
V2	3	3,33	3	2,96	3,04	3,26	3,11	2,96	3,11	3,15	2,96
V3	3,23	2,92	3,08	2,38	2,77	2,88	2,65	2,69	2,88	2,96	2,81
AVG	2,96	3	2,89	2,54	2,81	3	2,8	2,75	2,91	2,89	2,8

5. CONCLUSION

This research could indicate a difference between the types of interactivities and the effectiveness of the advertising message, in a practice that has seen a growth in use, such as the opinion of players that it is important for integration to be used. However, the difference between the opinion on the integration of advertising in games is small, so it is possible that the integration of the game will not affect the opinion of advertising integrations in games. Therefore, we propose the questions mentioned at the beginning of the study for future research to develop further knowledge in this area, considering the proposed factors.

Other predominant issues will be the effect of the platform itself, whether it is where the game is presented, for example, there may be a difference between a mobile game or a computer game, and also the platforms used by the players, a mobile player may or may not have a more favorable opinion of advertising in a game and/or may remember it better on the platform they use most. Lastly, we briefly looked at how respondents who play games in their free time may be influenced differently. In this study, they had worse results in terms of the effectiveness of advertising, although this difference is minimal, but their opinion is also more positive compared to the opinion of non-players, but neutral in general, which may indicate that previous experiences may have influenced this opinion, and that future experiences may be all the more important for the opinion of this practice, and advertising agents and game developers will have to take into account how advertising is integrated into their game. Another question proposed is how the types of games that the players surveyed usually play might affect their acceptance of this practice: games where there might be more advertising, such as sports games, might be more acceptable to their players, and if they are congruent, they also increase the realism of the game. Due to the scale of this topic, there are several limitations to the study. The first is obtaining sufficient data to be able to effectively investigate this topic, as there are several factors that can influence the effectiveness of advertising. In the same way, this study is exploratory in its descriptive analysis of the data collected, so it will not be possible to draw any definitive conclusions on this subject, which is still being debated, even about product placement in other media; during the literature review, the debate on its effectiveness and consequences, whether positive or negative, was visible.

Another limitation is the complexity of the subject, there are several variables that could influence the game, the advertising, and the players, such as exploring other possible types of advertising integration, such as auditory, which may or may not help visual advertising, requiring a larger sample. Other factors that are pertinent, but which were not carried out due to the complexity of the project, are the analysis of the type of game, other types of games may be more acceptable, as well as the platforms on which they are found, the players who play, each community around a game has different expectations of their game. This study serves as a basis for future studies, and may be very relevant to this, the suggestions proposed here, which are: to integrate advertising of different levels of interaction in future research, this may increase the cost of research relevant to the topic, but we think it is an important factor that can influence the outcome of research, and these increasingly have to have the level of interaction in their analysis, since games today apply advertising messages in a more involved way.

Future analyses will have to realistically simulate these integrations, and not just apply a static 2D logo in which you can't interact with the advertising message beyond a simple mention of a brand. Another perspective for future projects is the use of other factors, such as the variability of opinion and effectiveness of the advertising message and its integration into other platforms and other types of games, and how they differ from each other. It is important to know which and where is the best implementation, to mitigate the risks for all the players involved. Another desire of this project is to effectively serve as a basis for future projects and perhaps raise the questions initially proposed, such as deepening the investigation into the different existing advertising implementations, and perhaps also studying their best form of monetization, if any.

REFERENCES

Amaral, G., Bushee, J., Cordani, U. G., KAWASHITA, K., Reynolds, J. H., ALMEIDA, F. F. M. D. E., de Almeida, F. F. M., Hasui, Y., de Brito Neves, B. B., Fuck, R. A., Oldenzaal, Z., Guida, A., Tchalenko, J. S., Peacock, D. C. P., Sanderson, D. J., Rotevatn, A., Nixon, C. W., Rotevatn, A., Sanderson, D. J., … Junho, M. do C. B. (2013). CAN EVERY BRAND WIN WITH IN-GAME ADVERTISING? THE ROLE OF BRAND FAMILIARITY Gunnar. Journal of Petrology, 369(1), 1689–1699. https://doi.org/10.1017/CBO9781107415324.004

Chohan, U. W. (2021). Non-Fungible Tokens: Blockchains, Scarcity, and Value.

de Pelsmacker, P., Dens, N., & Verberckmoes, S. (2019). HOW AD CONGRUITY AND INTERACTIVITY AFFECT FANTASY GAME PLAYERS' ATTITUDE TOWARD IN-GAME ADVERTISING. In Journal of Electronic Commerce Research (Vol. 20).

Faelens, L., Hoorelbeke, K., Cambier, R., van Put, J., van de Putte, E., de Raedt, R., & Koster, E. H. W. (2021). The relationship between Instagram use and indicators of mental health: A systematic review. Computers in Human Behavior Reports, 4, 100121. https://doi.org/10.1016/j.chbr.2021.100121

Fryman, S., & Romine, W. (2021). Measuring smartphone dependency and exploration of consequences and comorbidities. Computers in Human Behavior Reports, 4, 100108. https://doi.org/10.1016/j.chbr.2021.100108

Garcia, J. E., Rodrigues, P., Simões, J., & Serra da Fonseca, M. J. (2022). Gamification Strategies for Social Media. Advances in Marketing, Customer Relationship Management, and E-Services - Implementing Automation Initiatives in Companies to Create Better-Connected Experiences, 137-159. http://dx.doi.org/10.4018/978-1-6684-5538-8.ch007

Heckler, S. E., & Childers, T. L. (1992). The Role of Expectancy and Relevancy in Memory for Verbal and Visual Information: VVhatIsIncongruency? http://jcr.oxfordjournals.org/

Hussain, Z., & Wegmann, E. (2021). Problematic social networking site use and associations with anxiety, attention deficit hyperactivity disorder, and resilience. Computers in Human Behavior Reports, 4, 100125.

Kim, D., & Ko, Y. J. (2019). The impact of virtual reality (VR) technology on sport spectators' flow experience and satisfaction. Computers in Human Behavior, 93, 346–356. https://doi.org/10.1016/j.chb.2018.12.040

Kowert, R., & Daniel, E. (2021). The one-and-a-half sided parasocial relationship: The curious case of live streaming. Computers in Human Behavior Reports, 4, 100150. https://doi.org/10.1016/j.chbr.2021.100150

Lee, M., & Faber, R. J. (2007). Effects of product placement in on-line games on brand memory: A perspective of the limited-capacity model of attention. Journal of Advertising, 36(4), 75–90.

Makuch, E. (2021, February 3). EA Earnings Report: Billions In Microtransaction Revenue, Star Wars Reaches 52 Million Sold, BioWare Comments, More - GameSpot. https://www.gamespot.com/articles/ea-earnings-report-billions-in-microtransaction-revenue-star-wars-reaches-52-million-sold-bioware-comments-more/1100-6487042/

Mau, G., Silberer, G., & Constien, C. (2008). Communicating brands playfully: Effects of in-game advertising for familiar and unfamiliar brands. International Journal of Advertising, 27(5), 827–851.

Moorman, M., Neijens, P. C., & Smit, E. G. (2007). The effects of program involvement on commercial exposure and recall in a naturalistic setting. Journal of Advertising, 36(1), 121–137. https://doi.org/10.2753/JOA0091-3367360109

Sloman, K. N. (2011). Research Trends in Descriptive Analysis. In The Behavior Analyst Today (Vol. 11, Issue 1).

Sunday, O. J., Adesope, O. O., & Maarhuis, P. L. (2021). The effects of smartphone addiction on learning: A meta-analysis. Computers in Human Behavior Reports, 4, 100114. https://doi.org/10.1016/j.chbr.2021.100114

DEVELOPMENT FRAMEWORK BASED ON OPENVSLAM FOR WEB-BASED VR TOURS USING 360VR VIDEOS

Yoshihiro Okada, Kosuke Kaneko and Wei Shi
Innovation Center for Educational Resources (ICER), Kyushu University Library, Kyushu University, Japan
Academic Research and Industrical Collaboration Management Office, Kyushu University, Japan
Research Institute for Information Technology, Kyushu University, Japan

ABSTRACT

This paper proposes new development framework based on OpenVSLAM for web-based VR tours using 360VR videos. Although the authors have already proposed the development framework for web-based VR tours as navigation contents of 360VR videos and as walkthrough contents of 360VR images, it is not easy to prepare 360VR images because the authors took over 300 360VR images at different locations for the walkthrough contents of 360VR images introduced in this paper. Therefore, in this paper, the authors propose new development framework for web-based VR tours as both navigation contents and walkthrough contents from 360VR videos. For walkthrough contents of 360VR images, 360VR videos of navigation contents can be used instead of 360VR images because required 360VR images can be extracted from 360VR videos of the same scene. In this case, only 360VR videos of a portable 360VR camera like Insta360 ONE X2 are enough. The development framework for navigation VR tours of 360VR videos need their moving path information and for walkthrough VR tours of 360VR images need their location information. The authors have created them manually so far. For generating them automatically, the authors decided to employ OpenVSLAM. This paper shows evaluation results how accurate moving paths and location information can be generated by OpenVSLAM.

KEYWORDS

VR Tours, 360VR, Development Framework, Educational Materials, OpenVSLAM

1. INTRODUCTION

This paper treats activities of ICER (Innovation Center for Educational Resources), Kyushu University, Japan. The missions of ICER are to provide educational materials using the latest ICT and to support teachers for creating such educational materials. In this paper, we treat development frameworks for web-based VR tours of 360VR images/videos as the activities of ICER. Recently, many types of VR goggles have been released as commercial products and many entertainment applications for them have been created. However, there have been few educational VR contents so far because the creation of VR contents needs much time and human resources. In the near future, our center ICER has to create many educational VR contents to enhance educational efficiency using VR technology. On the other hand, many types of scanning devices have been researched and developed so far, e.g., lidar cameras, 360VR cameras and so on. ICER has these scanning devices. Using these scanning devices, we can obtain 3D data like Point Cloud Data (PCD), 3D model data, 360VR images/videos. To use such 3D data for educational VR contents, we have already proposed the development framework for web-based VR tours that support VR goggles and also developed many web-based VR tour contents (Okada, et al, Feb. 2023 and Okada, et al, July 2023).

Although we have proposed the development framework for navigation contents of 360VR videos and for walkthrough contents of 360VR images, it is not so easy for us to prepare 360VR images. For example, in the VR tours introduce in this paper, we prepared over 300 locations' 360VR images. Therefore, in this paper, we propose new development framework for web-based VR tours as both navigation contents and walkthrough contents from 360VR videos. The development framework for navigation VR tours of 360VR videos need their moving path information and for walkthrough VR tours of 360VR images need their location information that were created manually so far. For generating them automatically, we tried to employ OpenVSLAM(Open Visual SLAM: Simultaneous Localization and Mappting). In this paper, we show evaluation results how accurate moving paths and location information can be generated by OpenVSLAM and clarify the usefulness of OpenVSLAM for our development framework.

The remaining parts of this paper are as follows: In next section 2, we describe related work. Section 3 introduces our previous work and Section 4 describes the development framework based on OpenVSLAM. In this section, we introduce OpenVSLAM and show how accurate moving paths and location information can be generated by OpenVSLAM. Finally, we conclude the paper in Section 5.

2. RELATED WORK

There are many toolkit systems for creating interactive 3D graphics applications and such educational materials. As a research system of our laboratory, we have proposed IntelligentBox (Okada and Tanaka, 1995) as one of the interactive 3D graphics software development systems, and there have been many desktop applications including educational materials (Okada and Ogata, 2017, Kosuki et al, 2012, Nomi et al, 2021, 2022) practically developed using IntelligentBox so far. Indeed, we have also proposed the web-version of IntelligentBox (Okada, 2013) and there have been its web-based 3D graphics applications. However, these web-based 3D graphics applications cannot support native VR goggles such as Meta Quest 2. We need to use other toolkit systems for educational VR contents that support VR goggles. Unity is one of the most popular game engines in the world (https://unity.com/). We have developed a couple of serious games for education purposes using Unity (Sugimura, et al, 2014). Although Unity is very powerful and sophisticated, it requires programming knowledge and skills of its operations for developers. Therefore, the use of Unity is not easy for common end-users like teachers. We have developed several web-based 3D educational materials using our development frameworks (Okada. et al, 2016, 2016, 2017, Ma. et al, 2018, Hirayama. et al, 2019, Yamamura. et al, 2020) based on Three.js, one of the popular WebGL-based 3D graphics JavaScript library systems (https://threejs.org/). Our development frameworks treated in this paper for web-based VR tours of 360VR images/videos and PCD also uses Three.js (https://threejs.org/).

For 360VR images/videos and PCD, there are several commercial services for creating interactive web VR contents using them. The service of RICOH (https://www.theta360.biz/) does support 360VR images but not 360VR videos nor PCD. As one of the remarkable points, this service provides a web-based editing function that enables even end-users to create their own interactive contents of 360VR images. Unfortunately, our frameworks do not provide such a function. The service of Matterport (https://matterport.com/) does support 360VR images and PCD but not 360VR videos. As one of the remarkable points, this service provides a powerful tool based on AI technology called Matterport capture application that automatically generates a location map from 360VR images and PCD. Unfortunately, our previous framework does not provide such a tool so that we propose the use of OpenVSLAM to generate moving paths and location information in this paper.

3. PREVIOUS WORK

As previous work, we introduce web-based VR tours of 360VR images/videos in this section.

3.1 360VR Cameras and their Dedicated Software

For developing web-based VR tours of 360VR images/videos, first of all, we have to prepare such media files. As a sensing device for 360VR images/videos, we use Insta360 Pro because it has six fish-eye lens cameras and we can obtain high quality 360VR videos/images such as up to 8K 360VR. For 360VR videos, we use a portable 360VR camera like Insta360 ONE X2 or Ricoh Theta shown in the left part of Figure 1. It is easy to take 360VR image/video by walking around wearing a helmet with 360VR camera on its top as shown in the right part of the figure. After we take fish-eye lens image/video shown in the left part of Figure 2, we can obtain equirectangular image/video shown in the right part of the figure using the dedicated software such as Insta360 STITCHER. Finally, by mapping an equirectangular image/video onto the inside surface of a sphere in a 3D space using the texture mapping technique, 360VR image/video contents become available.

Figure 1. Portable 360VR cameras, Insta360 ONE X2 and Ricoh Theta, and a helmet with 360VR camera on its top

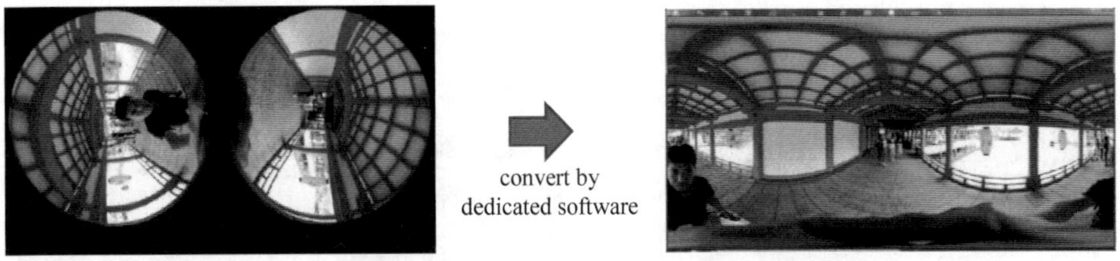

Figure 2. Converting fish-eye images into equirectangular images using a dedicated software

3.2 Development Framework for VR Tours of 360VR Images/Videos

Although in this paper, we mainly treat our development framework for VR tours using 360VR images/videos, it includes three individual systems for walkthrough contents and navigation contents using 360VR images/videos, and for walkthrough contents using PCD. The all JavaScript and HTML files of the three systems are shown in Figure 3.

walk_map.html
video_map.html
pcd_map.html
JS {
    walk_map.js,
    walk_map_controls.js,
    video_map.js,
    video_map_controls.js,
    pcd_map.js,
    pcd_map_controls.js
}
	JSM {
	    Several JS files from Three.js library
	  }
	Assets
	  Images { 360VR images, optional images }
	  Videos { 360VR videos }
	  Models { PCD files }
	  Movies { optional movie files }
	  Sounds { optional sound files }

Figure 3. All files of the three systems

Each of the three systems consists of one HTML file like *_map.html, i.e., {walk_map.html, video_map.html and pcd_map.html}, one main JavaScript file like *_map.js, i.e., {walk_map.js, video_map.js and pcd_map.js}, and one subsidiary JavaScript file like *_map_controls.js, i.e., {walk_map_controls.js, video_map_controls.js and pcd_map_controls.js}. *_map.js works with several functions derived from Three.js library. For creating new contents, you do not need to change these programs. Only the things you need to do are to prepare required media files, i.e., 360VR images/videos and PCD files those are included in Assets directory, and just to modify *_map_controls.js appropriately to read required media files into each of the three main JavaScript programs.

Actually, we created VR tours of the university library building for our open campus event to appeal that the building is one of the biggest university libraries in Japan. In the followings, we explain two development systems for navigation and walkthrough contents individually using these VR tours.

3.2.1 Walkthrough Content of VR Tour of 360VR Images

Figure 4 includes three screen shots of the walkthrough content and the map of Library Building 3F using 360VR images. The map of the left upper part of the figure is also located in the left upper part of each screen shot. As you can see, there are many orange dots on the map totally over 100. Each indicates the location where its corresponding 360VR image was taken by 360VR camera, Insta 360 Pro. By clicking on one of the orange dots, its corresponding 360VR image will be displayed as the next 360VR scene. Similarly, by clicking on one of the thin gray cylinders in a 360VR scene, the corresponding 360VR image taken at the same location will be displayed as the next 360VR scene. Furthermore, the framework supports multimedia like standard images and movies. For example, the right upper part of the figure shows one of the standard images, an explanation panel appears in the middle of the screen shot, and the right lower part of the figure shows one of the standard movies appears in the middle of the screen shot these are displayed by clicking on the corresponding red sphere object.

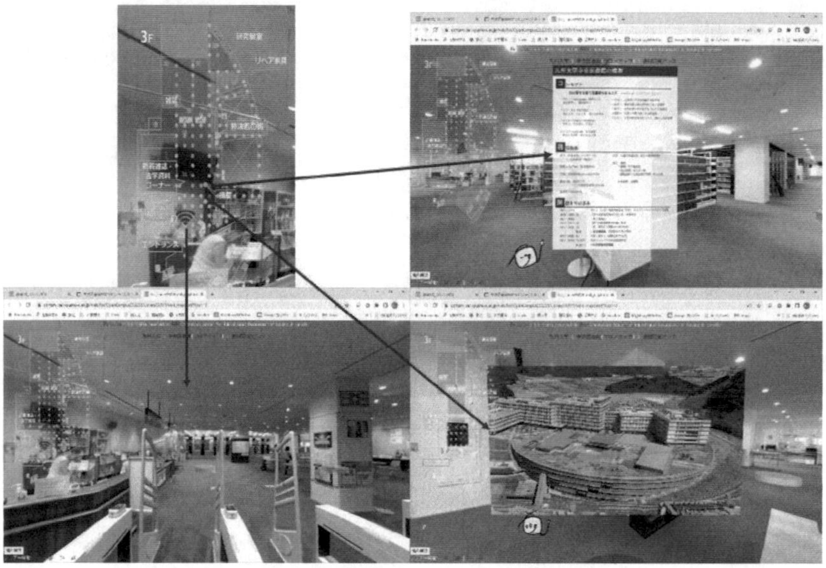

Figure 4. Three screen shots of the walkthrough content using 360VR images and the map of 3rd floor of the library building

3.2.2 Navigation Contents of 360VR Videos

Figure 5 includes three screen shots of the navigation content and the map of Library Building 3F using 360VR video. The map of the left upper part of the figure is also located in the left upper part of each screen shot. As you can see, there is a control panel in the lower middle part of each screen shot for controlling the 360VR video, i.e., play, pause, backward, forward, etc. Also, you can see a cyan color closed polyline that means the moving path actually the person wearing a helmet with 360VR camera on its top walked through when taking this 360VR video. By clicking on the polyline, the 360VR video moves to the corresponding position of the video. Similar to the system for walkthrough contents, this system also supports multimedia like standard images. For example, in the right upper and the right lower parts of the figure, there are image files displayed on their center. The 360VR scene automatically changes according to the current playing point of the 360VR video. Therefore, we call this type of contents are navigation ones.

Figure 5. Three screen shots of the navigation content using 360VR video and the map of 3rd floor of the library building

4. OPENVSLAM BASED DEVELOPMENT FRAMEWORK FOR WEB-BASED VR TOURS USING PORTABLE 360VR CAMERA

Although we have proposed the development framework for navigation contents of 360VR videos and for walkthrough contents of 360VR images, it is not so easy to prepare 360VR images if the number of images is too large. For example, in the above Library Building 3F case, we prepared 360VR images of over 100 locations by spending much time. Therefore, in this paper, we propose new development framework for web-based VR tours of both navigation contents and walkthrough contents using only 360VR videos. Both navigation and walkthrough contents need their map information. So far, we have created such map information manually by spending much time. Instead, we tried to generate such map information automatically from 360VR videos as moving paths by using OpenVSLAM. In the following, we introduce OpenVSLAM and show its evaluation results to clarify the usefulness of OpenVSLAM. After that, we show new 360VR tours of navigation mode and walkthrough mode using only 360VR videos.

4.1 OpenVSLAM and Evaluation Results

To obtain the walking path of the person wearing a helmet with 360VR camera on its top when taking a video, we have to use any tools like SLAM (Simultaneous Localization and Mapping). We decided to use OpenVSLAM(Open Visual SLAM), one of the Visual SLAM algorithms because it supports 360VR videos and its tool can be downloaded from https://github.com/OpenVSLAM-Community/openvslam.git.

Figure 6 is a screen shot of OpenVSLAM execution about the 360VR video of Library Building 3F. The right part is one frame of 360VR video of Library Building 3F and the left part shows moving paths simultaneously generated by VSLAM algorithm. There are many feature points called Landmarks and the walking path (purple polyline) with key frame locations (green triangles).

When you use the following command with the parameter '–eval-log-dir eval' to execute OpenVSLAM tool, you can obtain key frame location data as one text file 'keyframe_trajectory.txt' in 'eval' directory. The contents of the file are shown below. Each line includes time_stamp(system time), x-, y- and z-coordinate, and quaternion values.

Figure 6. Screen shot of OpenVSLAM executing for the 360VR video of Library Building 3F

Command:
./run_video_slam -v /vocab/orb_vocab.fbow -m library3F.mp4 -c equirectangular.yaml --no-sleep --map-db-out library3F.msg --eval-log-dir eval

File 'keyframe_trajectory.txt':
1692445872.59002 -0 -0 -0 0 0 0 1
1692445873.99002 0.0035851773 -0.000222045069 -0.000110629381 -0.000992051701 -0.0146692998 -0.000758150407 0.99989162
…
1692446093.95648 1.30501332 -0.102533099 6.09009006 -0.0161551557 0.99928409 0.0232693377 0.0250770024

Figure 7 shows several evaluation results of the moving path information generated by OpenVSLAM. We evaluated OpenVSLAM about VR tour of 360VR videos of the library building introduced in previous section. Our library building has four floors so that there are four 360VR videos. The figure includes four pairs of the map with moving path created manually and the moving path information generated by OpenVSLAM. Each moving path information of OpenVSLAM was generated from the all x- and z-coordinate values written in each 'keyframe_trajectory.txt' file. By comparing the left map and right map of each pair, it can be said that the moving path information generated by OpenVSLAM is very accurate. Although we have to adjust the scale and orientation, the moving path generated by OpenVSLAM can be used as the moving path of navigation VR tour and as the location information of walkthrough VR tour.

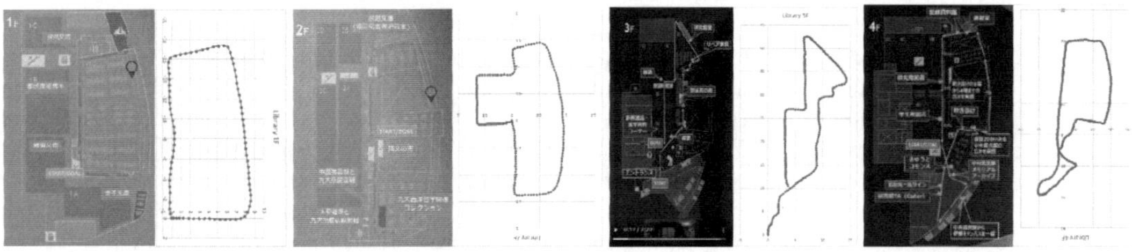

Figure 7. Four pairs of the map with moving path created manually and the moving path information generated by OpenVSLAM

4.2 New 360VR Tours of Navigation Mode and Walkthrough Mode Using 360VR Videos

We modified the development framework a little to employ the moving paths generated by OpenVSLAM instead of manually created maps. Then, we will not need to create maps manually. Figure 8 shows two screen shots of new 360VR tours of navigation mode (upper) and walkthrough mode (lower) using 360VR video of Library Building 3F. There is the moving path generated by OpenVSLAM in their left upper part. By clicking on one of the orange dots, current 360VR frame will be changed into the 360VR frame of the corresponding position of the video. In the navigation mode, you can see the control panel for controlling a video like 'play', 'pause' and so on. Instead, you can see many gray thin cylinder objects in the walkthrough mode. By clicking one of them, current 360VR frame will be changed into the 360VR frame of the corresponding position of the video.

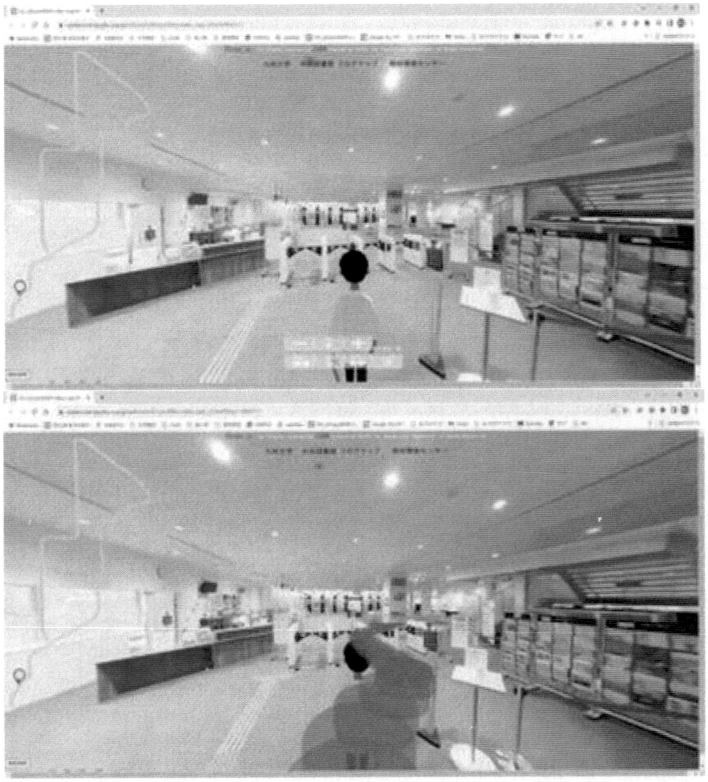

Figure 8. New 360VR tours of navigation mode (upper) and walkthrough mode (lower) using 360VR video of Library Building 3F

5. CONCLUSIONS

Recently, many types of scanning devices have been researched and developed, e.g., lidar scanners, 360VR cameras and so on. Using these scanning devices, we can obtain 3D data like Point Cloud Data (PCD), 3D model data, 360VR images/videos more easily rather than ever. To use these 3D data as educational VR contents, we have already proposed the development framework for web-based walkthrough and navigation contents using 360VR images/videos and PCD. Although we have proposed the development framework for them, it is tedious work to prepare 360VR images if the number of the images is too large. Therefore, in this paper, we proposed new development framework based on OpenVSLAM. From the evaluation results, it can be said that the moving paths generated by OpenVSLAM are very accurate and then we decided to employ them instead of manually created maps and moving paths. As future work, we will make more and more VR tour contents practically using the proposed development framework to justify the usefulness of it. Also, we will try to implement an editing function similar to the web-based editing function of the service of Ricoh theta .

ACKNOWLEDGEMENT

This research was partially supported by JSPS KAKENHI Grant Number JP22H03705 and VISION EXPO Project of Kyushu University.

REFERENCES

Hirayama, D. et al, 2019. Web-Based Interactive 3D Educational Material Development Framework and Its Authoring Functionalities, Proc. of the 22nd International Conference on Network-Based Information Systems (NBiS-2019), ISBN 978-3-030-29028-3, pp. 258-269.

Kosuki, Y. and Okada, Y. 2012. 3D visual component based development system for medical training systems supporting haptic devices and their collaborative environments. Proc. of 6th International Conference on Complex, Intelligent, and Software Intensive Systems, CISIS 2012, pp. 687-692, https://doi.org/10.1109/CISIS.2012.131

Ma, C. et al, 2018. E-Learning Material Development Framework Supporting VR/AR Based on Linked Data for IoT Security Education, Proc. of 6th International Conference on Emerging Internet, Data & Web Technologies (EIDWT 2018), ISBN: 978-3-319-75928-9, pp. 479-491.

Nomi, M. and Okada, Y. 2021. Improvement of Dental Treatment Training System Using a Haptic Device. Proc. of the 15th International Conference on Broad-Band and Wireless Computing, Communication and Applications, BWCCA 2020, pp. 143-153, Lecture Notes in Networks and Systems; Vol. 159 LNNS.

Nomi, M. and Okada, Y. 2022. Dental Treatment Training System Using Haptic Device and Its User Evaluations. Proc. of the 16th International Conference on Complex, Intelligent and Software Intensive Systems CISIS-2022, pp. 569-580, Lecture Notes in Networks and Systems; Vol. 497 LNNS.

Okada, Y. 2013. Web Version of IntelligentBox (WebIB) and Its Integration with Webble World, Vol. 372 of the series, Communications in Computer and Information Science, Springer, pp. 11-20.

Okada, Y. and Tanaka, Y, 1995. IntelligentBox: a constructive visual software development system for interactive 3D graphic applications, Proc. of Computer Animation '95, IEEE CS Press, pp. 114-125.

Okada, Y. el al, 2016. Interactive Educational Contents Development Framework Based on Linked Open Data Technology, 9th annual International Conference of Education, Research and Innovation, pp. 5066-5075.

Okada, Y. et al, 2016. Framework for Development of Web-based Interactive 3D Educational Contents, 10th International Technology, Education and Development Conference, pp. 2656-2663.

Okada, Y. et al, 2017. Interactive Educational Contents Development Framework and Its Extension for Web-based VR/AR Applications, Proc. of the GameOn 2017, Eurosis, ISBN: 978-90-77381-99-1, pp. 75-79.

Okada, Y., Kaneko, K., Shi, W. (Feb 2023, Development Framework Using 360VR Cameras and Lidar Scanners for Web-Based XR Educational Materials Supporting VR Goggles. In: Barolli, L. (eds) Advances in Internet, Data & Web Technologies. EIDWT 2023. Lecture Notes on Data Engineering and Communications Technologies, vol 161. Springer, pp. 401-412.

Okada, Y., Kaneko, K., Shi, W. (July 2023). Development Framework for Web-based VR Tours and Its Examples. 27th International Conference Information Visualisation (IV), pp. 420-425.

Okada, Y., Ogata, T. el al, 2017, Component-based approach for prototyping of Tai Chi-based physical therapy game and its performance evaluations. Computers in Entertainment, 14(1), https://doi.org/10.1145/2735383

Sugimura, R., et al, 2014. Mobile Game for Learning Bacteriology, Proc. of IADIS 10th Int. Conf. on Mobile Learning 2014, pp.285-289.

Sumikura,S., Shibuya, M. and Sakurada, K., 2019, OpenVSLAM: A Versatile Visual SLAM Framework, MM '19: Proceedings of the 27th ACM International Conference on MultimediaOctober 2019Pages 2292–2295.

Yamamura, H. et al, 2020. A Development Framework for RP-type Serious Games in a 3D Virtual Environment, VENOA 2020 in Proc. of the 14th International Conference on Complex, Intelligent, and Software Intensive Systems (CISIS-2020), pp. 166-176.

PROPOSAL OF A KNOWLEDGE GRAPH USING INTERNATIONAL SEMANTIC STANDARDS IN THE OIL AND GAS AREA

Elvismary Molina de Armas[1], Geiza Maria Hamazaki da Silva[2], Yenier Torres Izquierdo[1], Melissa Lemos Cavaliere[1] and Eduardo Thadeu Leite Corseuil[1]

[1]*Instituto Tecgraf - Pontifícia Universidade Católica do Rio de Janeiro (PUC-RIO)*
Rio de Janeiro, RJ, Brazil
[2]*Universidade Federal do Estado do Rio De Janeiro (UNIRIO)*
Rio de Janeiro, RJ, Brazil

ABSTRACT

In the last decade, Knowledge Graphs (KGs) have increased their use as a tool to represent knowledge and query data. Some industrial solutions use KGs to allow the integration between the systems, to use artificial intelligence, or to facilitate communication between humans and the systems. DANKE is a platform developed by Tecgraf Institute at PUC-Rio University to support key searches over preprocessed and integrated data. It was configured and used for searching over data related to real-world operation and maintenance activities of an Oil and Gas production scenario. The Knowledge Graph of this system, called DOnG-KG (DANKE Oil and Gas - Knowledge Graph), is its core and allows searching and linking information from concepts collected from diverse data sources. However, it was developed under agile methodology, sacrificing some modeling decisions to empower performance. Moreover, it does not consider existing data models and core ontologies like ISO15926-part 14 for life-cycle data for process plants to guide the graph construction. This work proposed a refactoring of the DOnG-KG using well-known ontologies like SKOS, DC, OntoCape, ISO15926 part 2 (Reference Data Library), and part 14 (Upper Ontology) to define some concepts. We also extend the graph, including more concepts previously treated as data properties. In that way, the graph was adequate to an international semantics standard for life-cycle data for process plants, including Oil and Gas production facilities, allowing the inclusion and linking of new terms in the graph and different standards-subgraph for specific subdomains without inconsistency and ambiguity. Finally, the KG resulting from this work could be extended by plugging new sources and even used for other applications in the Oil and Gas context.

KEYWORDS

Knowledge Graph, Oil and Gas, ISO15926, CFIHOS

1. INTRODUCTION

In the last decade, Knowledge Graphs (KGs) have increased their popularity and use in scientific communities in different research fields such as Machine Learning, Artificial Intelligence, and Databases, for instance, and big industrial players, giving a powerful tool for the company. A "Knowledge Graph" can be defined succinctly as "a graph of data with the intent to compose knowledge" (Bonatti et al., 2018), in which the nodes could be composed by the "concepts" of the described world, and the arcs represent the relations between the concepts that define the world. As a tool to represent knowledge, KG allows us to describe the formal semantics of terms used in the graph through (for example) model theory, contributing with a machine-interpretability of the underlying graph and allowing for formal reasoning methods that can infer new data, detect inconsistencies, and enabling query answering over implicit knowledge (Bonatti et al., 2018).

The Oil and Gas industry has not been left out of the advantages of using KGs (Brewton, 2023; Huang, Wang & Yu, 2020; Tang et al., 2022). By using KGs to store and organize data about the life-cycle data of the plant, such as prospection data, drilling data, design, construction, production rates of oil and gas wells, operations and maintenance activities, companies can register the knowledge, understand in a better way their assets and make better decisions about how to increase the company's profitability from an economic and environmental point of view.

In parallel, the Oil and Gas community has been involved in the specification of standards, such as ISO15926 and CFIHOS, to formalize and to improve the organization of data in this process, like IOJP (https://www.iogp.org) members and consortia like POSC-Caesar (https://www.posccaesar.org), to give a semantic and well-defined interpretation of the concepts associated with the domain and process in this industry.

DANKE (Izquierdo et. al., 2021) is a platform, developed by Tecgraf Institute at PUC-Rio University in partnership and founded by Petrobras, that provides an intelligent data extraction mechanism for searching, retrieving, exploring, and summarizing data. It was configured for searching over real-world data from operation and maintenance activities of an Oil and Gas production scenario. The KG of this system, called DOnG-KG (DANKE Oil and Gas - Knowledge Graph), is the system's core, allowing for searching and linking information from concepts collected from different data sources. However, it was developed giving up some modeling decisions in favor of optimizing query time, and there needs to be a well-established vocabulary of the terms. It lacks a core foundational vocabulary that allows the insertion of new specialized terms and the identification of similar terms through a hierarchical structure coherently and consistently.

In this context, this work proposes a verification and remodeling of the DOnG-KG, contributing with (i) a well-specified definition of the concepts, (ii) use of the core-ontology ISO15926 to define the concepts of the graph, (iii) use of well-known ontologies like SKOS, DC, OntoCape, to define some concepts, (iv) extension of the graph, including more concepts previously treated as data properties. In that way, the graph was adequate to the ISO15926 international standard for life-cycle data for process plants, including Oil and Gas production facilities, opening the company to the international corporate world. Since it is used ISO15926 - Part 14 (upper ontology) and ISO15926 - Part 4 (Reference Data Library), it is possible to incorporate and link new terms in the graph, respecting the identification of equal (semantically) terms and the logical rules laid from the relationships between them, and also use the shared definitions of the terms. Moreover, ISO15926 maintains a Memorandum of Understanding (MOU) with other international standards, for instance, CFIHOS[1]; therefore, the new graph can incorporate different standards for specific subdomains without inconsistency and ambiguity. Finally, the KG resulting from this work could be extended by plugging new sources and even used for other applications.

2. BACKGROUND

2.1 SAP-ERP and DOnG-KG

SAP-ERP is an enterprise resource planning software used to manage maintenance and inspection activities regarding service management, maintenance history, and costs (SAP, 2023). Some Oil and Gas companies use this system to manage maintenance activities, offering flows for attending to and monitoring maintenance demand, including the register of principal documents such as maintenance notes, plans, orders, inspection technical reports, and the identification of technical objects.

DANKE[2] is a data and knowledge extraction platform that offers keyword-based searching over preprocessed and integrated data. Using DANKE, the users can refrain from knowing the specific structure of the data sources and the language to consult them. The DOnG-KG (DANKE Oil and Gas - Knowledge Graph) is the system's core of the DANKE configuration to support data searching over the operation and maintenance activities data for Oil and Gas production plants. It allows searching and linking information from concepts collected from diverse data sources.

Originally, the DOnG-KG was built by modeling concepts from five management systems, where the concepts originating from SAP-ERP are the most representative. Nevertheless, it was born with the perspective to be extended for including data from other systems in upcoming releases. Among the concepts included from SAP-ERP, we found some concepts related to the plan breakdown, like TECHNICAL OBJECT, PLATFORM and TAG, and others associated with maintenance documents such as MAINTENANCE PLAN, PLAN ITEM,

---

[1] CFIHOS: https://www.jip36-cfihos.org, accessed on 07/24/2023

[2] DANKE: https://danke.tecgraf.puc-rio.br/, accessed on 07/24/2023

MAINTENANCE NOTE, MAINTENANCE ORDER, and TECHNICAL INSPECTION REPORT (RTI, by its acronyms in Portuguese). Each concept has many attributes, all modeled as data properties using string data type. Figure 1 shows an overview of the concepts related to SAP-ERP as nodes and the relations among them. However, the concepts definitions were not formalized and the relations were not labeled.

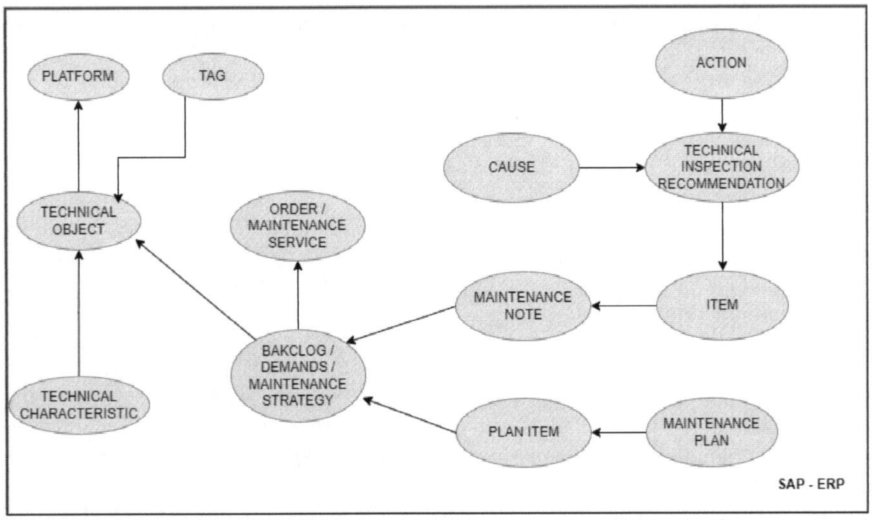

Figure 1. The DOnG-KG. Section related to the concepts from SAP-ERP

The DOnG-KG was developed using a subset of concepts of enterprise systems, guided by iterative and incremental user requirements, and implemented using an agile software development methodology. Therefore, the implementation of the graph was conducted mainly by the user functional requirements, and some decisions about the KG were subdued in favor of optimizing the search response time. Consequently, the concepts definitions were not very well-formalized, and no domain vocabulary was established. Moreover, the SAP-ERP follows its own-private data model, with no intersection with some validated and well-established data representation standard in the Oil and Gas industry. The current KG also lacks core foundational vocabulary that allows plugging in new specialized terms and helps identify similar terms through the top of the hierarchical structure. This fact limits the application and extension of this graph to incorporate new concepts from other systems and linking them with the previous existing coherently and consistently.

2.2 International Standards to Represent Data in Oil and Gas Domain

ISO15926[3] standard, "Integration of life-cycle data for process plants including oil and gas production facilities", was proposed to promote the development of open specifications to be used as standards to enable the interoperability of data, software and related matters. Currently composed of fourteen parts, the ISO15926 initially proposes a language consisting of syntactic and semantic parts. The syntactic part and the domain terminology can be used to develop ontologies for the different functional domains. ISO15926-Part8 provides rules for implementing the superior ontology specified by ISO15926-Part2 and the model methodology defined by ISO15926-Part7 in the RDF and OWL languages, including models for reference data specified by ISO15926-Part3 and Part4. More recently, with the advent of OWL 2 (W3C, 2012), there has been interest in OWL versions of the top-level ontology. This resulted in ISO/TS 15926-Part14. The objective of the latter part is to meet the needs of OWL 2 ontologies based on ISO15926-Part2, which allow efficient reasoning and capture life-cycle information.

The Joint Industry Project (JIP) READI[4] (REquirement Asset Digital life-cycle Information) project (Project, n.d.) was a digitalization project in the Oil and Gas area that aims at the standardization and automation of critical business processes in the disposal of assets, maintenance, operations, the transformation

[3] ISO15926: https://www.iso.org/standard/29556.html, http://15926.org, accessed on 07/24/2023.

[4] READI project, https://readi-jip.org, accessed on 08/31/2023.

of business processes and a common digital language and structure. It proposes domain modeling in computational ontologies with the objective that inconsistencies and deviations are detected instantly, reducing future problems. The fundamental parts of READI are: 1-Digital reference data library based on ISO15926-Part14; 2-Reference Designation System for Oil and Gas; and 3-The asset information modeling structure.

The ISO15926-Part14[5]; was implemented and published by the POSC Caesar Association as a result of the READI project, as well as independent ontologies of the upper domain. The RDL was effectively implemented as an ontology using the OWL language, which incorporates the ISO15926-Part4 terminology and the ISO/IEC 21838-2 BFO standards. Additionally, this ontology was extended with other modules (ontologies) for specific domains such as processes, equipment, documents, etc.

CFIHOS[6], an acronym for Capital Facilities Information HandOver Specification, is an industry-standard developed to improve how information is exchanged between companies that own, operate, and build equipment for the process and energy sectors. It also aims to offer standardized specifications and practices for the transfer of information that work for any person involved in the construction, operation, maintenance, or decommissioning of industrial facilities, or so on, all in the information supply chain - operators, entrepreneurs, and equipment manufacturers and suppliers.

Starting from a common taxonomy of equipment nomenclature and support specifications, its objective is to become a common language for exchanging information that must be delivered when a project passes from development to operations. The Reference Data Library, or "RDL", is at the heart of CFIHOS. This library provides a standard and unified naming convention for equipment, its attributes, disciplines, and documents. The CFIHOS RDL includes: a) a list of classes for Tag and Equipment (what the equipment does and what it is); b) a list of properties (attributes, measures, characteristics, etc.); c) lists of requirements by class (data and document requirements); d) unique data pattern encoding to facilitate digital design and other workflows; e) a list of document types; and f) a list of subjects. To facilitate implementation, CFIHOS defines five templates that reflect typical contracting scenarios and that can be adapted to reflect the scope of information to be delivered by a Contractor.

3. FORMALIZATION OF THE KNOWLEDGE GRAPH CONCEPTS

As one of the main contributions of this work, we present the formal definitions of the concepts in the graph from SAP-ERP listed in Table 1.

Table 1. Concept names and definitions of the initial DOnG-KG

Concept name	Definition
PLATFORM	A PLATFORM consists of a set of equipment that performs a physical or chemical process, including production, transport, and storage.
TECHNICAL OBJECT	A TECHNICAL OBJECT is a term used to denote both EQUIPMENT and INSTALLATION PLACE. An EQUIPMENT is a physical object for which there is a need for technical history and traceability of movements by Maintenance or Inspection. An INSTALLATION PLACE is a location of a given operational unit where one or more pieces of equipment can be installed and where the Maintenance or Inspection services are carried out.
TAG	A TAG is a unique alphanumeric number that defines an object designed for performing functional requirements and serving as a specification for equipment.
MAINTENANCE NOTE	A MAINTENANCE NOTE is a service request made by a customer for Maintenance or Inspection. Notes are the beginning of a flow of information and actions under the responsibility of Maintenance, triggered by a service need for a customer. They are applied to INSTALLATION PLACE and EQUIPMENT.

[5] PCA Reference Data and Services. ISO 15926-14 PCA RDL, https://rds.posccaesar.org/doc/presentations/presentation_intro_plmrdl/, accessed on 08/31/2023.
[6] CFIHOS: https://www.jip36-cfihos.org, accessed on 08/31/2023.

Concept name	Definition
MAINTENANCE PLAN	A MAINTENANCE PLAN is a set of information that allows planning and scheduling interventions with pre-defined frequencies and standardized tasks, to ensure continuity and operational safety of facilities and preservation of equipment and materials.
MAINTENANCE PLAN/ ITEM	A MAINTENANCE PLAN ITEM is a set of data that is part of the structure of the MAINTENANCE PLAN and associates a task list with the TECHNICAL OBJECT, specifies the execution priority of the MAINTENANCE ORDERs, and informs the planning and cost allocation data.
TECHNICAL INSPECTION RECOMMENDATION (RTI)/ MEASURE	A TECHNICAL INSPECTION RECOMMENDATION (RTI), also called MEASURE, is a type of note used by the inspection to record the measures (recommendations) to be taken to remedy problems identified during the inspection.
BACKLOG / DEMANDS/ MAINTENANCE STRATEGY	BACKLOG, also known as DEMANDS or MAINTENANCE STRATEGY, consists of the union of information present in the concepts MAINTENANCE NOTE, RTI, and MAINTENANCE PLAN.
ITEM	An ITEM is part of a MAINTENANCE NOTE. The link to the RTI represents a reference to an affected part.
CAUSE	A CAUSE represents the reason why the problem reported in the RTI happened.
ACTION	An ACTION defines the activity to be executed to resolve a problem reported in an ITEM.
MAINTENANCE ORDER	A MAINTENANCE ORDER is a document used to plan and monitor maintenance and inspection actions in order to respond to service requests made by customers or to comply with preventive or predictive maintenance and inspection routines of MAINTENANCE PLANs. It could contain the planned human resources, materials and services, and their respective costs.
TECHNICAL CHARACTERISTIC	A TECHNICAL CHARACTERISTIC is a characteristic of a TECHNICAL OBJECT that identifies one of its inherent properties.

Writing the concept definition must be done in parallel while the nodes are inserted on the graph. A formalized definition helps to identify equal entities that may use different names. Even more, it can help establish relations between the domain concepts. The definitions of the terms allow us to see two groups of nodes: those related to the plant breakdown structure and those associated with maintenance documents that are used to manage the maintenance process.

4. ISO15926 MAPPING AND GRAPH REFACTORING

After formalizing the concepts definitions of the initial version of the DOnG-KG, we start mapping them with concepts existing in models proposed by well-established standards for the Oil and Gas industry, using the ISO15926 as a foundational ontology. During this process, we also use another well-known ontologies and vocabularies such as SKOS, OBO, READI ontology modules, and Cartesian Coordinate Ontology. To represent entities from ISO15926, we use the prefix "*lis14*". We also create a Reference Data Library for SAP (SAP RDL) concepts that could not be mapped to any pre-existing concept in the international standards reviewed using the prefix "*rdlsap*" to denote them.

In the case of TECHNICAL OBJECT, as the definition clarified, it was represented as the grouping of two concepts: INSTALLATION PLACE and EQUIPMENT. Therefore, we created these new concepts. The EQUIPMENT concept is mapped as *lis14:InanimatePhysicalObject*, allowing the use of properties associated with the latter. In the case of INSTALLATION PLACE, an appropriate concept in the standards to map it was not found, so it is inserted as a new term in the SAP RDL. However, given the close similarities, it is declared as *skos:closeMatch* to *lis14:Site*. The properties associated with EQUIPMENT that would also be necessary for the INSTALLATION PLACE are included in the *rdlsap* namespace and set through property inheritance.

A new concept is also added to represent a point in space associated with a TAG, mapped as *lis:PointInSpace*. It allows searching by the position of a TECHNICAL OBJECT, using a property *cartCoord:hasPlacement* from the Cartesian Coordinate Ontology[7]. The TAG concept is represented through a data property as a *xsd:string* value. It was associated with TECHNICAL OBJECT, using *rdlsap:hasTAG* for EQUIPMENT and *rdlsap:hasIdentification* for INSTALLATION PLACE.

[7] Cartesian Coordinate Ontology: HTTP://DIARMUIDR3D.GITHUB.IO/CARTCOORD/

The TECHNICAL CHARACTERISTIC concept was re-modeled through existing concepts in ISO15926/READI and their properties. A characteristic is represented through a PHYSICAL QUANTITY (*lis14:PhysicalQuantity*) associated with a value (*lis14:QuantityDatum)* using the *lis14:qualityQuantifiedAs* relationship. The *lis14:QuantityDatum* has a value data and optionally a unit of measure (*lis14:UnitOfMeasure*). Later, an EQUIPMENT could be associated with a technical characteristic using the *lis:hasPhysicalQuantity* relationship while an INSTALLATION PLACE using the *rdlsap:hasPhysicalQuantity* relationship.

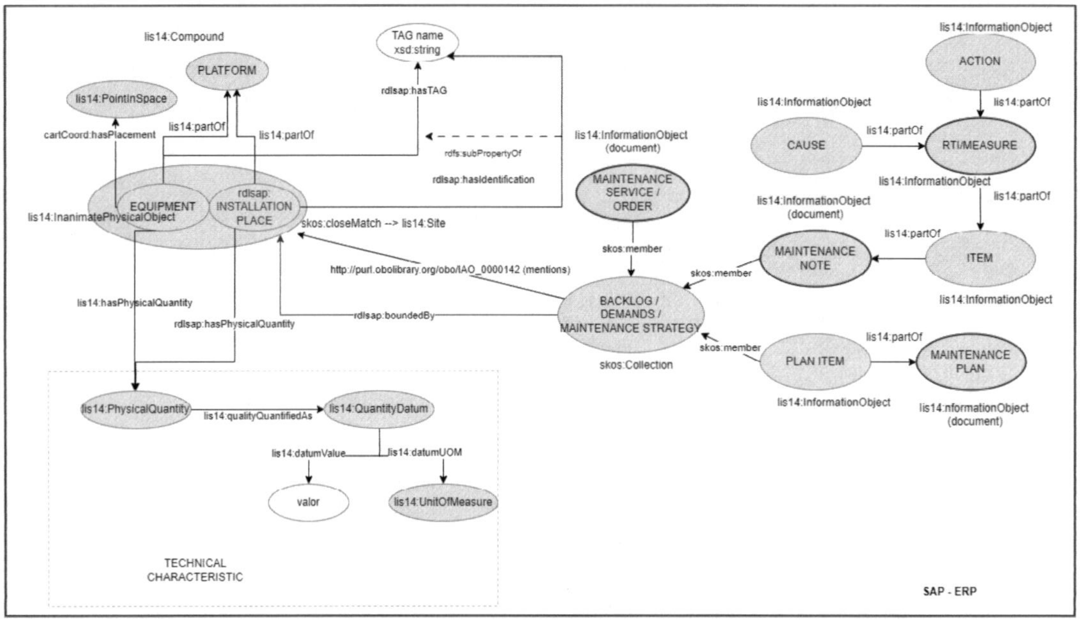

Figure 2. Concepts present in the SAP subset mapped to ISO15926 Part 14 (ontology foundation)

The concepts related to documents: MAINTENANCE NOTE, MAINTENANCE PLAN, and MAINTENANCE ORDER are mapped as *lis14:InformationObject* and fitting as documents in the ontology module of READI http://rds.posccaesar.org/ontology/plm/ont/document. The BACKLOG concept was modeled as *skos:Collection* that keeps as members the previous ones mentioned. The BACKLOG is related to TECHNICAL OBJECT through two properties, one to refer to the technical object that is affected and must be attended by the demand, using *rdlsap:boundedBy*, and the second for other technical objects mentioned in the demand (*http://purl.obolibrary.org/obo/IAO_0000142*), which are related with the bounded equipment and are used to reference it.

ITEM was modeled as *lis14:InformationObject* and part of (*lis14:partOf*) the MAINTENANCE NODE. Similarly, the RTI concept was mapped as *lis14:InformationObject* as well as CAUSE and ACTION. The *lis14:part* was used to establish the relation of inclusion between those concepts.

After analyzing the primary concepts presented in the graph, we start to analyze all the attributes of each concept to pick out if it should be modeled as a concept or as an attribute (data property). This activity allowed the graph to grow and mature the concepts and relations existing in the first version.

Figure 3 shows how it is possible to extend the graph by plugging extensions of other data models as proposed by CFIHOS. CFIHOS proposes a common taxonomy of equipment nomenclature and support specifications for an equipment class and the properties associated with each class. For instance, the EQUIPMENT concept was modeled as *lis14:InanimatePhysicalObject*. The last is extended by Equipment ontology (READI) as *Artefact* concept, which is specialized by concepts like *Valve*, *Pump*, *Compressor*, etc. These concepts are linked to CFIHOS class using *skos:closeMatch* property, see an example for the *Valve* concept in Figure 3. In this sense, it is possible to link an equipment (READY) with its Equipment class, Tag Type, and the Property list concepts from CFIHOS data model.

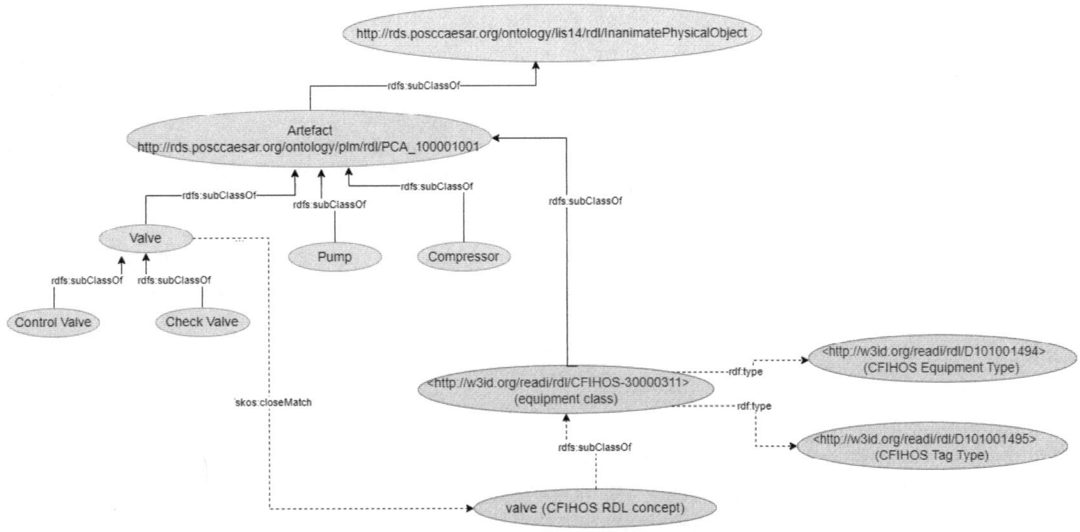

Figure 3. CFIHOS extension from *lis14:InanimatePhysicalObject*. CFIHOS Equipment class and Tag Type

Starting from the PLATFORM concept, the Asset, Business Unit, and Maintenance Center attributes were modeled as concepts. New particular properties for the SAP RDL were used to describe the relation between some concepts like *rdlsap:managedBy* and *rdlsap:attendedBy*. A hierarchy of centers was introduced to detail all types of centers involved with the SAP concepts modeled, not only those directly related to PLATFORM. Therefore, the Maintenance Center became a specialization of the Center concept. Moreover, the Organization Ontology (https://www.w3.org/TR/vocab-org/) was used to describe organization units (*org:OrganizationalUnit*) like Asset, Management, Center, and Business unit, and to establish relations between them using the property *org:hasSubOrganization*. A detailed diagram of the PLATFORM and its attributes model is shown in Figure 4.

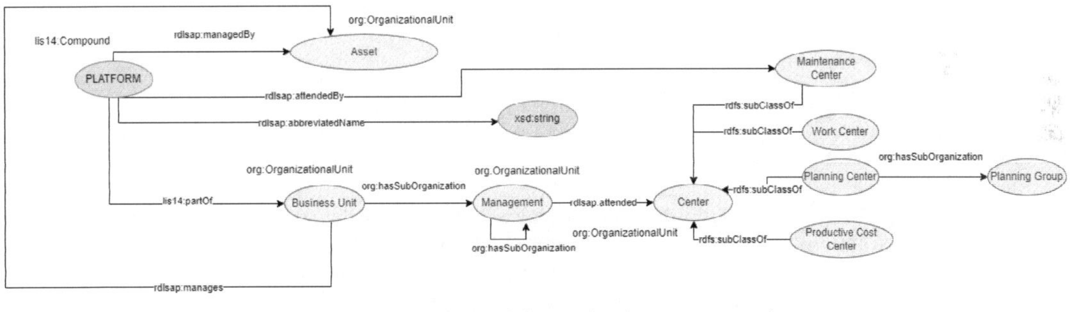

Figure 4. PLATFORM and direct related concepts overview

A similar process was applied for each concept and its attributes to extract new concepts and their relationships.

Significantly, we can mention the use of *skos:Collection* to map many attributes as concepts, for example, attributes related to the Status of the user and the Status of the system, Type of, Class of, Situation of, and Category. The relationship between some attributes could now be expressed as concepts, relations, and hierarchies. Some attributes shared by more than one concept could be modeled as one new concept. Other well-known ontologies were used, for example Dublin Core, to specify descriptions of the concepts and OntoCAPE for the cost of a MAINTENANCE ORDER. Nevertheless, many specific attributes were represented as data types using properties in the SAP RDL because the terms are used with a unique semantic in SAP-ERP, and we could not map to international standards and well-known ontologies.

The representation resulting from the analysis of each main concept's attributes is available at https://github.com/emolina85/DOnG-KG-model.

5. CONCLUSION

A relevant contribution of this work is the formal definition of the concepts in the DOnG-KG originating from SAP-ERP. Defining the terms helps us see two groups of nodes: those related to the plant breakdown structure and those associated with maintenance documents used to manage the maintenance process. Moreover, this facilitates mapping with ISO15926 entities as foundational ontology and other well-known ontologies.

The main concepts modeled in DOnG-KG from SAP-ERP were mapped using ISO15926 terms. The TECHNICAL OBJECT concept was represented as the grouping of two concepts, EQUIPMENT and INSTALLATION PLACE, represented as *lis14:InanimatePhysicalObject* and *skos:closeMatch* to *lis14:Site,* respectively. To define the technical characteristics of a TECHNICAL OBJECT, the classes to represent physical quantities and their values and units of measure in ISO15926 could be used. Similarly, the *InformationObject* class from ISO15926 was used to map the SAP documents and their parts. This mapping gives us a clear vision of the concepts and their coherence with the ISO15926 data model.

For each concept, the attributes were analyzed and remodeled, generating new concepts and data properties. In that way, the graph was extended with new concepts and relations. As a result, it was possible to establish hierarchy and relationship rules between some attributes that previously did not exist. Moreover, it was possible to identify repeated attributes that are only one and modeled as one concept. The mapping process allowed us to standardize the terms using well-known ontologies like SKOS, DC, and OntoCape. We also created an SAP RDL approach, containing the concepts and relationships inherent to SAP-ERP as *rdlsap* prefix term. The latter helps us to meet the industry's demands for a standard data model for ERP.

Finally, the graph was adequate to an international standard for life-cycle data for process plants, including Oil and Gas production facilities, opening the company to the international corporate world. Since ISO15926 - Part 14 is an upper ontology, it is possible to incorporate and link new terms in the graph and incorporate different standards for specific subdomains compatible with ISO15926, all of this without the risk of losing consistency and generating ambiguity. Finally, as a relevant result of this work, the DOnG-KG could be extended by plugging new sources and even used by integrating other applications.

ACKNOWLEDGEMENT

This work was partly funded by Petrobras within the ANP R&D levy as a commitment to research and development investments.

REFERENCES

Bonatti, P. A. et al, 2018. Knowledge Graphs: New Directions for Knowledge Representation on the Semantic Web. *Report from Dagstuhl Seminar*, *8*(09), 18371. Retrieved from http://www.dagstuhl.de/18371

Brewton, B., 2023. How Using Knowledge Graphs can Optimize the Oil and Gas Industry. Retrieved from *Linked in*: https://www.linkedin.com/pulse/how-using-knowledge-graphs-can-optimize-oil-gas-industry-jon-brewton#

Huang, S., Wang, Y., & Yu, X., 2020. Design and Implementation of Oil and Gas Information on Intelligent Search Engine Based on Knowledge Graph. *Journal of Physics: Conference Series*, *1621*(1). https://doi.org/10.1088/1742-6596/1621/1/012010

Izquierdo, Y. T. et al, 2021. A Platform for Keyword Search and its Application for COVID-19 Pandemic Data. *Journal of Information and Data Management,* 12(5). doi: 10.5753/jidm.2021.1904.

SAP, 2023. SAP-ERP. Retrieved from *SAP official site*: https://www.sap.com/brazil/index.html

Tang, X. et al, 2022. Construction and application of an ontology-based domain-specific knowledge graph for petroleum exploration and development. *Geoscience Frontiers*, 14(5), 101426. https://doi.org/10.1016/j.gsf.2022.101426

W3C, 2012. OWL 2 Web Ontology Language Quick Reference Guide (Second Edition). Retrieved from *W3C Recommendation* official site: https://www.w3.org/TR/owl2-quick-reference/

NATURALMSEQUERIES - A NATURAL WAY TO QUERY MATERIAL SCIENCES ENGINEERING DATA EXPERIMENTS

André Valdestilhas[1*], Soudeh Javamasoudian[1], Ghezal Ahmad Jan Zia[1], Thilo Muth[1], Thomas Hanke[2] and Horst Fellenberg[2]
[1]Federal Institute for Materials Research and Testing (BAM), Germany
[2]Fraunhofer Institut for Mechanics of Materials IWM, Germany

ABSTRACT

Materials science experiments involve complex data that are often very heterogeneous and challenging to reproduce. Challenges with materials science data were observed, for example, in a previous study on harnessing lightweight design potentials via the Materials Data Space for which the data from materials sciences engineering experiments were generated using linked open data principles, e.g., Resource Description Framework (RDF) as the standard model for data interchange on the Web. However, detailed knowledge of formulating questions in the query language SPARQL is necessary to query the data. It was noticed that domain experts in Materials Science lack knowledge of querying the data using SPARQL queries. With this work, we aim to develop NaturalMSEQueries an approach for the material science domain expert where instead of SPARQL queries, the user can develop expressions in natural language, e.g., English, to query the data. This will significantly improve the usability of Semantic Web approaches in materials science and lower the adoption threshold of the methods for the domain experts. We plan to evaluate our approach, with varying amounts of data, from different sources. Furthermore, we want to compare with synthetic data to assess the quality of the implementation of our approach. The repository is available online at https://github.com/Mat-O-Lab/KnowledgeUI.

KEYWORDS

Materials Science, Natural Language Processing, Semantic Web, Knowledge Graph, Predictions

1. INTRODUCTION

Experiments in materials science contain complex data that is difficult to replicate and sometimes redundant. Due to heterogeneous and challenging to work with detailed knowledge from Materials Science experiments such as data with concrete or aluminum, requiring a specific way to be interpreted by the user.

Challenges with materials science data were observed, for example, in a previous study on harnessing lightweight design potentials via the Materials Data Space (Huschka et al., 2022) for which the data from materials sciences engineering experiments were generated using linked open data principles (Berners-Lee et al., 2001), e.g., Resource Description Framework (RDF) as the standard model for data interchange on the Web. However, detailed knowledge of formulating questions in the query language SPARQL is necessary to query the data. It was noticed that domain experts in Materials Science lack knowledge of querying the data using SPARQL queries.

This complex materials science data can be represented as directed graphs - Directed graphs are defined in the preliminaries section. In this way, the most suitable way found to represent this data was using RDF and SPARQL query is needed to work with RDF data. Here is a need for more specific knowledge of SPARQL queries by the MSE domain experts.

Several Materials Science approaches use Semantic Web Technologies to obtain FAIR (Himanen et al. 2019; Valdestilhas et al., n.d.; Wilkinson et al., 2016) data. In most cases, creating ontologies, converting tabular data to RDF, etc. Therefore, SPARQL query language is needed to formulate questions, and domain experts in material science need to gain this knowledge.

* Corresponding author: andre.valdestilhas@bam.de

Querying the data using Natural Language, e.g., English, would be easier than querying the data using SPARQL queries. Instead of SPARQL queries, the user can develop expressions in natural language, e.g., English, to query the data. With this work, we aim to develop NaturalMSEQueries, an approach for the ma- terial science domain expert, in which instead of SPARQL queries, the user queries the data using Natural Language.

NaturalMSEQueries aims to provide a framework for querying Material Science data using Natural Lan- guage, e.g., English. The resources described here must be properly maintained, both short-term and long-term. Our approach, including a video demonstration, is available in a GitHub repository - *https://github.com/Mat-O-Lab/KnowledgeUI*

2. RESEARCH QUESTIONS

Our main problem is to remove the complexity of SPARQL queries and provide a Natural Language alternative to query the data, motivating us to unfold the following research questions:

RQ1 How to query semantic mse data easier than using SPARQL queries?

RQ2 How much will the framework help the Materials Science Engineering domain? RQ3 What is the best way to organize Material Sciences Methods data?

– **Axiom(RQ3)**: *MSE Methods can be represented as a directed graph, and RDF Knowledge graphs are directed graphs; therefore, RDF Knowledge Graphs can be used to represent MSE Methods graphically, which is the best approach to our case.*

The contributions of this work are listed below:

- Alternative to query MSE data with Natural Language.
- A rank of entities from the dataset represented using an interactive sunburst diagram.
- Predefined queries, to help users enhance the queries and learn our methodology.
- Query history, allowing the user to store and execute previous queries.
- Graph visualization of the query output data.

3. PRELIMINARIES

Here we describe and define terms used in this paper.

API: Computer programs can communicate with each other via an Application Programming Interface - *https://en.wikipedia.org/wiki/API*

FAIR Data: The application of the FAIR principles (Wilkinson et al., 2016) - *https://www.go-fair.org/fair-principles/* is aimed at increasing the Findability, Accessibility, Interoperability, and Reusability of (research) data.

IRI: Internationalized Resource Identifier - *https://www.rfc-editor.org/rfc/rfc3987* can be used instead of a URI to identify resources uniquely.

MSE: Quoting "Materials Science and Engineering combine engineering, physics, and chemistry principles to solve real-world problems associated with nanotechnology, biotechnology, information technology, energy, manufacturing, and other major engineering disciplines." - Quoting from *https://mse.umd.edu/about/what-is-mse/*

Ontology: Gruber defines "An ontology is an explicit specification of a conceptualization" (Gruber, 1993). Ontology creation involves the description of knowledge through specified terms (formalized vocabularies) and their relationships to other terms, usually covering a specific domain rep- resented by a community of users. The semantic web languages OWL - *https://www.w3.org/OWL/* (Web Ontology Language) and its revised extension OWL2 - *https://www.w3.org/TR/2012/REC-owl2-overview-20121211/* enable the creation and sharing of ontologies over the Web aiming at making Web content more accessible to machines.

RDF: The Resource Description Framework - *https://www.w3.org/RDF/* is a standard model for data interchange on the Web. In the RDF model, each statement consists of three components, subject, predicate, and object, and is represented by URIs. Statements are made in the form of RDF triples - *https://www.w3.org/TR/rdf-concepts/#section-triples/*, such as,

```
1 <http://example.org/#specimen> <http://www.perceive.net/schemas/relationship/isMadeOf>
2 <http://example.org/#material> .
```

An RDF graph - *https://www.w3.org/TR/rdf-concepts/#section-rdf-graph/* is defined by a set of RDF triples, which can be stored in RDF Triple Stores - *https://www.w3.org/2001/sw/wiki/Category:Triple_Store*. Serialization of RDF graphs is enabled by syntaxes such as Turtle - *https://www.w3.org/TR/turtle/*. The query language SPARQL - *https://www.w3.org/TR/rdf-sparql-query/* allows information retrieval from RDF graphs based on Turtle syntax. RDF itself does not provide any vocabulary related to the schema. RDFS - *https://www.w3.org/2001/sw/wiki/RDFS* (RDF Schema) can be used to represent simple RDF vocabularies on the Web. Other vocabulary definition technologies, such as OWL, OWL2, or SKOS - *https://www.w3.org/TR/skos-reference/*, provide language for defining structured, Web-based ontologies. In this regard, a reasoner is a soft- ware that can draw logical conclusions from a collection of axioms or claimed facts on ontologies.

SWT: Refers to Semantic Web Technologies that apply linked data and RDF concepts from Berners-Lee et al., 2001, aiming to provide RDF graphs from Material Sciences Engineering (MSE) knowledge data. **URI:** Universal Resource Identifier - *https://www.w3.org/wiki/URI/* is used to identify resources on the SW.

W3C: The World Wide Web Consortium - *https://www.w3.org/* provides standards for the World Wide Web.

4. RELATED WORK

The state-of-the-art includes approaches that endeavored to implement the ability to translate the natural language to the SPARQL query. We only concentrate on some of them here, which have proved the best performance compared to others. In this research, the main focus is on SPARKLIS, a pure JavaScript project which is compatible with other languages.

FREyA (Damljanovic et al., 2012) is a Java-based chatbot framework with a natural language to SPARQL (SPARQL Protocol and RDF Query Language) assessment module. This module allows the chatbot to com- prehend natural language user inquiries and translate them into SPARQL queries for searching RDF (Re- source Description Framework) data sources. To utilize this module in FREyA, you must first construct a set of intent definitions that translate natural language questions into SPARQL queries. These intent definitions may be articulated using FREyA's Domain Specific Language (DSL). When establishing the intent definitions, you may assess user requests using the natural language of the SPARQL module.

Neural SPARQL Machines (NSPM) (Soru et al., 2017; Soru et al., 2018) is a deep learning-based neural machine translation (NMT) system that learns the mapping between natural language inquiries and SPARQL queries. Overall, NSpM is an effective tool for improving the accuracy and efficiency of query creation in the Semantic Web. It can potentially change how data is queried and analyzed, allowing users to extract important information from large-scale RDF databases more easily.

Sparnatural (Marlet et al. 2019) is a Javascript component that lets users compose SPARQL searches to explore an RDF Knowledge Graph following a graph of properties and entities. Unfortunately, it was impossible to reproduce in our software environment due to technical limitations.

The Semantic PARaphrase Acquisition from Large-scale Knowledge-intensive Sources (SPARKLIS) (Ferré 2017) is a framework for natural language processing (NLP) which is the approach we use for querying RDF data using SPARQL. It allows users to enter queries in natural language and translates them into SPARQL queries, which can then be executed against a SPARQL endpoint. The tool also provides a graphical interface for browsing and exploring RDF data with the ability to enter the endpoint dynamically. It was designed to automatically learn paraphrases (i.e., phrases or sentences that convey the same meaning as other phrases or sentences) from large-scale knowledge resources, such as text corpora, semantic networks, and lexical databases. The framework uses distributional semantics and machine learning techniques to identify and extract paraphrases, which can be used to improve various NLP applications, such as information retrieval, machine translation, and text summarization.

5. GENERATION RDF KNOWLEDGE GRAPHS FROM MSE DATA

As we saw in the introduction on Axiom (RQ3), RDF Knowledge Graphs can be used to represent MSE Methods, and this way to work is spreading with the adoption of FAIR (Wilkinson et al., 2016) data by the MSE community. There are several ways to generate this data, and now we show approaches from our knowledge.

The ontopanel (Chen et al., 2022) aims to create domain ontologies and method graphs that adhere to MSE testing criteria. Ontopanel was built as a plugin for the popular open-source graphical editor diagrams.net to enable graphical ontology editing to meet the project's genuine expectations from domain experts. It provides pipeline tools to promote ontology creation in diagrams.net, such as ontology imports and re-use, diagram conversion to Web Ontology Language (OWL), diagram verification using OWL rules, and data mapping.

Besides that, more initiatives and projects are included in the project Innovations-Plattform MaterialDigital - *www.materialdigital.de* highlighting different ways to generate RDF Knowledge Graphs, all in an initial development phase, but very promising and pioneer initiative. The data used in our experiments with NaturalMSEQueries comes from those initiatives.

We chose SPARKLIS over FREyA (Damljanovic et al. 2012), NSpM (Soru et al., 2017; Soru et al., 2018), and SparNatural Marlet et al. 2019 because the semantic accuracy that generates semantically accurate paraphrases. It uses syntactic and semantic analysis techniques to ensure that the meaning of the original sentence is preserved in the paraphrases. This is important because it ensures that the generated paraphrases are diverse but also accurate and meaningful. Also, the domain specificity of SPARKLIS can be trained on specific domains to produce specific paraphrases. This means that it can be customized to generate paraphrases relevant to a particular application or field of study, in our case, the Materials Science domain.

6. THE METHODOLOGY

We develop a framework specific for the MSE community, in which instead of SPARQL query, you use NLP. We have integrated a prediction framework in which it we use SLAMD (Völker et al., 2022), allowing users to have a completely automated workflow. We also provide a sunburst diagram that helps users identify entities in the dataset, which is an RDF Knowledge Graph in our case.

The components of NaturalMSEQueries are listed as follows:

- SPARQL endpoint selection: An input text for the SPARQL endpoint URL containing the dataset.
- SunBurst Diagram: Illustrate a rank of entities from the selected SPARQL endpoint in an interactive Sunburst diagram, where the user can select an entity from the dataset.
- Predefined queries: Provides predefined queries which help the user improve the query.
- YASGUI: Provides an environment where the user can edit and execute the query converted to a SPARQL query.
- Graph Visualization: If a graph can represent the results, the user can visualize this graph.
- Prediction Framework. An environment that uses Artificial intelligence (AI) and Machine Learning (ML) to give building materials research a new dynamic. Sequential Learning (SL) promises a breakthrough by quickly identifying promising experiments and discarding unfavorable experimental paths early on. Allows the development of new materials with significantly fewer experiments overall.

We assume that the user of our approach is a domain expert in the area of Materials Science Engineering. Using our approach, the workflow can be folded into five steps described in the next paragraphs and illustrated at Figure 1.

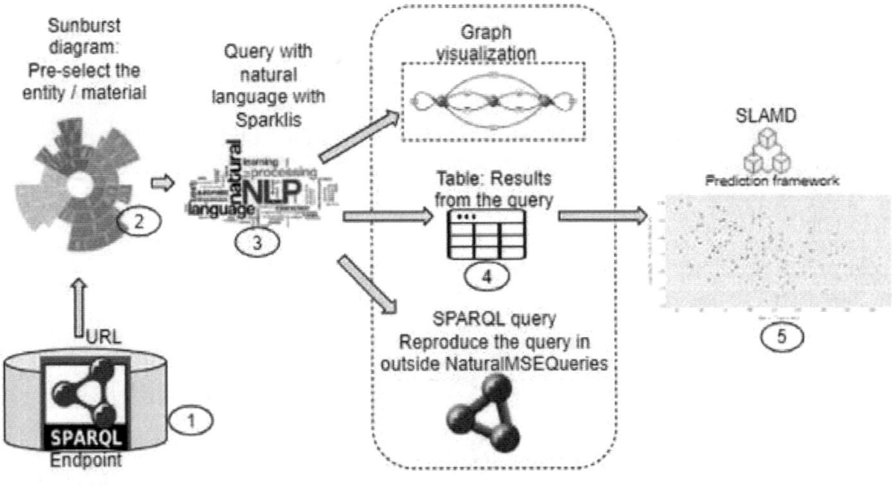

Figure 1. The workflow using our approach to query Material Science data using Natural Language

1. Given a dataset contained in a SPARQL endpoint provided by the user.
2. The entities are extracted from the data provided by the SPARQL endpoint and a rank of representativity illustrates the information using an interactive Sunburst diagram where the user can select the entity to start formulating queries.
3. The first query is given, in Natural Language, to obtain all information about the selected entity. The user can now develop the query by selecting more related entities, filtering information, visualizing the graph, if the results are graphs, and converting the Natural Language query into a SPARQL query to execute out of the NaturalMSEQueries environment.
4. The query results can be exported to CSV format or parsed to be used straight in our integrated prediction framework for prediction framework use - The user can also use the results in CSV format to use in another implementation of the prediction framework, e.g., *https://slamd-demo.herokuapp.com/*
   • The query is stored, allowing us to have a history of queries to be used later or executed straight in the SPARQL endpoint.
5. The parsed results allow the use of the prediction framework SLAMD to obtain predictions and im- prove their materials science experiments. SLAMD framework provides several ways to visualize the outcoming predictions. Once the natural language query process is done, another component can be used for prediction aims which use a sequential learning model (SLAMD). The underlying idea is to find useful experiments with more information. It is notable to say that promising experiments are the ones that are preferred over others, and their outcome is known. The output of this step is a prediction framework that enhances the validation of material experiences. SLAMD uses machine learning models like Decision Tree Regression, Scikit Random Forest Regression, Lolopy Random Forest Regression, and Gaussian Process Regression.

7. USAGE EXAMPLE

As a usage example, we have the Alutrace dataset (Huschka et al., 2022), which contains data about harnessing lightweight design potentials via the materials data space. The data model for our approach is RDF, in which all data is available in a SPARQL endpoint.

Figure 2 and Figure 3 illustrate our approach, together with the following list of steps.

1. The user provides the Alutrace SPARQL Endpoint URL - Available at *https://fuseki.matolab.org/alutrace/sparql*, illustrated in Figure 2.
2. The Sunburst diagram is loaded illustrating a rank of entities from the dataset, illustrated in Figure 2.
3. The user chose an Entity from the diagram by clicking on it with the mouse pointer, illustrated in Figure 2.

4. The first Natural Language query is automatically created, which is “give me every material entity”, illustrated in Figure 2.
5. The user goes the predefined queries to improve the query, e.g., “Process chain of a given TechnologicalProduct”, illustrated in Figure 3.
6. The user converts the Natural Language query to SPARQL with YASGUI to verify the complexity avoided, illustrated in Figure 3.

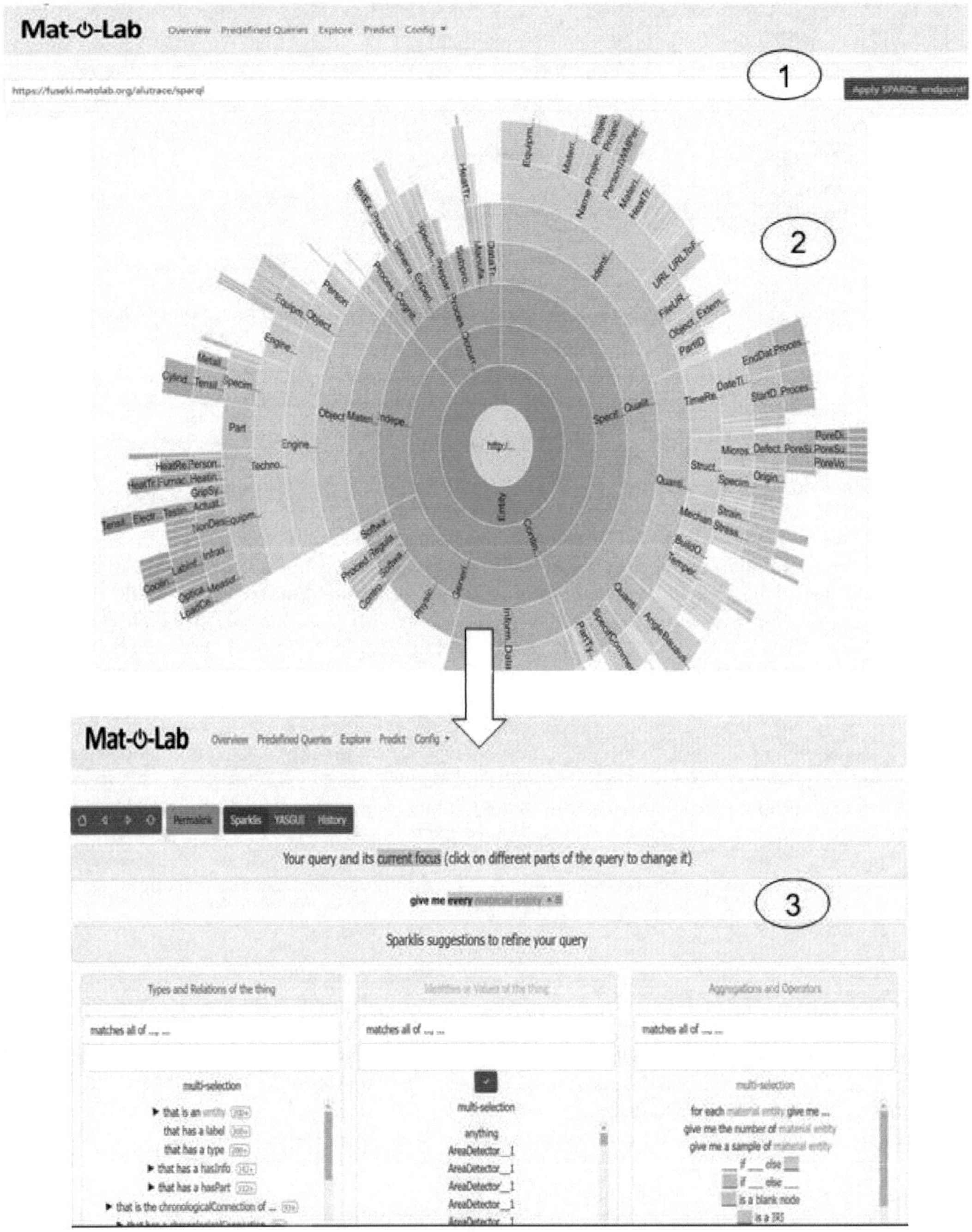

Figure 2. SPARQL endpoint, SunBurst diagram and Natural Language Processing interface

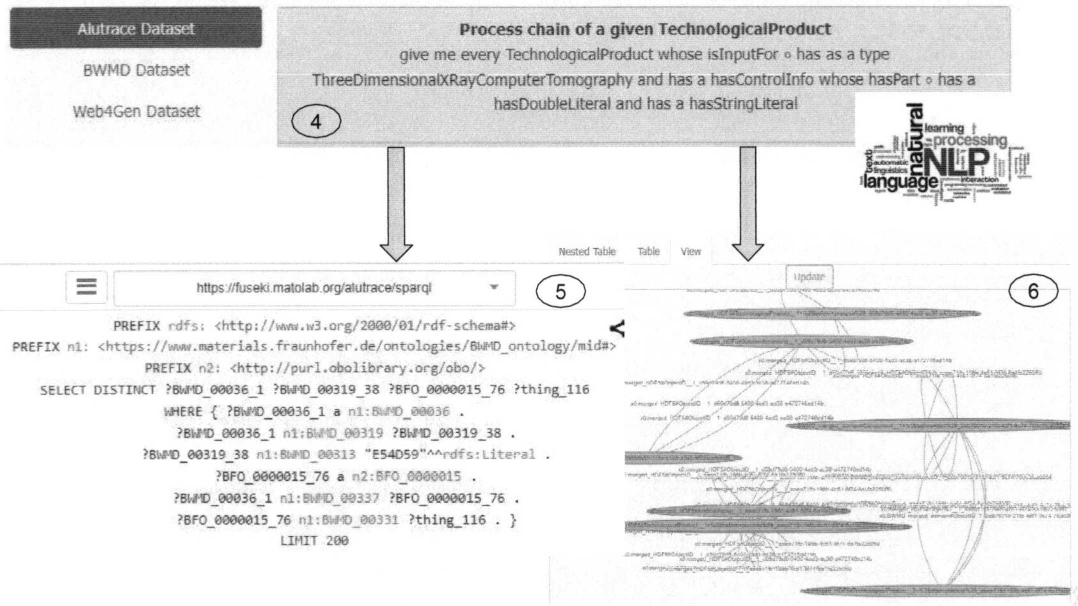

Figure 3. Natural Language to SPARQL query and graph visualization of the query results

8. SUSTAINABILITY PLAN

NaturalMSEQueries aims to provide a framework for querying Material Science data using Natural Langue, e.g., English. The resources described here must be properly maintained, both short-term and long-term.

In the short term, NaturalMSEQueries is being actively developed by Bundesanstalt für Materialforschung und -prüfung (BAM) and Fraunhofer Institute within the Mat-o-Lab project. The NaturalMSEQueries soft- ware is essential for the future of BAM and the Fraunhofer Institute. It is being successfully used in several European projects, which requires and ensures maintenance on the short term. The short-term implementation and maintenance issues are tracked using the GitHub project boards. All new features and fixes are tracked using issues and pull requests, which makes the development of NaturalMSEQueries available for anyone to follow and collaborate.

BAM and Frannhoufer Institute are dedicated to providing high-quality research output and ensuring sustainability. In the Long-term, BAM and Frannhoufer Institute guarantee the maintenance of this project for five years after initiation. This means that anyone willing to contribute can maintain its fork of the software, which voids any legal barriers towards long-term maintenance - Sustainability plan based on a success case available at https://github.com/firmao/wimuT/wiki/Sustainability-plan.

9. CONCLUSION

We use our approach in real word cases with the Alutrace dataset, which shows a lightweight design. We link data across institutions, e.g., BAM and Fraunhofer allowing us to exploit heterogeneous material data. We also realize that data space is needed for design purposes.

We plan to evaluate our approach, with varying amounts of data, from different sources. Furthermore, we want to compare with synthetic data to assess the quality of the implementation of our approach. Our evaluation shows that our work can significantly improve the usability of Semantic Web approaches in materials science and lower the adoption threshold of the methods for domain experts.

Due to a recent trend for using the novel Artificial Intelligence ChatGPT (Eloundou et al., 2023) chatbox in our upcoming work, we plan to incorporate Large Language Models with ChatGPT to enable the querying of RDF Knowledge Graphs through Natural Language Processing.

ACKNOWLEDGEMENT

Funding provided by Bundesanstalt für Materialforschung und-prüfung (BAM) is gratefully acknowledged.

REFERENCES

Berners-Lee, T., Hendler, J., and Lassila, O. (2001). "The semantic web," Scientific american (284:5), pp. 34–43.

Chen, Y., Schilling, M., Hartrott, P. von, Nasrabadi, H. B., Skrotzki, B., and Olbricht, J. (2022). "Ontopanel: A Tool for Domain Experts Facilitating Visual Ontology Development and Mapping for FAIR Data Sharing in Materials Testing," Integrating Materials and Manufacturing Innovation (11:4), pp. 545–556.

Damljanovic, D., Agatonovic, M., and Cunningham, H. (2012). "FREyA: An interactive way of querying Linked Data using natural language," in The Semantic Web: ESWC 2011 Workshops: ESWC 2011 Work- shops, Heraklion, Greece, May 29-30, 2011, Revised Selected Papers 8, Springer, pp. 125–138.

Eloundou, T., Manning, S., Mishkin, P., and Rock, D. (2023). "Gpts are gpts: An early look at the labor market impact potential of large language models," arXiv preprint arXiv:2303.10130 ().

Ferré, S. (2017). "Sparklis: An expressive query builder for SPARQL endpoints with guidance in natural language," Semantic Web (8:3), pp. 405–418.

Gruber, T. R. (1993). "A translation approach to portable ontology specifications," Knowledge acquisition (5:2), pp. 199–220.

Himanen, L., Geurts, A., Foster, A. S., and Rinke, P. (2019). "Data-driven materials science: status, challenges, and perspectives," Advanced Science (6:21), p. 1900808.

Huschka, M., Dlugosch, M., Friedmann, V., Trelles, E. G., Hoschke, K., Klotz, U. E., Patil, S., Preußner, J., Schweizer, C., and Tiberto, D. (2022). "The "AluTrace" Use Case: Harnessing Lightweight Design Potentials via the Materials Data Space®," Workshop: Data Spaces & Semantic Interoperability ().

Marlet, O., Francart, T., Markhoff, B., and Rodier, X. (2019). "OpenArchaeo for usable semantic interoperability," in ODOCH 2019@ CAiSE 2019,

Soru, T., Marx, E., Moussallem, D., Publio, G., Valdestilhas, A., Esteves, D., and Neto, C. B. (2017). "SPARQL as a Foreign Language," arXiv preprint arXiv:1708.07624 ().

Soru, T., Marx, E., Valdestilhas, A., Esteves, D., Moussallem, D., and Publio, G. (2018). "Neural machine translation for query construction and composition," arXiv preprint arXiv:1806.10478 ().

Valdestilhas, A., Bayerlein, B., Moreno Torres, B., Zia, G. A. J., and Muth, T. (n.d.). "The Intersection Between Semantic Web and Materials Science," Advanced Intelligent Systems (n/a:n/a), p. 2300051. eprint: https://onlinelibrary.wiley.com/doi/pdf/10.1002/aisy.202300051.

Völker, C., Kruschwitz, S., Moreno Torres, B., Firdous, R., Zia, G., and Stephan, D. (2022). "Accelerating the search for alkali-activated cements with sequential learning," in FIB Conference 2022, pp. 1–9.

Völker, C., Torres, B. M., Zia, G. A., Rafia Firdousc, T., Böhmerd, F., Stephanc, D., and Kruschwitz, S. (2023). "Searching for the needle in the haystack - how machine learning couldhelp to find ideal sustainable building materials," Proceedings of the RSC-CMSS23 Conference, Rabat ().

Wilkinson, M. D., Dumontier, M., Aalbersberg, I. J., Appleton, G., Axton, M., Baak, A., Blomberg, N., Boiten, J.-W., Silva Santos, L. B. da, Bourne, P. E., et al. (2016). "The FAIR Guiding Principles for scientific data management and stewardship," Scientific data (3:1), pp. 1–9.

Zunger, A. (2018). "Inverse design in search of materials with target functionalities," Nature Reviews Chemistry (2:4), p. 0121.

THE SOLID DEVELOPMENT EXPERIENCE: GIVING DEVELOPERS THE TOOLS THEY NEED

Koen Luyten, Gregory Van Seghbroeck, Wannes Kerckhove, Thomas Dupont,
Filip De Turck and Bruno Volckaert
Ghent University - IMEC
Technologiepark-Zwijnaarde 126, B-9052 Ghent, Belgium

ABSTRACT

The Solid protocol aims to let people take back control over their personal data by allowing them to store this data in personal data vaults called pods. While this has advantages in terms of data ownership, it also imposes new challenges when developing applications that use the protocol for data storage. Some auxiliary software libraries already exist in most popular programming languages for handling functions like authentication or basic file management, however, to the best of our knowledge, there is currently no toolkit available that provides a more integrated developer environment with features like data validation, code completion, and package management. In this paper a Solid Development Experience or SDX is presented, which uses SHACL shapes and GraphQL as the basis to provide a type-safe programming environment for both Javascript and Java projects. SHACL shapes can be downloaded and installed, after which GraphQL schemas can be generated based on them. Next, queries can be defined on these schemas to retrieve RDF data stored in a pod. The use of SHACL and GraphQL allows a mapping of dynamically typed RDF models to statically typed Java/Typescript constructs, with the goal of leveraging full type-safety when interfacing with RDF data. This mapping was found to incur a limited overhead during performance testing, the results of which are presented in this paper. Additionally, a detailed overview of the main components that make up the SDX and the design and technology choices that were made for each of them is provided.

KEYWORDS

Linked Data, Solid, Software Development, RDF, SHACL, GraphQL

1. INTRODUCTION

The Solid protocol ('Solid Protocol', 2022) is a proposal that aims to let people take back control over their data. This is achieved by storing personal data inside so-called pods, which are personal data vaults of which an individual can have one or more, instead of the current situation where almost all personal data is stored in data silos controlled by private corporations. While the use of Solid pods for data storage provides advantages in the sense of improved data ownership of end-users personal data, it also represents a significant shift in the way applications are developed for this new protocol as opposed to the current paradigm of centralized data storage (from the point of view of the private corporation holding the data). One of the major differences is the use of RDF as the main data format to store and communicate data between the pod and the application. While RDF as a data format has many advantages because of its graph approach to storing information, it poses some unique challenges precisely because of this graph-oriented format. An additional problem arises from the fact that there is currently no system to efficiently query a Solid pod server side. When trying to build applications using a new protocol like this, efficient tooling is a major factor in deciding the success of software projects (Maxwell, Van Wassenhove and Dutta, 1996). These tools can range from advanced auto-completion features to entire frameworks which provide an abstraction over lower-level concepts, so developers do not need to worry about them anymore. In this paper, such a toolkit is presented: the Solid Development Experience (SDX)[1]. It can be used for developing applications on top of the Solid protocol in both the Java and Javascript ecosystem and contains several features which contribute to a more productive development experience and in

[1] https://github.com/SolidLabResearch/sdx,
https://github.com/SolidLabResearch/solidlab-sdx-jdk

turn greater adoption of the protocol outside of academia (Von Nostitz-Wallwitz, Krüger and Leich, 2018). Its main feature is the use of ('Shapes Constraint Language (SHACL)', 2017) shapes to generate a ('GraphQL', 2018) schema, which can then be used to query a Solid pod client side and map the dynamically typed RDF data to statically typed Java or Typescript constructs, providing a type-safe environment when interfacing with a Solid pod.

First, an overview is given of the related work and how the work presented differs. In Section 3, the main components of the SDX are reviewed in detail, highlighting their benefits to developers, and evaluating their performance in the prototype implementation where applicable. Afterwards the SDX is discussed as a whole, providing insight into why certain design choices were made over others. Finally, a conclusion is given along with a look at the future work ahead.

2. RELATED WORK

While there have been some efforts to provide tools for developing on the Solid protocol specifically, like the libraries listed on the official Solid project webpage[2] or those from Inrupt[3], these all have a different scope, mostly solving one specific problem, instead of providing a fully integrated solution. Some provide a basic client for interacting with files on the pod, others provide authentication functionality for Solid OIDC, with additional, more general linked data libraries like LDFlex or Tripledoc being suggested to process the RDF data stored on the pod. The work presented here tries to go beyond the current state of the art by providing a more integrated developer experience, which provides tools for both interacting with the pod in an easy, straightforward way, as well as managing the linked data resources retrieved from them in an accessible and typesafe manner.

(Leinberger et al., 2019) is similar in that it recognises the ability of SHACL shapes to be used not only to validate linked data, but also for type checking program code. Our methodology differs, because it defines GraphQL queries and types based on pre-existing shapes, while Leinberger infers shapes from SPARQL queries and uses these inferred shapes to generate types against which program code can be checked. Their formal underpinning of such a type checking system based on SHACL shapes, with a proof of type safety, also differs from our more pragmatic approach of using existing tools like GraphQL schemas to provide a type-safe programming environment. Instead of having to implement a type checking system from scratch based on this formal logic, we can leverage such systems for GraphQL which are already available in most IDEs.

The work done by (Angele et al., 2022) is of note because it shows that GraphQL can be used to retrieve data from arbitrary SPARQL endpoints, without much loss of expressiveness or performance, while being less complex than SPARQL.

Several commercial graph databases offer various levels of support for using GraphQL to query RDF data. Although they are not applicable in the context of development for the Solid protocol, they show the relevance of being able to effectively query RDF data using GraphQL. Stardog[4] offer a graph database called the "Enterprise Knowledge Platform", which as of version 5.1 supports the use of schema enforced GraphQL queries. Although the data contained in the database is still schema-less RDF data, when queried through the provided GraphQL endpoint, the returned data is validated against a GraphQL endpoint and serialized as GraphQL data. A similar commercial solution is "TopBraid Enterprise Data Governance (EDG)" by TopQuadrant[5], which stores RDF data and allows for the definition of data schemas in RDF Schema, SHACL, and OWL as well as GraphQL schemas, after which the data can be queried using GraphQL.

The GOO (which stands for "Graph Oriented Objects") framework (Salvadores et al., 2013) is similar in its effort to provide a framework to abstract away most of the complexity querying RDF data by using a REST interface. This differs from the approach presented here, which heavily relies on the use of GraphQL.

---

[2] https://solidproject.org/developers/tools/
[3] https://www.inrupt.com/products/dev-tools
[4] https://www.stardog.com/
[5] https://www.topquadrant.com/resources/querying-topbraid-edg-with-graphql

3. SOLID DEVELOPER EXPERIENCE

3.1 Overall Description

When developing an application on the Solid protocol using the SDX, one of the first steps is determining the application's data model. Application data is preferably stored on a pod as RDF, in fact this is one of its main advantages, as it allows for greater data interoperability and referring to data stored in other locations, which can be other solid pods or other hosts, through URI's.

RDF data, although structured, is not necessarily validated. In its most basic form, it describes a knowledge graph as a set of triples, but it gives no guarantee about which triples should or should not be included, and what datatypes should be used as the object of those triples. The Shape Constraint Language (SHACL) is a language which allows for the validation of an RDF graph against a set of constraints, called shapes. These shapes can be used to describe our data model. To facilitate the use of shapes in this way, a Shape Catalog was built, which indexes an arbitrary number of shape packages, which bundle related shapes. The catalog should replace the current situation, where shape files are published at ad-hoc locations and developers are mostly left to their own devices to find them. The catalog can then be queried for the desired shapes or shape packages, after which they can be easily installed into a development environment along with their related shapes as illustrated in step 1 of Fig. 1. This enables developers to install shapes from trusted sources with the possibility of features like semantic versioning and dependency management for dependent shapes.

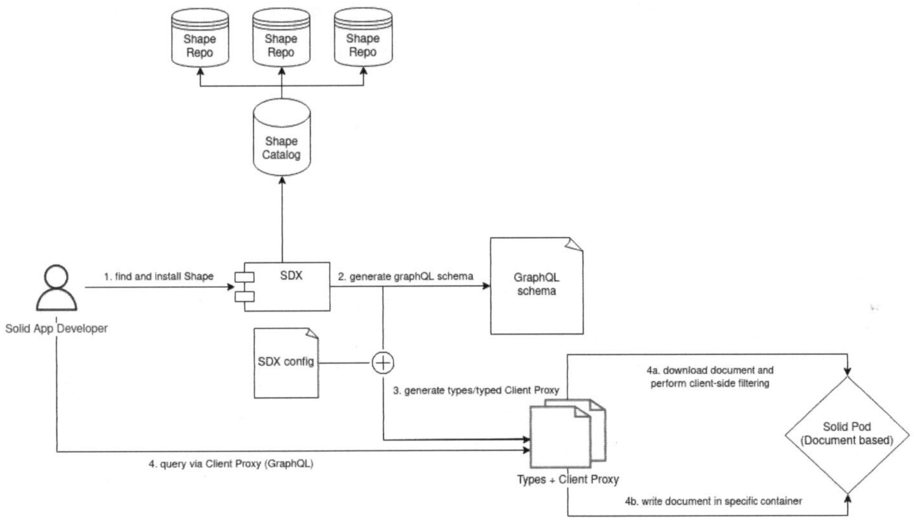

Figure 1. High level overview of the SDX workflow

While SHACL shapes can be used to validate RDF data, this does not automatically enable querying of the data. GraphQL is a query language for API's, as well as a runtime for executing these queries using a type system based on a predefined schema. Based on the installed shapes, the SDX generates a GraphQL schema, which defines an object type for each shape, shown in step 2 and 3 of Fig. 1. These object types can then be used in the development environment as regular domain objects with full type safety.

Finally, queries can be written to fetch, store or mutate RDF data on the pod. These queries are handled by a client proxy, as shown in step 4a en 4b of Fig. 1, which interfaces with the pod to retrieve the applicable RDF document and performs the actual selection or mutation of the contained graph client side. This client proxy is the main interaction point with the SDX in a developer's own code. It can be instantiated in a projects code, after which the queries ran against it return fully typed results, based on the object types defined in the GraphQL schema. Fig. 2 gives an example using a SHACL shape, which describes a simple contacts shape. This shape is transformed into a GraphQL Contact object type that can finally be used to define queries against.

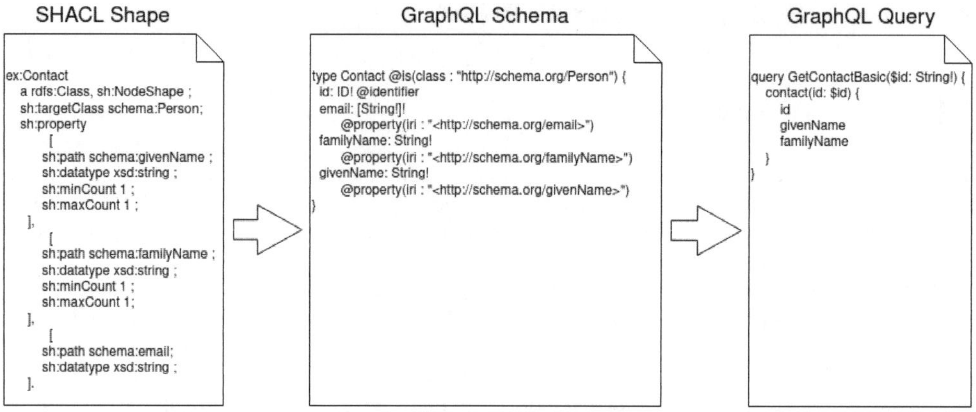

Figure 2. Example of the transformation of SHACL shape for contact data into a GraphQL schema. The type declared in the schema can be used in the definition of GraphQL queries

The implementation differs slightly for the Java and Javascript platform. For the Java platform implementation, a Gradle plugin was chosen, which is a popular build tool for the Java ecosystem[6]. This plugin downloads the shapes and generates the GraphQL schema file. Afterwards, the Apollo Gradle plugin is activated by the SDX plugin to generate Java class files based on the GraphQL schema. These generated classes can be used by the developer to define additional queries, which are executed by the client proxy. The client proxy queries the pod on predetermined locations, using a URL the developer provides at the instantiation of the client. For Javascript developers, the SDX is made available as an npm package, which can be run using a Command Line Interface (CLI) to download shape files and generate the GraphQL schema6. Based on this schema and any additional queries the developer defines, a fully-typed Solid client is generated that can query predetermined locations on the pod, using a URL the developer provides when the client is created. At the moment, this is the only way to determine where to fetch or store a document on the pod, although more advanced resolvers are on the roadmap.

3.2 Shape Catalog

To facilitate the use of reusable shapes, a Shape Catalog is used as an index for reusable shape packages. A shape package is a collection of SHACL shapes that are intended to be used together. At the moment, developers can add a package to the catalog by uploading a turtle file containing the SHACL shapes to be included in the package, although the indexing of complete repositories has been planned for future development. The catalog can easily be queried to discover specific shape packages or packages containing a specific shape, download and install them in the development environment. This is done in a way that is similar to how each respective ecosystem handles dependency management. The Gradle plugin has configuration options where necessary shapes can be declared as either part of a shape package from the catalog using its catalog id or from another legacy source using a URI for the shape file, while the CLI for the Typescript ecosystem has built-in commands which allow for the querying and installation of packages from the catalog directly from the command line.

3.3 GraphQL Schema

The generated GraphQL schema is the basis for most functionality of the SDX, in both the Java and Javascript implementation. They are used to leverage full type safety in the programming environment and to write queries and mutations for the data in the pod. GraphQL schemas are generated by parsing installed SHACL shapes using the Apache Jena[7] libraries or the N3[8] libraries for the Java implementation or the Javascript

[6] https://gradle.org/
[7] https://jena.apache.org/
[8] https://github.com/rdfjs/N3.js/

implementation, respectively, after which the schema is defined using the standard GraphQL API for programmatically generating schemas. The GraphQL object types are generated for each SHACL NodeShape defined in the SHACL file. Each of this NodeShape's properties is translated into a GraphQL field with the name corresponding to the property's path, minus its IRI prefix. RDF literals are represented using the applicable data types in GraphQL. Nested shapes are allowed, but only if their respective SHACL shapes are also installed in the project, otherwise they are ignored in the generation of the schema. Because the possible properties of a given Shape therefore correspond either to GraphQL primitive types or other SHACL shapes, we can easily generate a GraphQL object type based on any arbitrary SHACL shape, provided we have access to any necessary nested SHACL shapes as well. This shows that GraphQL can easily model any arbitrary SHACL shape. Therefore, this abstraction comes at no cost regarding expressiveness.

3.4 Proxy Client

The main entry point for the SDX in an applications code is the proxy client. It stores or fetches the necessary RDF data from the pods, after which it performs the requested query client side and returns their result. At the moment, the prototype implementation requires a developer to provide a static URL from which the RDF data can be fetched or stored. The target of this URL is a Solid resource on the pod. Solid resources are published in a hierarchical manner. A resource can be either a container or a document. A container is defined by a URL ending in a '/', so as to resemble a directory in a traditional path, whereas a document is defined by a URL lacking such a trailing slash, therefore referring to a specific document in the parent container. When storing data in document mode, the client proxy stores all the data validated by a certain shape in one document at the provided URL, whereas in container mode, the proxy creates a separate document for each shape in the provided container. Although the current implementation is limited to resolving the location of the relevant documents on the pod through a developer provided URL, the SDX can be easily modified to use more advanced resolvers, as will be discussed in the future work section of the paper.

3.5 Drawback: RDF Marshalling into GraphQL

Using GraphQL in this manner has one important drawback: at runtime the marshalling of RDF data into GraphQL types might entail significant overhead, when compared to the traditional approach of using RDF wrappers like Apache Jena. To evaluate this, a limited performance test was performed on the Java implementation to compare it to a baseline implementation which does not perform such marshalling, but instead queries the retrieved RDF graph directly using Apache Jena.

A micro benchmark was run on the Java implementation of the SDX. For the experiment, an RDF document containing contact data for 896 contacts was queried for one specific contact, using both the SDX and a baseline implementation. The baseline implementation only fetches a document and queries it using traditional Jena methods. The average execution time was then compared for each method. The results can be found in Table 1.

Table 1. Result of SDX micro benchmark. the experiment was run for a set amount of time, which explains the different number of samples given the mean execution time of each

Implementation	Mean time (ms)	Standard deviation (ms)	# Samples
SDX	31.43	6.93	812
Baseline	18.43	5.08	1373

A t-test confirmed the means for the two are different with 99.9% confidence. Therefore a 13 ms (70%) overhead resulting from the marshalling of the RDF data into type-safe objects is observed, for the Java implementation. The implications of these results are analysed in detail in the discussion part of this paper.

4. DISCUSSION

This section presents the major design choices that were made throughout development and explains the reasoning for them.

4.1 General Design Choices

The first major design choice was which platforms and programming languages to support. One of the main requirements was providing support for both backend and frontend development, with the possibility for two separate implementations. For supporting frontend development, this meant the decision quickly fell on the Javascript ecosystem, which is by far the most popular frontend ecosystem, and it is also used heavily by the Solid community already (more specifically: the statically typed Typescript). Since the advent of Node.js, Javascript can also be used for backend development. Its popularity in that context is not as dominant however, and to increase the possible reach of the toolkit, it was decided to build a separate additional implementation for the Java platform, as this is a very popular platform for backend development, with the additional benefit that this covers the Kotlin and Scala programming languages as well, the former of which is also popular for development of mobile applications on the Android platform.

For the actual packaging of the toolkit, and how it would be offered, the decision fell on a npm package for the Javascript implementation and a Gradle plugin for the Java implementation. The choice for npm was obvious given its popularity, ease of use, and heavy integration in the Javascript ecosystem. For the Java ecosystem, the choice was between a Maven or a Gradle plugin. Gradle was chosen because it has slightly better integrations with the Kotlin programming language, which was used for the implementation, but possibility of such a plug-in in the future is not yet ruled out, given that Maven is slightly more popular as a build tool.

4.2 SHACL and Shape Catalog

After determining the supported platforms and the packaging of the toolkit, the focus turned more on its inner workings. First, the choice to work with a shape-based system. The Solid protocol is heavily focused on RDF data, and therefore it was decided to focus on this for the toolkit as well. (Verborgh, 2023) has written extensively about the advantages of using shapes when developing for the Solid Protocol and since shape languages like SHACL and SHeX are explicitly designed for validation of RDF and don't need additional semantics like some of the attempts that were made to allow for defining constraints in OWL (Tao *et al.*, 2010), they were more suited for this application. SHACL was ultimately picked, as it is a W3C recommendation as opposed to SHeX.

To increase the reusability of these SHACL shapes, a Shape Catalog was built. Its purpose is analogous to software package repositories, like npm or Maven Central, or container image registries like Docker Hub. The use of such repositories is beneficial to both individual developers and the programming language ecosystem in a variety of ways. First of all, it improves productivity and code quality through reuse of existing software assets (Chowdhury et al., 2022). Second, the ubiquity of such reusable assets can be a driving factor for the popularity of a programming language ecosystem, as has been the case with npm for the Node.js ecosystem (Cox, 2019) or The Comprehensive R Archive Network (CRAN) in the R ecosystem (Bogart et al., 2016). Finally, the availability of a multitude of reusable assets with similar functionality from which developers can choose, creates a healthy competition between them, which in turn results in high quality reusable assets (Bogart et al., 2016).

4.3 GraphQL

Arguably the main feature of the SDX is the generation of the GraphQL schema on which the other features rely. The choice for GraphQL as such a central part of the architecture, is the result of weighing many factors: the availability of supporting libraries, ease of use for the developer and the ability to query retrieved data client side.

SPARQL was considered, as it is also a W3C recommendation. It does not provide additional tooling, however, that could be leveraged for features like type checking program code. GraphQL can be used to abstract away the complexity of SPARQL, without losing much functionality (Angele *et al.*, 2022).

Furthermore, GraphQL has been shown (Brito and Valente, 2020) to be relatively easy to learn for both experienced and novice developers, with the type safety of GraphQL being mentioned as one of its main advantages. This type safety is also one of the main advantages leveraged by the SDX, as traditional libraries for interfacing with RDF like Apache Jena or N3 only provide a wrapper around the data, with no guarantees about the actual structure of the contained data. Programming in a type-safe environment has been shown to increase productivity and leads to less code smells and error-prone code (Bogner and Merkel, 2022). Moreover, it allows us to leverage the tools of most modern IDEs for code completion and suggestion, which also increases developer productivity (Maxwell, Van Wassenhove and Dutta, 1996).

An additional advantage of using GraphQL in this manner, is that it provides an abstraction for the data retrieval process, similar to what most Object Relational Mapping (ORM) libraries provide for the persistence of software objects in relational databases. This abstraction frees developers from having to write code to parse and query the raw data returned from the pod and provides a clear and concise interface to interact with the data, similar to the GOO framework for the Ruby ecosystem (Salvadores et al., 2013).

Finally, GraphQL also has wide support for most programming languages, providing libraries we could easily re-use to implement client side querying in both the Java and Javascript implementations, and for most modern IDE's providing functionality like syntax checking and code completion of the GraphQL documents themselves. Ultimately, the combination of these factors led to the decision for GraphQL as the central technology on which the SDX relies.

While the overhead associated with using GraphQL in this way as measured in a preliminary benchmark is not insignificant, the tested code was a very specific part of application code. Processing of the queried data may result in far longer runtimes, relative to which a mean difference in query time of 13 ms might not be impactful. The difference is also still well below the threshold for human responsiveness, which is around 300 ms (Nielsen, 2010), so when displaying the results of the query, there is no perceivable difference in speed between the two implementations. Considering this, we conclude that the slight overhead (in absolute terms) is worth the trade-off considering all the advantages the use of GraphQL has.

5. CONCLUSION AND FUTURE WORK

The ability to use installed SHACL shapes to seamlessly transform a developers programming environment into one that is type-safe and supports most modern IDE features, while also abstracting away aspects of the Solid protocol with which most developers might not be familiar, removes a major hurdle for the widespread adoption of and development on the Solid protocol itself. While still in a prototype phase, the implementation of the SDX shows very promising results, both performance wise and in usability.

For future work, the ability to infer a SHACL shape from a GraphQL schema is worth investigating. This allows developers to define and upload new shapes to the Catalog when existing ones are not sufficient for their needs, without having to write SHACL files themselves and it could even be leveraged by existing applications which already use GraphQL to integrate the application with Solid. Another focal point is the implementation of more advanced resolvers than the current static resolver used by the prototype implementation of the client proxy. The plan is to integrate support for both the type index and the shape tree specifications, as they are compatible with the Solid specification as is. This would allow the proxy client to resolve the location of documents associated with certain shapes on the pod automatically. However, the possibility for more advanced interfaces which might become part of the Solid specification (Dedecker et al., 2022), is also considered. This is why special attention was paid to the ability to easily plug in more advanced resolvers, anticipating future developments. Finally, benchmarking the toolkit in both the Java and Javascript implementation, to get a more detailed understanding of its performance at runtime as well as performing usability studies to evaluate the increased ease of development are on the roadmap.

ACKNOWLEDGEMENT

Supported by SolidLab Vlaanderen (Flemish Government, EWI and RRF project VV023/10). I would like to thank Jasper Vaneessen from SolidLab for his contributions to the Shape Catalog.

REFERENCES

Angele, K. et al. (2022) 'GraphSPARQL: a GraphQL interface for linked data', in Proceedings of the 37th ACM/SIGAPP Symposium on Applied Computing. SAC '22: The 37th ACM/SIGAPP Symposium on Applied Computing, Virtual Event: ACM, pp. 778–785. Available at: https://doi.org/10.1145/3477314.3507655.

Bogart, C. et al. (2016) 'How to break an API: cost negotiation and community values in three software ecosystems', in Proceedings of the 2016 24th ACM SIGSOFT International Symposium on Foundations of Software Engineering. FSE'16: 24nd ACM SIGSOFT International Symposium on the Foundations of Software Engineering, Seattle WA USA: ACM, pp. 109–120. Available at: https://doi.org/10.1145/2950290.2950325.

Bogner, J. and Merkel, M. (2022) 'To type or not to type?: a systematic comparison of the software quality of JavaScript and typescript applications on GitHub', in Proceedings of the 19th International Conference on Mining Software Repositories. MSR '22: 19th International Conference on Mining Software Repositories, Pittsburgh Pennsylvania: ACM, pp. 658–669. Available at: https://doi.org/10.1145/3524842.3528454.

Brito, G. and Valente, M.T. (2020) 'REST vs GraphQL: A Controlled Experiment'. arXiv. Available at: http://arxiv.org/abs/2003.04761 (Accessed: 24 May 2023).

Chowdhury, M.A.R. et al. (2022) 'On the Untriviality of Trivial Packages: An Empirical Study of npm JavaScript Packages', IEEE Transactions on Software Engineering, 48(8), pp. 2695–2708. Available at: https://doi.org/10.1109/TSE.2021.3068901.

Cox, R. (2019) 'Surviving software dependencies', Communications of the ACM, 62(9), pp. 36–43. Available at: https://doi.org/10.1145/3347446.

Dedecker, R. et al. (2022) 'What's in a Pod? – A knowledge graph interpretation for the Solid ecosystem', in. Online, pp. 81–96.

'GraphQL' (2018). Facebook Inc. Available at: https://spec.graphql.org/June2018/.

Leinberger, M. et al. (2019) 'Type Checking Program Code using SHACL (Extended Version)'. arXiv. Available at: http://arxiv.org/abs/1907.00855 (Accessed: 24 May 2023).

Maxwell, K.D., Van Wassenhove, L. and Dutta, S. (1996) 'Software development productivity of European space, military, and industrial applications', IEEE Transactions on Software Engineering, 22(10), pp. 706–718. Available at: https://doi.org/10.1109/32.544349.

Nielsen, J. (2010) Usability engineering. 3.Nachdr. Amsterdam Heidelberg: Kaufmann.

Salvadores, M. et al. (2013) 'Boosting RDF Adoption in Ruby with Goo', in WaSABi@ISWC.

'Shapes Constraint Language (SHACL)' (2017). W3C. Available at: https://www.w3.org/TR/shacl/.

'Solid Protocol' (2022). W3C. Available at: https://solidproject.org/TR/protocol.

Tao, J. et al. (2010) 'Integrity Constraints in OWL', in Proceedings of the National Conference on Artificial Intelligence.

Verborgh, R. (2023) 'Shapes for machine-readable and -writable data', Shaping Linked Data apps, 1 May. Available at: https://ruben.verborgh.org/blog/2019/06/17/shaping-linked-data-apps/#shapes.

Von Nostitz-Wallwitz, I., Krüger, J. and Leich, T. (2018) 'Towards improving industrial adoption: the choice of programming languages and development environments', in Proceedings of the 5th International Workshop on Software Engineering Research and Industrial Practice. ICSE '18: 40th International Conference on Software Engineering, Gothenburg Sweden: ACM, pp. 10–17. Available at: https://doi.org/10.1145/3195546.3195548.

TOWARDS A MACHINE-LEARNING ARCHITECTURE FOR EFFICIENT RESOURCE MANAGEMENT

Alexandros Kostopoulos[1*], Ioannis P. Chochliouros[1], John Vardakas[2], Christos Verikoukis[2,3], Arifur Rahman[4], Andrea P. Guevara[5], Robbert Beerten[5], Philippe Chanclou[6], Simon Pryor[7], Emmanouel Varvarigos[8] and Polyzois Soumplis[8]

[1]Hellenic Telecommunications Organization S.A., 99 Kifissias Avenue, Maroussi, Athens, Greece

[2]IQUADRAT Informatica, Calle Doctor Rizal 10, Barcelona, Spain

[3]University of Patras, University campus, 26504, Rio, Patras, Greece

[4]IS-Wireless, Ulica Pulawska 45, Warsaw, Poland

[5]Katholieke Universiteit Leuven, Oude Markt 13, Leuven, Belgium

[6]Orange S.A., Rue Olivier de Serres 78, Paris, France

[7]Accelleran, Heerstraat 12, Geel, Belgium

[8]Institute of Communications and Computer Systems (ICCS) Patission 42, Athens, Greece

ABSTRACT

5G mobile networks will soon be available to handle all types of applications and to provide services to massive numbers of users. In this complex and dynamic network ecosystem, an end-to-end performance analysis and optimisation will be "key" features to effectively manage the diverse requirements imposed by multiple vertical industries over the same shared infrastructure. To enable such a challenging vision, the MARSAL EU-funded project (MARSAL, 2021) targets the development and evaluation of a complete framework for the management and orchestration of network resources in 5G and beyond by utilizing a converged optical-wireless network infrastructure in the access and fronthaul/midhaul segments. In this paper, we present the network architecture of the MARSAL, as well as how the cell-free experimentation scenarios are mapped to the considered architecture.

KEYWORDS

Cell-Free, Distributed Cloud, Network Automation, Machine Learning, Secure Multi-Tenancy

1. INTRODUCTION

Communication networks currently undergo a high number of structural and functional changes that are associated with the need to support current and future demands (e.g., mobile traffic is expected to grow three-fold within 2025, as a result of predicted 10 million devices per km^2 and 100 billion devices worldwide), and with the commitment for the provision of ultra-low latency and reliability (Cisco, 2019). With the advancement of technology, the communication nodes will be inseparable from human social activities. To truly realize the diverse connection and interaction needs "at any-time and anywhere", future networks need to have specific characteristics, such as: Omnipresence (covering air, ground, space and sea); All-in-one (Internet of Everything); Omniscience (with the help of various sensors), and All-purpose (based on big data and deep learning). The same circumstances are also forecasted for other fields, such as Industry 4.0, health sectors,

*Corresponding author email: alexkosto@oteresearch.gr

manufacturing industries, and autonomous industries, where revolutionary changes are underway. Another major challenge of the future 6G networks is to reach climate goals by reducing CO2 emissions. This will be achieved through improved operational and management efficiency and energy consumption reduction.

To tackle these challenges, several steps should be taken from the perspective of network concepts and technological aspects, to ensure economic developments, reliability and increased energy efficiency (Chochliouros, 2021). Key advances are required both at the network design and network management levels, as well as at the network security level to accommodate highly dynamic traffic demand, achieve energy reduction and provide cost-effective multi-level resource pooling in a secured way. Specifically, the network should support multiple distributed edge nodes and a multitude of access points (APs) coordinated by entities in a low-cost and near-zero latency manner. A unified and hierarchical infrastructure is essential to provide intelligent management of communication, computation and storage resources. The incorporation of efficient Machine-Learning (ML) algorithms (Boutaba, 2021) can further improve network efficiency. Additionally, infrastructure sharing is a sustainable way of lowering the network's capital and operating expenditures. Furthermore, support of multiple tenants is the key enabler of the new sharing economy business models in the telecommunication industry. Novel mechanisms for resourceful and efficient management of shared networks are necessary to enable a plethora of use-cases and industry verticals targeted in beyond-5G (B5G) and 6G systems.

In this context, MARSAL proposes a novel converged optical-wireless configuration based on the Cell-Free (CF) concept that targets flexible connectivity of a massive number of Radio Units (RUs) and aims to unlock the potential of user-centric CF deployments in 6G networks, while aligned with the O-RAN initiative (ORAN, 2023). The paper is organized as follows: In *Section 2*, we present the MARSAL overall architecture. *Section 3* presents use cases enabling cell-free networking in dense and ultra-dense hotspot areas. In particular, *Section 3.1* focuses on dense user-generated content distribution with mmWave fronthauling, while *Section 3.2* presents ultra-dense video traffic delivery in a converged fixed-mobile network. Each experimentation scenario is mapped to the MARSAL architecture. We conclude our remarks in *Section 4*. We built on our previous paper (Kostopoulos, 2022), where we presented the main use cases and the involved stakeholders. Our innovation is focused on how these use cases are applied to our proposed ML network architecture.

2. NETWORK ARCHITECTURE

The proposed approach is illustrated in Fig.1 and consists of an evolved 3GPP NG-RAN (3GPP, 2021), (3GPP, 2017) that is extended with emerging CF technologies, and of an innovative optical transport domain that deploys a distributed edge infrastructure with Data Centres (DCs) structured in 2 tiers, featuring Regional Edge and Radio Edge nodes.

At the radio edge, the proposed radio network configuration is based on two radio access solutions. The first solution is based on the interconnection of multiple RUs (Radio Units) with the DU (Distributed Unit) via a sequential fronthaul (upper right part of Fig.1) which then iteratively decode the received signal. This approach aims at addressing the of limited fronthaul capacity at the DU; thus, enabling CF deployment in beyond 5G RANs (Radio Access Networks) (Saha, 2018), (Agarwal, 2021), (Niknam, 2022), based on the utilization of dynamic cluster-formation algorithms. The dynamic feature of such RU clustering algorithms is based on the dissaggregation of the CPU from the CF literature into multiple DUs and the Near-RT RIC, which will enable the support of distributed computation and coordination between RUs and between DUs. Under this networking configuration, clusters of RUs, connected to multiple DUs, jointly transmit and receive users' signals. MARSAL is the first to address inter-DU and RU-DU coordination, while also considering fronthaul and midhaul constraints. The optimal cooperation levels between RUs and DUs and between DUs can be guaranteed through the application of dynamic adaptability algorithms of the involved entities' coordination levels.

The second solution for MARSAL's radio edge is based on an mmWave Hybrid Fronthaul for CF networks. Massive MIMO fronthauling solutions have been already proposed in the literature (Demirhan, 2022) targeting efficient interconnection of multiple RUs to the CPU, by considering CF-based network configurations (Blandino, 2019). MARSAL's novel Hybrid MIMO fronthauling approach targets to provide support to CF networks through advanced beamforming solutions. In this way, various RU topologies can be supported, where RUs can be reassigned to different DUs on demand. For the provision of this point-to-multipoint (PtMP) connectivity, MARSAL targets a new design of a mmWave radio node, by utilizing RFIC (Radio Frequency

Integrated Circuit) mmWave beamforming transceiver and phased-array antenna module (Zhang, 2018). In this way, diverse innovations can be provided by the MARSAL partners, related to optimal RU deployment strategies, new formulations of dynamic RU clustering and adaptive coordination problems, and studying the effect of functional splitting in the context of the CF fronthauling compatible with 3GPP's scope. As in the first radio-edge solution, MARSAL's mmWave Hybrid fronthaul approach also considers inter-DU coordination, targeting to introduce the interface for direct interconnection of DUs for the first time.

At the regional node, two SDN (Software Defined Network) controllers are considered, for managing the optical and wireless networking resources, respectively. The controllers at the edge are coordinated by the Network-Slicing-as-a-Service (NSaaS) subsystem at the core-tier Network Function Virtualization Orchestrator (NFVO), communicating via the OR-Vi interfaces (ETSI, 2018). Thus, intelligent traffic management and load balancing among PtP (Point to Point) and PtMP traffic via the appropriate scheduling of the two SDN controllers can be implemented, while improved power consumption can be achieved via traffic rerouting and shutting down individual SFP-OLTs (Small-Formfactor Pluggable – Optical Line Terminals) during light loads. Additionally, the implementation of predictive slice reconfiguration that provides traffic fluctuations' prediction can trigger slice reconfiguration, thus increasing statistical multiplexing while minimizing the impact on Service Level Agreement (SLAs).

At the core, the orchestrator is integrated to the NFV infrastructure and supports coordinated resource allocation for MEC (Multi-access Edge Computing) applications and network functions by coordinating two diverse management and orchestration subsystems (i.e., the NFVO and the MEC Application Orchestrator (MEAO)) (ETSI, 2018). Moreover, MARSAL aims at achieving self-driven and closed-loop autonomy for the Virtual Elastic Infrastructure to enable dynamic orchestration and management of networking and computing resources. To this end, MARSAL incorporates a distributed approach that involves Analytic Engines (AEs) at all tiers of the Edge infrastructure, and Decision Engines (DEs) in the two Core-Tier orchestration subsystems, targeting to overcome the isolation and underutilization of resources deployed at Edge nodes, through resource sharing.

For the network security pillar of MARSAL, three main contributions are considered in the overall architecture. Firstly, the solution for private and secure exchange of data among tenants through decentralized framework for confidentiality and trust that is based on novel data privacy representation techniques that are integrated into a smart contract platform. Secondly, the solution for ensuring data security through different policies and distributed storage of the data. Finally, the solution for network security protection through two different technologies that allow the analysis of the data transferred by the network in real time. Thus, MARSAL do not limit itself to the typical network security (also covered using accelerated hardware ML), but it also aims at protecting the data stored in the cloud, allowing secure multi-party computation and distributed data storage, while also it allows the cooperation among tenants by allowing them to automatically sign smart contracts and share data in a privacy preserving way.

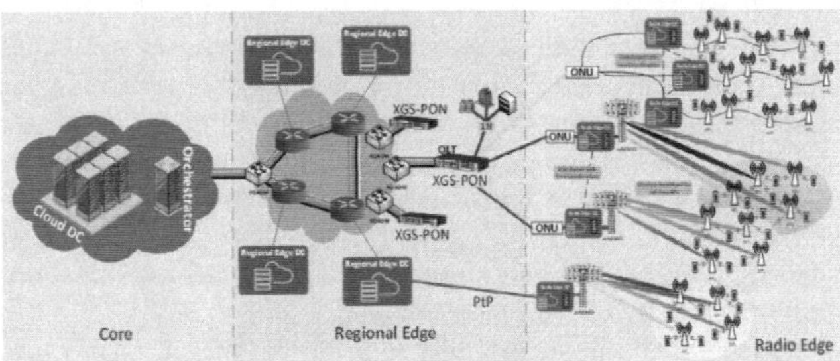

Figure 1. The MARSAL network architecture

3. CELL-FREE NETWORKING IN ULTRA-DENSE HOTSPOT AREAS

During high-popularity events, both indoors and outdoors, a large number of users tend to stream high volumes of content from multiple handheld devices, thus creating a heavy burden to the network infrastructure both in the uplink and in the downlink. In CF massive MIMO, users are simultaneously served by multiple cooperating

RUs (with a low number of antennas) instead of associating each user terminal to a cell with a gNB (next generation NodeB) equipped with a large number of antenna elements. Thus, the cell boundaries almost vanish, which can significantly reduce or even eliminate inter-cell interference. Therefore, canonical cell-free mMIMO (massive MIMO) (Elhoushy, 2022) shows a 2.5X improvement over Small Cell Networks (SCNs) in terms of per-user UL (Uplink) network throughput and it can achieve performance up to 8 Mbits/s (Ngo, 2017) for the 5% worst users on a 20 MHz bandwidth. This makes cell-free networking, an emerging 6G technology, extremely suitable for hotspot areas, as it can offer seemingly infinite capacity and fully mitigates data rate problem of the cell edge users. Like 5G, the SCN which uses non-cooperative base stations (BSs), can only serve up to a 200-meter cell-radius, reduce power in signal transmission up to 10 Watts, and achieve a mean spectral efficiency of 3 Mbits/s/Hz. The network densification through small-cell deployment, even with cellular MIMO, still does not match cell-free massive MIMO in terms of spectral efficiency (Liu, 2014). This is because of the interference generated by neighboring cells, increasing numbers of uncoordinated and lightly loaded small cells in the network. An in-depth analysis of small cell deployment is provided in (Mowla, 2017). We will overcome the Inter-Cell Interference (ICI) problem (Hamza, 2013) and uncoordinated deployment of such SCN by the cell-free RAN solution of MARSAL where dynamic adaptability algorithms enable RU-DU and DU-DU coordination. Such a coordinated solution can further improve the system capacity/spectral efficiency of future 6G networks.

3.1 Dense User-Generated Content Distribution with mmWave Fronthauling

The main objective of this scenario is to demonstrate and evaluate MARSAL's distributed cell-free RAN in terms of sum capacity and spectral efficiency gains, and the adaptivity of dynamic clustering and RRM (Radio Resource Management) mechanisms in managing connectivity resources in a dynamic environment with varying hotspots areas. Furthermore, an additional objective of this scenario is to evaluate the Hybrid MIMO Fronthaul (Femenias, 2019) in terms of its ability to offer a dynamic AP topology.

This experimentation scenario shows the potential of deploying cell-free networking in 6G networks with RUs massive AP deployments (Kassam, 2023). Here the MARSAL innovations focus on distributed processing, with clusters of RUs and DUs coordinating via fronthaul links. In this experimentation scenario, we evaluate the performance of dynamic data driven clustering algorithm. This scenario will also explore and evaluate the effect of inter-DU coordination spectral efficiency (Zhang, 2017) and propose dynamic adaptability of the coordination levels jointly addressing RU-DU and DU-DU coordination, for the first time. The cell-free vRAN (virtualised RAN) components in this experimentation scenario will validate the design of cell-free enabled vO-DU, cell-free MAC (Medium Access Control) scheduler, PHY (Physical layer) sub-layer. Moreover, it will also validate appropriate modification of the CP (Control Plane) protocols and O-RAN specified interfaces (i.e., E2, O1) (ORAN, 2023), to support practical cell-free operation (Vardakas, 2022) and fully distributed processing.

The investigated experimental scenario represents an event with a high density of users and RUs. It can be an indoor venue (e.g., a concert) or an outdoor setting (e.g., a football stadium). During this kind of event, it is common for dense UGC (User Generated Content) to be streamed by spectators via their handheld devices and consumed locally in real-time (RT). Moreover, there may be users with very different requirements: for instance, a UAV (Unmanned Aerial Vehicle) controlled by law enforcement or security agent vs. a regular user/spectator. In general, this use case is characterized by high user density and the users generate high traffic.

The involved stakeholders in this experimentation scenario are: *cell-free mMIMO infrastructure provider*, *cell-free vRAN VNFs provider*, *RAN intelligent controller* and *xAPPs provider*, *mmWave fronthaul provider*, *mmWave transport network* and *network equipment manufacturer*.

In this scenario, O-RUs will be interconnected with O-DU (ORAN DU) nodes serving the users in a coordinated manner. Furthermore, MARSAL's Hybrid MIMO fronthaul solution (Rommel, 2018) will be leveraged for the interconnection of O-RUs (O-RAN Radio Units) and O-DUs. The performance of the cell-free NG-RAN (Next Generation RAN) will be evaluated via pre-recorded video content that will be uploaded and downloaded by UEs (User Equipment) to/from a video streaming MEC application (app) deployed at the Regional Edge node, to emulate Dense UGC streaming both in the uplink and in the downlink (DL) direction.

To support the abovementioned experimentation scenario, MARSAL CF NG-RAN will include cell-free clustering solution, mmWave fronthaul, CF MAC scheduler as a part of the CF vRAN to provide mMIMO support in the MARSAL architecture. The cell-free vRAN, especially the vO-DU and vO_CU-UP will be deployed as VNFs (Virtual Network Functions) at the radio edge data centre. The mmWave transport network will be providing distributed cell-free coordination amongst the VNFs deployed in radio edge DCs (data centers) and regional edge DCs. A MEC platform be deployed both at the regional and radio edge DCs and a pre-recorded video will be used during the PoC (Proof-of-Concept) evaluation. Moreover, Near-RT RIC (RAN Intelligent Controller) will be hosted at the regional edge DCs, and it will relate to the XGS-PON (10 Gigabit Symmetrical - Passive Optical Network) of the MARSAL architecture.

Fig.2 depicts the mapping of this scenario into the MARSAL architecture. To deploy the cell-free vRAN solution on the radio edge data centre we consider the higher and lower layer split suggested by 3GPP (3GPP, 2021), O-RAN (ORAN, 2023), and Small Cell Forum (SCF, 2023). Such flexible split options together with the utilization of a converged optical wireless network will allow us to deploy the cell-free vRAN solution in a cost-effective manner for future 6G networks. Furthermore, the O-RAN (ORAN, 2023) introduces a near Real-Time RAN Intelligent Controller (RT-RIC), which implements radio resource management, measurement, and telemetry.

The proposed configuration deploys the vO_CU-UP and vO-DU at the Radio Edge, while the vO_CU-CP near-RT RIC is deployed at the Regional Edge. The split inside the physical layer will simplify the data mapping by limiting the required associated control messages and it will also allow us to enable transport bandwidth scalability based allowing usage of a higher number of antennas without asking for extra transport bandwidth. The O-RAN compliant vO-CU and vO-DU components are incorporated in the form of RAN Virtual Network Functions, while the APs serve as the RUs (MARSAL, 2021).

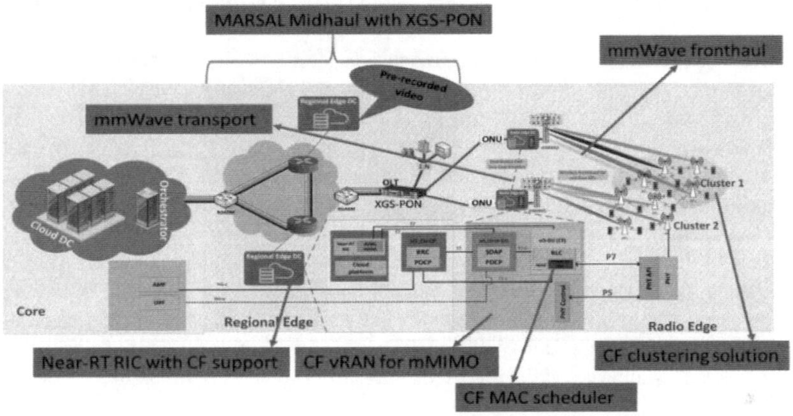

Figure 2. Overview of the dense UGC distribution with mmWave fronthauling scenario, mapped into the MARSAL architecture

3.2 Ultra-Dense Video Traffic Delivery in a Converged Fixed-Mobile Network

This scenario showcases MARSAL's solution towards Fixed-Mobile Convergence (FMC) in an ultra-dense indoors context like campus, stadium, malls, etc. Mobile clients served by a distributed Cell-Free RAN will be sharing the Optical Midhaul (Pfeiffer, 2015) with third party fixed clients. The Fixed-Mobile Convergence in an Ultra-dense indoors scenario will be operated based on two operation modes, that is Fixed operation (Passive Optical LAN (Local Area Network)) and Mobile operation (small/pico cell with optionally Distributed Antenna System - DAS), respectively. The mobile clients served by a distributed cell-free RAN will be sharing the Optical Midhaul with third party FTTH (Fiber-to-the-Home) clients. The optical fiber access equipment (Optical Line Terminal - OLT) will relate to PON and PtP interfaces where the Network urbanism organization, e.g., OLT and CU co-localized and DU at the end face of the optical termination.

Here we would like to highlight the motivation of this work by considering the 5G status and the 6G needs. So first, 5G carriers and equipment are emitted and localized at the regular antenna locations with previous generations (2G/3G/4G). The pressure of coverage based on the requirements of the regulator is the main reason to have such deployment engineering rules. Concerning the mobile backhaul, 5G deployment coincides with a massive use of optical fiber to achieve the required backhaul throughput up to 10GEth. The fixed access network is based on PtP topology to achieve the connectivity between antenna site and the first aggregation node (central office). Due to the fact that in parallel of 5G, FTTH is under deployment, we have more and more central offices equipped with OLT shelf. 5G backhauling could be addressed either by direct PtP connection to aggregation switch/router or through OLT PtP ports & cards. To address the increase of 6G cells, the preferred fixed technology to collect multiple spots is the PtMP also named PON based on "tree" fiber infrastructure. 6G transport challenges concern the coordination between RAN and FAN (Radio & Fixed Access networks) networks to address throughput, latency, availability issues.

MARSAL's distributed cell-free RAN Radio Unit is deployed based on a Serial Fronthaul topology (Furtado, 2022), (Farias, 2016). The Serial Fronthaul allows a large number of cell-free APs to be interconnected in a bus topology, significantly increasing Spectral Efficiency, but with minimal cabling requirements. The technology of transmission considered to support serial fronthaul is Wavelength Division Multiplexing (WDM) (Song, 2018). A passive fiber network infrastructure is preferred using passive optical multiplexer. Serial Fronthauling is considered an ideal solution for indoor venues.

Secondly, in this scenario, Radio Edge nodes, that host the vRAN elements, are interconnected via PtP and PtMP (PON technology like G-PON (gigabit capable) and XGS-PON (10 gigabit capable)) midhaul links with the Regional Edge. The Regional Edge nodes, interconnected in a WDM ring topology, will host the Near-RT RIC and vCU_CP VNFs. The SDN-Transmission controller and Near-RT RIC SDN function will also be deployed at the Regional Edge nodes. The performance of this scenario will be evaluated via pre-recorded 4K/HDR (High Dynamic Range) video that will be uploaded and downloaded by UEs to/from a video streaming MEC application deployed at the Regional Edge node. Fixed clients will be included as well in this scenario that will be served by the same infrastructure via PtMP (PON) links sharing capacity with the Radio Edge node.

The involved stakeholders in this experimentation scenario are: *optical access networks and fiber infrastructure provider, radio intelligent controller provider, RAN components provider, and network equipment manufacturer.*

To support this experimentation scenario, we include an Optical Access Network to serve the connectivity between radio edge data centers and cell sites equipped with DUs and RUs. We also propose coordination between the controllers dedicated to Fixed and Radio access networks. Fig.3 depicts the mapping of the scenario into the MARSAL architecture. It must be noted that we also use existing and next-generation PON technologies, to take advantage of their lower CAPEX (due to higher reuse of commodity Fiber-to-the-x (FTTx) equipment) and shared OPEX options, to demonstrate 5G midhaul and backhaul traffic over PON (Levi, 2020). The PON solution also provides a management interface to the network operators. When used for mobile networks, PONs already make use of a Dynamic Bandwidth Allocation (DBA) algorithm to prioritize certain flows. The development of network slicing could be proposed by dynamic creation/edition/deletion of slice instances (Hexa, 2021).

This scenario demonstrates an on-the-fly reconfiguration of the PON DBA parameters, to be managed from an SDN controller in coordination between fixed and radio networks, used for mid- and back-haul of 5G traffic with integrated RU/DU. We also consider PTPv2 (Precision Time Protocol v2) and SyncE (Synchronous Ethernet) protocols (transportation over the different transport domain mentioned above will be demonstrated. To support this demonstration, video services of various flavors (e.g., downstream HD/4K streams and/or conversational video) will been selected as representative vertical services that the Edge and Core DCs will also host the 5G NFs (e.g., the 5G Core VNFs), while resource sharing will be accomplished via MARSAL's innovative MEO. This will allow disaggregating the AR (Augmented Reality), scene analysis, and activity recognition application functions in multiple tiers (i.e., Regional Edge, Radio Edge, on-device).

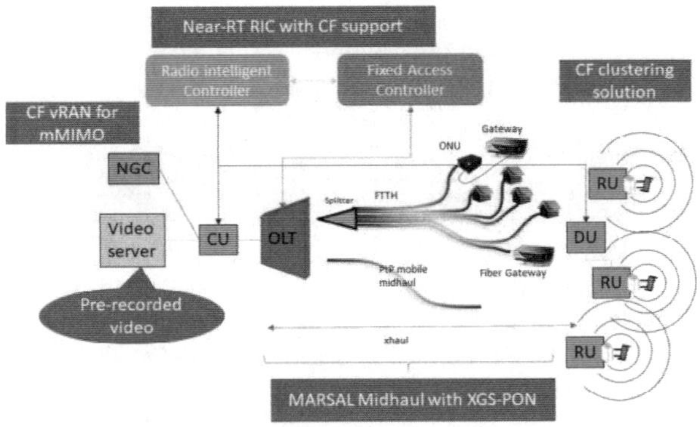

Figure 3. Overview of the ultra-dense video traffic delivery in a converged fixed-mobile network scenario, mapped into the MARSAL architecture

4. DISCUSSION

In this paper, we presented the main architectural components of MARSAL, as well as how the applied cell-free use cases are mapped into the proposed architecture. In particular, the first scenario is focused on cell-free networking in dense and ultra-dense hotspot areas. We consider dense User-Generated Content (UGC) distribution with mmWave fronthauling. The main objective of this scenario is to demonstrate and evaluate MARSAL distributed cell-free RAN in terms of increased capacity and spectral efficiency gains, and the adaptivity of dynamic clustering and RRM mechanisms in managing connectivity resources in a dynamic environment with varying hotspots areas. The second experimentation scenario investigates ultra-dense video traffic delivery in a converged fixed-mobile network. This showcases MARSAL's solution towards Fixed Mobile Convergence in an ultra-dense indoors context. Mobile clients served by a distributed Cell-Free RAN will be sharing the Optical Midhaul with third party FTTH clients. Our future work focuses on the evaluation process, as well as on a set of preliminary targeted KPIs.

ACKNOWLEDGEMENT

The paper has been based on the context of the "MARSAL" ("Machine Learning-Based, Networking and Computing Infrastructure Resource Management of 5G and Beyond Intelligent Networks") Project, funded by the EC under the Grant Agreement (GA) No.101017171.

REFERENCES

3GPP (2017). *Study on new radio access technology; Radio access architecture and interfaces* (Release 14), TS38.801

3GPP (2021). *NG-RAN Architecture*, https://www.3gpp.org/news-events/2160-ng_ran_architecture

Agarwal, V., Sharma, C., Shetty, R., Jangam, A., and Asati, R. (2021). *A Journey Towards a Converged 5G Architecture & Beyond.* In Proceedings of IEEE *5GWF'21,* pp.18-23

Blandino, et *al.* (2019). *Multi-User Hybrid MIMO at 60 GHz Using 16-Antenna Transmitters*. IEEE Transactions on Circuits and Systems I, Regular Papers 66(2), 848-858

Boutaba, R., Salahuddin, M., Limam, N., and Ayoubi, S. (2018). *A Comprehensive Survey on Machine Learning for Networking: Evolution, Applications and Research Opportunities*. Journal of Internet Services and Applications 9(1), 1--99

Chochliouros, I.P., Spiliopoulou, A.S., P. Lazaridis, Z. Zacharis, M.-A. Kourtis, C. Zarakovitis and A. Kourtis (2021). *Energy Efficiency Concerns and Trends in Future 5G Network Infrastructures. Energies (MDPI)*, 14(17), 5932

Cisco (2019). *Cisco Visual Networking Index: Forecast and Trends, 2017–2022*, White Paper

Demirhan, U., and Alkhateeb, A. (2022). *Enabling Cell-Free Massive MIMO Systems With Wireless Millimeter Wave Fronthaul.* IEEE Transactions on Wireless Communications 21(11), 9482-9496

Elhoushy, S., Ibrahim, M., and Hamouda, W. (2022). *Cell-Free Massive MIMO: A Survey.* IEEE Communications Surveys & Tutorials 24(1), 492-523

ETSI (2018). European Telecommunications Standards Institute. *Mobile Edge Computing (MEC); Deployment of Mobile Edge Computing in an NFV environment.* ETSI GR MEC-017 V1.1.1 (2018-02)

Farias, F., et *al.* (2016). *Cost- and energy-efficient backhaul options for heterogeneous mobile network deployments.* Photonic Network Communications 32, 422-437

Femenias, G., and Riera-Palou, F. (2019). *Cell-Free Millimeter-Wave Massive MIMO Systems With Limited Fronthaul Capacity.* IEEE Access 7, 44596-44612

Furtado, L., Fernandes, A., Ohashi, A., Farias, F., Cavalcante, A., and Costa, J. (2022). *Cell-Free Massive MIMO Deployments: Fronthaul Topology Options and Techno-Economic Aspects.* EuCAP'22, pp.1-5

Hamza, A.S., Khalifa, S.S., Hamza, H.S., and Elsayed, K. (2013). *A Survey on Inter-Cell Interference Coordination Techniques in OFDMA-Based Cellular Networks.* IEEE Com. Surveys & Tutorials 15(4), 1642-1670

Hexa-X Project: D1.2 (2021). *Expanded 6G vision, use cases and societal values – including aspects of sustainability, security and spectrum*, https://hexa-x.eu/wp-content/uploads/2021/05/Hexa-X_D1.2.pdf

Kassam, J., Castanheira, D., et *al.* (2023). *A Review of Cell-Free Massive MIMO Systems.* Electronics (MDPI) 12(4), 1001.

Kostopoulos, et *al.* (2022). *Experimentation Scenarios for Machine Learning-Based Resource Management.* In AIAI-2022, AICT, vol.652, pp.120-133. Springer, Cham

Levi, D. (2020). *The Case for Using PON for 5G Fronthaul.* Lightwave: https://www.lightwaveonline.com/5g-mobile/article/14188094/the-case-for-using-pon-for-5g-fronthaul

Liu, W., Han, S.,and Yang, C. (2014). *Energy efficiency comparison of massive MIMO and small cell network. IEEE GlobalSIP'14,* pp.617-621

MARSAL (2021). *Machine Learning-based Networking and Computing Infrastructure Resource Management of 5G and Beyond Intelligent Networks*, 5G-PPP/H2020 project, Grant Agreement No.101017171, https://www.marsalproject.eu/

MARSAL D2.1 (2021). *Description and definition of targeted PoCS*, https://www.marsalproject.eu/wp-content/uploads/2021/09/D2.1-Marsal-final.pdf

Mowla, M.M., Ahmad, I., et *al.* (2017). *A Green Communication Model for 5G Systems.* IEEE Transactions on Green Communications and Networking 1(3), 264-280

Ngo, H.Q., Ashikhmin, A., Yang, H., et *al.* (2017). *Cell-Free Massive MIMO Versus Small Cells.* IEEE Transactions on Wireless Communications 16(3), 1834-1850

Niknam, S., Roy, A., Dhillon, H.S., *et al.* (2022). *Intelligent O-RAN for Beyond 5G and 6G Wireless Networks. IEEE Globecom Workshops (GC Wkshps),* pp. 215-220

O-RAN (2023). Open Radio Accees Network Alliance e.V., https://www.o-ran.org/

O-RAN (2023). Open Radio Accees Network Alliance e.V.: *O-RAN Alliance Specifications*, https://www.o-ran.org/specifications

O-RAN (2023). Open Radio Accees Network Alliance e.V.: O-RAN Architecture Description. *TS "O-RAN.WG1.OAD-R003scription-v08.00"*, https://orandownloadsweb.azurewebsites.net/specifications

Pfeiffer, T. (2015). *Next generation mobile fronthaul and midhaul architectures.* Journal of Optical Communications and Networking 7(11), B38-B45

Rommel, S., Thiago Raddo, R., and Monroy, I.T. (2018). *The Fronthaul Infrastructure of 5G Mobile Networks.* IEEE CAMAD'18, pp.1-6

Saha, R.K., Nanba, S., Nishimura, K,. Kim, Y.-b., and Yamazaki, K. (2018). *RAN Architectural Evolution Framework toward 5G and Beyond Cellular-An Overview.* In Proc. *IEEE PIMRC'18,* pp.592-593. IEEE

SCF - Small Cell Forum (2023), https://www.smallcellforum.org/

Song, D., Zhang, J., Xiao, Y., Wang, X., and Ji, Y. (2018). *Energy Optimization with Passive WDM Based Fronthaul in Heterogeneous Cellular Networking.* IEEE ACP'18, pp.1-3

Vardakas, J.S., Ramantas, K., Vinogradov, E., *et al.* (2022). *Machine Learning-Based Cell-Free Support in the O-RAN Architecture: An Innovative Converged Optical-Wireless Solution Toward 6G Networks.* IEEE Wireless Communications 29(5), 20-26

Zhang, D., Wang, Y, Li, X., and Xiang, W. (2018). *Hybridly Connected Structure for Hybrid Beamforming in mmWave Massive MIMO Systems.* IEEE Transactions on Communications 66(2), 662-674

Zhang, J., et *al.* (2017). *Spectral and energy efficiency of cell-free massive MIMO systems with hardware impairments.* IEEE WCSP'17, pp.1-6.

HOW GOOD UX DESIGN ENHANCES THE VALUE OF QUALITY PRODUCTS: AN EXPERIENCE REPORT ON APPLYING INTEGRATED UX LEAN IN SCRUM

Sydhia Mara Valente Moreira[1], Bruno Araújo Bonifácio[1], Rafael Pedrozo de Araújo[1], Juarez Pará Neto[1] and Thiago Soares[2]
[1]*Eldorado Research Institute*
Manaus, Amazonas - Brazil
[2]*Jabil Circuit Inc.*
Betim, MG - Brazil

ABSTRACT

The software development process is an intrinsically human-focused activity, in which User Experience (UX) plays a fundamental role in the success and adoption of new software technologies. For this reason, several companies have been integrating UX design principles into process software development. However, adoption in practice creates essential challenges that influence successful project deliverables. This paper shares our experience integrating UX strategies into Scrum, using Lean UX. The adapted process improved requirement understanding, quality, and user satisfaction. This hybrid method was used in a real-world case study, and experimental evaluation showed increased team performance and customer satisfaction. However, the hybrid method led to higher discovered defects, re-works, and project duration compared to teams using only Scrum.

KEYWORDS

Scrum, UX Design, Lean UX, Human Computer-Interaction, Software Engineering

1. INTRODUCTION

The software development market has been experiencing exponential growth. This growth can be attributed to several factors, including development practices, rapid response to changes, and a lower software development cost for the creation of new services and businesses. Therefore, companies have combined methods and development with software technologies processes to enhance the quality of their deliveries (Pillay and Wing, 2019). In this scenario, the software industry faces the challenge of ensuring a quality product and determining the factors that guarantee its success and adoption. Consequently, it is crucial for the software development process to follow models that prioritize both quality and user needs (Hinderks *et al.* 2022).

In order to address this issue, many companies are incorporating User Experience (UX) design principles into their agile software development process (Pilz et al. 2021). Companies adapted their agile methodologies to integrate UX strategy into incremental and iterative life cycles. However, despite agile methods (e.g. Scrum, Extreme Programming - XP, and Kanban) guaranteeing efficient delivery, and reducing the time taken to develop a product available in the market there are shortcomings and challenges associated with the integration process related to time constraints, work balance modularization, feedback, prioritization, and documentation that prevent adherence to the best UX practices.

The integration between UX and the development cycle often does not deliver the desired benefits on the product developed (Da Silva *et al.* 2021). For this reason, UX design and Agile development are often needed together to ensure that the needs and requirements of the user and to ship the product faster. This, in turn, increases the likelihood of creating a successful and well-received product among its target audience.

The goal of this paper is to share our experience integrating UX strategies into the agile development process, using Scrum. Thus, Scrum and Lean UX frameworks were combined to investigate the effectiveness of using UX as a strategy for improving the quality of use on software projects. Our hypothesis was the result of adapting Scrum, using Lean UX before and after the development of the sprint life cycle help us to understand the requirements and functionalities built, and the construction of the application.

As a result, obtained from this case study we show that the above-adapted method led to an increase in team performance and customer satisfaction. However, considering the amount of discovered defects, re-works, and duration of the project implementation were higher in the team that used the adapted method than the other teams that only used Scrum UX. We hope with this experience report shares an alternative to achieve an integration between UX and Scrum processes without clashes that lead to compromising on either quality or time.

This paper is structured as follows: section 2 briefly summarizes the related work and presents a gap analysis. Section 3 presents our case study applying a method adapted using UX and Scrum, in a software development project in real context. Section 4 outlines the results and key findings of our study as well as the answers to our research question. The paper ends with ideas and future works.

2. BACKGROUND

Agile methods refer to activities relating to code creation or project management using an iterative and incremental approach, following the principles outlined in the Agile Manifesto (Alhammad and Moreno, 2022). The UX design methods, focus on the interactions and interface of the product with users. Moreover, Agile focuses on developing a minimum viable product, often overlooking usability and the involvement of end users during the development phase. In contrast, usability approaches emphasize the understanding of user needs (Cursio *et al.* 2018).

2.1 UX and Agile Integration

The integration of UX and Agile software development has been extensively addressed in the literature. This has resulted in the proposal of new methods and techniques aimed at merging these two domains, as well as discussions on the challenges associated with their integration. Thus, several studies have been published to propose and improve the integration between Agile and UX.

Da Silva *et al.* (2021) and Curcio *et al.* (2018) provide a comprehensive and high-level overview of the field, offering valuable insights into the evolution of Agile and UX over the past two decades. These studies successfully identify various strategies, forms, and challenges associated with integrating both disciplines. However, despite the abundance of integrated processes and techniques published in the literature, they are seldom implemented in practice (Hinderks *et al.* 2022).

Other approaches are considering the organization's culture, related collaboration, and communication issues during process integration (Alsaykhan et al. 2022). Moreover, research has highlighted the existence of a gap between the various roles involved in the Agile process and the consideration of UX factors, which hinders effective collaboration with UX professionals. Furthermore, the lack of UX knowledge among software developers is paralleled by a lack of understanding of Agile processes among designers (Cajander *et al.* 2022).

According to a literature review conducted by Hinderks *et al.* 2023, the integration between software development and UX design has garnered significant interest, and numerous researchers have identified various issues and proposed solutions. However, a common limitation of the proposed models is the lack of emphasis on UX activities related to product research and testing before development and after the development sprint cycle.

As a result, the research confirmed that Agile UX often yields inconclusive results regarding the applicability and generalizability of agile methodologies such as Scrum, XP, or Kanban in practical settings. These findings can be attributed to gaps in knowledge and the challenges associated with adapting Scrum processes, which can have a significant impact on the outcomes of such studies. Thus, it needed more studies in practice in a real environment to determine the applicability of new approaches and derivate methods.

2.2 UX Strategies and Resources

The user experience (UX) encompasses various quality criteria, including classical usability, as well as pragmatic qualities such as efficiency, controllability, learnability, novelty, and aesthetic aspects related to the design of the user interface. To develop a product that delivers a great user experience, it is crucial to establish proper user expectation management regarding UX. Faced with this, when applying UX principles, it is important to consider the UX goals, UX strategy, and available UX resources (Mckeown, 2020). This will provide a better understanding of how to manage and effectively apply UX practices.

By implementing UX strategies, it becomes feasible to accomplish specific UX-related goals. However, executing these strategies requires essential resources such as surveys, questionnaires, and usability tests, among others (Schrepp, 2019). In this context, one of the primary challenges lies in identifying UX strategies that can be effectively integrated into iterative development methodologies, considering that the traditional UX process often follows a linear approach.

In this context, various UX methods have been incorporated into the Agile process to ensure a better user experience. As suggested by Alsaykhan et al. 2022, these strategies can be categorized into different approaches, including Little Design Up Front, Prototypes, Personas, Workshops, Usability Testing, and Lean UX as shown in Table 1.

Table 1. UX Strategies based Methods [adapted from Alsaykhan et al. 2022]

Category	Description	Methods related
Design Up Front	Is known as a process of modeling small subsystems of a product before coding. Traditionally, upfront design practices, such as the "sprint zero" approach, were commonly used. However, the adoption of Little Design Up Front has gained prominence as a more iterative and flexible approach within the Agile framework.	Design Thinking, User Story Mapping, Information Architecture
Prototypes	Prototypes are often used for testing and validating designs. They allow designers and stakeholders to gather feedback, evaluate usability, and identify potential improvements before moving forward with the development process.	Low-fidelity sketches, wireframes, interactive mockups
Personas	It is a usability tool that uses fictional people to represent users. This method is substantially used in user-centered projects to provide the development team with a user perspective, helping to define objectives of real users.	Personas
Workshops	Workshop can be used by developers and designers to discuss their work, ideas, and feedback in order to have a common understanding of the product. The contribution is to assist product managers, development teams and stakeholders understand how to handle the development process in an agile environment.	Design Studio, Product Discovery
Usability Testing	The usability testing is used to evaluate each system iteration with a variety of participants in order to identify and address usability problems early on. Its primary focus is on producing usable prototypes of high quality.	Think-aloud, Usability testing, User Trial
Lean UX	The method aims to sketch ideas and create a skeletal design output that can be used in time-boxed sprints until the minimum viable product (MVP) is produced, while considering usability aspects.	Lean inception, User Centered Design (UCD).

According to Alsaykhan et al. 2022, each category of UX strategies focuses on a UX goal during the development life cycle. Little Design Up Front is commonly used at project start, through defining user flows, and briefing mapping information used to create UI from the product. In this approach, the UX designer needs to collaborate closely with the agile team and the project manager, especially on the kickoff project. During each interaction, UI is improved and accepted by the client. In this case, the product owner must develop and evaluate the design artifacts to assist in the analysis, verification, and validation.

In their study by Ananjeva *et al.* (2020), the researchers employed a prototyping technique to enhance the team's understanding of the design by visualizing the prototype sketch. According to results, prototypes serve as valuable tools for making design decisions, particularly when multiple design solutions are being considered.

Workshops and usability testing are approaches used to assess the integration of each UI flow, with a focus on identifying and improving usability issues during the development process (Alhammad and Moreno, 2022). Various studies propose new integration approaches between the Agile process and UX by incorporating workshops and usability testing. However, these approaches may not be efficient when it comes to discovering user profiles or meeting user expectations (Alsaykhan et al. 2022). In such cases, the development team may need to refactor and enhance the UI throughout the process, as these approaches are typically applied after the sprint cycle.

Another important strategy is to incorporate Lean UX, which combines Lean principles with UX strategies (Alsaykhan et al. 2022). Multiple studies have emphasized the significance of this approach in elevating UX to a central concept throughout the planning, creation, monitoring, execution, verification, and validation stages of development processes. Consequently, the integration of lean transformation and agile software development has effectively positioned UX and UX-related documentation at the forefront of planning and goal-setting activities.

3. ENHANCING AGILE SOFTWARE DEVELOPMENT PROCESS WITH UX DESIGN STRATEGIES

In the next section, we present a motivation scenario to integrate UX design strategies into the agile software development process.

3.1 Motivating Scenario

An essential requirement to integrate User Experience (UX) in agile software development is understanding how to measure or determine successful UX management, during the development process. Our company is a Research Institute of Technologies located in the Amazon Region. We are entrusted with the responsibility of developing software solutions and driving innovation for various industries situated in the Industrial Amazon Region of Brazil. One of our partner companies required improvement in an internal process, utilizing software technology, to ensure the proper functioning of its globally distributed units across various global centers. However, the project owners and stakeholders had a limited understanding of the product vision, and there was a tight deadline for developing a Minimum Viable Product (MVP).

In order to address these challenges, the development team decided to adopt agile methods, specifically Scrum, to ensure efficient and effective product development. However, it was crucial to integrate UX strategies into the process to meet both functional quality and usability criteria.

Firstly, we adopted as a UX strategy the use of the Design Up Front technique. Thus, we create a kick-off project where we met with sponsors, stakeholders, and user keys to understand the problem and elaborate the project based on the User-Centered Design approach (UCD). During the development process, the Designer used Low-fidelity sketches to validate user flows and UI design with the product owner. So when we realized sprint planning the designer established tasks to produce design UI in high fidelity, during each sprint. After each UI is already done, at the end of the Sprint, the Designer validates with stakeholders and user keys. All improvements were sent to the sprint backlog to realize new improvements and modifications. The design UI flow approved was estimated to develop by the developer team.

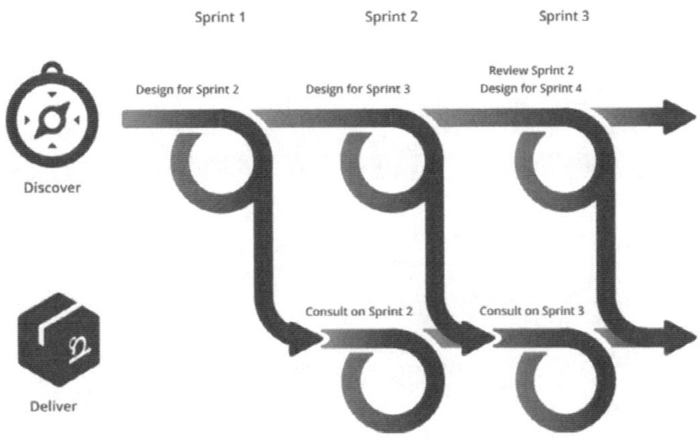

Figure 1. Scrum process adapted with UX process

According to Figure 1, following the recommendations found in the literature, we implemented the Scrum process, with adaptations to incorporate the UX cycle. One sprint was dedicated to validating the high-fidelity UI prototypes in collaboration with stakeholders and key users. Their feedback and insights were crucial in refining the design. In the subsequent sprint, the approved design was taken into development, following the incremental iterative cycle.

This approach allowed us to ensure that the UI prototypes were thoroughly evaluated and refined before moving forward with development. By involving stakeholders and key users in the validation process, we gained valuable insights and feedback that contributed to the overall quality of the product. The incremental iterative cycle in development facilitated continuous improvement and integration of the UX design throughout the project. However, during validation, we found several usability and UX issues that cause refactoring and improvements.

In this context, we opted for the Lean UX approach because Agile UX is a methodology that aims to rationalize UX development processes so that your work gains speed without losing quality (Ghanmi et al. 2020). This integrative approach has not yet received sufficient critical attention in the scientific literature (Alhammad and Moreno 2022).

3.2 Adapting Lean UX and Scrum

To address usability and refactoring issues encountered during the process, we made adaptations to the Scrum process by introducing an intermediate phase dedicated to validating and testing prototypes with key users. Each iteration encompassed product discovery, design, formative evaluation, and testing, following the sprint development cycle.

The process started with a thorough exploration of the problem, conducting extensive research to gain insights and establish a comprehensive understanding. The Designers and product owners actively engaged in ideating and testing potential solutions, considering user interaction flows in collaboration with key users. Feedback from testing sessions played a vital role in refining and improving the design. Subsequently, the design was finalized and approved, with stakeholders and key users actively participating in the validation process at the end of each sprint.

The design specification was then transferred to the sprint backlog for implementation by the development team. Figure 2 presents the process workflow integrating UX Lean and Scrum.

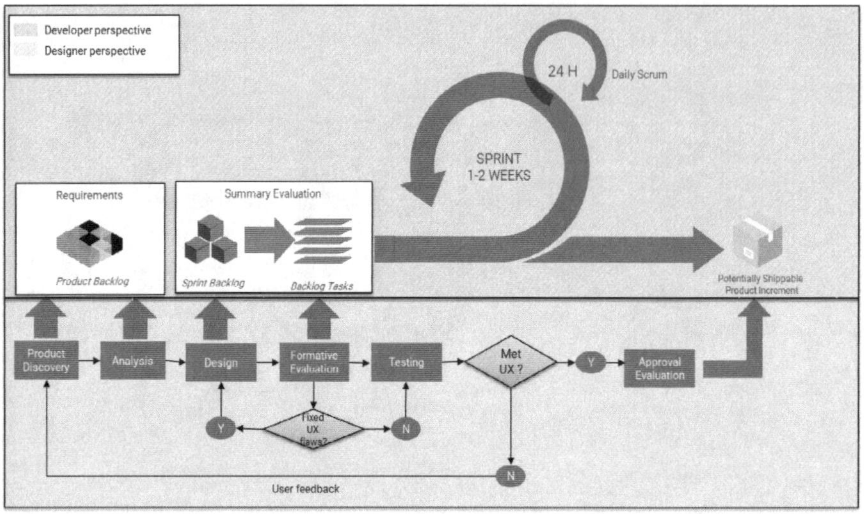

Figure 2. Lean UX process integrated with Scrum (adapted from Ghanmi et al. 2020)

Figure 2 shows the process conducted by our team, from two perspectives: designer and developer team. The adaptations inserting product discovery, formative evaluation, and testing during the sprint cycle allowed us to address usability issues proactively and incorporate user feedback into the design process. By involving key users in the validation and testing phases, we ensured that the final design met their expectations and needs. The iterative approach of the Scrum process, coupled with the integration of user-centered activities, facilitated continuous improvement and enhanced the overall quality of the product. In the next section, we present results obtained with the scrum process adapted with Lean UX, during project execution.

4. RESULTS

To analyze our approach, we used a software project in the review automated industry material process domain. To evaluate the effectiveness of the hybrid methodology, the following variables were considered and gathered during the Sprints implementation.

1. **Number of usability defects in each Sprint:** we consider usability defects all problems found by the team and feedback collected from users with each delivery performed.
2. **Amount of re-work:** we considered as re-work, the user stories transferred from the previous to the current Sprint) and necessary adjustments found during the validations carried out by the test team.
3. **Team performance:** resulting from the number of user stories, improvements, and features selected and delivered in each Sprint.
4. **Amount of customer satisfaction:** customer self-reporting in the Sprint review meeting.

Considering the contract negotiations with the customer, it should be noted that the length of the Sprints of this project was considered to be 10 working days. The product backlog remained consistent throughout the project, and the team selected user stories from this backlog based on customer preferences.

The above-mentioned project was implemented in the form of two separate teams, each one with six members. The composition of these teams was considered by the senior management of the company before the project onset. In this composition, attempts were made to keep teams at the same level of workability and engineering.

Initially, we followed a specific four-sprint approach, dedicating one sprint to design validation with the development of wireframes and improvements to be implemented and the subsequent sprint to development. Additionally, we implemented our alternative approach for the remaining four sprints, incorporating discovery, design validation, and testing activities into each sprint. Team 1 used the traditional scrum approach and team 2 used scrum adapted with Lean UX.

In the following, the results of data collection concerning the variables of this research are addressed. From one point of view, the defects discovered in each Sprint indicate the team's accuracy in performing its tasks. The more the team can obtain a degree of executive quality where fewer defects are observed, the higher the quality of the development process implementation. Figure 3 shows the statistics about variables considered in this case study.

Figure 3. Results obtained considering 1) number of defects; 2) number of re-work; 3) team performance and; 4) Customer satisfaction

The statistics mentioned above show that the total of the defects observed in Team 1 is in total less than that of the other team. Considering usability issues, Team 1 has been on a downward trend, indicating that this team has outperformed the other team (Team 2). However, as we tested the prototype during Sprint, Team 2 detected previously release a new product increment after development Sprint. These results impacted directly the approval evaluation of product increment during Sprint Review.

Regarding the re-work rate, this criterion shows the extent to which teams are required to perform things again. This variable usually is caused by performing inspections and considering the evaluation criteria. In this paper, we consider the number of user stories that teams have to implement again in the next Sprint as re-work. The lower the volume of the user stories, the higher the team's accuracy in performing tasks.

As can be observed, the amount of re-works in Team 1 is greater than in the other team. This is probably caused by the use of measurements and evaluations required during sprint execution by our approach adopted. To achieve using Scrum with the Lean UX approach adapted, the team seems to be sometimes forced to do more things. May be regarded as a negative point, but is justifiable about achieving higher quality and customer satisfaction.

Considering team performance percentage, as can be observed, the team performance in Team 1 is higher than the other team. This increase indicates that additional activities during the sprint can impact team performance by a team that uses Scrum with Lean UX adapted. However, the customer satisfaction rate, using our approach with Lean UX and Scrum is greater than traditional Scrum UX integration. This result is because Learn Ux is an interactive construction process that is based on feedback regarding what was built to incorporate new features into the product and solve problems as interactions take place.

5. CONCLUSION AND FUTURE WORKS

To increase competitiveness and ensure high-quality software products, software engineers often employ a combination of methodologies and adapt them to their specific needs. This merger encompasses various quality and management methodologies, approaches, and standards. Among them, Scrum has gained significant popularity and is widely adopted by software teams. However, teams also strive to leverage the strengths of other methodologies and patterns. Lean Ux can complement and enhance the Scrum methodology by offering more user-centric approaches focused on generating value for the customer.

This paper aimed to present our experience during the integration of Lean UX with Scrum in the software development process. By combining these approaches, we can observe that the insertion of a multidisciplinary model work methodology, that is, the collaboration of several team members and the insertion of the client in the process, results in a more agile and responsive process, with deliveries that are capable of generating greater customer and end-user satisfaction.

Overall, this research contributes to understanding how Lean UX can complement and improve the Scrum methodology, emphasizing continuous user feedback, and ensuring that the developed features are useful and aligned with their needs. The integration of Lean UX with Scrum improves the software development process, making it more user-centric, agile, collaborative, and efficient, resulting in a high-quality product that better meets the needs and expectations of end users.

In future work, we intend to apply and validate this adaptation in other projects comparing it with other UX methods and hybrid methodologies to analyze the efficiency and effectiveness delivery of project artifacts.

REFERENCES

Alhammad M. Moreno, A. M. 2022. Integrating user experience into Agile: an experience report on lean UX and Scrum. In: *44th International Conference on Software Engineering Software Engineering Education and Training (ICSE-SEET 22).* Pages 146–157

Alsaykhan et al. 2022. Challenges of Integrating Agile and UX/UCD: Systematic Literature Review. *International Journal of Computer Applications.* Volume 184 – No.33 p. 40 – 51

Ananjeva A, Persson J.S., Brunn A., 2020. Integrating UX work with agile development through user stories: An Action research study in a small software company. *In: Proceedings of the 16th International Conference on Web Information Systems and Technologies (WEBIST 2020)* Vol 170. P. 14-24

Cajander A., Larusdottir M., Geiser J., 2022. UX professionals' learning and usage of UX methods in agile, *Information and Software Technology*, Volume 151, 2022, p 1-9.

Curcio K., Santana R., Reinehr S., and Malucelli A., 2019. "Usability in agile software development: A tertiary study," *Comput. Stand. Interfaces*, vol. 64, no. December 2018, pp. 61–77.

Da Silva T. S., Silveira M. S., Maurer F., and Silveira F. F., 2018. "The evolution of agile UXD," *Information and Software Technology*, vol. 102, no. March, p. 1–5.

Hinderks, A. Mayo J. D., Thomaschewski J., Escalona M. J., 2022. Approaches to manage the user experience process in Agile software development: A systematic literature review, *Information and Software Technology Journal*, Volume 150, 2022, p. 12 – 26. 106957, ISSN 0950-5849.

Mckeown M. 2020. *The Strategy Book: How to Think and Act Strategically to Deliver Outstanding Results* (third ed.), Pearson, Harlow, England.

Nora Khaled Al Ghanmi, Nor Shahida Mohd Jamai 2020. Integrating Scrum development process with UX design flow *In: Bulletin of Electrical Engineering and Informatics* Vol. 9, No. 6, December 2020, p. 2630~2636 ISSN: 2302-9285, DOI: 10.11591/eei.v9i6.248

Pillay N. and Wing J., 2019. "Agile UX: Integrating good UX development practices in Agile," *Conference on Information Communications Technology and Society (ICTAS)*, Durban, South Africa, 2019, p. 1-6.

Pilz, J., Deutschländer, J., Thomaschewski, J. and Schön, E. 2021. Integrating Agile Human-Centered Design with Lean UX and Scrum. In Proceedings of the 17th International Conference on Web Information Systems and Technologies (WEBIST 2021), p. 467-473

Schrepp M., Thomaschewski J.2019. Handbook for the Modular Extension of the User Experience Questionnaire. Available in: https://ueqplus.ueq-research.org/Material/UEQ+_Handbook_V2.pdf

UX im Scrum-Team – Kann es Liebe werden? 2017. Available in: https://tech.jobvalley.com/blog/ux-im-scrum-team

THE INFLUENCE OF CYBERSECURITY VULNERABILITY PERCEPTION ON E-GOVERNMENT ADOPTION BY CITIZENS IN DEVELOPING COUNTRIES

Willard Munyoka
The University of Venda, Department of Business Information Systems,
Faculty of Management, Commerce, and Law
P. Bag X5050, Thohoyandou, Limpopo, Province, South Africa

ABSTRACT

With the rapid advancements in technology and the increasing digitization of government services, e-Government adoption has emerged as a crucial factor in developing and modernizing countries, particularly in the context of developing nations. However, cybersecurity concerns have been recognized as a significant barrier to the widespread adoption of e-Government services. This paper explores the relationship between the perception of cybersecurity vulnerability and e-Government adoption by citizens in developing countries, focusing on three selected countries, South Africa, Zambia, and Botswana. Underpinned by the technology threat avoidance theory (TTAT), the protection motivation theory (PMT), and UTAU2 as the theoretical lens and the quantitative research, this study proposed a Research framework. The model was tested using survey data from 600 selected respondents who accessed local municipality services using online-administered questionnaires. Regression analysis was used to analyze the data and test the hypotheses. The findings reveal that perceived susceptibility, distrust, risk, and uncertainty propensity significantly influence e-government adoption. The results of this study have implications for decision-makers and practitioners involved in e-government matters seeking better ways to improve online services to citizens.

KEYWORDS

Cybersecurity Vulnerability, E-Government Adoption, Developing Countries

1. INTRODUCTION

Digital technologies are indispensable in upholding and connecting societies, supporting the essential public service provision in health, education, safety, security, government ministries, and local government services to the general public (United Nations, 2022). The COVID-19 pandemic has exposed the over-reliance on in-person access to these essential services and amplified the wake-up call for embracing electronic government (e-government henceforth) and digital transformation as indispensable tools in accessing government services. To survive in this hybrid digital society, governments should embrace change as an inevitable force and create an innovative culture where all stakeholders can engage, experiment, learn and develop (United Nations, 2022). E-government facilitates the effective and efficient exchange and flow of information, communications, and transactions among various governmental stakeholders. Thus, e-government has become a fundamental building block for practical, accountable, resilient, and inclusive for all players in local, regional, national governmental, and international collaborations. This aligns with the United Nations Sustainable Development Goals number 16 on peace, justice, and strong institutions.

Despite its vast potential for transforming societies through smart and seamless services, the adoption of e-government by the civic society during and post-COVID-19 in the Southern Africa region remains suboptimal (Munyoka, 2020; Verkijika & De Wet, 2018). Various scholars (Rose et al., 2015; Castro & Lopes, 2022; Chen & Aklikokou, 2020) attributed this low adoption to several factors, chief among them being the lack of awareness, perceived digital mistrust, perceived lack of security, perceived ease of use, social value, economic value, uncertainty, transaction cost, and agency costs. However, the impact of these factors on adoption varies from country to country, region to region, and individual to individual, depending on the prevailing socio-economic, level of education, and the factors mentioned above. This study focuses on the effect of cybersecurity-related factors on e-government adoption by citizens in three countries from the Southern Africa region (i.e., Botswana, South Africa, and Zambia). The focus will be on local municipal services accessed by citizens in these three countries.

The UNDESA's UN E-government Survey (United Nations, 2022) is a comprehensive and reliable report for measuring a country's progress in e-government transformation using three aggregated core development indexes on ICT, infrastructure development, and e-government adoption. These are the telecommunications infrastructure development index (TII), online services index (OSI), and Human Capital Index (HCI).

The infrastructure development index (IDI) measures a nation's ICT infrastructure development level. The major barometers used to measure the IDI index are ICT readiness, ICT intensity, and ICT impact (ITU, 2023). The ICT readiness sub-index assesses a country's ICT readiness using five infrastructure and access indicators, which are fixed-telephone subscriptions, mobile-cellular telephone subscriptions, international Internet bandwidth per Internet user, households with a computer, and households with Internet access (ITU,2023). According to the UN E-government Survey (2022), South Africa attained an average score of 0.6850 on IDI, 0.6814 for Botswana, and 0.3909 for Zambia.

Online Service Index (OSI) assesses government portals using five criteria: the institutional framework (IF), services provision (SP), content provision (CP), technology (TEC), and e-participation (EPI) (UN, 2022). OSI is therefore calculated as a normalized value of these five subindexes. To attain a good OSI value, a country should have an ICT framework that guides its e-government initiatives. Similarly, providing services online, with frequently updated content, is a big attraction for e-government adoption. E-participation (EPI) is a collection of various tools and features used to assess the engagement of multiple stakeholders, including marginalised people, with government entities online. Chief among these features includes the availability of open government data (OGD) to all the sectors of the economy, collaborative services provision, active citizen participation in policy formulation and adoption, and evidence of online consultations with citizens via e-forums, e-polls, e-questionnaires (UN, 2022). Rwanda is leading the African continent with an OSI index score of 0.7935, while South Africa is in second place with a score of 0.7487. Zambia and Botswana are among the top sixteen performers in Africa, with OSI index scores of 0.4414 and 0.2740, respectively. Krishna and MP (2021) suggest cybersecurity influences stakeholders' decisions to adopt e-government services. As such, governments worldwide should work tirelessly to ensure that e-government services, data, and transactions are secure.

Human Capital Index (HCI) consists of the "knowledge, skills, and health that the people and nations invest in and accumulate throughout their lives, enabling them to realize their potential as productive members of society" (World Bank, 2022). In other words, it measures children's productivity and human capital potential in each country, given optimal health and education conditions. Major building blocks for evaluating HCI for a nation include the adult literacy rate; the combined primary, secondary, and tertiary gross enrolment ratio; expected years of schooling; and the average years of education for a nation. Only three African countries, Seychelles (0.7758), South Africa (0.7733), and Mauritius (0.7733), have HCI scores above the world average score of 0.7000. Botswana scored 0.6932, while Zambia scored 0.6744.

The E-government development index (EGDI) assesses a country's e-government development and inclusion of the civic society and various stakeholders in the values chain. It is a composite index based on the weighted average of IDI, OSI, and HCI. Mauritius is the best African performer, with an average EGDI score of 0.7196, followed by Seychelles (0.6920) and South Africa (0.6891). Botswana and Zambia scored 0.5383 and 0.4242, respectively, well below the world average of 0.6201. These EGDI for the three countries falls far short of those for the European top performer (i.e., Denmark's 0.9717), the Asian top performer (Republic of Korea's 0.9529), and the Americas top performer (USA's 0.9151).

E-government Outreach - this speaks of the status and efforts of various government agencies in educating the general public about the existence of public services online. Lee, and Porumbescu (2019) suggest that e-government services are only helpful if people know their existence, are motivated, and can use them effectively. The three indicators for assessing e-government outreach and demand are citizens' access to ICTs, use patterns, and citizens' level of education. E-participation in e-government remains suboptimal across the African continent.

These statistics show that some headway and effort have been made in South Africa, Botswana, and Zambia toward attaining a knowledge society through e-government adoption. However, several factors influence the adoption of e-government in these countries. Thus, this study seeks to:

- establish the effect of perceived susceptibility on e-government adoption.
- establish the effect of distrust propensity on e-government adoption.
- establish the effect of risk propensity on e-government adoption.
- establish the effect of uncertainty propensity on e-government adoption.

2. RESEARCH MODEL AND HYPOTHESES

This study is underpinned by three theoretical frameworks: the technology threat avoidance theory (TTAT), the protection motivation theory (PMT), and UTAU2.

The technology threat avoidance theory (TTAT) explains a system user's behavior of avoiding the threat of malicious information technologies (Liang and Xue, 2009). If one perceives themselves as vulnerable when engaging with an online system, it influences their motivation and behavior to avoid using such a system. Thus, the construct of perceived susceptibility from the TTAT theory is pertinent to this study. Several scholars (Ma and Zheng, 2019; Malodia et al., 2021) established perceived susceptibility as a predictor of digital service adoption. The Commitment-Trust Theory (CTT) asserts that successful relationship marketing requires relationship commitment and trust (Morgan and Hunt, 1994). It is widely used to assess the effect of electronic trust (e-trust) on adopting e-commerce. The CTT theory posits that commitment and trust lead directly to cooperative behaviors conducive to relationship marketing success. This theory is pertinent to the e-government context since it involves e-trust and commitment from all stakeholders to engage online. Thus, the CTT theory provides the distrust propensity construct to this study. Conspiracy Theories are a "subset of false beliefs in which the ultimate cause of an event is believed to be due to a plot by multiple actors working together with a clear goal in mind, often unlawfully and in secret" (Swami and Furnham, 2014, p. 220). The conspiracy theories provide the 'distrust propensity' construct for this study to understand how trust or their lack affects one's decisions to adopt e-government services.

However, several factors influence the adoption.

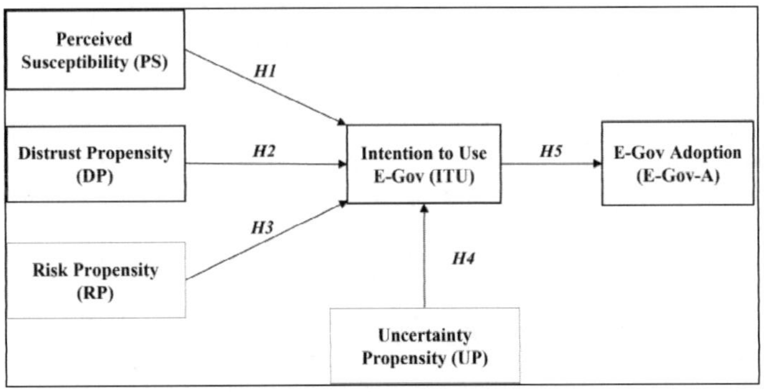

Figure 1. E-Government Research Model

Based on the five constructs in Figure 1five hypotheses underpins this study:

H1: Perceived Susceptibility (PS) positively influences the intention to use e-government (ITU).
H2: Distrust Propensity (DP) positively influences the intention to use e-government (ITU).
H3: Risk Propensity (RP) positively influences the intention to use e-government (ITU).
H4: Uncertainty Propensity (UP) positively influences the intention to use e-government (ITU).
H5: Intention to use e-government (ITU) positively influences e-government adoption (E-Gov-A).

3. METHODOLOGY

A quantitative research approach was adopted in this study as it facilitated the validation of the proposed research model to establish the significance of the five predictor variables of e-government adoption (E-Gov-A). A structured questionnaire was administered online to 600 respondents across the three countries (South Africa, Zambia, and Botswana) using survey monkeys and various social media platforms (489 were suitable and used in the final data analysis). Respondent-driven sampling (RDS) strategy was used to collect data from the 600 respondents. The RDS sampling technique was the best choice due to the complexity of identifying e-government users from the capital cities of these countries (South Africa, Zambia, and Botswana). Government agencies dealing with d-government matters, mobile phone companies, chiefs, and university student representatives were used as seedings in identifying the participants for this study. The IBM Statistical Package for the Social Sciences (SPSS) version 29 was used to capture, validate, verify, and analyze the collected data using regression analysis.

4. RESULTS AND DISCUSSION

Various approaches were adopted in this study to establish the reliability and validity of the measurement scales, as outlined next.

4.1 Reliability Analysis

Cronbach's Alpha (Cronbach, 1951) was used to establish the reliability of the measurement scales of the survey instrument. The rule of thumb is that all Cronbach's Alpha values should be at or above 0.70 to demonstrate good internal consistency (Hair et al., 2018). Table 1 shows that all five constructs of the survey instrument had their Cronbach's Alpha values above 0.70, thus, demonstrating good internal consistency in line with Hair et al. (2018) recommendation.

Table 1. Construct Reliability

Construct	**Number of Items**	**Cronbach's Alpha (α)**	**Comment**
Perceived Susceptibility (PS)	4	0.826	High Reliability ($\alpha >= 0.70$)
Distrust Propensity (DP)	4	0.878	High Reliability
Risk Propensity (RP)	4	0.778	High Reliability
Uncertainty Propensity (UP)	4	0.857	High Reliability
Intention to use e-government (ITU)	3	0.798	High Reliability

4.2 Validity Analysis

Validity analysis was done by establishing the sampling adequacy and unidimensionality of measurement scales using Exploratory Factor Analysis (EFA). This study used the Kaiser-Meyer-Olkin (KMO) to measure sampling adequacy, i.e., the suitability of data for factor analysis. KMO values for this study are above 0.8 and below 1.0 (see Table 2), thus, demonstrating sampling adequacy (Shrestha, 2021). The Chi-Square values for all five construct variables were significant with $p < 0.05$, thus demonstrating construct validity (Hair et al., 2018).

Table 2. Validity Analysis

Construct	Kaiser-Meyer-Olkin (KMO)	Chi-Square (χ^2)	significant ($p < 0.05$)
Perceived Susceptibility (PS)	0.895	297.231	$p < 0.001$
Distrust Propensity (DP)	0.973	197.825	$p < 0.000$
Risk Propensity (RP)	0.801	178.504	$p < 0.001$
Uncertainty Propensity (UP)	0.804	331.479	$p < 0.000$
Intention to use e-government (ITU)	0.821	385.123	$p < 0.000$

The factor loading values for the five constructs were above the cut-off level of 0.70 (Hair et al., 2018), thus suitable for regression analysis.

4.3 Regression Analysis

Regression analysis used the incremental fit measure, R Square, and ANOVA test. The incremental fit measure, R Square (R^2), is a ratio of the difference in the response variable and uses the null model (i.e., a flexible tool to statistically benchmark the finding) to compare the study results against the hypothesized model (Alexopoulos, 2010). The closer the value of R^2 to 1, the better the good fit of the research model. The R^2 was used to assess the incremental fit of the model. Multicollinearity occurs when one or more independent variables in a regression model are strongly correlated (Shrestha, 2021).

Regression analysis for the e-government adoption (E-Gov-A) shows that correlation coefficients (r) values, significant at 0.00 levels (2-tailed), ranged between -0.087 to 0.805. This finding confirms the absence of the problem of multicollinearity. Multiple regression tests show that the model of the independent variable explains about 15 percent of the variance in the dependent variable, with an R-square equal to 0.152 (see Table 3).

Table 3. Regression Analysis Results

Model	R	R Square	Adjusted R Square	Std. Error	R Square Change	F Change	df1	df2	Sig. F Change
1	0.348 a	0.152	0.141	0.557	0.152	14.102	6	496	0.000

a. Predictors: PS, RP, UP, ITU

ANOVA test results confirm that the research model is significantly better at predicting the outcome than the mean, with F = 14.102 and p = 0.000. The relationship between the dependent variable (e-government adoption- E-Gov-A) and the independent variables (PS, RP, UP, and ITU) was shown by the β-value and the significance of the t-test. The model confirmed a significant relationship between ITU and E-Gov-A with $\beta = 0.358$, significant at p = 0.000. The regression analysis demonstrated a significant relationship between the PS variable (PS with $\beta = 0.217$ and $p = 0.000$) and ITU. Likewise, a positive and significant relationship between DP and ITU was achieved with $\beta = 0.234$ and p = 0.001. Moreover, the ANOVA test confirms RP as a strong and positive predictor of ITU (i.e., $\beta = 0.198$; p = 0.011). Uncertainty propensity positively influenced the intention to use e-government with $\beta = 0.227$ and $p = 0.000$. Overall, the results show a significant F-Change value of 0.000.

Table 4 summarizes the hypotheses testing results as either supported or not by the findings. Perceived susceptibility positively influences citizens' intention to adopt e-government. Thus, hypothesis H1 was accepted. Similarly, distrust propensity, risk propensity, and uncertainty propensity influenced citizens' intention to adopt d-government. Thus, H2, H3 and H4 were accepted. Equally, the intention to use e-government positively influences e-government adoption. Thus, H5 is supported by the findings of this study.

Table 4. Hypotheses Testing Summary

Hypothesis Number	Hypothesis Item	Hypothesis Supported?
H1	Perceived Susceptibility (PS) positively influences the intention to use e-government (ITU).	Yes
H2	Distrust Propensity (DP) positively influences the intention to use e-government (ITU).	Yes
H3	Risk Propensity (RP) positively influences the intention to use e-government (ITU).	Yes
H4	Uncertainty Propensity (UP) positively influences the intention to use e-government (ITU).	Yes
H5	Intention to use e-government (ITU) positively influences e-government adoption (E-Gov-A).	Yes

Figure. 2 shows the final research model with validated predictor variables for the use behaviour independent variable.

Perceived Susceptibility - hypothesis (H1) was supported by the findings of this study. In the G2C setup, a person's subjective perception of the risk of being vulnerable when accessing government services via an e-government system. The results of this study reveal that people's fears of being exposed to hacking have a positive and significant effect on their intention to use e-government. This aligns with previous studies (Ma and Zheng, 2019; Malodia et al., 2021), which establish the perceived vulnerability as a strong predictor of intention to adopt e-government.

Distrust Propensity - the findings of this study supported hypothesis (H2). In the G2C setup, the customer's engagement with the e-government system is anchored on the trust that the transaction will be secure from cyberattacks and hacking. However, cyberattacks, hacking, and phishing on e-government systems lead to a lack of faith. This, in turn, leads to transaction abandonment and eversion. This finding aligns with previous studies (Hansen et al., 2018; Morgan and Hunt, 1994), establishing distrust propensity as a strong predictor of intention to adopt online services.

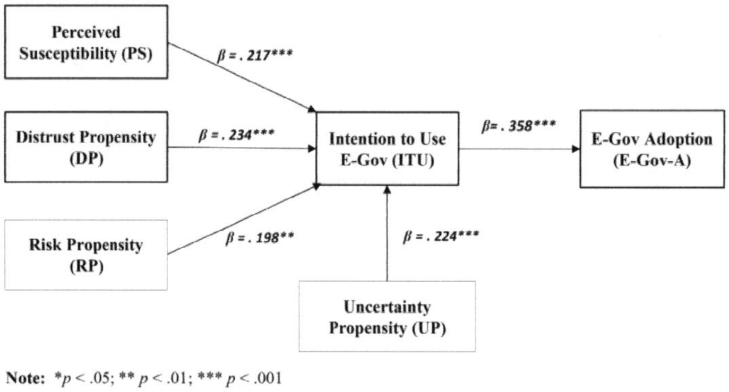

Figure 2. Research model showing significant constructs

The finding of this study confirmed Risk Propensity (hypothesis H3) as having a positive significant effect on citizens' intention to adopt e-government. Various studies establish that citizens' propensity to use e-government systems is driven by trust in the providers of the services (Hansen et al., 2018, Xie et al., 2017). Once users perceive being vulnerable and losing confidential personal details or money, they will likely avoid using such a system. Thus, the government should ensure that e-government systems are secure to build citizens' confidence and encourage adoption.

Uncertainty Propensity - the findings of this study confirmed hypothesis (H4). Nowadays, engagement on online services is associated with personal vulnerabilities and risks of being hacked and losing valuable personal information that could be used again via ransomware. The findings of this study concur with conclusions of previous scholars who establish uncertainty propensity as a salient determinant of e-government adoption (Venkatesh et al., 2016; Alkraiji and Ameen, 2022). Thus, government agencies should work tirelessly to secure e-government systems and create awareness programs on how system users can circumvent online attacks through phishing and other basic cyberattacks.

Hypothesis (H5) on citizens intention to use e-government was confirmed as a significant determinant of e-government adoption in this study. This finding concurs with findings of Khan et al., (2021) who establishes intention to use as a determinant of e-government adoption. Citizens' intention to adopt e-government is influenced by a range of factors, i.e., a person's subjective perception of the risk of being vulnerable when accessing government services and distrust perceptions due to previous attacks. Thus, to promote e-government adoption, governments should secure e-government systems and educate system users, especially from marginalized communities on various ways to avoid the traps of online phishing and hacking.

5. CONCLUSION

The findings of this study draw attention to the crucial role played by perceived susceptibility, distrust, risk, uncertainty propensity, and behavioural intention in shaping the adoption of e-government by citizens in developing nations. All five factors played a positive significant role in influencing the use behaviour of e-government. Citizens are most likely to adopt e-government services if they feel less vulnerable to cyber-attacks and that the systems are secure. Overall, the empirical findings of this study provide some basis for validating the five predictor variables of the proposed e-government research model. Therefore, the results of this study provide citizens' insights and views to policymakers on e-government-related matters on their sentiments on the effect of cyberattack vulnerabilities on decisions to adopt e-government. Lastly, by knowing those factors that prevent e-service adoption, governments will be better positioned to roll out secure e-government services to the citizens.

This study focused on the effects of five predictor variables on e-government adoption in the G2C setup in the context of three Southern African countries without paying attention to other construct variables and moderator variables like age, gender, and user experience. This constitutes one of the limitations of this study and should be investigated further. Similarly, caution should be taken when generalizing the findings of this study to different contexts. In the future, more predictor variables and moderating factors should be considered beyond the Southern African region.

ACKNOWLEDGEMENT

This work is an extension of my Ph.D. work, so no acknowledgment is worth noting.

REFERENCES

Alexopoulos, E.C., 2010. Introduction to multivariate regression analysis. *Hippokratia, 14(1), pp. 23–28.*

Alkraiji, A. and Ameen, N., 2022. The impact of service quality, trust, and satisfaction on young citizen loyalty towards government e-services. Information Technology & People, 35(4), pp.1239-1270.

Castro, C. and Lopes, C., 2022. Digital government and sustainable development. *Journal of the Knowledge Economy*, *13*(2), pp.880-903.

Chen, L. and Aklikokou, A.K., 2020. Determinants of E-government adoption: testing the mediating effects of perceived usefulness and perceived ease of use. International Journal of Public Administration, 43(10), pp.850-865.

Cronbach, L.J., 1951. Coefficient alpha and the internal structure of tests. *psychometrika*, *16*(3), pp.297-334.

Hair, B.J.F., Black, W.C. and Anderson, R.E., 2018. Multivariate Data Analysis, 8th, illustration ed.

Hansen, J.M., Saridakis, G. and Benson, V., 2018. Risk, trust, and the interaction of perceived ease of use and behavioral control in predicting consumers' use of social media for transactions. *Computers in human behavior*, *80*, pp.197-206.

International Telecommunication Union [ITU], "The ICT Development Index (IDI): conceptual framework and methodology"; May. 2023, [online] Available: https://www.itu.int/en/ITU-D/Statistics/Pages/publications/mis2016/methodology.aspx

Khan, S., Umer, R., Umer, S. and Naqvi, S., 2021. Antecedents of trust in using social media for E-government services: An empirical study in Pakistan. *Technology in Society*, *64*, p.101400.

Krishna, B. and MP, S., 2021. Examining the relationship between e-government development, nation's cyber-security commitment, business usage and economic prosperity: A cross-country analysis. *Information & Computer Security*, *29*(5), pp.737-760.

Lee, J.B. and Porumbescu, G.A., 2019. Engendering inclusive e-government use through citizen IT training programs. *Government Information Quarterly*, *36*(1), pp.69-76.

Liang, H. and Xue, Y., 2009. Avoidance of information technology threats: A theoretical perspective. *MIS Quarterly*, pp.71-90.

Ma, L. and Zheng, Y., 2019. National e-government performance and citizen satisfaction: a multilevel analysis across European countries. *International Review of Administrative Sciences*, *85*(3), pp.506-526.

Malodia, S., Dhir, A., Mishra, M., and Bhatti, Z.A., 2021. Future of e-Government: An integrated conceptual framework. *Technological Forecasting and Social Change*, *173*, p.121102.

Morgan, R.M. and Hunt, S.D., 1994. The commitment-trust theory of relationship marketing. *Journal of Marketing*, *58*(3), pp.20-38.

Munyoka, W., 2020. Electronic government adoption in voluntary environments–a case study of Zimbabwe. *Information Development*, *36*(3), pp.414-437.

Rose, J., Persson, J.S., Heeager, L.T. and Irani, Z., 2015. Managing e-Government: value positions and relationships. *Information Systems Journal*, *25*(5), pp.531-571.

Rose, J., Persson, J.S., Heeager, L.T. and Irani, Z., 2015. Managing e-Government: value positions and relationships. *Information Systems Journal*, *25*(5), pp.531-571.

Shrestha, N., 2021. Factor analysis as a tool for survey analysis. *American Journal of Applied Mathematics and Statistics*, *9*(1), pp.4-11.

Swami, V., and Furnham, A. (2014). Political paranoia and conspiracy theories, in *the Power Politics, and Paranoia: Why People Are Suspicious of Their Leaders*, eds J. P. van Proijen and P. A. M. van Lange (Cambridge: Cambridge University Press), 218–236. doi: 10.1017/CBO9781139565417.016

United Nations (2022) E-Government Survey 2022: The Future of Digital Government, New York, USA.

Venkatesh, V., Thong, J.Y., Chan, F.K. and Hu, P.J., 2016. Managing citizens' uncertainty in e-government services: The mediating and moderating roles of transparency and trust. *Information systems research*, *27*(1), pp.87-111.

Verkijika, S.F. and De Wet, L., 2018. E-government adoption in sub-Saharan Africa. *Electronic Commerce Research and Applications*, 30, pp.83-93.

World Bank, 2022. The Human Capital Project: Frequently Asked Questions. Available at: https://www.worldbank.org/en/publication/human-capital/brief/the-human-capital-project-frequently-asked-questions (Accessed: 25 May 2023)

Xie, Q., Song, W., Peng, X. and Shabbir, M., 2017. Predictors for e-government adoption: integrating TAM, TPB, trust and perceived risk. *The Electronic Library*, *35*(1), pp.2-20.

ADDRESSING ACCESSIBILITY, AFFORDABILITY AND SUSTAINABILITY BARRIERS FOR BROADBAND INTERNET ACCESS AND PENETRATION IN RURAL AREAS

Sicelokuhle Oscar Ngwenya[1], Reolyn Heymann[2], Theo G. Swart[2] and Albert A. Lysko[3]
[1]Postgraduate School of Engineering Management
University of Johannesburg, South Africa
[2]Department of Electrical and Electronic Engineering Science
University of Johannesburg, South Africa
[3]CSIR NextGen Enterprises and Institutions (NGEI)
Council for Scientific and Industrial Research (CSIR), South Africa

ABSTRACT

It has been said that the spread of Information and Communications Technology (ICT) and global interconnectedness has a great potential to accelerate human progress, to bridge the "digital divide" and to develop knowledge societies, in countries where it is available. However, it has also been determined that certain barriers, more prevalent in rural communities, pose an incessant impediment to the access and penetration trends of broadband internet networks and infrastructure in rural areas. These barriers have been identified as 'accessibility', 'affordability', and 'sustainability'. It is hereby asserted, therefore, that a concerted effort is required to address these barriers, with great deliberation and haste, if digital inclusion is to be achieved in rural areas. This paper proposes a broadband internet system that is aimed at addressing these barriers, through a proposed model, which is intended to be implemented as a Proof of Concept (PoC) in the rural area of Mbazwana, located in the province of KwaZulu-Natal (KZN), South Africa (SA). The model has been presented to the community, and subsequently followed by a survey to determine the feasibility of the implementation thereof. This paper will present the proposed model, as well as the results obtained from the research conducted.

KEYWORDS

Accessibility, Affordability, Broadband, Digital Divide, ICT, Internet, Mbazwana, Rural, South Africa, Sustainability, Urban

1. INTRODUCTION

Accessibility, affordability, and sustainability are three of the main barriers to broadband internet access and penetration in rural areas (Ngwenya *et al.*, 2023). These barriers are the main contributing factors to the so-called "Digital Divide", which is described as "the gap between individuals, households, businesses and geographic areas at different socio-economic levels with regard both to their opportunities to access ICTs and to their use of the internet for a wide variety of activities" (Souter *et al.*, 2009). In the current economic and social epoch, this is deemed to be non-progressive by several papers and studies, as the world moves into a digital era, where the internet is an essential enabler and tool for participation (Stork, Calandro and Gamage, 2014) (Institute of Electrical and Electronics Engineers, 2009) (Mosenthal, Nleya and Manthoko, 2009) (Rully *et al.*, 2005) (Su and Caballero, 2010). As a result, the demand for ICT has risen sharply as countries continually recognise the benefits and potential of it as a tool for social and economic development.

This connectivity is typically achieved by providing broadband access to the general population. Broadband penetration is considered an important factor for economic growth in a society, by improving productivity of businesses, accelerating innovation and providing opportunities for new products and services (Stork, Calandro and Gamage, 2014). The primary beneficiaries of this development at present, however, are the developed countries, referred to as 'First World' countries. Statistics show that broadband penetration has occurred vastly and much more rapidly in these countries than in their 'Third World' country counterparts. First world countries are characterised by the definition of being "industrialised" and are often leading the way in the ICT sector, including the provision of broadband infrastructure and access to most of their respective populations, who typically reside in suburban and urban areas. In third world countries, however, in most cases, a significant percentage of the population resides in underdeveloped and underserved areas, often associated with rural areas. In these areas, the same trend for ICT services, including internet access, is not seen. Generally, rural, and isolated areas of the developing world are still largely disconnected in terms of internet services. This is epitomized in some countries, like Tanzania, for example, where the majority of the population lives in rural areas (Byanyuma *et al.*, 2013). These same countries are normally characterised by poor infrastructure and services (or the complete lack thereof), low income, illiteracy and poverty amongst the population, as well as highly scattered and low-density landscape and terrains (Byanyuma *et al.*, 2013). It is therefore concluded that unequal access to internet services directly relates to unequal access to opportunities, jobs, and the ability to deal with unexpected events such as emergencies and disasters. As a result, the need to connect rural areas using broadband internet becomes more and more crucial. This paper aims to recommend a feasible proposal that will address the broadband access and penetration trends in rural areas that will be ***affordable, accessible,*** and ***sustainable*** for rural communities while stimulating economic participation and growth.

In Section 2 of the paper, the problem statement is presented. Section 3 describes the research methodology that was employed to conduct this research. The research design, done in two parts, is expanded upon, where the process and objective thereof are described. This is followed by a presentation and analysis of the results obtained, in Section 4, and a discussion of the results in Section 5. Finally, the paper is concluded with a summary of the outcome of the research, including recommendations and proposed future work.

2. PROBLEM STATEMENT

Based on statistics published in January 2021, there were 4.66 billion active internet users worldwide, which makes up approximately 59.5% of the global population (Hassan *et al.*, 2021). The unfortunate news is that the other 40% of the global population remains offline, and most of this "other half" resides in developing countries where, on average, 45% of the population has access to the internet. Most of these digitally excluded communities are situated in emerging economy countries with large rural populations (Mekuria *et al.*, 2021). Some of the main, generally agreed upon, attributes that prevent the adoption of ICTs in rural areas, according to work done in some academic papers such as (Henry, 2019a) and (Vemu, Bhatnagar and Hemachandra, 2007), are depicted as "Affordability", "Accessibility" and "Sustainability", and ultimately the problem statement that is intended to be addressed by this paper.

3. RESEARCH METHODOLOGY AND DESIGN

The methodology that was employed to conduct the research for this paper is based on public surveys and in-person interviews. This was done with the objective to consult with the community with respect to the specific challenges that they face as a community, which uphold, if not exacerbate, the digital divide. Following a visit to the rural community of Mbazwana on the 18th of March 2023, 176 community members were engaged by the research team with respect to broadband internet access barriers in the community. The first step was a proposal for a community incentive-based data package sales model, to address the challenges of accessibility, affordability, and sustainability of rural broadband systems. This is proposed to be implemented as part of a Proof of Concept (PoC) using a Television White Space based Broadband Network (TVWS) (Mzyece, Mfupe and Mekuria, 2018), to be deployed in the community of Mbazwana. The choice of TVWS was based on the excellent propagation properties of TVWS waves and the cost efficiency of the TVWS setup. The locations of the access points (APs) were identified in collaboration with the community, based on the footfall trends, on a daily basis at these sites. This system is meant to be a bespoke solution for the community of Mbazwana, with the intention to follow the same approach with other rural areas in the future. The second and final step included the distribution of a questionnaire, which consisted of non-intrusive, concise questions, presented mostly in a multiple-choice format. Participation and completion of this questionnaire excluded minors (under the age of 18 years) in accordance with the university ethics committee's guidance.

3.1 Community Incentive Based Sales Model and PoC

The community incentive-based sales model is a proposal with the intention of addressing accessibility, affordability, and sustainability barriers to internet access, as identified by the research team. The sales model, depicted in Figure 1, includes data packages that are relatively more affordable compared to those currently offered by traditional Internet Service Providers (ISPs). These data bundles, however, will be valid for shorter periods. The internet access would be provisioned by a Television White Space (TVWS) broadband network pilot, with access points situated in four locations that have been identified by the research team, in consultation with the community. These four locations include two high schools (Mpiyakhe High School and King Moses Secondary School), a local clinic and an art centre. These locations have been chosen due to the proximity to the main economic hub of the village, as well as the number of potential users that are present at the locations, on a regular basis. These locations are also aligned with those identified as part of the objective and targets stipulated in South Africa's National Broadband Policy (NBP), the SA Connect Policy (*South Africa's Broadband Policy*, 2013).

Additionally, the community incentive-based sales model proposes that all proceeds of the data voucher sales be kept in a central repository, that will be overseen by democratically elected members of the community, by the community. The broadband system portal is to be bespoke to the community of Mbazwana with the ability to advertise local small businesses. The resellers of the data vouchers, who are proposed to be community members, are also offered an incentive to advertise their services on the platform. Finally, the tribal council is also entitled to advertise communications pertinent to the issues of the community, including social and political events, as and when they arise. The model also proposes three options for regular users, where the biggest monthly data user(s) is offered a reward of free data bundles.

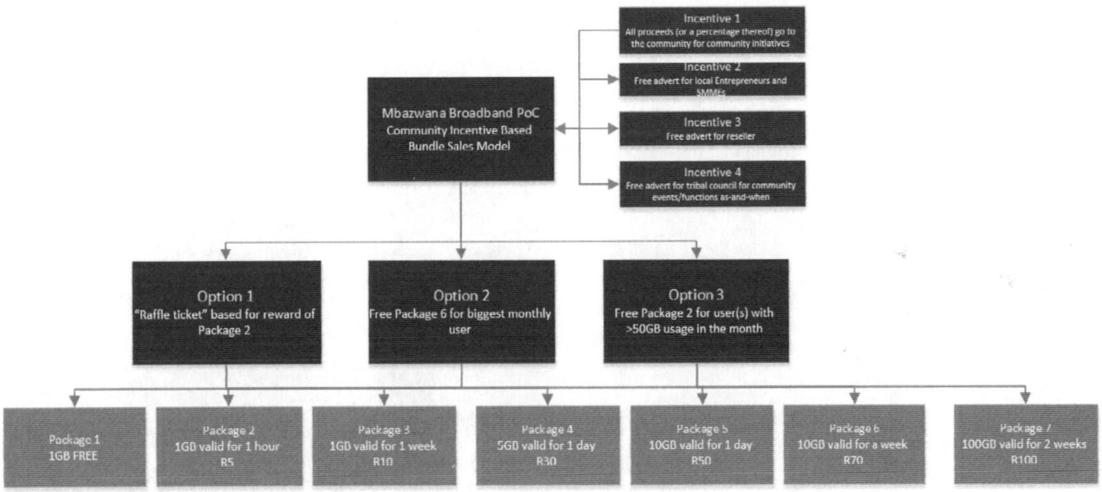

Figure 1. Community Incentive-Based Sales Model

3.2 Questionnaire

The questionnaires were distributed in physical form to all the 176 attendees. Prior to this, consent forms were distributed to all participants, in accordance with the UJ ethics committee approval. The objective of the questionnaire was to elicit the extent to which the three above-mentioned barriers are prevalent, specifically in the rural area of Mbazwana. The envisaged outcome of the questionnaire was to use the information obtained, in conjunction with the feedback received from the community incentive-based model presented, to propose/recommend the most suitable broadband system that is accessible to all in the community (all ages, genders, races, etc.), and that is also affordable and sustainable. It was anticipated, as has been done in papers such as (Mekuria *et al.*, 2021) and (Mzyece, Mfupe and Mekuria, 2018), that the involvement of the community in this process would ensure that the community members would protect and preserve the broadband system, in recognition that it would greatly benefit them, by providing readily accessible, affordable, always-on and high-speed internet, which will in turn provision access to ICT services. The results of the questionnaire are discussed in the next section.

4. RESULTS AND ANALYSIS

4.1 Age and Employment Status

Although all age groups were represented, the responses on the age profile of the participants indicate that the majority is between the ages of 18 and 29. The employment status of the participants indicates that the majority of the participants are in fact unemployed. These results are depicted in Figures 2 and 3.

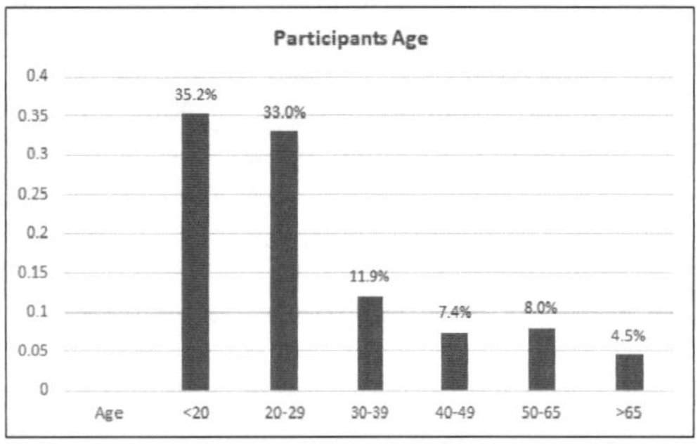

Figure 2. Age Profile

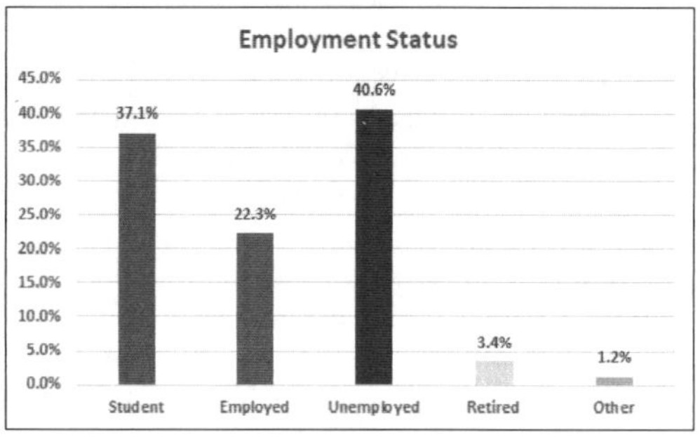

Figure 3. Employment Status

4.2 Internet Access

The majority of the participants claimed to have access to the internet, with over 90% reporting that they own a smartphone, as a primary means of their internet access. This is depicted in Figures 4 and 5.

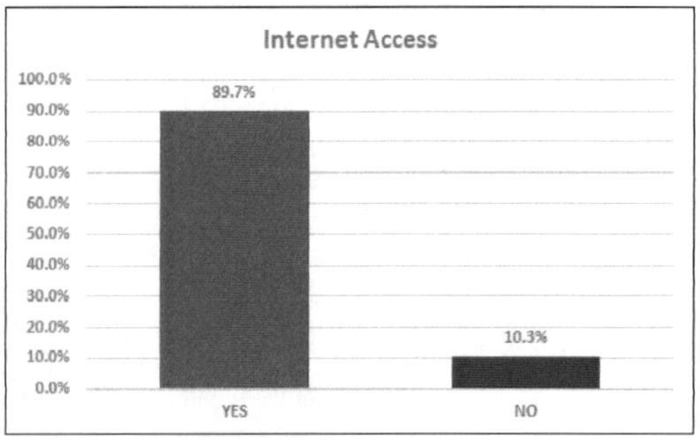

Figure 4. Internet Access

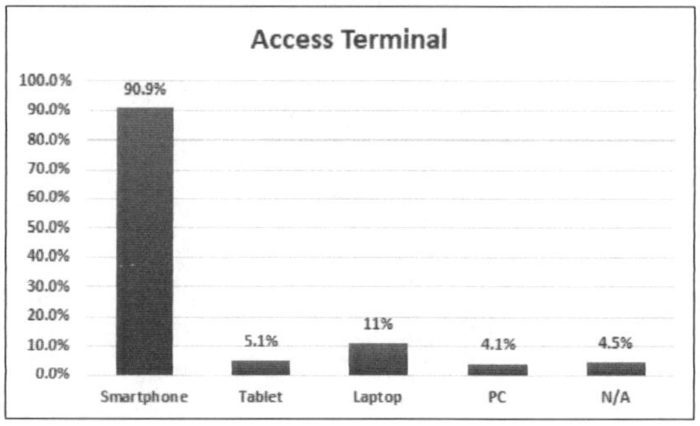

Figure 5. Internet Access Terminal

4.3 Internet Access Location

Currently, the majority of the participants claim to be able to access the internet at their homes, followed by the workplace and school. When asked where they would prefer to access the internet, should a community-based broadband system be introduced, the participants reported that their preferred location to be their home, followed by school and workplace. These results are depicted in Figure 6.

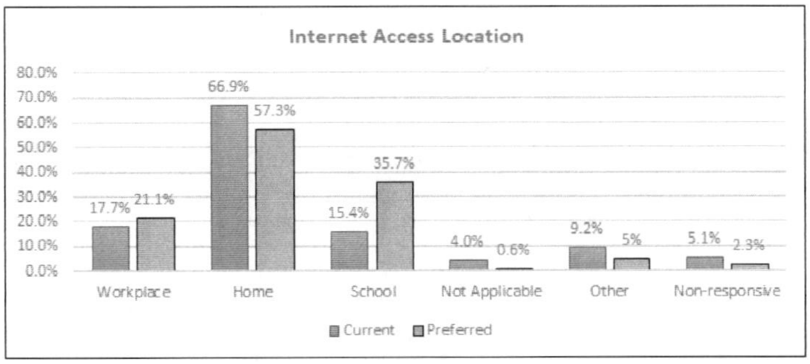

Figure 6. Current Internet Access Location

4.4 Internet Access Limitations

The participants were asked what kind of limitations they experience with their current internet access. The majority reported that money constraints are the most prevalent issue. This was followed by the quality of the broadband service, with respect to connection speeds and availability thereof. A significant number of the participants also cited distance and use time constraints as a limitation. This result is depicted in Figure 7.

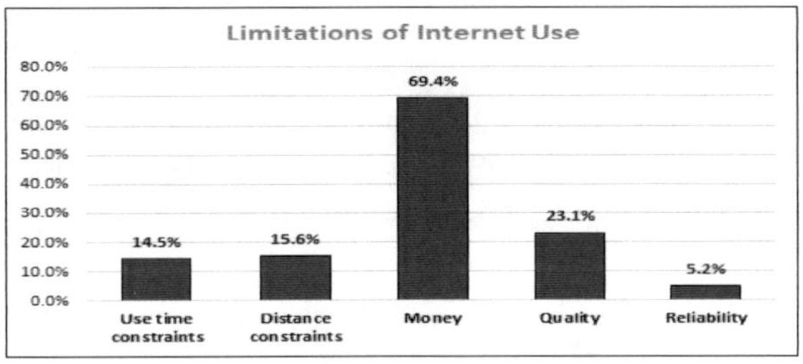

Figure 7. Internet Use Limitations

4.5 Monthly Data Spend

Currently, the majority of the participants reported to be spending the minimum amount of money, from the options presented to them. The participants further reported that they would be willing to pay a little more for monthly data if they deemed the data bundle package to be reasonably priced. This result is depicted in Figure 8.

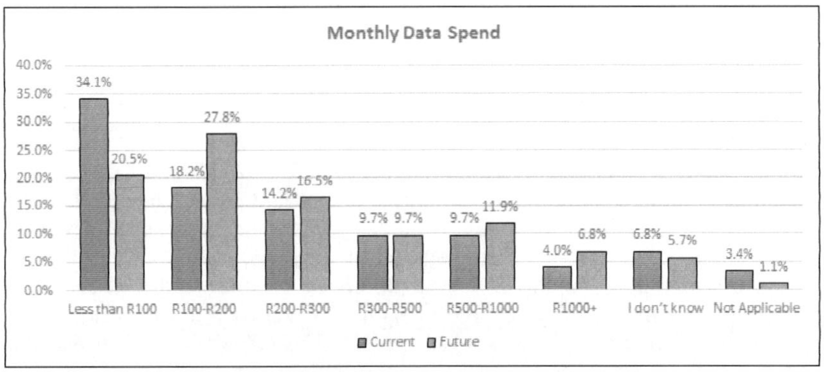

Figure 8. Current and Future Monthly Data Spend

4.6 Monthly Data Usage

The result from the previous data in Section 4.5 translates to the majority of the participants using the least amount of monthly data, from the options presented and preferring to spend a little more for a larger amount of data, should it be made available at what they perceive as a more palatable cost. This result is depicted in Figure 9.

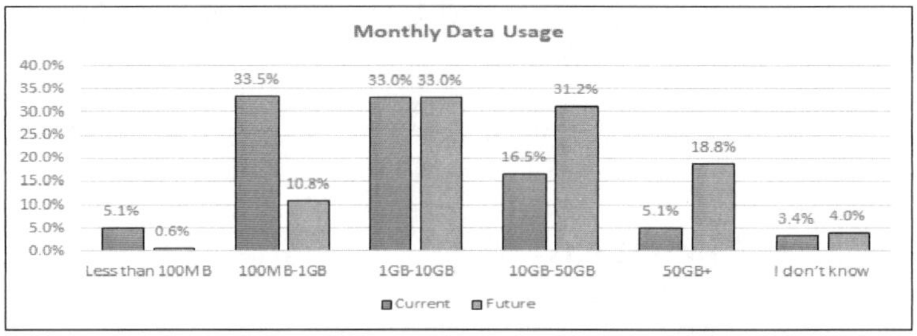

Figure 9. Current and Future Monthly Data Usage

4.7 Support

The majority of the participants reported that they are in support of the proposal as presented by the research team, as they indicated that they believe the proposal would work in their community, if implemented as per the research teams' proposal. The majority, however, also indicated that there is a concern of potential corruption if the correct individuals are not allocated to oversee this proposal. These results are depicted in Figures 10 and 11.

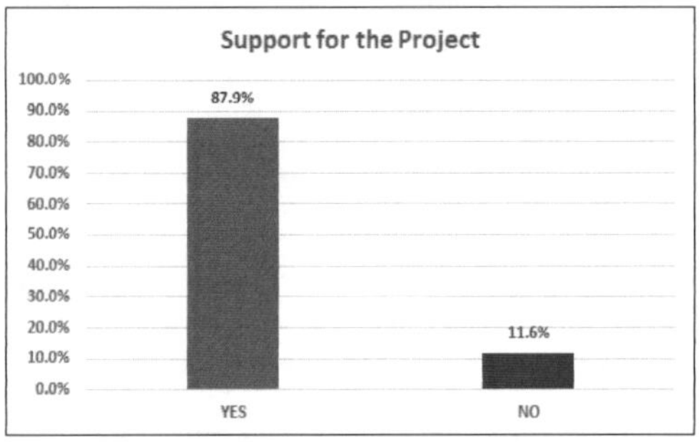

Figure 10. Support for the Proposal

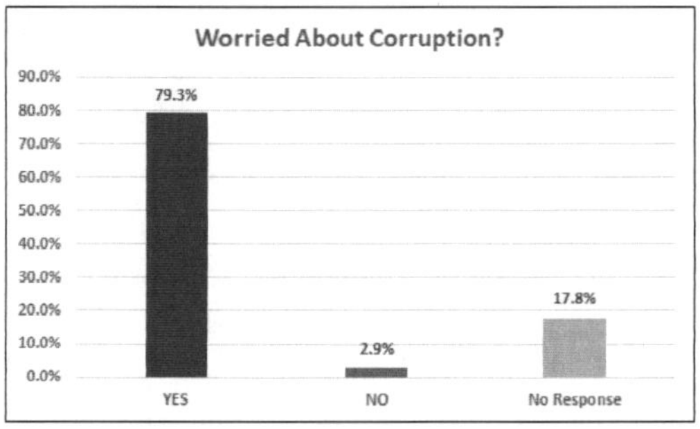

Figure 11. Concerns about Corruption

5. DISCUSSION OF RESULTS

All age groups, from the sample of respondents who participated, are represented in this survey. It has been noted, however, that young people are more represented, more than any other age group, which alludes to the interest in ICT services per age group. Unemployment amongst the group is clearly demonstrated, as the majority of the participants are unemployed. This result reflects the affordability barrier. The majority of the participants have also reported that they do have access to the internet and own smartphones, however, they have also reported that there are limitations to this access. The majority has cited that there are financial constraints which pose an impediment for regular and continuous internet access. Some have cited distance constraints, i.e., they are required to travel long distances to access the internet, and some have cited the quality of the network that is provisioned by ISPs. Some have indicated that they have time constraints imposed on them, especially where their internet access relies solely or partially on public amenities such as internet cafes, local libraries, and local community centres. This result reflects the accessibility barrier that has been identified. The participants have also reported that they use and spend the minimum amount of internet data and money from the options presented to them, respectively. This is expected as the majority is unemployed, and so affordability becomes an issue, especially since the internet data costs in SA are considered to be relatively exorbitant by the rural community. The participants, who are largely considered to be representing the views of the community, have indicated that the proposal of a bespoke community broadband network would work, as the incentive-based model, as well as the affordable internet data offers, are deemed acceptable. The community members have also expressed their approval for the different incentives offered, particularly Option 3 in Figure 1. This is further strengthened by the fact that all proceeds will be under the auspices of the community, for further expansion of the scalable system, as well as other community development initiatives. The main concern that was expressed by the participants regarding this proposal is the embezzlement of funds, should the individuals elected to oversee the sales not be cautiously elected.

6. CONCLUSION

Following the visit to Mbazwana, the research team concluded that the community incentive-based sales model using television white space (TVWS) technology would best address the three barriers of accessibility, affordability, and sustainability. The location of the four APs that have been selected are in alignment with SA's National Broadband Policy (SA Connect Policy) and are accessible to the majority of the community members of Mbazwana. The data packages that have been offered are palatable to the community members, who have expressed interest in, and approval for the above-mentioned proposal made by the research team, which will be implemented as a proof of concept. The community has expressed its concern about corruption and mishandling of funds and has asked the research team to formulate a framework on how the sales should be conducted, to minimise the potential of corruption. As of the publication of this paper, the proof of concept, under the auspices of the University of Johannesburg (UJ), South Africa, has been approved and is to be implemented during the second half of the current year, 2023. The research team has further formulated an economic market structure proposal to the community of Mbazwana, to be used to regulate sales by the local resellers of the internet data vouchers, aimed to minimise corruption. These proposals are deemed to be sufficient to address the barriers to internet access and penetration in rural areas, and in turn bridge the digital divide in the area. For future work, it is recommended that the implementation and operation of this model is closely monitored in order to determine if it fulfils the intended objectives of an accessible, affordable and sustainable rural broadband model.

REFERENCES

Byanyuma, M. *et al.* (2013) 'Affordable Broadband Connectivity For Rural Areas', in *2013 Pan African International Conference on Information Science, Computing and Telecommunications, PACT 2013*. Institute of Electrical and Electronics Engineers Inc., pp. 62–65. Available at: https://doi.org/10.1109/SCAT.2013.7055090.

Department of Communications (2013) *Republic Of South Africa South Africa Connect: Creating Opportunities, Ensuring Inclusion South Africa's Broadband Policy*. Available at: www.gpwonline.co.za.

Hassan, S.M.M. *et al.* (2021) 'Bridging the Digital Divide in Malaysia using Fixed Wireless Access', in *Proceeding - 2021 26th IEEE Asia-Pacific Conference on Communications, APCC 2021*. Institute of Electrical and Electronics Engineers Inc., pp. 74–78. Available at: https://doi.org/10.1109/APCC49754.2021.9609825.

Henry, L. (2019a) *'Bridging the urban-rural digital divide and mobilizing technology for poverty eradication: challenges and gaps'*. St Augustine, Trinidad and Tobago. Available at: https://www.un.org/development/desa/dspd/wp-content/uploads/sites/22/2019/02/Henry-Bridging-Digital-Divide.pdf.

Institute of Electrical and Electronics Engineers. (2009) *ISABEL 2009 : 2nd International Symposium on Applied Sciences in Biomedical and Communication Technologies, November 24-27, 2009, Bratislava, Slovak Republic.* IEEE.

Mekuria, F. *et al.* (2021) 'Affordable connectivity and digital entrepreneurial ecosystem for rural Africa', in *IEEE AFRICON Conference*. Institute of Electrical and Electronics Engineers Inc. Available at: https://doi.org/10.1109/AFRICON51333.2021.9570984.

Mosenthal, J.T., Nleya, B. and Manthoko, N.G. (2009) 'Broadband / future generation network services deployment in rural and remote areas', in *ICAST 2009 - 2nd International Conference on Adaptive Science and Technology*, pp. 128–132. Available at: https://doi.org/10.1109/ICASTECH.2009.5409736.

Mzyece, M., Mfupe, L.P. and Mekuria, F. (2018) *Innovating for Broadband: The Case of Television White Space Networks in Sub-Saharan Africa*. Johannesburg. Available at: https://researchspace.csir.co.za/dspace/bitstream/handle/10204/12462/Mfupe_2018.pdf?sequence=1&isAllowed=y.

Ngwenya, S.O. *et al.* (2023) 'A Comparative Analysis Of Urban And Rural Broadband Penetration And Access Trends In South Africa', in *International Association for Development of the Information Society, 17th Multiconference on Computer Science and Information Systems*, p. 10.

Rully, A. *et al.* (2005) 'Addressing digital divide: Experiment on tele-medicine applications using broadband wireless system in rural areas', in *2005 International Conference on Wireless and Optical Communications Networks*, pp. 98–101. Available at: https://doi.org/10.1109/wocn.2005.1435997.

Souter, D. *et al.* (2009) *The APC ICT Policy Handbook*. Available at: www.apc.org.

Stork, C., Calandro, E. and Gamage, R. (2014) 'The future of broadband in Africa', *Info*, 16(1), pp. 76–93. Available at: https://doi.org/10.1108/info-10-2013-0055.

Su, Y. and Caballero, I. (2010) 'Deployment of broadband wireless access for e-health in Chinese rural areas', in *2010 2nd International Conference on Communication Systems, Networks and Applications, ICCSNA 2010*, pp. 34–37. Available at: https://doi.org/10.1109/ICCSNA.2010.5588948.

Vemu, K.R., Bhatnagar, S. and Hemachandra, N. (2007) 'Link route pricing for enhanced QoS', *Proceedings of the IEEE Conference on Decision and Control*, 2(2), pp. 1504–1509. Available at: https://doi.org/10.1109/CDC.2007.4434595.

UNLOCKING THE VALUE OF CULTURAL HERITAGE IMAGES THROUGH SEMANTIC TECHNOLOGIES – TAKE "MISS" AS EXAMPLE

Yang Xin[1], Zhang Junjie[1], Fu Yaming[2] and Chen Tao[1*]
[1]School of Information Management, Sun Yat-Sen University
Guangzhou 510006, China
[2]School of Cultural Heritage and Information Management, Shanghai University
Shanghai 200444, China

ABSTRACT

The preservation of cultural heritage through the concept of "activation" represents a pivotal approach to unlocking its intrinsic value. Images, serving as a fundamental medium for manifesting and transmitting cultural heritage, frequently encounter formidable challenges related to sharing and reusability. These challenges stem from the limited interoperability among cultural institutions, resulting in the depreciation of these images and the establishment of isolated "image silos." Nevertheless, the application of advanced semantic web technologies for knowledge organization offers a viable solution. Semantic web technologies offer a way to facilitate standardized descriptions, streamline semantic retrieval, enhance interactive sharing, and establish robust knowledge associations with cultural heritage image resources. In this context, this paper introduces the Multi-dimensional Image Smart System (MISS), constructed upon the 'LIBRA technology stack', encompassing Linked Data, IIIF (International Image Interoperability Framework), Big Data, RDF (Resource Description Framework), and AI (Artificial Intelligence). MISS is structured into resource, system, and application layers, enabling the accomplishment of four core functions: dynamic Optical Character Recognition (OCR), multi-layer image annotation, cultural discovery, image reuse, and re-aggregation. Consequently, MISS plays a pivotal role in infrastructure building and the dissemination of cultural heritage images. Its practical implementation has been successfully demonstrated across multiple institutions dedicated to the preservation of cultural heritage images, effectively broadening, and enriching the presentation and utilization of these valuable image resources. Furthermore, MISS holds significant promise for application in digital humanities research and various pertinent academic domains.

KEYWORDS

International Image Interoperability Framework, Cultural Heritage, Image Management, Digital Humanities, Semantic Web

1. INTRODUCTION

Preserving and passing down cultural heritage to future generations effectively and efficiently poses a considerable challenge in the realm of cultural heritage protection and inheritance. Thanks to advancements in information technology (IT), digitizing cultural heritage now offers enhanced possibilities for both preservation and transmission. Among various data formats, images, when treated with the same level of interactivity and shareability, have the potential to greatly facilitate cultural transmission and inspire new creative endeavors. However, the effective transmission, sharing, and interoperability of cultural heritage images face significant obstacles due to the lack of a universal system among image databases that follows standard data rules. This limitation hinders the reuse and semantic exploration of cultural heritage image resources.

To enable cross-institutional sharing and interoperability of image resources, the International Image Interoperability Framework (IIIF) was proposed by galleries, libraries, archives, and museums (GLAM) in 2015. The IIIF Consortium, now with 65 members, including prestigious institutions like Harvard University, the British Library, the Vatican Library, and the Bodleian Library, mainly consists of GLAM institutions and

*Corresponding author: chent283@mail.sysu.edu.cn

universities. Increasingly, GLAM institutions and projects are adopting IIIF as their image infrastructure. For instance, Julien A. R. proposed measures for deploying IIIF in Swiss cultural heritage institutions (Raemy & Schneider, 2019), OCLC's digital collection supports IIIF access via CONTENTdm, the Bodleian Library at Oxford University uses IIIF for displaying medieval manuscripts (Gomez, Allen, Matney, et al., 2020), and the Library of Congress released IIIF image resources of the Yongle Encyclopedia.

Moreover, given the vast repositories of cultural heritage images in the digital realm, there is an immediate need to convey the information and knowledge encapsulated within them, particularly from a knowledge organization perspective. Leveraging the distinct advantages of semantic web technology in knowledge representation, description, and organization, research in the field of digital humanities has increasingly turned to the design of ontologies, RDF, linked data, SPARQL, and related semantic web technologies to address these challenges. For instance, Chen et al. introduced an image semantic relation model grounded in web-based knowledge (Chen, Guo & Dong, 2013). They employed semantic web technology to semantically annotate the content of digital images, aiming to enhance image retrieval, integration, and knowledge discovery within digital image collections (Chen & Qu, 2021).

In general, the utilization of semantic web technology and IIIF in digital humanities has progressively advanced, and their collaborative integration in image research is steadily gaining traction. Gene Loh proposed that by combining Linked Data with IIIF specifications, which becomes feasible to achieve semantic annotation of images and delve deeper into image content (Loh, 2017). Through IIIF and Linked Data, the Cultural Japan project has released over one million collections in the form of linked data. Similarly, the Europeana project employs IIIF as a foundational infrastructure to seamlessly integrate digital images with EDM metadata. Currently, their combined application plays a significant role in the cross-modal aggregation of images and metadata and is experiencing expanding usage.

Against this backdrop, the development of the Multi-dimensional Image Smart System (MISS) was undertaken to enhance the knowledge and semantics associated with images, facilitated by their improved interoperability. This system serves as a crucial link connecting images with knowledge. Currently, the MISS platform offers a range of functionalities, including image uploading, reuse, organization, annotation, collaboration, and sharing. MISS harnesses the support of the 'LIBRA technology stack', which encompasses Linked Data, the International Image Interoperability Framework (IIIF), Big Data, the Resource Description Framework (RDF), and Artificial Intelligence (AI) (Chen, Li, Zhang, et al., 2022).

2. DESIGN CONSIDERATIONS AND INNOVATIONS

2.1 MISS Architecture

Figure 1 illustrates the architecture of the MISS platform, primarily constructed upon the 'LIBRA technology stack'. Its primary objective is to establish a comprehensive ecosystem for image applications, enriching the semantic dimensions of cultural heritage images in a multi-faceted manner, and fostering innovation in humanities and art research. The architecture mainly consists of the following three layers.

(a) The bottom layer, known as the resource layer, predominantly consists of image resources provided by a wide range of collection institutions in the form of IIIF manifests.

(b) The middle layer encompasses key functionalities of the MISS platform, encompassing object and text recognition, semantic annotation and association, cultural discovery, and online re-aggregation of cultural heritage images.

(c) The top layer, the application layer, showcases the MISS platform's capacity to offer features such as image annotation and sharing.

It is worth noting that IIIF does not constitute a standalone application system; instead, it provides six programmable APIs designed for the sharing and interoperability of images across different platforms. These APIs include the Image API, Presentation API, Search API, Authentication API, Change Discovery API, and Content State API (Shan, Chen, Liu, et al., 2021). The first five APIs have already been integrated into the MISS platform, while the latest API, a stable version was released last year, and will be incorporated in its future developments.

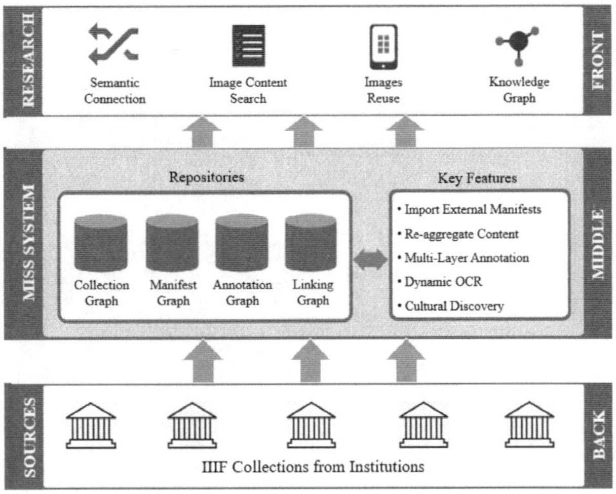

Figure 1. The architecture of MISS

2.2 Innovation Opinions

2.2.1 Dynamic OCR

Chinese characters are the only ideographic characters in existence, which is rich in connotations. In cultural heritage images, art forms such as calligraphy, painting, and seals interpret each other in symbiosis, generating diverse dimensions of meaning. The OCR result separated from the original images will lack the soul of Chinese characters, therefore, the idea of dynamic OCR is proposed. The OCR function on MISS is supported by a third-party OCR tool (Unihan online OCR API) to perform dynamic OCR and manual proof reading of text in images. Text generated from OCR is not only an important source of image semantic annotation, but also can be taken as a useful machine learning corpus to improve the OCR recognition rate. Dynamic OCR reduces the complexity of images and text conversion, providing a solid foundation for semantic organization of images.

The traditional OCR method involves performing OCR on the entire image. In contrast, the concept of dynamic OCR entails selecting a suitable image area for OCR based on researchers' specific requirements. This approach is motivated by several factors. Firstly, cultural heritage images are often large, with some reaching several gigabytes, posing challenges for comprehensive OCR across the entire image. Secondly, cultural heritage images normally contain non-text image content, which is inherently challenging to OCR. Presently, the platform provides support for third-party company OCR interfaces and has established a collaboration with Unihan company (https://www.unihan.com.cn/) to facilitate OCR processes for East Asia ancient books.

2.2.2 Multi-Layer Image Annotation

According to the characteristics of cultural heritage images, this paper proposed a five-layer semantic annotation model shown in figure 2 which includes spectrum layer, image layer, object layer, semantics layer and smart layer. The model forms an image knowledge chain from surface layer to inner layer, from explicit to invisible, and from perception to cognition, in order to enrich image content, cluster and link objects in images, by which the users can quickly retrieve, obtain, and understand the extrinsic and intrinsic meaning of images.

(a) Spectral layer mainly superimposes hyperspectral images in existing images to present multi-dimensional features of images from different angles, especially the image features of invisible light parts. Hyperspectral images are often used in the archaeological process of cultural relics, and are often used in the process of dating and forgery of cultural relics.

(b) The image layer is the metadata organization of the image through ontology, such as the title, author, creator, carrier, creation time, external description information, etc., which information is usually

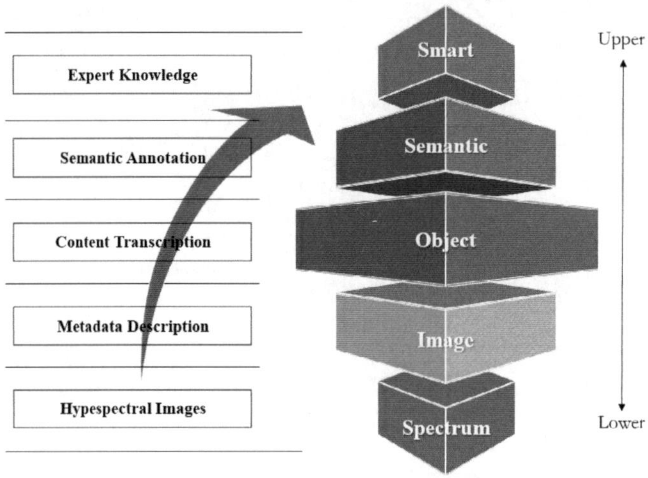

Figure 2. Multi-layer Annotation of Images

provided by the collection institution that holds the image. The function of image layer is to describe and explain the theme, content, attributes, and characteristics of cultural heritage images, to organize and retrieve them more conveniently and quickly.

(c) The object layer is aiming to transcriptions or annotations. Image often contains different objects which author use to express themselves. Person, object, entity, character, and even every pixel in the image can be considered as an object that can help with the annotation and understanding of the image. When annotating, objects in the image can be automatically identified in combination with the VoTT (Visual Object Tagging Tool). Identified tags can be organized using the W3C's recommended WADM (Web Annotation Data Model).

(d) The semantics layer is based on the image layer and object layer, aiming to extend the cultural content or establish connection between images. On the one hand, metadata and objects annotated in an image can be associated with entities in other open datasets, such as DBPedia, WIKIDATA, Freebase and so on, through the object property of ontologies. On the other hand, objects annotated can be associated with the same objects in other images within MISS.

(e) The smart layer is mainly the interpretation of the image content from experts and scholars with their background knowledge and professional evaluation. This layer will raise annotations of images from the perceptual to the cognitive level to a certain extent, providing more research possibilities for image researchers.

2.2.3 Cultural Discovery

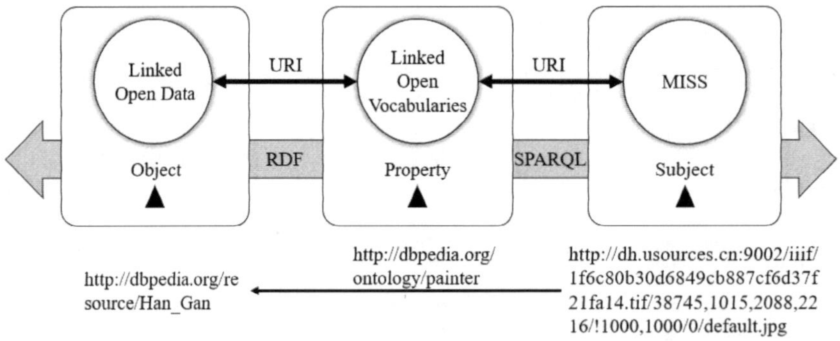

Figure 3. Knowledge discovery through semantic annotation

The main purpose of cultural discovery is to obtain diverse dimensions of cultural knowledge by establishing links between images within MISS with existing open datasets. For metadata information, such as creator, the federated query provided by SPARQL (Zhang, Yu & Wang, 2021) is used to query the same entities from local and external SPARQL endpoints. The SPARQL endpoint is a simple interface that allows users to obtain RDF data available on the server by executing SPARQL queries, thus solving the problem of the lack of semantic processing (Mosser, Pieressa, Reutter, et al., 2022).

With the semantic annotation in the five-layer annotation model, the connection between local objects in the image and the linked open dataset can be realized, to obtain more data to achieve knowledge discovery. Figure 3 shows the process of semantic annotation. The local area of the annotated image in MISS has a unique URI address, which can be used as the subject. For the predicate part of the connection, the appropriate property in the ontology is selected, which can be queried and used in the LoV (Linked Open Vocabularies). The object part is primarily the resource URI in the target dataset to be connection. After the connection is established, a large amount of RDF data in the target dataset can be obtained.

2.2.4 Image Online Re-Aggregation

Within IIIF, the image API facilitates image-centric interactions and responses through web services, while the presentation API offers interface specifications for organizing and presenting image URIs. These APIs greatly simplify the acquisition and interaction with images across different institutions. Many collection institutions share their image resources online through manifest.json files. Each manifest typically provides instructions on how to render a single composite object, whether it is an image (such as a page from a manuscript), or a collection of multiple images (such as a book). Scholars often require the ability to curate relevant content from different manifests to create new research topics, like assembling songs from different music albums to create a personalized playlist. In the context of MISS, users can import manifests from different organizations and select the images they wish to combine within each manifest to construct new manifest files.

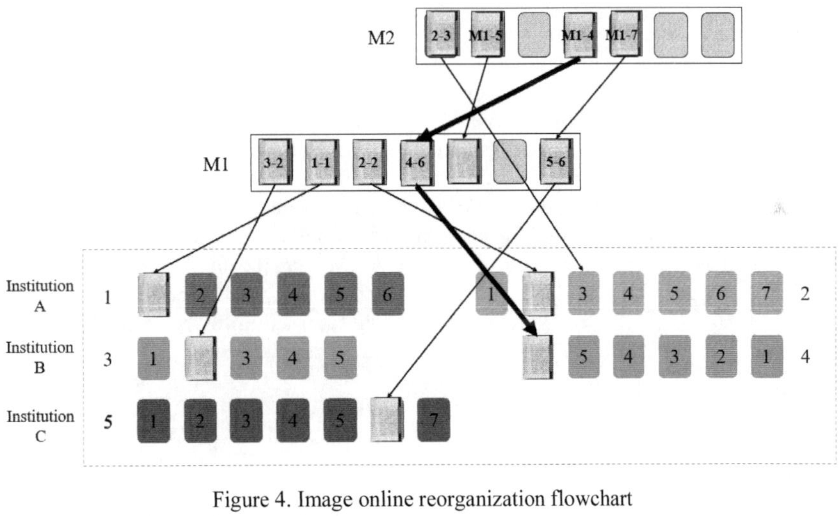

Figure 4. Image online reorganization flowchart

Figure 4 presents the flowchart of image reorganization, assuming the three institutions possess lists of 5 manifests, each containing multiple images. Upon importing these manifests into MISS, researchers gain the ability to reuse specific images, such as 3-1, 2-2, and so on, to construct their individual research topics, denoted as M1 for one researcher and M2 for another. Importantly, the platform meticulously records the complete path of original image reuse. For example, image M1-4 within M2 corresponds to image 4 within manifest M1, with the same image in M1 originally reused from image 6 within manifest 4 of institution B. Looking ahead, we are also contemplating the inclusion of NFTs (Non-Fungible Tokens) within the image reuse process to help with tracking the owner of the image and protect the non-interoperable asset (Stublić, Bilogrivić & Zlodi, 2023).

In this way, the platform realizes reuse of cultural heritages images, but also plays an important role in digital regression of discrete archives. Take the *Yongle Encyclopedia* as an example, one of China's most precious ancient books, which is distributed in more than 30 collection institutions in eight countries. In recent years, the Library of Congress, Harvard University Library, Bodleian Library and other institutions have successively released the IIIF images of it. By invoking and re-aggregation the above images, the MISS platform has realized the digital regression of *Yongle Encyclopedia*.

3. CASE STUDY

Take *The White-Shining Night* as an example, which is a traditional Chinese painting created by painter Han Gan in Tang dynasty, and describes the favorite horse of Emperor Xuanzong. The painting is collected by the Metropolitan Museum of America and can be accessed online. Many historical celebrities have left their inscriptions and seals in the painting, increasing the historical, literary, and calligraphic value of the painting.

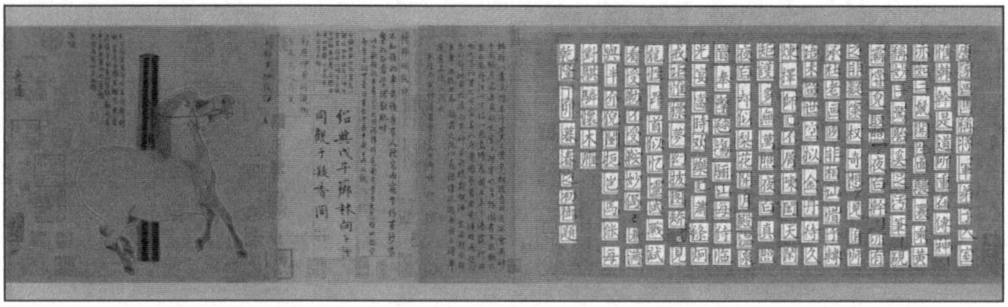

Figure 5. Object Annotations in *The White-Shining Night*

As mentioned above, the image annotation in MISS mainly applies the middle three layers of the 5-layer annotation model, namely the image layer, the object layer, and the semantic layer. All the annotation content is primarily organized using RDF and WADM, which provides an extensible, interoperable framework for expressing annotations so that they can be easily shared between platforms. Figure 5 shows the specific annotation information, in which the inscription on the right calls the external OCR recognition interface for automatic recognition. The whole process mainly has the following steps. Firstly, MISS calls and reconstructs its IIIF manifest file in JSON-LD, descripting its metadata such as title, author, creation time, collection institutions and so on. Secondly, all the objects in it were annotated in a manual way, including horse, seals, calligraphy, etc., and these objects are descripted by WADM (Sanderson, Ciccarese & Sompel, 2013), which consists of target and content. Finally, the image part that needs to be recognized by OCR is sent to the third-party API interface, and the recognition result will be returned in JSON format as follows.


```
{
  "words_result": [
   {
    "words": "唐",
    "location": {
     "top": 7,
     "left": 4833,
     "width": 159,
     "height": 197
    }
   }
   ,{
    "words": "家",
    "location": {
     "top": 216,
     "left": 4858,
     "width": 152,
     "height": 203
    }, ......
```

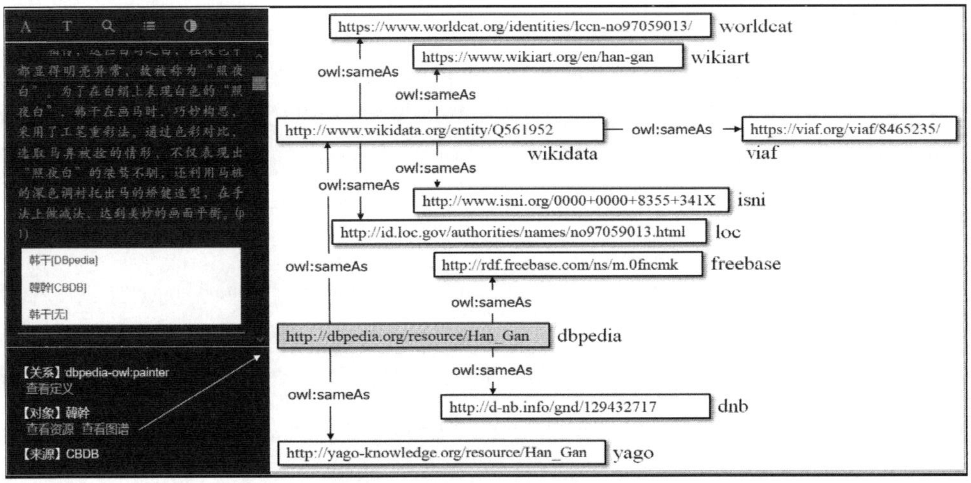

Figure 6. “Han Gan” is connected with dbpedia and other resources

In addition, the author *Hangan* is linked with his URI in DBPedia through the object property “dbo:painter”, while the latter provides dozens of URIs of him from linked open datasets through the property “owl:sameAs”, such as WIKIDATA, WIKIART, LOC, Freebase, Yago, CBDB, etc. More information about *Hangan* can be obtained from these datasets. Information about dynasty and title can be linked in the same way, as is shown in figure 6.

4. CONCLUSION AND PROSPECTS

MISS facilitates the semantic organization and interactive utilization of images, culminating in the creation of an all-encompassing ecosystem for cultural heritage image resources management. This achievement is attributable to the synergy of semantic technologies, artificial intelligence (AI), and IIIF. Text content is the most important information to enrich the semantics of images, but the excavation of cultural heritage takes time to achieve.

At present, the platform has been applied to public cultural institutions and scientific research institutions to assist them in displaying special collection resources, such as ancient books, manuscripts, newspapers, and periodicals. In terms of public GLAM institutions, in the historical and humanistic big data platform of Shanghai Library, MISS is used in the presentation of old newspapers. From the academic perspective, MISS has been considered as a tool for humanities scholars to conduct image research. Researchers are using the MISS platform to annotate images in depth. For example, researchers in Nantong University have used MISS to annotate Erya phonogram, and match their self-designed Erya ontology with the corresponding images in Erya phonogram. Furthermore, in MISS, the basis for re-aggregation is various and changeable, which depends on users' creation. MISS does not store images, so it will not damage the ownership of image storage institutions. In short, it can not only help the humanities research, but also provide a reasonable way to preserve the value in ancient books and help with the aggregation of lost documents.

In the future, we plan to integrate multi-modal data into the MISS platform, including audio and video forms; and plan to further combine vision transformer (ViT) (Dosovitskiy, et al., 2020) for computer vision analysis and apply it in other image research such as image classification and image segmentation.

ACKNOWLEDGEMENT

This work was supported by the General Program of National Social Science Foundation of China, "Research on Knowledge Representation Model and Smart System Construction of Multi-modal Cultural Heritage Data" (No. 23BTQ088).

REFERENCES

Chen, J. J., & Qu, S. Y. (2021). Development and Application of the Semantic Annotation Framework for Digital Images. *Electronic Library*, 39(6):824-845.

Chen, S., Guo, X., & Dong, Y. (2013). Computer Engineering and Applications, Semantic annotation method for images by Web background knowledge. *Jisuanji Gongcheng yu Yingyong (Computer Engineering and Applications)*, 49(4):166-169.

Chen, T., Li, H., Zhang, Y. J., & Sun, A. (2022). LIBRA Technology Theory and Its Application in Historical Image Resources. *Journal of Academic Libraries*, 40(4):64-74.

Dosovitskiy, A., et al. (2020). An Image is Worth 16x16 Words: Transformers for Image Recognition at Scale. In *Ninth International Conference on Learning Representations*. Vienna, Austria:1-21.

Gomez, J., Allen, K., Matney, M., Awopetu, T., & Shafer, S. (2020). Experimenting with a Machine Generated Annotations Pipeline. *Code4Lib Journal*, (48).

Loh, G. (2017). Linked Data and IIIF: Integrating Taxonomy Management with Image Annotation. In *2017 Pacific Neighborhood Consortium Annual Conference and Joint Meetings (PNC)*. Tainan, China:50-55.

Mosser, M., Pieressa, F., Reutter, J. L., Soto, A., & Vrgoč, D. (2022). Querying Apis with SPARQL. *Information Systems*, 48(105):101650.

Raemy, J. A., & Schneider, R. (2019). Suggested Measures for Deploying IIIF in Swiss Cultural Heritage Institutions (White paper). In *Zenodo (CERN European Organization for Nuclear Research)*. European Organization for Nuclear Research. https://doi.org/10.5281/zenodo.2640416

Sanderson, R., Ciccarese, P., & Sompel, H. (2013). Designing the W3C open annotation data model. In *Proceedings of the 5th Annual ACM Web Science Conference*. New York, United States:366-375.

Shan, R. R., Chen, T., Liu, W., & Xia, C. J. (2021). International Image Interoperability Framework and Extended Applications. *Library Journal*, 40(5):89–95.

Stublić, H., Bilogrivić, M., & Zlodi, G. (2023). Blockchain and NFTs in the Cultural Heritage Domain: A Review of Current Research Topics. *Heritage*, 6(4): 3801-3819.

Zhang, Y., Yu, B., & Wang, J. (2021). Research on SPARQL SEMANTIC Query Technology Based on Knowledge Hybrid Storage. In *Proceedings of the 5th International Conference on Algorithms, Computing and Systems*. New York, United States:74-9.

DIGITAL AND DIALOGIC LOOP PRINCIPLE IN OFFICIAL WEBSITES OF THE PORTUGUESE COMMUNICATION AGENCIES

Ana Pereira[1] and Adriana Oliveira[2]
[1]ISCAP, Polytechnic of Porto
Rua Jaime Lopes Amorim, s/n 4465-004 S. Mamede de Infesta, Portugal
[2]CEOS, ISCAP, Polytechnic of Porto
Rua Jaime Lopes Amorim, s/n 4465-004 S. Mamede de Infesta, Portugal

ABSTRACT

The digital transformation introduced the web into the organizational context. The web has become one of the most important communication channels for organizations, particularly with regard to the dialogue established between organizations and their different stakeholders, who are now more autonomous, active in their exposure to the content published on the internet. In this context, interactivity has become one of the elements capable of providing a more direct and continuous communication with stakeholders. Aware of these transformations, organizations, namely communication agencies, make use of dialogical principles in order to provide more efficient communication with stakeholders. Among these principles is the Dialogic Loop, which in this article is assumed as the main one. To study the adoption of the Dialogic Loop principle, an analysis was carried out on the websites of the finalist communication agencies of the Marketeer 2023 Awards in Portugal. The results showed that there is no significant adoption of the Dialogic Loop Principle.

KEYWORDS

Digital Transformation, Dialogic Communication, Communication Agencies, Websites, Portugal

1. INTRODUCTION

The introduction of the web in the organizational context has opened up the possibility of faster and more direct communication between organizations and their most different stakeholders. In this context, interactivity has assumed a leading role, namely because it can also be understood as a concept of communication and capable of providing a linear and non-linear interaction (Kiousis, 2002), carried out in face-to-face, mediated or quasi-mediated contexts (Thompson, 1998). This scenario gains greater visibility if we consider that stakeholders today are more autonomous, active and capable of deciding what information they want to see and when they want it; that is: interactivity ends up being the foundation for an annulment of passive stakeholders and imposing active behaviour in the face of exposure to information conveyed by the Internet (Silva 2001: 2; Alsoud, Al-Muani, & Alkhazali, 2022). In this sense, the main objective of this article was to study and analyze the role of the Dialogic Link principle on the websites of the finalist communication agencies of the Marketeer 2023 Awards. As specific objectives we defined the following: specific objectives were defined: 1) analyze the degree of adoption of the sixteen indicators by the organizations' websites; 2) identify which of the sixteen indicators is most adopted by the organizations' websites; 3) identify which of the sixteen indicators is least adopted by the organizations' websites; 4) identify which organization adopts the most indicators on its website; 5) identify which organization has the least adoption of indicators on its website. Analyzing the data allows us to conclude that there is no significant adoption of the Dialogical Connection Principle.

2. BACKGROUND

2.1 Digital and Interactivity

Conceived in 1963 by Larry Roberts, the Internet would be responsible for changes in the organizational, institutional and media fields, in society in general, or in the individual in particular; it would enable access to and organization of diverse content and could be used for the most diverse reasons, in the most diverse places, contexts and by diverse consumers (Negroponte, 1996; Korgaonkar and Wolin, 1999; Castells, 2005). The Internet would become a good example of what could be called the "information superhighway" (Negroponte, 1996) and honoured as "the most revolutionary technological medium of the Information Age" (Castells, 2005:54), "a formidable system for transmitting and accessing an incalculable number of information" (Wolton, 1999: 92).

In this context, interactivity seems to assume a pertinent role, namely because it can be understood as a communication concept rather than a computer concept; that is: interactivity can mean communication between individuals, between man and machine or between user and service (Silva, 2001; Alsoud, Al-Muani, & Alkhazali, 2022). There is evidence here that the individual is invited to participate actively in the communication process, either in the emission of content or as (co)creator of the content itself. Faced with this reality, the audience began to expose itself in a more autonomous, active way, and to obtain more protagonism in the exposure to the contents transmitted by the Internet, choosing how, when and what it wanted to see (McQuail, 2003: 122; Johnstone, 1974). There is room for the user to "listen, watch, read, record, go back, go forward, select, process and send any kind of message anywhere. In short, interactivity allows us to move beyond the condition of passive spectator to that of operative subject" (Silva 2001: 2). Thus, "interactivity" can be understood as the variable capable of providing the opportunity to establish "one-to-one, one-to-many and many-to-many" communication, whether in a synchronous or asynchronous perspective. According to the author, communication can be expressed through a "simple transfer of information to sophisticated movements in video games or through the world wide web, thus encompassing linear and non-linear communication" (Kiousis, 2002). This framework brings us back to the thinking formulated in the late nineties by John Thompson (1998) when he set out three typologies of interaction: "face-to-face interaction"; "mediated interaction"; and "quasi-mediated interaction". The "face-to-face interaction" the actors in the communication process are physically present in the same space and at the same time as the communication act takes place, having a "dialogical" character, with the use of mixed communication. The "mediated interaction" does not require the actors in the communication process to be physically present in the same space and the interaction takes place through the use of "a technical medium (paper, electrical cables, electromagnetic waves, etc.)". The "quasi-mediated interaction" is oriented towards an undefined number of receivers and assumes a monological character, with no obligation for the receiver to respond or for reflexive control of the response (Thompson, 1998). "Interactivity" can also be thought of from a "functional" and "contingency" perspective (Sundar, Kalyanaraman and Brown, 2003). "Functional interactivity" refers to the different resources made available to users, producing the ability to establish the possibility of "interactivity". From the authors' words, it can be concluded that "interactivity" allows for states of "low interactivity", if it does not provide the user with resources to establish communication, "medium interactivity", if it provides, for example, a link to access extra information, or "high interactivity" if it provides, for example, an e-mail that gives the individual the possibility to send a message. This conceptualization was developed by the authors from a website promoting a fictitious political candidate. Differences were found between those with "low", "medium" and "high "interactivity". Participants who were provided with resources that enabled them to engage in "medium" and "high interactivity behaviour showed a more "caring" and "sensitive" feeling towards the candidate than participants who were exposed to "low interactivity". "High interactivity" also enabled affinity with the candidate on the part of participants who showed no interest in politics but alienated those who were politically savvy. In contrast, 'medium interactivity' would be the desired level for enlightened participants because it would provide affinity between them and the candidate. It seems, therefore, that for the authors it is necessary not only to make the resources available, but also to ensure the interconnection of the messages facilitating the act of "interactivity". In turn, "contingent interactivity" expresses that the message is dependent on another message. Thus, this perspective understands the exchange of messages between different users, so it is imperative that dialogue is established and that there is feedback (Sundar, Kalyanaraman and Brown, 2003). This is what happens in the exchange of messages that are made, for example, in chats, in the different digital platforms of which facebook, Google+, hi5, Twitter, blogs, or Linkedin or websites that present themselves as a world where "interactivity" is exercised, allowing the sharing of content between people. And it is in this conception of "contingent" interactivity that our research is done.

After the exposition of the thought, the next section presents a brief dissertation on the concept of dialogic communication.

2.2 Dialogic Loop Principle

The trend of globalization has led to the transformation of many aspects of society, namely redefining the meaning of cultural identity and civil society, requiring a new form of intercultural interaction (Alawi, 2021), with new social media emerging as the foundation of this transformation creating, for example, new social networks and activities (Lagoa, 2021; Vural, Değirmen & Ünüvar, 2022). In this context, dialogic communication plays a vital role within organizations, as it allows the organization "any negotiated exchange of ideas and opinions" (Kent & Taylor, 1998, p. 325), and allows the organization to get involved in an open, honest and ethical relationship with its publics; this scenario gives organizations opportunities to listen to stakeholders and adapt to their needs (Pang et al., 2018). Dialogic communication theory was proposed by Kent and Taylor (1998) as a way to develop and maintain effective relationships between organizations and their publics. These authors referred to dialogic communication as any negotiated exchange of ideas and opinions. And, they proposed that by using websites, organizations have the opportunity to build dialogic relationships with publics. Their theory consists of five underlying principles that provide guidelines on how to integrate dialogic relationships and the internet, and they are: Dialogic loop; usefulness of information; return visits; ease of interface; visitor retention. The Dialogic Loop is the most important principle of dialogic communication and refers to providing opportunities for users to ask questions and get answers from the organization (Kent and Taylor, 1998). It is the dialogic loop that focuses on the opportunity that an online environment offers, feedback. The dialogic loop enables direct communication between the organization and stakeholders, namely by providing answers to the public's questions, concerns and problems (Gonçalves, 2017). The Dialogic Loop will be the principle studied by this research, and for its objective to be achieved, websites must make available tools such as: Chat (Hinson, Osabutey, & Kosiba, 2018); Space for comments (Kent & Taylor, 2003); Forum (Kent, Taylor and White, 2001); Sharing experiences of holidaymakers (texts) (Augusto, 2015); Sharing experiences of holidaymakers (photos) (Augusto, 2015); Possibility to send messages, comments (McAllister-Spooner, 2010); Links and contacts to directly contact employees, departments of the organization (McAllister-Spooner & Kent, 2009); Possibility to subscribe to newsletter (Karkin & Janssen, 2014); Possibility of transactions, requesting services (Feeney & Brown, 2017); Links to social networks (Fietkiewicz, Mainka & Stock, 2017); Texts of response to the public (Reber & Kim, 2006); Possibility to request information (Ingenhoff e Koelling, 2009); Possibility for users to ask questions (McAllister-Spooner, 2010); Questionnaire (to give opinion on issues (McAllister-Spooner, 2010); Engaging and interactive online environment (Hinson, Osabutey, & Kosiba, 2018); Possibilities for community interaction (Hinson, Osabutey, & Kosiba, 2018). Information usefulness refers to the provision of information in various formats that is valuable and appropriate to the needs of different stakeholders, and it is necessary to establish relationships with various publics in order to fulfil public relations objectives and address the values and concerns of the publics involved. By prioritizing the usefulness of information, organizations can communicate effectively by contributing to the knowledge and understanding of the general public. Therefore, organizations should strive to provide relevant, accurate and meaningful information that aligns with their objectives and serves the interests and concerns of the general public (Kent & Taylor, 1998, 2002). Generating return visits relates to the idea of organizations incorporating elements that increase their attractiveness and usefulness to encourage users to return to, for example, the organization's website. A simple but effective method of promoting such a return is, for example, to provide a comprehensive compilation of frequently asked questions (FAQ) for users to access on the organization's website, as they can meet the needs of their audience by answering common questions and concerns. This not only saves users time and effort, but also improves their overall browsing experience (Wilkinson, 2019). In addition, incorporating features such as search functionalities and user-friendly navigation can also contribute to making the website more engaging and appealing, further increasing the likelihood of repeat visits

(Wilkinson, 2019). The fourth principle, ease of interface, refers to the ease of the user interface, highlighting the importance of designing interface options such as telephone lines, workshops, websites that are intuitive and userfriendly in order to promote dialogue between the organization and its audiences in an efficient and effortless manner (Kent & Taylor, 1998, 2002). This principle recognizes the importance of minimizing barriers and maximizing efficiency in order to create an enjoyable experience for the public. Visitor retention refers to what is being done to encourage users to stay on the page (Haro-De-Rosario, Sáez-Martín, & Gálvez-Rodríguez, 2017) and maintaining the attention and interest of different audiences is crucial to ensure their continued engagement with the organization. To do so, it is pertinent to provide relevant and engaging information, encouraging exploration by the audience. By offering comprehensive and valuable resources, organizations can minimize the likelihood that users will seek information from external sources (Kent & Taylor, 1998, 2002). In this sense, digital media dialogues allow the public to provide feedback on organizational practices, provide opportunities for organizations to respond to public concerns and include their opinions. Online interactivity can facilitate the quality of organization-public dialogues and generate positive outcomes, with increased trust, improved product knowledge and increased profits (Ihlen & Levenshus, 2017b; Zhou & Xu, 2021). In addition to relationships at the organizational level, dialogic communication can play a key role in developing and enhancing an organization's image, because while traditional media are useful in image management, digital media have been contextualized as the "new virtual landscape" (Vernuccio, 2014, p.214).

This framework of thought highlights the role of new media in disseminating verbal and non-verbal messages from the organizational context, namely communicating its activities, practices of responsibility and/or involvement with users in real time, promoting its activities (Camilleri, 2018; Dwivedi et al., 2021). Having said this, the following section presents the methodology, followed by the presentation and discussion of the data.

3. CASE STUDY OF OFFICIAL WEBSITES OF COMMUNICATION AGENCIES

3.1 Research Objective and Methodology

The literature review highlighted the active and dominant role of the Internet in the organisational context, enabling the transmission of large amounts of information quickly and to many recipients at the same time (Negroponte, 1996; Wolton, 1999, Korgaonkar and Wolin, 1999; Castells, 2005). The literature also emphasises the autonomous, active role of the audience (Johnstone, 1974; McQuail, 2003). And in this context, interactivity has a pertinent role, as it allows the audience to show this active role (Silva 2001). This framework of thought gains greater prominence if we also take into account the fact that we are facing new media that present themselves with characteristics that end up supporting the active actions of the audience. In this context, dialogic communication plays a vital role within organisations (Kent & Taylor, 1998, p. 325), providing opportunities to listen to stakeholders and adapt to their needs (Pang et al., 2018). Given this context, the following research question was formulated: what is the role of the dialogic bond in the online context of communication agencies? To answer the question, we will try to identify and analyse the degree to which the Dialogic Bond principles are adopted on the websites of the finalist communication agencies of the Marketeer 2023 Awards. The sample thus consists of the websites of the Adagietto; CV&A; Global Press; Hill+Knowlton Strategies; Lift Consulting; LLYC; LPM agencies; it should be noted that the CorpCom agency website was undergoing maintenance and was therefore excluded from the analysis - see table 1. For the analysis, we used descriptive statistics and frequency distribution.

Table 1. Communication Agencies' Websites

Communication Agencies	Websites
Adagietto	https://www.adagietto.pt/home
CV&A	https://h-advisors.global/network/cva/
Global Press	https://global-press.com/en/homepage/
Hill+Knowlton Strategies	https://www.hkstrategies.pt/pt-pt/
Lift Consulting	https://lift.com.pt/
LLYC	https://www.llorenteycuenca.com/pt/
LPM	https://www.lpmcom.pt/

Marketeer Awards is an initiative of Marketeer magazine and has been seeking, for 15 years, to recognise the brands, companies and personalities that make a difference in Portugal in different areas. We chose to analyse websites because it is understood that in the context of digital communication they play a vital role in allowing to reach the various audiences and guarantee the development of the company. At the same time, it is considered to be one of the most important elements with which to start digital communication since it has been established as an instrument that synthesises the company's strategy effectively (Grewal et al., 2022). Websites play a key role in the online communication strategy of a company or organisation. They serve as a central platform to present information, promote products or services and interact with the target audience, as shown in the figure below. As already mentioned, we aim to study the adoption of the Dialogic Loop, the main dialogic principle (Kent & Taylor, 1998) by testing sixteen indicators indicated by the following authors - see table 2.

Table 2. Dialogic Loop - sixteen indicators

	Indicators	Authors
Dialogic Loop	Chat	Hinson, Osabutey, & Kosiba, 2018
	Space for comments	Kent & Taylor, 2003
	Forum	Kent, Taylor and White, 2001
	Sharing experiences of holidaymakers (texts)	Augusto (2015)
	Sharing experiences of holidaymakers (photos)	Augusto (2015)
	Possibility to send messages, comments	McAllister-Spooner, 2010
	Links and contacts to directly contact employees, departments of the organization	McAllister-Spooner & Kent, 2009
	Possibility to subscribe to newsletter	Karkin & Janssen (2014)
	Possibility of transactions, requesting services	Feeney & Brown (2017)
	Links to social networks	Fietkiewicz, Mainka & Stock (2017)
	Texts of response to the public	Reber & Kim (2006)
	Possibility to request information	Ingenhoff e Koelling (2009)
	Possibility for users to ask questions	McAllister-Spooner (2010)
	Questionnaire (to give opinion on issues)	McAllister-Spooner (2010)
	Engaging and interactive online environment	Hinson, Osabutey, & Kosiba, (2018)
	Possibilities for community interaction	Hinson, Osabutey, & Kosiba, (2018)

That said, the following specific objectives were defined: 1) analyze the degree of adoption of the sixteen indicators by the organizations' websites; 2) identify which of the sixteen indicators is most adopted by the organizations' websites; 3) identify which of the sixteen indicators is least adopted by the organizations' websites; 4) identify which organization adopts the most indicators on its website; 5) identify which organization has the least adoption of indicators on its website.

3.2 Results

The results of the analysis of the adoption of the Dialogic Loop, the main dialogic principle (Kent & Taylor, 1998), on the websites of the finalist communication agencies of the Marketeer 2023 Awards are presented.

Thus, the analysis of the data presented in Table 3 shows that the communication agencies under study, in general, do not expressively adopt the Dialogical Loop principle. The data allow us to draw this conclusion, because, as shown in Table 3, there is not a strong adherence on the websites of the communication agencies to the sixteen indicators that are part of the Dialogical Loop principle. However, among the sixteen indicators, Global Press 63% of the indicators (10), followed by Lift Consulting with 56% (9). Agencies LLYC and LPM use 50% of the indicators (8 each), followed by Hill+Knowlton Strategies using only 44% (7). It should be noted that Adagietto and CV&A use only 38% of the indicators (6) – see table 3.

Table 3. Frequency of indicators by communication agencies

Communication agencies	Frequency of indicators	%
Adagietto	6	38%
CV&A	6	38%
Global Press	10	63%
Hill+Knowlton Strategies	7	44%
Lift Consulting	9	56%
LLYC	8	50%
LPM	8	50%

Thus, despite being communication agencies, there is not a wide adoption of the sixteen indicators associated with the Dialogic Loop principle, so the Dialogic Loop principle, considered the most important principle of dialogic communication (Kent and Taylor, 1998), has no strong adoption by institutions. It is understood that low adoption can jeopardize direct communication between the organization and stakeholders, namely given answers to public questions, concerns and problems (Gonçalves, 2017).

Regarding the indicators, data analysis reveals that there are 3 indicators - Links to social networks; Possibility of requesting information; Possibility of questioning by users - which are adopted in 100% by all communication agencies studied - see table 4. The indicators Possibility of sending messages, comments (86%), Possibility of subscribing to the newsletter, news and Forum reach a considerably high percentage of adhesion (71%) – see table 4. On the other hand, table 4 also shows that there are indicators that are never offered by institutions to their audiences, they are: Sharing experiences lived by users (texts); Sharing experiences lived by users (photographs); Possibility of transactions, request for services; Questionnaire (to give an opinion on the subjects); Possibilities of interaction with the community. And only 1 agency provides chat, 2 space for comments, 3 response texts to the public – see table 4.

Table 4. Indicators used

Communication agencies	Frequency of indicators	%
Chat	1	14%
Space for comments	2	29%
Forum	5	71%
Sharing experiences of holidaymakers (texts)	0	0%
Sharing experiences of holidaymakers (photos)	0	0%
Possibility to send messages, comments	6	86%
Links and contacts to directly contact employees, departments of the organisation	7	100%
Possibility to subscribe to newsletter	5	71%
Possibility of transactions, requesting services	0	0%
Links to social networks	7	100%
Texts of response to the public	3	43%

Possibility to request information	7	100%
Possibility for users to ask questions	7	100%
Questionnaire (to give opinion on issues)	0	0%
Engaging and interactive online environment	4	57%
Possibilities for community interaction	0	0%

These data allow us to state that there is no significant adoption of these sixteen indicators that are part of the Dialogic Loop Principle; that is: there is a poor practice regarding dialogic communication and, therefore, the development and improvement of the organization's image may be compromised (Vernuccio, 2014, p.214).

4. CONCLUSION

Internet has assumed a relevant role in the context of organizations (Negroponte, 1996; Korgaonkar and Wolin, 1999; Silva, 2001; Castells, 2005; Alsoud, Al-Muani, & Alkhazali, 2022). In this context, dialogic communication assumes vital importance, namely based on five principles: Dialogic Loop; usefulness of information; return visits; ease of interface; visitor retention. The Dialogical Loop is the most important principle of dialogical communication (Gonçalves, 2017) and websites are one of the most fundamental means of transmitting the message. In this sense, this article aimed to identify and analyze the degree of adoption of the Dialogic Loop principle on the websites of communication agencies shortlisted for the 2023 Marketeer Award. It can be concluded that there is not a strong adherence on the websites of the communication agencies of the sixteen indicators that are part of the Dialogic Loop principle. However, among the sixteen indicators, Global Press and Lift Consulting are the two agencies that most adopt the dialogic principle. It can also be concluded that the indicators Links to social networks, Possibility of requesting information, Possibility for users to ask questions are the most used indicators on the institutions' websites. On the other hand, the indicators Sharing experiences lived by users (texts), Sharing experiences lived by users (photographs), Possibility of transactions, requesting services Questionnaire (to give an opinion on subjects) and Possibilities of community interaction are never not used by the agencies. In short, the finalist communication agencies for the Marketeer 2023 awards do not make significant use of the Dialogic Loop principle.

In this sense, the data allow us to state that the communication agencies need to improve their capacity for dialogue with regard to the website, as the dialogic dimension is fundamental for interaction, dialogue and relationships between organizations and their publics (Kent and Taylor, 1998). It is understood that failure to develop dialogic communication will jeopardise the ability to control the communication of messages with the public, organization-public interaction, the very reputation of the organization's image, and given the characteristics of the organizations under study, they show little credibility to "handle" the image, the communication of future clients (Kiptinness & Mbatha, 2023). The introduction of indicators relating to the Dialogic Loop will allow for more dialogue with their audiences, who, given that they are communication agencies, can show greater credibility in their work. That said, we recognise that it would be valuable to continue working on this line of research, analyzing more agencies in order to have a larger sample and therefore more data. In this way, it will be possible to draw conclusions that are even more representative of communication agencies in Portugal.

REFERENCES

Alawi, A., 2021. Media and Intercultural Communication Shifts: A Semiotic Analysis of the Cultural Identity in Two International Films. In Croatian International Relations Review, Vol. XXVII, No. 88, pp. 1-13.

Alsoud, M. et al, 2022. Digital platform interactivity and Jordanian social commerce purchase intention. In International Journal of Data and Network Science, Vol. 6, No. 2, pp. 285-294.

Augusto, L., 2015. Comunicação e Turismo: relações públicas, dialogismo e imagem nos media digitais (Doctoral dissertation).

Camilleri, M. A., 2018. Unlocking Corporate Social Responsibility through Digital Media. In A. Lindgreen, J. Vanhamme, F. Maon & Watkins, R. (Eds.), Communicating Corporate Social Responsibility in the Digital Era. Routledge.

Castells, M., 2005. A sociedade em rede, Vol. 1, No. 6. Paz e terra, São Paulo.

Dwivedi, Y. et al, 2021. Setting the future of digital and social media marketing research: Perspectives and research propositions. In International Journal of Information Management, Vol. 59, pp. 1-37.

Gonçalves, G., 2017. Os hospitais são nossos amigos? Um estudo sobre o papel do Facebook na comunicação dialógica das organizações hospitalares. In T. Ruão, R. Neves & J. Zilmar (Eds.), A Comunicação Organizacional e os desafios tecnológicos: estudos sobre a influência tecnológica nos processos de comunicação nas organizações. CECS, Braga, pp. 15-33.

Grewal, D. et al, 2022. The Future of Digital Communication Research: Considering Dynamics and Multimodalit. In Journal of Retailing, Vol. 98, No. 2, pp. 224-240.

Haro-de-Rosario, A. et al, 2017. Papel do conselho de administração na ética empresarial em países da América Latina. In Rev. adm. empres., Vol. 57, No. 5, pp. 426-438.

Hinson, R. E. Et al., 2018. Exploring the dialogic communication potential of selected African destinations' place websites. In Journal of Business Research.

Ingenhoff, D. and Koelling, A. M., 2009. The potential of web sites as a relationship building tool for charitable fundraising NPOs. In Public Relations Review, Vol. 35, No. 1, pp. 66–73.

Ihlen, Ø. and Levenshus, A., 2017. Digital Dialogue. In social media and Crisis Communication. pp. 389-400.

Kent, M. L. and Taylor, M., 1998. Building dialogic relationships through the World Wide Web. In Public Relations Review, Vol. 24, No. 3, pp. 321-334.

Kent, M. L. and Taylor, M., 2002. Toward a dialogic theory of public relations. In Public Relations Review, Vol. 28, No. 1, pp. 21-37.

Kent, M. L. and Taylor, M., 2003. Maximizing media relations: A Web site checklist. In Public Relations Quarterly, Vol. 48, No. 1, pp. 14–20.

Kiousis, S., 2002. Interactivity: a concept explication. In New media & society, Vol. 4, No. 3, pp. 355-383.

Korgaonkar, P. K. and Wolin, L. D., 1999. A multivariate analysis of web usage. In Journal of advertising research, Vol. 39, No. 2, pp. 53-53.

Lagoa, A., 2021. A comunicação interna como ferramenta de gestão - um Estudo de caso no Agrupamento de Escolas Fontes Pereira de Melo. Dissertação de Mestrado em Educação. Especialização em Administração das Organizações Educativas. Escola Superior de Educação, IPP.

McAllister-Spooner, S. M., 2010. Whose site is it anyway? Expectations of college Web sites. In Public Relations Journal, Vol. 4, No. 2.

McAllister-Spooner, S. M. and Kent, M. L., 2009. Dialogic public relations and resource dependency: New Jersey community colleges as models for web site effectiveness. In Atlantic Journal of Communication, Vol. 17, No. 4, pp. 220–239.

McQuail, D., 2003. Media accountability and freedom of publication. Oxford University Press, USA.

Negroponte, N., 1996. Books without pages. In ACM SIGDOC Asterisk Journal of Computer Documentation, Vol. 20, No. 3, pp. 2-8.

Pang, A. et al, 2018. Building relationships through dialogic communication: organizations, stakeholders, and computer-mediated communication. In Journal of Marketing Communications, Vol. 24, No. 1, pp. 68–82.

Silva, B. D. D., 2001. A tecnologia é uma estratégia.

Sundar, S. S. et al, 2003. Explicating web site interactivity: Impression formation effects in political campaign sites. In Communication research, Vol. 30, No. 1, pp. 30-59.

Taylor, M. et al, 2001. How activist organizations are using the Internet to build relationships. In Public Relations Review, Vol. 27, No. 3, pp. 263–284.

Thompson, J. B., 1998. A mídia e a modernidade, Vol. 8. Vozes, Petrópolis.

Vernuccio, M., 2014. Communicating Corporate Brands Through Social Media: An Exploratory Study. In International Journal of Business Communication, Vol. 51, No. 3, pp. 211-233.

Vural, Z. et al, 2022. Social Media as a Dialogical Communication Tool: Izmir Metropolitan Municipality Examp. In Online Journal of Communication and Media Technologies, Vol. 12, No. 1, p. e202210.

Wilkinson, J., 2019. When to Build an FAQ: A Case Study. In Public Services Quarterly, Vol. 15, No. 2, pp. 142-150.

Wolton, D., 1999. A comunicação no centro da modernidade. Um debate teórico fundamental. In Internet, e depois?: uma teoria crítica das novas mídias, pp. 35-67.

THE LEGAL FRAMEWORK GOVERNING HEALTHCARE INFORMATION SYSTEMS: A COMPARATIVE STUDY BETWEEN SMALL MACAO AND MAJOR JURISDICTIONS

Victor K. Y. Chan
Faculty of Business, Macao Polytechnic University,
Rua de Luís Gonzaga Gomes, Macao, China

ABSTRACT

Today, information systems are crucial for efficient, effective, and timely healthcare service delivery. Notwithstanding, they process sensitive healthcare-related and personal data and thus are subject to legal governance under local and sometimes international legal frameworks and so are the healthcare institutions and the staff developing and/or using the systems. This article identifies general legal regulation of healthcare information systems, privacy and security, and legal liabilities as the key perspectives of such legal governance and, from a healthcare information system developer's and/or user's viewpoint as opposed to a traditional comparative law researcher's standpoint, examines each perspective of such legal governance under the legal frameworks of Macao in comparison to major jurisdictions like the United States, the United Kingdom, and Hong Kong. Relevant statutes, regulations, and academic literature are analyzed to highlight key similarities and dissimilarities between the jurisdictions. Macao is underscored in this article with a view to exemplifying the legal regimes in typical small jurisdictions in respect of healthcare information systems. The analysis shows that Macao's legal framework is still developing in this area, with relatively fewer specific laws governing healthcare information systems vis-à-vis the United States, the United Kingdom, and Hong Kong. The former jurisdiction's framework in this area is also less prescriptively stringent and punitively more lenient than the latter jurisdictions'. Subject to confirmation by further research, in all likelihood, these phenomena are true of many small jurisdictions other than Macao in view of their limited populations and thus inadequate scale economies of and relevant court cases from the local healthcare industry to justify specialization of the law. However, Macao's current legal framework at least provides a baseline of protection for the patients whose healthcare data resides in the local healthcare information systems. Managing the legal aspects of healthcare information systems will require continued legal developments in Macao or most other small jurisdictions alongside vigilant governance and administration of the systems.

KEYWORDS

Legal Framework, Healthcare Information Systems, Comparative Study, Macao, Major Jurisdictions

1. INTRODUCTION

1.1 Healthcare Information Systems

Information systems are essential for modern healthcare services, enabling the collection, storage, communication, analysis, and other processing of vast volumes of healthcare data about patients, treatments, equipment, medicines, and other inventories (Ebnehoseini et al, 2019; Farzandipour et al, 2019). However, collection, storage, communication, analysis, and other processing of such healthcare data and personal data are subject to legal governance under local and sometimes international legal frameworks. As with the variation of legal systems across jurisdictions, healthcare information systems' legal governance differ from place to place. In particular, small and large jurisdictions possess substantially disparate populations, scale economies of the local healthcare industry, numbers of court cases, and thus prioritizations (Boar et al, 2020). Therefore, the former bloc of jurisdictions may evolve legal landscapes that contrast sharply with those of the latter bloc. This article singles out Macao as the quintessence of small jurisdictions and, from a healthcare information system developer's and/or user's viewpoint as opposed to a traditional comparative law researcher's standpoint, analyzes the legal framework regulating healthcare information systems in the small enclave in comparison with those in major and presumably large jurisdictions, namely, the United States, the United Kingdom, and Hong Kong. The ultimate purpose is to uncover the similarities and dissimilarities between the legal frameworks in typically small jurisdictions and quintessential major and large jurisdictions. Macao was so selected for this comparative study not only because the author's affiliation with a university there but also because the city somewhat typifies small jurisdictions, so that any findings from the study can likely serve as an analogy for comparison between legal framework regulating healthcare information systems in small jurisdictions and those in major and large jurisdictions.

Whenever one considers the feasibility of any project, be it for healthcare information systems or otherwise, there are five key aspects, namely, technical, economic/financial, legal, operational, and scheduling (Mukherjee and Roy, 2017). Being one of the five key aspects, the legal feasibility can never be denigrated. In summary, for the development and/or usage of any healthcare information system, its legal aspect is at least as determining as the technical, economic/financial, operational, and scheduling aspects. This is why it is worthwhile to conduct this comparative study on the legal aspects of healthcare information systems.

1.2 Macao

Macao, also spelled as "Macau" (probably, due to its Portuguese etymology) and formally referred to as the Macao Special Administrative Region (SAR) of the People's Republic of China, is a jurisdiction with a unique system of laws and regulations. The paramount governance is based on the Basic Law of the Macao SAR. Throughout its past history of Portuguese administration, Macao developed its own legal system by derivation from Portuguese civil law. Since China resuming its exercise of sovereignty over Macao toward the turn of the millennium, Chinese law has been integrated, ending up with a blended system. Albeit this arrangement is in a sense akin to that of the relatively more notable Special Administrative Region Hong Kong, which integrates English common law with Chinese law (Castellucci, 2012), this legal framework of Macao blending Portuguese and Chinese laws happens to be distinct and unique, paralleled by virtually no other jurisdiction worldwide. Appertaining to its geography, the enclave lies on the southern coast of the country, has a population of approximately 694,400 people, and spans an area of 33 square kilometers (Britannica Academic, 2023; CIA, 2023).

1.3 The Present Article

This rest of this article will analyze each key perspective of the legal framework regulating healthcare information systems and the healthcare institutions developing and/or using them in the small jurisdiction Macao in comparison with major jurisdictions like the United States, the United Kingdom, and Hong Kong. These perspectives are identified as general legal regulation of healthcare information systems, privacy and security, and legal liabilities. Therefore, the analysis in essence boils down to the following questions:

1. What laws generally regulate healthcare information systems in Macao? How do these laws compare to those in major jurisdictions?
2. What are the key privacy and security concerns of healthcare information systems under Macao law versus the laws of major jurisdictions?
3. What legal liabilities may arise regarding healthcare information systems in Macao in contrast to major jurisdictions?

On top of being an academic treatise, this article may additionally double as guidelines and a checklist for healthcare information system developers and/or users, who are much concerned about legal compliance during the development and/or usage of these systems in major jurisdictions around the globe and some small jurisdictions as epitomized by Macao.

2. GENERAL LEGAL REGULATION OF HEALTHCARE INFORMATION SYSTEMS

2.1 Macao

Macao does not yet have comprehensive legislation tailored specifically to healthcare information systems. The tangentially relevant statutes are Act 8/2005: Personal Data Protection Act. (PDPA) (Macao Special Administrative Region, 2023a). Originally not being any law specific to healthcare information systems, the PDPA does somehow collaterally serve as legal regulation of healthcare information systems one way or another, so this subsection will focus on its relevance to such healthcare information systems whilst its original emphasis on privacy and security will be illuminated in Section 3. The PDPA establishes general data protection principles based on the European approach. It covers public and private organizations processing personal data, with exemptions for households and news reporting. Healthcare data is considered sensitive personal data under Article 7 of the Act. The PDPA prohibits transferring sensitive personal data outside Macao except to jurisdictions with equivalent protections.

The PDPA is enforced by the Office for Personal Data Protection (GPDP). However, compliance remains challenging given the law's general nature. Overall, Macao lacks a bespoke legal framework for healthcare information systems at present.

2.2 United States

In contrast, the United States has enacted several important healthcare privacy and security laws and rules. The Health Insurance Portability and Accountability Act of 1996 (HIPAA) (Centers for Disease Control and Prevention, 2023a) and the HIPAA Privacy Rule (Centers for Disease Control and Prevention, 2023b) are the core federal law and rule. HIPAA requires the establishment of national standards to protect sensitive patient health information from being disclosed without patients' consent or knowledge. The United States Department of Health and Human Services (HHS) promulgated the HIPAA Privacy Rule to implement the HIPAA's requirements. The HIPAA Privacy Rule covers the national standards governing the use and disclosure of individuals' health information by individuals and organizations subject to the HIPAA Privacy Rule. The HIPAA Privacy Rule also contains the national standards for individuals' rights to understand and control how their health information is used. A major goal of the HIPAA Privacy Rule is to make sure that individuals' health information is properly protected while allowing the flow of health information necessary for the provision and promotion of high-quality healthcare and for the protection of the public's health and well-being. The Privacy Rule permits important uses of information while protecting the privacy of people who seek healthcare and healing. (Centers for Disease Control and Prevention, 2023c)

In addition, the Health Information Technology for Economic and Clinical Health Act (HITECH) being part of the American Recovery and Reinvestment Act (ARRA) of 2009 provides incentives to apply healthcare information technology, including incentives for using electronic health record (EHR) systems among healthcare providers. As HITECH gives rise to an expansion in the exchange of electronic protected health information (ePHI), it also broadens the scope of privacy and security protections under the HIPAA by, for example, increasing legal liability for non-compliance and more enforcement actions. (American Speech-Language-Hearing Association, 2023) Other federal laws like the Computer Fraud and Abuse Act (CFAA), codified at Title 18, United States Code, Section 1030, counters cyber-based crimes, including those dealing with health records (United States Department of Justice, 2023).

Violations of these laws and rules can result in substantial civil and criminal penalties. Overall, the United States has a complex ramification of laws regulating healthcare information systems.

2.3 United Kingdom

In the United Kingdom, the Health and Social Care Act 2012 (HSCA) is the primary legislation regulating healthcare information security (National Archives, 2023a). The Act concerns powers to publish healthcare information standards, details of the healthcare information standards, the establishment and duties of the

Health and Social Care Information Centre (HSCIC), powers to direct the HSCIC to establish healthcare information systems, powers to request the HSCIC to establish healthcare information systems, the collection of confidential healthcare information by the HSCIC, the powers of the HSCIC to require and request provision of healthcare information, the publication and, otherwise dissemination of healthcare information by the HSCIC, the HSCIC's preparation and publication of a code of practice on the collection, analysis, publication, and other dissemination of confidential information related to the provision of health services or of adult social care, the healthcare-related Information Register maintained and published by the HSCIC, the HSCIC's assessment of quality of healthcare information, and the power to establish accreditation scheme of healthcare information service providers (National Archives, 2023a).

All in all, like the United States, the United Kingdom has a specialized legal regime for healthcare data, presumably on healthcare information systems, built up incrementally over the years.

2.4 Hong Kong

Hong Kong's legal framework combines general data protection law with sector-specific healthcare legislation. The Personal Data (Privacy) Ordinance (PDPO) (Office of the Privacy Commissioner for Personal Data, 2023) governs public and private organizations processing personal data, of course inclusive of healthcare data of individuals. Under PDPO, the likelihood is that higher penalties apply to mishandling healthcare data than most other personal data given the former's sensitivity though particular court case judgements are dependent on the context of the corresponding cases. The Electronic Health Record Sharing System (eHRSS) Ordinance (Chapter 625) (eHRSSO) (Electronic Health Record Sharing System, 2023) governs the collection, sharing, use, and safekeeping of data shared through the eHRSS, Hong Kong's centralized electronic health record system. It restricts access to authorized healthcare providers, requires consent for participation, and establishes offences for violations. Additionally, the Hong Kong Hospital Authority (HA) has extensive policies and guidelines for managing patient records and information technology security based on international standards, given its governance of public hospitals (Tsui, 2017).

By and large, Hong Kong relies on general data protection law in regulating healthcare information systems, much like Macao, but the former complemented its legal framework in this aspect by tailored healthcare laws and bespoke regulations of its public hospital administration.

2.5 Comparative Summary

The foregoing Subsections 2.1 to 2.4 indicate that Macao currently has minimal legal provisions specific to healthcare information systems compared to the more comprehensive regimes in the United States, the United Kingdom, and Hong Kong. Macao's PDPA provides baseline privacy protections but lacks healthcare-specific rules or dedicated oversight agencies like those established elsewhere. However, many jurisdictions originally relied on general data protection laws before gradually developing tailored regulations on healthcare information systems once new technologies emerged. Macao's legal framework remains in its infancy regarding healthcare information systems.

3. PRIVACY AND SECURITY

Despite Macao's limited laws specific to healthcare information systems at present, the collection, storage, communication, processing, and otherwise use of patient data must still conform to privacy and security laws. As detailed in Subsection 2.1 above, Macao's PDPA is the key and practically only legislation on privacy and security. Some key aspects of the PDPA are examined below in comparison to major jurisdictions.

3.1 Data Breaches

Unauthorized access and theft of patient records present a universal risk across jurisdictions. Such data breaches can lead to fraud, identity theft, and reputational damage. Macao's PDPA holds data controllers (usually, healthcare institutions in this context) responsible for implementing security safeguards proportionate to the data sensitivity. Breaches must be reported to the GPDP. The author is not aware of any explicit requirement of such breaches being reported to the data subject (usually, the affected patients in this context).

By contrast, the United States' HIPAA and Hong Kong's PDPO impose mandatory breach notification, requiring notification of the data subjects by the data controllers (United States Department of Health and Human Services, 2023; Office of the Privacy Commissioner for Personal Data, 2023). HIPAA refers to such breach notification practice as the Breach Notification Rule (United States Department of Health and Human Services, 2023). By virtue of Section 68 of the Data Protection Act 2018 (National Archives, 2023b) of the United Kingdom, the data controllers mush notify the data subjects (usually the affected patient in this context) of such data breaches, which are referred to as "personal data breaches" in the United Kingdom.

3.2 Weak Consent Processes

The author is not aware of any explicit and extra requirement under Macao's legal framework for data controllers (usually, the healthcare institutions in this context) to attain express consent from data subjects (usually, the patients in this context) to lawfully collect, store, communicate, process, and/or otherwise use healthcare data vis-à-vis other personal data. In contrast, United States' HIPAA and HIPAA Privacy Rule expressly mandate such consent from the patients to the healthcare institutions (Centers for Disease Control and Prevention, 2023a; Centers for Disease Control and Prevention, 2023b; Centers for Disease Control and Prevention, 2023c). Similarly, pursuant to Section 35 of the United Kingdom's Data Protection Act 2018, processing of healthcare data is subsumed under "sensitive processing," which necessitates the corresponding data subjects' consent to the processing (National Archives, 2023b). Likewise, Hong Kong's PDPO demands such explicit consent by virtue of its Data Protection Principle 3 (Office of the Privacy Commissioner for Personal Data, 2023). PDPO being applicable to personal data in the SAR's eHRSS (Electronic Health Record Sharing System, 2023), any electronic healthcare data could not have been in the eHRSS without such prior explicit consent from the corresponding patients.

Macao may consider strengthening consent requirements to better protect patient autonomy and minimize privacy violations.

3.3 Comparative Summary

In summary, Macao's current legal framework addressing privacy and security of healthcare data in healthcare information systems is less compendious than those in major jurisdictions. Developing Macao's legal framework to match those in major jurisdictions may be an ongoing way forward for the SAR.

4. LEGAL LIABILITIES

Violations of laws governing healthcare information systems precipitate civil, criminal, and administrative penalties across most jurisdictions. However, Macao has seen minimal enforcement actions to date compared to the proliferating litigation and prosecutions in the United States and Hong Kong. A brief overview of Macao's potential legal liabilities is provided below in contrast to other jurisdictions.

4.1 Civil Liability

Article 14 of Macao's PDPA enables data subjects to receive compensation for damages from data controllers' unlawful collection, storage, communication, analysis, and processing of personal data, be it related to healthcare or not (Macao Special Administrative Region, 2023a). More likely than not, data controllers contravening the PDPA when healthcare data is entailed are confronted with heavier damages compensation than when the data is not about healthcare in view of healthcare data being considered sensitive personal data under Article 7 of the Act (Macao Special Administrative Region, 2023a). Nonetheless, there have been only very limited number of PDPA court cases throughout the years.

By comparison, the United States has witnessed rampant class action litigation against healthcare institutions under HIPAA, resulting in settlements of hundreds of millions of dollars (HIPAA Journal, 2023).

Given Macao's historically restrained civil litigation culture, American-style civil liabilities seem unlikely currently but could emerge over time.

4.2 Criminal Offences

Macao's PDPA prescribes fines and 1 to 2 years of imprisonment for criminally violating its provisions plus some additional imprisonment for exceptional serious cases (Macao Special Administrative Region, 2023a). The penalties are light compared to the 5-year maximum sentence under Hong Kong's PDPO (Hong Kong Special Administrative Region, 2023). However, Macao's Amended Act 11/2009: Anti-computer Crime Act provides for stiffer penalties of up to 10 years imprisonment for illegal access to, interference with, and frauds on computer systems and their data (Macao Special Administrative Region, 2023b). Prosecutions in Macao have been rare but may increase with wider adoption of electronic healthcare data. The United States stands apart with its assertive prosecution of healthcare data breaches. HIPAA cases have resulted in multi-million dollar fines at the federal level, and additional punitive damages at the state level may be even more burdensome (HIPAA Journal, 2023).

Macao is unlikely to pursue similar punitive enforcement in the near future given cultural differences. Nonetheless, the possibility of criminal sanctions adds an important deterrent against healthcare data misuse.

4.3 Administrative Fines

Macao's PDPA authorizes administrative fines of up to 100,000 Macao Patacas (MOP) for administrative violations as distinct from criminal violations (Macao Special Administrative Region, 2023a). As per a public announcement in 2020, the GPDP exercised this power, fining a beauty company MOP1,080,000 in total, presumably for multiple data breaches (Macao Special Administrative Region, 2023c). Though not a traditional healthcare institution, the beauty company's operation in this case resembles and represents that of such institutions. As the watchdog for the PDPA, the GPDP can be expected to rely more on fines to enforce compliance as awareness and capacity increase. By comparison, U.S. regulators have imposed massive administrative fines reaching hundreds of millions of dollars upon healthcare institutions for HIPAA contraventions, alongside requiring corrective actions under binding resolution agreements (HIPAA Journal, 2023). At the other extreme of the continuum, Hong Kong seldom sanctioned healthcare institutions like hospitals and clinics under its PDPO and eHRSS. Macao's fines are likely to remain modest at present but add an additional means of accountability.

In summary, Macao has various civil, criminal, and administrative remedies for violations of laws governing healthcare information systems on par with other jurisdictions. However, enforcement has been extremely limited. Building up Macao's legal accountability will be vital as healthcare information systems expand.

5. CONCLUSION AND DISCUSSION

This comparative analysis reveals that Macao currently lacks a specialized legal framework for regulating healthcare information systems, in contrast to the much larger regimes in the United States, the United Kingdom, and Hong Kong. However, Macao's healthcare information systems are prone to such legal issues as privacy, security, etc. in a way similar to that in the much larger regimes. Further constructing Macao's healthcare legal infrastructure may be advisable.

To be specific, the only legislation somewhat related to health information systems is its PDPA originally meant to govern personal data protection in general. In contrast, the United States, the United Kingdom, and Hong Kong all enact laws specific or at least partly specific to healthcare information systems whilst the United Kingdom and Hong Kong at the same time practice their own general personal data protection laws. As far as what the author is cognizant of, Macao does not specify any explicit requirement for healthcare institutions' patient data breaches being reported to the affected patients. Similarly, Macao does not mandate healthcare institutions obtaining express consent from patients to lawfully collect, store, communicate, process, and/or otherwise use healthcare data of the patients while this is a necessity in the United States, the United Kingdom, and Hong Kong. However, Macao's current legal framework at least provides a baseline of protection for the patients whose healthcare data resides in the healthcare information systems of the local healthcare institutions. Macao's legal landscape is also characterized by comparatively lenient penalties and minimal litigation and prosecutions. Table 1 briefly summarizes the comparison of the legal framework for healthcare information systems between Macao and major jurisdictions.

Table 1. Comparison of the legal framework for healthcare information systems between Macao and major jurisdictions

	General Legal Regulation for Healthcare Information Systems	Privacy and Security	Legal Liabilities
Macao	No comprehensive legislation.	PDPA: Healthcare data = sensitive personal data; no mandatory breach notification of the data subjects (as far as the author is aware); data subjects' consent to the data controller as with other data.	PDPA: Minimal enforcement actions to date; heavier civil liabilities with healthcare data than other data; lighter criminal penalties than elsewhere; administrative fines. Anti-computer Crime Act: stiffer penalties.
United States	HITECH.	CFAA.	HIPAA: Rampant civil class action litigation; heavy criminal penalties; heavy administrative fines and corrective actions under binding resolution agreements.
	HIPAA: Breach notification of the data subjects. HIPAA and HIPAA Privacy Rule: Data subjects' consent to the data controller.		
United Kingdom	HSCA.	Data Protection Act: Breach notification of the data subjects; data subjects' consent to the data controller.	
Hong Kong	eHRSS Ordinance.	PDPO: Breach notification of the data subjects PDPO and eHRSS: Data subjects' consent to the data controller.	Seldom sanctioned healthcare institutions under its PDPO and eHRSS.

For small jurisdictions, there may be insufficient populations and thus limited scale economies of and relevant court cases from the local healthcare industries to justify specialization of their legal frameworks to cater for the healthcare information systems. Macao's legal framework regulating healthcare information systems is generally shared with all sectors in society handling personal data, and the provisions therein sound like a simplified version of larger jurisdictions' counterparts. It may be reasoned that such traits of Macao's legal framework may be found in many other small jurisdictions around the world. In fact, this phenomenon of specialization versus economies of scale is universally true in virtually all industries in society (Daraio et al, 2015), and it comes as no surprise to see the same in the legal frameworks governing healthcare information systems. Nevertheless, further statistical research across more jurisdictions is essential in order to theorize this phenomenon of specialization versus scale economies of the legal regime associated with healthcare information systems.

Lastly, the author would underline the disclaimer that despite the plausibility of this article serving as practical guidelines or a checklist for healthcare information system developers and/or users concerned about legal compliance worldwide, formal consultation with qualified legal professionals of the corresponding jurisdictions is strongly advised whenever specific legal issues are to be addressed.

REFERENCES

American Speech-Language-Hearing Association (2023). *Health Information Technology for Economics and Clinical Health (HITECH) Act*. American Speech-Language-Hearing Association. Retrieved August 12, 2023 from https://www.asha.org/practice/reimbursement/hipaa/hitech-act/#:~:text=The%20Health%20Information%20Technology%20for,(EHR)%20systems%20among%20providers.

Boar, C., Holden, H., and Wadsworth, A. (2020). Impending Arrival – A Sequel to the Survey on Central Bank Digital Currency. *In Bank for International Settlements Paper No 107*. Retrived August 11, 2023 from https://papers.ssrn.com/sol3/papers.cfm?abstract_id=3535896

Britannica Academic (2023). Macau. *In Britannica Academic*. Retrived May 4, 2023 from https://academic.eb.com/levels/collegiate/article/Macau/49619

Castellucci, I. (2012). Legal hybridity in Hong Kong and Macau. *In McGill Law Journal*, Vol. 57, No. 4, pp. 665–720.

Centers for Disease Control and Prevention (2023a). *Health Insurance Portability and Accountability Act of 1996 (HIPAA)*. Centers for Disease Control and Prevention Retrieved August 12, 2023 from https://www.cdc.gov/phlp/publications/topic/hipaa.html

Centers for Disease Control and Prevention (2023b). *HIPAA Privacy Rule*. Centers for Disease Control and Prevention Retrieved August 12, 2023 from https://www.cdc.gov/phlp/publications/topic/hipaa.html

Centers for Disease Control and Prevention (2023c). *Public Health Professionals Gateway: Public Health Law*. Centers for Disease Control and Prevention. Retrieved August 12, 2023 from https://www.cdc.gov/phlp/publications/topic/hipaa.html

CIA (2023). *The World Factbook: Macau*. CIA. Retrived May 4, 2023 from https://www.cia.gov/the-world-factbook/countries/macau/

Daraio, C., Bonaccorsi, A. and Simar, L. (2015). Efficiency and economies of scale and specialization in European universities: A directional distance approach. *Journal of Informetrics*, Vol. 9, No. 3, pp. 430-448.

Ebnehoseini, Z., Tabesh, H., Deldar, K., Mostafavi, S. M., and Tara, M. (2019). Determining the Hospital Information System (HIS) Success Rate: Development of a New Instrument and Case Study. *In Open Access Macedonian Journal of Medical Sciences*, Vol. 7, No. 9, pp. 1407–1414. Retrieved August 11, 2023 from https://www.ncbi.nlm.nih.gov/pmc/articles/PMC6542404/

Electronic Health Record Sharing System (2023). *Electronic Health Record Sharing System Ordinance*. Retrieved August 12, 2023 from https://www.ehealth.gov.hk/en/whats-ehealth/ordinance.html#:~:text=The%20Electronic%20Health%20Record%20Sharing,data%20shared%20through%20the%20eHRSS.

Farzandipour, M., Meidani, Z., Jabali, M. S., and Bnadaki, R. D. (2019). Designing and Evaluating Functional Laboratory Information System Requirements Integrated to Hospital Information Systems. *In Jornal of Evaluation in Clinical Practice*, Vol. 25, No. 5, pp. 788-799. Retrived August 11, 2023 from https://onlinelibrary.wiley.com/doi/abs/10.1111/jep.13074

HIPAA Journal (2023). HIPAA Violation Cases. *HIPAA Journal*. Retrieved August 13, 2023 from https://www.hipaajournal.com/hipaa-violation-cases/

Hong Kong Special Administrative Region (2023). *Pesonal Data (Privacy) (Amendment) Ordinance 2021*. Retrieved August 13, 2023 from https://www.gld.gov.hk/egazette/pdf/20212540/es12021254032.pdf

Macao Special Administrative Region (2023a). *Act 8/2005: Personal Data Protection Act*. Macao SAR Government. Retrieved June 23, 2023 from https://www.gpdp.gov.mo/file/Laws%20and%20Regulations/%E5%80%8B%E4%BA%BA%E8%B3%87%E6%96%99%E4%BF%9D%E8%AD%B7%E6%B3%95_EN.pdf

Macao Special Administrative Region (2023b). *Amended Act 11/2009: Anti-computer Crime Act*. Macao Special Administrative Region. Retrieved August 13, 2023 from https://bo.io.gov.mo/bo/i/2020/17/lei04_cn.asp

Macao Special Administrative Region (2023c). *The Office for Personal Data Protection Penalizes and Censures a Company (in Chinese)*. Macao Special Administrative Region. Retrieved August 14, 2023 from https://www.gov.mo/zh-hant/news/336617/

Mukherjee, M. and Roy, S. (2017). Feasibility Studies and Important Aspect of Project Management. *In International Journal of Advanced Engineering and Management*, Vol. 2, No. 4, pp. 98-100. Website: https://ijoaem.org/00204-25

National Archives (2023a). *Health and Social Care Act 2012*. National Archives. Retrieved August 12, 2023 from https://www.legislation.gov.uk/ukpga/2012/7/contents/enacted

National Archives (2023b). *Data Protection Act 2018*. National Archives. Retrieved August 12, 2023 from https://www.legislation.gov.uk/ukpga/2018/12/part/3/enacted

Office of the Privacy Commissioner for Personal Data (2023). *The Personal Data (Privacy) Ordinance*. Office of the Privacy Commissioner for Personal Data. Retrieved August 12, 2023 from https://www.pcpd.org.hk/english/data_privacy_law/ordinance_at_a_Glance/ordinance.html

Tsui, W. (2017). *IT in Hospital Authority: IT Career Role Models Platform*. Hospital Authority. Retrieved August 12, 2023 from https://www.ogcio.gov.hk/en/our_work/business/industry_support/ict_manpower/student_it_corner/motion_corner/2017/itcrmp/doc/presentation_slide_by_hait_20171123.pdf

United States Department of Health and Human Services (2023). *Breach Notification Rule*. Retrieved August 12, 2023 from https://www.hhs.gov/hipaa/for-professionals/breach-notification/index.html

United States Department of Justice (2023). *The Computer Fraud and Abuse Act ("CFAA"), Title 18, United States Code, Section 1030*. The United States Department of Justice. Retrieved August 12, 2023 from https://www.justice.gov/jm/jm-9-48000-computer-fraud

DOES IT WORK ON CONTENT MARKETING WITH SHORT-VIDEO IN CHINA?

Chun-Chi Chen*
Department of Marketing and Distribution Management
School of Business, Xiamen Institute of Technology, China, P.R.C.

ABSTRACT

The monthly active users of the short video industry were reached 905 million in China (Quest Mobile, 2022). In 2021, the average daily time for online audiences to watch short videos has been to 125 minutes (CNNIC, 2022). Even it, over 90% of audience remain rejects the marketing method of "short video + content marketing" used by enterprises (iResearch Consulting Group, 2022). Starting from the content dimension, what try to construct a theoretical model with effective explanation and generalization in this study. A total of 750 valid samples were obtained by questionnaire research method. AMOS v. 18 is used as an analysis tool for testing measurements and structural models. The test results are as follows: (a) Social interaction content positively and significantly affects psychological distance; (b) Self-actualization content positively and significantly affects psychological distance; (c) Psychological distance has a positive and significant impact on brand trust; (d) Brand trust has a positive and significant impact on purchase intention; (e) Product involvement has a negative and significant moderating effect between content marketing and purchase intention. Finally, this study points out the corresponding theoretical and managerial implications based on the data analysis results.

KEYWORDS

Short Video, Content Marketing, Psychological Distance, Brand Trust, Product Involvement

1. INTRODUCTION

In 2021, the scale of Internet usage in China has reached 1.011 billion people (CNNIC, 2022). The monthly active users of the short video industry reached 905 million (Quest Mobile, 2022). Short video content marketing is not limited by time and can be flexibly presented in the eyes of consumers in fragmented time. In 2021, the average daily time for online audiences to watch short videos has been to 125 minutes (CNNIC, 2022). Even it, over 90% of audience remain rejects the marketing method of "short video + content marketing" used by enterprises (iResearch Consulting Group, 2022). This study is different from the focus of previous research. Starting from the content dimension, this study explores the differences in the impact of content marketing in various dimensions on purchase intentions, and introduces three important behavioral decision-making variables, including psychological distance, brand trust, and product involvement, what try to construct a theoretical model with effective explanation and generalization.

2. LITERATURE REVIEW AND HYPOTHESIS

2.1 Content Marketing, CM

Holliman (2014) believes that content marketing is a kind of marketing strategy that can deliver value and help audiences solve problems, transforming sales into helping audiences solve problems. There is no uniform standard for the division of content marketing dimensions in the literature. Users watch short videos to learn about products and news, which are functional content. In order to watch interesting content, relax and pass the time, it belongs to entertainment content. In order to broaden the social circle, it belongs to social interaction

* Corresponding author: ashin1229@gmail.com

content. In order to pay attention to stars and idols, it belongs to brand interactive content. In order to learn some useful knowledge and skills, it belongs to self-actualization content (iResearch Consulting Group, 2022). Content marketing has a positive and significant impact on purchase intention (Zhang, 2020). In summary, this study proposes a causal hypothesis.

H1a: Functional content has a positive and significant impact on consumers' purchase intention;

H1b: Entertainment content has a positive and significant impact on consumers' purchase intention;

H1c: Social interaction content has a positive and significant impact on consumers' purchase intention;

H1d: Brand interactive content has a positive and significant impact on consumers' purchase intention;

H1e: Self-actualization content has a positive and significant impact on consumers' purchase intention.

2.2 Psychological Distance, PD

Psychological distance is an individual's subjective perception of the similarity between a product and himself (Yu, 2011). The level of psychological distance will affect the audience's cognition, feeling, behavior, and way of explaining things (Liberman etal., 2002; Wang, 2020). When the audience recognizes the company's content marketing, it will be more beneficial Enterprises shorten the psychological distance between the audience and the product (Wang, 2020; Yu, 2011). When the psychological distance is closer, the audience's trust in the brand gradually increases (Li etal., 2017). Therefore, this study proposes causal hypothesis.

H2a: Functional content has a positive and significant impact on psychological distance;

H2b: Entertainment content has a positive and significant impact on psychological distance;

H2c: Social interaction content has a positive and significant impact on psychological distance;

H2d: Brand interactive content has a positive and significant impact on psychological distance;

H2e: Self-actualization content has a positive and significant impact on psychological distance;

H3: Psychological distance has a positive and significant impact on brand trust.

2.3 Brand Trust, BT

Brand trust is a psychological subjective attitude of the audience, and it is an expression of confidence in a certain product or service, which is mainly reflected in the audience's trust in the brand's product quality, recognition of its service attitude, corporate culture, etc. (Delgado-Ballester etal., 2003; Yang, 2020). Brand trust is a key direct factor affecting purchase intention (Moorman etal., 1992; Yang, 2020). Therefore, this study proposes a causal hypothesis.

H4: Brand trust has a positive and significant impact on purchase intention

2.4 Product Involvement, PIT

Product involvement is not only related to its own factors, but also closely related to the nature of the product itself. Products that are more important to the audience will have higher involvement than products that are not so important. For the audience, high product Involvement means that the audience will pay more attention and care when searching for product performance, utility, precautions, and price comparisons (Traylor, 1981). High or low product involvement will interact to stimulate purchase intentions (Wang, 2020). Therefore, this study proposes a causal hypothesis.

H5: Product involvement has a negative and significant moderating effect between content marketing and purchase intention.

3. METHODOLOGY

3.1 Research Design

The comprehensive research of Muijs (2011) is helpful to understand the participants' consumption motivation for China's "Short Video + Content Marketing" business model. The data collection is based on the cross-sectional design conducted by Sedgwick (2014). The sample data is obtained at a single point in time, usually from multiple groups or types of people. This study used AMOS software for structural equation modeling (SEM). The software uses a structural equation model based on the covariance-based method. In terms of sample size, distribution assumptions, and model complexity, it is not as restrictive as other software (such as LISREL) (Hair etal., 2013). A two-stage analysis method was adopted (Anderson and Gerbing, 1988), which the confirmatory factor analysis (CFA), fitness among the variables of the structural model and test for causality (Anderson and Gerbing, 1988).

3.2 Sample and Data Collection

Battaglia (2011) pointed that a part of the population called a sample may estimate certain conditions of the entire population. Purpose sampling is used to determine respondents based on selection criteria, that is, respondents must be consumers who have received the "Short Video + Content Marketing" business model for online consumption. Wright (2005) mention that the online surveys make it easier to obtain the interests, attitudes and values of specific groups of people. A total of 827 questionnaires of official were distributed and 750 valid samples were received. The response rate was 90.6%.

4. DATA ANALYSIS AND RESULTS

4.1 Measurement Model

In the reliability analysis, all observed variables were required to have a factor loading (Hair etal., 2013) and squared multiple correlation (SMC) greater than .5 (Bagozzi and Yi, 1988). In the convergent validity analysis, the reliability, composite reliability, and average variance extracted (AVE) of each individual item was considered (Hair etal., 2013), as shown in Table 1. In the discriminate validity analysis, the square root of the average variance extracted (SQAVE) was required to be greater than the correlation coefficients of other dimensions (Hair et al., 2013), as indicated in Table 2.

Table 1. Reliability and convergent validity analysis

Construct	Indica tor	Factor loading (λ)>0.5 (Hair et al., 1992)	AVE>0.5 (Fornell & Larcker, 1981)	Cronbach's alpha (α)>0.7 (Cronbach, 19 51)	Composite reliability (CR)>0.7 (Hair et al., 1998)
Functional content, FC	FC1	0.81	0.653	0.848	0.849
	FC2	0.87			
	FC3	0.74			
Entertainment content, EC	EC1	0.75	0.653	0.754	0.849
	EC2	0.76			
	EC3	0.65			
Social interaction content, SIC	SIC1	0.80	0.653	0.803	0.805
	SIC2	0.77			
	SIIC3	0.71			
Brand interactive content, BIC	BIC1	0.64	0.547	0.772	0.783
	BIC2	0.79			
	BIC3	0.78			
Self-actualization content, SAC	SAC1	0.81	0.651	0.846	0.848
	SAC2	0.81			
	SAC3	0.80			
Psychological distance, P D	PD1	0.79	0.583	0.809	0.807
	PD2	0.74			
	PD3	0.76			
Brand trust, BT	BT1	0.78	0.624	0.829	0.832
	BT2	0.88			
	BT3	0.70			
Product involvement, PIT	PIT1	0.79	0.651	0.848	0.848

	PIT2	0.80			
	PIT3	0.83			
Purchase intention, PI	PI1	0.75	0.679	0.859	0.863
	PI2	0.94			
	PI3	0.77			

Table 2. Discriminate validity analysis

Construct	PI	PIT	BT	PD	SAC	BIC	SIC	EC	FC
PI	0.824								
PIT	0.869	0.807							
BT	0.739	0.839	0.790						
PD	0.631	0.685	0.771	0.764					
SAC	0.599	0.639	0.658	0.734	0.807				
BIC	0.590	0.660	0.659	0.679	0.843	0.740			
SIC	0.537	0.621	0.589	0.719	0.720	0.805	0.808		
EC	0.401	0.472	0.473	0.641	0.537	0.648	0.770	0.808	
FC	0.414	0.530	0.476	0.551	0.464	0.525	0.672	0.754	0.808

4.2 Structural Model

4.2.1 Fitness Assessment of the Theoretical Model

This study was referred to Bagozzi and Yi (1988), Bentler (1995), Hair (2009), etc. for model fit analysis and verification of the overall structure model. The results show that the theoretical model has a good model fit (as shown in Table 3).

Table 3. the Model fit of theoretical model

Model fit index	Suggestion	This study
$\chi 2$	The smaller the better (Bagozzi and Yi, 1998)	846.64
df (Degree of Freedom)	The bigger the better (Bagozzi and Yi, 1998)	230
$\chi 2$/df	$1<\chi 2/df<5$(Bagozzi and Yi, 1998)	3.68
AGFI	$>$ 0.90(MacCallum and Hong, 1997)	0.90
RMSEA	$<$ 0.08(Schumacker and Lomax, 2004)	0.05
SRMR	$<$ 0.08 (Bentler, 1999)	0.04
TLI(NNFI)	$>$ 0.90(Cheung and Rensvold, 2002)	0.93
CFI	$>$ 0.90(Hair et al., 1998)	0.94

4.2.2 Structural Model and Hypothesis Test

Through the calculation of AMOS, the path coefficients of H2c, H2e, H3, H4 in the structural model are shown to be significant and reach the significant standard ($p < 0.05$) (see Figure 1).

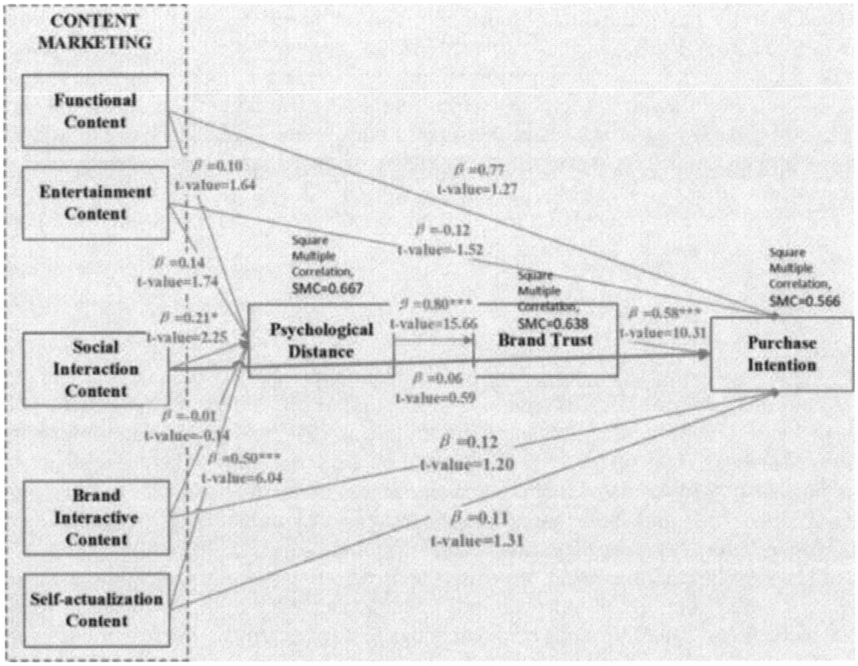

Figure 1. The Full structural model path test

4.3 Moderation Effect Test

According to Joreskog and Sorbom (1996), this study uses the multi-group structural equation model (AMOS) to analyze second-order model of identical concept in both high group and low group, and to test whether the model presented moderator effect (See Table 4).

Table 4. Identical test results of two sample path coefficients

Model	Explanation	Chi-square value	Degree of freedom	the Difference of chi-square value with model 1
Model 1	Baseline model	1731.22242	654	
Model 2	Moderating model	1735.158	655	3.93558

The path coefficient of the low group is greater than the path coefficient of the high group (see Table 5.). The difference of the chi-square value between Baseline Model and Moderating Model is greater than 3.84 (α=0.05) under 1 degree of freedom. The H5 of this study was supported.

Table 5. Moderating path analysis results of high and low group

Path		Content marketing → Purchase intention
the Estimated value	Low group	0.373
	High group	0.235

5. DISCUSSION

5.1 Theoretical Implications

First, the direct impact of each dimension of content marketing on consumers' purchase intention are not supported in this study. In recent years, deceptive short video content such as fake and shoddy products, false propaganda, etc., and the arrival of the post-epidemic period have caused audiences to face a series of negative information. Under the business model of short video content marketing, the audience will not be like Believe blindly as before (Zhao, 2022). Changes in the external environment and the psychological adjustment of the audience have jointly reshaped the new consumption awareness, and rational consumption has been generally valued (Yao, 2022). Furthermore, according to the data analysis results of this study, only social interaction content and Self-actualization content have the support on psychological distance. This is just in line with the survey of iResearch Consulting Group (2022), 51.9% of short video users watch short videos to learn something useful Knowledge and skills, which belong to Self-actualization content. 29.5% of users want to broaden their social circle, which belongs to social interaction content. These two items respectively represent the top two purposes of audience watching short videos.

5.2 Managerial Implications

The first thing that enterprises are struggling and feeling confused is trying to create truly valuable content while not embedding too obvious advertising information in the content. This is actually quite difficult. Spending precious time promoting content, but you have to give up sales-oriented information, which runs counter to the purpose of making a profit. However, users are very smart. If there is a "content advertisement" hidden in the content, that is, when there is an advertisement placed in it and tries to sell a product or service, they will quickly see through it. Some users are very sensitive and disgusted by unexpected advertising content or excessive sales information, so the ratio of the two should be used with caution. Often in the early stages, when businesses try to market content, they use the same one-way communication approach as traditional marketing and advertising, ignoring community engagement rates and not further engaging with users. Traditional marketing is usually a single ad or campaign that either arouses interest or does not arouse interest. Businesses use the A/B Test advertising method to compare which ad resonates more and leads to more sales. Relatively speaking, content marketing generally does not lead to immediate sales, because if done correctly - you will not sell anything. This indirect strategy helps to hit the heart and build a solid loyalty of users. Good content marketing must be a consistent, patient, and uninterrupted long-term investment. Content marketing is not a quick fix. When doing content marketing, companies should uphold the spirit of selfless dedication, constantly think about who their users are, what content is closely related to the lives of users, and focus on producing user-centered content. In the process of continuously giving practical and valuable information to the main target customer groups or potential users, cultivate them to become potential consumers of the brand in the future.

6. CONCLUSION

In the post-epidemic era, consumers are more cautious about consumption, and audiences abandon impulsive consumption, online celebrity economy and other perceptual consumption demands will return to rational consumption, which indicates that external factors such as the epidemic have catalyzed Chinese consumers to enter the stage of rational consumption. Consumers form an initial perception of content in the process of watching short videos, that is, psychological distance, and brand trust, as an attitude, will affect consumers' purchase intentions. Therefore, consumers do not immediately generate purchase intentions after seeing the content marketing of short videos, but go through a series of psychological mechanisms. When the audience obtains product information, the higher the product involvement, the more important the value of the product is to itself, and because the risk is higher, the audience will pay more attention, and the decision-making will be more rational and more concerned. The internal and external attributes of the product. Therefore, when the product involvement is high, the audience tends to only agree with the product, and the purchase intention will be stimulated, and the purchase decision becomes relatively complicated. At this time, the direct impact of content marketing on the purchase intention will be smaller; on the contrary, When the product involvement is lower, the purchase decision process is simpler, and the direct impact of content marketing on purchase intention is higher.

7. LIMITATIONS AND FUTURE DIRECTIONS

There is still no uniform standard for the division of content dimensions in the literature now, and with changes in the external environment, the audience's purpose of watching short video content may change, and new content dimensions emerge. Therefore, follow-up studies can expand it based on this concept in China, and even make a cross-country comparisons research. Furthermore, this study conducted a cross-sectional study at a specific point in time, although it has its theoretical and practical contributions. However, such conclusions are not sufficient to infer that the longitudinal study can show with environmental change factors. Therefore, follow-up research can carry out periodic empirical discussion.

REFERENCES

Anderson, J. C. and Gerbing, D. W., 1988. Structural equation modeling in practice: A review and recommended two-step approach. *Psychological Bulletin*, 103, 411-423.

Bagozzi, R.P., 2007. The legacy of the technology acceptance model and a proposal for a paradigm shift. *J. Assoc. Inf. Syst.* 8, 244–254.

Bagozzi, R.P., Dholakia, U., 1999. Goal setting and goal striving in consumer behavior. *J. Mark.* 63, 19–32.

CNNIC, 2022. Statistical Report on China's Internet Development. Retrieved from https://www.cnnic.net.cn/6/86/88/index.html

CTR Market Research, 2022. Short Video Full Link Marketing White Paper. Retrieved from https://www.ctrchina.cn/product/KWP/xfzmjyxlmx

Delgado-Ballester E., Munuera-Aleman J. L., Yague-Guillen M. J., 2003. Development and validation of a brand trust scale. *International Journal of Market Research*. 45(1): 35-54.

Hair, J.F., Jr, Hult, G.T.M., Ringle, C., Sarstedt, M., 2013. *A Primer on Partial Least Squares Structural Equation Modelling (PLS-SEM)*. Sage Publications, Thousand Oaks, California, CA.

Holliman G, Rowley J. 2014. Business to business digital content marketing: marketers'perceptions of best practice. *Journal of research in interactive marketing.* 8(4): 269-293.

iResearch Consulting Group, 2022. 2022 Overseas TMT Internet Annual Strategy Report: The Second Half of Standardization, New Opportunities from Virtual to Reality. https://www.iresearchchina.com/insights/report.html

Liberman, N., Sagristano, M., and Trope, Y., 2002. The effect of temporal distance on level of construction. *Journal of Experimental Social Psychology.* 38(6), 523-535.

Li Tingting, Li Yanjun, 2017. The Formation Mechanism of Continuous Trust in Farmers' Purchase Decision-Making in Different Psychological Distance Situations. *Journal of Finance and Economics*. Vol. 9, 83-93.

Moorman C, Zaltman G, Deshpande R., 1992. Relationships between providers and users of market research: The dynamics of trust within and between organizations. *Journal of Marketing Research*. 29(29):314-328.

Quest Mobile, 2022. 2020-2021 Scale Trend of Monthly Active Users in the Short Video Industry. Retrieved from https://www.questmobile.com.cn/research/reports

Traylor, 1981. Product involvement and brand commitment. *Journal of Advertising*. 51-56.

Yao Yao, 2022. The Impact of the New Coronary Pneumonia Epidemic on the Consumption Behavior of Urban Residents in Kunming and Suggestions. *China Market*, vol. 9:5-10.

Zhao Xinran, 2022. On the new consumption concept and consumption policy in the post-epidemic period. *China Market*. vol. 3:129-130.

SHORT

PAPERS

DECLARATIVE PROGRAMMING IN MODERN IMPERATIVE LANGUAGES

Lutz Hamel
Dept. of Computer Science & Statistics
University of Rhode Island
Kingston, Rhode Island, USA

ABSTRACT

Declarative features provide new ways of solving programming problems in imperative programming languages. It is now a given that modern imperative programming languages support declarative features such as first-class functions and higher-order programming, and increasingly pattern matching. To further explore declarative programming and in particular pattern matching in the imperative programming paradigm we designed and implemented the Asteroid programming language. Asteroid is an imperative, dynamically typed programming language that not only supports common declarative features, but also supports pattern matching to a degree not found in many imperative languages and, in particular, it supports first-class patterns. In this short paper we briefly review some common declarative programming techniques and then briefly survey programming in Asteroid with first-class patterns.

KEYWORDS

Declarative Programming, Pattern Matching, First-Class Patterns, First-Class Functions, Higher-Order Programming

1. INTRODUCTION

Declarative features provide new ways of solving programming problems in imperative programming languages. It is now a given that modern imperative programming languages support declarative features such as functions as first-class citizens. This includes anonymous functions and higher-order programming features such as the map function. Also supported by many imperative programming languages are declarative features such as list comprehensions and generator expressions. However, from our perspective the most interesting development is the increasing adoption of pattern matching, a declarative programming technique. This not only includes structural matching on structures like lists and tuples but also conditional pattern matching and pattern matching on objects. The latter is particularly interesting because it stands in direct conflict with the classical object-oriented notion of encapsulation and protection of object members. Pattern matching provides novel ways of solving problems analogous to the way higher-order programming provides novel ways of accomplishing things.

To explore declarative programming and in particular pattern matching in the imperative programming paradigm further we designed and implemented the Asteroid programming language (asteroid-lang.org). Asteroid is an imperative, dynamically typed programming language that not only supports common pattern matching features like the match and let statements, but it also supports pattern matching on function arguments in the style of functional programming languages like ML (Milner, 1997). Furthermore, Asteroid supports first-class patterns (Jay & Kesner, 2009). The latter opens whole new avenues of programming language research such as pattern reusability, patterns as constraints, and patterns as enhancement to type systems. The contributions of this short paper are (1) the placement of our current research into the context of the current declarative evolution of modern imperative programming languages and (2) a brief demonstration of the utility of first-class patterns including our pattern scope operator and our improved conditional pattern matching operator which allows the developer to use patterns as constraints on other patterns.

Our notion of first-class patterns is related to the ideas of first-class dynamic types developed in (Homer et al., 2019) but drastically differs from first-class patterns in Haskell (Tullsen, 2000) where they are treated as anonymous functions. The first-class patterns in F#, also known as active patterns (Syme, 2020), are limited in their application compared to our more general notion of first-class pattern.

An imperative language similar to ours that also implements first-class patterns is Thorn (Bloom & Hirzel, 2012). Unfortunately, that language is no longer under development. Furthermore, our ideas of patterns constraining patterns as well as our pattern scope operator seem to be novel.

The remainder of the paper is structured as follows. Section 2 is a brief survey of the most common declarative features found in today's imperative programming languages and places our work in the context of those features. Section 3 introduces first-class patterns and highlights some of our findings with regards to programming with first-class patterns. The features discussed here will be available in our upcoming 2.0 release. Section 4 presents our conclusions and points to some interesting directions for further work.

2. DECLARATIVE PROGRAMMING

Declarative programming features are now implemented to varying degrees by almost every modern, popular programming language. We define popularity of a programming language as being in the top ten programming languages on indexes like TIOBE (www.tiobe.com/tiobe-index) and IEEE (spectrum.ieee.org/top-programming-languages-2022) and we define modern by the fact that a programming language was initially designed/release from the 1990's onward. This includes languages like Go (go.dev), Java (www.java.com), JavaScript (Severance, 2012), Python (www.python.org), R (www.r-project.org), Rust (www.rust-lang.org), and Swift (www.swift.org).

The power of declarative features is that they provide new ways of accomplishing programming task in imperative programming languages. Consider the task of transforming a list. Higher-order programming techniques allow this to be done without explicit looping as in this JavaScript code snippet that transforms an integer list into a list of squared values by mapping an anonymous function onto the integer list,

```
const numbers = [1, 2, 3, 4, 5];
const squaredNumbers = numbers.map((num) => num * num);
```

Here the anonymous function (num) => num * num transforms a number into its square and the map function applies this function to each member of the list producing a new list. The reduce or fold function available in virtually all functional languages and many of today's imperative languages is a variation on the map function. Here, a given list is reduced or folded into a single value. Consider the problem of checking whether all elements on a list are positive values. Instead of writing a loop which traverses the list and checks whether the elements fulfill the constraint, the reduce function allows us to accomplish this with a single expression,

```
Asteroid 2.0.1
(c) University of Rhode Island
Type "help" for additional information
ast> [1, 2, 3, 4, 5] @reduce (lambda with (acc,i) do (i > 0) and acc, true)
true
ast> [1, 2, 3, -4, 5] @reduce (lambda with (acc,i) do (i > 0) and acc, true)
false
ast>
```

In this Asteroid example the first list is reduced to the value true, and the second list is reduced to the value false. List comprehensions and generator expressions are another feature that is available in many modern imperative programming languages. These expressions allow us to construct lists again without explicit looping constructs. The following is a code snippet in Swift demonstrating list comprehensions by computing a list of squares,

```
let squaredNumbers = [number * number for number in 1...5]
```

The construction on the right of the let statement is a list comprehension. In languages that do not support list comprehensions directly, higher-order programming techniques like we have seen in the above JavaScript example can usually be employed in order to achieve similar results.

This brings us to pattern matching, an increasingly important part of declarative programming in imperative languages. For example, the match statement, which supports full structural pattern matching, was added to Python very recently (Kohn et al., 2020). The simplest form of pattern matching is found in let/assignment statements. The following Rust code snippet illustrates accessing the components of a Point object using pattern matching (also called destructuring),

```
struct Point { x: i32, y: i32 } // define a Point structure
let p = Point { x: 5, y: 10 }; // instantiate a Point object using a constructor
let Point { x: a, y: b } = p;  // destructure a Point object using a pattern
assert_eq!(a, 5);
assert_eq!(b, 10);
```

The construction on the left of the equal sign on the third line of the code above is called a pattern. The power of this declarative programming techniques derives from the fact that a pattern mirrors the structure of the object to be destructured; in this case it is the Point object whose structure is defined on the first line. Notice that the pattern-match instantiates the two variables a and b with the contents of the given object—therefore the notion of destructuring.

In general, more advanced pattern matching techniques are available in match statements. The following Python code snippet demonstrates the use of the match statement applied to a list structure,

```
def f(data):
  match data:
    case []:
      return("Empty list.")
    case [x, *_] if isinstance(x, int) and x > 0:
      return("List whose first element is a positive integer.")
    case _:
      return("Unknown object.")
```

Here we define a function f that uses the match statement and pattern matching to analyze the list passed to the function. The first case clause uses an empty list pattern to detect whether the data variable contains an empty list. The second case clause is interesting in that the pattern can match non-empty lists of any length and then uses a conditional pattern-match to only match lists whose first element is a positive integer. The last case clause uses a wild-card pattern which matches any object and works as a default case. All the above declarative programming features are also available in our Asteroid programming language.

Before we move on to first-class patterns it is interesting to look at function invocation. The imperative languages mentioned above except for Asteroid look at function invocation as a "function call" with a function name and a list of parameters to pass to the function. This is different from the more mathematically motivated view of function invocation as "function application" in the declarative paradigm. Here a function is applied to a single object. This single object could be a member of a cross-product set to accommodate multivariate functions. The imperative view of function invocation as function call has unexpected implications at function invocation sites. For example, in Python this means that for calls to a function foo which expects two parameters we have foo(1,2)≠foo((1,2)), that is, parenthesizing an expression changes its semantics at the function call site. In the declarative view of function invocation as function application to a single object this paradoxical problem does not occur. Consider the snippet of Asteroid which supports function application,

```
Asteroid 2.0.1
(c) University of Rhode Island
Type "help" for additional information
ast> function foo with (a,b) do a+b end. -- define foo
ast> foo(1,2) == foo((1,2))
true
ast>
```

Since Asteroid looks at function invocations as function applications, parenthesizing the object (1,2) has no impact on the semantics of the function application.

3. FIRST-CLASS PATTERNS

To further explore pattern matching in imperative programming we implemented patterns as first-class entities in Asteroid. In Asteroid, first-class patterns are introduced with the keyword pattern and patterns themselves are first-class values that we can store in variables, amongst other things, and then reference them when we want to use them like so,

```
let p = pattern (x,y).
let *p = (1,2).
```

The first let statement assigns a pattern value to the variable p and on the left side of the second let statement we dereference the pattern stored in variable p and use it to match against the term (1,2) on the right side. The match introduces the bindings $x \rightarrow 1$ and $y \rightarrow 2$ into the current scope.

Promoting patterns to first-class status separates pattern definition points from pattern usage points enabling new use-cases for pattern matching. Consider the following Asteroid code snippet,

```
let pos_int = pattern x if (x is %integer) and (x > 0).
let neg_int = pattern x if (x is %integer) and (x < 0).

function fact
  with 0 do return 1.
  with *pos_int do return x*fact(x-1).
  with *neg_int do throw Error("illegal value: "+tostring(x)).
end

function sign
  with 0 do return 1.
  with *pos_int do return 1.
  with *neg_int do return -1.
end
```

The first two lines define first-class patterns for positive and negative integers, respectively. Next, we define the function fact which computes the factorial of an integer. We use pattern matching on the function argument to determine what value to return. Most notably, we use the patterns defined earlier to accomplish this. The first two with-clauses define the usual behavior for a factorial computation. Observe that the constant 0 is also considered a pattern. The last with-clause matches if the function is called with a negative integer and throws an exception indicating so. If the function is called with a value that does not match any of the patterns, then the runtime system will throw an exception indicating that the function was called with a value that the function does not recognize.

Next, we define the mathematical sign function which returns the value 1 for integer input values greater than or equal to zero. Otherwise it returns the value -1. Again we use pattern matching on the function argument and, most notably, we reuse our positive and negative integer patterns.

First-class patterns promote pattern reuse and encourage developing interesting and perhaps complex patterns since they are no longer "one shot deals" but can be reused in many different contexts. We leverage this insight in our current library design for Asteroid where we plan to publish a pattern module containing reusable patterns.

It is interesting to observe that by restricting the scope of the variables instantiated by a pattern to just the pattern itself using the %[...]% scope operator, patterns essentially become constraints and as such behave almost like data types. The latter is particularly appealing in dynamically typed languages like Asteroid as it allows the developer to recover some sort of type safety. The following Asteroid code snippet demonstrates this,

```
let nat = pattern %[x if (x is %integer) and (x >= 0)]%.

function nat_add with (a,b):(*nat,*nat) do
  return a+b.
end
```

The first line defines a first-class pattern for the natural numbers. Observe the %[...]% scope operator which ensures that x will not be bound into the current scope when the pattern is used but is only visible within the pattern.

The function definition for nat_add needs some explanation. First observe that the function expects a pair of values given by the pattern (a,b). Next, we use our colon pattern construction which is a shorthand notation for a conditional pattern match: The match of pattern (a,b) is only successful if this pattern matches a pair of natural numbers (*nat,*nat). In that way, the pattern (*nat,*nat) acts like a data type restricting the values that can be passed to the function. Note, here we have patterns constraining other patterns. The pattern (*nat,*nat) also demonstrates that first-class patterns allow us to construct patterns in a modular fashion by assembling complex patterns from simpler ones.

4. CONCLUSIONS

We discussed declarative programming in today's imperative languages. Many declarative features have been seamlessly adopted and enable new problem solutions in the imperative paradigm. One interesting note is that function invocations in imperative languages have resisted the shift to declarative programming. Function invocations are still viewed as function calls with a function name and a parameter list. This leads to paradoxical issues as shown above. We should note that Asteroid supports the more declarative view of function invocation via function application.

Pattern matching is being increasingly adopted by imperative languages and first-class patterns as implemented in the Asteroid programming language are a natural extension to the current declarative programming evolution within modern, imperative programming languages. Pattern reuse and patterns viewed as constraints are interesting applications of first-class patterns.

We are currently implementing a pattern library to be shipped with the next release of Asteroid. One of the more intricate patterns in this library is a pattern that describes integer lists,

```
pattern %[(x:%list) if x @reduce (lambda with (acc,i) do (i is %integer) and acc, true)]%
```

For dynamically typed languages where lists are inherently polymorphic this is an important pattern because it allows for some type safety on lists. Also notice that as a first-class pattern we only have to specify it once and then use it wherever we need it.

Another topic we are exploring are parameterized patterns. That is, patterns that take other patterns as parameters. The integer list pattern above is clearly a good candidate for this, where the data type of the list elements specified as the built-in pattern %integer could be replaced by a pattern parameter specifying the element type.

REFERENCES

Bloom, B. and Hirzel, M.J., 2012. Robust scripting via patterns. *ACM SIGPLAN Notices*, *48*(2), pp. 29-40.

Homer, M., Jones, T. and Noble, J., 2019, October. First-class dynamic types. In *Proceedings of the 15th ACM SIGPLAN International Symposium on Dynamic Languages* (pp. 1-14).

Jay, B. and Kesner, D., 2009. First-class patterns. *Journal of Functional Programming*, *19*(2), pp. 191-225.

Kohn, T., van Rossum, G., Bucher II, G.B. and Levkivskyi, I., 2020, November. Dynamic pattern matching with Python. In *Proceedings of the 16th ACM SIGPLAN International Symposium on Dynamic Languages* (pp. 85-98).

Milner, R., Tofte, M., Harper, R. and MacQueen, D., 1997. *The definition of standard ML: revised*. MIT press.

Severance, C., 2012. Javascript: Designing a language in 10 days. *Computer*, *45*(2), pp. 7-8.

Syme, D., 2020. The early history of F#. *Proceedings of the ACM on Programming Languages*, *4*(HOPL), pp. 1-58.

AN IOT VIRTUAL SENSOR FOR INDOOR HEALTH RISK ASSESSMENT

Lorenzo Calisti[1], Paolo Capellacci[1], Giuditta Schiavano[2], Asja Conti[3], Giulia Amagliani[3], Cecilia Papalini[4], Giorgio Brandi[3] and Emanuele Lattanzi[1]
[1]*Department of Pure and Applied Science, University of Urbino Carlo Bo, 61029 Urbino, Italy*
[2]*Department of Humanities, University of Urbino Carlo Bo, 61029 Urbino; Italy*
[3]*Department of Biomolecular Sciences, University of Urbino Carlo Bo, 61029 Urbino, Italy*
[4]*Papalini Spa, Via Paolo Borsellino, 9 61032 Fano (PU), Italy*

ABSTRACT

Indoor environments have a significant impact on human health and well-being. With the increasing urbanization and the amount of time individuals spend indoors there is a growing need for accurate and real-time monitoring of air quality and health risks. Moreover, the mere presence of people in enclosed spaces, apart from saturating the environment with gases typically produced by human respiration, leads to microbiological contamination due, for example, from exhaled aerosols which can contain several pathogens.

In this study, we propose an Internet of Things virtual sensor for indoor health risk assessment that integrates several physical sensors measuring various parameters related to indoor air quality, including temperature, humidity, carbon dioxide levels, volatile organic compounds, and particulate matter with the purpose to indirectly estimate the bacterial load present in the air. Preliminary results, obtained in a real testbed, demonstrate, from the qualitative point of view, the appropriateness of the proposed device.

KEYWORDS

IoT Sensor, Health Risk Assessment, Air Bacterial Load Estimation

1. INTRODUCTION

Indoor air quality plays a crucial role in human health, and accurate assessment of potential health risks is essential for maintaining a safe and healthy indoor environment. The World Health Organization (WHO) coined the term Sick Building Syndrome (SBS) to describe a set of symptoms including irritation of the eyes, nose, and throat, dry mucous membranes and skin, mental fatigue, frequent respiratory infections as well as nausea. Numerous epidemiological and experimental studies have been published in recent years regarding the correlation between these symptoms and various factors, such as building age, ventilation system type, room temperature, static electricity, particulate matter, and microbial contamination (Babaoglu, U. T. et al, 2022) (Sarkhosh, M et al, 2021).

In this study, we present a new Internet of Things (IoT) virtual sensor for indoor health risk assessment that leverages IoT technology to collect real-time environmental data, such as temperature, humidity, particulate matter, volatile organic compounds, and carbon dioxide levels whit the aim to indirectly estimate the bacterial load present in the air of indoor environments. In particular, the collected data is transmitted to a Cloud-server, where, by means of fusing data coming from different sensors, and using advanced data analysis techniques, it is possible to identify potential health hazards and promptly alert occupants of conditions that may pose risks to their well-being. Additionally, the virtual sensor provides insights into long-term trends and correlations between different environmental factors, enabling proactive measures for mitigating health risks (Ha, Q. P., et al, 2020).

Traditional IoT monitoring systems focus on measuring physical quantities to evaluate indoor air quality with respect to the admissible concentration limits provided by government laws (Dai, X et al, 2023), while we present a work in progress that introduces a novel approach to indoor health risk assessment by offering an indirect estimation of bacterial load. In particular, the main purpose of this work is to explore the relationship between physical measurements and bacterial contamination in the indoor environment to define an empirical model capable of inferring air quality from the microbiological point of view.

Preliminary results obtained from a real testbed deployed inside a public building suggest the validity of the proposed device which can represent a valid starting point to develop a virtual sensor for indirectly measuring air bacterial load.

2. THE VIRTUAL SENSOR

From the hardware point of view, the entire platform is built around the Espressif ESP32 which is a feature-rich System on Chip (SoC) with integrated Wi-Fi and Bluetooth connectivity for a wide-range of applications (Espressif, 2023). The ESP32 provides a dual-core MCU with 520 KB of ram and 4MB of persistent memory for firmware storage. The communication interface is built around 48 pins with multiple functions including Analog-to-Digital Converter (ADC), SPI interfaces, UART interfaces, I2C interfaces, and several general-purpose input/output pins (GPIOs), through which it can manage the physical sensors. In particular, we make use of a MH-Z19B NDIR infrared gas module to detect the CO_2 air concentration (Winsen, 2023), a SPS30 particulate matter sensor to measure the exhaled aerosols (Sensiron, 2023), and a SPG30 multi-gases sensor to assess the concentration of VOCs - Volatile Organic Compounds (Sensiron spg30, 2023). Finally, the platform is completed by a DHT11 which measures air temperature and humidity (Osepp, 2023).

Figure 1. A picture of the proposed virtual sensor mounted on a wall of a university classroom

Figure 1 shows a picture of a prototype of the proposed virtual sensor mounted in a classroom at Urbino University. All the electronic components have been assembled by means of a prototyping PCB board contained within a self-3D-printed enclosure. The platform shown in the picture is also provided with a 0.96″ RGB display to notify room occupants of the air quality status in real-time.

The sensor firmware has been developed on top of the Espressif IoT development framework base on the FreeRTOS operating system. The main goal of the proposed firmware is to build a reliable low-power platform granting a high level of interoperability ad reconfigurability to host several kinds of physical sensors. Moreover, the software stack should be light enough to maintain reduced response times and future expandability.

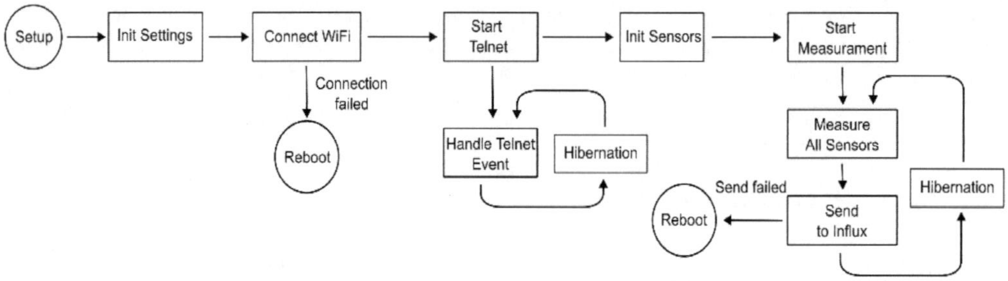

Figure 2. A diagram illustrating the firmware's main functionalities

Figure 2 reports a flow diagram of the main functionality of the developed firmware. In particular, the software is composed of two main tasks (represented by the two self-loop) each of which can run in parallel using one of the two available cores. The first task is defined by a Telnet service that is waiting for events and its main purpose is to allow a remote control and configuration of the sensor. The second task, on the other hand, is the proper monitoring task which periodically collects data from the sensors, elaborates, and remotely sends it to the cloud-end server.

In order to guarantee a high level of reliability, several watchdog points have been foreseen to trigger a software reset in the event of a failure in the remote connection, data collection, or data transmission to the cloud. To avoid continuous resets in case of persistent problems a conspicuous delay has been introduced in the reboot routine.

The software flow starts with a boot sequence which, after a basic initialization, tries to establish a remote connection. In case of failure, the system schedules a delayed reboot to retry a new fresh start in the future. On the contrary, if a valid connection has been created, the Telnet loop can be started together with the measurement task. Sampling parameters, sensor configurations, and elaboration criteria are stored on the internal storage memory and can be remotely configured by means of built-in Telnet commands.

Finally, the proposed platform implements low-power features by providing support to the hibernation during long waiting phases. For instance, if the system configuration expects to collect data every five minutes, the device can shut down most electronic circuits to save power.

As a cloud server, the proposed IoT system makes use of InfluxDB which is one of the most widespread time series databases (TSDBs) developed by the company InfluxData (InfluxData, 2023). Here the collected data can be easily stored, retrieved, and analyzed to infer the current air quality and attempt to predict future values. Moreover, it also allows for extracting meaningful statistics and other characteristics of the data.

3. EXPERIMENTAL RESULTS

Several prototypes of the proposed virtual sensor have been installed inside as many classrooms hosting the degree program in Informatics - Science and Technology at the University of Urbino in Italy. Figure 3 plots, as a representative example, the concentration levels (continuous line) of CO_2 (a) and VOCs (b) measured during a written exam taken by 14 students in a classroom of about 100 m^2 on 22 June 2023.

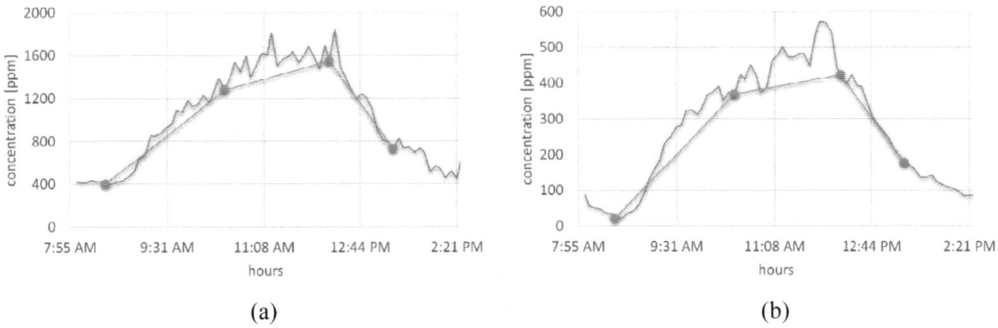

Figure 3. CO_2 (a) and VOCs (b) levels measured during a written exam on June 22, 2023. The orange line connects the points representing the time instants in which the bacterial load has been measured using a Surface Air System sampler (SAS)

Both CO_2 and VOCs concentrations showed a rapid increase upon student arrival (around 9.00 am) which continues, even if more slowly, until the end of the exam (about 12.00 am). Notice that the classroom has not a mechanical heating ventilation and air conditioning (HVAC) system, and only one window was slightly open during the exam, so the gas concentration tends to reach a constant value which roughly represents the balance between production and dispersion. On top of the concentration plots, a broken line is drawn which connects four points representing the time instants in which the bacterial load has been measured using traditional techniques. For the evaluation of aero-dispersed bacterial load, several air samples were collected with a Surface Air System (SAS) sampler before students entered (08:30 am), during the exam (10:30), at the end of the exam (12:00 am), and after an hour from the exit of the students (01:20 pm).

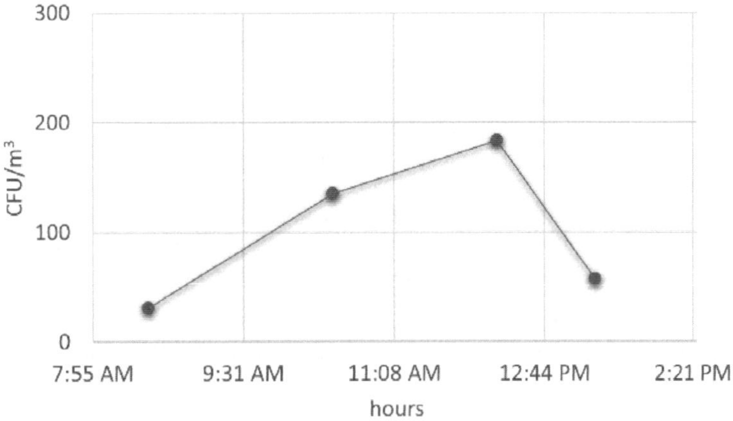

Figure 4. CFU levels measured during a written exam on June 22, 2023

For this purpose, Figure 4 plots the Colony Forming Units (CFU) per m^3 measured in the room during the exam. The concentration of bacterial load shows a shape that quite faithfully reflects those already shown as regards the concentration of CO_2 and VOCs suggesting that the proposed IoT sensor can be a valid starting point for future investigation to build and validate a virtual sensor that could, indirectly, estimate the indoor bacterial load.

4. CONCLUSION

It is becoming more and more important to supervise and control indoor environments, especially when they are overcrowded, due to the severe health effects caused by poor indoor air quality. In addition to regularly checking for the presence of microbes, it is crucial to utilize monitoring devices that can quickly gather relevant data about the air we breathe.

In this paper, we present an IoT virtual sensor for indoor health risk assessment which is the result of a work in progress. The main purpose is to explore the relationship between physical measurements and bacterial contamination in the indoor environment by applying modern IoT technologies. Preliminary results suggest that the proposed approach can be a valid starting point to develop a virtual sensor for indirectly measuring air bacterial load. This technology, when validated, can be employed in various indoor settings, including residential, commercial, and public buildings, to enhance occupant safety and well-being.

Future research will focus on validating the proposed virtual sensor against traditional bacterial load measurement techniques.

REFERENCES

Andualem, Z., Gizaw, Z., Bogale, L. et al, 2019. Indoor bacterial load and its correlation to physical indoor air quality parameters in public primary schools. *Multidiscip Respir Med* Vol. 14, No. 2, pp. 1-7.

Babaoglu, U. T., Milletli Sezgin, F., & Yag, F. 2020. Sick building symptoms among hospital workers associated with indoor air quality and personal factors. *Indoor and Built Environment*, Vol. 29, No. 5, pp. 645-655.

Dai, X., Shang, W., Liu, J., Xue, M., & Wang, C., 2023. Achieving better indoor air quality with IoT systems for future buildings: Opportunities and challenges. *Science of The Total Environment*, Vol. 895, pp. 1-14.

Espressif, 2023. Esp32-c3-wroom-02 datasheet, last accessed 2023-07-18. Available online: https://www.espressif.com/en/support/documents/technical-documents

Ha, Q. P., Metia, S., & Phung, M. D., 2020. Sensing data fusion for enhanced indoor air quality monitoring. *IEEE Sensors Journal*, Vol. 20, No. 8, pp. 4430-4441.

InflusData, 2023. Introducing InfluxDB 3.0, last accessed 2023-07-18. Available online: https://www.influxdata.com/products/influxdb-overview/

Megahed, N. A., Ghoneim, E. M., 2021. Indoor Air Quality: Rethinking rules of building design strategies in post-pandemic architecture. *Environmental research*, Vol. 193, pp. 1-9.

Osepp, 2023. DHT11 Humidity & Temperature Sensor, last accessed 2023-07-18. Available online: https://www.osepp.com/downloads/pdf/DHT11-Technical-Data-Sheet-Translated-Version.pdf

Sarkhosh, M., Najafpoor, A. A., Alidadi, H., Shamsara, J., Amiri, H., Andrea, T., & Kariminejad, F., 2021. Indoor Air Quality associations with sick building syndrome: An application of decision tree technology. *Building and Environment*, Vol. 188, No. 107446, pp. 1-16.

Sensiron sgp30, 2023. SGP30 - Multi-gas (VOC and CO_2eq) sensor, last accessed 2023-07-18. Available online: https://sensirion.com/products/catalog/SGP30/

Sensiron, 2023, PM2.5 Sensor for HVAC and air quality applications, last accessed 2023-07-18. Available online: https://sensirion.com/products/catalog/SPS30/

Winsen, 2023. Intelligent Infrared CO2 Module, last accessed 2023-07-18. Available online: https://www.winsen-sensor.com/d/files/infrared-gas-sensor/mh-z19b-co2-ver1_0.pdf

WHAT COULD POSSIBLY GO WRONG? *OR: HOW TO LIVE WITH AI?*

Alessandro Rigutto
Owner, Legal Issue Management B.V.
Oegstgeest, The Netherlands
https://www.limbv.com

ABSTRACT

The risks inherent in AI and its current pace of development and launch are increasingly acknowledged by industry leaders. These risks force us to reflect on AI's role in society, and what regulatory framework we need avoid undesired developments. This paper addresses (1) the crossroads we are at and (2) why we should act now, and (3) discusses regulatory efforts afoot or under consideration in China, the US and the EU. It concludes that particularly article 4a (1) of the (draft) EU AI law, which is based on a clear and coherent vision of AI's role in society and sets legally enforceable standards for AI developers and professional AI users, may turn out to be an effective, technology neutral tool to ensure these developers and users err on the side of caution in developing and deploying new AI tools.

KEYWORDS

Artificial Intelligence, Risks, Law, EU, US, China

1. INTRODUCTION

"*What you're doing has enormous potential and enormous danger*" (McCabe, 2023). This comment of US President Biden made in a brief meeting with tech CEO's echoes warnings prompted by the release, late 2022, of Open AI's Chat GPT and the competitive race to market that followed it. These events highlighted Big Tech's inabilities to fully understand its products and their inherent risks, and to resist the commercial pressure to release not fully matured products to market. They have prompted calls for government intervention.

In a recent hearing before a subcommittee of the US senate's judiciary committee, Open AI's CEO Sam Altman joined the choir of advocates for government regulation and oversight (Kang, 2023). Some see that call as self-serving, noting that government intervention now in ways that are consistent with Open AI's own safety practices will only help Open AI to consolidate its current market-lead (Heikkilä, 2023). That may well be so: but motive may not matter much, as even current AI-developments raise *broadly acknowledged risks* that may significantly impact individuals and society at large, and that AI-developers have nevertheless been willing to take.

Accordingly, our problem statement (PS) is threefold:

PS1 - what are the (acknowledged or perceived) *risks* of AI?
PS2 - what *legislative steps* are being proposed to check these risks?
PS3 - are these steps *adequate and robust*?

These points will be addressed below, focusing on legislative efforts underway in China, the US and the EU. The manuscript was closed end July 2023.

2. INDUSTRY WARNS, AND WHY THAT MATTERS

On 22 March 2023, the Future of Life Institute published an open letter (Future of Life institute, 2023) warning about the dangers of the race to the market triggered by the release of Chat GPT 4.0, and calling for a *voluntary*

6-month moratorium in order to agree joint protocols to ensure the safety of even more powerful AI going forward. Greeted with skepticism at first by those who disagreed with (different aspects of) the letter, its core message is now echoed by leading minds throughout the industry.

This call for help is not without precedent. Some thirty years ago, Shell published "*Climate of concern*" (Shell, 1991), an in retrospect eerily accurate documentary about global warming and the effects it might have on society thirty years hence. After analyzing the issue and its impact, Shell calls on politicians and society at large to rethink existing societal arrangements in an effort to counter the threat of global warming.

This well-reasoned warning and call for action went mostly unheeded. Perhaps we should listen now.

3. SO, WHAT COULD POSSIBLY GO WRONG?

In an interview with *The New York Times* published in May 2023 (Tavernise, et al., 2023), Geoffrey Hinton explains why recent developments have caused him to change his mind about the risks of AI. The core of Hinton's concerns lies in the ever-increasing speed at which, and the (unchecked and uncheckable) facility with which, linked neural networks learn by copying, and building on, learnings from other neural networks in the chain. He further notes that as their learning progresses, AI-systems will increasingly and unavoidably take independent decisions that will not readily be recognizable to, or controllable by, their human operators. Finally, Hinton sees a risk that AI-systems may come to learn the relevance of control to their efficient operation and may (inadvertently, or deliberately through the actions of bad actors) acquire the capability to act on that learning. This analysis then leads Hinton to call for *reflection and (self)regulation.*

So what, then, are the currently identified (perceived) risks of unchecked AI? Hinton identifies and discusses several of them, grouped by imminence:

1. **current**: bias, disinformation;
2. **mid-term**: mass-unemployment;
3. **long(er)-term**: "autonomous killer robots" and AI-dominance, understood as described above.

That list is fairly comprehensive, and reflects concerns expressed by a range of field-experts over time. Henry Kissinger, in a recent interview (The Economist, 2023), adds a further mid-term risk when he warns of the risk of AI-driven shifts in the world order without any settled principle on which countries can rely to maintain peace. Additional (mostly: current) risks identified so far center around privacy-related individual and societal concerns (e.g. fully automated decision-taking; social scoring; video surveillance; unwitting interaction with AI-systems; etc.) and, in relation to generative AI, on copyright infringement

Some of the more immediate risks identified above are fairly widely acknowledged: in the US Senate judiciary subcommittee meeting mentioned earlier, for example, Sam Altman stressed the need for urgent action to address the risk of election-manipulation through the use of AI.

Other identified risks are more controversial. This includes the risks of mass-unemployment and, specifically, of AI dominance. On this last topic, Meta's Joelle Pineau, for example, strongly disagrees with Hinton's warnings (Heikkilä, 2023):

"When you start looking at ways to have a rational discussion about risk, you usually look at the probability of an outcome and you multiply it by the cost of that outcome. [The existential-risk crowd] have essentially put an infinite cost on that outcome," (…) *"When you put an infinite cost, you can't have any rational discussions about any other outcomes. And that takes the oxygen out of the room for any other discussion, which I think is too bad."*

This statement evidences a *fundamental misunderstanding of the concerns* of Hinton and others who advocate caution. Current developments in high capability AI are so fast, and the drive to market is so strong, that even today, risks are no longer recognized or addressed upfront. To illustrate this point: Chat GPT learned coding, not as a programmed or taught skill, but as *emergent behavior* (Roose, 2023); Microsoft Bing's chatbot displayed disturbing behavior akin to a *split personality* when red teamed (Roose, 2023b); and Alphabet's chatbot BARD was found to *hallucinate* (Grant and Metz, 2023). Sure, these flaws have since been addressed, but when it comes to safety, "*no harm no foul*" is clearly the wrong attitude, as safety experts in mature high-risk industries like the oil and gas and medical industries will tell you.

In these circumstances, legislation is warranted to ensure that industry is reminded to err on the side of caution when releasing new products to market. Such legislation should on the one hand be flexible enough to cover future developments, but on the other hand be underpinned by a robust vision on AI's role in society so that it can still guide such future developments.

4. CURRENT LEGISLATIVE THOUGHTS AND INITIATIVES

Three leading economic blocks (China, the US and the EU) are all working on legislation that seeks to balance these competing objectives. What steps are they taking to check the risks identified above?

4.1 China

Unlike the US and the EU, who are working on encompassing AI-legislation, China has opted for an *incremental approach*, gradually building its regulatory framework in line with AI developments. Currently, the core building blocks of that framework are the 2021 regulation on recommendation algorithms (PRC regulation I), the 2022 rules for synthetically created content (PRC regulation II) and a draft regulation for generative AI launched in March 2023 that China aims to enact into law by the end of this year (PRC draft regulation III).

The drivers behind China's legislative initiatives differ fundamentally from those of the US and the EU as well. Where the US and EU seek to *protect democratic values,* China seeks to check the threat AI may pose to the Chinese state's *ability to control* public information, public discourse and ultimately, the state itself. Still, some of the solutions adopted in these Chinese regulations are not too different from those envisaged in the US and the EU. This holds true, for example, for the requirements (1) that synthetically generated or altered content is labeled as such; (2) that algorithms falling within the scope of these regulations are registered in a dedicated register; and (3) that such algorithms undergo a security self-assessment that must be reported to the relevant government-agency. Although interpretations and monitoring practices of these and similar safety provisions will differ between China, the US and the EU, these similarities could prove relevant to eventual efforts at international or global regulation, should it come to that (Sheehan, 2023; PRC regulations I and II and PRC draft regulation III).

4.2 The US

Whilst China's legislative initiatives aim to keep pace with current developments, US legislators are scrambling to catch up. At the US Senate subcommittee meeting mentioned earlier (*Oversight of A.I.: Rules for artificial intelligence | United States Senate Committee on the Judiciary*, 2023), solutions explored included the potential use of scorecards and prescribed labels showing a model's operation and inaccuracies; mandatory disclosures on training-data; mandatory labeling of AI generated content; disclosure of the fact that people are communicating with an AI-system; licensing requirements for (certain types of) AI; establishment of an independent government agency exercising oversight over AI developers; establishment of an international intergovernmental body to set standards for the tech industry; prohibitions on development or use of certain specific capabilities or functionalities in models; the need to establish rules to protect intellectual property; and, finally, whether the US should adopt European style privacy or AI legislation.

In his speech of 21 June 2023, US Senate majority leader Chuck Schumer set out his thoughts on a potential framework for AI (*Majority Leader Schumer Delivers Remarks To Launch SAFE Innovation Framework For Artificial Intelligence At CSIS | Senate Democratic Leadership*, 2023). This *"SAFE Innovation Framework for AI"* recognizes AI-innovation as a crucial driver of the US economy, but also acknowledges that in order to ensure public safety and trust, that innovation requires guardrails in the areas of Security, Accountability, protecting Foundational values of the US and Explainabilty (captured in the acronym SAFE). The speech outlines how Mr. Schumer intends to proceed in formulating and enacting legislation built on these principles, but the details of and timeline for enactment that legislation are as yet unclear.

4.3 The EU

In contrast, the EU is moving fast. On 14 June 2023, the European Parliament adopted a proposal for amendment (*Artificial Intelligence Act – Text adopted -Wednesday, 14 June 2023*, hereafter the "Act") of the European Committee's original proposal for an AI Act. The 771 amendments so approved significantly expand the scope of protection of the Act and align it with AI-developments since the European Committee released its original proposal in 2021. They also seek to make the Act (more) technology neutral, and stress the need for developers and professional users of AI-systems to ensure the inherent safety of their AI-systems.

Structurally, the Act remains a typical EU product-safety regulation, classifying AI-systems by risk category according to their scope:

1. AI-systems posing *unacceptable risks* (e.g., social scoring systems) will be banned, subject only to some limited exceptions;
2. AI-systems that fall into one or more of eight listed areas (e.g., biometric ID; critical infrastructure; law-enforcement and legal aid) and that pose a significant risk of harm to the health, safety or fundamental rights of people or to the environment are considered *high risk*. Such systems will have to be registered in an EU database and will have to undergo safety-assessments throughout their lifecycle.
3. Providers of *foundation models* as defined in the Act must assess and mitigate possible risks to health, safety, fundamental rights, the environment, democracy and rule of law and must register their models in the EU database before these can be released on the EU market. *Generative AI systems* must have inbuilt safeguards against generating illegal content, must disclose that their products are AI-generated, and will be subject to requirements on public disclosure of copyrighted data they have been trained on.
4. Finally, *limited risk* AI systems must comply with minimal transparency requirements that would allow users to make informed decisions about their (continued) use.

As part of its proposed amendments the European Parliament introduced *a new Article 4a (1)* that sets generic, substantive standards for all AI falling within the scope of the Act. Specifically, Article 4a (1) requires developers and professional users of such AI to use best efforts to ensure that they develop or use AI in accordance with principles of *'human agency and oversight*; *'technical robustness and safety'*; *'privacy and data governance'*; *'transparency'*; *'diversity, non-discrimination and fairness'*; and *'social and environmental well-being',* all as outlined in that provision.

5. CONCLUSION

AI fundamentally impacts individuals and societies globally, and AI development is moving fast, and will likely move faster in future. At the same time, recent events have shown that even the most sophisticated AI developers no longer fully grasp their own products, and that without government regulation, they may release immature products to market. China, the US and the EU have recognized this and are rightly working on regulating AI on the basis of a comprehensive view of AI's desired place in society. Given the similarities in the AI related risks they face, it is not surprising that in spite of significant (ideological) differences, the measures being considered by China, the US and the EU show substantial similarities.

Work on this paper has led me to change my views on the EU's Act. Initially skeptical, I now believe that the Act, and particularly Article 4a (1), will be a useful instrument to ensure AI developers and users err on the side of caution in development and use of AI. Compliance with Article 4a (1) may be costly, but no more so than getting it wrong – and it should be well achievable, as Sam Altman's draft written testimony before the US senate's subcommittee aptly illustrates (Altman, 2023).

The world faced a crossroads before when Shell called on it to consider climate-change and its response thereto. *We missed a turn then; perhaps we'll find our way now.*

ACKNOWLEDGEMENT

The author would like to thank Professor emeritus Dr. H. Jaap van den Herik for his review of, and constructive feedback on, an earlier, more extensive version of this paper.

REFERENCES

Altman, S. (2023). "Written Testimony of Sam Altman Chief Executive Officer OpenAI Before the U.S. Senate Committee on the Judiciary Subcommittee on Privacy, Technology, & the Law". Available at: https://www.judiciary.senate.gov/imo/media/doc/2023-05-16%20-%20Bio%20&%20Testimony%20-%20Altman.pdf

Artificial Intelligence Act – Text adopted -Wednesday, 14 June 2023. Available at: https://www.europarl.europa.eu/doceo/document/TA-9-2023-0236_EN.html

Future of Life Institute (2023). Pause Giant AI Experiments: An Open Letter - Future of Life Institute. Available at: https://futureoflife.org/open-letter/pause-giant-ai-experiments/

Grant, N. and Metz, C. (2023). "Google releases Bard, its AI chatbot, a rival to ChatGPT and Bing," The New York Times, 21 March. Available at: https://www.nytimes.com/2023/03/21/technology/google-bard-chatbot.html.

Heikkilä, M. (2023). "Meta's AI leaders want you to know fears over AI existential risk are 'ridiculous,'" MIT Technology Review, 20 June. Available at: https://www.technologyreview.com/2023/06/20/1075075/metas-ai-leaders-want-you-to-know-fears-over-ai-existential-risk-are-ridiculous/

Kang, C. (2023). "Sam Altman, ChatGPT creator and OpenAI CEO, urges Senate for AI regulation," The New York Times, 16 May. Available at: https://www.nytimes.com/2023/05/16/technology/openai-altman-artificial-intelligence-regulation.html.

Majority Leader Schumer Delivers Remarks To Launch SAFE Innovation Framework For Artificial Intelligence At CSIS | Senate Democratic Leadership (2023). Available at: https://www.democrats.senate.gov/news/press-releases/majority-leader-schumer-delivers-remarks-to-launch-safe-innovation-framework-for-artificial-intelligence-at-csis.

McCabe, D. (2023). "White House unveils initiatives to reduce risks of AI," The New York Times, 4 May. Available at: https://www.nytimes.com/2023/05/04/technology/us-ai-research-regulation.html.

Oversight of A.I.: Rules for artificial intelligence | United States Senate Committee on the Judiciary (2023). Available at: https://www.judiciary.senate.gov/committee-activity/hearings/oversight-of-ai-rules-for-artificial-intelligence.

PRC draft regulation III, "Measures for the Management of Generative Artificial Intelligence Services" of April 2023. English translation available at https://digichina.stanford.edu/work/translation-measures-for-the-management-of-generative-artificial-intelligence-services-draft-for-comment-april-2023/.

PRC regulation I, "Provisions on the Management of Algorithmic Recommendations in Internet Information Services" of 1 March 2022. English translation available at https://www.chinalawtranslate.com/en/algorithms/; https://www.chinalawtranslate.com/en/deep-synthesis/.

PRC regulation II, "Provisions on the Administration of Deep Synthesis Internet Information Services" of 10 January 2023. English translation available at https://www.chinalawtranslate.com/en/deep-synthesis/.

Roose, K. (2023). "How to Use Chatbots, like ChatGPT, in Your Daily Life and Work," The New York Times, 8 April. Available at: https://www.nytimes.com/2023/03/30/technology/ai-chatbot-chatgpt-uses-work-life.html.

Roose, K. (2023b). "Why A conversation with Bing's chatbot left me deeply unsettled," The New York Times, 17 February. Available at: https://www.nytimes.com/2023/02/16/technology/bing-chatbot-microsoft-chatgpt.html.

Sheehan, M. (2023). "China's AI regulations and how they get made," Carnegie Endowment for International Peace [Preprint]. Available at: https://carnegieendowment.org/2023/07/10/china-s-ai-regulations-and-how-they-get-made-pub-90117.

Shell (1991). "Climate of concern". Available at: https://www.youtube.com/watch?v=vTlYYlRN0LY.

Tavernise, S. et al. (2023). "The Godfather of A.I. has some regrets," The New York Times, 1 June. Available at: https://www.nytimes.com/2023/05/30/podcasts/the-daily/chatgpt-hinton-ai.html.

The Economist (2023). "Henry Kissinger explains how to avoid world war three," The Economist, 29 June.

A NO-CODE WEB APP FOR SUPPORTING DECISION MODELLING OF CLUSTERING PROBLEMS

Helder Gomes Costa[1] and Leonardo Fernandes Costa[2]
[1]Universidade federal Fluminense
Rua Passos da Pátria, 156, São Domingos, Niterói, Rio de Janeiro, Brasil
[2]Instituto Federal Fluminense
Rua Dr. Siqueira, 273, Parque Dom Bosco, Campos dos Goytacazes, Rio de Janeiro, Brasil

ABSTRACT

There are various attempts to encourage coding in the field of machine learning, which significantly boost expertise in this area. On the other hand, there is an opportunity to create apps to enhance learning and decision-making for professionals who do not have programming experience. In this paper, we describe a no-code clustering web tool that seeks to address this void. It now implements k-means unsupervised clustering. Our app was created to be a user-friendly interface for supporting decision-makers do deal with cluster modeling, even those without programming skills.

KEYWORDS

Clustering, No-Code, Decision Making, Python, K-Means

1. INTRODUCTION

Data analysis has experienced an explosion in recent years, due to the introduction of a wide range of electronic devices, algorithms, methods, datasets, and programs. Th highlight this, we mention: sources that provide datasets (as UCI Machine Learning Repository, Mendeley Data, and Kaggle), open packages to enable data analysis (pandas, numpy, sci-kit learn, Matplotlib, GGplot2, Altair, Bokeh, and Vega, among others), the git protocol that made versioning control easier and allowed collaborative code building. Also, there are worthily initiatives that help to popularize web coding for data analysis, such as Django, Flask, Streamlit, and Shiny communities. In the same vein of assisting "devs" in developing code for data analysis and machine learning, there are IDEs (such as Visual Studio and R Studio), environments for building notebooks (such as Jupyter and Google Collab), and even the Anaconda Navigator, which facilitates the creation and management of virtual machines to support code development, including those for data analysis and machine learning. We also highlight the W3-schools effort in the e-learning stream, which provides access to tutorials on many programming languages, including Python and R

As one can see, there is powerful support for those experts devoted to developing and deploying machine learning-based apps and scripts. On the other hand, this powerful world should be supplemented by tools aimed for persons who are unfamiliar with coding but are interested in employing machining learning approaches to do consistent data analysis and gain fresh and dazzling insights from data analysis.

In other words, there are professionals from various fields such as medicine, economics, management, nursing, biology, architecture, law, and marketing who are not familiar with coding processes and methods but have extensive knowledge in their field and can use machining learning tools to perform consistent data analysis and gain new and shiny insights.

In this study, we describe a web tool to assist this type of professional with data analysis. We hope that our contribution will be useful in bringing folks from non-coding domains to the realm of data analysis. At this time the web was constuucted by using Python 3 language (Van Rossum & Drake, F.L. (2009)), and the packages Mathplotlib (Harris et al (2020), Pandas (Mckinney (2010)) , Numpy (Hunter(2007)), Scikitlearn package (Pedregosa et al (2019)) and Streamlit (Streamlit Team (2023)).

2. THE PROPOSAL

This section outlines the structure of a web app that we propose as a framework to allow modeling data. Instead of using an UML representation, we choose to show though the flow chart in Figure 1 to make it more legible for those who have not coding skills. It is followed by a description of the app's core features.

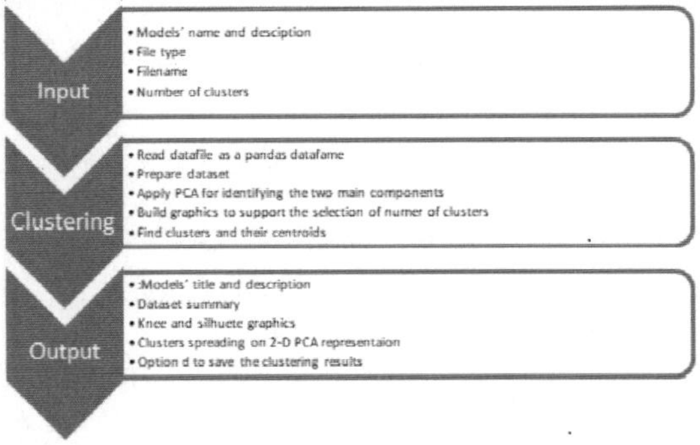

Figure 1. Flow chart illustrating the input, clustering, and output flows

2.1 Input Screen

All model parameters have to be entered on the left side of the framework's interface. These criteria are:

a) Model title. The title or name by which the user refers to its own model
b) Model description. A concise description of the model's characteristics, including the objective of the modeling, constraints, limitations, and other important characteristics
c) The data set's format. In the current version, one should can select either CSV XLSX files
d) Datafile. A file containing the data set.
e) Clustering parameters. The user can select the number of clusters and the clustering algorithm to employ.

2.2 Clustering

The backend of the app Visual Clustering is comprised of the following steps:

a) To read the data set contained in the data file as the Pandas data frame proposed by Mckinney (2010)
   - To prepare the dataset by: eliminating from the data frame any column containing all blank cells; eliminating from the data frame any rows with at least one vacant cell; and, transforming the data frame into a numpy (Harris et al., 2020) matrix X
b) To construct graphics for supporting the choice of the number of clusters (k):
   - Silhouette graphic. A two-dimensional array that stores the Silhouette Coefficient Avg (Rousseeuw, 1987) metric as a function of the number of clusters. Using the kmeans++ library, the Scikitlearn package (Pedregosa et al., 2019) supported the computation of this coefficient.
   - Elbow or Knee graphic. A two-dimensional array that stores the SSE metric as a function of the number of clusters. This matrix's calculation was supported by the Scikitlearn program utilizing the kmeans++ library.
c) To run the Principal Component Analysis (PCA) to identify the two principal components of the dataset, producing a two-dimensional array containing projections of the instances on the first and second principal components of the dataset. In this step, the PCA library of the Scikitlearn package was.
d) To identify clusters and their centers by applying the kmeans++ library, from the Scikitlearn to the dataset.

2.3 Output

The output screen displays:

a) Models' title and description

b) Dataset summary
c) The knee and silhouette graphics
d) Each observation and its assigned cluster
e) The centroids of the clusters
f) The projection of each observation on the APC axis
g) A button that enables the user to save the subsequent results

3. APP USAGE

The purpose of this section is to demonstrate some features of input and output interfaces appear to the user and how the user can interact with the application as a whole.

3.1 Visual K-Means as a No-Code Webpage

Figure 2 depicts the visual appearance of the initial screen of the app, operates as a webpage dashboard, organized into two sections:

- The Input screen: on the left side of the screen, one can input dataset and all model's parameters.
- The Output or Main screen: at the right side of the screen, it is shown the results of the modeling.

As the app is loaded, a sample model launches to provide the user an overview of the app features. Deails about the sample dataset, are described in Duarte and Costa (1920) and Costa and Duarte (2020.

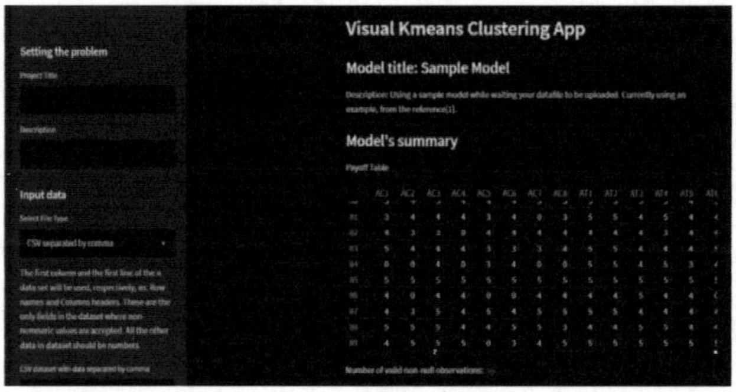

Figure 2. Initial screen

3.2 Input and Output Screens

3.2.1 Inputting Model's Metadata

As shown in Figure 3, the user can define its own model's "Title" and "Description". Just after updating these (Title and Description), the application updates the output screen.

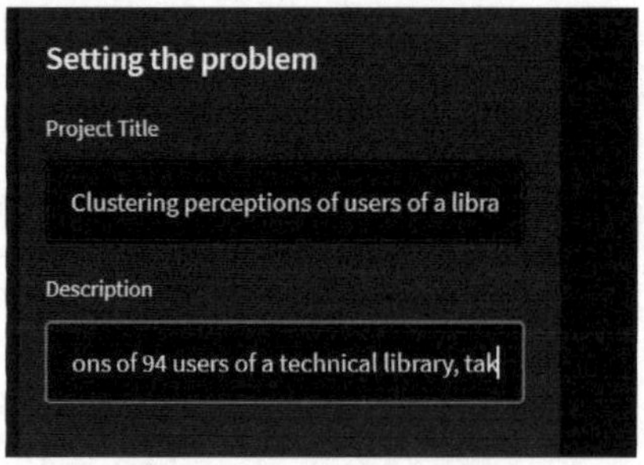

Figure 3. Entering the title and description for a model+

3.2.2 Supporting the Choice of the Number of Clusters

Figure 4 displays a screen that shows a graphic building according SSE and silhouette metrics, which assist the decision maker in selecting an appropriate number of clusters to use in the modeling.

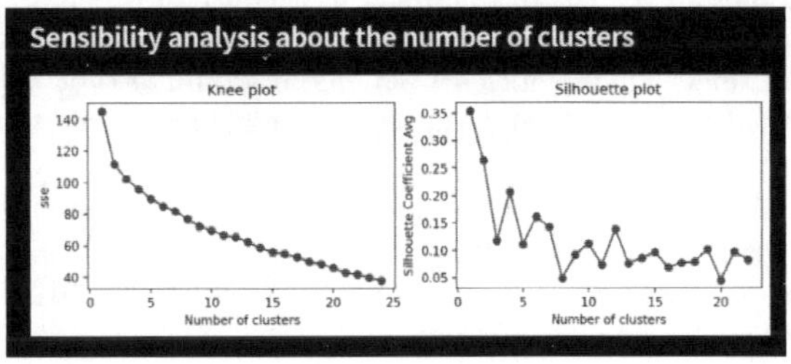

Figure 4. Graphics to support the selection of the number of clusters

3.2.3 A Two-Dimensional View of the Clusters' Distribution

Figure 5 illustrates the clusters spreading by using the two main components or factors of the dataset as the graphic's axes. In this picture, the user can enlarge the image by hovering the mouse over the double expansion arrow symbols that appear on the screen at the upright corner of the dataset view, and the user can save the image of the graphics by hovering the mouse over the left bottom of the mouse.

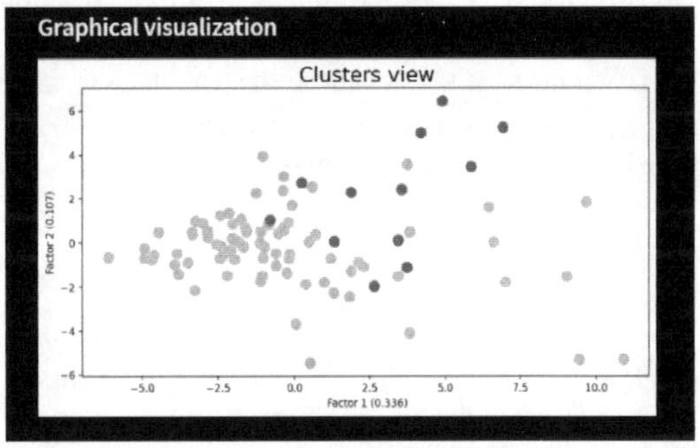

Figure 5. Spreading of the clusters

3.2.4 Viewing the Clusters Assignments and Centroids

Figure 6 displays the cluster to which each instance it is assigned, as well as the locations of the centroids for each variable.

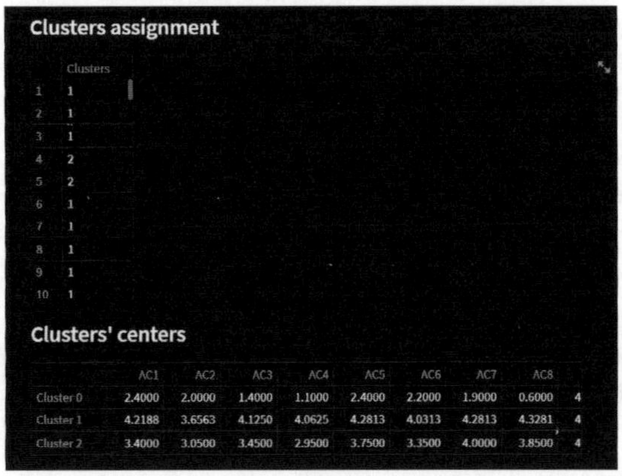

Clusters assignment

	Clusters
1	1
2	1
3	1
4	2
5	2
6	1
7	1
8	1
9	1
10	1

Clusters' centers

	AC1	AC2	AC3	AC4	AC5	AC6	AC7	AC8	
Cluster 0	2.4000	2.0000	1.4000	1.1000	2.4000	2.2000	1.9000	0.6000	4
Cluster 1	4.2188	3.6563	4.1250	4.0625	4.2813	4.0313	4.2813	4.3281	4
Cluster 2	3.4000	3.0500	3.4500	2.9500	3.7500	3.3500	4.0000	3.8500	4

Figure 6. Linking instances to the clusters and clusters' centers

4. CONCLUSION

The primary objective was to develop a user-friendly, no-code web application to aid non-programmers in making clustering-based decisions. We conclude that this objective was met because the approach designed for non-programmers was able to centralize interactions on a single screen and divide this screen into two frameworks: one for user inputs and one for user outputs. It should also be emphasized that the use of visual objects and classes provided by Streamlit and Matplotlib made the user interface friendlier.

As the main limitations of the current version of this app, we mention that it does not support:

- the integration of clustering with assignment of weights (or constant of scales, as mentioned in Keeney and Raiffa (1993) to the model variables,
- the ranking of clusters, as it was proposed in Souza and Costa (2021i) that ranked k-means clusters through a multicriteria, and,
- the implementation of supervised learning models.

As future works, we plan to address the aforementioned limitations by adding additional clustering features, such as the option to use supervised learning, the use of weights, and the ability to rank clusters based on multiple criteria.

ACKNOWLEDGEMENT

This research was supported in part by: Conselho Nacional de Desenvolvimento Científico e Tecnológico (CNPq, Brazil) – Grant ´ Number: 421779/2021-7; Conselho Nacional de Desenvolvimento Científico e Tecnologico ´ (CNPq, Brazil) – Grant Number: 314953/2021-3; Coordenação de Aperfeiçoamento de Pessoal de Ensino Superior (CAPES, Brazil) – Grant Number: 001; and Fundação Carlos Chagas Filho de Amparo a Pesquisa no Estado do Rio de janeiro (FAPERJ, Brazil) – Grant number: ` E-26.200.974/2022.

REFERENCES

Costa, H., Duarte, M.B.T., 2019. Applying ELECTRE TRI ME for Evaluating the Quality of Services Provided by a Library. *Proceedings of the 2019 11th International Conference on Education Technology and Computers*, Association for Computing Machinery (ACM). Amsterdam Netherlands, pp 278–281. https://doi.org/10.1145/3369255.3369313

Bodorik P. et al, 1991. Deciding to Correct Distributed Query Processing. *In IEEE Transactions on Data and Knowledge Engineering*, Vol. 4, No. 3, pp 253-265.

Duarte, M.B.T., Costa, H.G., 2017. A model for mapping users per-ceptions about the services supplied by a specialized library. In *Perspectivas em Ciencia da Informacao* , Vol. 22, No. 2, pp 232–243. https://doi.org/10.1590/1981-5344/2463

Harris, C.R. et al., 2020. Matplotlib: A 2D graphics environment. *In Nature*, Vol. 585, pp 357-362. https://doi.org/10.1038/s41586-020-2649-2

Hunter, J.D., 2007. Array programming with NumPy. *In Computing in Science and Engineering*, Vol. 9, No. 3, pp. 90-95. https://doi.org/10.1109/MCSE.2007.55

Keeney, R. and Raiffa, H. 1993. *In Decisions with multiple objectives: preferences and value tradeoffs.* Cambridge University Press, London, UK.

Mckinney, W., 2010. Data Structures for Statistical Computing in Python. *Proceedings of the 9th Python in Science Conference.* Austin, Texas, USA, Vol. 445, pp 56-61. http://doi.org/10.25080/Majora-92bf1922-00a

Pedregosa, A. et al., 2011. Scikit- learn: Machine Learning in Python. *In Journal of Machine Learning Research*, Vol. 12, No. 85, pp 2825–2830.

Rousseeuw, P.J., 1987. Silhouettes: A graphical aid to the interpretation and validation of cluster analysis. *In Journal of Computational and Applied Mathematics*, Vol. 20, pp 53–65. https://doi.org/10.1016/0377-0427(87) 90125-7

Souza, R.L.S. de, Costa, H.G. (2021). K-Means and Multicriteria Decision Aid Applied to Sustainability Evaluation. P*roceedings of the Intelligent Systems Design and* Applications. World Wide Web, pp 1198–1208. https://doi.org/10.1007/978-3-030-71187-0_111.

Streamlit Team. 2023. *Streamlit documentation*. 2023. https://docs.streamlit.io. Accessed in: July, 24th 2023.

Van Rossum, G. and Drake, F.L. 2009. *Python 3 Reference Manual.* CreateSpace, Scotts Valley, CA, USA.

HUMAN IN FOCUS: EVALUATION WITH ELECTRO GRAPHIC METHODS AND ARTIFICIAL INTELLIGENCE

Melanie Steiner and Dieter Meiller
Ostbayerische Technische Hochschule (OTH) Amberg-Weiden
Kaiser-Wilhelm-Ring 23
92224, Amberg, Germany

ABSTRACT

Perception, emotions and human reactions during the use of interactive applications are important factors for the evaluation of the user experience. The optimal evaluation of applications with augmented, mixed, virtual reality concept, or those with persuasive design usually consists of a standard user experience method mix. In addition to the classic usability test, survey or observation, psychophysical methods can also be used. This paper gives hints to help choosing the optimal measurement method mix for evaluation in giving a short description on 5 electro graphic methods. It compares the electro graphic methods electrooculography (EOG) and electroencephalography (EEG) and shows pros, cons, technical details and knowledge to perform the procedures. Both methods are combinable and can give a more detailed view in human reactions. The idea behind the study was to analyze and interpret typical user reactions. One insight learned during the development of the research design was the missing literature with specific EEG atlas for user experience context. Therefore, we show result cases out of the study and discuss the idea to simplify analysis and interpretation of data with a specified user EEG atlas and an image based artificial intelligence algorithm we will work on in future.

KEYWORDS

User Experience, Human Centered-Computing, Evaluation, Electro Graphic Method, Artificial Intelligence

1. INTRODUCTION

For ethical reasons, user experience (UX) evaluation methods should be designed to be as accessible as possible and to involve minimal effort for participating users. In terms of study design efficiency, effort and applicability must be kept in mind. As well the quality of the measurement results. With just about 5 users we can find out 80 percent of main problems (Nielson, 2000).

The nature of human being is complex and so is the complexity of measurement methods too. For several years bio-signal measurement is being made usable for a lot. This seems to be due to the simplification of the technologies, the process practicability, optimized interaction, and result visualization of the systems. Such bio-signal measurement methods and technologies have been used so far primarily in medicine, psychology or neuromarketing (Blume et al. 2013, Braeutigam 2005, Zavaglia et al. 2006).

In the meantime, access to relevant measurement technologies has become massively easier. Devices are available via online-shop, as single- or multi-systems. They can measure multiple types of body reactions simultaneously. The quality of the measurement results is usually suitable enough for the user experience context. Human reactions can be measured by a lot of different procedures (Steiner 2023). Systems developed specifically for the user experience context can be purchased to measure body reactions before, during, and after a usage. Researchers and user experience professionals may be interested in this following 5 electrographic measurement methods. The following methods are of fundamental interest to bio-signal measurement and can be combined:

- Electrocardiography (ECG) – measures the electrical activity of the heart
- Electrodermal Activity (EDA) – measures the electrical skin activity
- Electroencephalography (EEG) – measures the electrical activity of the brain
- Electromyography (EMG) – measures the electrical muscles activity
- Electrooculography (EOG) – measures the electrical activity of the retina

Electrographic methods capture minimal body signals. There are also quantitative approaches such as quantitative EEG (QEEG). It serves as a basis for tomographic photo mapping in 2D and 3D representations (Teplan, 2002).

Several of the mentioned electrographic methods can be used to analyze the primary visual modality. Eye tracking methods have already established themselves in the context of user experience evaluation. When using mobile eye trackers, the cornea reflex method is usually used. Another eye tracking method that is used less frequently in user experience evaluation is the electrooculography, called EOG. EOG serves as a comparative method to EEG.

2. THE MEASUREMENT OF ELECTRICAL ACTIVITY

Electrical activity is always present in the human body. Cells communicate with each other with the help of electrical impulses. Electrograph procedures, such as ECG, EDA, EEG, EMG, EOG, are image processing techniques. They are capable to visualize the electrical impulses and their differences. This facilitates the analysis, is the basis for the interpretation and makes it also interesting for the user experience context.

Willem Einthofen (1902) developed the bipolar conduction at the heart: the electrocardiography (ECG). This basis method measures voltage differences between two measurement points of arms. A reference electrode reduces external interferences. It provides information about the heart beat (Hoth, 2021). If tension arise in cells. we call it action potentials. This action potentials can be measured on the skin.

3. BRIEF OVERVIEW OF THE METHODS EEG AND EOG

The basics of bipolar derivation have been transferred to other methods such as EEG and EOG. Body surface potentials can also reveal brain activity in EEG or retinal activity in EOG. Both methods therefore are suitable to measure the activity of the visual sense during use of interactive products.

Electrical activity is measured in millivolts (mV) for EOG method and microvolts (μV) for EEG method. The methods use a period observation. They can also be used over several hours during a user experience evaluation. Milliseconds are considered to obtain qualitative results and to detect the smallest patterns.

Until a few years ago, both methods be used in the clinical setting with heavy, large and expensive hardware. Systems designed for user experience evaluation are now easy to obtain. Modern EEG and EOG technologies can be used in complex, non-mobile and mobile context. Static positioning of users is no longer necessary.

The technical setup for EEG and the EOG procedure contains almost the same technical components. Specific electrodes and sensors are needed for qualitative results. An amplifier with additional filters, an analog-digital converter, and a device for recording the measurements are required. The derivation is accomplished with the help of electrodes. They must be fixed at specific points on the head. The procedure can be used invasive (with needle electrodes) or non-invasive.

A revised list based on the summary by Teplan (2002) shows which electrodes are able to be used:

- Self-adhesive and non-adhesive disposable gel electrodes
- Disposable disc electrodes and reusable disc electrodes
- Saline based electrodes
- Needle electrodes (invasive)

A simplification is offered by ready-made solutions with special wearables. A wearable in the form of EOG glasses has already been developed for EOG method (Bulling et al. 2008). EEG wearables, for example, are available as head mounted variants. They work with integrated electrodes and can be used as electrode cap, headset, or headband. With three electrodes for three measurement points, all requirements are fulfilled for bipolar recording. Two of the electrodes derive the action potentials, while the reference electrode minimizes artifacts caused by external interferences. For the calculation of the results, the same transformation formula can be used (EEG 2023, EOG 2023):

$$EEG(V),\ EOG(V) = \frac{\left(\frac{ADC}{2^n} - \frac{1}{2}\right) \cdot VCC}{G} \quad (1)$$

The formula (1) contains values of the analog digital converter (ADC), the resolution (n) in Bit, the signal amplification of the sensor (G) and the operative voltage (VCC). The analysis of the results these must be considered with different scales in voltage. Details can be found in the following chapters of the article (see formula 2, 3).

4. SPECIFIC ASPECTS OF THE ELECTROENCEPHALOGRAPHY

In EEG, the use of 10-20 measurement points is standardized. As early as 1958, the International Federation for Electroencephalography and Clinical Neurophysiology adopted the standard for placement of electrodes according to the 10-20 system (Jasper 1958). Electrode placement is based on brain regions: frontal (F), central (C), temporal (T), posterior (P), and occipital (O). However, an EEG can also be minimized to three electrodes, taking into account the limitations in quality and the results. The derivation of brain activity is shown in wave patterns. It is given by extending the transformation formula (1) in microvolt (EEG 2023):

$$EEG(\mu V) = EEG(V).1 \times 10^6 \quad (2)$$

A measurement takes place from wave peak to wave peak. The power spectrum has a continuous character and is measured in heart (Hz). It ranges from 0 Hz to half of the sampling frequency for brain waves. The results are assigned to the following five frequency rhythms: alpha (7- 13 Hz), beta (13 - 30 Hz), delta (0.5 - 4 Hz), gamma (> 30 Hz) and theta (4 - 7 Hz).

It requires an amplitude of +/- 0.5 - 30 Hz to detect all frequency bands, rhythms. Specific human states are attributed to these frequency bands when analyzed. The alpha rhythm is particularly visible in the occipital region, at the back of the head. The beta rhythm corresponds to the relaxed, active, normal state. It can be measured well in the frontal cortex (Halgren et al. 2019). Hans Berger was already able to demonstrate this with the so-called "Berger effect". This means that relaxed subjects change from the α-rhythm to the β-rhythm when opening their eyes (Berger 1929). The α-waves are blocked to a certain extent (Stöhr 2002). From the perspective of neurofeedback therapy, brain waves are specifically changed from β-waves to α-waves to reach human calmness and balance (Schmid 2016).

5. SPECIFIC ASPECTS OF THE ELECTROOCULOGRAPHY

Electrooculography can record eye movements as well as the resting potential of the eyes and its changes. It shows how we use our eyes. The electrical dipole between the retina and the cornea is measured at least two action potentials and its difference is calculated (Heide et al. 2005).

This measurement of the voltage difference leads back to Schott's discovery in 1922 (Schott 1922). It was introduced in clinical diagnostics and is still used there today as a non-invasive standard method for measuring the oculomotor system. If an AC amplifier is used for the EOG, the method also appears in the literature of clinical diagnostics as electronystagmography (ENG) method (Heide et al. 2005).

An EOG allows the measurement of non-willingly as well as willingly eye movements. Measurements with closed eyes and slight rotation of the head are also possible. By placing the electrodes on the right and left side at the eyes, movements can be recorded horizontal. Vertical eye movements can be recorded by placing the electrodes above and below the eye. The field of vision is not restricted when measuring with single electrodes. The cornea is positively charged while the retina has a negative charge (Heide et al. 2005).

A bandwidth of 0.8 - 49 Hz is necessary to detect retinal activity. The signal amplification of the sensor with 2040 turns out to be much lower than with EEG with 40000. It is expressed in millivolts by extending the transformation formula (1) (EOG 2023):

$$EOG(\mathrm{m}V) = EOG(V) * 1{,}000 \quad (3)$$

If the eye position does not change, the EOG visualization get nearly linear. If the gaze moves vertically from bottom to top, a positive wave is generated. By moving from top to downwards a negative wave gets reflected. If the electrodes are placed horizontally, the waves are more differentiated. The negative pole is placed on the right and the positive pole on the left, a gaze movement from right to left results in a positive peak and vice versa. The EOG behaves in exactly the opposite way if the electrodes are swapped.

6. RESULTS OF EOG AND EEG MEASURMENT STUDY

In order to demonstrate the applicability of the two methods presented, a practical test was conducted with classic usability cases for evaluation. In the first case, a user was asked to fix a certain point on the mobile phone and then to press a button above the fixation point in response to a given audio signal. To create first a resting situation before starting, the fixation time was 30 seconds.

For the EOG method, the arrangement of self-adhesive gel electrodes above and below the right eye was chosen. The electrodes were placed on points F1 and F2 frontally on the forehead. The measurement was performed at 1000 Hz, with 16 Bit as a single channel measurement with a bio-signal multisystem.

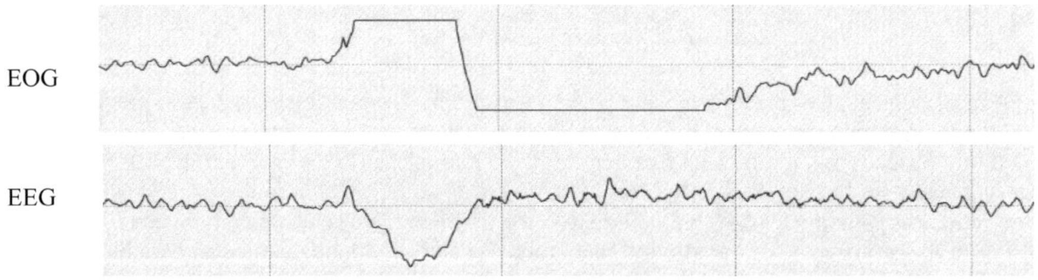

Figure 1. Berger-effect and eye movement in a usability use case on a mobile phone

Figure 1 shows in the upper image the spontaneous gaze movement upwards and back again. The bottom image shows a change from the α- to the β-rhythm with negative deflection of the amplitude (y-axis). The time span is exactly one second (x-axis). During the debrief in the interview, the participant explained that he had first been calm then started an active search, pressed the button, waiting then calmly for further instructions.

A second example from the study shows a typical user behavior: Reading a short product description while visiting the website. The three-line text was read by the user from left to right and line changes were registered using both EOG and EEG (see figure 3). A font size of 11 pt area with single line spacing was displayed on a 17.3 inch notebook monitor in daylight. The displayed time slot ranged from 13 seconds to 23 seconds at 3.2 second intervals. Amplitude was measured for EEG in microvolts with a range of +/- 35 μV. For EOG a range of +/- 70 mV was set. The average reading time was 5.8 seconds for the presented sequence of 239 characters with 36 words. Basically, the waveform of the beta band appears on the participant when his eyes are open and he concentrates on the content of the text. During reading, the measurement points F1 and F2 (frontal cortex) appear inconspicuous. The respective saccade into the next reading line is clearly visible in figure 2. The differentiation of a change of gaze into a new reading section could also be registered. Activation of the frontal region begins and ends simultaneously with the pupillary movement from right to left recorded in the EOG. Here, an early normalization can be seen in the EEG. In the medical context, the results of figure 3 would be declared as artifacts and excluded from the data. For the context of UX evaluation the results provide indications for further statements.

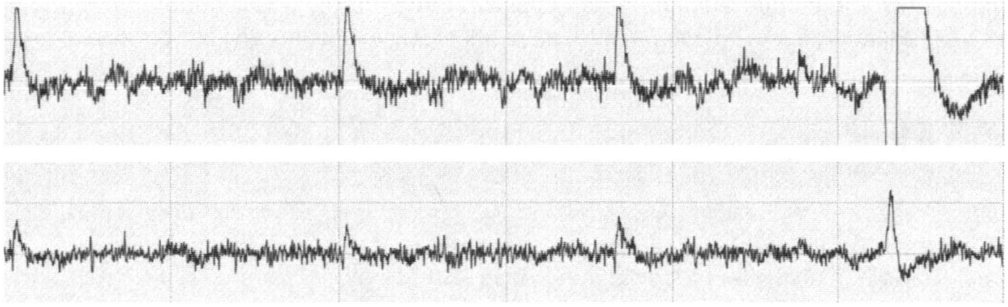

Figure 2. Reading-effects of product descriptions while reading on a website

7. CONCLUSION

If the two methods, EEG and EOG, are used in the context of user experience evaluation, it becomes apparent that the required effort for preparation and implementation remains manageable. This leads to positive effects for the study management, user experience professionals as well as for the participating users in time, costs and participation barriers.

Electroencephalography and electrooculography are methods which can show complex interrelationships of human machine interaction simplified and with a strong focus on the human being. Due to the simple acquisition with multi-systems, complex cases of a usage can also be evaluated. This concerns the periods before, during, and also after a use and a usage over more hours.

The quality of the results is usually sufficient even with simple systems and for supplementary aspects in the user experience evaluation. Usability scenarios with closed eyes or a usage context with reading and much more cases can be captured with both methods. Systems with a specific orientation for the evaluation of the UX are available in the retail. The two methods are particularly practical in their application for an evaluation of visual modality.

However, EEG in particular is also suitable for drawing conclusions about additional sensory responses.

The placement of electrodes requires basic physical knowledge of the human body. An analysis results requires higher effort in terms of time, good evaluation tools and at least minor basic medical knowledge.

The methods are similar in many aspects and are therefore suitable as comparison methods to verify results and identify artifacts, but the information to interpret the results must be gathered from many reference sources to work in the context of the user experience. In summary both methods can be recommended as complementary methods in the context of user experience evaluation.

8. OUTLOOK

For medical diagnostics, there exist catalogs of specific EEG images to interpret the results (Blume et al. 2013, Gibs 1941). They list images of characteristic EEG signals for various diagnoses. For example, images of the signals in epilepsy. Here, physicians can compare the pictures of the signals of patients with those listed in the catalog and make a corresponding diagnosis. The actual step in progress is the creation of an EEG atlas for specific evaluation context for UX design. This would allow to catalog specific patterns for certain user behavior and emotions. If enough labeled data, i.e., patterns with the corresponding classes of user behavior or emotions, were available, the evaluation could be automated using machine learning methods. With the data, a neural network could be trained for classification. This could then be used to evaluate the bio-signals in real time. This would not only make it possible to analyze user behavior in real time, but also to create new types of user interfaces that respond to the thoughts and emotions of users. To make the process of training and using the neural networks efficient, a suitable processing method should be chosen. The plotted graphs could be evaluated using image recognition methods. Veiga et al. (2017) have already successfully applied this to assign sensor data to specific fitness exercises. In this way, the large amount of data generated by the measurements could be efficiently projected onto an image and classified using a Convolutional Neural Network. Another next consequential step will be to measure more appropriate amounts and collect data.

REFERENCES

Beck K., Ralph J. (1994). Patterns Generates Architectures. *Proceedings of European Conference of Object-Oriented Programming*. Bologna, Italy, pp. 139-149.

Berger H. (1929). Uber das Elektrenkephalogramm des Menschen. *Psychiatrie und Nervenkrankheiten*. vol. 87, pp. 527–570.

Blume W. T., Holloway G. M., Kaibara M., Young G. B. (2013). EEG-Atlas.

Braeutigam S. (2005). Neuroeconomics. *Brain Research Bulletin*. vol. 67, no. 5, pp. 355–360.

Brown C. C. (1967). A proposed standard nomenclature for psychophysiologic measures. *Psychophysiology*. 4, pp. 260–264.

Bulling A., Roggen D., Tröster G. (2008). It's in Your Eyes – Towards Context-Awareness and Mobile HCI Using Wearable EOG Goggles. *In: UbiComp 2008. Proceedings of the 10th International Conference on Ubiquitous Computing*. September 21–24, 2008, Seoul, Korea. Association for Computing Machinery, New York NY 2008

Diepgen P., Goerke H. (1960). Kurze Übersichtstabelle zur Geschichte der Medizin. 7, pp. 64.

Electroencephalography (EEG). (2023). Data Sheet - EEG 26012018. Members Pluxbiosignals company. Retrived June 6, 2023 from https://www.pluxbiosignals.com/products/electroencephalography-eeg.

Electrooculography (EOG). (2023). Data Sheet - EOG 10102018. Members Pluxbiosignals company. Retrived June 6, 2023 from https://www.pluxbiosignals.com/products/electrooculography-eog-sensor-1.

Einthoven, W. (1902). Galvanometrische registratie van het menschelijk electrocardiogram. *In: Herinneringsbundel Professor S. S. Rosenstein*. Leiden, Netherlands: Eduard Ijdo. pp. 101–106.

Gibbs F. A., Gibbs E. L. (1941). Atlas of electroencephalography. F. A. Gibbs, Boston City Hospital.

Halgren, M., Ulbert, I., Bastuji, H., Fabó, D., Erőss, L., Rey, M., ... & Cash, S. S. (2019). The generation and propagation of the human alpha rhythm. *Proceedings of the National Academy of Sciences,* 116(47), pp. 23772-23782.

Heide W., Siebold C., Kömpf D. (2005). Okulographie. In Referenz-Reihe Neurologie. pp. 216-217.

Hoth M., Wischmeyer E. (2021). Extremitätenableitung nach Einthofen. *Duale Reihe Physiologie* 2021.

Jasper S. H. H. (1958). The ten-twenty electrode system of the International Federation. *Electroencephalography and Clinical Neurophysiology*, pp. 371-375.

Nielson J. (2000). Why You Only Need to Test with 5 Users, https://www.nngroup.com/articles/why-you-only-need-to-test-with-5-users/, reviewed 11.08.2023.

Schmid N. (2016). Neurofeedback und Biofeedback in der Praxis: Selbstkontrolle von Körper und Gehirnwellen. *In Psychologie in Österreich*, May 2016. pp. 350-355.

Schott A. (1922). Die chemische Contractor des Säugetiermuskels bei erhaltener und fehlender „elektrischer Erregbarkeit ". *Pflüger's Archiv für die gesamte Physiologie des Menschen und der Tiere*, 194, pp. 271-292.

Steiner M., Meiller D. (2023, 16. July). Simple measurement of user response. Conference on Interfaces and Computer Interaction IHCI. Porto, Portugal, https://www.ihci-conf.org.

Stöhr M., Kraus R. (2002). Einführung in die klinische Neurophysiologie. EMG, EEG, evozierte Potenziale., pp. 60.

Teplan M. (2002). Fundamentals of EEG measurement. *In Measurement science review*, 2(2), 4.

Veiga D. et al. (2017). Feature-Free Activity Classification of Inertial Sensor Data With Machine Vision Techniques: Method, Development, and Evaluation. JMIR Mhealth Uhealth, 5, p.e115. [Online]. doi:10.2196/mhealth.7521.

Weber T. (2010). Journal of Hypertension 2010. *Grundlagen: Zentraler Blutdruck, Pulswellenreflexion, Pulswellengeschwindigkeit*, vol. 14 (2), pp. 9-13.

Zavaglia M., Astolfi L. , Babiloni F., Ursino M. (2016). Use of a neural mass model for the analysis of effective connectivity among cortical regions based on high resolution EEG during cognitive or motor tasks. *Journal of Neuroscience Methods*, vol. 157, no. 2, pp. 317–329.

IMPROVING ALGEBRAIC EXPRESSION GENERATION USING CROW SEARCH BASED GENETIC ALGORITHM

Praful Kumar Prajapati, Alisha Raj and Jitendra Pradhan
IIT Kharagpur, India

ABSTRACT

This research paper proposes the integration of the Crow Search Algorithm (CSA) which is a metaheuristic optimization algorithm into GP to enhance its effectiveness in generating high-quality functions. The results obtained from the experiments demonstrate the effectiveness of CSA-GP in improving the function generation process, particularly focusing on algebraic expressions investigating the potential benefits in terms of performance time and accuracy.

KEYWORDS

Genetic Algorithm, Crow Search Algorithm, Awareness Probability, Optimization, Adaptive Mechanisms, Mutation, Cross Over, Expression Generation, Evolutionary Algorithm

1. INTRODUCTION

Genetic Programming (GP) is a powerful subfield of evolutionary computation that automatically generates programs or functions to solve specific tasks, including symbolic regression, classification, and control problems. One critical aspect is the generation of high-quality functions that accurately model complex relationships within data. To address challenges in GP's search effectiveness and convergence speed, we propose integrating the Crow Search Algorithm (CSA) (Wang, et al., 2022) into GP for function generation. CSA's intelligent foraging behavior offers an efficient exploration- exploitation balance, making it a promising candidate for enhancing GP's search capabilities. Through experiments, we evaluate the performance of the proposed CSA-integrated GP approach (CSA-GP) and compare it with traditional GP algorithms on benchmark problems. The results provide insights into CSA-GP's solution quality, convergence, and robustness across algebraic equation domains.

2. RELATED WORK

Researchers have explored techniques to enhance function generation in Genetic Programming (GP), including integrating different search algorithms, incorporating domain-specific knowledge, adapting fitness evaluation strategies, and utilizing surrogate models and parallel computing (Khamprapai, et al., 2021). DEAP is an innovative framework that leverages the Genetic Algorithm (GA) for symbolic regression, serving as a benchmark in GP research (Koza, 1992). Symbolic regression is widely applied in real-life distributions, where conventional regression methods may face limitations. Evolvability, related to diversity and redundancy, has been extensively studied in Genetic Engineering (GE). Recent research has explored the impact of genetic code degeneracy and the significance of redundancy in GE evolvability (O'Neill & Ryan, 1999). Symbolic regression, also known as Automatic Function Definition (AFD), excels in discovering optimal symbolic functions, but it may have limitations in identifying necessary coefficients for accurate fitting (Koza, 1992). Studies have compared reinforcement learning-based and genetic algorithm-based approaches for symbolic regression (Zhang & Zhou, 2021). A hybrid approach combining genetic algorithms and reinforcement learning aims to enhance symbolic regression's performance and applicability in real- world scenarios. The Crow Search Algorithm (CSA) with parameters like flight length (FL) and awareness probability (AP) plays a crucial role in problem optimization (Cheng et al., 2021). By incorporating CSA features (FL and AP) into a standard genetic algorithm, improved outcomes have been observed. However, no definitive conclusion on Genetic Engineering's effectiveness can be drawn, as it has shown success in various problem domains. Diversity is crucial in the evolvability of GP, and CSA provides effective measures to control it.

3. METHODOLOGY

3.1 Preliminary Concepts on Genetic Programming Using DEAP

DEAP (Distributed Evolutionary Algorithm in Python) is an open-source Python library primarily designed for evolutionary algorithms like Genetic Programming, Genetic Algorithms, and Multi-objective Evolutionary Algorithms such as NSGA-II and SPEA-2. It offers built-in data structures, algorithms, and operators for creating custom genetic algorithm code. DEAP is developed to enable users to craft their evolutionary loops while supporting concurrency, distributing work across multiple CPU cores to significantly reduce execution time. This speed advantage allows for more generations to be processed within a given time frame, enhancing the exploration of a larger search space and leading to more optimized results. For more information about how DEAP has implemented Genetic programming you can refer to (Fortin et al., 2012).

3.2 Improved GP Using Concepts of Crow Search Optimization Algorithm

3.2.1 Function Generation/Symbolic Regression

The task involves Symbolic Regression (SR), which aims to uncover hidden relationships within data using genetic programming (GP). Our focus is on generating compact mathematical expressions for improved interpretability. This poses a challenge for accuracy, often requiring iterative expansion of solution sizes. We chose the DEAP library, a widely-used open-source tool for genetic algorithms, to support our research in this context.

3.2.2 Defining the Primitive Sets of Functions and Terminals

A primitive set is a collection of functions and terminals used to construct genetic programming individuals. We use three primitive sets from DEAP: the main set (pset) for our expression, one for the 'x' variable (psetX), and another for the 'y' variable (psetY). These sets define the available building blocks, including operators, terminals, and arguments, for creating expressions or trees in the genetic programming process.

3.2.3 The Mutate Function in Genetic Algorithm

This function conducts manual uniform mutation on an individual in genetic programming, influenced by the flight length parameter from the crow search algorithm. The mutation process is guided by three input parameters: the individual to be mutated, the expression generator (expr), and a set of available functions and terminals (pset).

The mutation process involves:

1. *Mutation Probability Calculation:* Calculate the mutation probability 'n' based on the flight_length parameter and the length of the individual. Flight_length (ranging from 0 to 1) controls the proportion of the individual's length to be mutated.

2. *Index Selection*: Generate 'n' distinct random indices within the range of the individual's length. These indices indicate which nodes within the individual's tree structure will undergo mutation.

3. *Mutation Process:* For each index in the generated set of indices, the code checks if it falls within the valid range of the individual's length. If valid, it proceeds with the mutation. The code identifies the type of node at the selected index and replaces the subtree rooted at that index with a newly generated expression using the expr function. This newly mutated individual is returned as the function's output (Hong & Wang, 1992).

This mutation process balances exploration and exploitation, enhancing solution quality and convergence characteristics in genetic programming.

3.2.4 Improved GP With Crow Search Optimization Algorithm Flow

The Crow Search Algorithm (CSA) is a recently developed meta-heuristic model inspired by the intelligent behavior of crows in storing food in secretive locations for future retrieval (Burke et al., 2004). This code implements a genetic programming algorithm to find a solution that accurately fits an expected expression.

Initialization: It sets the number of runs and initializes a population of individuals with a size of 500.

Evolution Loop: The algorithm iterates for a specified number of generations (200). Each generation explores and improves solutions, balancing exploration and exploitation (Winkler, 2010).

Variation Operators: Offspring individuals are created through crossover and mutation, controlled by an awareness probability. Crossover combines two individuals, while mutation modifies a single individual. This balances diversity and focus in the search.

Tree Repair: Individuals are checked to ensure they contain variables 'x' and 'y' in their tree structure. If not, mutations are applied to introduce them.

Fitness Evaluation: Each individual's fitness is evaluated based on the expected expression.

Parent Selection: The best individuals from the current and offspring populations are selected for the next generation.

Termination Criteria: The algorithm terminates if a desired fitness value is reached, indicating a solution. It tracks the number of solutions found and the average generations needed.

Best Individual: After the evolution loop, the best individual is selected and its corresponding mathematical function is compiled for demonstration.

This process mimics natural evolution to find an accurate expression fit.

4. EXPERIMENTAL SETUP

4.1 Dataset

We have created a dataset of ranges from -n to n for every X, Y and Z coordinate and it output, given in the experimental setup.

4.2 Performance Metrics and Evaluation Criteria

The algorithms are evaluated using several key performance metrics:

1. *Fitness Value:* This quantifies solution quality, with a focus on minimizing the value. It reflects how well the algorithm meets problem criteria, indicating improved performance when lower fitness values are achieved.
2. *Average Generation*: It measures how quickly the algorithm converges to a correct mathematical expression. It's calculated as the sum of generations needed to find a solution divided by the number of successful solution discoveries.
3. *Accuracy Rate:* This metric assesses the balance between exploration and exploitation. It's calculated as the number of successful solution discoveries divided by the total number of algorithm runs.
4. *Average Deviation*: This measures the fitness scores of individuals when a solution is not found, providing insight into convergence quality. It's calculated as the sum of fitness scores for unsuccessful solutions divided by the total number of unsuccessful attempts.
5. *Execution Time:* This metric evaluates algorithm efficiency and speed. It's crucial for resource optimization and selecting the right algorithm for time-sensitive tasks. Faster execution times are preferred, especially for larger datasets or time-critical applications.

4.3 Experimental Procedures

Parameter Settings: The algorithms are executed with the following parameter settings: Population size: 500, number of runs: 100, number of generations: 200, crossover rate: 0-1, mutation rate: 0-1,flight Length: 0-1, awareness Probability: 0-1

Testing Mathematical Expression: We have selected 6 random different equations:

5x^2, x^4+2x^2, 50x^6+4x^4+22x^3+11x^2+12x+2x^5, 12*(x^3)*(y^2)

By following this experimental setup, we ensure transparency and reproducibility of the experiments conducted to evaluate the algorithms. It provides a clear description of the dataset, performance metrics, and evaluation procedures, enabling accurate comparison and analysis of the algorithmic performance.

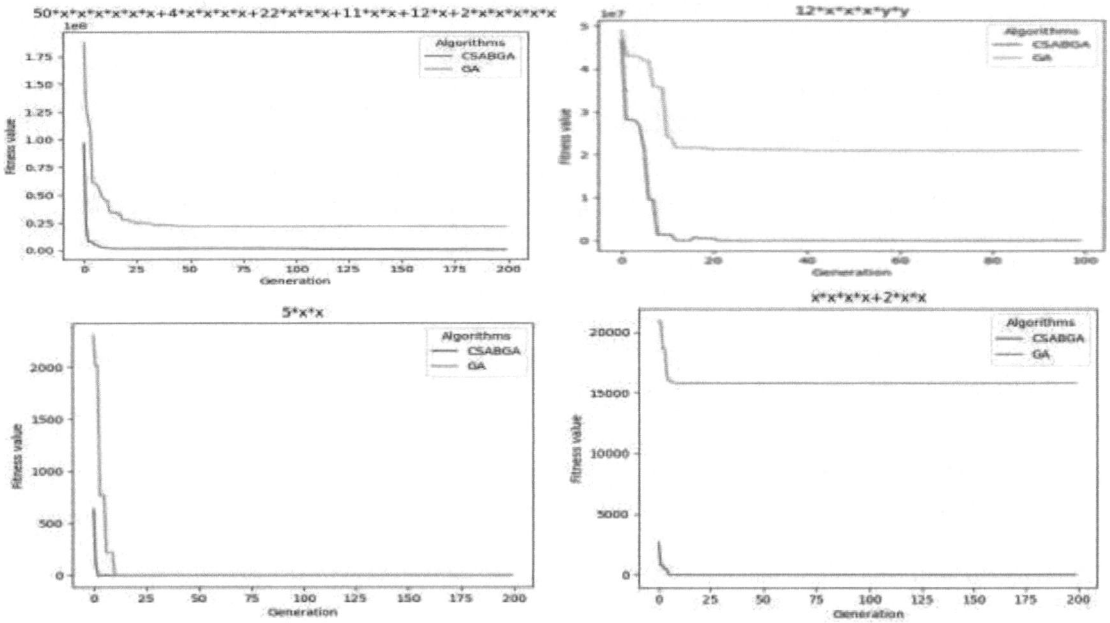

Figure 1. Fitness value trend over generations for GA and CSBGA

5. RESULT AND ANALYSIS

Fitness Value: CSBGA consistently outperforms GA as we plotted the graphs (Figure 1) of GA and our modified CSA (CSBGA). It converges faster to the solution, while GA often gets trapped in local minima, leading to constant fitness values. CSBGA excels in both speed and accuracy.

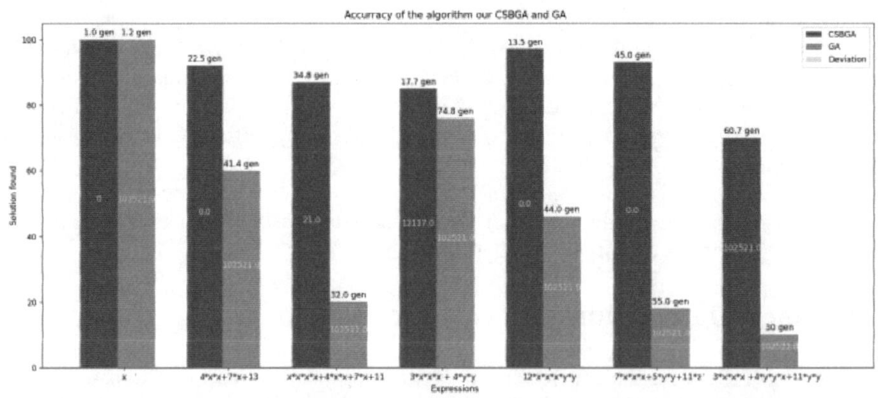

Figure 2. Accuracy, generation rate and deviation comparison for GA andCSBGA

Accuracy: CSBGA demonstrates superior accuracy as we can see from the Figure 2 maintaining over 90% accuracy for most cases. In contrast, GA's accuracy decreases with higher equation complexity. CSBGA consistently performs well, highlighting its robustness.

Average Generation Rate: CSA generally converges faster than GA, indicating efficient performance. However, CSA may require more generations for complex expressions, partly due to GA getting stuck in local minima.

Table 1. Execution time comparison for GA and CSBGA

Expression	Time Taken byGP(in seconds)	Time Taken by CSA	Time Difference
5x^2	53s	60s	7s
x^4+2x^2	67s	128s	51s
12*(x^3)*(y^2)	56s	108s	52s
50x^6+4x^4+22x^3+11x^2+12x+2x^5	100s	180s	80s

Deviation: CSA exhibits lower deviations, implying more consistent solutions closer to the optimal value. GA tends to have higher deviations, indicating less consistency and more variation in results.

Execution Time: GA is faster than CSA for completing 500 iterations on various algebraic expressions. CSA's added manual mutation and population differences contribute to its slightly longer execution time, especially for higher-powered expressions.

In summary, CSBGA demonstrates superior performance in terms of speed, accuracy, and solution consistency, while GA struggles with complex expressions and can get trapped in local minima. The execution time difference between the two algorithms is relatively small.

6. DRAWBACKS

While our model has shown promising results compared to genetic programming, there are still notable drawbacks that present opportunities for future enhancement. In terms of expression generation, our model performs well for large powers up to 6-7; however, its accuracy deteriorates significantly beyond this range. Also, the current benchmarking with random simple mathematical expressions can be improved with the solutions of existing benchmarking multi-modal functions such as Rastrigin function, Rosenbrock functions etc. Addressing these limitations and improving the model's accuracy and scalability for higher powers, as well as incorporating domain-specific knowledge, are crucial areas for future research and development in the field of mathematical expression generation.

7. FUTURE SCOPE

Enhancing Accuracy for Higher Powers: Address the model's limitations in accurately generating high-powered expressions (>6-7) by exploring advanced mutation strategies and mathematical techniques.

Incorporating Domain-Specific Knowledge: Improve efficiency by integrating domain-specific knowledge into the algorithm, leveraging mathematical properties and relationships.

Fine-tuning Awareness Probability and Flight Length: Optimize awareness probability and flight length parameters for a better balance between exploration and exploitation, enhancing convergence towards global optima.

Algorithmic Enhancements: Investigate selection methods, advanced crossover and mutation operators, and tailored evolutionary operators to refine the model's performance.

Evaluation and Comparison: Conduct comprehensive evaluations comparing the model with other algorithms, providing insights into its strengths, weaknesses, and performance relative to state-of-the-art methods.

By addressing these limitations and focusing on the future scope of work, significant advancements can be made in the field of mathematical expression generation.

8. DISCUSSION AND CONCLUSION

In conclusion, this research introduced the CSBGA, a hybrid algorithm combining Crow Search Behavior with Genetic Algorithm, to enhance algebraic mathematical expression generation. We investigated its impact on convergence rate, solution quality, and diversity maintenance, comparing it with other metaheuristic algorithms. Adaptive mechanisms for CSA parameter adjustment were explored and validated through experiments. Our contributions include insights into leveraging CSA for genetic algorithms and advancing optimization techniques.

Results demonstrate CSBGA's superiority over GA in accuracy, and solution quality, albeit with a slightly longer execution time. Future work should address limitations in handling higher powers and scalability, fine-tune parameters, and explore further algorithmic enhancements. These efforts promise advancements in mathematical expression generation, benefiting various domains requiring efficient mathematical modeling and problem-solving algorithms.

REFERENCES

Burke, E. K, Gustafson, S., Kendall, G. (2004, February 19). "Diversity in genetic programming: an analysis of measures and correlation with fitness". IEEE Trans Evolut Comput 8(1): pp 47–62. Doi: https://doi.org/10.1109/TEVC.2003.819263

Chen and Guestrin (2016). "Improving Model-based Genetic Programming for Symbolic Regression of Small Expressions". In: Genetic programming theory and practice XIV, Springer.

Fortin, E.-A., De Rainville, F.-M., Gardner, M-A., Parizeau, M., and Gagne, C. (2012). {DEAP}: "Evolutionary Algorithms Made Easy", Journal of Machine Learning Research.

Syswerda, G. (1992). BBN Laboratories BBN Systems and Technologies Corporation, 10 Moulton Street, Cambridge, MA 02138 "Simulated Crossover in Genetic Algorithms". Appl Soft Comput 62: pp. 1003– 1018.

Zhang, H. and Zhou, A. (2021). "RL-GEP: SymbolicRegression via Gene Expression Programming and Reinforcement Learning". International Joint Conference on Neural Network 2021, pp. 1-8.

Hidalgo, J. I, Colmenar J. M., Risco-Martín J. L, Cuesta-Infante A, Maqueda E, Botella M, Rubio J. A (2014). "Modelling glycemia in humans by means of grammatical evolution". Appl Soft Comput 20: pp. 40–53.

Koza, J. (1992). "Genetic Programming". MIT Press, Cambridge, MA.

O'Neill, M., Ryan, C. (1999). "Genetic code degeneracy: implications forgrammatical evolution and beyond". In: Floreano D, Nicoud JD, Mondada F (eds) Advances in artificial life. Vol 1674, Springer, Berlin, pp. 149– 153.

Cheng, Q., Huang, H., and Chen. M. (2021, October 26). "A Novel Crow Search Algorithm Based on Improved Flower Pollination". Mathematical Problems in Engineering. Vol. 2021.

Teotima Evangelista Gorres-Abato (2021). "Symbolic Regression via Genetic Programming"; Philippines Population Prediction: 2010-2020.

Wang, T., Zhang, C., He, A., and Dong, W. (2022). "Overview of Crow Search Algorithm". Journal of Physics: Conference Series.

Hong, T.-P., Wang, H.-S. (1992). "A dynamic mutation genetic algorithm".

Khamprapai, W., Tsai, C.-F., Wang, P. and Tsai, C.-E. (2021, July 27). "Performance of Enhanced Multiple-Searching Genetic Algorithm for Test Case Generation in Software Testing". In: Proceedings of the workshop on advancesin machine learning for computational finance, London, UK.

Winkler S. M (2010). "Structural versus evaluation based solutions similarity in genetic programming based system identification". In: González JR, Pelta DA, Cruz C, Terrazas G, Krasnogor N (eds) Natureinspired cooperative strategies for optimization NICSO 2010, studies in computational intelligence, vol 284, Springer, Granada, Spain, pp. 269–282.

A PROPOSED DRONE-ENABLED PLATFORM FOR HOLISTIC DISASTER MANAGEMENT

Eleni Aretoulaki, Stavros T. Ponis, George Plakas, Dimitra Tzanetou and Antonios Kitsantas
School of Mechanical Engineering, National Technical University Athens
Heroon Polytechniou 9, Zografos 15780, Athens, Greece

ABSTRACT

Lack of available data acts as a serious bottleneck in performing humanitarian logistics operations. This paper proposes a drone-enabled integrated humanitarian logistics platform, called "AIRDROP", for holistic well-informed disaster management, aiming to assist first responders and operational decision-makers, before, during and after the strike of a disaster. AIRDROP aims to be a scalable, modular and flexible solution which will consist of an array of drones of different sizes and payload capabilities, able to provide different humanitarian logistics services addressing a broad range of disaster types (natural or human-made) and stages, from mitigation and preparedness (pre-disaster) to response and recovery (post-disaster). These services are manifold and include but are not limited to the monitoring and mapping of the disaster area to provide continuous situation awareness through the use of various drone-mounted sensors, physical operations, such as the delivery of medical care and emergency relief supplies and last, the serving as communication nodes in ad-hoc networks to provide undisrupted coverage. The description of the platform's scope and services sets the stage for future research steps including the establishment of the platform's requirements to be assessed for relevance and viability, thereby ensuring the fulfillment of all potential stakeholders' demands and contributing to AIRDROP's future development.

KEYWORDS

Humanitarian Logistics, Disaster Management, Unmanned Aerial Vehicles, Drones; Internet of Things, Machine Learning

1. INTRODUCTION

Humanitarian Logistics (HL) refers to the process of planning, conducting and controlling the efficient, cost-effective flow and storage of goods and materials as well as related information from the point of origin to the point of consumption with the aim of mitigating the suffering of those who are most in need (Tomasini 2018). The latter represents one of the most significant challenges in HL due to the limited availability of data, which acts as a bottleneck in understanding various hazards needing to be tackled. Without adequate data, gaining knowledge about risk dynamics, scenario planning, informed decision-making, and implementing risk reduction practices becomes problematic. The use of emerging digital technologies, including drones, has been proved pivotal in improving data availability in HL operations. In this paper, to address the aforementioned challenges, a drone-enabled platform, henceforth called "AIRDROP", is proposed incorporating various heterogeneous data sources into disaster management. Several pertinent projects have made significant contributions to HL operations, including ResponDrone (Friedrich et al. 2022), ASSISTANCE (Perez et al. 2020), and FASTER (Katsadouros et al. 2022), each of which has focused on critical particular aspects of HL operations, contributing to the advancement of the field. Even though humanitarian crises cannot all be approached the same way due to their intrinsically different characteristics and complexities (Aretoulaki et al. 2020), the proposed platform aims to provide an integrated approach to HL offering a comprehensive solution that encompasses a wide range of disaster types both pre- (Mitigation & Preparedness) and post-disaster (Response & Recovery), thereby marking a significant milestone in the field of HL.

2. AIRDROP SCOPE & SERVICES

AIRDROP aims to be a scalable, modular and flexible solution which will employ an array of unmanned vehicles (Unmanned Aerial Vehicles-UAVs, Unmanned Ground Vehicles-UGVs, Unmanned Surface Vehicles-USVs) of different sizes and payload capabilities that will be able to provide different HL services to assist first responders and operational decision-makers, before, during and after the strike of a disaster. The platform's essential services are discussed below.

Control System: This service refers to the planning, management and supervision of the response mission. Two human-machine interfaces commanding the drones are provided, the Command Center Web Application (CCWA) and the First Responder Mobile Application (FRMA). The CCWA visualizes the results provided by the Decision Support System (DSS) and is meant to fuse multiple source data and integrate it into an aggregated operational picture to be used by a mission commander with the authorization of making mission-relevant decisions. The primary purpose of the CCWA is to manage the mission by supervising drone missions, assigning tasks for the first response units in the field or creating incident reports, in order to gather, store and provide collected data to all stakeholders as well as actionable business insights. These reports can refer to various aspects of the mission, including incident description and classification, impact assessment, response actions takes, resources exploited, event timelines, information about stakeholder coordination, recommendations, communication logs etc. This interface also provides information about the status of the vehicles (e.g., battery level, GNSS strength signal, camera model) and the rescue teams/systems (e.g., number and type of available first responders or helicopters for emergency medical services). Events relevant to the situation assessment are also reported, such as hospital operational status, departments and capacity, updates on infrastructure status (e.g., bridges, roads) and areas at risks. Last, the CCWA interface provides information relevant to the mission KPI assessment (e.g., response time, task completion rate, incident report generation time).

On the other hand, the FRMA is used by first response units operating in the disaster area. On the FRMA, the first response units in the field can access a tailored visualization of the disaster situation based on the type of unit using it (e.g., medical emergency services, fire and rescue services, law enforcement teams). They can receive the tasks they are assigned with, create incident reports, see the live video stream from the optical sensors mounted on the drones, and request drone missions. First responders are also able to interact with one another and the operational decision-makers via a dedicated chat function.

Mission Planning System (MPS): Once a mission is requested by the CCWA-operator or by a unit in the field via the FRMA, it is sent to MPS for processing. Hereby, MPS takes as input information from the mission-relevant components to compute a more detailed flight plan, to be approved by the CCWA-operator. Once approved, the flight plan is being processed further by the MPS, which computes and verifies de-conflicted trajectories and forwards them to the Ground Control Station (GCS). Based on the needs as well as the available resources, the locations to be visited by the drones are determined and prioritized accordingly. As far as the UAVs are concerned, the parameters that can be set for each waypoint are speed, altitude, aircraft heading, loiter, gimbal pitch angle, cornering, sensor measurement Start/Stop and last, end-mission action, i.e., return, hover, or land. Similar parameters are set for the UGVs and USVs deployed.

This service is also meant to define a specific area of flight and enforce geo-fencing restrictions (no fly zones near the flight area) for safety purposes. If the UAV approaches the boundaries of the area, it will hover and trigger a notification. Through this service, conflicts between 4D trajectories of different UAVs can also be identified and prevented. Each point on a 4D trajectory denotes the UAV's presence at a specific location in 3D space at a certain moment in time. Correspondingly, the same service applies to the UGVs and USVs for the de-confliction of their 3D trajectories.

Last, through this service, the UAVs should be able to land on specific static and moving targets (e.g., platforms attached to UGVs) by interpreting visual cues through the use of Machine Learning (ML) algorithms. Additionally, in case of an emergency, autonomous flight to the nearest emergency landing site and geo-fence removal will take place. Multiple missions can be deployed at once or paused, resumed and terminated.

Area Scanning System: The Area Scanning System allows for scanning an area through a variety of sensors and cameras attached to the UAVs, UGVs and USVs. Depending on the type of the disaster, this system can perform a multitude of tasks. All the tasks mentioned below can be carried out when the UAV is hovering or even static (fixed point observation) and swarms of drones can also be used to accelerate the scanning process.

For starters, the first area scanning task can be exploited in the event of a fire outbreak, in which UAVs and UGVs equipped with electro-optical and infrared cameras can be employed. These cameras feature an on-board real-time video analytics system, leveraged by ML algorithms for detecting fire or smoke. The vehicles are also equipped with gas sensors which can be used to detect carbon monoxide (CO) and carbon dioxide (CO2) leakage. For industrial or nuclear disasters as well as atmospheric pollution monitoring, the next task utilizes UAV/UGV-mounted gamma radiation sensors for the radiological mapping of post-disaster nuclear environments and chemical sensors for the detection of hazardous chemicals (e.g., PM2.5, PM10, SO2, NH3).

In the event of a flood, the UAV-mounted camera featuring a real-time video analytics system can leverage ML algorithms for detecting the locations of (potentially) flooded areas. Similarly, in the event of an earthquake, landslide, hurricane, tsunami or any disaster that can result in infrastructure damage, the UAVs/UGVs can detect the locations where possible victims could be trapped (e.g., voids) as well as damaged infrastructure in general. Such system, trained accordingly, can also be used for the detection of missing persons or vehicles. Alternately, the UAV/UGV can be equipped with acoustic sensors for the identification of human sounds (e.g, speaking, footsteps, breathing noises, or other vocalizations) or a monitoring UAV can be used in tandem with miniature UGVs equipped with chemical sensors which can detect the presence of specific organic compounds emitted by humans (e.g., volatile organic compounds).

Multiple parameters can be measured through weather sensors attached to the UAV, such as wind speed and direction, air pressure, temperature and relative humidity. Mission planning heavily relies on weather forecasts, which however have to be verified in-situ, since drones are difficult to operate in humid, foggy, rainy, windy or snowy environments and results can be adversely affected. Extreme temperatures can also have detrimental effects on batteries, motors and radio monitoring equipment.

Finally, the last task helps extend the field of view of first responders using the FRMA through Augmented Reality (AR) devices, visualizing important data resulting from the Area Scanning Service (e.g., live sensor data) and the DSS for real-time data overlay (e.g, warning the first responders about approaching the danger zone, in all phases of the emergency).

Communication System: The Communication System takes various mission aspects into account. First, it ensures that the drone swarms can be reconfigured in case one of them stops working. When a failure occurs in a drone, such as loss of communication or sensor malfunction, the others should become aware of the issue by exchanging information through wireless communication protocols. Through swarm management algorithms, the swarm should dynamically redistribute the tasks and responsibilities among the operational drones (e.g., reallocating the surveillance areas, or reassigning specific tasks previously performed by the failed drone). Second, it ensures that critical control commands are processed without delay by requiring UAVs, UGVs, and USVs to prioritize C2 messages, i.e., messages responsible for the management and control of the drone, over telemetry messages, i.e., messages used to transmit data related to the status, performance, and measurements of the drone or its components, and maintain low latency for both, between the vehicles and the GCS.

Third, it supports communication relaying capabilities, enabling UAVs to act as relays and extend the communication range and coverage in scenarios where direct communication links are not feasible, thereby enhancing the overall connectivity and information sharing capabilities of the platform. The communication range must be enough, so the C2 link is necessary to provide very long-range transmission and reception, since it is charged with ensuring connectivity for information exchange across all flight phases. Additionally, with integration of Wi-Fi access points, connectivity interfaces (e.g., Bluetooth, Wi-Fi) in sensors, and support for offloading data to cloud servers, the Communication System fosters network connectivity and facilitates seamless information sharing among the disaster management platform components, hence enabling real-time data exchange, collaborative decision-making, and enhanced situational awareness. It also employs redundancy in data storage and efficient bandwidth management strategies, including data compression techniques, to ensure reliable optimized data transfer and utilization. To guarantee data integrity and dependability and avoid data loss in the event of server failure or network outages, copying data across different cloud servers or using distributed storage systems is crucial. To make the best use of the network's available resources and enable effective data offloading, it is important to give priority to crucial data streams, dynamically distribute bandwidth based on application requirements, and reduce data congestion. Compressing the data can help in optimizing bandwidth usage and improving transmission efficiency.

The Communication System also leverages Received Signal Strength Indication (RSSI)-based techniques and Wi-Fi connectivity to carry out crowd counting services, allowing for the estimation of crowd sizes and densities in affected areas, providing valuable insights for resource allocation and emergency response planning. Finally, by utilizing multiple GNSS receivers, Real-Time Kinematic (RTK) GPS technology, and multi-frequency receivers, it ensures high position accuracy for the UAVs, UGVs, USVs (lower than 1m) and First Responders (lower than 5m). This enables precise localization and mapping of the affected areas, enhances mission planning, and supports effective response coordination.

Social Media Sensing: This service focuses on the extraction and gathering of real-time observations on the status of a disaster from online social media platforms (i.e., Twitter, Instagram, Facebook, Youtube), including text, photographs, and videos. Language-agnostic text extraction and classification, image analysis, and video content analysis will all be carried out using ML approaches. The material can be divided into different categories, including information on casualties, missing people, damage assessment, relief operations progress, and irrelevant or useless content.

Geotags, message metadata, user profiles, connections, message content, photos, videos, and the spatiotemporal distribution of messages can all be used to extract location information from social network posts. Before proceeding with further processing, pre-processing operations, such as text normalization and image/video de-noising, will be conducted. The results will then be communicated to the DSS for validation.

Rescue: This service is divided into five distinct modules, i.e., package delivery, patient care, evacuation, extinguishing and first responder risk status monitoring. In the first module, UAVs are responsible for delivering various commodities (e.g., water, food, clothing, blankets and bedding, hygiene products, masks, gloves, waste disposal bags, hand sanitizers) by identifying the positions of relief item delivery trucks using ML techniques, and determining optimized delivery routes based on supply allocation algorithms. In the second module, drone-mounted medical sensors are utilized for the real-time monitoring of victims' vital signs (e.g., heart rate monitor, infrared thermometer, glucose monitor, respiration rate monitor, ECG monitor, blood pressure monitor). Furthermore, UAVs also carry necessary medical supplies for patient care (e.g., first aid kits, medical drugs, and blood samples) and are equipped with cold transport capabilities for delivering life-saving vaccines.

The third module has to do with the evacuation of stranded people. It enables users to input ad-hoc evacuation areas and shelters (location and capacity) and calculates safe evacuation routes, real-time routes status, access times to the emergency points as well as approximate evacuation times through the use of emergency particular parameters and historical demographic data. A UAV equipped with a megaphone to assist the evacuation of stranded people can also be utilized. For fire-related scenarios, drones will be equipped with firefighting mechanisms, i.e., a water-based fire extinguishing agent which they will use to put out a fire in a forest or building, a fire suppression system, a tank etc.

The last module revolves around the monitoring of the risk status of first responders through wearable sensors. These sensors can include personal video cameras, CO detection sensors, temperature sensors, GPS trackers, gas detectors, and radiation sensors.

The Rescue Service communicates with the DSS and depending on the rescue task described above, the information communicated can be emergency type and location, location, type and risks of infrastructure damage, commodity demand, location of victims needing immediate medical care and the type of care, sensor measurements etc.

Virtual Reality (VR) Training: This service includes the combined use of 3D VR, unmanned vehicles and cloud computing, where data sets generated by the observations of the robotic systems are used to create a realistic VR environment able to reflect actual conditions and facilitate the preparation of rescue scenarios to be tackled by the first response units within an acceptable time window. Integrating immersive technologies, such as VR and potentially including AR and gamification, is one of the prerequisites for the training service. The training should be conducted in small groups, with an equal distribution of theoretical and practical components, and should be specifically designed to meet the needs of first responders. Systems of rating and feedback are essential for assessing performance. The training sessions should be organized according to participant availability, with the training materials and support being offered in English. Setting up data management systems to safely preserve training data and evaluation outcomes for later analysis is a crucial aspect of this service.

Reconstruction: The Reconstruction service refers to the steps taken after the immediate threats of a disaster have been mitigated, to restore the living conditions of stricken areas by rebuilding damaged infrastructure. Attaching UAVs to remotely operated construction machines is a significant step to ensuring safety and security during reconstruction operations as well as for surveillance and progress monitoring. Also, construction supplies can be delivered by UAVs to inaccessible locations. Integration with the DSS will achieve effective data interchange and coordination.

Decision Support System (DSS): The final proposed service, the DSS, serves as the central hub for data integration and exchange, seamlessly connecting the functionalities of the entire AIRDROP platform. It collaborates effectively with the CCWA, FRMA, MPS, Area Scanning, Communication, Social Media Sensing, Rescue, VR Training and Reconstruction services, enriching the platform with coherence and insight through comprehensive data exchange. Figure 1 depicts the data flow diagram illustrating information exchange between the DSS and the other AIRDROP services. The DSS will provide an API REST service for data insertion and consultation as well as support video streaming and photo access. Moreover, it will incorporate a GIS-based system for geospatial analysis, including the identification of danger zones, uncertainty and hazard position calculations, sensor position optimization, scenario planning, as well as performance and progress evaluation. The DSS should additionally validate social media data, determine optimal resource allocation, and provide insights for reconstruction efforts (e.g., through the identification of damaged infrastructure, affected areas, and potential hazards) and communication (e.g., through communication effectiveness analyses and network traffic analyses).

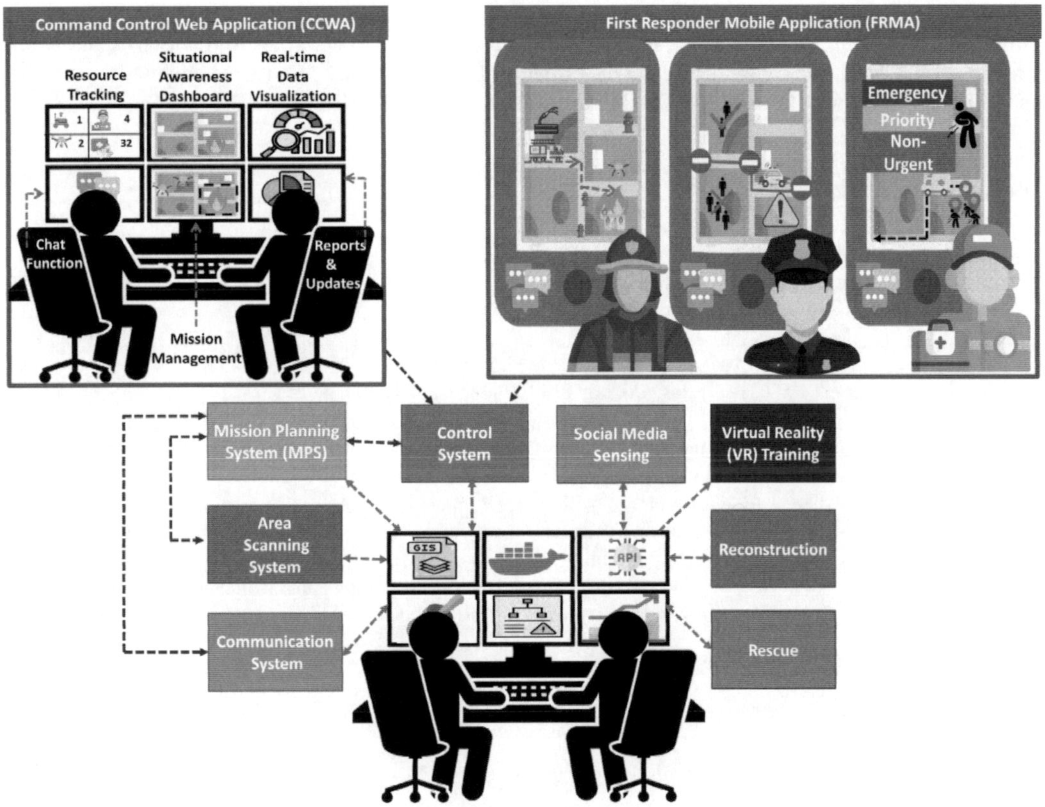

Figure 1. Data Flow Diagram: Information exchange between DSS and the rest of the AIRDROP services

3. CONCLUSION

By aspiring to address all four disaster stages and a wide variety of disaster types, AIRDROP offers a substantial advantage to the HL community by proposing a complete and holistic disaster management solution. However, the platform's described complexity in managing several areas, such as data integration, interoperability, and real-time decision-making represents a crucial limitation. These factors need to be carefully considered and coordinated to maintain smooth and seamless operations. For that purpose, future work will concentrate on carrying out a thorough requirements specification study to highlight the precise requirements of AIRDROP's services and functionalities. The results of this investigation will be used in a requirements analysis questionnaire which will be created to elicit opinions and insights with regard to the proposed requirements from a variety of stakeholders, including subject matter and technology experts, academics, as well as specialists in disaster management and professional first responders. Their insightful opinions will be used to validate the requirements' relevance and viability, guaranteeing that the platform will satisfy the demands of all HL stakeholders. This process shall contribute to shaping the architectural design and development of the platform and ultimately, may pave the way for new processes, organizational structures, and managerial frameworks for HL operations.

ACKNOWLEDGEMENT

This research has been co-financed by the European Regional Development Fund of the European Union and Greek national funds through the Operational Program Competitiveness, Entrepreneurship and Innovation, under the call RESEARCH – CREATE – INNOVATE (project code: T2EDK-03478).

REFERENCES

Aretoulaki, Eleni, Stavros Ponis, George Plakas, and Konstantinos Agalianos. 2020. "A Systematic Meta-Review Analysis of Review Papers in the Marine Plastic Pollution Literature." *Marine Pollution Bulletin* 161 (December): 111690. https://doi.org/10.1016/j.marpolbul.2020.111690.

Friedrich, Max, Teemu Joonas Lieb, Annette Temme, Eduardo N. Almeida, André Coelho, and Helder Fontes. 2022. "ResponDrone - A Situation Awareness Platform for First Responders." In *2022 IEEE/AIAA 41st Digital Avionics Systems Conference (DASC)*, 1–7. https://doi.org/10.1109/DASC55683.2022.9925792.

Katsadouros, Evangelos, Dimitrios G. Kogias, Charalampos Z. Patrikakis, Gabriele Giunta, Anastasios Dimou, and Petros Daras. 2022. "Introducing the Architecture of FASTER: A Digital Ecosystem for First Responder Teams." *Information* 13 (3): 115. https://doi.org/10.3390/info13030115.

Perez, Debora Robles, Manuel Esteve Domingo, Israel Perez Llopis, and Federico J. Carvajal Rodrigo. 2020. "System and Architecture of an Adapted Situation Awareness Tool for First Responders." In *Proceedings of the He 17th ISCRAM Conference*.

Tomasini, Rolando M. 2018. "The Evolutions of Humanitarian-Private Partnerships: Collaborative Frameworks Under Review." In *The Palgrave Handbook of Humanitarian Logistics and Supply Chain Management*, edited by Gyöngyi Kovács, Karen Spens, and Mohammad Moshtari, 627–35. London: Palgrave Macmillan UK. https://doi.org/10.1057/978-1-137-59099-2_21.

A BLOCKCHAIN-BASED APPLICATION FOR FOOD WASTE REDUCTION

Stavros T. Ponis, George Plakas, Eleni Aretoulaki, Dimitra Tzanetou and Antonios Kitsantas
School of Mechanical Engineering, National Technical University Athens
Heroon Polytechniou 9, Zografos 15780, Athens, Greece

ABSTRACT

Food waste is a major global concern and engenders profound ramifications of environmental and socio-economic dimensions, while on the other hand, food insecurity affects a significant part of the global population. The co-existence of food waste and food insecurity in urban environments is a paradox of modern cities. The research project presented in this paper introduces a solution using blockchain technology to address both of these issues, simultaneously. The project aims to develop a decentralized mobile application (dApp), which facilitates the reduction of food waste and provides safe and nutritious meals to food-insecure individuals. The tokenization capability provided by the blockchain technology, through the utilization of smart contracts, is used to incentivize food waste reduction and track surplus availability. Citizens use the project's token as currency to purchase food portions, while the participating food service establishments from the retail sector, receive the tokens in exchange for the saved surplus. In this paper the architectural design and all the components of the decentralized application are outlined and described and a holistic view of their interconnection into an IT architecture is provided. This description is followed by an initial discussion of the tokenization process of the proposed ecosystem and its main characteristics that are going to guide the development of the project's tokenomics, by taking into account token's supply, distribution, utility and market demand to estimate the token's value.

KEYWORDS

Blockchain, Smart Contracts, Tokens, Tokenization, System Architecture, Food Waste

1. INTRODUCTION

Food waste is an increasingly critical issue worldwide, impacting environment and society in a multi-dimensional way. It contributes to greenhouse gas emissions and depletes water and land resources (Munesue & Masui, 2019). If food waste was a country, it would be the third largest emitting country in the world, after China and USA (UNEP, 2021). Economically, it causes $936 billion per year in economic damages (FAO, 2014) and socially, it exacerbates inequalities, especially in metropolitan areas where it occurs along food insecurity. Food waste takes place in every link of the food supply chain (Parfitt et al., 2010) from primary producers and processing to retail stores and final consumers. Especially in hospitality and food service sector, according to studies, nearly one third of all food is wasted and almost half of the waste, can be avoided (Papargyropoulou et al., 2019). The level of the food supply chain that includes among others, the restaurants and eateries in the cities, i.e., the retail sector, plays significant role in arising food waste. Initiatives to mitigate the phenomenon include improved supply chain management, innovative packaging and storage solutions, redistribution of surplus food to those in need, and educational campaigns that aim to shift consumer attitudes and behaviors (Attiq et al., 2021; Strotmann et al., 2017; Wikström et al., 2019). The efforts of the project presented in this paper target those in need, that suffer from food insecurity, as the recipients of the food surplus generated by the retail sector, in order to try to effectively tackle the repercussions emerging from food waste, with the utilization of the blockchain technology and its derivatives, i.e., smart contracts and tokens.

2. SYSTEM ARCHITECTURE

The core objective of the project presented in this paper, namely BLOCKFOODWASTE, is to develop a mobile application based on blockchain, for reducing food waste from the food service establishments of the retail sector, such as restaurants, eateries, bakeries etc. The users of the application are divided in two categories: a) the Food Service Establishments (FSEs) that offer their food surplus (supply) and the citizens that suffer from food insecurity or are willing to help the mitigation of food waste problem (demand). The IT architecture is critical in the development of any information system no matter of its size, development approach, structural type and domain of application and the same applies to this project's case. The technical components that are used to build the project's decentralized application (dApp) help to ensure that it is secure, scalable and interoperable with other dApps and systems. The research team decided to treat the development efforts of the discrete components separated, in order to rationalize software development processes and gain time. This decision separated the first two large building blocks of the architecture i.e., BFW blockchain from the Application system. The software development follows an agile approach, because agile methods are suited to develop systems whose requirements are not completely understood since the beginning, or tend to change, as it is this case. The choice for the public blockchain network that will be utilized in the Proof-of-Concept phase of this project is the Ethereum blockchain, but due to its high gas fees, it may not be the blockchain of the project's final product. Based on the above, an initial take of the high-level system architecture is depicted in **Figure 1**. For figure clarity purposes, interconnections between nodes in the blockchain component have not drafted, yet they are implied. All the nodes are connected to each other, and they continuously exchange the newest information on the blockchain with each other. This ensures all nodes are updated.

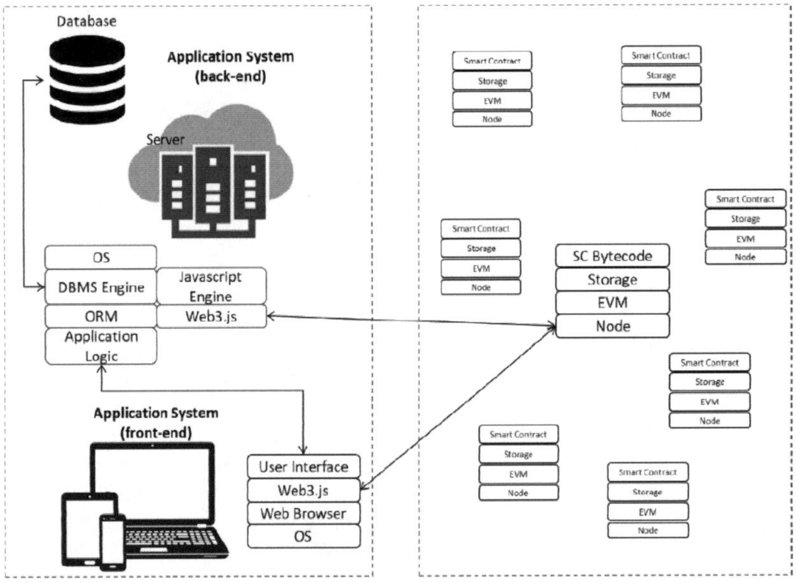

Figure 1. High Level IT Architecture of the BFW Distributed Application

The Application system is composed of a software system running on mobile devices and/or on servers, exchanging information with users and external devices. Its User Interface (UI) runs on a Web browser and in a mobile app interface. The server component stores data that cannot be stored in the blockchain and performs business computations. As shown in **Figure 1**, interaction between Ethereum nodes and the system application (mostly managing the creation and dispatches of transactions) will be carried out using Web3.js through HTTP, IPC, or WebSocket. Object-relational mapping (ORM) is a programming technique in which a metadata descriptor is used to connect object code to a relational database. Object code will be written in object-oriented programming (OOP) languages such as Java or C#. Finally, in the blockchain component, EVM (Ethereum Virtual Machine) is the runtime environment that executes Ethereum smart contracts. Ethereum contracts are written in Ethereum's proprietary Turing-complete scripting language, called Solidity, which will be used to develop the project's smart contracts and their embedded business logic.

Further drilling down in the dApp architecture, at this point, outlining the interaction of the two discrete blocks of **Figure 1** is in order. In **Figure 2**, a simplified version of the interaction between the two components is presented, along with available software tools for creating the smart contracts (VScode and Remix IDEs), cloud service providers such as Microsoft Azure and Amazon Web Services and finally Ethereum wallets, such as MetaMask and Exodus.

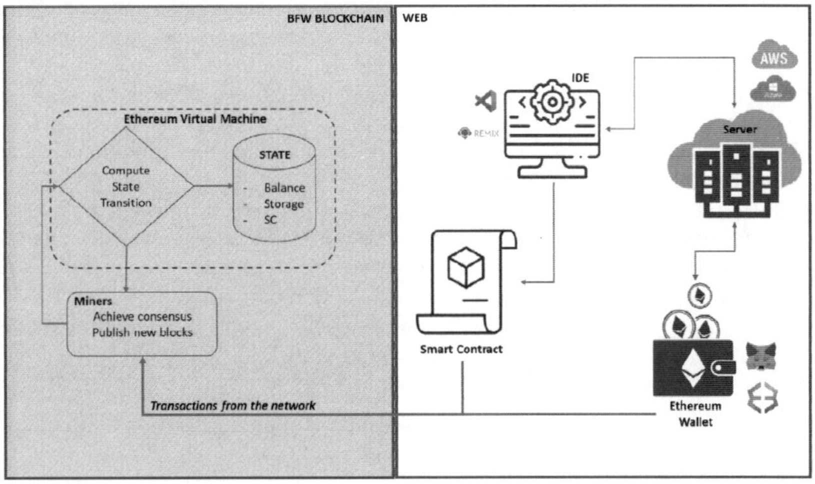

Figure 2. Component Interaction

Having determined the upper-level architecture of the project's dApp and in order to provide more details of the proposed approach, an outline of the iterative software development process is provided. The high-level expectations (requirements) for each discrete component, are the following:

Mobile App: The mobile app should have a user-friendly interface for citizens to browse and place an order for surplus food from participating FSEs. It should have integration with blockchain to securely record transactions and track food waste reduction and use GPS or other location-based services to show available surplus food nearby the interested citizens.

Web Platform: The web platform should provide an interface for food service establishments to manage their surplus food inventory and track food waste reduction. It should have integration with blockchain to securely record transactions and track food waste reduction. Additionally, it should have an analytics dashboard to monitor food waste reduction and track the performance of participating FSEs and a reporting system to generate reports, such as on food waste reduction goals.

Blockchain: The blockchain should be used to securely record transactions and track food waste reduction. It should provide transparency and immutability in recording the transactions and food waste reduction and allow for the creation of smart contracts to automate the process of surplus food distribution and food waste tracking.

Database: The database should store the information about participating food service establishments, surplus food inventory, citizen orders, and food waste reduction tracking. It should be scalable to accommodate the growing number of transactions and data as the food waste reduction platform grows and should be securely managed to protect sensitive information.

The information above, constitutes the generic requirements of the BFW project so it can efficiently reduce food waste while providing a free, secure and transparent solution for both citizens and FSEs. Additionally, the research will decide later in the project for the inclusion of an advertising system, as a result of a full-blown cost and sustainability analysis. The advertising system should be integrated into the mobile app and web platform to provide funding for the food waste reduction initiative and should display relevant and non-intrusive advertisements to customers, which can provide the necessary funding to support the free food waste reduction platform.

Finally, data architecture is also an important aspect in the development of a dApp because it defines how data is stored, organized, and managed within the dApp. A well-designed data architecture helps ensure data integrity, security, scalability, and accessibility, all of which are critical for the success of a dApp. Additionally, a clear and consistent data architecture makes it easier for developers to build and maintain the dApp, and for users to interact with the dApp and its data. Ultimately, a strong data architecture is essential for the long-term viability and success of a dApp. In the case of this project, the proposed data architecture for the BFW dApp has the following dimensions:

Data Storage: The blockchain would be used to securely store data such as food types, food inventory levels, expiration dates, and any transactions related to food waste reduction. This data would be immutable and transparent, ensuring that all stakeholders can have trust in the information stored.

Data Access: The data stored on the blockchain and processed by the backend system would be accessible to all users and FSEs for free, in line with the goal of reducing food waste and making a positive impact on the environment. Access to the data would be controlled through secure authentication and authorization mechanisms to ensure that only authorized users can access the data.

Data Processing: A backend system would process the data stored on the blockchain and generate reports and insights for both citizens and FSEs.

Data Visualization: The mobile app and web platform would provide interactive visualizations of the data to help eating citizens and FSEs understand the impact of their actions on food waste reduction. These visualizations would include graphs, charts, and maps that provide insights into the sources and causes of food waste and highlight the successes of food waste reduction efforts.

Data API: A REST API would be provided to allow mobile app and web platform users to access the data stored on the blockchain and processed by the backend system. This API would enable users to see real-time information about food waste reduction efforts in their area and take action to support these efforts.

3. TOKENIZATION

The first step in the tokenization process is to identify the asset that will be represented by the digital token that is going to be created. In the context of the BFW project, tokenization is used to track and incentivize the reduction of food waste with the cooperation of participating citizens and FSEs. As such, the asset that is represented by the digital token is the surplus food available to the ecosystem everyday by the FSEs. The project's token, which is named BFW, will be created using a smart contract that outlines the terms and conditions of the token, such as its value, ownership, and transferability and will be added in a blockchain. As it was mentioned, for the proof-of-concept phase of the project, the smart contract will be added in Ethereum blockchain that supports token creation and management. So, the project's smart contract will be used to manage the allocation, transfer, and redemption of the BFW tokens. A detailed description of the smart contract building process in Ethereum follows:

– The smart contract will be deployed on the Ethereum blockchain, making it available to all participants in the above-mentioned network. The smart contract will define the rules and conditions for the allocation, transfer, and redemption of tokens.

– Tokens will be issued through the smart contract, and the contract will determine the number of tokens that will be issued and the conditions under which they can be issued to FSEs and citizens, based on their food waste reduction efforts.

– The contract will be monitored by all parties on the Ethereum blockchain, providing transparency and accountability for the tokenization process. For example, citizens and FSEs will be able to view the terms of the contract and the status of token transfers and trades on the blockchain ledger.

– The smart contract will manage the allocation of tokens to eating establishments and users based on predefined conditions.

– The smart contract will validate and execute token transfers and will ensure that tokens are transferred only in accordance with predefined conditions.

– The smart contract will define the conditions under which tokens can be redeemed and the rewards that will be provided.

– The contract could be updated as needed by the BFW consortium, allowing for flexibility and adaptation to changes in the food waste reduction efforts. Contract updates will be validated by the Ethereum network and recorded on the blockchain ledger.

– The code for the smart contract in Ethereum will be designed to be secure and transparent, and to enforce the terms of the agreement for reducing food waste. The contract will be publicly available on the Ethereum blockchain for review and auditing. The code will be free for everyone to use, allowing for widespread adoption and participation in reducing food waste.

The novel ecosystem is built around the BFW token, so the token's smart contract will automatically issue the tokens to participating FSEs and citizens based on their food waste reduction efforts. Tokens will be used as a currency to purchase surplus food or other products from participating business entities. This incentivizes users to participate in food waste reduction and aligns their interests with the goals of the platform. For example, for every kilogram (or portion) of food saved from going to waste, the participating establishment would receive a certain number of BFWs. FSEs can redeem their tokens in exchange for free access or discounts on platform services (e.g. ads), access to analytics and resources and other incentives, or even donate the tokens back to food insecure citizens, directly or through other organizations. This aligns the interests of eating establishments with the goals of the platform, as they will have an interest in reducing food waste to earn more tokens. The same applies to citizens who place an order from their mobile App, to receive meals from participating FSEs.

The BFW tokens will be managed using a blockchain wallet, integrated into the mobile app to provide customers and restaurants with a secure and convenient way to manage their tokens and track food waste reduction. Traditionally, the equivalent of one token would depend on the value assigned to the token by market demand and supply. In that sense, the exact value of one (1) BFW token can only be determined through market dynamics, i.e., the use of the token within the food waste blockchain ecosystem, and the overall success of the food waste reduction efforts. In the beginning, a potential approach could be to set the initial value of one BFW token based on the cost of preventing a certain amount of food waste, for example, 1 BFW token could represent the cost of preventing 1 kilogram of food waste. This value could then fluctuate over time based on market demand and supply. Ultimately, the value of one BFW token would be determined by a combination of factors, including the success of the food waste reduction efforts, the adoption of the food waste blockchain application, and the demand for the token within the ecosystem. The project's initial take on the subject has produced three alternatives, which can also can be used in combination, as follows:

– Mass of food not wasted (kg): Assign a fixed value to each kilogram of food waste prevented, for example, 1 BFW token per kilogram of food waste prevented. This approach would directly reflect the environmental impact of the food waste reduction efforts and incentivize users to reduce as much food waste as possible.

– Food portions: Assign a fixed value to each portion of food waste prevented, for example, 1 BFW token per portion of food waste prevented. This approach would be more accessible for consumers and could be more easily translated into everyday actions.

– Food market value: Assign a fixed value to each dollar of food waste prevented, for example, 1 BFW token per dollar of food waste prevented. This approach would reflect the economic impact of the food waste reduction efforts and incentivize users to reduce food waste in a cost-effective manner.

The blockchain can enforce rules and conditions for token transfer, such as minimum food waste reduction goals, to ensure that the tokens are used effectively to incentivize food waste reduction. The tokenization process within the ecosystem has to be designed meticulously, as the main objective is to keep the platform sustainable, so it's important to carefully consider all revenue sources and how they align with the project's mission against food waste. In the future, project partners will consider all available options in terms of initiating alternative revenue streams, in order to remain sustainable such as: Advertising, Sponsored content, E-commerce, Data licensing etc. The initial token supply and exchange rate depends on several factors such as the purpose of the token, the target audience, market demand, and competition. The purpose of the token will dictate the total supply and the exchange rate. In the project's case, the token will be used as a medium of exchange and as such, its supply should be large enough to meet the demand. The market demand for the token will also play a role in determining the initial supply and exchange rate. The token's exchange rate should be in line with the market demand. Since, BFW will operate in a closed market, the need for the token exchange rate to be in line with similar tokens in the market is absent.

The next step in the project for the research team, is to decide the overall tokenomics of the system and then use financial modeling and market analysis tools to estimate the potential value of the BFW token. The tokenomics will be decided considering the following parameters:

– Token supply: The total number of tokens that will be created and set in circulation.

– Token distribution: The allocation of tokens to various stakeholders, including project partners (in essence the founders and early investors) and community members.

– Token utility: The function of the token within the food waste blockchain application, such as serving as a medium of exchange, reward, or governance mechanism.

– Token economics: The underlying economic model, such as inflationary or deflationary, and how it affects token supply and demand.

– Network effects: The potential for the value of the token to increase as more people use the food waste blockchain application.

– Market demand: The potential demand for the token from various groups, such as food waste reduction organizations, consumers and later investors. Competition as expressed by the presence of other food waste blockchain solutions and how they compare in terms of tokenomics will be evaluated but not considered as decisive factor at this stage of business model development.

4. CONCLUSION

Food waste is a challenge that calls for collaborations, in order to create a more equitable, efficient and sustainable food system. By understanding the multifaceted nature of food waste, technology can be utilized to significantly reduce waste, alleviate hunger and conserve resources. The high level of the BLOCKFOOWASTE project's technology landscape and baseline data, provided in this paper, aligns with the above-mentioned goals, by minimizing food waste, and contributing to the well-being of food insecure individuals in urban areas. The project's system and data architecture aspire to provide a secure, transparent, and scalable solution for reducing food waste from restaurants and other eating establishments. It can enable the members of the community to work together towards a common goal, leveraging the strengths of blockchain, to make a positive impact on the environment. By using tokenization, the project's application can incentivize participating FSEs and citizens to reduce food waste, track their progress, and reward them for their efforts. Blockchain technology offers an anonymous and automated manner to accomplish the food donations from the FSEs, using smart contracts. The use of smart contracts provides a secure way to manage the tokenization processes (token issuance, allocation, transfer, trading, and redemption), allowing for widespread adoption and participation in reducing food waste.

ACKNOWLEDGEMENT

This research has been co-financed by the European Regional Development Fund of the European Union and Greek national funds through the Operational Program Competitiveness, Entrepreneurship and Innovation, under the call RESEARCH – CREATE – INNOVATE (project code: T2EDK-05051).

REFERENCES

Attiq, S., Chau, K. Y., Bashir, S., Habib, M. D., Azam, R. I., & Wong, W. K. (2021). Sustainability of household food waste reduction: A fresh insight on youth's emotional and cognitive behaviors. International Journal of Environmental Research and Public Health, 18(13), 7013.

Munesue, Y., & Masui, T. (2019). The impacts of Japanese food losses and food waste on global natural resources and greenhouse gas emissions. Journal of Industrial Ecology, 23(5), 1196-1210.

Papargyropoulou, E., Steinberger, J. K., Wright, N., Lozano, R., Padfield, R., & Ujang, Z. (2019). Patterns and causes of food waste in the hospitality and food service sector: Food waste prevention insights from Malaysia. Sustainability, 11(21), 6016.

Parfitt, J., Barthel, M., & Macnaughton, S. (2010). Food waste within food supply chains: quantification and potential for change to 2050. Philosophical transactions of the royal society B: biological sciences, 365(1554), 3065-3081.

Strotmann, C., Friedrich, S., Kreyenschmidt, J., Teitscheid, P., & Ritter, G. (2017). Comparing food provided and wasted before and after implementing measures against food waste in three healthcare food service facilities. Sustainability, 9(8), 1409.

UNEP (2021). UNEP food waste index report 2021. Nairobi. Retrieved from: https://www.unep.org/resources/report/unep-food-waste-index-report-2021

Wikström, F., Williams, H., Trischler, J., & Rowe, Z. (2019). The importance of packaging functions for food waste of different products in households. Sustainability, 11(9), 2641.FAO. (2014). Food wastage footprint. Full-cost accounting. Final Report. Retrieved from: https://www.fao.org/3/i3991e/i3991e.pdf

A SMART ENVIRONMENT MONITORING SYSTEM FOR MITIGATING MARINE LITTERING

Dimitra Tzanetou, Stavros T. Ponis, George Plakas, Eleni Aretoulaki and Antonios Kitsantas
School of Mechanical Engineering, National Technical University Athens
Heroon Polytechniou 9, Zografos 15780, Athens, Greece

ABSTRACT

Environmental monitoring and management have received remarkable attention in recent years, since climate change constitutes a ubiquitous issue that needs to be tackled, as soon as possible. Especially, marine plastic pollution has been widely described as tremendously threatening, considering it has deleterious impacts on the planetary boundaries leading to the jeopardization of various ecosystems and subsequently, human life. To that end, the proposed paper demonstrates an innovative technology system based on Smart Environment Monitoring (SEM), which utilizes advanced technologies, such as Unmanned Vehicles and state-of-the-art sensors, in order to collect optical data (images and videos) about the accumulated debris and monitor, measure and analyze essential environmental parameters about the air, water, and noise pollution of the supervised area. The solution's integrated management methodology is structured according to the information collected by the independent system's components, as well as numerous bins equipped with smart scales that are distributed across the coastal region. Lastly, the data processed by the project's subsystems are employed for the development of a Serious Game, in which all involved beaches compete with each other, aiming at the active participation of both citizens and tourists in cleaning and recycling activities, thus reinforcing marine sustainability.

KEYWORDS

Marine Littering, Internet of Things (IoT), Wireless Sensor Networks (WSNs), Unmanned Vehicles (UVs), Smart Environment Monitoring (SEM), Serious Game

1. INTRODUCTION

Anthropogenic-caused marine pollution remains an omnipresent problem that keeps getting deteriorated in the course of time, exacerbating climate change on a noticeable scale and causing adverse consequences on a plethora of ecosystems. More specifically, it has been documented that plastic waste accounts for 60% to 95% of the total marine debris from surface waters to deep sea sediments (Le Guern, 2018), while at the same time only 9% and 12% of plastic waste is recycled and incinerated respectively (OECD, 2022; Greenpeace, 2022). To make matters worse, tiny particles of microplastic have been detected by scientists in human blood, hence sounding the alarm about the detrimental effects of marine plastic pollution on public health (Leslie et al., 2022). Furthermore, the economic damage of the aforementioned catastrophic problem should not be neglected, as it is estimated to rise rapidly throughout the upcoming years, impacting three valuable domains; shipping, fishery/aquaculture and marine tourism (McIlgorm, 2022). In 2011, numerous amounts of waste ended up on the surrounding beaches of a touristic island in South Korea, leading to the significant decrease of the beach users by 50% (Jang et al., 2014). As a result, the coordination and implementation of activities aiming at the organized cleaning of the coastlines, as well as the monitoring and evaluation of their maintenance can negatively influence the overall quality of a seaside country, rendering its effective management a critical issue (IUCN, 2021). Especially, since the sustainable use of oceans, seas and marine resources is considered more urgent than ever for the UN Sustainable Development Goals (SDGs) (United Nations, 2022).

In light of the above, it comes as no surprise that it is now imperative to take preventive countermeasures, utilizing state-of-the-art technologies for managing the plastic waste produced, before it ends up in the marine environment. Particular emphasis is placed on Smart Environment Monitoring (SEM), which enables the optimal detection and measurement of a wide range of environmental indicators and consequently, contributes to the adoption of effective methods that tackle the emerging challenges stemming from the high levels of hazardous pollutants, e.g., CO, O_3, NO_2, SO_2, Persistent Organic Pollutants (POPs), toxic metals, etc. (Ullo & Sinha, 2020; Sarkar et al., 2006). In general, SEM plays a cardinal role in early detecting environmental problems, improving safety and enhancing sustainability, since it provides valuable insights and information about the inspected area (Paessler, 2023). Internet of Things (IoT), Wireless Sensor Networks (WSNs), as well as up-to-date sensors which employ Artificial Intelligence (AI) are described, as the most essential components of the SEM systems, which can lead to marine preservation and successful prevention of environmental disasters (Bhoomika et al., 2016; Ullo & Sinha, 2020).

More particularly, IoT technological solutions reinforced with the appropriate software and sensors could be the most suitable solution for collecting and processing the necessary data, even in inaccessible or dangerous regions. Their distinctive feature is that they have the ability to integrate connectivity mainly in a cloud computing technology network (Cloud-IoT) and analyze all the information gathered, leading to the optimization of the collected data and rendering possible the transmission of real-time data not only to computers, but also to mobile device applications (mobile apps) (Gubbi et al., 2013). Therefore, IoT technologies have emerged as a promising tool, gradually expanding on diverse sectors, such as the environment, industry, medicine, agriculture, transportation, etc. (Kumar et al., 2019) and providing assurance, security, and interoperability (Gatsis & Pappas, 2017).

Even so, for the effective implementation of an IoT application, a wireless solution is needed in order to support all participated devices in the network and ensure that the applications run seamlessly and smoothly. The network of sensors, some of which are equipped with special technologies, e.g., spectrometers and fluorometers, should be deployed in key spots in order to accumulate information regarding specific pollutants, including chemical contaminants, toxic gases, and plastic litter, as well as monitor various alterations in water and air quality (Shin et al., 2021). It is also, worth mentioning that the vast majority of sensors integrated into drones, such as cameras, Lidar (LIght Detection And Ranging) systems, which rely on the emission of pulsed radiation, as well as Dynamic Vision Sensors (DVS) (Gallego et al., 2019; Mostafa, 2018) are responsible for their proper operation and informing the project's supervisor at any time.

Last but not least, nowadays drones are constantly being exploited in applications related to the protection of the environment. Such applications could be the study of climate change, the melting of glaciers, the high concentration of greenhouse gases in the earth's atmosphere or even the biodiversity in different ecosystems, such as rainforests and marine environments. In China, small drones have already been used to measure air pollution (Xuefeng, 2015), while sensors collect air pollution data, generate geographic air quality information and measure substances such as CO, CO_2, O_2, O_3, NO, NO_2, SO_2, NH_3, CH_4, H_2, H_2S, HCl, HCN, PH_3, EtO, Cl_2, but also the particle sizes (PM1, 2.5 and 10). In addition, another environmental implementation could be the real-time monitoring of mountains in order to map them, visualize pollution hotspots and derive results that will predict through algorithms natural disasters, such as landslides and soil flows. Especially, Unmanned Aerial Vehicles could be successfully applied in oceans to study marine organisms, detect oil spills and plastic waste due to their embedded video cameras, which show high-resolution and can take thousands of aerial photographs, over the sea and across coastlines (Koski et al., 2009).

2. THE PROPOSED SOLUTION

The project presented in this paper demonstrates a holistic management methodology for preventing marine littering. The methodology is based on a Smart Environment Monitoring aiming at the extraction of collected data and measurement of various environmental indicators that demonstrate the existing pollution across the beach. The basic infrastructure of the project installed in the beach premises is the Wireless Sensor Network, which collects a plethora of data from multiple sensor categories (imaging, environmental, etc.) leading to their transmission to the project's dedicated cloud platform, for analysis and reporting.

The main component of the integrated system is a pair of Unmanned Vehicles, one Unmanned Aerial Vehicle (UAV) and one Unmanned Surface Vehicle (USV), reinforced with imaging/optical and environmental sensors, audiovisual equipment and wireless communication capability, in order to visually monitor the supervised area. The project's UAV exemplifies a quadricopter configuration, featuring four arms, each equipped with an individual electric motor, thus enabling vertical take-off and landing (VTOL) capabilities, while fostering stabilized flight for supporting multiple air operations. This particular UAV is able to operate with minimal manpower and operational footprint under harsh environmental and electromagnetic conditions, using advanced algorithms tailored to the needs of each mission. On the other hand, the chosen USV is built according to hydrodynamic principles to achieve high speeds and provide increased stability and designed in a way that eliminates water leaks that could potentially harm the inside electronic devices. The vehicles' imaging sensors collect images and videos from the area of interest that are processed at a later stage, as soon as the material is uploaded to the cloud platform. Especially, for the traceability of plastic waste floating on the sea surface or being located underwater, it has been established that optical technology utilizing high-definition video cameras can be exploited for its effective detection. Land- and sea-based station pads are installed across the beach for vehicles' recharging and maintenance, but most importantly for the wireless transmission of the collected field data to the cloud central server. Finally, for the identification and calculation of the litter quantities, image recognition technology is accompanied by Artificial Intelligence algorithms that are applied in order to detect and quantify the plastic debris through the material collected by the imaging sensors and classify them into some main categories, e.g., bags, bottles, cups, etc.

For the safety of the equipment, the Unmanned Vehicles are furthermore reinforced with sensors that identify other vehicles in the aerial and surface/underwater areas, leading to the relentless execution of their mission. Subsequently, the drones are equipped with a LIDAR sensor capable of mapping their surroundings in three dimensions in order to create a contour map of the environment and avoid obstacles. Of course, Global Positioning System (GPS) sensors are also, used for providing and recording accurate information about a point's position (longitude and latitude), altitude, speed, and direction of movement. The drone's design incorporates a digital compass, providing a convenient method of positioning it away from sources of interference that may exist in the drone's range. As a consequence, GPS sensors are embodied in both Unmanned Vehicles, since their type of mission requires accurate location determination. Subsequently, the data about the movements of the vehicles is stored in the recorder's internal memory and is available to the end user for further processing.

Tackling plastic marine littering lies in the epicenter of the project's holistic methodology for beach management, but it is not the only piece, as more attributes are taken into account in order for a beach to be ranked as the highest one. More specifically, air and water quality, as well as, noise levels during visiting hours, are all important aspects in the service provided by a beach to its visitors and are also, connected with marine environment preservation. As a result, ground and underwater environmental sensors are utilized in order to collect relevant data from the coastal area. These sensors constitute another key component of the integrated solution, as they provide valuable data about the air and underwater quality of the inspected region, by monitoring and analyzing various environmental parameters, including temperature, humidity, atmospheric pressure, concentration of CO_2, CO, O_2, CH_4, NH_3, O_3, etc. Lastly, the project utilizes noise level sensors, through which the citizens can be informed of the noise levels of any beach during any hour of the day and choose the most suitable one. The above-mentioned environmental sensors connected to the project's WSN contribute to the documentation of any environmental measurement and provide both citizens and tourists with significant information about the cleaning status of the beach.

The data collected by the imaging sensors of the drones is the most essential metric for the project's effort to develop its final product, i.e., a competitive Serious Game, aiming at the adoption of beach cleaning methods and supporting citizens' behavioral change. Nonetheless, the changes in the game's leaderboards due to the efforts of the citizens will not be immediately visible through the data analyzed by the imaging sensors, as the change of attitude is a process that needs time and scalability. So, in order to amplify citizens' engagement in preserving the marine ecosystem, the project's methodology includes also a subsystem quantifying the citizens' efforts for proper waste disposal. More specifically, smart scales are placed under every bin which lies on the beach area, both under regular and recycling bins, which measure in real-time the weight of the waste and transmit their data to the cloud platform, through the project's WSN. The enhanced bins are distributed across the coastline, upgrading the region's waste management system into an innovative solution, that not only quantifies the total waste that is disposed by beach visitors in bins, but also quantifies the ratio of recyclables to regular waste, thus incentivizing recycling on a great scale.

Consequently, all data collected by Unmanned Vehicles, environmental sensors and bins are analyzed in the project's cloud platform. The data extracted from the sensor network is filtered and evaluated through a suite of software tools and Machine Learning algorithms, which is further processed and analyzed. Lastly, the presented project implements a beach networking platform where two-way communication with citizens takes place through an easy-to-use gamified mobile application. The platform processes the results of each beach and is responsible for informing citizens, through the mobile application and solar powered screens installed on each beach, about the ranking of the beaches participating in the ecosystem, based on their cleaning progress and total clean status. A schematic of the aforementioned management system is demonstrated in Figure 1:

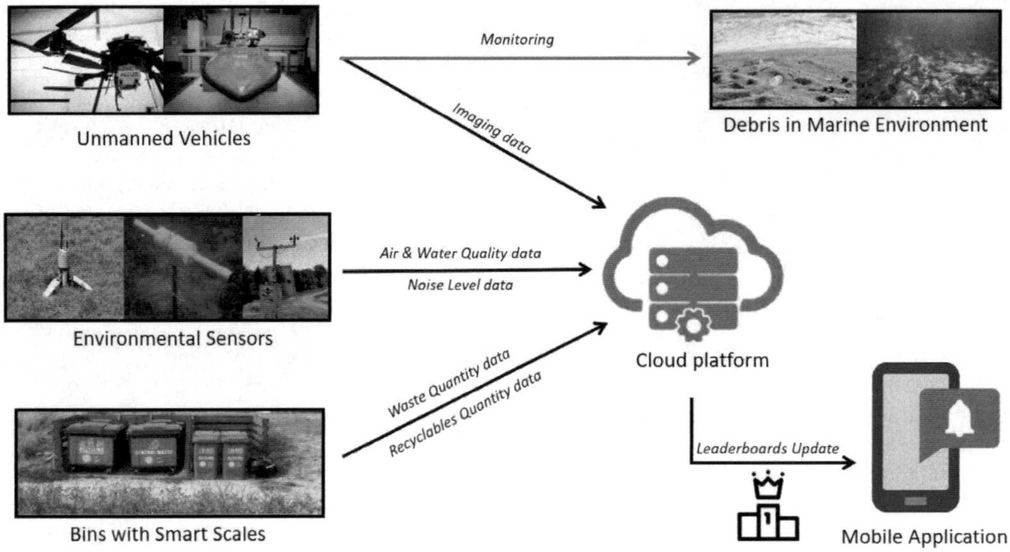

Figure 1. Data Collection

After data analysis, the results are visualized in the project's mobile application and are available for anyone to get informed and take the appropriate actions. The mobile application is actually the monitoring mechanism of the Serious Game that takes place on the beach every day. Through the application, the beach visitors can browse through multiple leaderboards and see the metrics for every participating beach. Some of the leaderboards are simple based on one or two metrics (e.g., Percentage of Beach Covered by Waste leaderboard, Air Quality leaderboard, Noise Level leaderboard, Total Waste leaderboard, Recycling Ratio leaderboard, etc.), but the main leaderboard contains all the metrics and is heavily dependent on the imaging data from the Unmanned Vehicles, as this is exactly the project's ultimate goal, preserving the beach as clean as possible.

The research team is currently in the phase of developing the final technical design of all the subsystems analyzed in this paper, and at the same time the authors try to identify ways for design improvements about the project's Serious Game. The research team's future objective is to produce a fully customized and pilot tested Proof of Concept of the integrated solution.

3. CONCLUSION

The research project outlined in this paper introduces a novel beach management methodology through the implementation of Smart Environment Monitoring, and by incorporating cutting-edge technologies, it aims to progressively address the issue of marine littering. Comprising two categories of Unmanned Vehicles enhanced with advanced optical and environmental sensors, the integrated solution acquires visual data concerning shoreline debris and surface/underwater waste. Simultaneously, it monitors vital environmental indicators to assess the coastal region's air and water quality. In order to further engage the citizens, the project employs dedicated bins across the beach, equipped with weight sensors to accurately quantify the disposed waste. The processed information from all the project elements is harnessed to develop an engaging Serious Game. This innovative game encourages both local residents and tourists to actively participate in clean-up and recycling endeavors and through the efforts of the integrated solution, the project makes significant strides in combatting marine pollution, reinforcing sustainable practices, as well as fostering circular economy habits.

ACKNOWLEDGEMENT

This research has been co-financed by the European Regional Development Fund of the European Union and Greek national funds through the Operational Program Competitiveness, Entrepreneurship and Innovation, under the call RESEARCH – CREATE – INNOVATE (project code: T2EDK-03478)

REFERENCES

Bhoomika, K. N., Deepa, C., Rashmi, R. K., & Srinivasa, R. (2016). Internet of things for environmental monitoring. Int. J. Adv. Netw. Appl, 497-501.

Gallego, E., Folch, J., Teixidor, P., Roca, F. J., & Perales, J. F. (2019). Outdoor air monitoring: Performance evaluation of a gas sensor to assess episodic nuisance/odorous events using active multi-sorbent bed tube sampling coupled to TD-GC/MS analysis. Science of the total environment, 694, 133752.

Gatsis, K., & Pappas, G. J. (2017, April). Wireless control for the IOT: Power, spectrum, and security challenges. In Proceedings of the Second International Conference on Internet-of-Things Design and Implementation (pp. 341-342).

Greenpeace, 2022. Why burning plastic won't solve the plastic crisis. Retrieved from: https://www.greenpeace.org.uk/news/incineration-burning-plastic-crisis/

Gubbi, J., Buyya, R., Marusic, S., & Palaniswami, M. (2013). Internet of Things (IoT): A vision, architectural elements, and future directions. Future generation computer systems, 29(7), 1645-1660.

IUCN, 2021. Marine plastic pollution. Retrieved from: https://www.iucn.org/resources/issues-brief/marine-plastic-pollution

Jang, Y. C., Hong, S., Lee, J., Lee, M. J., & Shim, W. J. (2014). Estimation of lost tourism revenue in Geoje Island from the 2011 marine debris pollution event in South Korea. Marine pollution bulletin, 81(1), 49-54.

Koski, W. R., Abgrall, P., & Yazvenko, S. B. (2009). A review and inventory of unmanned aerial systems for detection and monitoring of key biological resources and physical parameters affecting marine life during offshore exploration and production activities. IWC paper SC/61 E, 9.

Kumar, S., Tiwari, P., & Zymbler, M. (2019). Internet of Things is a revolutionary approach for future technology enhancement: a review. Journal of Big data, 6(1), 1-21.

Le Guern, C. (2018). When the mermaids cry: the great plastic tide. Santa Anguila Foundation.

Leslie, H. A., Van Velzen, M. J., Brandsma, S. H., Vethaak, A. D., Garcia-Vallejo, J. J., & Lamoree, M. H. (2022). Discovery and quantification of plastic particle pollution in human blood. Environment international, 163, 107199.

McIlgorm, A., Raubenheimer, K., McIlgorm, D. E., & Nichols, R. (2022). The cost of marine litter damage to the global marine economy: Insights from the Asia-Pacific into prevention and the cost of inaction. Marine Pollution Bulletin, 174, 113167.

Mostafa, M., Zahran, S., Moussa, A., El-Sheimy, N., & Sesay, A. (2018). Radar and visual odometry integrated system aided navigation for UAVS in GNSS denied environment. Sensors, 18(9), 2776.

OECD, 2022. Plastic pollution is growing relentlessly as waste management and recycling fall short. Retrieved from: https://www.oecd.org/environment/plastic-pollution-is-growing-relentlessly-as-waste-management-and-recycling-fall-short.htm

Paessler, The monitoring experts. Smart Environmental Monitoring, 2023. Retrieved from: https://www.paessler.com/it-explained/smart-environmental-monitoring

Sarkar, A., Ray, D., Shrivastava, A. N., & Sarker, S. (2006). Molecular biomarkers: their significance and application in marine pollution monitoring. Ecotoxicology, 15, 333-340.

Shin, Y. H., Gutierrez-Wing, M. T., & Choi, J. W. (2021). Recent progress in portable fluorescence sensors. Journal of The Electrochemical Society, 168(1), 017502.

Ullo, S. L., & Sinha, G. R. (2020). Advances in smart environment monitoring systems using IoT and sensors. Sensors, 20(11), 3113.

United Nations, 2022. Conserve and sustainably use the oceans, seas and marine resources for sustainable development. Retrieved from: https://sdgs.un.org/goals/goal14

Xuefeng Zhang, 2015. China uses drones to monitor pollution problem from above. Retrieved from: https://www.thethirdpole.net/en/pollution/china-uses-drones-to-monitor-pollution-problem-from-above/

PIONEERING WOMEN IN COMPUTING: A CULTURAL WEBSITE BASED ON INFORMATION ARCHITECTURE

Lina García-Cabrera[1], José-María Serrano[1] and Irene Pedrosa-García[2]
[1]*Dpt. Computer Science, University of Jaén*
Edificio A3 - Campus Las Lagunillas, 23071, Jaén, Spain
[2]*El Valle High School, Junta de Andalucía*
Carr. de Madrid, 2, 23009, Jaén, Spain

ABSTRACT

In an effort to acknowledge the eminent role of a number of relevant women, pioneers in the field of Computer Science, an exposition was developed as part of a cultural project hosted by the University of Jaen (Spain). In order to establish a permanent, virtual, version of this exhibition, a website has been created, as a way to allow visitors to know more about these pioneers, about their life and history, and their many contributions to the field. In addition, the site serves as a record of all events related to the exhibition, as well as multimedia galleries in order to improve the experience. In this work, we provide an analysis about the development of this site, which features information architecture guidelines, as well as accessibility and usability issues.

KEYWORDS

Accessibility, Usability, Information Architecture, Gender Gap, Female Computer Pioneers

1. INTRODUCTION

In recent decades, a noticeable gender gap has persisted in computer-related fields, often dominated by men. Only in recent years have studies (Misa, 2011) acknowledged the significance of women in computer science, aiming to promote girls' involvement in computer engineering careers. "Pioneering Women in Computing Science" ("Pioneras Informáticas" in Spanish) (García-Cabrera et al., 2021, 2023), led by the University of Jaén (Spain), is a cultural initiative dedicated to bridging this gender gap in Computer Science. The project takes the form of a traveling exhibition titled "Pioneering Women Computer Scientists: Recognizing the Contributions of Women in Computer Engineering." This exhibition invites visitors to explore the lives of several influential 20th-century women who made crucial contributions to Computer Science. For each of these Computer Pioneers, the project has created expressive comic-style posters. These posters succinctly and engagingly highlight their most notable contributions to Computer Science, share anecdotes, motivational quotes, and significant moments from their lives, including the social challenges they faced. Schools, institutes, and educational institutions can request this exhibition. Additionally, a promotional video (UJA, 2022) has been developed to support the exhibition's objectives and the broader cultural project.

In order to promote this physical exhibition, support it and progressively expand it with more educational and informative content, a website was also developed. In addition, this website serves as a permanent, virtual exhibition, and it keeps the project alive. The website can be viewed also as a historical log of all the events that have taken place related to the cultural project: the original exhibition at the University of Jaén, roundtables and conferences, external exhibitions in other educational institutions, etc. Our objective is also to gradually incorporate more protagonists and additional, richer contents to offer and maintain a digital museum about pioneering women computer scientists.

Information architecture (IA) is a critical aspect in the designing of a website that significantly impacts its usability, user experience, and overall success (Gullikson et al., 1999, Hasegawa, 2021). In particular:

- It organizes content, ensuring it to be easily found and hence reducing user frustration.
- It establishes consistent navigation patterns, making it easier for users to browse the site.
- It designs user flow and journeys, helping users to efficiently accomplish their goals.

- It prevents content overload, avoiding overwhelming users with too much information.
- It ensures scalability, making it easier to manage and maintain the website as it grows.
- It considers accessibility, ensuring the site is usable by people with disabilities.
- It improves conversion rates, as an intuitive IA leads to better user engagement and interaction.
- It effectively provides an intuitive user experience, meeting user needs and expectations.

In cultural and promotional websites, IA plays a significant role to present information in a clear, engaging, and accessible manner, the design of these websites must pay attention to:

- Categorization and Organization: IA assists in organizing content into logical categories, simplifying navigation and enabling visitors to explore cultural information and events efficiently. Grouping related content enhances user experience.
- Storytelling and Narrative: Cultural websites often feature captivating stories about history, society, biographies, or artistic endeavors. Effective IA structures and presents these narratives coherently, creating a seamless flow that captivates and engages visitors.
- Navigation: A clear and logical navigation structure is essential. IA helps users understand the website's hierarchy, improving usability. A well-structured IA reduces frustration and encourages users to explore more content through links and internal references.
- Emphasizing Key Events: IA can highlight featured events or cultural exhibits to ensure they receive appropriate attention. This may involve prominent placement on the homepage or a dedicated section for upcoming events.
- Multilingual and Multicultural Considerations: For global audiences, IA should consider multilingual and multicultural aspects. Providing clear navigation in multiple languages and localized content options is essential for success.
- Easy Access to Practical Information: Cultural websites often include practical details like event schedules, venue locations, and contact information. A well-structured IA ensures easy access to such information, helping visitors plan their participation effectively.
- Visual Hierarchy and Design: IA and design work together. Establishing a clear visual hierarchy through typography, colors, and layout choices helps users quickly identify important information or promotional offers on the website.
- Integration of Multimedia Content: Cultural websites frequently incorporate multimedia content, such as images, videos, and audio recordings, to convey cultural experiences. IA ensures these media elements are appropriately placed, enhancing storytelling and engagement.
- Performance and Accessibility: A well-structured IA contributes to overall website performance and accessibility. It optimizes load times and adheres to accessibility standards, ensuring that the website is usable by all users, including those with disabilities.

In this contribution, we present how the design of the Computer Pioneers website has been approached with all these considerations in mind. The aim is to share this experience so that it can serve as a pattern or guide when designing the IA of cultural and educational information spaces. Section 2 describes the process followed for the design of the information architecture. In section 3 interaction, style and accessible issues are discussed. Finally, conclusions and future tasks can be found in section 4.

2. DESIGNING AN USABLE CULTURAL & PROMOTIONAL WEBSITE

The website aims to close the gender gap in Computer Science by highlighting the inspiring journeys of pioneering women who overcame obstacles to make substantial contributions to the field. Its target audience encompasses a wide range of individuals, notably schools and colleges. To fulfill its goals, the website must provide captivating, narrative-style content to engage visitors effectively. It should also incorporate multimedia elements related to the featured historical figures and include clear call-to-action design elements.

2.1 Technologies Involved in the Development of the Website

A headless architecture was considered for the development and implementation of the website. The frontend has been decoupled from the backend, allowing the use of different technologies and programming languages for each part, content management flexibility, improved performance, scalability and enhanced security.

In the internal layer, an SQLite database stores and maintains all the necessary information about the website. For the backend section, the headless Strapi CMS was considered. It can be used along with SQLite to obtain efficient results in the management of the website. ReactJS Javascript library has been used for the frontend development. Finally, Nginx has offered an efficient and secure solution as a web server.

2.2 Structured Contents: Female Computer Pioneers and Events

The core contents of our website are obvious: the story of these female computer pioneers and the events log around the traveling exhibition. Both types of contents are structured and ready to be increased over time, with new content-page for each new pioneer and event. According to this, gallery pages and formal ways to organize and filter these information spaces are needed (section 2.3). All the documentation and research project is described in depth in (García-Cabrera et al., 2021). Maintaining attention about a historical figure on a webpage requires a well-crafted approach that must combine engaging content, an appealing design, and interactive elements. Previously, fixed layouts need to be determined regarding the essentials and relevant contents about each computer pioneers:

- Short formal description. Her name, place of birth, birth-death dates.
- In two sentences. A couple of key phrases or sentences that define or characterize their most significant contributions.
- Summary: A brief summary of who they are and what they have done.
- Life. A description of their LIFE in a brief list of chronologically ordered milestones: date of birth, training, relevant social events…
- Achievements. An enumeration of contributions both in the field of Computer Science and social, especially if they have contributed to break the gender gap, chronologically ordered.
- Acknowledgements. A list of awards and recognitions related to their contributions.
- Quotes. A series of inspirational quotes or anecdotes that reflect personal or challenging circumstances they had to deal with according to their gender.
- Documentary Sources. Consulted documents, websites, books, papers, etc.
- Multimedia Material. Embedded videos or interactive content related to the female CS pioneer.

The events section serves a dual purpose: to inform visitors about the locations and details of the traveling exhibition and to engage schools and institutes, fostering their involvement in the project. This section provides simplified information, including event type, hosting institution and location, event description, and event photos (https://pionerasinformaticas.ujaen.es/en/events/exposicion-colegio-generalcastanos-bailen-en).

Furthermore, a glossary has been integrated as a third structured content component. It's designed to assist exhibition visitors, especially those less familiar with computer science terminology, in comprehending and appreciating the achievements of these pioneering women in computing. The glossary includes CS and technical terms sorted alphabetically, making them searchable by keyword or filterable by classification tags. Additionally, whenever these terms appear in website texts, they are linked to the glossary for easy reference.

2.3 Multimedia Galleries Pages

To facilitate access, search and filtering of computer pioneers and events, two gallery pages have been included. Women pioneers gallery (https://pionerasinformaticas.ujaen.es/en/computer-women-pioneers) displays each pioneer as a multimedia element with her portrait, name, place of birth, birth-death date. The gallery includes accurate sorting and filtering schemes such as A-Z index, chronological timeline and other ambiguous ones like research or career fields (software engineering, game design, artificial intelligence, and so on), nationalities, awards and companies (https://pionerasinformaticas.ujaen.es/en/events#all-events). Events gallery includes the same accurate sorting and filtering schemes and only one ambiguous: type of event.

2.4 Unstructured Contents

To ensure the success of the website it is vital to incorporate other unstructured contents but with a clear layout and visual hierarchy:

- Website and sections purpose. Texts that explain "what is the website about" in the home page (https://pionerasinformaticas.ujaen.es/en/) and the aim of each section of the website (giant drop-down menu).
- All about and How to. Texts with detailed description of the material that is part of the traveling exhibition, how to order it (events section).
- About us: Information about what is the Female Computer Pioneers cultural project, what has been its trajectory (https://pionerasinformaticas.ujaen.es/en/about-us), the work team in charge of the project and the institutions that support us (https://pionerasinformaticas.ujaen.es/en/team-sponsors), the press coverage, contact information in order to offer transparency and generate trust.
- Branding and Identity: The webpage incorporates branding elements like logos, taglines, or brand colors to reinforce the identity of the website or organization.

3. INTERACTION, STYLE, AND ACCESSIBILITY ISSUES

The preliminary study of the IA has made it possible to design a user-friendly navigation with well-organized content, a coherent hierarchy of sections/subsections, intuitive tags and usable filters. In order to attract the attention of the user, it is designed with several call-to-action elements such as:

- Buttons (https://pionerasinformaticas.ujaen.es/en/events) to directly access the computer pioneers, request the exhibition, request the visitor's opinion, etc.
- Cards to show the most relevant data of the computer pioneer and the event (https://pionerasinformaticas.ujaen.es/en/computer-women-pioneers/mary-kenneth-keller-en).
- Carousel-type elements to show videos, timeline, the Life-Achievements-Acknowledgement-Quotes of the computer pioneer.
- Icons that allow to show and/or hide elements like texts and filters (https://pionerasinformaticas.ujaen.es/en/computer-women-pioneers).

Some key style elements have been adopted that positively influence the usability of a web site:

- Typography: clear and legible typography, easy to read fonts have been chosen, with appropriate font sizes for the different sections of the website and with sufficient contrast between text and background colors to improve readability.
- White space (negative space): Proper use of white space helps create a clean, uncluttered design, making it easier for users to focus on the content.
- Color Scheme: A simple, attractive color scheme has been used that complements the brand identity.
- Consistent design elements: Buttons, call-to-action, links, headers, footers and navigation have a consistent design that promotes familiarity and helps users to navigate the site in an easier way.
- Navigation and Menus: Intuitive and easy-to-use navigation menus have been designed. Clear, descriptive labels for menu items and a navigation bar that remains visible as users scroll down the page (sticky navigation) have been considered.

In addition, different aspects have been taken into account with respect to the accessibility of the website, with the idea of favoring a suitable navigation from any type of device, and, at the same time, enriching the experience of all types of visitors:

- The website implements a responsive design, so that the content is visually attractive regardless of the screen size and resolution of the device from which it is accessed.
- In order to establish the different elements of the web interface, certain guidelines have been followed regarding the appropriate use and combination of color. For example, the interface supports both day and night modes for viewing.
- Break down the content into short paragraphs and use bullet points to present key facts or highlights. This makes the content more scannable and accessible.
- The website is hosted within the domain of the University of Jaén. This fact has made it possible to make use of some plugins as is the case of webReader (https://www.readspeaker.com/), which has been embedded in the site, making it accessible for visually impaired visitors.
- The content of the site is currently available in different languages (Spanish, English, French, German, Portuguese, Italian...), with the possibility of adding new languages in the future.

Currently, we keep working to make all multimedia material, like images and videos, accessible. In particular, we intend to develop an online version of the pioneers' posters accessible by offering audio-text descriptions. Actually, the goal is more ambitious. The aim is to offer the posters of the pioneers in video format in order to narrate their stories to make the content more engaging and relatable to the audience. The idea is to develop subtitled videos, audio-narrated and with transcriptions describing the poster and the pioneer's panels. For now, only a very preliminary prototype is offered for Computer Pioneer Chieko Asakawa (https://pionerasinformaticas.ujaen.es/en/computer-women-pioneers/chieko-asakawa-en).

4. CONCLUSION AND FUTURE TASKS

In this work, we have presented our proposal for the Female Computer Pioneers website. It is an usable website because it is based on the principles of IA: core-structured content has been identified, it offers a limited upper hierarchy that offers the really relevant options for the users, it has organized the content in a progressive way, trying to catch the audience's attention, it offers multiple criteria for sorting and filtering information, it has designed a rich and contextualized navigation and it is prepared to grow in content while keeping it well-structured and organized.

Our future plans include the maintaining of the website, while we develop and upload new contents for a new batch of Female Computer Pioneers. As the main objective of the website is to keep alive the exhibition, within these new contents we plan to develop interactive and playable versions of the exhibition posters.

ACKNOWLEDGEMENT

The present work has been sponsored by the Vice-Rector's Office for Projection of Culture and Sports (University of Jaén, Spain). Call for Cultural Projects 2020-22.

REFERENCES

García-Cabrera, L. Pedrosa-García I. & Serrano J.M., 2021. Posters about Women Pioneers in Computer Science to Break the Gender Gap: A Preliminary Method *International Conference on Computational Science and Computational Intelligence (CSCI)*, Las Vegas, NV, USA, pp. 1117-1120, doi: 10.1109/CSCI54926.2021.00072.

García-Cabrera, L., Pedrosa-García, I., & Serrano, J. M., 2023. An Experience in Breaking the Gender Gap in Computer Science by means of Comic Panels about Female Pioneers. In *INTED2023 Proceedings* IATED, Valencia, SPAIN, pp. 3521-3526. doi: 10.21125/inted.2023.0953

Gullikson, S., Blades, R., Bragdon, M., McKibbon, S., Sparling, M., & Toms, E. G. (1999). The impact of information architecture on academic web site usability. *The Electronic Library*, 17(5), 293-304.

Hasegawa, A., 2021. *Information Architecture Do* (道). In: Resmini, A., Rice, S.A., Irizarry, B. (eds) Advances in Information Architecture. Human–Computer Interaction Series. Springer, Cham. https://doi.org/10.1007/978-3-030-63205-2_15.

Misa, T.J. (ed.) (2011). Gender codes: Why women are leaving computing. John Wiley & Sons.

UJA (University of Jaén) (2022) Pioneras informáticas. Reconociendo las aportaciones de la mujer en la Ingeniería Informática, YouTube. Available at: https://www.youtube.com/watch?v=qcxd580XJdE

AUGMENTED REALITY AS A SUPPORT FOR THE TEACHING-LEARNING PROCESS IN THE SUBJECT OF ENTERPRISE ARCHITECTURE

Nelson Salgado-Reyes, Suyana Arcos-Villagomez and Susana Masapanta-Carrión
Pontificia Universidad Católica del Ecuador
12 de octubre 1076, Quito, Ecuador

ABSTRACT

Augmented reality represents an innovative technological tool that greatly contributes to the teaching-learning process of students at any educational level. In this context, the student can discover the real environment "augmented" by certain virtual elements. The primary focus of the research is focused on the evaluation of a proposal based on augmented reality in order to support the teaching-learning of the business architecture subject in the information systems career taught at the Pontifical Catholic University of Ecuador (PUCE). In this context, a quasi-experimental study was carried out with two independent groups, taken as control and experimental groups with 30 students each. In the experimental group, the subjects of the subject were taught according to the methodological strategy designed, while in the control group the classes were carried out as usual. During the different phases of the investigative process, two instruments were applied; on the one hand, a knowledge test in both groups in post-test and, on the other hand, a survey applied to the experimental group to evaluate the satisfaction of the students on the proposed methodological strategy.

KEYWORDS

Augmented Reality, Methodological Strategy

1. INTRODUCTION

In the era of digital technology, emerging technologies are reshaping education, revolutionizing teaching and learning across various fields, and offering new avenues to enhance learning experiences (Cabero J. &., 2019). Technology, when used in education at all levels, should cater to students' learning needs while always prioritizing knowledge acquisition as the core of educational activities, rather than technology itself. Information and communication technologies (ICT), as suggested by Lopes, Sartor, Pozzebon, and Ferenhof (2019), serve to create innovative pedagogical strategies in the educational domain. Aznar, Romero, and Rodríguez (2018) further emphasize that technology can foster stronger connections between students and their subjects, contingent upon the perspectives of both educators and students. While integrating technological innovations into the classroom poses challenges for teachers, it provides valuable learning opportunities for students. Nonetheless, teachers continually face the challenge of innovating through technology to meet students' needs and implement novel pedagogical strategies (Cabero, García, Cabero, and García, 2016; Zamora, 2018).

One particularly promising technology is Augmented Reality (AR), which merges the real world with virtual elements to create interactive and immersive learning experiences, thereby enhancing the learning process. This concept involves the integration of computer-generated data onto real-world objects or locations and offers three primary features: the fusion of the real and virtual, real-time interactivity, and 3D representation (Abero, Fernández, & Marín, 2017; De la Horra, 2017).

Numerous authors highlight the advantages of augmented reality in the teaching-learning process, stimulating kinesthetic learning, aiding in the comprehension of abstract phenomena, and facilitating the inspection of three-dimensional objects and educational materials from multiple perspectives (Blázquez, 2017; Cabero, Vásquez, & López, 2018; Ierache, et al., 2014). Augmented reality also enhances students' prior knowledge, increasing engagement in classes (Aguirre, García, Guevara, & Erazo-Álvarez, 2020; Astudillo, 2019; Saltan, 2017). In the context of Business Architecture, which involves designing and managing organizational structures, Augmented Reality has emerged as a valuable tool, enriching the teaching-learning process and offering numerous benefits. Augmented Reality enables students to explore and manipulate business models in three dimensions, providing a practical and visual understanding of theoretical concepts (Aznar, Romero, & Rodríguez, 2018; Barroso, Cabero Almenara, Leiva, López, & Moreno, 2017). Students can use devices like tablets or headsets to interact with virtual business models, visualizing their structures and relationships, leading to a deeper understanding of Enterprise Architecture concepts that can be applied in real-life situations.

Furthermore, Augmented Reality allows the simulation of complex business scenarios, enabling students to apply their knowledge and skills in a controlled virtual environment (Mesquida & Pérez, 2017; Ruiz, Jiménez, & Barón, 2018). This fosters critical thinking, problem-solving skills, and informed decision-making, preparing students to face real-world business challenges effectively.

2. MATERIALS AND METHODS

2.1 Design of the Investigation

In a quasi-experimental study, we divided participants into two groups: a control group and an experimental group, comprising students from the Information Systems program at the Pontifical Catholic University of Ecuador (PUCE) who were studying enterprise architecture. Initially, students explored the fundamentals of Enterprise Architecture (EA) and Augmented Reality (AR), understanding their applications in business and education, setting course objectives, and introducing fundamental EA concepts.

The study then shifted focus towards an extensive exploration of AR technologies, covering aspects like tracking, markers, and spatial mapping. Practical workshops provided hands-on experience in AR development, enhancing technical skills for interactive content creation. Simultaneously, we delved into core Enterprise Architecture concepts, including components, architectural layers, and methodologies like TOGAF and Zachman.

Midway through the course, students engaged in pedagogical design for AR content, learning to create engaging educational experiences and collaboratively designing AR modules for teaching Enterprise Architecture. Group presentations enabled them to showcase their designs and receive feedback from peers and instructors.

A pivotal phase revolved around the discussion of AR implementation in education. This phase examined seamless integration strategies, technical aspects, and incorporated insights from experienced guest speakers in AR education implementation. As the course concluded, students refined and presented their AR modules, effectively communicating Enterprise Architecture concepts and showcasing active learning. The final assessment, whether it be an exam or a project, evaluated their understanding and application of EA and AR.

In summary, this traditional approach seamlessly merges theory and practical application, providing a comprehensive understanding of Enterprise Architecture and Augmented Reality. Through interactive tasks, real-world examples, and AR content creation, students developed technical and pedagogical skills, preparing them for the effective application of AR in both educational and business contexts. In the reference group, classes followed a conventional teaching approach, whereas the experimental group implemented activities using a methodological strategy grounded in augmented reality. At the conclusion of the course, a post-assessment was administered to both groups to measure the outcomes of the teaching-learning process.

2.2 Participants

The participating sample consisted of two courses of 30 students each from the subject of business architecture of the Information Systems career in the 7th semester.

Table 1. Description of the groups formed

Grups	men		women		Total	
Control	23	80,0%	7	20,0%	30	100,0%
Experimental	21	70,0%	9	30,0%	30	100,0%

As can be seen in Table 1, the absolute frequency of students in the experimental group is similar to those in the control group, with a predominance of men over women; Therefore, the groups are heterogeneous in their composition with respect to sex.

2.3 Instruments

During the investigation two instruments were applied; In the first stage, a knowledge test consisting of 10 questions was applied to each group. Then, in a second stage, a survey consisting of 7 questions was applied to the experimental group that allowed obtaining information about the satisfaction of the students about the use of augmented reality in business architecture classes during the teaching-learning process. Accordingly, "the test and the survey" were taken as data collection techniques.

Knowledge assessment test. A questionnaire with 10 qualitative questions was elaborated and applied; with a maximum score of 10 points and an individual score of 1 point. The test was subjected to a content validity analysis, where experts intervene, in which a concordance coefficient of 0.87 was obtained, which is considered acceptable when it is above 0.8.

On the other hand, the reliability of the instrument was verified through Cronbach's alpha internal concordance coefficient, for which a value of 0.826 was obtained, which implies a reliable result.

Satisfaction instrument of the methodological strategy. A survey was developed and applied that allowed measuring the satisfaction of the methodological strategy in the teaching-learning process, which consisted of 7 items with an ordinal qualitative scale. The instrument was validated through the criteria of experts whose concordance coefficient was 0.88 and the reliability verified with the calculation of Cronbach's alpha internal concordance coefficient, where a value of 0.856 was obtained.

2.4 Data Analysis

The data collected through the applied instruments was inputted into SPSS v25, a statistical software, for analysis. Initially, the data underwent purification, including the identification and handling of atypical and missing values. Subsequently, a descriptive analysis was conducted on all items using central tendency statistics such as the mean and median, as well as variability statistics such as the standard deviation.

To compare the potential differences between the scores obtained in the post-test knowledge assessment of the control and experimental groups, the Mann-Whitney U non-parametric test for independent samples was employed. This choice was made due to the violation of assumptions required for the application of parametric tests.

3. PROPOSAL

Next, the proposed methodological strategy elaborated with the use of augmented reality for the subject of business architecture for the Information Systems career of the Pontifical Catholic University of Ecuador (PUCE) is presented. The design is based on constructivist and connectionist theories as a methodological approach to develop the teaching-learning process.

Below are the six activities that are part of the proposal and use augmented reality technology as a tool to support the educational process.

Methodological strategy proposal for the subject of business architecture:

1. **Theoretical introduction.** The class begins with a theoretical explanation of some important concepts of enterprise architecture and its importance in a business environment. It provides students with a general description of the elements related to the vision of companies, technology, management of the organizational structure and processes. It also highlights how enterprise architecture provides a comprehensive framework for improving organization and business performance.

2. **Exploration of business models in augmented reality**. The student group is divided into several sub-groups which are provided with a tablet device or augmented reality headset. Students can explore and manipulate 3D business models through an application, visualizing the structure of different companies, as well as the interrelationship of their components.

3. Analysis and group discussion. After the exploration and interaction of the students with the business models through augmented reality, a group analysis and discussion session is organized. This activity encourages the active participation of the students, where they share observations, questions and reflections on the different models displayed. In addition, this stimulates the debate and the perspectives of the sub-groups, enriching the collective understanding.

4. Business simulations. Business simulations are designed using augmented reality. For this, scenarios are created where students simulate the creation of a company, identify and solve organizational processes, design growth strategies, assume roles in the organization and make decisions in a controlled virtual environment. This encourages critical thinking.

5. Resolution of business problems. Activities are developed where students solve problems related to reorganization, efficiency using augmented reality

6. Assessment based on enterprise architecture. Augmented reality elements are used to assess student learning. This allows for a hands-on assessment of your enterprise architecture knowledge and skills.

4. RESULTS

The results were analyzed in two dimensions, on the one hand, the evaluation of the effectiveness of the proposal through the non-parametric Mann-Whitney U test and, on the other hand, the results of the applied satisfaction survey.

Results of the test in the post-test

Next, graph 1 presents the results obtained in the applied knowledge test, which was measured at 0.5 points for each question in a total of 20 items.

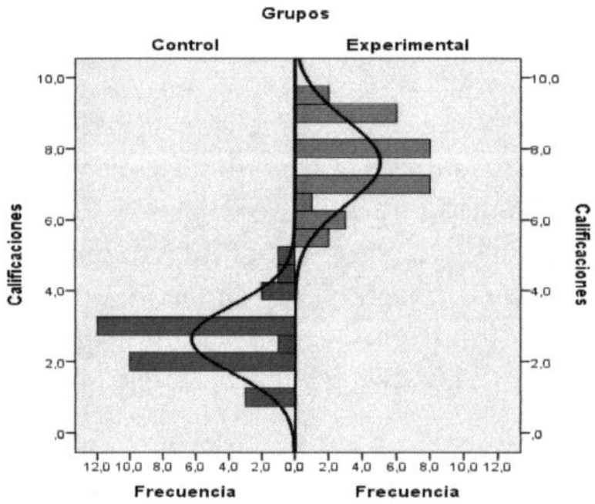

Graph 1. Histogram of the scores obtained in the test in both groups

As shown, in the control group scores between 1 and 4.5 points were obtained, with scores between 2 and 3 prevailing; with a mean of 2.63 and a standard deviation of 0.956. These results show shortcomings in learning when using a traditional methodology in the business architecture subject since the scores are low. According to the histogram, the grades are quite homogeneous, not finding students who reach half of the total grade.

On the other hand, the results obtained in the experimental group, which received the classes under the methodological strategy based on augmented reality, were generally good. In this sense, scores between 5.5 and 9.5 points were obtained, with an arithmetic mean of 7.62 and a standard deviation of 1.1867.

Finally, to test whether there were significant differences in both groups, the non-parametric Mann-Whitney U test for independent samples was used; whose results can be seen in graph 2.

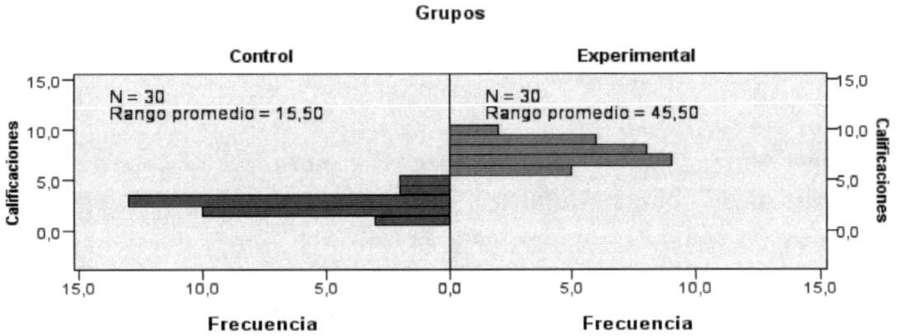

N total	60
U de Mann-Whitney	900,000
W de Wilcoxon	1.365,000
Estadístico de prueba	900,000
Error estándar	67,011
Estadístico de prueba estandarizado	6,715
Significación asintótica (prueba bilateral)	,000

Graph 2. Mann-Whitney U test results

As observed, the bilateral asymptotic significance was 0.000; Therefore, it was concluded that there were statistically significant differences in the results of the qualifications between the group where a traditional methodology was followed and the group where the methodological strategy based on augmented reality was applied.

The results of the conducted survey are presented in Table 2, which displays the mean values and standard deviations obtained for all survey items related to students' perception of augmented reality usage during the teaching-learning process. Overall, it is evident that the average scores achieved were 4.28, indicating a favorable perception above the scale's central value. Notably, the highest scores were observed for indicators 5, 4, and 1, which correspond to the level of satisfaction derived from the implemented methodological strategy and the desire for its continued integration within the subject.

Table 2. Statisticians of the items of the applied survey

Items	Mean	Dev.
1. Does the use of augmented reality seem attractive to you as part of a methodological strategy?	4,75	0,78
2. Does the information provided by augmented reality in the classes arouse or increase interest in the course?	4,56	1,24
3. Was the interaction with augmented reality useful to me in learning the business architecture course?	4,48	1,61
4. Are you satisfied with teaching and learning enterprise architecture through an augmented reality methodology strategy?	4,86	0,67
5. Based on the experiences acquired in your classes, would you like to permanently use augmented reality as a learning tool?	4,88	0,23
6. How familiar are you with the Augmented Reality Enterprise Architecture class?	3,42	1,37
7. Do you think your teachers are prepared to effectively use augmented reality in class?	3,02	1,62

5. CONCLUSIONS

The following were the conclusions of the investigation:

- ✓ Currently, the teaching of the business architecture subject in the Information Systems major at the Pontificia Universidad Católica del Ecuador follows a traditional approach using didactic resources such as texts and presentations. However, the need to evaluate the effectiveness of a more updated methodological strategy based on augmented reality has been recognized.

- ✓ The use of augmented reality has a high potential to be used in educational environments, facilitating its integration in the classroom, favoring the teaching-learning process.
- ✓ It was found that all students in the experimental group reached important knowledge in the subject after applying the methodological strategy, in contrast to the control group.
- ✓ Positive levels of satisfaction and acceptance of the students who received the course were obtained through the methodological strategy.
- ✓ Although the incorporation of augmented reality tools in the teaching-learning process is not complex, teachers must develop the necessary pedagogical skills and abilities to carry out their classes mediated by this technology.

REFERENCES

Abero, J., Fernández, B. & Marín, V., 2017. Dispositivos móviles y realidad aumentada en el aprendizaje del alumnado universitario. RIED. Revista Iberoamericana de Educación a Distancia, 20(2), pp. 167-185.

Aguirre, R. G., García, D. G., Guevara, C. F. & Erazo-Álvarez, J. C., 2020. Realidad aumentada y educación en el Ecuador. Revista Arbitrada Interdisciplinaria Koinonía, 5(5), p. 415–438.

Astudillo, M. P., 2019. Aplicación de la Realidad Aumentada en las prácticas educativas universitarias. Revista Latinoamericana de Tecnología Educativa - RELATEC, 18(2), pp. 203-216.

Aznar, D., Romero, R. & Rodríguez, G., 2018. La tecnología móvil de Realidad Virtual en educación: una revisión del estado de la literatura científica en España. EDMETIC, Revista de Educación Mediática y TIC, pp. 256-274.

Barroso, J. y otros, 2017. Realidad aumentada y educación: Innovación en contextos formativos. s.l.:Ediciones Octaedro.

Blázquez, S., 2017. Realidad aumentada en educación. Universidad Politécnica de Madrid Gabinete de Tele-Educación. Madrid: Campus de Excelencia Internacional.

Cabero, A., Vásquez, C. & López, M., 2018. Uso de la Realidad Aumentada como recurso didáctico en la enseñanza universitaria. Formación Universitaria, 11(1), pp. 25-34.

Cabero, J. &. R. R., 2019. La Motivación de Escenarios Tecnológicos en Realidad Aumentada (AR): Resultados de Diferentes Experimentos. Applied Sciencies, 9(14).

Cabero, J., García, F., Cabero, J. & García, F., 2016. Realidad aumentada. Tecnología para la formación. s.l.:Editorial Síntesis S.A..

De la Horra, I., 2017. Realidad aumentada, una revolución educativa. Edmetic, pp. 9-22.

Ierache, J. y otros, 2014. Herramienta de Realidad Aumentada para facilitar la enseñanza en contextos educativos mediante el uso de las TICs. Revista Latinoamericana de Ingeniería de Software, 2(6), pp. 365-368.

Lopes, L. M., Sartor, K. N., Pozzebon, E. & Ferenhof, H., 2019. Inovações educacionais com o uso da realidade aumentada: uma revisão sistemática. EDUR. Educação em Revista.

Mealy, P., 2018. Virtual y augmented reality for Dummies. New Jersey: John Wiley y Sons.

Mesquida, J. & Pérez, A., 2017. Estudio de Apps de realidad aumentada para uso en campos de aprendizaje en un entorno natural. Edutec. Revista electrónica de tecnología educativa, pp. 19-33.

Ruiz, H., Jiménez, F. & Barón, M., 2018. Aplicaciones y desafíos para su uso en el aula de clase. Revista Educación y ciudad, pp. 137-148.

Saltan, F. a. A. Ö., 2017. The Use of Augmented Reality in Formal Education: A Scoping Review. Eurasia Journal of Mathematics, Science & Technology Education, 13(2), pp. 503-520.

Siti, N. y otros, 2018. A review of multimodal interaction technique in augmented reality environment. International Journal on Advanced Science Engineering Information Technology, 8(4), pp. 1460-1469.

Zamora, R., 2018. Realidad aumentada: Rol del docente y modelos pedagógicos en el proceso educativo. Ingenio, 1(1), pp. 34-47.

WHAT IF CHINA'S HEALTH CODE SYSTEM WERE LAUNCHED IN OTHER COUNTRIES, IN PARTICULAR, MAJOR WESTERN COUNTRIES?

Victor K. Y. Chan
Faculty of Business, Macao Polytechnic University
Rua de Luís Gonzaga Gomes, Macao, China

ABSTRACT

This article explores the potential legality and legitimacy issues if the mobile phone-based health code system, a distinctive eHealth system, as adopted in China during the COVID-19 pandemic were mandatorily deployed in such major Western or Western-style countries as the United States and the European Union (i.e., its member countries). It first dwells on an overview of China's health code system, including how China required citizens to install a health code app on their mobile phones that could then display colored QR codes indicating the citizens' corresponding freedom of movement permitted, and what personal data was taken into account by the system's algorithm in determining the code color. While this system succeeded in containing the virus spread to an extent, this article identifies and elucidates some key legality and legitimacy perspectives, namely, privacy and other personal rights, discrimination, accuracy and reasonableness, and security risks that might concern the above countries in the hypothetical scenario of the system being mandatorily launched there one day. The article further analyzes the specific perspectives especially accentuated by each of these countries' laws. Findings are that in the United States, constitutional challenges to the deprivation of the personal right of liberty would be the emphases. In the European Union, constitutional challenges to the deprivation of the personal right of liberty, discrimination, and accuracy and reasonableness (especially, the consequential fair trial issues) and legal queries about privacy would be the highlights.

KEYWORDS

China, Health Code Systems, Major Western or Western-Style Countries, Hypothetical

1. INTRODUCTION

During the COVID-19 pandemic, many countries implemented technology-based tracking and monitoring eHealth systems to help control the spread of the virus. One of the most prominent one in the media worldwide was China's health code system (Davidson, 2020). While broadly accepted in China, similar systems might raise legality and legitimacy issues over privacy, other personal rights, etc. if adopted elsewhere. This article provides an overview of China's health code system and analyzes the potential legality and legitimacy issues if it were, in a hypothetical scenario, mandatorily launched in such major Western or Western-style countries as the United States and the European Union (i.e., its member countries or states). Please note that despite the seeming comparison between various countries in respect of health code systems, this article is neutral, refrains from being judgmental, and does not incline to any correctness, incorrectness, superiority, or inferiority of any countries, any legal systems, any social systems, any political systems, or even any ideologies.

1.1 Overview of China's Health Code System

In February 2020, the Chinese government introduced a mandatory (or nearly mandatory depending on the context) mobile phone-based health code system to manage citizens' trajectories of movement during the COVID-19 outbreak (Mozur et al, 2020; Yu, 2022). People were required to input personal particulars and other information into the app for storage on central server(s), which then assigned them via the app a colored QR code in green, yellow, or red, indicating their risk of having been infected as determined by certain algorithm taking cognizance of the overlap between each person's past trajectory and those of the infected people, etc. A green code permitted free movement, yellow mandated some restrictions (e.g., to stay home for seven days and/or others), and red precipitated even more stringent restrictions (e.g., two weeks of quarantine and/or others) (Mozur et al, 2020; Yu, 2022).

The system sourced big data from various government departments, organs, public transportation operators, healthcare institutions, etc. for the above algorithm to work. Such big data for each person included the identity document type and number, the domicile address, the contact telephone number, the brief medical history, the recent trip history, the infection records, the infection test records, the body temperature, any current symptoms, the self-declared health condition, public transportation rides, and proximity to infected (high-risk) areas or people, among other less relevant data (Mozur et al, 2020; Yu, 2022; Zhang, 2022). Real-time tracking of location was also incorporated (Yu, 2022). Authorities and public transportation operators scanned the QR codes to control access to public places like malls, restaurants and trains (Mozur et al., 2020).

The health codes played a key role in regulating and tracking citizen movement during lockdowns in China. Over 300 cities were using the system with nearly 900 million Chinese citizens being so covered (Liang, 2020).

2. KEY PERSPECTIVES OF LEGALITY AND LEGITIMACY

2.1 Privacy and Other Personal Rights

A prime perspective is concerns about privacy and other personal rights as a result of personal data collected by the health code system and the expanded government surveillance and digital tracking such a system could enable (Zhang, 2022), as detailed in Subsection 1.1. In some countries and regions, these governmental practices might be prohibited by privacy or other personal rights laws like the European Union's General Data Protection Regulation (GDPR), which limits collection, storage, communication, analysis, and other processing of personal data (European Parliament & Council, 2023a). For instance, Articles 12 to 14 of GDPR requires transparency to the data subject (the natural person whom the personal data is about) and the data subject's consent to personal data collection. In other words, the data subject is supposed to be able to understand how his/her personal data is to be processed. As per Mozur et al (2020),

> "'T[t]he broad rules aren't public,' Mr. Lei said. 'How it assigns red or yellow codes isn't public. And there's no clear way to make your code turn green.'"

The author is not in a position to comment on the veracity of the above statements as reported by Mozur et al. (2020). After all, it is true that if any such doubt ever appears in European Union countries adopting any health code system one day, it would likely be up to the court to rule on the question whether the situation lives up to, for example, the transparency requirements of the GDPR. Other personal rights like liberty could also be contested if any health code system is put into practice in some countries.

2.2 Discrimination

Another potential legality and legitimacy issue is discrimination if health code colors restrict freedom of movement based on the medical history, the recent trip history, the infection records, the infection test records, the body temperature, any current symptoms, the self-declared health condition, public transport rides, and proximity to infected (high-risk) areas or people. Denying individuals' access to public spaces due to health conditions or background might violate anti-discrimination laws in some countries (Von Hirsch and Shearing, 2001). Having said that, restrictions based solely on infection risk and prevention might be legally defensible as public health measures during a serious epidemic outbreak, but coded systems that share personal data with a broad range of authorities and organizations might precipitate longer-term discrimination. All these might again be subject to the court's decision in the corresponding country.

2.3 Accuracy and Reasonableness

Determining a person's right to access public spaces by some health code system's algorithms might lead to fair trial issues in some countries, i.e., the issues as to whether the decision on the person's right to access public spaces is made after a fair and public hearing, within a reasonable time, by an independent and impartial court (Council of Europe, 2023; Fair Trials International, 2023). Restricting access to public places or other freedom of movement simply by virtue of a health code's color on a mobile phone app would likely trigger legal appeals to contest inaccurate or unreasonable determinations of the color by the health code system (Council of Europe, 2023; Fair Trials International, 2023).

2.4 Security Risks

Centralized health code systems could also be beset by security concerns. Hacking could expose citizens' utterly sensitive health and location information, facilitating identity theft or stalking (Batra et al, 2020; van de Weijer, et al, 2019). The situation is aggravated by the fact that such data is provided directly to governments, which are often subject to different laws than business entities. Strong cybersecurity protections would be helpful, though not always reliable (Lavrov et al, 2018).

3. SPECIFIC PERSPECTIVES ESPECIALLY ACCENTUATED BY EACH MAJOR COUNTRY'S LAWS

3.1 United States

Any nation-wide mandatory health code system in the U.S. would likely spark off constitutional challenges under Fifth and Fourteenth Amendment "due process guarantees." The Fifth Amendment (Legal Information Institute, 2023a) reads as:

"No person… nor be deprived of life, liberty, or property, without due process of law..."

The Fourteenth Amendment (Legal Information Institute, 2023b) contains a similar phrase.

Therefore, the challenge would not lie in the health code system itself but the subsequent actions taken based on the health code color on the app, for example, restricting the access of any person with a yellow or red code to public places, which might constitute deprivation of liberty, a kind of personal right. Government's defense might concentrate on the "due process of law" if there is some legislation in place to institutionalize due legal processes to enforce restriction in accordance with the health code color.

3.2 European Union

In the European Union, any mandatory health codes system would rather clearly contravene the GDPR. Apart from the transparency issue of the GDPR's Articles 12 to 14 as exemplified in Subsection 2.1 above, the system might breach the GDPR's Article 8 on children's consent given that the system's operation as per Mozur et al (2020), Yu (2022), Zhang (2022), and Davidson (2020) does not seem to implement the kind of extraordinary treatment of children's consent as stipulated in the Article.

It also remains a grey area as to whether the system could infringe Article 5: Right to Liberty and Security under the European Convention on Human Rights (European Court of Human Rights, n. d.). Defense of governments might make use of the exception point (e) in the Article, which permits detention of persons for the prevention of the spreading of infectious diseases. However, whether the algorithms of the system to generate a yellow or red code are adequately confirmative in respect of the person concerned being substantially related to any spreading of infectious diseases is disputable and subject to the court's view.

Discrimination delineated in Subsection 2.2 above is outright forbidden by Article 14: Prohibition of Discrimination under the European Convention on Human Rights (European Court of Human Rights, n. d.). Likewise, the fair trial issues mentioned in Subsection 2.4 above are also highlighted in Article 6: Right to a Fair Trial under the European Convention on Human Rights (European Court of Human Rights, n. d.).

4. CONCLUSION AND DISCUSSION

The mandatory launch of China's health code system or any of its variants in major Western or Western-style countries would be prone to contests in such legality and legitimacy perspectives as privacy and other personal rights, discrimination, accuracy and reasonableness, and security risks. Specifically, the perspectives especially accentuated by each of the United States' and the European Union's laws can be summarized as follows: In the United States, constitutional challenges to the deprivation of the personal right of liberty would be the emphases. In the European Union, constitutional challenges to the deprivation of the personal right of liberty, discrimination, and accuracy and reasonableness (especially, the consequential fair trial issues) and legal queries about privacy would be the highlights. Table 1 juxtaposes the potentially prime legality and legitimacy perspectives to be contested in the United States and those in the European Union

Table 1. Juxtaposing the potentially prime legality and legitimacy perspectives to be contested in the United States and those in the European Union

	United States	European Union
Privacy and other personal rights	Fifth and Fourteenth Amendment "due process guarantees": Access restriction may constitute deprivation of liberty.	GDPR: The health code app may not be sufficiently transparent and may not have extraordinary treatment of children's consent. European Convention on Human Rights: Probable infringement if detention is based on the health code.
Discrimination		European Convention on Human Rights: Probable infringement on Prohibition of Discrimination.
Accuracy and reasonableness		European Convention on Human Rights: The fair trial issues.
Security risks		

Finally, it is absolutely essential to underline the disclaimer that in spite of this article's probable practical value as a reference for the authorities in these major Western or Western-style countries to evaluate the feasibility of using any system similar to China's health code system in combating any future pandemics, formal consultation with qualified legal and/or other professionals of the corresponding country is strongly recommended in the face of any specific legality and/or legitimacy issues in any particular context for any particular purposes, especially, when confounded by other factors. Also, whereas this articles cites quite extensively the literature, be it academic, journalistic or otherwise, the author does not necessarily approve of or disapprove of any political and societal stances or ideologies that might be embedded and/or advocated implicitly or explicitly in the cited works. Instead, the citations would rather focus on the scientific and factual contents, for example but not limited to, the statistical figures, law provisions, etc.

REFERENCES

Batra, S., Gupta, M., Singh, J., Srivastava, D., and Aggarwal, I. (2020). An Empirical Study of Cybercrime and its Preventions. *Proceedings of 2020 Sixth International Conference on Parallel, Distributed and Grid Computing (PDGC).* Waknaghat, India, pp. 42-46. Retrieved August 19, 2023 from https://ieeexplore.ieee.org/abstract/document/9315785?casa_token=L_9se0JqWiQAAAAA:LbXppVzyQp4runIiLGytZFTVTRk4amZyrwvw846aWBe1rVhhnfATiBLDZZ62cPairPl-6nKtIOp8aQ

Centers for Disease Control and Prevention (2023a). *Health Insurance Portability and Accountability Act of 1996 (HIPAA).* Centers for Disease Control and Prevention Retrieved August 12, 2023 from https://www.cdc.gov/phlp/publications/topic/hipaa.html

Centers for Disease Control and Prevention (2023b). *HIPAA Privacy Rule.* Centers for Disease Control and Prevention Retrieved August 12, 2023 from https://www.cdc.gov/phlp/publications/topic/hipaa.html

Council of Europe (2023). Impart of the European Convention on Human Rights: Right to a Fair Trial. Retrieved August 19, 2023 from https://www.coe.int/en/web/impact-convention-human-rights/right-to-a-fair-trial

Davidson, H. (2020). China's coronavirus health code apps raise concerns over privacy. *The Guardian*. Retrieved August 17, 2023 from https://www.theguardian.com/world/2020/apr/01/chinas-coronavirus-health-code-apps-raise-concerns-over-privacy.

European Court of Human Rights, n. d. *European Convention on Human Rights*. Council of Europe. Retrieved August 20, 2023 from https://www.echr.coe.int/documents/d/echr/convention_ENG

European Parliament & Council (2023a). Regulation (EU) 2016/679 of the European Parliament and of the Council of 27 April 2016 on the protection of natural persons with regard to the processing of personal data and on the free movement of such data, and repealing Directive 95/46/EC (General Data Protection Regulation). Official Journal of the European Union, L 119, 1–88. Retrieved June 25, 2023 from https://eur-lex.europa.eu/legal-content/EN/TXT/PDF/?uri=CELEX:32016R0679

Fair Trials International (2023). *The Right to a Fair Trial*. Fair Trials International. Retrieved August 19, 2023 from https://www.fairtrials.org/the-right-to-a-fair-trial/#presumption-of-innocence-94

Lavrov, E. A., Volosiuk, A. A., Pasko, N. B., Gonchar, V. P., and Kozhevnikov, G. K. (2018). Computer Simulation of Discrete Human-Machine Interaction for Providing Reliability and Cybersecurity of Critical Systems. *Proceedings of 2018 Third International Conference on Human Factors in Complex Technical Systems and Environments (ERGO)s and Environments (ERGO)*. St. Petersburg, Russia, pp. 67-70. Retrieved August 20, 2023 from https://ieeexplore.ieee.org/abstract/document/8443846

Legal Information Institute (2023a). *Fifth Amendment*. Cornell Law School. Retrieved August 20, 2023 from https://www.law.cornell.edu/constitution/fifth_amendment

Legal Information Institute (2023b). *Fourteenth Amendment*. Cornell Law School. Retrieved August 20, 2023 from https://www.law.cornell.edu/constitution/amendmentxiv

Liang, F. (2020). COVID-19 and Health Code: How Digital Platforms Tackle the Pandemic in China. *Social Media and Society*, Vol 6, No. 3. Retrieved August 18, 2023 from https://www.ncbi.nlm.nih.gov/pmc/articles/PMC7424612/

Mozur, P., Zhong, R., and Krolik, A. (2020). In Coronavirus Fight, China Gives Citizens a Color Code, With Red Flags. *The New York Times*. Retrieved August 18, 2023 from https://www.nytimes.com/2020/03/01/business/china-coronavirus-surveillance.html

van de Weijer, S. G. A., Leukfeldt, R., and Bernasco, W. (2018). Determinants of reporting cybercrime: A comparison between identity theft, consumer fraud, and hacking. *European Journal of Criminology*, Vol. 16, No. 4. Retrieved August 19, 2023 from https://journals.sagepub.com/doi/abs/10.1177/1477370818773610

van de Weijer, S. G. A., Leukfeldt, R., and Bernasco, W. (2019). Determinants of reporting cybercrime: A comparison between identity theft, consumer fraud, and hacking. *European Journal of Criminology*, Vol. 16, No. 4, pp. 486–508. Retrieved August 19, 2023 from https://journals.sagepub.com/doi/abs/10.1177/1477370818773610

Von Hirsch, A. and Shearing, C. (2001). Exclusion from Public Space. *In: Von Hirsch, A., Garland, D., and Wakefield, A. Eds. Ethical Perspectives in Situational Crime Prevention*, Oxford: Hart Pub, pp. 77-96. Retrieved August 19, 2023 from https://www.researchgate.net/profile/Clifford-Shearing/publication/304246143_Exclusion_from_Public_Space/links/576a471a08ae1a43d23b3de4/Exclusion-from-Public-Space.pdf

Yu, H. (2022). Living in the era of codes: a reflection on China's health code system *Biosocieties*, pp. 1–18. Retrieved August 18, 2023 from https://www.ncbi.nlm.nih.gov/pmc/articles/PMC9713107/

Zhang, X. (2022). Decoding China's COVID-19 Health Code Apps: The Legal Challenges. *Healthcare (Basel)*. Retrieved August 18, 2023 from https://www.ncbi.nlm.nih.gov/pmc/articles/PMC9408613/

REFLECTION

CYBER ETHICS OF BLOCKCHAIN, AI AND WORLDCOIN

Dario Elias Félix de Oliveira Rodrigues
Instituto Politécnico de Santarém, Santarém, Portugal

ABSTRACT

This paper discusses the evolution of cyber ethics steered by blockchain technology (BT), artificial intelligence (AI), and, perhaps, Worldcoin, which is an ambitious global project to build a decentralized "proof-of-personhood" encrypted in an anonymous "World ID" for each human being. To investigate the digital conundrum and evaluate the ethical implications of BT, Explainable AI (XAI), and Worldcoin, the "Cyberethics-Mix" framework will be a compass oriented to four cardinal points of ethics in cyberspace: Privacy (data protection), Property (data ownership), Precision (data accuracy), and Pervasiveness (data access). The paper's main conclusion is the ethical desirability of an inclusive and decentralized policy in cyberspace.

KEYWORDS

Cyber Ethics, Blockchain Technology, Explainable Artificial Intelligence (XAI), Worldcoin, Proof-of-Personhood, Cyberethics-Mix Framework

1. INTRODUCTION

Technology poses ethical challenges in today's digital landscape, requiring new ethical frameworks. Rodrigues's "Cyberethics-Mix" (2011) proposed a template to navigate these ethical waters, foregrounding four pivotal elements encapsulated by the letter "P": data's property, precision, privacy, and pervasiveness. Blockchain promotes decentralized trust (Rodrigues, 2021a), while AI stresses the importance of explainability (Gunning & Aha, 2019). Worldcoin, combining cryptography and AI, aims to balance privacy and convenience, including a guarantee of a worldwide equitable coin distribution (Gent, 2023, p.42).

2. BLOCKCHAIN'S ETHICAL IMPLICATIOS AND TRUST DYNAMICS

Historically, trust expanded from tribal groups to the nation-state "Leviathan" (Hobbes, 1996). Blockchain technology (BT) extends the trust genesis through distributed consensus (Xiao et al., 2020, p. 1432), introducing the "Internet of Value" (Lacity, 2022, pp. 326, 327). Originating decentralized (Nakamoto, 2008), BT changes ethical dynamics and may drive innovation. The cybernetics-mix compass (Rodrigues, 2011, 2021) underscores the following ethical challenges.

2.1 Privacy

Blockchain's cryptographic security ensures transparency and quasi-anonymity in transactions, though identities could be traced raising ethical concerns. Despite this, blockchain enhances accountability, deterring fraud, and strengthens privacy by safeguarding sensitive data (Zyskind & Nathan, 2015). This focus on privacy can be advantageous, as consumers prefer companies that manage data responsibly (Bleier et al., 2020).

2.2 Property

The internet's early phase favored new intermediaries, leading to predatory digital business models exacerbating agency costs (Loureiro et al., 2021). As blockchain enhances property rights and eases asset transfers (Tan & Saraniemi, 2022), cryptocurrencies, NFTs, and smart contracts streamline intellectual property monetization (De Filippi & Wright, 2018), reshaping business models and prompt an ethical reevaluation of ownership rights dynamics that may include monetary systems, suggesting an ethical shift to bridge individual goals with sustainable collective action (Rodrigues, 2021b).

2.3 Precision

Digital content accuracy is crucial in cyber ethics. Blockchain ensures data authenticity and integrity via collective validation, utilizing digital signatures and hash functions (Nakamoto, 2008; Pierro, 2017). This fosters trust in sectors like logistics and healthcare. Blockchain's principles align with the early internet's democratic ideals, reflecting Surowiecki's "crowd wisdom" (2004) and modern tools like "Twitter Community Notes" (Kim, 2023), emphasizing decentralized truth validation.

2.4 Pervasiveness

Blockchain technology (BT) brings forth transformative ethical implications, especially evident in decentralized finance (DeFi) sectors, which aim for broader financial inclusivity by bypassing traditional banking constraints (Abdulhakeem & Hu, 2021). BT's inherent features champion transparency, diversity, and fairness, echoing the principles of democratic systems (Gupta et al., 2023, p. 556). Rodrigues underscores the ethical importance of securely sharing information, highlighting that such openness fosters innovation (2011, p. 335). With advancements like the "Orb" eye-scanner (Worlcoin, 2023) combined with Privacy Preserving Cryptographic Technologies (PPCT, Gupta et al., 2023), there is an amplification in digital accessibility, further solidifying democratic ethical underpinnings. However, the promise of BT is two-sided. Its transformative potential largely depends on political will and societal understanding. Barriers such as the digital divide, technological illiteracy, and ambiguous regulations might limit its reach.

3. THE ETHICAL LANDSCAPE OF EXPLAINABLE AI (XAI)

Explainable AI (XAI) represents a paradigm shift in artificial intelligence. There were no trust concerns while humans operated with early hardware and software. With straightforward algorithms, these systems executed the tasks they were programmed to do. In a sense, they represented the purest form of trust. However, ethical dilemmas arose with machine learning evolution, especially with "deep learning," the architecture that powers advanced Generative AI and Natural Language Processing models (like the GPT series).

> *A machine incapable of autonomy was not a threat and could be easily trusted, and people could easily believe more in a machine's output than human output. However, the advent of Machine Learning (ML) and the successful implementation of the concept of making machines think and perform tasks autonomously has resulted in a breach of the trust that existed, as machines can now operate and act independently. (Chamola et al., 2023)*

XAI seeks to ethically restore trust in mathematical models eroded by business algorithms' pragmatism by ensuring AI's transparency. This endeavor is a considerable challenge, and the cyberethics-mix framework will now be used for investigating its ethical implications.

3.1 Privacy

XAI aims for transparency but can expose personal data used in AI models, potentially risking re-identification. While useful for audits, such clarity might overshare data details. "Differential privacy" counters this by adding controlled noise to data, preserving individual privacy while allowing overall analysis (Utaliyeva et al., 2023, p. 3). "Privacy-preserving machine learning" (PPML) further enables confidential model training (Hulsen, 2023, p. 657). EU's GDPR strengthens the "data minimization" principle, ensuring only necessary data processing (Oprescu et al., 2022, p. 59). Additionally, "layered explanations" vary AI detail based on user access (Guesmi et al., 2022, p. 177), and "synthetic data" provides computer-generated data for secure AI training (Oblizanov, 2023, p. 5).

3.2 Property

XAI's transparency can expose AI models to potential replication and reverse-engineering, posing intellectual property challenges. However, XAI can also identify possible infringements within copyrights or patents, allowing for rectifications. While the focus remains on AI's outputs, the intellectual property aspects of AI inputs, like training data, are often overlooked. Datasets may include copyrighted works, raising legal questions. Since AI relies on public or copyrighted data representing societal knowledge, should its creations be communal? Moreover, AI's inventiveness stirs debate about recognizing it as a creative entity.

> *It must be kept in mind that there are also many AI systems that appear to have independent hypothesis generation and testing capabilities, which in patent parlance might lead to independent invention by the intelligent system, i.e., without any direct action by humans. The question here is whether the owner, user, or programmer of the robot or an AI system is entitled to patent protection for an invention developed directly by AI. (Laukyte & Lucchi, 2022, p.177)*

As AI assumes new societal roles, its legal identity becomes an issue. If AI undertakes human tasks, should it receive similar legal rights? Intellectual property laws might expand beyond human-only contributions. The European Parliament's 2017 resolution suggests an "electronic personhood" for advanced robots (Pagallo, 2018, p. 2), and more research is needed to align machines' property rights with ethical data usage.

3.3 Precision

XAI aims for clearer AI decisions, aligning with demands for transparency (Gerlings & Constantiou, 2020, p. 1284). However, "post-hoc" explanations might not reflect true model logic (Vale et al., 2022, p. 826), and there's a risk of favoring simpler models (Rudin, 2019) or crafting explanations to fit regulations (Wachter et al., 2017). Thorough research and oversight are vital to ensure XAI's authenticity.

3.4 Pervasiveness

XAI promotes AI understanding, which invites ethical input. However, simplifying complex AI decisions might misrepresent their intricacy (Doshi-Velez & Kim, 2017). Geoffrey Hinton suggests valuing performance over explainability (Ridley, 2022a), but although unexplained practical algorithms can have their merits, a thorough evaluation of AI systems is still vital (Arrieta et al., 2020, p. 83).

4. WORLDCOIN AT THE ETHICAL CONUNDRUM

Led by OpenAI's CEO, Sam Altman, Worldcoin aims to revolutionize identity verification by combining a unique World ID with cryptocurrency rewards (Worldcoin, 2023). The cyberethics-mix lens will now focus on that.

4.1 Privacy

Differentiating between humans and AI is vital, making it crucial to confirm humanness online without exposing personal details, balancing online ease with privacy. WLD, the currency behind World ID, demonstrates such unique utility, which proves cryptocurrency's multidimensional value (Rodrigues, 2021b), emphasizing transparency and user autonomy. Worldcoin's authentication process is based on an eye scan that determines human uniqueness and then, allegedly, immediately erases the users' data, producing only an encrypted code called a zero-knowledge proof (ZKP). This method hides ledger input data while allowing validation (Morais et al., 2019), offering "proof of personhood" by giving each person a unique "World ID." Rather than verifying identity, this ID asserts its holder's digital uniqueness. Hence, users can skip password memorization using their World ID to reaffirm their unique status, simplifying online interactions. The cyberethics-mix compass will be used to discern Worldcoin's ethical implications.

4.2 Property

World ID, a nuclear element of the Worldcoin project, redefines digital identity by granting human users a unique digital stamp, affirming their individuality. WLD tokens act as a currency and symbolize users' stake and involvement in the Worldcoin project. This dual approach amplifies the users' sense of ownership and belonging, bridging the gap between individual and collective rights. Cryptocurrency may encourage an organic collective action rooted in a principle of individual freedom and unique contribution, as stated by Rodrigues (2021a) and Worldcoin (2023). As put by George and colleagues, Worldcoin's ambition is more than to create a new currency; it is a pioneering endeavor to mitigate economic disparities and champion financial inclusion globally, regardless of an individual's location or socio-economic standing (2023, p. 136).

4.3 Precision

Reliance on AI underscores the need for accurate information and genuine human input verification. World ID counters AI-driven misinformation by confirming human authors using the iris's unique biometric traits (Sehrawat & Sankhyan, 2016, p. 437), ensuring unparalleled precision and preventing fraud.

4.4 Pervasiveness

Worldcoin aims to democratize online verification and finance access, bridging the digital divide. However, diverse cultural and regional trust challenges arise. Verifying individual uniqueness promotes equal digital access and deters abuse, emphasizing the potential for Universal Basic Income via World ID.

5. CONCLUSION

Distributed technologies may foster transparent, secure ecosystems to improve the world. For ethical engagement, user education is crucial. Worldcoin and World ID embody this digital evolution's opportunities and concerns. Once upholding transparency and biometric data privacy, as promised in Worldcoin's white paper, this worldwide initiative may result in a safe global decentralization. Thus, continuous scrutiny is essential. While blockchain and AI redefine cyber ethics, and Worldcoin addresses users' convenience and security challenges, well-informed political decisions are paramount for a promising future.

REFERENCES

Abdulhakeem, S.A. and Hu, Q. (2021). Powered by Blockchain technology, DeFi (Decentralized Finance) strives to increase financial inclusion of the unbanked by reshaping the world financial system. Modern Economy, 12(01), pp. 1.

Arrieta, A.B., Díaz-Rodríguez, N., Del Ser, J., Bennetot, A., Tabik, S., Barbado, A. and Herrera, F. (2020). Explainable Artificial Intelligence (XAI): Concepts, taxonomies, opportunities and challenges toward responsible AI. Information Fusion, 58, pp. 82-115.

De Filippi, P. & Wright, A. (2018). Blockchain and the law: The rule of code. Harvard University Press.

Doshi-Velez, F. & Kim, B. (2017). Towards a rigorous science of interpretable machine learning. arXiv preprint, [online] Available at: https://arxiv.org/abs/1702.08608.

European Parliament (2017). Recommendations to the Commission on Civil Law Rules on Robotics (2015/2103(INL)). Official Journal of the European Union, C 252, pp. 239-257.

George, A. S., George, A. H. & Baskar, T. (2023). Worldcoin: A Decentralized Currency for a Unified Global Economy. Partners Universal International Research Journal, 2(2), pp. 136-155.

Gerlings, J., Shollo, A. & Constantiou, I. (2020). Reviewing the need for explainable artificial intelligence (xAI). arXiv preprint arXiv:2012.01007.

Guesmi, M. et al. (2022). Explaining user models with different levels of detail for transparent recommendation: A user study. In Proceedings of the 30th ACM Conference on User Modeling, Adaptation and Personalization, pp. 175-183.

Gupta, R. et al. (2023). A Voting System Using Block Chain A Deep Survey. In 2023 3rd International Conference on Advance Computing and Innovative Technologies in Engineering (ICACITE). IEEE, pp. 556-561.

Hobbes, T. (1996) (1651). Leviathan. Oxford University Press.

Hulsen, T. (2023). Explainable Artificial Intelligence (XAI): Concepts and Challenges in Healthcare. AI, 4(3), p. 652. Lacity, M.C., 2022. Blockchain: From Bitcoin to the Internet of Value and beyond. Journal of Information Technology, 37(4), pp. 326-340.

Kim, J. (2023). When Partisans Fly: Twitter Community Notes and the Political Economy of Social Media Disinformation.

Laukyte, M. & Lucchi, N. (2022). Creative AI: The Complex Relationship between Human Inventiveness and Intellectual Property. BioLaw Journal-Rivista di BioDiritto, (3), pp. 169-183.

Loureiro, M., Pêgo, A. and Raposo, I. G. (2021). The Real Blockchain Game Changer: Protocols and DAOs for Coordinating Work to Provide Goods and Services. In: D. Rodrigues, ed., Political and Economic Implications of Blockchain Technology in Business and Healthcare. IGI Global, pp. 160-172.

Morais, E., Koens, T., Van Wijk, C. & Koren, A. (2019). 'A survey on zero knowledge range proofs and applications', SN Applied Sciences, 1(1), pp. 1-17.

Oblizanov, A. et al. (2023). Evaluation Metrics Research for Explainable Artificial Intelligence Global Methods Using Synthetic Data. Applied System Innovation, 6(1), p. 26.

Oprescu, A.M. et al. (2022). Towards a data collection methodology for Responsible Artificial Intelligence in health: A prospective and qualitative study in pregnancy. Information Fusion, 83(84), pp. 53-78.

Pagallo, U. (2018). Apples, oranges, robots: four misunderstandings in today's debate on the legal status of AI systems. Philosophical Transactions of the Royal Society A: Mathematical, Physical and Engineering Sciences, 376(2133), p. 20180168.

Di Pierro, M. (2017). What is the blockchain?. Computing in Science & Engineering, 19(5), pp. 92-95.

Rodrigues, D. (2011). Cyberethics of E-Business Social Networking. In M.M. Cruz-Cunha et al. eds. Handbook of Research on Business Social Networking: Organizational, Managerial, and Technological Dimensions. IGI Global – Business Science Reference Publishers, pp. 314-338.

Rodrigues, D.D. (2021b). Blockchanging Money: Reengineering the Free World Incentive System. In D.D. Rodrigues, ed. Political and Economic Implications of Blockchain Technology in Business and Healthcare. IGI Global, pp. 69-117.

Rodrigues, D. D. and Lopes, P. S. (2021a). Blockchanging Politics: Opening a Trustworthy but Hazardous Reforming Era. In: D. Rodrigues, ed., Political and Economic Implications of Blockchain Technology in Business and Healthcare. IGI Global, pp. 118-159.

Rodrigues, D. D. (2021). Blockchanging Trust: Ethical Metamorphosis in Business and Healthcare. In D.D. Rodrigues, ed. Political and Economic Implications of Blockchain Technology in Business and Healthcare. IGI Global, pp. 1-41.

Ribeiro, M.T., Singh, S. & Guestrin, C. (2016). "Why should I trust you?" Explaining the predictions of any classifier. Proceedings of the 22nd ACM SIGKDD conference on knowledge discovery & data mining, pp. 1135-1144.

Ridley, M. (2022a). Explainable Artificial Intelligence (XAI). INFORMATION TECHNOLOGY AND LIBRARIES.

Rudin, C. (2019). Stop explaining black box machine learning models for high stakes decisions and use interpretable models instead. Nature Machine Intelligence, 1(5), pp. 206-215.

Selbst, A. & Barocas, S. (2018). The intuitive appeal of explainable machines. Fordham Law Review, 87(3), pp. 1085-1139.

Sehrawat, J.S. and Sankhyan, D. (2016). Iris Patterns as A Biometric Tool For Forensic Identifications: A Review. Brazilian Journal of Forensic Sciences, Medical Law and Bioethics, 5(4), pp. 431-440.

Surowiecki, J. (2004). The Wisdom of Crowds. Lisboa: Lua de Papel.

Utaliyeva, A., Shin, J. & Choi, Y. H. (2023). Task-Specific Adaptive Differential Privacy Method for Structured Data. Sensors, 23(4), p. 1980.

Vale, D., El-Sharif, A. & Ali, M. (2022). Explainable artificial intelligence (XAI) post-hoc explainability methods: Risks and limitations in non-discrimination law. AI and Ethics, 2(4), pp. 815-826.

Xiao, Y., Zhang, N., Lou, W. and Hou, Y. T. (2020). A survey of distributed consensus protocols for blockchain networks. IEEE Communications Surveys & Tutorials, 22(2), pp.1432-1465.

Wachter, S., Mittelstadt, B. & Russell, C. (2017). Counterfactual explanations without opening the black box: Automated decisions and the GDPR. Harvard Journal of Law & Technology, 31(2), pp.841-887.

Worldcoin (2023). Worldcoin Whitepaper. [online] Available at: https://whitepaper.worldcoin.org/.

Worldcoin.org (2023b). Worldcoin open source and public goods. [online] Available at: https://worldcoin.org/open-source.

Worldcoin (2023a). Worldcoin tokenomics. Available at: https://whitepaper.worldcoin.org/tokenomics.

AUTHOR INDEX